ŚRĪ ŚRĪ GURU-GAURĀṄGAU JAYATAḤ

THE UDDHAVA-GĪTĀ

of

Kṛṣṇa-Dvaipāyana Vyāsa

एतांस आस्थायपरात्मनिष्ठामध्यासितांपूर्वतमैर्महर्षिभिः
अहंतरिष्यामिदुरन्तपारंतमोमुकुन्दाङ्घ्रिनिषेवयैव

etāṁ sa āsthāya parātma-niṣṭhām adhyāsitāṁ pūrvatamair maharṣibhiḥ
ahaṁ tariṣyāmi duranta-pāraṁ tamo mukundāṅghri-niṣevayaiva

I shall cross over the insurmountable ocean of nescience by being firmly fixed in the service of the lotus feet of Kṛṣṇa. This was approved by the previous ācāryas, who were fixed in firm devotion to the Lord, Paramātmā, the Supreme Personality of Godhead.

Publications by Touchstone Media:

Gītā Mahātmya and Śrīmad Bhāgavatam Mahātmya
Prārthanā
Amrta Vani
Śrī Bhaktivinoda Vāṇī Vaibhava Volume 1, Sambandha
Śrī Bhaktivinoda Vāṇī Vaibhava Volume 1, Abhideya and Prayojana
Śrī Prema Bhakti-candrika
Sārvabhauma Śataka
Hari Bhakti Kalpa Latika
Śrī Nityānanda-caritāmṛta
Pada Sevana
Sweet Pastimes of Damodara
Dog and the Wolf
Epic Characters of Mahabharat Series
Krishna Pocket Guide
Prema Vilasa
Adventures of India Series
Mahabharat

If you are interested in the purchasing or the distributing of this book or any of the above publications, you may contact the publisher at:

Touchstone Media
Block FE 2/3, Sector 3
Salt Lake, Kolkata 700106
India
E-mail : isvara99@gmail.com
Website: www.touchstonemedia.com

THE UDDHAVA-GĪTĀ

KṚṢṆA SPEAKS TO UDDHAVA HIS SEQUEL TO BHAGAVAD GĪTĀ

Original Sanskrit Text, Roman Transliterations, and Translations

Featuring

***Sārārtha Darśinī* Commentary by**
Śrīla Viśvanātha Cakravartī Ṭhākura
Chapter Summaries and *Gauḍīya Bhāṣya* Purport by
Śrīla Bhaktisiddhānta Sarasvatī Ṭhākura

Produced and Published by Īśvara dāsa
Translated by Bhūmipati dāsa
Edited by Pūrṇaprajña dāsa

Touch stone media

The Uddhava Gītā

Sārārtha Darśinī Commentary by Śrīla Viśvanātha Cakravartī Thākura
Chapter Summaries and *Gauḍīya Bhāṣya* Purport by
Śrīla Bhaktisiddhānta Sarasvatī Ṭhākura
Produced and Published by Īśvara dāsa
Translated by Bhūmipati dāsa
Edited by Pūrṇaprajña dāsa
Typeset by Caitanya devī dāsī
Editorial Input by Sāmba dāsa
Proofread by Kṛṣṇa-kṛpa dāsa
Index by Grahila dāsa
Cover Painting by Añjana dāsa
Layout and Design by Īśvara dāsa

First Printing 2007, 2000 copies
2nd Printing 2009, 2000 copies

ISBN 81-87897-13-3

We are greatly thankful to the Bhaktivedanta Book Trust for their English edition of the Eleventh canto of the *Śrīmad Bhagavatam*, which served as a guide for this book.

Printed in India by
CDC Printers Pvt. Ltd., Kolkata

DEDICATION

THIS BOOK IS DEDICATED TO

HIS DIVINE GRACE
A. C. BHAKTIVEDANTA SWAMI PRABHUPĀDA
FOUNDER ĀCĀRYA INTERNATIONAL SOCIETY FOR KRISHNA CONSCIOUSNESS
WHO REVEALED TO THE WORLD BHAGAVAD-GĪTĀ AS IT IS

CONTENTS

Introduction

oṁ ajñāna-timirāndhasya jñānāñjana-śalākayā
cakṣur unmīlitaṁ yena tasmai śrī-gurave namaḥ
śrī-caitanya-mano-'bhīṣṭaṁ sthāpitaṁ yena bhū-tale
svayaṁ rūpaḥ kadā mahyaṁ dadāti sva-padāntikam

I was born in the darkest ignorance, and my spiritual master opened my eyes with the torch of knowledge. I offer my respectful obeisances unto him. When will Śrīla Rūpa Gosvāmī Prabhupāda, who has established within this material world the mission to fulfill the desire of Lord Caitanya, give me shelter under his lotus feet?

vande 'haṁ śrī-guroḥ śrī-yuta-pada-kamalaṁ śrī-gurūn vaiṣṇavāṁś ca
śrī-rūpaṁ sāgrajātaṁ saha-gaṇa-raghunāthānvitaṁ taṁ sa-jīvam
sādvaitaṁ sāvadhūtaṁ parijana-sahitaṁ kṛṣṇa-caitanya-devaṁ
śrī-rādhā-kṛṣṇa-pādān saha-gaṇa-lalitā-śrī-viśākhānvitāṁś ca

I offer my respectful obeisances unto the lotus feet of my spiritual master and unto the feet of all Vaiṣṇavas. I offer my respectful obeisances unto the lotus feet of Śrīla Rūpa Gosvāmī along with his elder brother Sanātana Gosvāmī, as well as Raghunātha Dāsa and Raghunātha Bhaṭṭa, Gopāla Bhaṭṭa, and Śrīla Jīva Gosvāmī. I offer my respectful obeisances to Lord Kṛṣṇa Caitanya and Lord Nityānanda along with Advaita Ācārya, Gadādhara, Śrīvāsa, and other associates. I offer my respectful obeisances to Śrīmatī Rādhārāṇī and Śrī Kṛṣṇa along with Their associates Śrī Lalitā and Viśākhā.

he kṛṣṇa karuṇā-sindho dīna-bandho jagat-pate
gopeśa gopikā-kānta rādhā-kānta namo 'stu te

O my dear Kṛṣṇa, You are the friend of the distressed and the source of creation. You are the master of the gopīs and the lover of Rādhārāṇī. I offer my respectful obeisances unto You.

tapta-kāñcana-gaurāṅgi rādhe vṛndāvaneśvari
vṛṣabhānu-sute devi praṇamāmi hari-priye

I offer my respects to Rādhārāṇī, whose bodily complexion is like molten gold and who is the Queen of Vṛndāvana. You are the daughter of King Vṛṣabhānu, and You are very dear to Lord Kṛṣṇa.

vāñchā-kalpatarubhyaś ca kṛpā-sindhubhya eva ca
patitānāṁ pāvanebhyo vaiṣṇavebhyo namo namaḥ

I offer my respectful obeisances unto all the Vaiṣṇava devotees of the Lord. They can fulfill the desires of everyone, just like desire trees, and they are full of compassion for the fallen souls.

śrī-kṛṣṇa-caitanya prabhu-nityānanda
śrī-advaita gadādhara śrīvāsādi-gaura-bhakta-vṛnda

I offer my obeisances to Śrī Kṛṣṇa Caitanya, Prabhu Nityānanda, Śrī Advaita, Gadādhara, Śrīvāsa and all others in the line of devotion.

hare kṛṣṇa hare kṛṣṇa kṛṣṇa kṛṣṇa hare hare
hare rāma hare rāma rāma rāma hare hare

Uddhava-gītā is a hidden treasure practically unknown to the people of the world, and the reason for this is certainly a great mystery. *Uddhava-gītā* was personally spoken by Lord Śrī Kṛṣṇa just prior to His disappearance from this material world, more than five thousand years ago. It is the Lord's final instructions, imparted to His dear devotee, Śrī Uddhava. His Divine Grace A. C. Bhaktivedanta Swami Prabhupāda wrote about the *Uddhava-gītā:*

"Lord Śrī Kṛṣṇa is factually the spiritual master of the three worlds, and He is the original source of all Vedic knowledge. It is very difficult, however, to understand the personal feature of the Absolute Truth, even from the *Vedas*. His personal instructions are needed in order to understand the Personality of Godhead as the Supreme Absolute Truth. *Bhagavad-gītā* is the evidence of such transcendental knowledge in gist. One cannot know the Supreme Lord unless one is graced by the Lord Himself. Lord Kṛṣṇa exhibited this specific mercy towards Arjuna and Uddhava while He was in the material world. Undoubtedly *Bhagavad-gītā* was spoken by the Lord on the Battlefield of Kurukṣetra just to encourage Arjuna to fight, and yet to complete the transcendental knowledge of *Bhagavad-gītā*, the Lord instructed Uddhava. The Lord wanted Uddhava to fulfill His mission and disseminate knowledge which He had not spoken even in *Bhagavad-gītā*."

From this we can understand that although *Uddhava-gītā* contains instructions similar to those imparted to Arjuna on the battlefield of Kurukṣetra, it also contains very confidential teachings that are not available even in *Bhagavad-gītā*. The five truths that embody the teachings of *Bhagavad-gītā*—*īśvara* (the Supreme Lord), *jīva* (the living entities), *prakṛti* (material nature), *kāla* (time), and *karma* (activities)—are fully elaborated upon in the *Uddhava-gītā*.

The Vedic literature offers us many *gītās*, or songs. There are the *Gītā Govinda*, *Venu-gītā*, *Bhramara-gītā*, *Gopi-gītā*, *Avanti-gītā*, *Bhagavad-gītā*, *Uddhava-gītā* and many more. All of these *gītās* have one thing in common: they are either songs of the Lord Himself, or of His devotees. In either case, the purpose of these songs is to invoke our forgotten eternal loving relationship with the Supreme Lord. Thus, the songs found in the Vedic literature are not like the ordinary songs of this material world, which are compared to the croaking of frogs, simply inviting the snake of death.

Near the end of Lord Kṛṣṇa's manifested pastimes in this material world five thousand years ago, the demigods, headed by Brahmā and Śiva, went to see Him at Dvaraka. At that time, they submitted this appeal:

"My dear Lord, previously we had requested You to remove the burden of the earth. O unlimited Personality of Godhead, that request has now been fulfilled. You killed innumerable demons in order to protect Your devotees, and You re-established the religious principles that had been forgotten in the course of time. You have certainly broadcast Your glories throughout the world, so that everyone can easily become purified simply by hearing about You. Descending into the dynasty of King Yadu, You have manifested Your unique transcendental form, and for the benefit of the entire universe, You have executed magnanimous transcendental pastimes. My dear Lord, pious and saintly persons, who, in the age of Kali, hear and chant narrations of Your transcendental pastimes, will easily cross over the dense darkness of that terrible age. O Supreme Personality of Godhead, O my Lord, You have descended into the Yadu dynasty, and thus You have spent one hundred and twenty-five autumns with Your devotees. My dear Lord, there is nothing remaining for Your Lordship to do on behalf of the demigods. O Lord, You are the basis of everything and if You so desire, then kindly return to Your own abode in the spiritual world."

Lord Śrī Kṛṣṇa replied, "I have very well understood your prayers. I have certainly executed My duty of removing the burden of the earth, but if I depart for My own abode at this time, the members of the Yadu dynasty will constitute another great burden. Therefore, before I depart from this world, I shall arrange for the withdrawal of the Yadu dynasty."

Thereafter, Lord Kṛṣṇa inspired Durvāsā Muṇi and other sages to curse the members of the Yadu dynasty, so that while quarrelling with each other, they would be annihilated. Lord Kṛṣṇa then met the elder members of the Yadu dynasty and informed them, "Because of the curse of the *brahmaṇas*, I see many inauspicious omens foreboding great disturbances and destruction. We should therefore go to Prabhāsa-tīrṭha, which is a very sacred place. There, we will be able to counteract the ill effects of all our sinful activities by satisfying the *brāhmaṇas* with gifts of charity."

Then, in obedience to the Lord's desire, the members of the Yadu dynasty went to Prabhāsa-tīrṭha, and a fire sacrifice was performed. At that time the men of the Yadu dynasty drank an intoxicating beverage that made them forget everything, even the identities of their mothers, brothers, fathers, children, and friends. Being intoxicated, by the will of the Lord, they fought with each other, and the result was the annihilation of the Yadu dynasty. Actually, the annihilation of the Yadu dynasty was a display of the Lord's illusory energy, *maya*. The Yādavas are eternal associates of the Lord, and are therefore eternally liberated souls. When He had contemplated winding up His pastimes within the material world, the Lord considered how, in His absence, the members of the Yadu dynasty would suffer greatly in separation from Him. It is for this reason that the Lord arranged for their return to His supreme abode before His own departure from the material world.

Thereafter Lord Balarāma appeared in His form Śeṣa Nāga and departed from this world. Lord Śrī Kṛṣṇa then sat underneath a banyan tree, meditating upon Himself. At that time, Uddhava came before Him and prayed, "My dear Lord, I know that You want to return to Your eternal abode in the spiritual sky. I cannot bear to live without You, and so please take me with You."

Lord Śrī Kṛṣṇa replied, "There is something remaining for you to do on My behalf in this world, and so you must stay here for some time. I will now disclose to you the most confidential understanding of religious principles, whereby even a blind man can easily follow the path and ultimately attain pure love for Me. After understanding this most confidential subject matter, it will be your duty to impart it to the sages residing at Badarikāśrama, headed by Nara-Nārāyaṇa Ṛṣi."

The reason for the Lord's descent into the material world was revealed by the Lord Himself in the *Bhagavad-gītā* (4.9):

yadā yadā hi dharmasya glānir bhavati bhārata
abhyutthānam adharmasya tadātmānaṁ sṛjāmy aham

Whenever and wherever there is a decline in religious practice, O descendant of Bharata, and a predominant rise of irreligion—at that time I descend Myself.

The Lord executed His will Himself, as well as through the agency of His dear devotees. It is explained by the Lord in the *Bhagavad-gītā* (4.3) that only His pure devotees are fit to receive His revelation and pass it on to others:

sa evāyaṁ mayā te 'dya yogaḥ proktaḥ purātanaḥ
bhakto 'si me sakhā ceti rahasyaṁ hy etad uttamam

That very ancient science of the relationship with the Supreme is today told by Me to you because you are My devotee as well as My friend and can therefore understand the transcendental mystery of this science.

The Lord had already delivered the science of the Supreme to His dear friend and devotee, Arjuna. Now, before enacting His pastime of disappearance from the material world, He desired to deliver more confidential understandings, and He considered Śrī Uddhava to be the fit candidate for receiving these instructions. The unique qualification of Śrī Uddhava was revealed by the Lord Himself in a verse of the *Uddhava-gītā*:

na tathā me priyatama ātma-yonir na śaṅkaraḥ
na ca saṅkarṣaṇo na śrīr naivātmā ca yathā bhavān

No one is as dear to Me as you, O Uddhava, not My son Brahmā, not Śiva who was born out of My very body, not My brother Saṅkarṣaṇa, not Lakṣmī, My consort, who dwells eternally on My chest. Even My own body is not as dear to Me as you are.

asmāl lokād uparate mayi jñānaṁ mad-āśrayam
arhaty uddhava evāddhā sampraty ātmavatāṁ varaḥ

Now I shall leave the vision of this mundane world, and I see that Uddhava, the foremost of My devotees, is the only one who can be directly entrusted with knowledge about Me.

His Divine Grace A. C. Bhaktivedanta Swami Prabhupada commented on this verse as follow: "*Jñānaṁ mad-āśrayam* is significant in this verse. Transcendental knowledge has three departmental divisions, namely knowledge of impersonal Brahman, knowledge of the all-pervading Supersoul and knowledge of the Personality of Godhead. Out of the three, transcendental knowledge of the Personality of Godhead has special significance and is known as *bhagavat-tattva-vijñāna*, specific knowledge of the Personality of Godhead. This specific knowledge is realized by pure devotional service and no other means. *Bhagavad-gītā* (18.55) confirms this: *bhaktyā mām abhijānāti yāvān yaś cāsmi tattvataḥ*. 'Only persons engaged in devotional service can factually know the transcendental position of the Lord.' Uddhava was considered to be the best amongst all devotees of that time, and therefore he was directly instructed by the Lord's grace, so that people might take advantage of Uddhava's knowledge after the disappearance of the Lord from the vision of the world. This is one of the reasons why Uddhava was advised to go to Badarikāśrama, where the Lord is personally represented by the Nara-Nārāyaṇa Deity."

As Uddhava was being instructed by the Lord in this most confidential understanding of the science of the Supreme, he posed the following question:

"The entire world is entangled in household-life. How can the worlds' population be liberated and develop attachment for You."

The Lord knew that soon after His departure the earth would be consumed by the powerful effects of Kali-yuga, and so He advised His dear devotee not to remain in household life, but instead take to a life of renunciation and go to a place in the Himalayas where great sages reside.

One might ask, "Why was Uddhava instructed to renounce the material world and go to the forest? After all, he was already a liberated devotee and a dear associate of the Lord."

The answer is that just as Arjuna was put into illusion on the battlefield of Kuruksetra so that the Lord could speak the *Bhagavad-gītā* to him, and thus to the entire world, similarly, Uddhava was advised to stay in this world after the Lord's departure, just so that he could deliver these final and most confidential instructions to the sages at Badarikāśrama, and thus to the entire world.

This conversation between the Lord and His dear devotee has been appropriately named *Uddhava-gītā*, although Lord Krsna is the speaker and Uddhava is the listener of the divine song. *Uddhava-gītā* begins by citing an ancient conversation that took place between Māharāja Yadu and a wandering mendicant, who, although naked, appeared quite healthy and self-satisfied.

The *Śrīmad Bhāgavatam* (1.2.6) reveals how one can be happy in this world:

sa vai pumsam paro dharmo yato bhaktir adhoksaje
ahaituky apratihata yayatma suprasidati

The supreme occupation for all humanity is that by which men can attain to loving devotional service unto the transcendent Lord. Such devotional service must be unmotivated and uninterrupted to completely satisfy the self."

Such a self-satisfied person always engages in remembering Lord Śrī Kṛṣṇa's transcendental pastimes. Yadu Māharāja offered his respects to the contented and naked wandering mendicant and said, "I would like to know something. You are naked and you have no possessions. You do not beg for your subsistence, and you roam freely throughout the world. How is it that you look so happy and healthy? I want to know about this."

In response, the naked sage explained how he had attained the state of self-realization by accepting twenty-four teachers. By observing their characteristics, he had attained his exalted spiritual status as an unattached and self-satisfied person.

Uddhava-gītā contains unparalleled instructions of the Lord that are not found anywhere else in this world. Many subjects were briefly discussed by Lord Kṛṣṇa when He spoke the *Bhagavad-gītā* to Arjuna. In the *Uddhava-gītā* these subjects are dealt with more elaborately, and they are explained in a way that they can be practically applied. We can understand that although Lord Kṛṣṇa spoke *Bhagavad-gītā* on the battlefield of Kurukśetra in just about forty-five minutes, He spoke to Uddhava while comfortably seated beneath a banyan tree and thus was able to impart more detailed and confidential instructions. Being at ease, Uddhava was free to pose numerous technical questions on a variety of subject matters pertaining to the perfection of spiritual life, and the Lord replied without constraints.

It is our great fortune to be able to present the *Uddhava-gītā*, which is contained within the Eleventh Canto of *Śrīmad-Bhāgavatam*, as a separate book. Eleventh Canto of *Śrīmad-Bhāgavatam* has been described as the crown on the head of the Lord. *Śrīmad-Bhāgavatam* is the literary incarnation of the Supreme Personality of Godhead, and beginning the study of that great literature with the First Canto is considered to be meditation upon the lotus feet of the Lord.

This present edition presents the commentaries of two great Vaiṣṇava masters in our disciplic succession—that of Śrīla Viśvanātha Cakravartī Ṭhākura and that of Śrīla

Bhaktisiddhānta Sarasvatī Ṭhākura, the spiritual master of His Divine Grace A. C. Bhaktivedanta Swami Prabhupāda, who revealed Lord Kṛṣṇa to the entire world while distributing His sacred teachings, culminating in the *Uddhava-gītā*. Both these great Vaiṣṇava masters, Śrīla Viśvanātha Cakravartī Ṭhākura and Śrīla Bhaktisiddhānta Sarasvatī Ṭhākura, need no introduction as their names speak volumes for the followers of Śrī Caitanya Mahāprabhu. They played prominent roles in the movement to propagate the teachings of Lord Kṛṣṇa and Lord Caitanya throughout the modern world.

Although I am a most insignificant creature, I pray that the publication of this book will bring delight to the dear devotees of the Lord, and shed some enlightenment upon the bewildered people of this world. In this way, I hope to be greatly benefited.

Hoping to remain the servant of the servant of those who are aspiring to be the servants of the Lord.

Īśvara dāsa.

Completed in Śrī Māyāpur Dhām, Rāma Navami, 2007.

Chapter 1

Lord Kṛṣṇa Instructs Uddhava

CHAPTER SUMMARY

This chapter describes how Uddhava requested the Lord to grant him permission to go back to Godhead, and how in response, the Lord suggested that he take to the renounced order of life. It also deals with the *avadhūta*'s description of twenty-four spiritual masters.

After hearing the prayerful request of Uddhava, Śrī Kṛṣṇa revealed to him His desire to return to His eternal abode since the purpose of His appearance in this world had been fulfilled. The Lord also indicated that soon after His disappearance, Kali will create great disturbances in the world. So Uddhava should take *sannyāsa*, fix his mind upon Him, and live in this temporary world without attachment, while acting as the benefactor of all living entities. Uddhava replied by saying that apart from devotees of the Lord, detachment from matter, which is the cause of spiritual advancement, is extremely difficult for those who are very attached to sense gratification. He requested the Lord to give him some instructions so that materialistic people who consider the body as the self could attain perfection.

Uddhava told the Lord that he had taken shelter of Him as the only instructor because He is free from all faults, omniscient, the Lord of Vaikuṇṭha, and the friend of all living entities. After hearing Uddhava's request, the Supreme Lord said that the spirit soul is himself can act as his spiritual master and thus the human form of life is very dear to Him. In this connection, the Lord related to Uddhava a conversation between an *avadhūta* and King Yadu that took place long ago.

Once, King Yadu, the son of Yayāti, happened to see an *avadhūta* who was happily wandering about here and there, sometimes acting like a materialist, sometimes like a madman, and sometimes like one haunted by a ghost. When King Yadu asked the *avadhūta* about the cause of his ecstatic wanderings, he replied that he was traveling throughout the world as he liked, after having received instructions from twenty-four spiritual masters, such as the earth, air, sky, water, and fire. Due to these instructions, he was able to wander over the earth in a liberated condition of life.

From the earth, he learned how to become steady. He also learnt from the mountains and trees of the earth how to do good to others—how to live in this world only for the sake of other's benefit.

From the life air, he learned how to remain satisfied with whatever is easily achieved for keeping the body and soul together. In addition, from the external air, he learned how to remain aloof from bodily sense enjoyment.

From the sky, he learned that the spirit soul, which is all-pervading throughout the body, is always pure and free from any contamination.

From water, he learned how to remain naturally pure and sanctified.

From fire, he learned to eat anything and yet not become contaminated. He also learnt that a charitable person will never face inauspiciousness. He learned that the spirit soul is that which illuminates every material body, and that the appearance and disappearance of the living entity at the times of birth and death is unseen.

From the moon, he learned how the material body develops and then dwindles.

From the sun, he learned how, despite remaining in contact with the objects of enjoyment, one can remain unentangled. He also learned to see how the spirit soul is unchangeable while the material body is simply a designation.

From the pigeon, he learned about the consequences of too much affection for one's family. A person who, in spite of receiving the human form of life, which is considered the gateway to liberation, becomes attached to family life like a pigeon, will certainly fall down, even though he has attained a superior platform after much struggle.

TEXT 1

श्रीभगवानुवाच
यदात्थमांमहाभागतच्चिकीर्षितमेवमे ।
ब्रह्माभवोलोकपालाःस्वर्वासं मेऽभिकाङ्क्षिणः ॥१॥

śrī-bhagavān uvāca
yad āttha māṁ mahā-bhāga tac-cikīrṣitam eva me
brahmā bhavo loka-pālāḥ svar-vāsaṁ me 'bhikāṅkṣiṇaḥ

The Supreme Lord said: O most fortunate Uddhava, what you have ascertained about My desire to destroy the Yadu dynasty and then return to Vaikuṇṭha is correct. This is actually My desire, and Brahmā, Śiva, and the other demigods are praying for Me to return to My abode in Vaikuṇṭha.

[1]COMMENTARY BY ŚRĪLA VIŚVANĀTHA CAKRAVARTĪ ṬHĀKURA

The word *svarvāsa* in this verse means "residence in Vaikuṇṭha."

PURPORT BY ŚRĪLA BHAKTISIDDHĀNTA SARASVATĪ ṬHĀKURA

The word *svarvāsa* refers to the planets where the demigods reside. Although Lord Viṣṇu is sometimes counted among the demigods, His residence is in Vaikuṇṭha. The heavenly planets created by the Lord's external potency, *maya*, are different from His abode. Lord Viṣṇu is the supreme controller of all controllers. From Him all the demigods have manifested, but they are under the control of *maya*, whereas Lord Viṣṇu is the controller of *maya*. The Supreme Lord, Viṣṇu, is the root of all existence and the material world is just a dim reflection of His eternal, spiritual abode. He is one without a second and the original source of all spiritual and material manifestations. Lord Viṣṇu is a plenary expansion of Lord Kṛṣṇa, the original source of all *viṣṇu-tattva* and *jīva-tattva* expansions.

TEXT 2

मयानिष्पादितंह्यत्रदेवकार्यमशेषतः ।
यदर्थमवतीर्णोऽहमंशेनब्रह्मणार्थितः ॥२॥

mayā niṣpāditaṁ hy atra deva-kāryam aśeṣataḥ
yad-artham avatīrṇo 'ham aṁśena brahmaṇārthitaḥ

The mission for which I descended on this earth, along with My plenary portion, Balarāma—the noble act of diminishing the burden of the earth because of the prayerful request of Brahmā—has now been fulfilled.

COMMENTARY

The world *aṁśena* means, "with Balarāma."

---

1 From now on, all commentaries are by Śrīla Viśvanātha Cakravartī Ṭhākura, and all purports are by Śrīla Bhaktisiddhānta Sarasvatī Ṭhākura.

PURPORT

The word *aṁśena* generally means "incomplete." It indicates an incompatible situation within the material kingdom. But, in the realm of spiritual variegatedness, this word refers to the inseparable portions of the Supreme Lord.

TEXT 3

कुलंवैशापनिर्दग्धंनंक्ष्यत्यन्योन्यविग्रहात् ।
समुद्रःसप्तमेह्येनांपुरींचप्लावयिष्यति ॥३॥

kulaṁ vai śāpa-nirdagdhaṁ naṅkṣyaty anyonya-vigrahāt
samudraḥ saptame hy enāṁ purīṁ ca plāvayiṣyati

Now, as a result of the *brāhmaṇas'* curse, the Yadu dynasty will be annihilated in a fratricidal war, and on the seventh day from today, the ocean will overflood the city of Dvārakā.

TEXT 4

यर्ह्येवायंमयात्यक्तोलोकोऽयंनष्टमङ्गलः ।
भविष्यत्यचिरात्साधोकलिनापिनिराकृतः ॥४॥

yarhy evāyaṁ mayā tyakto loko 'yaṁ naṣṭa-maṅgalaḥ
bhaviṣyaty acirāt sādho kalināpi nirākṛtaḥ

O saintly Uddhava, I will soon abandon this earth. Thereafter, being overwhelmed by the age of Kali, the earth will become bereft of all piety.

PURPORT

Simply by the advent of Kṛṣṇa, the entire world became filled with all kinds of auspiciousness. Wherever there is no existence of the Supreme Lord, the path of argument is prominent and the path of disciplic succession is attacked. Śrī Kṛṣṇa, who enjoys variegated spiritual pastimes, is an ocean of nectarean mellows. Wherever a relationship with Kṛṣṇa is absent, useless mental speculation becomes prominent, which creates quarrel due to the influence of Kali. If the existence of the Supreme Lord is not realized, people who are deceived by the illusory energy of the Lord are made to run after the path of mental speculation and dry argument.

TEXT 5

नवस्तव्यंत्वयैवेहमयात्यक्तेमहीतले ।
जनोऽभद्ररुचिर्भद्रभविष्यतिकलौयुगे ॥५॥

na vastavyaṁ tvayaiveha mayā tyakte mahī-tale
jano 'bhadra-rucir bhadra bhaviṣyati kalau yuge

My dear Uddhava, you should not remain on the earth after I return to My eternal abode in the spiritual sky because Kali-yuga will influence human beings so that they will become accustomed to performing all kinds of sinful activities. For this reason, you should not remain here.

PURPORT

Human beings in the age of Kali are very interested in pursuing sinful propensities because they are unaware of the advent of the Supreme Lord. So, the devotees of the Supreme Lord, who are sober and gentle, do not wish to live in this world, which is covered by the darkness of ignorance and is devoid of a loving relationship with the Supreme Lord. One of the symptoms of a devotee is that he takes pleasure in residing at a place where the Lord enacts His pastimes. Thus, Lord Kṛṣṇa advised Uddhava not to remain on earth in Kali-yuga.

TEXT 6

त्वंतुसर्वंपरित्यज्य स्नेहंस्वजनबन्धुञु ।
मय्यावेश्यमनःसंयक् समदृग्विचरस्वगाम् ॥६॥

tvaṁ tu sarvaṁ parityajya snehaṁ sva-jana-bandhuṣu
mayy āveśya manaḥ saṁyak sama-dṛg vicarasva gām

Now, you should completely give up all attachment to your friends and relatives and fix your mind on Me. Thus being always conscious of Me, you should observe all things with equal vision while wandering throughout the world.

COMMENTARY

Lord Kṛṣṇa thought as follows: "While remaining on the earth, I satisfied the desires of all those who sincerely wanted to see Me. I married many thousands of women, headed by Rukmiṇī, whom I had kidnapped, and I killed many demons in various places and by various contrivances. I attended the religious functions organized by

My friends and relatives, so that I have performed many wonderful pastimes for the satisfaction of My devotees."

"I gave My personal association to all the great devotees in the lower planets. Just to please My mother, Devakī, I returned her six dead sons, who had been killed by Kaṁsa, I went to Sutala and blessed My great devotee, Bali Mahārāja. To return the dead son of My spiritual master, Sāndīpani Muni, I personally went to Yamarāja, and thus gave him My audience. I even benedicted the residents of heaven with My personal association when I went there to take the *pārijāta* flower for My wife, Satyabhāmā. I traveled to Mahā-vaikuṇṭhaloka, to recover the dead children of a *brāhmaṇa*. In this way, all the devotees who sincerely desired to see Me received the fulfillment of their desires."

"However, Nara-Nārāyaṇa Ṛṣi and the great sages who reside with Him at Badarikāśrama, although hoping to see Me, never had their desire fulfilled. I have been on this earth for 125 years and so the duration of My stay has reached its limit. Being busy with My pastimes, I had no time to see these great sages. And yet, Uddhava is almost as good as Me. He is a pure devotee who has been awarded My transcendental opulence. I therefore consider him to be the right person for Me to send to Badarikāśrama. I shall impart transcendental knowledge to Uddhava, so that anyone who receives it from him will become detached from material existence. He is the right person to impart this knowledge to the sages at Badarikāśrama. He can teach them the procedures for rendering devotional service unto Me. Loving devotional service rendered to Me is the most valuable treasure available in this world. By receiving this knowledge, the desires of Nara-Nārāyaṇa and the other great sages will be fulfilled."

"The great souls who have surrendered unto Me are enriched with transcendental knowledge and detachment from the material world. Sometimes, being fully engaged in My devotional service, they may seemingly forget Me, but a pure devotee who possesses love for Me will always be protected by his sincere devotion. Even if such a devotee unexpectedly meets with death while forgetting to keep his mind fixed upon Me, his love for Me is so strong that it will give him protection so that he will eventually attain My lotus feet, which are beyond the vision of materialistic persons. Uddhava is My pure devotee because he can never give up My association."

While contemplating in this way, Śrī Kṛṣṇa inspired Śrīmān Uddhava to inquire about transcendental knowledge, renunciation, and devotional service to Him. He said to Uddhava, "You should give up affection for your relatives and friends in the Yadu dynasty." This affection of Uddhava towards the members of the Yadu dynasty are of two types.

1. Bodily relationship with the Yadus.
2. Relationship in regard to Kṛṣṇa.

Among the two, Uddhava is advised give up the former. The Lord will explain to Uddhava how to give up this attachment. As far as the latter relationship is concerned, Uddhava is incapable of giving it up. This relationship is not condemned. Uddhava is certainly aware of Kṛṣṇa's mentality.

PURPORT

The devotees of the Lord are equipoise because they see all material objects in relationship with Kṛṣṇa. Those whose hearts are steady do not become entangled in material affection, in the form of aversion to Kṛṣṇa, and thus do not consider their nondevotee relatives as the object of their sense gratification. Since those persons, who see everything in relation to Kṛṣṇa, wander about in this world while giving up the urges of the mind, speech, and body, they are fit to be called devotees of the Lord, or Gosvāmīs. The purport of the *brahmabhūta prasannātmā* verse of the *Bhagavad-gītā* is the perfect example of seeing all objects with equal vision.

TEXT 7

यदिदंमनसावाचाचक्षुर्भ्यांश्रवणादिभिः ।
नश्वरंगृह्यमाणंचविद्धि मायामनोमयाम् ॥७॥

yad idaṁ manasā vācā cakṣurbhyāṁ śravaṇādibhiḥ
naśvaraṁ gṛhyamāṇaṁ caviddhi māyā-mano-mayam

My dear Uddhava, know for certain that this material world which you perceive through your mind, speech, eyes, ears and other senses is an illusory creation that one imagines to be real due to the influence of *Maya.* **You should know that all of the objects of the material senses are temporary.**

COMMENTARY

The question may be raised, "What kind of equal vision should Uddhava have?" In reply to this, Lord Kṛṣṇa said, "O Uddhava, this material world, which is the object of the senses, such as the mind, speech, eyes, and ears, is temporary and perishable."

PURPORT

Any information received from this material body, which consists of the five knowledge-acquiring senses, the five working senses, and the mind, is limited and destroyed by time because of its temporary nature. The spirit soul coming in contact with the material body develops material designations and desires the insignificant enjoyment that is associated with this temporary material world. As a result of this misconception, he is bereft of the service of the Supreme Lord.

TEXT 8

पुंसोऽयुक्तस्यनानार्थोभ्रमःसगुणदोषभाक्।
कर्माकर्मविकर्मेतिगुणदोषधियोभिदा ॥८॥

puṁso 'yuktasya nānārtho bhramaḥ sa guṇa-doṣa-bhāk
karmākarma-vikarmeti guṇa-doṣa-dhiyo bhidā

That person whose mind is bewildered by illusion perceives many differences in value and meaning among material objects. Thus, one engages constantly on the platform of material good and evil and is bound by such conceptions. Absorbed in material duality, such a person contemplates the performance of compulsory duties, nonperformance of such duties, and the performance of forbidden activities.

COMMENTARY

An elaboration of the topics described in the previous verse is being given here. The living entities sometimes fall into the trap of duality. They think: "This is prescribed, therefore better; that is faulty, therefore inferior." This is the conception of ignorant people. For the fallen souls, what is superior and what is inferior? King Citraketu has said that all objects in this material world are insignificant. Therefore, it is difficult to ascertain which one is a curse, which one is a favor, which one is heaven, which one is hell, which one is happiness, and which one is distress. The faults and qualities of objects are attributed to them by the *Vedas* when it says that prescriptions are qualities and prohibitions are faults. This is a fact. The *Vedas* have described these subject matters for the benefit of the people who are in ignorance. Karma refers to those activities which are approved by the *Vedas*, *akarma* means to not perform those activities, and *vikarma* refers to those activities which are prohibited by the *Vedas*. Those who find faults and qualities are certainly ignorant.

PURPORT

Mental speculators distance themselves from the consideration of the Absolute Truth and engage in enjoying various sense objects, being bereft of the service of the nondual substance, the son of the king of Vraja. That is not the constitutional propensity of the spirit soul. That is the illusion of the unsuccessful yogis. Being controlled by the conception of faults and qualities, such people accept a few temporary activities as prescriptions, and a few activities as prohibition. In this way, they attribute superiority and inferiority to various objects. But, if all objects are seen in relation to Kṛṣṇa, such distinctions will not arise. In order to attain liberation from such conceptions that are based on finding faults and attributing qualities, the topic of *brahma-gāyatrī* has been described. Spiritual knowledge means knowledge with practical application. If one does not know the mystery of this, then he is sure to fall into illusion. Thus, he attributes faults and qualities to different persons and addresses them as *satkarmī*, *vikarmī*, and *kukarmī*.

TEXT 9

तस्माद्युक्तेन्द्रियग्रामोयुक्तचित्तइदम्जगत् ।
आत्मनीक्षस्वविततमात्मानंमय्यधीश्वरे ॥९॥

tasmād yuktendriya-grāmo yukta-citta idam jagat
ātmanīkṣasva vitatam ātmānaṁ mayy adhīśvare

Therefore, you should control your mind and senses and see this material world, which is full of happiness and distress, as situated within the self, and also see that this individual self is situated within Me, the Supreme Personality of Godhead.

COMMENTARY

Therefore, you should regulate your senses and understand that this material world, which is full of happiness and distress, is situated within the living entity as their object of enjoyment. You should also see this material world, as well as the spirit soul, as being under the full subordination of the Supersoul, which is one of My features.

PURPORT

By executing devotional service, all of one's senses become properly engaged. Then only can one realize that Kṛṣṇa is the controller of all, and that He is situated within everybody as the Supersoul. At that time, all the senses become engaged in the service of the master of the senses and thus become free from material designations. Impersonalists try to cease all sense enjoyment, thinking that in the perfectional stage, the living entities become inert. However, such self-abnegation simply denies one the opportunity to realize the Absolute Truth with transcendental senses. The fact is that the master of the senses, Kṛṣṇa, who is the only proper object of all the senses, is realized by rendering devotional service with all the senses.

Because the conditioned souls have rejected their constitutional position, and because they want to enjoy without God in this material world, which is created by the illusory energy of the Lord, they fall into bewilderment, thinking themselves as something other than eternal servants of the Supreme Lord, or as instruments for the Lord's service. That is why Śrī Kṛṣṇa, the Supreme Personality of Godhead, instructed His pure devotee, Uddhava, just as Prahlāda instructed his father, Hinranyakaśipu.

Attached householders, who do not see how everything is related to Kṛṣṇa, are perpetually deceived so that they cannot see the Supreme Lord as He is, because they are driven by their uncontrolled senses. Lord Viṣṇu is the ultimate goal of all the senses. The conditioned soul's propensity to enjoy the material senses is nothing but the spirit of enjoyment that is averse to devotional service.

When Kṛṣṇa, the son of the king of Vraja, who is one without a second, becomes the only object of all the senses then the temporary propensity of the material senses is checked and the spiritual propensity for serving the Supreme Lord with purified senses is awakened. Because there are no longer any material designations in that state of perfection, the distinction between the body and the self, between the form and the owner of the form, and between the qualities and the owner of qualities, cannot be experienced.

The Supreme Lord is the only object of worship for everyone. He is the object of service for everyone and the object of service of all the senses of everyone. The abomination in the form of unwanted conceptions that bring about inauspiciousness in the variegated activities of this material world cannot influence the servant of the Supreme Personality of Godhead, Vrajendra-nandana. On the spiritual platform, the considerations of *śuddha-dvaita*, *dvaitādvaita*, *viśiṣṭādvaita* and *śuddhādvaita* appear to be situated on the same platform so that the *ekāyana* system is not obstructed. When the philosophy of *acintyabhedābheda* is revealed, the spirit souls are not seen as distinct from the associates of the Lord who assist Him in His pastimes. On that platform, the pure spirit soul thinks himself as a servant of Kṛṣṇa and thus engages in His devotional service. Unless one sees all objects in relation to Kṛṣṇa, there is bound to be inauspiciousness. That is why the devotees of the Lord consider uninterrupted service to Kṛṣṇa as the constitutional and awakened propensity of the spirit soul.

People who cannot realize the Supreme Lord, the enjoyer of transcendental pastimes, become separated from Lord Acyuta and thus become faithful to temporary and imaginary objects. This is due to not understanding the essential characteristics of the Supreme Lord. In order to open the eyes of such blind people, the Lord, as the supreme instructor, expressed His desire to guide Uddhava, and other similar servants of Uddhava, who have no interest in the *karma-kāṇḍa* system of the *Vedas*, by giving them invaluable instructions.

TEXT 10

ज्ञानविज्ञानसंयुक्तआत्मभूतःशरीरिणाम् ।
अत्मानुभवतुष्टात्मानान्तरायैर्विहन्यसे ॥१०॥

jñāna-vijñāna-saṁyukta ātma-bhūtaḥ śarīriṇām
atmānubhava-tuṣṭātmā nāntarāyair vihanyase

Being fully endowed with conclusive knowledge of the *Vedas*, and having realized the ultimate purpose of such knowledge in practice, you will be able to perceive the pure self and become self-satisfied. In this way, you will become dear to all living beings, headed by the demigods, and you will never be obstructed by any impediment.

COMMENTARY

If one does not act with a mind fixed on Kṛṣṇa, then the demigods will create obstacles. This is being explained here. The word *jñāna* means, "ascertaining the purport of the *Vedas*." The word *vijñāna* means, "to realize that purport." One must possess both. When one is self-realized, one automatically becomes satisfied. In that condition, one becomes the object of affection of those who have demigod bodies. This is confirmed in the *Vedas* wherein it is stated, *ātmāhyeṣaṁ sa bhavatīti*, "such a soul is very joyful." Thereafter, the demigods no longer create any disturbance.

PURPORT

Due to lack of knowledge regarding the Supreme Personality of Godhead, Vrajendra-nandana, who is one without a second, the impersonalists cannot understand that both the object of worship and the worshipers are situated in the eternal spiritual kingdom. But, because the eternal devotees of Kṛṣṇa, who accept the personal form of the Lord and who are expert in seeing spiritual variegatedness, are blissful due to realizing their service to Kṛṣṇa, they become liberated from the conception of seeing the difference between the body and the owner of the body. In such a state, the insignificance of the four objectives of life is exposed. Those who are devoid of love for Hari, and who glorify the concept of impersonalism, which is a snare of Hari's illusory energy, *maya*, face an impediment in their path of self-realization. As a result, they bring about their own ruination, as did Kaṁsa, Jarāsandha, and so on. Theoretical knowledge can be purified when it is practically applied.

TEXT 11

दोषबुद्ध्योभयातीतोनिषेधान्ननिवर्तते ।
गुणबुद्ध्याचविहितंनकरोति यथार्भकः ॥११॥

doṣa-buddhyobhayātīto niṣedhān na nivartate
guṇa-buddhyā ca vihitaṁ na karoti yathārbhakaḥ

One who has attained the transcendental platform, beyond the influence of material dualities, such as good and evil, will automatically follow religious principles and avoid sinful acts. A self-realized soul acts in this way without separate endeavor, just like an innocent child, and not because he considers everything in terms of a materialistic conception of good and evil.

COMMENTARY

Less-intelligent people cannot act properly. Wise men, who are beyond the concept of finding faults and qualities, automatically give up activities that are prohibited by the scriptures, even though they no longer have such a dualistic outlook. And, they automatically act in a way that is approved by the scriptures. As an innocent child acts spontaneously and not under the influence of duality, the actions of a wise man are also spontaneous.

PURPORT

From the external point of view, an innocent child, not knowing the consequences of an action, may sometimes appear to reject sinful activities and be attracted to pious activities, as when a child spontaneously exhibits a generous nature. Similarly, transcendentalists do not become intoxicated by mundane knowledge. They are situated beyond the mentality of finding faults and qualities and realize that Kṛṣṇa alone is the object of service.

TEXT 12

सर्वभूतसुहृच्छान्तोज्ञानविज्ञाननिश्चयः ।
पश्यन्मदात्मकंविश्वंनविपद्येतवैपुनः ॥१२॥

sarva-bhūta-suhṛc chānto jñāna-vijñāna-niścayaḥ
paśyan mad-ātmakaṁ viśvaṁ na vipadyeta vai punaḥ

The self-realized souls who are firmly fixed in knowledge and realization, and who are equal to all living entities, know this material world as a manifestation of My energy, and thus do not again become entangled in the bondage of material existence.

PURPORT

Self-realized souls see all objects of this world to be related to Kṛṣṇa. They never fall into material existence on account of their spirit of enjoyment. They make friendship with all living entities, knowing them to be ingredients for Kṛṣṇa's worship. They are naturally peaceful and undisturbed because of their expertise in the field of knowledge and its practical application. No mundane temptation can distract their mind from the lotus feet of Kṛṣṇa. Those who fail to see this world as a house of happiness because of their unsuccessful attempt to enjoy this world, engage in fruitive activities to achieve material enjoyment. When they become disgusted with material enjoyment, they want to temporarily renounce such enjoyment. That is why Śrī Gaurasundara has instructed about *phalgu vairāgya* and *yukta vairāgya*, which are confidential purports of *Śrīmad-Bhāgavatam*, meant for the understanding of fortunate living entities.

TEXT 13

श्रीशुक उवाच
इत्यादिष्टोभागवत महाभागवतोनृप ।
उद्धवःप्रणिपत्याहतत्त्वंजिज्ञासुरच्युतम् ॥१३॥

śrī-śuka uvāca
ity ādiṣṭo bhāgavata mahā-bhāgavato nṛpa
uddhavaḥ praṇipatyāha tattvaṁ jijñāsur acyutam

Śrī Śukadeva Gosvāmī said: O King, after Lord Kṛṣṇa instructed Uddhava in this way, the mahā-bhāgavata, Uddhava, who had a desire to know the spiritual truth, offered obeisances to the Lord and spoke as follows.

TEXT 14

श्रीउद्धव उवाच
योगेशयोगविन्यासयोगात्मन्योगसम्भव ।
निःश्रेयसायमेप्रोक्तस्त्यागःसन्न्यासलक्षणः ॥१४॥

śrī-uddhava uvāca
yogeśa yoga-vinyāsa yogātman yoga-sambhava
niḥśreyasāya me proktas tyāgaḥ sannyāsa-lakṣaṇaḥ

Śrī Uddhava said: My dear Lord, You award the fruit of yoga, You are the knower of mystic yoga, You are the personification of yoga, and You are pleased by the execution of *bhakti-yoga*. For my ultimate benefit, You have explained to me the procedure for accepting the renounced order of life.

COMMENTARY

O my Lord, You are Yogeśvara because You are the controller of *karma-yoga*, *jñāna-yoga*, and *bhakti-yoga*. You are *yoga vinyāsa*, meaning that You are imparting to me the knowledge of yoga, although I am unqualified to receive it. O Yogātman, You are the personification of yoga. So, if I attain You, then I will attain all types of mystic yoga. Moreover, You will take birth in the house of a devotee because of his devotional service. Therefore, please award devotional service to me in a special way.

PURPORT

Uddhava has addressed Lord Kṛṣṇa in this verse as Yogeśa. Śrī Kṛṣṇa alone is the object of worship, and He alone is to be attained through the practice of devotional service. When one understands the characteristics of devotional service, one's propensity for enjoying mundane objects becomes vanquished.

Materialists are attached to hearing and chanting the topics of their wives and children. Learned scholars are attached to hearing and chanting the topics of scriptural debates. Yogīs are attached to the distress produced from controlling their life air. Ascetics are attached to their performance of austerities, and pseudo renunciates are attached to the cultivation of dry, speculative knowledge. But, the servants of Śrī Caitanya are always fixed in the path of *bhakti-yoga*. Because the devotees of the Lord have adopted the process of devotional service, which is inclusive of detachment, giving up other inferior attachments, they are real renunciates, or *yukta vairāgis*. That is why the Supreme Lord is addressed here as Yogeśa. Because the servants of Yogeśvara, like Uddhava, dovetail all other yoga processes in the execution of *bhakti-yoga*, the Lord is addressed here as *yoga-vinyāsa*.

Because the constitutional propensities of the living entities clearly manifest in the practice of *bhakti-yoga*, the Lord is called Yogātmā. In addition, because He is the source of all types of yoga, He is referred to as *yoga-sambhava*. Only persons who are situated in devotional service achieve the supreme benefit of life and thus are able to properly give up all non-devotional propensities. That is the most beneficial thing that can happen to a spirit soul. Śrī Kṛṣṇa had mercifully taught this *pāramahaṁsya-dharma*, in the form of *bhakti-yoga*, to Uddhava.

Renouncing the enjoyment of the fruits of one's karma and rejecting the fruits of *jñāna*, or the cultivation of impersonalism, cannot be the cause of the living entities' ultimate benefit because such activities are temporary and dependent. Those who have no interest in hearing the topics of the Supreme Lord are perpetually diverted from the transcendental mellows as a result of being misguided by different yoga processes, such as *haṭha-yoga*, *karma-yoga*, *rāja-yoga*, and *jñāna-yoga*. When mundane *rasa* displays prominence, then such people, in order to neutralize it, endeavor to practice different kinds of mystic yoga processes and thus are perpetually bereft of *bhakti-yoga*.

TEXT 15

त्यागोऽयंदुष्करोभूमन्कामानांविषयात्मभिः ।
सुतरांत्वयिसर्वात्मन्नभक्तैरितिमेमतिः ॥१५॥

tyāgo 'yaṁ duṣkaro bhūman kāmānāṁ viṣayātmabhiḥ
sutarāṁ tvayi sarvātmann abhaktair iti me matiḥ

My dear Lord, O Supersoul of all, I think that it is extremely difficult for those whose minds are attached to sense gratification, and who are bereft of devotion unto You, to renounce material desires.

COMMENTARY

If it is difficult to follow this process even for Your devotees whose minds are still attached to material enjoyment, then there is no doubt that it must be very difficult for the nondevotees.

PURPORT

Uddhava said: The devotees of the Supreme Lord never desire to accept anything that has not been first offered to the Lord. Therefore, apart from the ingredients of the Lord's service, it is natural for them to give up the desire for enjoying objects that are not related to the Lord. But, lusty nondevotees, who are busy collecting objects for sense gratification are fit to be called materialists because they have no propensity for the Lord's service. There is no possibility for such people to give up the desire for enjoying objects that are not related to the Lord. This is my opinion.

TEXT 16

सोऽहंममाहमितिमूढमतिर्विगाढस्त्वन्माययाविरचितात्मनिसानुबन्धे ।
तत्त्वञ्जसानिगदितंभवतायथाहंसंसाधयामिभगवन्नअनुशाधिभृत्यम् ॥१६॥

so 'haṁ mamāham iti mūḍha-matir vigāḍhas
tvan-māyayā viracitātmani sānubandhe
tat tv añjasā nigaditaṁ bhavatā yathāhaṁ
saṁsādhayāmi bhagavann anuśādhi bhṛtyam

My dear Lord, I am certainly foolish because I consider my body and bodily relations to be all and all, even though these things are simply products of Your illusory energy. Thus, I think, "I am this body and these relatives and possessions are mine." My Lord, please instruct Your foolish servant so that I can give up this illusion and surrender at Your lotus feet.

COMMENTARY

"My mind is absorbed in mundane conceptions because I am attached to my body, wife, and children, which are created by *maya*. The material body is just like a blind well. Therefore, it is my first duty to protect myself from that well. Then, the knowledge that will be gained by following the Lord's instructions will automatically follow." This is the sum and substance of this verse.

PURPORT

Those who are attacked by *nāmāparādha* in the form of maintaining the conception of "I and mine," pollute their real ego due to the influence of the illusory energy of the Lord of Vaikuṇṭha. At that time, they display no power to follow the instruction of the Supreme Lord because, due to lack of surrender, the living entities become bewildered by false ego. Due to the influence of false ego, the living entities become averse to the Supreme Lord and are then bound by the ropes of *maya*. On that platform, the constitutional position of the living entities becomes covered. In other words, their inclination towards the Lord's service slows down considerably. This is why Uddhava is praying to Kṛṣṇa to remain situated in the service propensity without deviation.

TEXT 17

सत्यस्यतेस्वदृश आत्मन आत्मनोऽन्यंवक्तारमीश विबुधेष्वपिनानुचक्षे ।
सर्वेविमोहितधियस्तवमाययेमेब्रह्मादयस्तनुभृतोबहिरर्थभावाः ॥१७॥

satyasya te sva-dṛśa ātmana ātmano 'nyaṁ
vaktāram īśa vibudheṣv api nānucakṣe
sarve vimohita-dhiyas tava māyayeme
brahmādayas tanu-bhṛto bahir-artha-bhāvāḥ

My dear Lord, You are the Supreme Personality of Godhead, and by Your mercy, You reveal Yourself to the hearts of Your pure devotees. Other than You, I do not see anyone who can impart to me perfect knowledge. You are the perfect teacher, and not the demigods in the heavenly planets. In fact, the demigods, even Lord Brahmā, are bewildered by Your illusory energy, maya. **The demigods are also conditioned souls who accept their material bodies and bodily expansions as ultimate reality.**

COMMENTARY

The word *satyasya* in this verse has been used in the dative case, which means that knowledge about the self has been produced from You because You are the basis of all time, place, and circumstances. You are the Supersoul and I am different from You.

PURPORT

Although the Supreme Lord is sometimes counted amongst the demigods, He is nevertheless the self-manifest Absolute Truth, the Supersoul, and the eternal Personality of Godhead. Although partial power of supremacy of the Supreme Lord is present in the Vaiṣṇava demigods, the moment they fail to display an eagerness for the service of the Supreme Lord, they fall down from the worship of the Lord and plunge into the ocean of forgetfulness. Therefore, if one is to consider the position of the demigods, who are devoid of service to the Supreme Lord, one will find that they lack self-manifest complete knowledge. From this, one can understand that the Supersoul, Lord Viṣṇu, is separate from the living entities, such as the demigods. Demigods like Brahmā, who are approachable by human knowledge, have a difference between their body and their self. All of them are bewildered by the illusory energy of Viṣṇu and consider the objects of the external world as the goal of their lives. The worshipers of the demigods, who are attracted to the material sense objects—sound, touch, form, taste, and smell—are similarly covered like their respective objects of worship, by the illusory energy of the Lord, *Maya*. Aversion to the service of the Supreme Lord is the proof of their non-devotional endeavors. This statement of Uddhava is greatly admired by the servants of Śrī Caitanya. They do not consider Śrī Caitanyadeva, who is nondifferent from the son of the king of Vraja, to be merely a spiritual master, like Ṛṣabhadeva or Vyāsadeva.

TEXT 18

तस्माद्भवन्तमनवद्यमनन्तपारं सर्वज्ञमीश्वरमकुण्ठविकुण्ठधिष्ण्यम् ।
निर्विण्णधीरहमु हे वृजिनाभितप्तो नारायणं नरसखं शरणं प्रपद्ये ॥१८॥

tasmād bhavantam anavadyam ananta-pāraṁ
sarva-jñam īśvaram akuṇṭha-vikuṇṭha-dhiṣṇyam
nirviṇṇa-dhīr aham u he vṛjinābhitapto
nārāyaṇaṁ nara-sakhaṁ śaraṇaṁ prapadye

Therefore, O Lord, feeling weary of material life and tormented by its distresses, I now surrender unto You because You are the perfect master. You are the same Nārāyaṇa, who is beyond the influence of material time and space. You are the unlimited, all-knowing Supreme Personality of Godhead, whose spiritual abode in Vaikuṇṭha is free from all disturbances. You are free from all faults and You are the sole benefactor of all living entities.

COMMENTARY

"O Lord, I am especially tortured by material miseries. Therefore, I surrender unto You."

Sometimes a person may possess all good qualities yet may commit sinful activities. So, how to give up all material association is being described here. The Lord is unlimited or He who has no end. In other words, the Lord is beyond the influence of material time and space.

"Some people are ungrateful but You are not so. You are omniscient. Some people cannot give protection but You are not like that. You are the supreme controller. Some people are a source of inauspiciousness but You are not like that. Your abode of Vaikuṇṭha is free from anxiety, and the material time factor. You are Nārāyaṇa. You are the supreme shelter of even the *puruṣāvatāras*. You are most compassionate because You are the ever well-wisher of all living entities. You appear in this world simply to exhibit Your mercy to the conditioned souls."

PURPORT

O Lord, the demigods fulfill our desires. Because the demigods who supply our necessities are not omniscient, rather they are limited living entities of this material world created by *Maya*, You are actually the true friend of all living entities. Because I have a tendency to commit sinful activities and I am greedy, I have no other alternative than to take shelter at Your lotus feet.

TEXT 19

श्रीभगवानुवाच
प्रायेणमनुजालोके लोकतत्त्वविचक्षणाः ।
समुद्धरन्तिह्यात्मानमात्मनैवाशुभाशयात् ॥१९॥

śrī-bhagavān uvāca
prāyeṇa manujā loke loka-tattva-vicakṣaṇāḥ
samuddharanti hy ātmānam ātmanaivāśubhāśayāt

The Supreme Lord said: Generally, persons who are able to understand the truth of this material world try to elevate themselves beyond such a life of inauspiciousness, which simply consists of gross sense gratification.

COMMENTARY

Lord Śrī Kṛṣṇa replied to Uddhava: You are thinking yourself to be a fool. But, I do not find a wise man like you among all learned persons. It is seen in this world that some people who are inferior to you attain spiritual knowledge on the strength of their own intelligence even without accepting instructions from their spiritual master. But, you are the crest jewel among all wise men. You know the spiritual science instructed by Me. Often many experienced people who are aware of the consequences of auspicious and inauspicious activities cannot deliver themselves from the inauspicious desire of material enjoyment.

PURPORT

Only those who give up all endeavors to satisfy the demands of the body and mind, which are opposite to their constitutional positions, are actually self-realized, and are able to deliver themselves from the desire for material enjoyment.

TEXT 20

आत्मनो गुरुरात्मैवपुरुषस्य विशेषतः ।
यत्प्रत्यक्षानुमानाभ्यांश्रेयोऽसावनुविन्दते ॥२०॥

ātmano gurur ātmaiva puruṣasya viśeṣataḥ
yat pratyakṣānumānābhyāṁ śreyo 'sāv anuvindate

O Uddhava, the self is the foremost spiritual master of the human beings because the self can attain supreme auspiciousness on the strength of his direct and indirect perceptions.

COMMENTARY

A person can sometimes achieve the highest auspiciousness directly, and sometimes through indirect perception.

PURPORT

The conditioned state can never create inauspiciousness to those who are self-realized. Therefore, self-realized souls accept the Supersoul as their spiritual master, without being entangled in the material conception of life. Such self-realized liberated souls, though living in this world, actually attain auspiciousness by using the two kinds of evidence—direct and indirect perception.

TEXT 21

पुरुषत्वेचमांधीराःसांख्ययोगविशारदाः ।
आविस्तरांप्रपश्यन्तिसर्वशक्त्युपबृंहितम् ॥२१॥

puruṣatve ca māṁ dhīrāḥ sāṅkhya-yoga-viśāradāḥ
āvistarāṁ prapaśyanti sarva-śakty-upabṛṁhitam

Those who are expert in the science of *sāṅkhya-yoga*, and are self-controlled, can directly see Me, along with all My potencies.

COMMENTARY

Many among such human beings can realize Me. Those who are sober and non-envious can certainly understand Me. Those who know *sāṅkhya-yoga* and *bhakti-yoga* can also realize Me. It is stated in the *śruti: puruṣatve cāvistarām ātmā sahita-prajñānena sampanna-tamo vijñātaṁ vadati vijñātaṁ paśyati veda śvastanaṁ veda lokālokau martyenāmṛtam īpsaty evaṁ sampanno 'thetareṣāṁ paśūnām āsanā-pipāse evābhijñānam.* "The human form of life is endowed with sufficient intelligence so that one can imbibe transcendental knowledge. While in the human form of life, one can speak about his realizations, see the truth of material existence, understand the future consequences of his actions, and thus appreciate the existence not only of this world, but also the next. By experiencing the futility of material existence, the soul in the human form can inquire about immortality. This is the purpose of human life because the human body can enable one to achieve perfection. When a human being becomes advanced by spiritual practice, he will see the futility of the activities of the animals, which are simply eating, sleeping, mating and defending."

PURPORT

People who are maddened by material enjoyment consider all visible articles as the objects of their temporary sense enjoyment. They consider the Supreme Lord to be impotent, and thus deny His existence. But, those steady and thoughtful people who have mastered the science of self-realization and devotional service realize that the all-powerful Supreme Lord is present in every object.

TEXT 22

एकद्वित्रिचतुस्पादोबहुपादस्तथापदः ।
बह्व्यःसन्तिपुरःसृष्टास्तासांमेपौरुषी प्रिया ॥२२॥

eka-dvi-tri-catus-pādo bahu-pādas tathāpadaḥ
bahvyaḥ santi puraḥ sṛṣṭās tāsāṁ me pauruṣī priyā

In this material world, there are varieties of created bodies—some with one leg, others with two legs, three legs, four legs, many legs, and still others with no legs. Among all such bodies, the human form is very dear to Me because it awards one the ultimate goal of life.

COMMENTARY

Now, the Lord is glorifying the human body by saying, "one leg, etc."

PURPORT

According to their karma, the conditioned souls receive different types of bodies. Because they are materially conditioned, they accept their material body to be their self. Among all such bodies, the human form is dear to the Supreme Lord because only in the human form is one capable of achieving the ultimate goal of life.

TEXT 23

अत्रमांमृगयन्त्यद्धायुक्ताहेतुभिरीश्वरम् ।
गृह्यमाणैर्गुणैर्लिङ्गैरग्राह्यमनुमानतः ॥२३॥

atra māṁ mṛgayanty addhā yuktā hetubhir īśvaram
gṛhyamāṇair guṇair liṅgair agrāhyam anumānataḥ

Although My form is not directly seen by ordinary sense perception, those situated in human life may use their intelligence and other faculties of perception to directly search for Me through both apparent and indirectly ascertained symptoms.

COMMENTARY

"The living entities who have received human forms can directly search for Me, the supreme controller of all. The devotees worship Me by the process of devotional service, beginning with hearing and chanting. I have already stated that I am known only through devotional service."

Now, the question may arise that since the Lord is the source of everything, including the intelligence, how can one realize Him through sense perception and mental speculation? The answer is that guesswork undertaken by use of intelligence is unacceptable. By such guesswork, the dependent living entity tries to reach a conclusion but the independent Supersoul is not fully realized by such a process. The Supreme Lord, Kṛṣṇa, is beyond the reach of dry arguments. His forms, qualities, pastimes, and opulence are all inconceivable. Therefore, He is not realized through indirect sense perception.

PURPORT

Only human beings can realize the existence of the Supreme Lord with the help of direct and indirect perception, after seeing cause and effect, temporary and permanent nature, and the external and internal causes in this material world.

TEXT 24

अत्राप्युदाहरन्तीममितिहासंपुरातनम् ।
अवधूतस्यसंवादंयदोरमिततेजसः ॥२४॥

atrāpy udāharantīmam itihāsaṁ purātanam
avadhūtasya saṁvādaṁ yador amita-tejasaḥ

Now I will relate to you a historical narration concerning a conversation between the greatly powerful King Yadu and a most intelligent avadhūta.

COMMENTARY

Now I will relate to you an ancient conversation that took place between an *avadhūta* and King Yadu, which will shed light on your understanding of the Supersoul.

TEXT 25

अवधूतंद्वियंकञ्चिच्चरन्तमकुतोभयम् ।
कविंनिरीक्ष्यतरुणंयदुःपप्रच्छधर्मवित् ॥२५॥

avadhūtaṁ dviyaṁ kañcic carantam akuto-bhayam
kaviṁ nirīkṣya taruṇaṁ yaduḥ papraccha dharma-vit

Once upon a time, Mahārāja Yadu, who himself was most learned in spiritual science, saw an *avadhūta brāhmaṇa* who appeared to be young and wise, wandering about fearlessly. Mahārāja Yadu took the opportunity and inquired from the *brāhmaṇa* as follows.

TEXT 26

श्रीयदुरुवाच
कुतोबुद्धिरियंब्रह्मन्नकर्तुःसुविशारदा ।
यामासाद्यभवाल्लोकंविद्वांश्चरतिबालवत् ॥२६॥

śrī-yadur uvāca
kuto buddhir iyaṁ brahmann akartuḥ su-viśāradā
yām āsādya bhavāl lokaṁ vidvāṁś carati bāla-vat

Śrī Yadu said: O *brāhmaṇa,* I can see that you are not practicing any kind of spiritual discipline and yet you have gained perfect understanding of everything and everyone within this world. Kindly tell me how you developed your extraordinary intelligence. Why do you wander over the earth, behaving as if you were a mere child?

TEXT 27

प्रायोधर्मार्थकामेषुविवित्सायांचमानवाः ।
हेतुनैवसमीहन्त आयुषोयशसःश्रियः ॥२७॥

prāyo dharmārtha-kāmeṣu vivitsāyāṁ ca mānavāḥ
hetunaiva samīhanta āyuṣo yaśasaḥ śriyaḥ

People in this world often cultivate religiosity, economic development, and sense gratification, and also the science of self-realization, and their usual motive is to achieve a long duration of life, acquire fame, and enjoy material opulence.

COMMENTARY

Although they desire to know about religiosity, economic development, sense gratification, and the self, people in general think that these will benefit them with a long duration of life, and so on.

TEXT 28

त्वंतुकल्पःकविर्दक्षःसुभगोऽमृतभाषणः ।
नकर्तानेहसेकिञ्चिञ्जडोन्मत्तपिशाचवत् ॥२८॥

tvaṁ tu kalpaḥ kavir dakṣaḥ su-bhago 'mṛta-bhāṣaṇaḥ
na kartā nehase kiñcij jaḍonmatta-piśāca-vat

Although you are able, wise, expert, handsome, and a sweet speaker, you are not engaged in doing anything. Rather, you appear to be acting like an inert madman, as if you were a ghostly creature.

COMMENTARY

Yadu, the son of Yayāti, is saying: You are not the performer of any action, and you do not want anything. It is not that you are not doing anything because of ignorance—you are capable. It is not that you lack expertise—you are expert in all activities. It is not that you are ugly and hence, you do not wish to associate with a woman—you are handsome. You speak less. It is not that you are not a learned person but you do not wish to converse with anyone. O *brāhmaṇa*, despite all these, why are you behaving like a dumb person?

TEXT 29

जनेषुदह्यमानेषुकामलोभदवाग्निना ।
नतप्यसेऽग्निनामुक्तोगङ्गाम्भःस्थइवद्विपः ॥२९॥

janeṣu dahyamāneṣu kāma-lobha-davāgninā
na tapyase 'gninā mukto gaṅgāmbhaḥ-stha iva dvipaḥ

Although human beings in this world are burning in the forest fire of lust and greed, you remain free and are not burned by that fire. You appear to be like a peaceful elephant in the midst of the water of the cooling Ganges.

COMMENTARY

You are young and still, you are not afflicted by lusty desires. What is the reason behind this? People in this world are always suffering from lust, greed, and so on. However, you are free from such suffering and thus appear to be like an elephant standing in the water of the Ganges.

PURPORT

There is abundance of water in the Ganges. The water of the Ganges can extinguish any fire. As the waves of the Ganges can extinguish the fire of lust of an intoxicated elephant and make him peaceful, although human beings in this world are always disturbed by enemies, such as lust, you are an *avadhūta*. And, because you are not overwhelmed by lusty desires, you are not disturbed by the fire of lust, like an elephant situated in the water.

TEXT 30

त्वंहिनःपृच्छतांब्रह्मन् आत्मन्यानन्दकारणम् ।
ब्रूहिस्पर्शविहीनस्यभवतःकेवलात्मनः ॥३०॥

tvaṁ hi naḥ pṛcchatāṁ brahmann ātmany ānanda-kāraṇam
brūhi sparśa-vihīnasya bhavataḥ kevalātmanaḥ

O great *brāhmāṇa*, I see that you are devoid of any contact with material enjoyment and that you are traveling alone, without any companions or wife and children. Therefore, because I am sincerely inquiring from you, please tell me the cause of the great ecstasy that you feel within yourself.

COMMENTARY

According to the logic that one who has a mouth will speak, I wish to know from where you are getting this unlimited happiness. You are completely aloof from sense enjoyment but still, you are receiving so much happiness.

PURPORT

The sense objects—form, taste, smell, sound, and touch—cannot attack those liberated souls who are fully engaged in the devotional service of the Supreme Lord, and who are freed from the desire for material enjoyment. Those who are attached to material form, taste, and so on, become entangled by the affection of their wife and children. You are an *avadhūta*, and so I want to know why you are experiencing transcendental bliss, even though you are not intoxicated by worldly happiness.

TEXT 31

श्रीभगवानुवाच
यदुनैवंमहाभागोब्रह्मण्येनसुमेधसा ।
पृष्टःसभाजितःप्राहप्रश्रयावनतंद्विजः ॥३१॥

śrī-bhagavān uvāca
yadunaivaṁ mahā-bhāgo brahmaṇyena su-medhasā
pṛṣṭaḥ sabhājitaḥ prāha praśrayāvanataṁ dvijaḥ

The Supreme Lord said: When the *avadhūta brāhmaṇa* was thus respected and spoken to in this way by the intelligent King Yadu, who was the benefactor of the *brāhmaṇas*, being pleased with the king's respectful attitude, he began to humbly reply.

COMMENTARY

The Supreme Lord said: O most fortunate Uddhava, when the wise King Yadu pleased the *avadhūta* by his service, he began to speak as follows.

TEXT 32

श्रीब्राह्मण उवाच
सन्तिमेगुरवोराजन् बहवोबुद्ध्युपश्रिताः ।
यतोबुद्धिमुपादायमुक्तोऽटामीहतान् शृणु ॥३२॥

śrī-brāhmaṇa uvāca
santi me guravo rājan bahavo buddhy-upaśritāḥ
yato buddhim upādāya mukto 'ṭāmīha tān śṛṇu

The *avadhūta brāhmaṇa* said: My dear King, I have received knowledge from the many spiritual masters who are present in this world. It is because of this that I am able to freely wander about in this world. Now, please hear as I describe these spiritual masters to you.

COMMENTARY

O King, I have many spiritual masters who I chose with the help of my intelligence. Although I did not formally receive instructions from them, I have accumulated much knowledge by observing them with the help of my intelligence. In this way, I have become free from the miseries of material existence and am wandering about freely in this world. Now, let me tell you the names of these spiritual masters.

PURPORT

Those who are averse to Kṛṣṇa and who are full of *anarthas* are always busy lording it over material objects. They spend their days accomplishing the three objectives of life—religiosity, economic development, and sense gratification. Their only aim is to enhance their duration of life, as well as their glories and beauty. Because Avadhūta Mahāśaya did not display any such behavior, King Yadu asked him the reason for his wandering about in this way. In reply, the *avadhūta* said: "Rather than accepting these twenty-four entities that are observed within this visible world as the means of my enjoyment, I have accepted them as my instructing spiritual masters, giving up the conception of accepting something and rejecting something else. I do not live like an ordinary human being, who is driven by mental speculation and thus bereft of the service of a spiritual master. I travel in this world under the shelter of my fixed intelligence. With a desire to surpass all *anarthas* and to always render loving service to the Supreme Lord, I have taken shelter of these twenty-four spiritual masters."

TEXTS 33–35

पृथिवीवायुराकाशमापोऽग्निश्चन्द्रमारविः ।
कपोतोऽजगरःसिन्धुःपतङ्गोमधुकृद्गजः ॥३३॥
मधुहाहरिणोमीनःपिङ्गलाकुररोऽर्भकः ।
कुमारीशरकृत्सर्प ऊर्णनाभिःसुपेशकृत् ॥३४॥
एतेमेगुरवोराजन् चतुर्विंशतिराश्रिताः ।
शिक्षावृत्तिभिरेतेषामन्वशिक्षमिहात्मनः ॥३५॥

pṛthivī vāyur ākāśam āpo 'gniś candramā raviḥ
kapoto 'jagaraḥ sindhuḥ pataṅgo madhukṛd gajaḥ

madhu-hā hariṇo mīnaḥ piṅgalā kuraro 'rbhakaḥ
kumārī śara-kṛt sarpa ūrṇanābhiḥ supeśakṛt

ete me guravo rājan catur-viṁśatir āśritāḥ
śikṣā vṛttibhir eteṣām anvaśikṣam ihātmanaḥ

O King, I have taken shelter of the following twenty-four things as my spiritual masters—the earth, air, sky, water, fire, moon, sun, a pigeon, a python, the sea, a moth, a honeybee, an elephant, a honey thief, deer, fish, the prostitute Piṅgalā, the kurara bird, a child, a young girl, an arrow maker, a serpent, a spider, and a wasp. My dear King, by studying their activities, I have learned the science of the self.

COMMENTARY

The earth, air, sky, water, fire, the moon, the sun, a pigeon, a python, the sea, a moth, a honeybee, an elephant, a hunter who steals honey, deer, fish, the prostitute named Piṅgalā, a kurara bird, a child, a young girl, an arrow maker, a serpent, a spider, and a wasp. I have learned many things from the behavior of these twenty-four things.

TEXT 36

यतोयदनुशिक्षामिचाथावानाहुषात्मज ।
तत्तथापुरुषव्याघ्रनिबोधकथयामि ते ॥३६॥

yato yad anuśikṣāmi yathā vā nāhuṣātmaja
tat tathā puruṣa-vyāghra nibodha kathayāmi te

Please listen, My dear son of Mahārāja Yayāti, a tiger among men, as I tell you what I learned from each of these spiritual masters.

TEXT 37

भूतैराक्रम्यमाणोऽपिधीरोदैववशानुगैः ।
तद्विद्वान् नचलेन्मार्गादन्वशिक्षंक्षितेर्व्रतम् ॥३७॥

bhūtair ākramyamāṇo 'pi dhīro daiva-vaśānugaiḥ
tad vidvān na calen mārgād anvaśikṣaṁ kṣiter vratam

A sober person, even when harassed by other living beings, should understand that his aggressors are acting helplessly under the control of providence. In this way, he should never be distracted from progress on his path. This principle of tolerance I have learned from the earth, which is always steady and tolerant, despite being repeatedly kicked by the living entities who dwell on her.

COMMENTARY

The *avadhūta* had learned the quality of tolerance from the earth—this is being described in this verse. Even though living entities continuously walk over the surface of the earth, the earth always remains steady and fixed. The *avadhūta* learned this quality from the earth. In the same way, an intelligent person should never give up following his prescribed path, whether he meets with happiness or distress brought about by the arrangement of providence.

PURPORT

People consider the earth to be an object of their enjoyment, rather than an instructing spiritual master. Every person tries to distract others from the path of eternal religion by causing various disturbances. Because of accepting the subordination of the demigods, who fulfill our material desires, the living entities become envious of each other. When living entities are overwhelmed with miseries caused by other living entities, there is very little chance for them to exhibit tolerance. Intolerant people invariably exhibit a great propensity toward material enjoyment in this world, due to lack of proper training. Nevertheless, the nature of the earth is tolerance. One can become tolerant if he considers the earth as a spiritual master and takes this lesson from her.

TEXT 38

शश्वत्परार्थसर्वेहः परार्थैकान्तसम्भवः ।
साधुः शिक्षेत भूभृत्तो नगशिष्यः परात्मताम् ॥३८॥

śaśvat parārtha-sarvehaḥ parārthaikānta-sambhavaḥ
sādhuḥ śikṣeta bhū-bhṛtto naga-śiṣyaḥ parātmatām

An intelligent person should learn from the mountain how to devote himself to the service of others, making their welfare the sole purpose for his existence. This is also the lesson to be learned as a disciple of the tree.

COMMENTARY

Two features of the earth are mentioned here—the mountains and the trees. What does one learn from the mountain? The mountain sustains the earth, produces streams that supply water, and produces various jewels. All these are meant for others' benefit. In the same way, all activities of a saintly person should be performed with the aim of benefiting others. This should be the nature of the devotees. Similarly, if someone uproots a tree and plants it somewhere else, the tree accepts it without any protest. One learns to do good to others from the tree. Therefore, a yogi should become like a tree. These are the teachings one should learn from the mountain and the tree.

PURPORT

The mountain is made of stone but clay is not so hard. That is why the hard mountain can sustain the soft soil but soft soil cannot sustain the burden of the mountain. The earth has two kinds of ingredients; the hard mountain and the soft clay. Everyone should learn how to perform welfare activities for others from the mountain. The principal characteristic of a saintly person is that he always desires supreme benefit for others. Otherwise, selfish interest captures the living entities and induces them to become envious of others.

The lesson to be learned from the tree, which grows on the earth, is to tolerate disturbances caused by others. The nondevotee materialistic enjoyer considers all items of this world to be objects of his enjoyment. But, a devotee considers all items as his spiritual masters, and learns from them different things. This is the nature of a devotee. Worship of Lord Hari is possible only if one becomes as tolerant as a tree, and as immovable and steady as a mountain. Otherwise, an intolerant person can never engage in the service of the Supreme Lord. That is why Śrī Gaurasundara has instructed everyone to be as tolerant as a tree in order to chant the holy name of Lord Hari.

TEXT 39

प्राणवृत्त्यैवसन्तुष्येन्मुनिर्नैवेन्द्रियप्रियैः ।
ज्ञानंयथाननश्येतनावकीर्येतवाङ्मनः ॥३९॥

prāṇa-vṛttyaiva santuṣyen munir naivendriya-priyaiḥ
jñānaṁ yathā na naśyeta nāvakīryeta vāṅ-manaḥ

As the life air moves within the body without expecting any support from the sense objects, a learned sage should take satisfaction in the simple maintenance of his existence, and should not seek satisfaction through gratifying the material senses. In other words, one should take care of his material body in a way that his cultivation of spiritual knowledge will not be disturbed, and his speech and mind are not distracted from his spiritual discipline.

COMMENTARY

Air is of two types: the life air that moves within the body, and the air of the external world, or wind. What we have to learn from the life air is being described here. The life air performs its duty and is simply satisfied with food and other bare necessities of life. As the senses enjoy various sense objects , such as form, taste, and so on, the life air does not. Similarly, thoughtful sages should remain satisfied even with just food and water, like the life air. One should eat only as much as is required to keep the body and soul together, so that the life air will not be disturbed. If one does not eat, his mind will not remain active, and as a result, his knowledge will be destroyed. Therefore, one should maintain his life properly so that his speech and mind are not disturbed. Moreover, by eating abominable, dry, and unclean foods, one's mind and words become disturbed.

Also, by eating palatable and rich foods, one becomes lazy, has an increase in the urge for sex, and becomes agitated in his speech and mind.

PURPORT

It is not the duty of thoughtful men to give up their tolerance and become restless in this rarely attained human form of life. By manipulating the senses under the influence of one's mental propensity, one becomes attracted to imperfect, temporary material objects. When one thus engages in material activities that are apparently pleasing to his senses, then the path of his material enjoyment becomes clearly laid out. As soon as one forgets the Supreme Lord, one desires to lord it over this material world, which was created by *maya*. As a result, his speech and mind become disturbed. Thus, he becomes situated in the darkness of ignorance and considers such ignorance or partial knowledge to be the attainment of full knowledge. This is how he falls down from the understanding of the Supreme Lord. Therefore, by adopting the path of liberation, and rejecting the path of sense gratification, there is no possibility of the speech and mind becoming covered by mixed knowledge, or ignorance. In addition, disturbance of the body and intelligence under the influence of pseudo renunciation does not help in diminishing the propensity for material enjoyment. Therefore, it is necessary to follow the path of proper renunciation and engage in the service of the Lord, which is the ultimate goal of life.

TEXT 40

विषयेष्वाविशन्योगीनानाधर्मेषुसर्वतः ।
गुणदोषव्यपेतात्मानविषज्जेतवायुवत् ॥४०॥

viṣayeṣv āviśan yogī nānā-dharmeṣu sarvataḥ
guṇa-doṣa-vyapetātmā na viṣajjeta vāyu-vat

The self-realized soul, whose heart is free from thoughts of happiness and distress, should always remain unattached, like the wind, despite coming in contact with material objects, which are full of material qualities.

COMMENTARY

Now, what can be learned from the wind is being described. Even if one is exposed to sense gratification, one should not become attached to it. One should not place too much importance in insignificant, great, superior, or inferior material objects. As the wind cannot enter a closed room, and thus does not help in the act of burning there, the introspective sage should not be the cause of any material activity.

PURPORT

As the unsteady, restless mind engages itself in enjoying form, taste, smell, sound, and touch, it nourishes various material conceptions of life. That is why subjects of thought, such as finding faults and attributing good qualities, display their mastery over the mind. As the wind blowing from various directions may create disturbances, the restless mind searching for varieties of material enjoyment destroys a conditioned soul's attempt for self-control. It is therefore essential for a devotee to serve Lord Hari by means of *ekāyana*, with the support of fixed intelligence.

TEXT 41

पार्थिवेष्विहदेहेषुप्रविष्टस्तद्गुणाश्रयः ।
गुणैर्नयुज्यतेयोगीगन्धैर्वायुरिवात्मदृक् ॥४१॥

pārthiveṣv iha deheṣu praviṣṭas tad-guṇāśrayaḥ
guṇair na yujyate yogī gandhair vāyur ivātma-dṛk

Just as the wind, although carrying varieties of aromas, does not mix with them, the self-realized soul, although living in a material body and apparently acting like an ordinary man, is never entangled.

COMMENTARY

One should remain unattached to bodily activities. This is the lesson one should learn from the wind. Although the wind may carry good or bad aromas, it is not affected by them, or does not mix with them. Similarly, even though a self-realized soul may live in a material body and act according to his acquired nature, he does not become entangled. By learning from the wind, a yogi should not become attached to his body or bodily activities. He should always know that the spirit soul is different from the material body.

PURPORT

Those who are able to understand the temporary nature of the material body and mind, as well as the fault of the conditioned soul's aversion to the Supreme Lord, are fit to be called self-realized yogis. Such yogis do not act due to being driven by the three modes of material nature, nor do they become entangled in activities that are pleasing to the body and mind. As the wind carries aromas but is not affected by any particular aroma, giving up its own nature, similarly, the self-realized soul engages in the service of the Lord while accepting the necessities of the body without attachment. In this way, he remains free from the results of activities performed by his gross and subtle bodies.

TEXT 42

अन्तर्हितश्चस्थिरजङ्गमेषुब्रह्मात्मभावेनसमन्वयेन ।
व्याप्त्याव्यवच्छेदमसङ्गमात्मनोमुनिर्नभस्त्वंविततस्यभावयेत् ॥४२॥

antarhitaś ca sthira-jaṅgameṣu
brahmātma-bhāvena samanvayena
vyāptyāvyavacchedam asaṅgam ātmano
munir nabhastvaṁ vitatasya bhāvayet

An introspective person, even while living in the material body, should consider himself to be an eternal spirit soul. He should see how eternal souls have entered all varieties of life-forms, both moving and non-moving, and that they are spread all over the universe. One should also understand that the Supreme Personality of Godhead, in His all-pervading feature as the paramātmā, **is present, along with the eternal souls, within all bodies. Both the individual soul and the Supreme Soul can be realized by contemplating the sky. Although the sky extends without limit, and everything rests within the sky, it does not mix with anything, nor is it divided.**

COMMENTARY

Although the Supersoul is situated both inside and outside all objects, He remains unattached, just like the sky. This is the lesson to be learned from the sky. In spite of remaining within the body, the Supersoul is all-pervading. By means of his transcendental realization, a yogi should think of the Supersoul as all-pervading, like the sky. Although present within all moving and non-moving living entities, He remains situated in His supreme position. Just as the all-pervading sky is present within a pot, and is also outside the pot, the Supersoul, although present within the material bodies of all living entities, is all-pervading.

PURPORT

There is always difference between the constitutional characteristics of an object and its unconstitutional characteristics. Persons who are acquainted with the science of the self never support the argument that the material body is the self. A self-realized soul never engages in accepting or rejecting material objects. He has no intention of either expanding his material enjoyment or minimizing it. Because the living entities are simultaneously one with and different from the Lord, they also possess the quality of all-pervasiveness. Similarly, if the concept of *acintya-bhedābheda* is accepted, it can be understood that the living entities simultaneously possess both the possibility for aversion to the Supreme Lord, and eternal service to the Supreme Lord. By directly or indirectly attaining knowledge of the self, one also realizes his self to be separate from the material objects he sees, just like the sky, which is present both inside and outside a pot. The natural characteristics of an object are realized by observing its interaction with other objects, both directly and indirectly.

TEXT 43

तेजोऽबन्नमयौर्भावैर्मेघाद्यैर्वायुनेरितैः ।
नस्पृश्यतेनभस्तद्वत्कालसृष्टैर्गुणैःपुमान् ॥४३॥

tejo-'b-anna-mayair bhāvairmeghādyair vāyuneritaiḥ
na spṛśyate nabhas tadvatkāla-sṛṣṭair guṇaiḥ pumān

Although powerful winds blow clouds across the sky, the sky itself is never disturbed. In the same way, the spirit soul is not transformed by contact with material nature. Although the spirit soul is awarded a body made of earth, water, and fire, and although his actions are dictated by the three modes of material nature, which are products of eternal time, his eternal nature is never affected.

COMMENTARY

Just as the sky remains aloof despite the presence of clouds being driven by the mighty wind, the spirit soul is always aloof from the material body made of fire, water, earth, and so on, which was created by the material time.

PURPORT

As clouds hover throughout the sky, being driven by the wind, the sky does not mix with the clouds, even though they appear so. Similarly, although the gross and subtle bodies seem merged with the spirit soul, the spirit soul is always distinct from them. When the spirit soul comes in contact with material nature, he is awarded a body made of the five gross elements. When the spirit soul is liberated from the bondage of the three modes of material nature, he has no more connection with the gross and subtle bodies. Eternal time factor is the original cause of the three modes of material nature. A differentiation in the three material qualities is made possible when the time factor becomes divided into past, present, and future. The conditional state produced by the material modes of nature, which are born of the divided time factor, is always distinct from the eternal spirit soul. Although clouds may appear to be part of the sky, the sky is distinct from the clouds, always maintaining its separate identity. Similarly, even though the spirit soul appears to be temporarily confined within the gross and subtle bodies, it is unaffected by them, just like the sky.

TEXT 44

स्वच्छः प्रकृतितः स्निग्धो माधुर्यस्तीर्थभूर्नृणाम् ।
मुनिः पुनात्यपां मित्रमीक्षोपस्पर्शकीर्तनैः ॥४४॥

svacchaḥ prakṛtitaḥ snigdho mādhuryas tīrtha-bhūr nṛṇām
muniḥ punāty apāṁ mitram īkṣopasparśa-kīrtanaiḥ

O King, a saintly person is naturally pure, free from all contaminations, well behaved, and a benefactor of all human beings. Just by seeing, touching, or hearing such an exalted soul, one is purified just as one is cleansed by bathing with pure water. A saintly person, like a holy place of pilgrimage, purifies all those who meet him, because he is always engaged in chanting the glories of the Lord.

COMMENTARY

Now the lesson to be learned from water is being described. Water is by nature pure and cooling. It is considered to be affectionate toward everyone. Water is sweet. Saintly persons are also sweet by nature, and they purify all living entities by instructing them about devotional service. Saintly persons should behave as the well-wishing friend of everyone, just like water. Devotees purify everyone, just as water purifies everything by its contact.

PURPORT

The people of this material world, who always desire happiness and yet simply suffer from distress, are very restless, and so they cannot be thoughtful. They are incessantly driven by their material conceptions of life and are firmly situated in the principle that material enjoyment is everything. Because they are exceedingly attached to material enjoyment, when their desires are not satisfied, they become angry. When they are in anxiety due to a lack of material enjoyment, they become afflicted with fear. However, the sages who are inclined to the Lord's service are not like this. They are as sanctified as water, they are naturally affectionate to everyone, and they are compassionate to all living entities. They are true friends of all living entities, they always speak very sweetly, and they are never interested in dry arguments. They are themselves places of pilgrimage because they are fully surrendered to the Supreme Lord, and thus they possess the twenty-six transcendental qualities. Such great souls are in direct contact with the Lord and thus, are never bereft of His association. Such saintly souls purify the entire world by their constant glorification of the Lord. Simply by their association, their faithful followers become liberated from their condition of material absorption.

By the phrase *apāṁ mitram*, the thoughtful sages have been compared with water. Within the water of the thoughtful sages, the three *puruṣa* incarnations—Kāraṇārṇavaśāyī Viṣṇu, Garbhodakaśāyī Viṣṇu, and Kṣirodakaśāyī Viṣṇu are manifest. There is no question of contamination in transparent water. By constant hearing and glorification of the Supreme Lord, liberated sages remain freed from material conceptions and thus become qualified to touch the Supreme Lord. Their association is the cause of the conditioned souls' liberation from their restlessness of mind and the resultant conditional life.

TEXT 45

तेजस्वीतपसादीप्तोदुर्धर्षोदरभाजनः ।
सर्वभक्ष्योऽपियुक्तात्मानादत्तेमलमग्निवत् ॥४५॥

tejasvī tapasā dīpto durdharṣodara-bhājanaḥ
sarva-bhakṣyo 'pi yuktātmā nādatte malam agni-vat

Saintly persons have become powerful by the execution of austerities. They do not endeavor to enjoy anything material of this world, and they accept food offered to them by destiny. If by chance they eat some contaminated food, they are not affected, just like fire, which burns up all contaminated substances that are offered to it.

COMMENTARY

The lesson to be learned from fire is herein being described. The next three verses are also concerning fire. Fire is very powerful, and no one has the ability to counteract it. Fire digests the food that enters the stomach. Those who are fire-like-yogis should not accumulate eatables for the future, but should be satisfied with what is easily available.

PURPORT

The lessons to be learned from fire are being described in this verse, and the following three verses. In this verse, it is said that when fire burns everything, it remains unaffected. Fire doesn't become contaminated, rather, it purifies everything. Similarly, saintly persons, even though given the opportunity to enjoy material objects, do not do so but instead, remain unattached. They are always transcendentally situated and so they do not take pleasure in temporary material objects. This is the characteristic of self-realized souls. Such persons do not accumulate things unnecessarily—they accept things only to the extent as is necessary for their maintenance and that also, without attachment. Saintly persons are always free from the contamination of sinful activities and thus they are the true moralists. They are not attracted to anything of this visible world, being driven by insatiable greed to attain spiritual perfection. These are the qualities to be learned from fire.

TEXT 46

क्वचिच्छन्नःक्वचित्स्पष्ट उपास्यःश्रेयइच्छताम् ।
भुङ्क्तेसर्वत्रदातॄणांदहन्प्रागुत्तराशुभम् ॥४६॥

kvacic channaḥ kvacit spaṣṭa upāsyaḥ śreya icchatām
bhuṅkte sarvatra dātṛṇāṁ dahan prāg-uttarāśubham

A pure devotee, just like fire, is sometimes not visible and at other times, he is seen. For the benefit of the conditioned souls who are desperately searching for happiness, a pure devotee may act as a spiritual master and thus like fire, burn his disciples' sinful reactions to ashes by mercifully accepting their service.

PURPORT

Devotees do not like to disclose their own glories and so they are like fire covered by ashes. Sometimes, in order to teach people, devotees reveal their glories, just like a blazing fire. Sometimes they act as a spiritual master for the benefit of ordinary people. As fire accepts gifts, such as ghee, offered by worshipers, devotees accept the glorification offered by their worshipers. In this way, they burn to ashes, just like fire, the most coveted objects possessed by materially absorbed worshipers, without exhibiting the slightest desire to enjoy them.

TEXT 47

स्वमाययासृष्टमिदंसदसल्लक्षणंविभुः ।
प्रविष्ट ईयतेतत्तत्स्वरूपोऽग्निरिवैधसि ॥४७॥

sva-māyayā sṛṣṭam idaṁ sad-asal-lakṣaṇaṁ vibhuḥ
praviṣṭa īyate tat-tat- svarūpo 'gnir ivaidhasi

The all-pervading Supersoul, having entered the bodies of the different species of life, which are created by His own energy, appears to have assumed such identities, just as fire appears to be manifest differently in pieces of wood of different sizes and shapes.

COMMENTARY

As fire is present within wood and manifests when there is friction, the Supreme Lord is present everywhere within this world and He reveals Himself when one cultivates devotional service, beginning with hearing and chanting.

PURPORT

Just as fire is present within the wood and generally manifests when there is friction, similarly, the object of worship remains with the worshiper as He displays various worldly forms. Because the living entities are by nature subordinate to the Supreme Lord, their perfection is attained when they take complete shelter of the object of their worship. Because the conditioned souls in this material world accept service from others rather than rendering service to their worshipable Lord, they forget their constitutional position as eternal servants of the Supreme Lord.

Although the conditioned souls, who are averse to the Lord's service, are situated within the temporary nature created by the supreme director, which causes their constitutional position to be covered and their service to the Lord forgotten, they remain fully spiritual.

TEXT 48

विसर्गाद्याः श्मशानान्ता भावा देहस्य नात्मनः ।
कलानामिव चन्द्रस्य कालेनाव्यक्तवर्त्मना ॥४८॥

visargādyāḥ śmaśānāntā bhāvā dehasya nātmanaḥ
kalānām iva candrasya kālenāvyakta-vartmanā

The stages of one's bodily condition, beginning with birth and ending with death, have no effect upon the eternal soul, just like our vision of the waxing and waning of the moon does not affect the moon itself. Such changes occur due to the imperceptible movements of time.

COMMENTARY

Birth and death, as well as the other transformations, are meant only for the material body and not the spirit soul, just as the apparent waxing and waning of the moon does not affect the moon itself. Such changes are enforced by the imperceptible movements of time.

PURPORT

The wheel of time is unseen. In the present conditional state, the living entities cannot understand what undivided, or eternal, time is. It is the time factor that causes the waxing and waning of the moon. From this example, it is understood that the pure spirit soul neither increases nor decreases. Rather, it is the material body, which is obtained from the temporary material nature, that develops and then dwindles. Under the influence of time, the material body is born, remains for some time, and then dies. As the waxing and waning of the moon is an effect of reflecting the rays of the sun, so all living entities are manifested in various species by the will of the Supreme Lord.

TEXT 49

कालेनह्योघवेगेनभूतानांप्रभवाप्ययौ ।
नित्यावपिनदृश्येते आत्मनोऽग्नेर्यथार्चिक्षाम् ॥४९॥

kālena hy ogha-vegena bhūtānāṁ prabhavāpyayau
nityāv api na dṛśyete ātmano 'gner yathārciṣām

The flames of a fire appear and disappear at every moment but this is not noticed by the casual observer. Similarly, the waves of time flow without stop, like the currents of a mighty river, and they imperceptibly cause the birth and death of the countless bodies of the living entities. And yet, the soul, who is thus forced to change his position again and again, cannot perceive how time is working.

COMMENTARY

Just like the logic of *siṁha avalokana*[2], this verse is teaching us the lesson to be learned from fire. As sparks continuously appear from a blazing fire, and then disappear, the material bodies of the spirit souls are constantly appearing and disappearing.

PURPORT

The birth and death of the living entities is caused by powerful time. As fire sometimes appears blazing and sometimes appears meek, the apparent conditions of the material body vary, but the spirit soul is unaffected.

---

2 After traversing some distance, the lion is said to look back at the tract that it has covered. This is called *simha-avalokana*.

TEXT 50

गुणैर्गुणानुपादत्तेयथाकालंविमुञ्चति ।
नतेषुयुज्यतेयोगीगोभिर्गा इवगोपतिः ॥५०॥

guṇair guṇān upādatte yathā-kālaṁ vimuñcati
na teṣu yujyate yogī gobhir gā iva go-patiḥ

Just as the sun evaporates a large quantity of water and then sends it back to the earth in the form of rain, so a saintly devotee accepts whatever is offered to him, and when a suitable person approaches him to beg for something, he gives such things up. Thus, both by accepting and renouncing the objects of the senses, a devotee is not entangled.

COMMENTARY

This verse, and the next verse, describe the lesson to be learned from the sun. The sun evaporates water and then distributes it, in the form of rain. In the same way, self-realized souls accept sense objects by means of their senses. Later on, if someone approaches them and asks for those objects, they give them away. The self-realized souls are not attached to anything. They do not think in terms of "I have gotten something," or "I have donated something."

PURPORT

Just as the sun evaporates water by its powerful rays, saintly persons accept all kinds of material enjoyment, but without attachment. Just as the sun does not take away the water from the earth, but ultimately gives it back, in the form of rain, the devotees of the Supreme Lord accept material enjoyment, but they do not become polluted by such actions.

TEXT 51

बुध्यतेस्वेनभेदेनव्यक्तिस्थ इवतद्गतः ।
लक्ष्यतेस्थूलमतिभिरात्माचावस्थितोऽर्कवत् ॥५१॥

budhyate sve na bhedena vyakti-stha iva tad-gataḥ
lakṣyate sthūla-matibhir ātmā cāvasthito 'rka-vat

Even though it is reflected in various objects, the sun is never divided, nor does it have anything to do with its reflection. Only dull-headed persons would consider the sun in this way. Similarly, although the soul is reflected through innumerable material bodies, it remains undivided and nonmaterial.

COMMENTARY

The sun may be reflected off various surfaces and thus appear in a variety of ways, but we know that the sun itself is far beyond such manifestations and has nothing to do with them. In the same way, the spirit souls are reflected through their material bodies, which exhibit myriad designations, such as white, black, male, female, young, and old. The soul's eternal constitutional position is something far beyond these temporary manifestations, however, and has nothing to do with them.

PURPORT

When the sun is reflected in many mirrors, it gives one the impression that there are many suns. Similarly, the illusory energy, *maya*, creates the impression that the conditioned souls have no resolute desire to serve the Supreme Lord. All living entities are eternal servants of the Supreme Lord. They have no other duty or destination than service to the Supreme Lord. But, foolish people give up the service of the Supreme Lord, under the control of false ego, and become busy for their own sense gratification. This is their foolishness. When the living entities are liberated from all gross and subtle designations, they constantly engage in the service of the Lord of Vaikuṇṭha. In Vaikuṇṭha, the living entities have no propensity whatsoever for sense gratification, unlike the conditioned souls. There is no question of any disturbance to the exchanges of happiness between the worshipable Lord and His eternal servants.

TEXT 52

नातिस्नेहःप्रसङ्गोवाकर्तव्यःक्वापिकेनचित् ।
कुर्वन्विन्देतसन्तापंकपोतैवदीनधीः ॥५२॥

nāti-snehaḥ prasaṅgo vā kartavyaḥ kvāpi kenacit
kurvan vindeta santāpaṁ kapota iva dīna-dhīḥ

One should never indulge in too much attachment for anything, or concern for anyone. Otherwise, this will lead one to great unhappiness, like the foolish pigeon.

COMMENTARY

The lesson to be learned from the pigeon is indicated in this verse. One should never have too much affection for anyone, nor should one become too attached to anything, nor should one be overly attached to maintaining his dependents.

PURPORT

Every living entity is an eternal servant of the Supreme Lord. If he gives up the service of the Lord and engages in the service of anyone else, for his own enjoyment, he will ultimately have to suffer like the pigeon who will be described in the following verses.

TEXT 53

कपोतःकश्चनारण्येकृतनीडोवनस्पतौ ।
कपोत्याभार्ययासार्धमुवासकतिचित्समाः ॥५३॥

kapotaḥ kaścanāraṇye kṛta-nīdo vanaspatau
kapotyā bhāryayā sārdham uvāsa katicit samāḥ

There once was a pigeon that lived in the forest, along with his wife. He built a suitable nest within a tree and lived there for several years in her association.

TEXT 54

कपोतौस्नेहगुणितहृदयौगृहधर्मिणौ ।
दृष्टिंदृष्ट्याङ्गमङ्गेनबुद्धिंबुद्ध्या बबन्धतुः ॥५४॥

kapotau sneha-guṇita hṛdayau gṛha-dharmiṇau
dṛṣṭiṁ dṛṣṭyāṅgam aṅgena buddhiṁ buddhyā babandhatuḥ

The two pigeons conscientiously performed their household duties. Their hearts were tied together by the rope of affection, and they were each attracted by each other's glances, bodily features, and moods. Thus, they completely bound each other with the tight knots of affection.

PURPORT

As a wife and husband are naturally attached to each other, the male and female pigeon were extremely attached to each other and in that way, they enjoyed sense gratification. They were so attached to each other that they could not bear separation from each other for even a moment. The main cause of such mundane affection and attachment is forgetfulness of the Supreme Lord. The living entities' affection for the Lord and their attachment to Him is eternal. When that relationship is disrupted, such pure affection and attachment is reflected in a perverted manner as affection for temporary objects of this material world. This creates a reflection of happiness, in the form of forgetfulness of the Supreme Lord.

TEXT 55

शय्यासनाटनस्थानवार्ताक्रीडाशनादिकम् ।
मिथुनीभूयविश्रब्धौचेरतुर्वनराजिषु ॥५५॥

śayyāsanāṭana-sthāna vārtā-krīḍāśanādikam
mithunī-bhūya viśrabdhau ceratur vana-rājiṣu

Innocently placing their faith in the future, the pigeons rested, sat, walked, stood, conversed, played, ate, and so on, as a loving couple in the trees of the forest.

COMMENTARY

As soon as the conditioned soul forgets the Supreme Lord, he begins to act in a different way and because of his enjoying propensity, he engages in activities such as sleeping, sitting, traveling, gossiping, playing, eating, simply for his personal sense gratification. However, these same activities are engaged in by the liberated servants of the Lord, for His pleasure. Liberated devotees have no other business than serving the Supreme Lord. All their activities, such as sleeping, traveling, and speaking, are performed with the aim of satisfying the Supreme Lord. The fallen condition of the living entities is due to their making a distinction between themselves and the Supreme Lord, who is eternal, full of knowledge and bliss.

TEXT 56

यंयंवाञ्छतिसाराजन्तर्पयन्त्यनुकम्पिता ।
तंतंसमनयत्कामंकृच्छ्रेणाप्यजितेन्द्रियः ॥५६॥

yaṁ yaṁ vāñchati sā rājan tarpayanty anukampitā
taṁ taṁ samanayat kāmaṁ kṛcchreṇāpy ajitendriyaḥ

O King, whenever the she-pigeon desired something, she would flatteringly cajole her husband with affectionate glances and conversation, and the he-pigeon, whose senses were not controlled, would provide everything she wanted, even with great personal difficulty.

COMMENTARY

O King, the wife of the pigeon pleased her husband with sweet gestures, smiles, glances, and pleasant conversation.

PURPORT

Materialistic persons who, instead of accepting the Supreme Lord as the only master of their senses, think themselves to be equal to Hṛṣīkeśa, engage in various activities in this world with a desire to gratify their senses and accumulate wealth. As the enjoyer pigeon acts whimsically to please the enjoyed pigeon, materialists are busy enjoying temporary material happiness with their gross and subtle bodies. The example of the male and female pigeons' happiness and distress has been cited to teach such materialists. The condition souls who maintain too much affection and attachment for material objects suffer in material existence, just like the male and female pigeon.

TEXT 57

कपोतीप्रथमंगर्भंगृह्णन्तीकाल आगते ।
अण्डानिसुषुवेनीडेस्तपत्युःसन्निधौसते ॥५७॥

kapotī prathamaṁ garbhaṁ gṛhṇantī kāla āgate
aṇḍāni suṣuve nīḍe sta-patyuḥ sannidhau sate

Then the female pigeon experienced her first pregnancy. When the time arrived, the chaste lady delivered a number of eggs within the nest in the presence of her husband.

TEXT 58

तेषुकालेव्यजायन्तरचितावयवाहरेः ।
शक्तिभिर्दुर्विभाव्याभिःकोमलाङ्गतनूरुहाः ॥५८॥

teṣu kāle vyajāyanta racitāvayavā hareḥ
śaktibhir durvibhāvyābhiḥ komalāṅga-tanūruhāḥ

When the time was ripe, baby pigeons, with tender limbs and feathers created by the inconceivable potencies of Śrī Hari, were born from those eggs.

COMMENTARY

The she-pigeon gave birth in due course of time.

PURPORT

When the conditioned souls become averse to the Supreme Lord, then the Supreme Lord spreads the network of illusion in all their activities, to increase their aversion to His service. Those who do not display an inclination for the service of the Supreme Lord are awarded suitable mentalities, according to their desires and activities. In this way, they pose themselves as enjoyers and become busy in trying to enjoy this material world.

TEXT 59

प्रजाःपुपुषतुःप्रीतौदम्पतीपुत्रवत्सलौ ।
शृण्वन्तौकूजितंतासांनिर्वृतौकलभाषितैः ॥५९॥

prajāḥ pupuṣatuḥ prītau dampatī putra-vatsalau
śṛṇvantau kūjitaṁ tāsāṁ nirvṛtau kala-bhāṣitaiḥ

The two pigeons became very affectionate to their children, and they took great pleasure in listening to their awkward chirping, which sounded very sweet to them. Thus, with love and affection, they began to raise the little birds who were born of them.

PURPORT

The conditioned souls, who are averse to the service of Kṛṣṇa, experience great pleasure by hearing the sweet words of their children, which are the fruit of their aversion to the service of the Lord. But, because that pleasure is not eternal, that very pleasure will one day become the cause of their distress.

TEXT 60

तासांपतत्रैःसुस्पर्शैःकूजितैर्मुग्धचेष्टितैः ।
प्रत्युद्गमैरदीनानांपितरौमुदमापतः ॥६०॥

tāsāṁ patatraiḥ su-sparśaiḥ kūjitair mugdha-ceṣṭitaiḥ
pratyudgamair adīnānāṁ pitarau mudam āpatuḥ

The mother and father pigeons became very happy while watching their children grow up. Their chirping, their childish movements around the nest, and their attempts to fly were all very pleasing to see. Seeing how their children were satisfied, the parents felt pleased.

COMMENTARY

The word *adīna* in this verse means that the pigeons were very joyful.

TEXT 61

स्नेहानुबद्धहृदयावन्योन्यंविष्णुमायया ।
विमोहितौदीनधियौशिशूनपुपुषतुःप्रजाः ॥६१॥

snehānubaddha-hṛdayāv anyonyaṁ viṣṇu-māyayā
vimohitau dīna-dhiyau śiśūn pupuṣatuḥ prajāḥ

In this way, being bewildered by the illusory energy of Lord Viṣṇu, the male and female pigeons, who were very much attached to each other, continued to nourish their offspring, even though this sometimes involved a great deal of difficulty.

COMMENTARY

Being overwhelmed by the illusory energy of Lord Viṣṇu, the male and female pigeons carefully maintained their young children.

TEXT 62

एकदाजग्मतुस्तासामन्नार्थंतौकुटुम्बिनौ ।
परितःकाननेतस्मिन्नर्थिनौचेरतुश्चिरम् ॥६२॥

ekadā jagmatus tāsām annārthaṁ tau kuṭumbinau
paritaḥ kānane tasminn arthinau ceratuś ciram

One day, the male and female pigeons, who had many dependent offspring, went out of their nest to find food for their children and thus wandered about within the forest for a long time.

TEXT 63

दृष्ट्वातान्लुब्धकःकश्चिद्यदृच्छातोवनेचरः ।
जगृहेजालमातत्यचरतःस्वालयान्तिके ॥६३॥

dṛṣṭvā tān lubdhakaḥ kaścid yadṛcchāto vane-caraḥ
jagṛhe jālam ātatya carataḥ svālayāntike

Then one day, a hunter who was wandering in the forest happened to see the baby pigeons walking near their nest. By spreading his net, the hunter gleefully captured them.

COMMENTARY

Upon seeing that the young pigeons were playing near their nest, the hunter spread his net and caught them all.

TEXT 64

कपोतश्चकपोतीचप्रजापोषेसदोत्सुकौ ।
गतौपोषणमादायस्वनीडमुपजग्मतुः ॥६४॥

kapotaś ca kapotī ca prajā-poṣe sadotsukau
gatau poṣaṇam ādāya sva-nīḍam upajagmatuḥ

The mother and father pigeon had always been very anxious to look after their helpless children, and they were wandering in the forest looking for food at that time. Having obtained something for their children to eat, they returned to their nest.

COMMENTARY

After collecting some food, the male and female pigeons returned to their nest.

TEXT 65

कपोतीस्वात्मजान्वीक्ष्यबालकान्जालसम्वृतान् ।
तानभ्यधावत्क्रोशन्तीक्रोशतोभृशदुःखिता ॥६५॥

kapotī svātmajān vīkṣya bālakān jāla-samvṛtān
tān abhyadhāvat krośantī krośato bhṛśa-duḥkhitā

When the female pigeon saw that her children were trapped within the hunter's net, she became overwhelmed with anguish. While crying out, she rushed toward them as they cried out to her in return.

TEXT 66

सासकृत्स्नेहगुणितादीनचित्ताजमायया ।
स्वयंचाबध्यतशिचाबद्धान्पश्यन्त्यपस्मृतिः ॥६६॥

sāsakṛt sneha-guṇitā dīna-cittāja-māyayā
svayaṁ cābadhyata śicā baddhān paśyanty apasmṛtiḥ

The female pigeon had wanted to be bound by the strong ropes of maternal affection and so when she saw the condition of her children, she became aggrieved. Being under the influence of the illusory energy of the Lord, she became practically mad. As she rushed to help her children, she also became bound up by the hunter's net.

COMMENTARY

When the mother pigeon saw her children trapped within the net, she became so overwhelmed with lamentation that she was also captured by the hunter.

TEXT 67

कपोतःस्वात्मजान्बद्धान् आत्मनोऽप्यधिकान्प्रियान् ।
भार्यांचात्मसमांदीनोविललापातिदुःखितः ॥६७॥

kapotaḥ svātmajān baddhān ātmano 'py adhikān priyān
bhāryāṁ cātma-samāṁ dīno vilalāpāti-duḥkhitaḥ

When the father pigeon saw his children, who he considered to be more dear than his very life, along with his wife, who he considered as equal to himself, fatally bound within the hunter's net, he became terribly distressed and began to lament most pathetically.

COMMENTARY

The usage of the word *ca* in this verse indicates that he began to lament for both his wife and children.

TEXT 68

अहोमेपश्यतापायमल्पपुण्यस्यदुर्मतेः ।
अतृप्तस्याकृतार्थस्यगृहस्त्रैवर्गिकोहतः ॥६८॥

aho me paśyatāpāyam alpa-puṇyasya durmateḥ
atṛptasyākṛtārthasya gṛhas trai-vargiko hataḥ

The male pigeon said: Alas, my life has been destroyed! What a fool I was, for never performed any pious activities. I neglected my own self-interest and thus failed to fulfill

the purpose of life. My family, which was the basis of my acts of religiosity, economic development, and sense gratification, is now vanquished.

TEXT 69

अनुरूपानुकूलाचयस्यमेपतिदेवता ।
शून्येगृहेमांसन्त्यज्यपुत्रैःस्वर्यातिसाधुभिः ॥६९॥

anurūpānukūlā ca yasya me pati-devatā
śūnye gṛhe māṁ santyajya putraiḥ svar yāti sādhubhiḥ

My wife and I were a loving couple. She faithfully served me as if I were her worshipable deity. Now, she has left me alone and gone to reside in the heavenly planets with our children.

TEXT 70

सोऽहंशून्येगृहेदीनोमृतदारोमृतप्रजः ।
जिजीविषेकिमर्थंवाविधुरोदुःखजीवितः ॥७०॥

so 'haṁ śūnye gṛhe dīno mṛta-dāro mṛta-prajaḥ
jijīviṣe kim arthaṁ vā vidhuro duḥkha-jīvitaḥ

I am a wretched person living alone in misery. My wife and children are dead. Why should I continue to live? My heart is so aggrieved on account of separation from my family that my life is nothing more than suffering.

TEXT 71

तांस्तथैवावृतान्शिग्भिर्मृत्युग्रस्तान्विचेष्टतः ।
स्वयंचकृपणःशिक्षुपश्यन्नप्यबुधोऽपतत् ॥७१॥

tāṁs tathaivāvṛtān śigbhir mṛtyu-grastān viceṣṭataḥ
svayaṁ ca kṛpaṇaḥ śikṣu paśyann apy abudho 'patat

As the foolish pigeon gazed upon his poor children trapped in the net, on the verge of death, struggling hopelessly to free themselves, he lost all good sense and also fell into the hunter's net.

COMMENTARY

Even after seeing that his children were entrapped within the net and were vainly struggling to get free, the male pigeon also fell into the trap.

TEXT 72

तंलब्ध्वालुब्धकःक्रूरःकपोतंगृहमेधिनम् ।
कपोतकान्कपोतींचसिद्धार्थःप्रययौगृहम् ॥७२॥

taṁ labdhvā lubdhakaḥ krūraḥ kapotaṁ gṛha-medhinam
kapotakān kapotīṁ ca siddhārthaḥ prayayau gṛham

After the cruel and greedy hunter had captured the attached male and female pigeons, and their children, he happily returned home.

TEXT 73

एवंकुटुम्ब्यशान्तात्माद्वन्द्वारामःपतत्रिवत् ।
पुष्णन्कुटुम्बंकृपणःसानुबन्धोऽवसीदति ॥७३॥

evaṁ kuṭumby aśāntātmā dvandvārāmaḥ patatri-vat
puṣṇan kuṭumbaṁ kṛpaṇaḥ sānubandho 'vasīdati

One who is too attached to family life becomes overburdened with grief and anxiety. Like the pigeon, his only hope is to find some tiny pleasure in sexual affairs. While busily engaged in maintaining his family, a materialistic person must suffer greatly, along with all his family members.

TEXT 74

यःप्राप्यमानुषंलोकंमुक्तिद्वारमपावृतम् ।
गृहेषुखगवत्सक्तस्तमारूढच्युतंविदुः ॥७४॥

yaḥ prāpya mānuṣaṁ lokaṁ mukti-dvāram apāvṛtam
gṛheṣu khaga-vat saktas tam ārūḍha-cyutaṁ viduḥ

If a person who, even after attaining the human form of life, which is like the gateway to liberation, becomes attached to household life, like the foolish bird in this story, then he is considered by the learned persons as one who has climbed to a high place only to trip and fall down.

PURPORT

Human beings are more qualified to achieve eternal benefit than the living entities in other forms of life. Living entities, such as animals and birds, are less-intelligent. It is easily seen by human beings that they are unable to give up attachment for their wife and children. In the same way, human beings who do not understand the consequences of a miserable materialistic life become attached to enjoying the association of their fellow humans and thus are just like the pigeon family. As long as human beings are alive, they should try to learn these lessons from the above-mentioned eight spiritual masters and thus attain life's ultimate goal. To see the earth, air, sky, water, fire, the moon, the sun, and the pigeon with mere knowledge of the external world will only increase one's thirst for sense gratification. But, with sharp internal vision, if one considers them as worshipable rather than objects of his enjoyment, then his inclination toward Kṛṣṇa will increase, and he will become eligible to attain liberation, even while living in this world.

Thus ends the translation of the First Chapter of the Uddhava-gītā, entitled "**Lord Kṛṣṇa instructs Uddhava**" *with the commentaries of Śrīla Viśvanātha Cakravartī Ṭhākura and chapter summary and purports by Śrīla Bhaktisiddhānta Sarasvatī Ṭhākura.*

Chapter 2

The Story of Pingala

CHAPTER SUMMARY

In this chapter, the Supreme Lord, Śrī Kṛṣṇa, describes to Uddhava what the *avadhūta brāhmaṇa* had learned from nine spiritual masters, beginning with the python. The *avadhūta brāhmaṇa* narrated to Mahārāja Yadu his experiences as follows.

1. The lesson to be learned from the python: It is the duty of intelligent persons to remain engaged in the worship of the Supreme Lord while maintaining their livelihood with whatever is easily available by the arrangement of providence. Even if no food is available, one who desires to worship the Supreme Lord should think that whatever is destined to him will certainly come, and that he should not waste his precious time uselessly endeavoring for the bodily necessities. In this way, he should maintain himself like a python, who does not endeavor for food. This practice will enable him to meditate on the Supreme Lord with undivided attention.

2. The lesson to be learned from the ocean: Self-realized souls, who are inclined towards the Supreme Lord, appear very pure and grave, just like the water of a calm ocean. As the ocean does not increase during the rainy season, even as many rivers flow into it, nor does it dry up in summer, when no water from the rivers enter it, a self-realized soul is neither elated when he receives objects of enjoyment, nor distressed when such objects are lacking.

3. The lesson to be learned from the moth: Just as a moth is enticed by a fire, flies into the fire, and dies, foolish people whose senses are not controlled are attracted by the form of a woman, her golden ornaments, and her dress, and thus fall down to the

darkest regions of hell. Chasing after these embodiments of the divine illusory energy of the Lord, one ultimately loses his life and falls down into the most horrible hell.

4. The lesson to be learned from the bee: There are two kinds of bees—the bumblebee and the honeybee. The lesson to be learned from the bumblebee is that a self-realized soul should maintain himself by begging a little bit from door to door. He should collect essential truths from all the scriptures, whether they be great or insignificant. The lesson to be learned from the honeybee is that a renounced person should not accumulate food, thinking that he will eat it later, in the evening or the next day. If he does so, he will be destroyed along with his accumulated food, just as a greedy honeybee is destroyed along with its honey.

5. The lesson to be learned from an elephant: The male elephant follows the female elephant with a desire to enjoy her, and thus falls into a ditch made by a hunter and is trapped. In the same way, one who is attached to the form of a woman is destroyed by falling deep into the well of material existence.

6. The lesson to be learned from the honey thief: Just as a man takes all the honey that was collected with hard labor by the honeybees, one in the renounced order of life has the privilege of enjoying before anyone else the food and other valuable things purchased by the hard-earned money of householders.

7. The lesson to be learned from the deer: Just as a deer loses his life after being attracted by the music of a hunter, the life of a person who is attached to worldly songs is wasted.

8. The lesson to be learned from the fish: Just as a fish meets with death when it tries to enjoy the baited fishhook, unintelligent people spoil their valuable human lives by being slaves to the demands of the insatiable tongue.

9. There was once a prostitute named Piṅgala who lived in the city of Videha and from her, the *avadhūta* learned a lesson. One day, Piṅgala dressed herself nicely and waited impatiently, from evening to midnight, for the arrival of her paramour. When he didn't come, Piṅgala became so disappointed that she developed detachment. Being inspired by her conscience, she abandoned her sinful desire born of the thirst for meeting her paramour. She then meditated on Śrī Hari and attained great peace in her mind. The instruction received from her is that desire for material enjoyment is the cause of our distress. Therefore, only one who has given up such desires can fix himself in meditation upon the Supreme Lord, and thus achieve transcendental peace.

TEXT 1

श्रीब्राह्मण उवाच

सुखमैन्द्रियकंराजन्स्वर्गेनरकएवच ।
देहिनांयद्यथादुःखंतस्मान्नेच्छेत तद्बुधः ॥१॥

śrī-brāhmaṇa uvāca

sukham aindriyakaṁ rājan svarge naraka eva ca
dehināṁ yad yathā duḥkhaṁ tasmān neccheta tad-budhaḥ

The *avadhūta brāhmaṇa* said: O King, just as material miseries come upon the living entities, whether in heaven or in hell, without endeavor, material happiness will automatically come without seeking it. For this reason, intelligent persons never endeavor for material enjoyment.

COMMENTARY

This chapter describes nine spiritual masters, beginning with the python. Later on, the disappointment that the prostitute, Piṅgala, experienced will be described as the cause of her happiness. One should not work very hard simply for bodily maintenance. In this regard, what can be learned from the python will be described in the following four verses. Just as distress comes without any endeavor, happiness will come to us of its own accord and so, what is the need to endeavor for it?

PURPORT

Intoxicated by material enjoyment, the conditioned souls try to gratify their senses by contact with temporary material objects. This enjoyment is of two types—worldly and heavenly. The conditioned souls enjoy sense gratification as long as they are alive, and then after death, according to their karma, pious souls enjoy heavenly pleasure while impious souls suffer in hellish conditions. Rather than pursue the path of fruitive activities for attaining the heavenly planets, or becoming sense enjoyers in contact with temporary material objects, intelligent people should become inclined towards the service of Kāmadeva Viṣṇu, who is the director and aim of our senses.

TEXT 2

ग्रासंसुमृष्टंविरसंमहान्तंस्तोकमेव वा ।
यदृच्छयैवापतितंग्रसेदाजगरोऽक्रियः ॥२॥

grāsaṁ su-mṛṣṭaṁ virasaṁ mahāntaṁ stokam eva vā
yadṛcchayaivāpatitaṁ grased ājagaro 'kriyaḥ

Like the python, one should give up material endeavors and accept for one's maintenance food that comes of its own accord, whether such food is delicious or tasteless, ample or meager.

COMMENTARY

The propensity of the python is to be inactive and make no endeavor for his maintenance.

PURPORT

The python is satisfied with whatever comes of its own accord. Instead of endeavoring for sense enjoyment, it remains satisfied with any condition of life. It does not try to eat palatable food, or too much food, and it does not try to manipulate the senses, mind, and speech for attaining happiness. Instead, the python always displays its gravity. The lesson to be learned from the python is that those who are inclining towards the service of Lord Kṛṣṇa should not be anxious to gratify their senses. They should not be bound up by the urges of the belly and genitals. One should remain indifferent to such propensities. Eating too much, collecting too much, and endeavoring too much are not favorable for the service of the Supreme Lord. Rather than seeing the python as a mere snake, one should consider it to be a spiritual master. Indeed, one who can see how the Supreme Lord is present everywhere must be considered a *mahā-bhāgavata*. Only those who are fully surrendered to the Supreme Lord are actually sober and qualified to serve the Supreme Lord. They are like the python, who is never agitated for sense enjoyment.

TEXT 3

शयीताहानिभूरीणिनिराहारोऽनुपक्रमः ।
यदिनोपनयेद्ग्रासोमहाहिरिवदिष्टभुक् ॥३॥

śayītāhāni bhūrīṇi nirāhāro 'nupakramaḥ
yadi nopanayed grāso mahāhir iva diṣṭa-bhuk

If food does not come of its own accord, a saintly person should simply fast without making any endeavor to fill his stomach. He should understand that his fasting is the arrangement of the Supreme Lord. Thus following the example of the python, he should patiently wait for the Lord to supply him food.

TEXT 4

ओजःसहोबलयुतंबिभ्रद्देहमकर्मकम् ।
शयानोवीतनिद्रश्चनेहेतेन्द्रियवान् अपि ॥४॥

ojaḥ-saho-bala-yutaṁ bibhrad deham akarmakam
śayāno vīta-nidraś ca nehetendriyavān api

A saintly person should remain in a peaceful condition of life by giving up all anxiety with regards to the maintenance of his body. Even though he may be very sound, both mentally and physically, he should never attempt to accumulate wealth like a materialistic man, but should always remain fixed in his real self-interest.

PURPORT

One should give up lethargy and always remain awake to his real self-interest by engaging in the devotional service to the Supreme Lord. One should not waste time accumulating more and more material assets. In this way, one should follow the example of the python.

TEXT 5

मुनिःप्रसन्नगम्भीरोदुर्विगाह्योदुरत्ययः ।
अनन्तपारोह्यक्षोभ्यःस्तिमितोदइवार्णवः ॥५॥

muniḥ prasanna-gambhīro durvigāhyo duratyayaḥ
ananta-pāro hy akṣobhyaḥ stimitoda ivārṇavaḥ

A saintly sage is happy and pleasing in his external behavior, whereas internally he is most grave and thoughtful. Because he is unfathomable, unconquerable, and unlimited, he is never disturbed, and thus in all respects he is like the tranquil waters of the unfathomable and unsurpassable ocean.

COMMENTARY

This and the next verse describe the lesson to be learned from the ocean. A self-realized soul is as grave as the ocean because he does not allow anyone to understand his intentions. A saintly person is thus unfathomable and does not reveal his mentality to others. He is unconquerable because his prowess is difficult to overcome. He is insurmountable because, even when put into great difficulty, he does not waver from his determination to remain in Kṛṣṇa consciousness. He does not reveal his mind to others and others do not agitate him because he has conquered the urges of the mind and senses.

TEXT 6

समृद्धकामोहीनोवानारायणपरोमुनिः ।
नोत्सर्पेतनशुष्येतसरिद्भिरिवसागरः ॥६॥

samṛddha-kāmo hīno vā nārāyaṇa-paro muniḥ
notsarpeta na śuṣyeta saridbhir iva sāgaraḥ

During the rainy season, raging rivers rush toward the ocean, and during the summer, the same rivers contain hardly any water. Still, the ocean does not increase in size during the rainy season, nor does it dries up in the summer. Similarly, a saintly person who has accepted the Supreme Lord as his goal of life should not become overjoyed when he receives material opulence, nor become morose when he has nothing.

COMMENTARY

Even though during the rainy reason the swollen rivers rush into the ocean, it does not become swollen. In the summer, the ocean does not dry up due to lack of water from the rivers, which have become shallow. Similarly, the transcendentalist should not become joyful when in a materially prosperous condition, and should not lament when he finds himself impoverished. Actually, the devotees of Lord Hari, who are fixed in devotional service, feel the sweetness of that service and lament when they feel a lack of devotional service.

PURPORT

The mind of the devotee who is always absorbed in devotional service is unfathomable, like the water of the ocean. Just as the ocean is very deep and therefore insurmountable, foolish conditioned souls are unable to understand the grave heart of a liberated soul. Those who are wise and are therefore inclined toward the Lord's service, and who desire their own welfare, should become as grave as the ocean by minimizing material activities. They should not become disturbed and restless like ordinary foolish people. Although the water of innumerable rivers constantly fills the ocean, it remains unchanged, just as devotees of the Supreme Lord, who are liberated souls, never are disturbed, even in the midst of a calamity.

TEXT 7

दृष्ट्वास्त्रियंदेवमायांतद्भावैरजितेन्द्रियः ।
प्रलोभितःपतत्यन्धेतमस्यग्नौपतङ्गवत् ॥७॥

dṛṣṭvā striyaṁ deva-māyāṁ tad-bhāvair ajitendriyaḥ
pralobhitaḥ pataty andhe tamasy agnau pataṅga-vat

Those whose senses are not controlled feel attracted to enjoy the form of a woman, which is created by the illusory energy of the Lord. Thus they fall into the darkness of material existence, just as the moth maddened by the fire rushes blindly into its flames.

COMMENTARY

When material beauty, especially the form of a woman, attracts a living entity, he becomes captivated. This is what is to be learned from the moth.

TEXT 8

योषिद्धिरण्याभरणाम्बरादिद्रव्येषुमायारचितेषुमूढः ।
प्रलोभितात्माह्युपभोगबुद्ध्यापतङ्गवन् नश्यतिनष्टदृष्टिः ॥८॥

yoṣid-dhiraṇyābharaṇāmbarādi-dravyeṣu māyā-raciteṣu mūḍhaḥ
pralobhitātmā hy upabhoga-buddhyā pataṅga-van naśyati naṣṭa-dṛṣṭiḥ

Foolish people are immediately aroused at the sight of a lusty woman who is beautifully decorated with golden ornaments, fine clothing, and other cosmetic features. Being eager to enjoy her, such foolish people lose all intelligence and are destroyed, just like the moth who rushes into the blazing fire.

COMMENTARY

Although a woman is attractive for all five senses, the perception of her form is mentioned first because of its prominence.

PURPORT

The conditioned souls, who are averse to the service of the Supreme Lord, are so attached to sense gratification that they always remain in the association of women, engaged in their service. Such persons are controlled by their wives, their fine dress, and their cosmetic arrangements, and they cannot understand that these are like a trap meant for their destruction. Foolish people who are driven by the desire to enjoy the objects of the senses, which are created by the illusory energy of Lord Viṣṇu, consider themselves to be enjoyers, just like moths attracted by a blazing fire. They endeavor to remain entangled in the material world because they think that it is a place of enjoyment. These restless and uncontrolled conditioned souls are attracted by the glaring form of material beauty and madly run towards it, just as a moth rushes towards a blazing fire.

As a result, they fall into the darkness of ignorance and lose all chance for spiritual happiness. Therefore, those who have material desires and are thus engaged in fruitive activities, and who have thus fallen into the trap of material enjoyment, should take this lesson from the moth.

TEXT 9

स्तोकंस्तोकंग्रसेद्ग्रासंदेहोवर्तेतयावता ।
गृहानहिंसन् आतिष्ठेद्वृत्तिंमाधुकरींमुनिः ॥९॥

stokaṁ stokaṁ grased grāsaṁ deho varteta yāvatā
gṛhān ahiṁsann ātiṣṭhed vṛttiṁ mādhukarīṁ muniḥ

The self-realized sage should accept only enough food to keep his body and soul together, taking just a little from different houses without giving trouble to the householders. In this way, one should take a lesson from the honeybee.

COMMENTARY

In this and the next verse, the lesson to be learned from the honeybee is being described. A honeybee may sometimes become attracted by the extraordinary aroma of a lotus flower and sit on it the whole day. However, when the lotus closes its petals at sunset, the honeybee is trapped. Similarly, an intelligent person should not become attracted by the generosity of a householder who gives him sumptuous food, and thus become ensnared in materialistic life. For this reason, a saintly person should collect a little food from many houses. By taking too much, again and again, a mendicant should not give trouble to householders.

PURPORT

A honeybee collects a small amount of honey from many flowers. A saintly devotee should take this lesson from his spiritual master, the honeybee. Instead of asking for a large quantity of alms from a particular householder, a saintly person should accept only that which is necessary for his maintenance by taking a small amount of food from many householders. Such behavior will not cause any difficulty to the householders. If a householder is regularly asked to give sumptuous food, he may certainly become displeased with the mendicant. Those who are mendicants should take this lesson of the honeybee. To accumulate vast assets for undertaking welfare activities is an impediment on the path of Kṛṣṇa consciousness.

TEXT 10

अणुभ्यश्चमहद्भ्यश्चशास्त्रेभ्यःकुशलोनरः ।
सर्वतःसारमादद्यात्पुष्पेभ्यैवषट्पदः ॥१०॥

aṇubhyaś ca mahadbhyaś caśāstrebhyaḥ kuśalo naraḥ
sarvataḥ sāram ādadyāt puṣpebhya iva ṣaṭpadaḥ

Just as a bee takes the nectar from all kinds of flowers, similarly, an intelligent person should take the essence of all the scriptures.

COMMENTARY

One should follow the example of the honeybee, accepting only the essence of life. An intelligent person should be prepared to take lessons from all religious scriptures, whether they be big or small, just as a honeybee collects honey from all kinds of flowers.

PURPORT

The symptom of an expert person is that he is able to extract the essence from both the small and large sources of knowledge. To collect the essence of the flowers is the act of an intelligent person, and not the taking away of the entire plant or bush. This is the lesson to be learned from the honeybee. An ass carries heavy loads but is ultimately cheated, whereas the honeybee, rather than carry the burden of a garden of flowers, simply collects the essential nectar from the flowers. By carefully noting the difference between the ass and the honeybee, an intelligent person should extract the essence from all scriptures that are favorable for the cultivation of devotional service. One should not be like an ass, carrying a heavy burden of useless knowledge. It is often seen that people deceive themselves by discussing useless topics, such as Śrī Gaurasundara's disappearance, and His traveling to Dvārakā.

TEXT 11

सायन्तनंश्वस्तनंवा नसङ्गृह्णीतभिक्षितम् ।
पाणिपात्रोदरामत्रोमक्षिकेवनसङ्ग्रही ॥११॥

sāyantanaṁ śvastanaṁ vā na saṅgṛhṇīta bhikṣitam
pāṇi-pātrodarāmatro makṣikeva na saṅgrahī

An introspective sage should not accumulate the food that he has collected by begging, thinking, "I will eat this in the evening, and I will save this for tomorrow." Rather, he

should accept only as much food as fits in his hands and store only that which fills his belly. He should not imitate a greedy honeybee who eagerly collects more and more honey.

COMMENTARY

The lesson to be learned from the honeybee is being described. A saintly person should not accumulate the food that he has collected by begging, thinking, "I will eat this in the evening, and I will eat that tomorrow." Then, what is the question of saving something for the next month? It is the opinion of some that one should not accept an invitation to eat at some future time. What kind of begging bowl should one employ? The answer is that one should use the palms of one's hands as his begging bowl. Where should one store his alms? The answer is that one should store whatever he collects in his stomach, and nowhere else. One who follows this advice is certainly a saintly devotee.

PURPORT

As a honeybee may meet with death after being stuck in the huge quantity of honey it has collected with great attachment, a mendicant may spoil his spiritual life by accumulating more than is required. However, for spreading Kṛṣṇa consciousness, one may accumulate unlimited material opulence.

TEXT 12

सायन्तनंश्वस्तनंवा नसङ्गृह्णीतभिक्षुकः ।
मक्षिका इवसङ्गृह्णन्सहतेनविनश्यति ॥१२॥

sāyantanaṁ śvastanaṁ vā na saṅgṛhṇīta bhikṣukaḥ
makṣikā iva saṅgṛhṇan saha tena vinaśyati

A saintly mendicant should not save any food for eating later in the day, or the next day. If he disregards this injunction and, like the honeybee, collects more than his immediate needs, he will be destroyed, along with his accumulated wealth.

COMMENTARY

What is the harm if one accumulates a great deal of wealth? The answer is that if a mendicant accumulates more than necessary, he will meet with destruction, along with his possessions.

TEXT 13

पदापियुवतींभिक्षुर्नस्पृशेद्दारवीमपि ।
स्पृशन्करीवबध्येतकरिण्या अङ्गसङ्गतः ॥१३॥

padāpi yuvatīṁ bhikṣur na spṛśed dāravīm api
spṛśan karīva badhyeta kariṇyā aṅga-saṅgataḥ

The introspective sage should never touch a young woman, or even a wooden doll in the shape of a woman with his feet. By bodily contact with a woman, he will become entangled and fall down into the pit of material enjoyment, just as an elephant is captured by the use of a she-elephant, due to his desire to touch her body.

COMMENTARY

A saintly person should not touch even a wooden form of a woman with his feet. Elephant hunters tempt and attract a male elephant by leading it to a pit covered by grass, showing it a female elephant at the far side. The enamored elephant then falls into the pit, and is thus captured.

PURPORT

The trick used for capturing wild elephants is herein described. Wild elephants are tempted by exhibiting a she-elephant in front of them. They are led to a well-guarded pit and thus captured. The madness of the elephant is compared to the arrow of Cupid. The maddened elephants are attached to enjoying the association of female elephants but intelligent devotees should adopt a mood contrary to this. As an elephant is attracted by the touch of a female elephant, a lusty man is attached to enjoying the association of women. Therefore, to see a woman on some pretext, or to even think about her, is totally prohibited for those who are renounced. One should not allow his mind to be lost in lusty dreams of sex pleasure. Sexual enjoyment is exhibited in various ways, such as by talking, by contemplating, by touching, and ultimately, by engaging in sexual intercourse. All of these constitute a network of illusion by which one is helplessly bound to material existence. Therefore, an intelligent person should not indulge in any form of sense enjoyment with women.

TEXT 14

नाधिगच्छेत्स्त्रियंप्राज्ञःकर्हिचिन्मृत्युमात्मनः ।
बलाधिकैःसहन्येतगजैरन्यैर्गजोयथा ॥१४॥

nādhigacchet striyaṁ prājñaḥ karhicin mṛtyum ātmanaḥ
balādhikaiḥ sa hanyeta gajair anyair gajo yathā

An intelligent person should never try to exploit the form of a woman for his sense gratification. Just as an elephant trying to enjoy a she-elephant may be killed by other bull elephants also enjoying her company, one trying to enjoy a lady's company can at any moment be killed by her other lovers who are stronger than he.

COMMENTARY

One should not think, "This woman is meant only for my enjoyment," because he may be killed by a stronger debauchee who wants to enjoy the same woman.

TEXT 15

नदेयंनोपभोग्यंचलुब्धैर्यद्दुःखसञ्चितम् ।
भुङ्क्तेतदपितच्चान्योमधुहेवार्थविन्मधु ॥१५॥

na deyaṁ nopabhogyaṁ ca lubdhair yad duḥkha-sañcitam
bhuṅkte tad api tac cānyo madhu-hevārthavin madhu

Greedy people earn wealth with great labor. But the person who has struggled so much to acquire this wealth is not always allowed to enjoy it himself or give it in charity to others. A greedy person is like a bee who works hard to make some honey, which is then stolen by someone who will either eat it or sell it. No matter how carefully one tries to protect his hard-earned wealth, there will always be someone who is able to steal it.

COMMENTARY

One may not be able to enjoy his hard-earned wealth, or give it in charity to others, because there is always the chance of it being stolen. This is the lesson that can be learned from the honey thief. Greedy people often earn money with great hardship but then are unable to enjoy it or give it away in charity because someone else has stolen it, just as a honey thief enjoys the honey that was accumulated by honeybees. Now, the question may arise, "How could another person know about one's hidden wealth?" The answer is that thieves can understand who has wealth by observing their behavior, just as a honey thief knows the whereabouts of honey by carefully observing the movement of the honeybees.

PURPORT

The conditioned souls, who are averse to the service of the Supreme Lord, fall into a life of inauspiciousness by accumulating material possessions for their own enjoyment. A honeybee works hard to collect honey, and yet it is enjoyed by someone else, and so an intelligent person should not allow himself to suffer the same fate. This is another lesson to be learned from the honeybee.

TEXT 16

सुदुःखोपार्जितैर्वित्तैराशासानांगृहाशिषः ।
मधुहेवाग्रतोभुङ्क्तेयतिर्वैगृहमेधिनाम् ॥१६॥

su-duḥkhopārjitair vittair āśāsānāṁ gṛhāśiṣaḥ
madhu-hevāgrato bhuṅkte yatir vai gṛha-medhinām

Just as a hunter takes away the honey laboriously produced by the honeybees, similarly the renounced mendicants first eat the food cooked by the attached householders who earn their wealth with great labor.

COMMENTARY

It is possible to enjoy sense gratification without personal endeavor. In this regard, I accept the honey thief as my spiritual master. The *brahmacārīs* and the *sannyāsīs* are entitled to be the first to enjoy the sumptuous food produced by householders. If a householder enjoys such food without first offering it in charity to the mendicants, he must purify himself by undergoing the atonement called *cāndrāyaṇam.*

PURPORT

Honeybees collect honey with a great deal of hardship. Just as a greedy hunter takes away the honey that was accumulated by the honeybees, renounced persons accept the first portion of the wealth accumulated by greedy and attached householders as alms. Although externally, it appears that saintly persons use the householders' wealth for their personal gratification, they actually employ it in the service of the Supreme Lord.

TEXT 17

ग्राम्यगीतंनशृणुयाद्यतिर्वनचरःक्वचित् ।
शिक्षेतहरिणाद्बद्धान्मृगयोर्गीतमोहितात् ॥१७॥

grāmya-gītāṁ na śṛṇuyād yatir vana-caraḥ kvacit
śikṣeta hariṇād baddhān mṛgayor gītā-mohitāt

A *sannyasī* who lives in the forest should never hear worldly songs promoting sense enjoyment. The consequence of becoming attached to worldly music can be understood by studying the example of the deer, who are bewildered by the sweet music of the hunter, and are thus captured and killed.

COMMENTARY

Attachment to mundane songs and music is an *anartha*. This should be learned from the deer. The *vānaprasthas* and the *sannyāsīs* should never hear mundane songs and music, which simply promote sense gratification. Instead, they should hear songs in glorification of the Supreme Lord.

PURPORT

Just as a deer becomes captivated by the hunter's enchanting music, *sannyāsīs* will certainly fall down from the path of renunciation by listening to songs promoting sense gratification. This is the lesson to be learned from the deer. It is well-known how Ṛṣyaśṛṅga Muni became ensnared by hearing the singing of beautiful women.

TEXT 18

नृत्यवादित्रगीतानिजुषन्ग्राम्याणियोषिताम् ।
आसांक्रीडनकोवश्यऋष्यशृङ्गोमृगीसुतः ॥१८॥

nṛtya-vāditra-gītāni juṣan grāmyāṇi yoṣitām
āsāṁ krīḍanako vaśya ṛṣyaśṛṅgo mṛgī-sutaḥ

Being attracted by the mundane singing, dancing and musical performances of beautiful women, even the great sage Ṛṣyaśṛṅga, the son of Mṛgī, came under their sway, just like a pet dog.

COMMENTARY

The most instructive example of a renounced person being attracted by songs of sense gratification is Ṛṣyaśṛṅga Muni, who came under the control of beautiful women in that way.

TEXT 19

जिह्वयातिप्रमाथिन्याजनोरसविमोहितः ।
मृत्युमृच्छत्यसद्बुद्धिर्मीनस्तुबडिशैर्यथा ॥१९॥

jihvayāti-pramāthinyā jano rasa-vimohitaḥ
mṛtyum ṛcchaty asad-buddhir mīnas tu baḍiśair yathā

Just as a fish, incited by the desire to enjoy its tongue, loses its life, being pierced by the fisherman's hook, foolish people meet with ruin, being disturbed by the urges of the uncontrollable tongue.

COMMENTARY

Attachment for enjoying varieties of taste is another *anartha*. This is the lesson to be learned from the fish. The fisherman places some meaty bait on a hook that easily attracts the unintelligent fish. Being greedy to enjoy its tongue, the fish tastes the bait and thus dies.

PURPORT

The fish invites its death by being attracted to the meat attached to the hook of the fisherman. Taking a lesson from the fish, the introspective sages should not indulge in eating palatable food, consisting of six kinds of taste. One cannot properly worship Kṛṣṇa if one remains a servant of his tongue and genital. In this regard, one should carefully consider the following verses.

jihvāra lālase yei iti-uti dhāya
śiśnodara-parāyaṇa kṛṣṇa nāhi pāya

One who is subservient to the tongue and who thus goes here and there, devoted to the genitals and the belly, cannot attain Kṛṣṇa.
(*Śrī Caitanya-caritāmṛta* Antya 6.227)

śamo man-niṣṭhatā buddher dama indriya-saṁyamaḥ
titikṣā duḥkha-sammarṣo jihvopastha-jayo dhṛtiḥ

The word *śama* or *śānta-rasa* indicates that one is attached to the lotus feet of Kṛṣṇa. *Dama* means controlling the senses and not being deviated from the Lord's service. Endurance of unhappiness is *titikṣā* and *dhṛti* means controlling the tongue and the genitals. (*Śrīmad-Bhāgavatam* 11.19.36)

TEXT 20

इन्द्रियाणिजयन्त्याशुनिराहारामनीषिणः ।
वर्जयित्वातुरसनंतनन्निरन्नस्यवर्धते ॥२०॥

indriyāṇi jayanty āśu nirāhārā manīṣiṇaḥ
varjayitvā tu rasanaṁ tan nirannasya vardhate

Intelligent people control all their senses, except the tongue, by fasting, because fasting causes one to be even more afflicted by the desire to taste delicious food.

PURPORT

Those who are attached to material enjoyment fulfill their desire for taste with the help of the tongue. If the tongue is denied its favorite tastes, it becomes greedy and agitated. An intelligent person, however, does not fall under the control of the tongue but instead tries to make progress in spiritual life.

The business of the tongue is to seek gratification with varieties of tastes. By visiting the twelve forests of Vṛndāvana, however, one can become released from the desire to enjoy the twelve kinds of mundane sense gratification. The five primary material relationships are neutrality, servitude, friendship, parental love, and conjugal love. The seven secondary material relationships are humor, astonishment, chivalry, compassion, anger, dread, and ghastliness. In their pure form, these twelve *rasas* are exchanged between the living entity and the Supreme Personality of Godhead in the spiritual sky. By visiting the twelve forests of Vṛndāvana, one can purify these twelve *rasas*, which are not manifested in a perverted form. In this way, one can become a liberated soul who no longer possesses material desires. If one artificially tries to renounce sense gratification, he will certainly fail. Indeed, such artificial renunciation generally results in inflaming one's material desires.

TEXT 21

तावज्जितेन्द्रियोनस्याद्विजितान्येन्द्रियःपुमान् ।
नजयेद्रसनंयावज्जितसर्वंजितेरसे ॥२१॥

tāvaj jitendriyo na syād vijitānyendriyaḥ pumān
na jayed rasanaṁ yāvaj jitaṁ sarvaṁ jite rase

Even if a person controls all his other senses, if he fails to control his tongue, he cannot be called a genuinely self-controlled man. On the other hand, if a person controls his tongue, it is to be understood that he has conquered all his senses.

COMMENTARY

The deer, elephant, moth, honeybee, and fish are attracted by sound, touch, form, taste, and smell and thus invite destruction. Human beings are also attracted to these five objects of the senses. If one becomes attached to sense objects, one's degradation is inevitable. The tongue, which is the leader of all the other senses and which induces the other senses, is potentially the most harmful. Therefore, one should take special care to conquer the tongue. The purport is that if one fasts, his other senses can be regulated but his tongue's demands will further increase. And, by indulging the tongue in sense gratification, all the other senses will become agitated. Therefore, one should control his tongue in such a way that all the other senses, which are subordinate to the tongue, are also controlled. What is the method of conquering the tongue? One should loudly chant the holy name of the Supreme Lord and thus experience the ecstasy of *kīrtana*. By honoring the remnants of the Supreme Lord's food, one can also control his tongue.

PURPORT

The senses of those in the bodily conception of life can never be controlled because such persons are bereft of the mellows of devotional service. Those with uncontrolled senses try to enjoy the objects of the senses, which are distinct from the spiritual realm of Vraja, and so they end up becoming devoted to their belly and genitals. Therefore, until one comes to the platform where he can see everything in relation to the Supreme Lord, he should utilize everything in his possession for the service of Kṛṣṇa, without attachment. Only in this way can one conquer his material desires, which are very difficult to subdue. A devotee who in the beginning is unable to traverse the path of attachment (*rāga-mārga*) must follow the regulative principles. One's desires for material enjoyment will not cease until they are replaced by desires to serve the Supreme Lord.

When a devotee attains the platform of *bhāva*, on the strength of his regulative devotional service, then as a result of becoming free of all *anarthas*, he becomes a traveler on the path of attachment. It is only then that one becomes liberated from the gross urges of the tongue, belly, and genitals, as well as from the subtle urges for profit, fame, and adoration. At that time, he is no longer bewildered by the flowery words of the *Vedas*, which tempt one to remain in this temporary world of material enjoyment. When one can control the urges of his body, mind, and speech, then all his *anarthas* are eliminated. In this regard, Śrīla Bhaktivinoda Ṭhākura has written the following song, the meaning of which should be discussed by everyone.

śarīra avidyā jāla, jaḍendriya tāhe kāla,
jīve phele viṣaya-sāgare
tā'ra madhye jihvā ati, lobhamāyā sudurmati,
tā'ke jetā kaṭhina saṁsāre
kṛṣṇa baḍa dayāmaya, karibāre jihvā jaya,
sva-prasāda-anna dila bhāi

sei annāmṛta khāo, rādhā-kṛṣṇa-guṇa gāo,
preme ḍāka caitanya-nitāi

O Lord! This material body is a lump of ignorance, and the senses are a network of paths leading to death. Somehow or other, we have fallen into the ocean of material sense enjoyment, and of all the senses, the tongue is the most voracious and uncontrollable. It is very difficult to conquer the tongue in this world, but You, dear Kṛṣṇa, are very kind to us for You have sent this nice ***prasāda*** to help us conquer the tongue. Therefore, let us take this ***prasāda*** to our full satisfaction and glorify Your Lordships Śrī Śrī Rādhā and Kṛṣṇa and in love call for the help of Lord Caitanya and Prabhu Nityānanda.

TEXT 22

पिङ्गलानामवेश्यासीद्विदेहनगरेपुरा ।
तस्यामेशिक्षितंकिञ्चिन्निबोधनृपनन्दन ॥२२॥

piṅgalā nāma veśyāsīd videha-nagare purā
tasyā me śikṣitaṁ kiñcin nibodha nṛpa-nandana

O son of kings, long ago, there lived a prostitute named Piṅgalā who resided in the city of Videha. Now, please hear what I have learned from her.

COMMENTARY

Now, the *brāhmaṇa* will describe what he learned from Piṅgalā, the prostitute, by narrating her story.

TEXT 23

सास्वैरिण्येकदाकान्तंसङ्केतुपनेष्यती ।
अभूत्कालेबहिर्द्वारिबिभ्रतीरूपमुत्तमम् ॥२३॥

sā svairiṇy ekadā kāntaṁ saṅketa upaneṣyatī
abhūt kāle bahir dvāre bibhratī rūpam uttamam

One night, the prostitute dressed herself attractively and sat outside her house, waiting for the arrival of a lover.

COMMENTARY

By dressing in attractive ways and making various sensual bodily gestures, the prostitute, Piṅgala, would attract her lovers.

TEXT 24

मार्ग आगच्छतोवीक्ष्यपुरुषान्पुरुषर्षभ ।
तान्शुल्कदान्वित्तवतःकान्तान्मेनेऽर्थकामुकी ॥२४॥

mārga āgacchato vīkṣya puruṣān puruṣarṣabha
tān śulka-dān vittavataḥ kāntān mene 'rtha-kāmukī

O foremost of men, this prostitute wanted desperately to get some money and for that purpose she stood by the side of the road at night, gazing at all the men as they passed by. She thought, "This man looks wealthy and I am sure that he would like to enjoy with me." In this way, she evaluated all men as they passed her by.

COMMENTARY

People who were attached to enjoying an intimate relationship with a woman would come to her house and pay a handsome amount.

TEXTS 25-26

आगतेष्वपयातेषुसासङ्केतोपजीविनी ।
अप्यन्योवित्तवान्कोऽपिमामुपैष्यतिभूरिदः ॥२५॥
एवंदुराशयाध्वस्तनिद्राद्वार्यवलम्बती ।
निर्गच्छन्तीप्रविशतीनिशीथंसमपद्यत ॥२६॥

āgateṣv apayāteṣu sā saṅketopajīvinī
apy anyo vittavān ko 'pi mām upaiṣyati bhūri-daḥ

evaṁ durāśayā dhvasta- nidrā dvāry avalambatī
nirgacchantī praviśatī niśītham samapadyata

As Piṅgalā stood in her doorway, many men passed her by. Her only means of support was her profession as a prostitute, and so she anxiously thought, "Maybe this man will enjoy my company. He looks like he has a lot of money. Here is another man who will surely pay me for my love. Alas! This man did not stop but someone else is coming

now who will surely want to pay me for my love." Thus, hoping against hope, Piṅgalā remained standing in her doorway, unable to earn enough money and thus retire for the night. Being very anxious, she sometimes went out into the street, and then again went back into her house. In this way, the night passed.

COMMENTARY

The word *niśīthaṁ* indicates that she waited till midnight but no one availed of her services.

TEXT 27

तस्या वित्ताशया शुष्यद्वक्त्राया दीनचेतसः ।
निर्वेदःपरमोजज्ञेचिन्ताहेतुःसुखावहः ॥२७॥

tasyā vittāśayā śuṣyad- vaktrāyā dīna-cetasaḥ
nirvedaḥ paramo jajñe cintā-hetuḥ sukhāvahaḥ

When it became very late, the prostitute, who badly wanted to get some money, became morose so that her face appeared withered. Being full of anxiety and greatly disappointed, she began to experience a sense of detachment from her situation, so that a kind of happiness arose within her mind.

COMMENTARY

Her entire night passed by thinking about wealth.

PURPORT

The prostitute, Piṅgalā, who was greedy for money, dedicated her life to satisfying lusty men. As a result of engaging in the service of conditioned souls with her body, mind, and speech, and forgetting the service of the Supreme Lord, her mind became extremely restless. Finally, she became so frustrated that she became indifferent to her situation, so that happiness began to arise within her mind.

TEXT 28

तस्या निर्विण्णचित्तायागीतंशृणुयथामम ।
निर्वेद आशापाशानांपुरुषस्ययथाह्यसिः ॥२८॥

tasyā nirviṇṇa-cittāyā gītāṁ śṛṇu yathā mama
nirveda āśā-pāśānāṁ puruṣasya yathā hy asiḥ

Detachment is the only means by which a person can destroy the network of material desires. The prostitute felt disgusted with her situation and this gave rise to indifference. Now, please hear from me the song sung by the prostitute in that situation.

COMMENTARY

Piṅgalā thought, "My ambitions are the cause of my material bondage. Detachment or indifference is the only weapon by which this network of bondage can be cut to pieces."

PURPORT

Those who cannot gain freedom from the bondage of their social position and family responsibilities, if they take up the trident of detachment, they can cut the knots of material bondage and attain auspiciousness. Those who are too attached to material enjoyment and are addicted to bodily pleasures cannot understand the messages of the self-satisfied Supreme Lord, being bound by the ropes of illusion.

TEXT 29

नह्यङ्गाजातनिर्वेदोदेहबन्धंजिहासति ।
यथाविज्ञानरहितोमनुजोममतांनृप ॥२९॥

na hy aṅgājāta-nirvedo deha-bandhaṁ jihāsati
yathā vijñāna-rahito manujo mamatāṁ nṛpa

O King, just as an ignorant person with no spiritual knowledge is never inclined to renounce his false sense of ownership, similarly, a person who has not developed a sense of detachment will never give up his attachment for his material body.

COMMENTARY

The *avadhūta* begins to explain the purpose of this narration.

TEXT 30

पिङ्गलोवाच
अहोमेमोहविततिंपश्यताविजितात्मनः ।
याकान्तादसतःकामंकामयेयेनबालिशा ॥३०॥

piṅgalā uvāca
aho me moha-vitatiṁ paśyatāvijitātmanaḥ
yā kāntād asataḥ kāmaṁ kāmaye yena bāliśā

Piṅgalā said: Alas! Just see how greatly illusioned I am, due to my uncontrolled senses. As a result, I have lost my power of discrimination and therefore desire satisfaction from similarly illusioned lusty men.

COMMENTARY

The word *kāma* means "lusty desires." Piṅgalā is in effect saying, "I desire to become satisfied in sex and thus I can understand that I am completely illusioned."

PURPORT

The senses of the conditioned souls are naturally attracted to the sense objects of this material world. This is the prime example of the conditioned soul's foolishness. Some people, who are actually averse to the Lord's service, try to artificially check their senses from engagement in sense gratification for some time, but this actually does more harm than good because of their misunderstanding regarding the Absolute Truth. Foolish people consider other sense enjoyers to be their masters, and thus they pray to them for the fulfillment of their own sense gratification. However, as soon as one becomes enlightened in spiritual understanding, his life of material enjoyment can be transformed into a life of spiritual perfection.

TEXT 31

सन्तंसमीपेरमणंरतिप्रदंवित्तप्रदंनित्यमिमंविहाय।
अकामदंदुःखभयाधिशोकमोहप्रदंतुच्छमहंभजेऽज्ञा ॥३१॥

santaṁ samīpe ramaṇaṁ rati-pradaṁ vitta-pradaṁ nityam imaṁ vihāya
akāma-daṁ duḥkha-bhayādhi-śoka- moha-pradaṁ tuccham ahaṁ bhaje 'jñā

I am so foolish that I have given up the service of the most beloved person, the Supreme Lord, who is always situated within my heart, and who can award me real pleasure and prosperity. I abandoned His service and engaged in the service of insignificant men who were unable to fulfill my real desires but instead brought me distress, fearfulness, anxiety, lamentation, and illusion.

COMMENTARY

Piṅgalā thought, "The Supersoul is sitting in my heart. Why do I not try to experience the pleasure of conjugal love with Him? Why am I earning money by allowing many sinful men to enjoy my body? Actually, all these rich men were unable to fulfill my lusty desires."

PURPORT

The material desires of the conditioned souls are aroused due to lack of God consciousness, or due to lack of seeing the Supreme Lord as the only worshipable person. Aversion to the Lord's service places the conditioned souls in an artificial condition of distress, fear, lamentation, and illusion. Being under the control of the material nature, they cannot understand that the Supreme Lord is the true object of worship in all respects, and that He is always present by their side. The Supreme Lord is the actual enjoyer of all that is enjoyable, and He is situated in the hearts of all living entities as their well-wishing friend. Because it is the natural propensity for a conditioned soul to befriend another conditioned soul, they should together engage in the service of the non-dual Supreme Person. The Supreme Lord is eternal, and He is the master of those who award material wealth and other benedictions. He alone awards transcendental happiness because He is the one supreme person, who is eternal, full of knowledge and bliss, who maintains all other, subordinate persons. One who gives up his relationship with the Supreme Lord and indulges in temporary material enjoyment is certainly fool number one.

TEXT 32

अहोमयात्मापरितापितोवृथासाङ्केत्यवृत्त्यातिविगर्ह्यवार्तया ।
स्त्रैणान्नराद्यार्थतृषोऽनुशोच्यात्क्रीतेनवित्तंरतिमात्मनेच्छती ॥३२॥

aho mayātmā paritāpito vṛthā sāṅketya-vṛttyāti-vigarhya-vārtayā
straiṇān narād yārtha-tṛṣo 'nuśocyāt krītena vittaṁ ratim ātmanecchatī

Alas! I have unnecessarily troubled myself by adopting this most abominable profession of prostitution, desiring to earn money and enjoy sexual pleasure by selling my body to lusty men, who themselves are to be pitied.

COMMENTARY

Piṅgalā laments that she tried to attain a most insignificant pleasure by selling her body to insignificant, useless men.

PURPORT

The art of arousing the spirit of enjoyment is called *saṅketya vṛtti*, and it involves employing sensual gestures and movements. Employing this art is one of the sinful ways of earning one's livelihood. Only the most condemned and greedy sense enjoyers are so attracted by the illusory beauty of a woman that they will spend their hard-earned money in exchange for a few moments of her association. If, somehow or other, a conditioned soul revives his inclination for Kṛṣṇa's service, he will come to understand that it was because of giving up the service of the Lord that he has been swallowed by the witches of material enjoyment and impersonal liberation.

TEXT 33

यदस्थिभिर्निर्मितवंशवंस्यस्थूणंत्वचारोमनखैःपिनद्धम् ।
क्षरन्नवद्वारमगारमेतद्विण्मूत्रपूर्णंमदुपैतिकान्या ॥३३॥

yad asthibhir nirmita-vaṁśa-vaṁsya-sthūṇaṁ tvacā roma-nakhaiḥ pinaddham
kṣaran-nava-dvāram agāram etad viṇ-mūtra-pūrṇaṁ mad upaiti kānyā

This material body is like a house wherein, I, the eternal spirit soul, am residing. My spine, ribs, and the bones of my arms and legs are like the beams and pillars of the house. This body, which is full of stool and urine, is covered by skin, hair, and nails. Foul secretions emanate from the nine doors of this body. Other than me, what woman would foolishly devote herself to this material body, thinking that she will find pleasure there?

COMMENTARY

Piṅgalā thought, "Alas! This is most strange! I have accepted this disgusting body, which is full of obnoxious substances, as the object of my conjugal pleasure. This house in the form of my body has nine gates. The spinal chord is the main bamboo pillar upon which the body is supported. The bones of the rib cage, as well as the hands and legs, are considered to be secondary beams, giving support. Who is more unfortunate than me to consider such a body as a source of love and pleasure?"

PURPORT

The gross body of the conditioned soul is compared to a house. Just as a house consists of many wooden beams that provide support to the structure, the physical body is an assembly of bones, flesh, hair, nails, and other component parts. This body excretes abominable substances, such as stool, urine, and perspiration. Therefore, it must be concluded that those who give up the service of Kṛṣṇa just to accept the perishable and disgusting objects of this material world as desirable, are certainly most unfortunate people.

TEXT 34

विदेहानांपुरेह्यस्मिन्नहमेकैवमूढधीः ।
यान्यमिच्छन्त्यसत्यस्मादात्मदात्काममच्युतात् ॥३४॥

videhānāṁ pure hy asminn aham ekaiva mūḍha-dhīḥ
yānyam icchanty asaty asmād ātma-dāt kāmam acyutāt

I rejected Śrī Hari, who awards self-realization and our original spiritual form, to enjoy sense gratification with many men. There is certainly no other woman in this city of Videha who is as foolish as myself.

COMMENTARY

Piṅgalā thought, "I am so unchaste that I desired the association of many useless men rather than Lord Acyuta, who gives Himself to His dear devotees."

PURPORT

The Supreme Lord is the personification of all transcendental mellows. There is nothing temporary or abominable in Him. If one desires to serve the Lord, one should give up the aspiration to be the enjoyer of the objects of the senses. To serve the temporary objects of this material world is certainly foolishness.

TEXT 35

सुहृत्प्रेष्ठतमोनाथ आत्माचायंशरीरिणाम् ।
तंविक्रीयात्मनैवार्हमेऽनेनयथारमा ॥३५॥

suhṛt preṣṭhatamo nātha ātmā cāyaṁ śarīriṇām
taṁ vikrīyātmanaivāhaṁ rame 'nena yathā ramā

Lord Hari is the well-wisher, the Lord, and the Supersoul of all living entities. I will purchase Him with the price of complete surrender and then enjoy with Him, just like Lakṣmīdevī.

COMMENTARY

Piṅgalā thought, " 'What should I do then?' If you ask me this, my answer is that I will dedicate my body to my most beloved Lord and enjoy His company."

PURPORT

Self-realized souls who are devoted to Lord Hari's service are the actual friends and best masters of the embodied souls. If the conditioned souls engage in the service of the Lord, like Lakṣmī, then their lives will become successful and they will attain eternal happiness. Piṅgalā realized that it is better to serve the Supreme Lord with one's body, mind, and speech, under the subordination of Lakṣmīdevī, than to sell one's body to the temporary men of this world. This realization alone can free the conditioned soul from his propensity for material enjoyment.

TEXT 36

कियत्प्रियंतेव्यभजन्कामायेकामदानराः ।
आद्यन्तवन्तोभार्यायादेवावाकालविद्रुताः ॥३६॥

kiyat priyaṁ te vyabhajan kāmā ye kāma-dā narāḥ
ādy-antavanto bhāryāyā devā vā kāla-vidrutāḥ

Men give women some satisfaction of their senses, but they are all destined to die, even the demigods in the heavenly planets. These men are temporary creations of the illusory energy of the Lord, who will be forcibly dragged away by time. Considering this, how much pleasure can men actually give to their women?

COMMENTARY

Piṅgalā thought, "All men, and even demigods, who endeavor to fulfill their lusty desires, are subject to birth and death. So, how can they please their wives? I therefore conclude that no one in this world, or in the next, other than the Supreme Lord, is worthy of my service."

PURPORT

Tempting objects of this world, proud men who are busily absorbed in their temporary material identifications, and demigods who cannot award any true benefit to their subordinates, are destroyed by time as a result of their karma.

TEXT 37

नूनंमेभगवान्प्रीतोविष्णुःकेनापिकर्मणा ।
निर्वेदोऽयंदुराशायायन्मेजातःसुखावहः ॥३७॥

nūnaṁ me bhagavān prīto viṣṇuḥ kenāpi karmaṇā
nirvedo 'yaṁ durāśāyā yan me jātaḥ sukhāvahaḥ

Although I was determined to enjoy this material world, because this most auspicious detachment has awakened in my heart, I think that Lord Śrī Hari must be pleased with me. Without even knowing it, I must have performed some activity that satisfied Him.

COMMENTARY

In this way Piṅgalā, praises her good fortune. Some learned authorities have said that when Dattātreya happened to come to Piṅgalā's house, she said to him, "O foremost sage, what have I done to have the good fortune of seeing you? Today, you have mercifully blessed my house. Please come in. Have some food and water and then rest awhile." Indeed, Piṅgalā even cleansed her courtyard when Dattātreya arrived there, out of his own sweet will.

PURPORT

In this regard, one should contemplate the purport of the following verse from the *Śrīmad-Bhāgavatam* (11.23.28):

nūnaṁ me bhagavāṁs tuṣṭaḥ sarva-deva-mayo hariḥ
yena nīto daśām etāṁ nirvedaś cātmanaḥ plavaḥ

The Supreme Lord, Hari, who is the Lord of lords, must have been pleased with me because, by His mercy, I have developed this mood of detachment, which is the means for my deliverance from the ocean of material existence.

TEXT 38

मैवंस्युर्मन्दभाग्यायाःक्लेशानिर्वेदहेतवः ।
येनानुबन्धंनिर्हृत्यपुरुषःशममृच्छति ॥३८॥

maivaṁ syur manda-bhāgyāyāḥ kleśā nirveda-hetavaḥ
yenānubandhaṁ nirhṛtya puruṣaḥ śamam ṛcchati

One who has developed detachment can give up the bondage of material existence, and one who undergoes great suffering gradually becomes, out of a sense of hopelessness, indifferent toward the material world. It was due to my great suffering that detachment awoke in my heart. If I were actually unfortunate, how could I have undergone such merciful suffering? I can only conclude that I am actually fortunate because, I have received the mercy of the Lord. Somehow or other, He must be pleased with me.

COMMENTARY

Piṅgalā thought, "Someone may ask me, 'Why are you suffering despite having wealth? Is it because Lord Viṣṇu is not pleased with you?' I would reply, 'Please do not say that. If Lord Viṣṇu was not pleased with me then I, who am an unfortunate prostitute, would not have developed a mood of indifference. Because of this indifference, I was able to give up all material aspirations and achieve satisfaction within my heart.' "

TEXT 39

तेनोपकृतमादायशिरसाग्राम्यसङ्गताः ।
त्यक्त्वादुराशाःशरणंव्रजामितमधीश्वरम् ॥३९॥

tenopakṛtam ādāya śirasā grāmya-saṅgatāḥ
tyaktvā durāśāḥ śaraṇaṁ vrajāmi tam adhīśvaram

Therefore, with all respect, I accept this favor of Śrī Hari upon my head. I will now surrender myself unto the lotus feet of the Lord of the universe, Śrī Hari, giving up all material desires.

COMMENTARY

Piṅgalā thought, "Therefore, I gladly welcome this favor of Lord Viṣṇu, which has resulted in my mood of detachment. Although I was fully attached to worldly enjoyment, I now take shelter at the lotus feet of the Lord of the universe, Śrī Hari."

TEXT 40

सन्तुष्टाश्रद्दधत्येतद्यथालाभेनजीवती ।
विहराम्यमुनैवाहमात्मनारमणेनवै ॥४०॥

santuṣṭā śraddadhaty etad yathā-lābhena jīvatī
viharāmy amunaivāham ātmanā ramaṇena vai

I have firm faith in the favor of Śrī Hari, and I am satisfied to accept whatever He provides for my maintenance. I will only enjoy the association of Śrī Hari, who is the actual source of all love and happiness.

COMMENTARY

Piṅgalā thought, "If someone were to ask, 'What will you do after surrendering to Śrī Hari?' the answer is that I will enjoy life with whatever I receive by His mercy. I will only enjoy the association of Śrī Hari, who alone is capable of giving me real pleasure."

PURPORT

One never commits any sin or offense if he utilizes all material objects in the service of Lord Kṛṣṇa, and accepts whatever comes of its own accord for his maintenance. Desire for material enjoyment arises as soon as there is an absence of the propensity to render loving service to the Supreme Lord. This is the root cause of all material miseries. While utilizing this natural propensity for serving the Supreme Lord, one is able to see everything within the material world as meant for the Lord's enjoyment, rather than his own enjoyment. Thus one sees the material world as an opportunity for engaging in the devotional service of the Lord. In Kṛṣṇa consciousness, one's conditional life is dissolved, and one become qualified to establish true friendship with other devotees in the course of rendering loving service to the Supreme Lord.

TEXT 41

संसारकूपेपतितंविषयैर्मुषितेक्षणम् ।
ग्रस्तंकालाहिनात्मानंकोऽन्यस्त्रातुमधीश्वरः ॥४१॥

saṁsāra-kūpe patitaṁ viṣayair muṣitekṣaṇam
grastaṁ kālāhinātmānaṁ ko 'nyas trātum adhīśvaraḥ

The intelligence of the conditioned souls is taken away by his activities of sense gratification. Thus, he falls into the dark well of material existence, where he is seized by the deadly serpent of time. Who else but the Supreme Personality of Godhead could save the poor living entity from such a hopeless condition?

COMMENTARY

One may argue, "Why did Piṅgalā surrender to Viṣṇu, instead of one of the demigods, like Brahmā?" The answer is that no one but Lord Viṣṇu is capable of delivering the living entities who are drowning in the dark well of material existence, and are thus blinded by their spirit of material enjoyment and devoured by the poisonous snake of time.

PURPORT

The conditioned souls are bitten by the snake of time because they consider themselves to be the enjoyers of this temporary material world, which is experienced by the senses as sound, touch, form, taste, and smell. This spirit of enjoying separate from the Lord is the reason for their falling into the dark well of material existence. Still, the all-merciful Supreme Lord has made many arrangements to deliver the fallen conditioned souls from the dark well of material enjoyment by engaging them in His devotional service.

TEXT 42

आत्मैवह्यात्मनोगोप्तानिर्विद्येतयदाखिलात् ।
अप्रमत्त इदंपश्येद्ग्रस्तंकालाहिनाजगत् ॥४२॥

ātmaiva hy ātmano goptā nirvidyeta yadākhilāt
apramatta idaṁ paśyed grastaṁ kālāhinā jagat

Only when one can see how this material world is being swallowed by the serpent of time does he become sober and thus come to his senses. Thus, he refrains from all types of material enjoyment and becomes qualified to act for his own protection.

COMMENTARY

One may ask, "By what means can one be delivered from the dark well of material existence?" The answer is that when one realizes that the entire material creation is being swallowed by the serpent of time, then he can become indifferent to all kinds of material enjoyment. Being endowed with this understanding, one becomes his own protector.

Piṅgalā replies, "Recently, this was my personal experience, and thus I became freed from the clutches of material existence without separate endeavor. Now, I will worship Lord Viṣṇu with love and devotion."

This is the sum and substance of this verse.

PURPORT

When a conditioned soul becomes self-realized and his natural propensity for the Lord's service is awakened, he receives the spiritual strength to protect himself from falling back down into material existence. As a result, he is no longer anxious to enjoy this material world, nor does he become intoxicated by thoughts of material enjoyment. It is only in forgetfulness of the Supreme Lord that a living entity indulges in sense gratification under the influence of the time factor. Such a materialistic life is the result of one's aversion to the Supreme Lord. One can be influenced by the material time factor, sense objects, and sense pleasure only as long as one is ignorant of his eternal constitutional position. The bodily conception of life separates the living entities from the cultivation of Kṛṣṇa consciousness and makes them falsely think of themselves as the enjoyers of material nature.

TEXT 43

श्रीब्राह्मणुवाच
एवंव्यवसितमतिर्दुराशांकान्ततर्षजाम् ।
छित्त्वोपशममास्थायशय्यामुपविवेशसा ॥४३॥

śrī-brāhmaṇa uvāca
evaṁ vyavasita-matir durāśāṁ kānta-tarṣa-jām
chittvopaśamam āsthāya śayyām upaviveśa sā

The *avadhūta brāhmaṇa* said: Thus, her mind completely made up, Piṅgalā cut off all her sinful desires to enjoy sex pleasure with so-called lovers, and so she became situated on the platform of perfect peace. Thereafter, she sat down on her bed.

TEXT 44

आशाहिपरमंदुःखंनैराश्यंपरमंसुखम् ।
यथासञ्छिद्यकान्ताशांसुखंसुष्वापपिङ्गला ॥४४॥

āśā hi paramaṁ duḥkhaṁ nairāśyaṁ paramaṁ sukham
yathā sañchidya kāntāśāṁ sukhaṁ suṣvāpa piṅgalā

Material desires are undoubtedly the causes of terrible misery, and freedom from such desires is the cause of the greatest happiness. While thinking in this way, Piṅgalā renounced all desires to enjoy the affection of materialistic men, so that she was able to peacefully go to sleep.

PURPORT

Sense enjoyers are always disturbed in this world of so-called enjoyment. Hiding somewhere nearby the path of renunciation, the threefold material miseries inspire careless transcendentalists to become enjoyers of perishable material objects whenever they get the slightest opportunity. The sinful desire for attaining fame even while tied by the ropes of desires for material enjoyment sometimes induces the conditioned souls to become servants of Rāvaṇa, Kaṁsa, Jarāsandha, Agha, Baka or Pūtanā. If the conditioned souls turn off the temporary lamp of material desires and become attached to the lotus feet of the inhabitants of Vraja, then all auspiciousness will be within their grasp. Pseudo renunciation makes a living entity very proud. On the other hand, proper renunciation places living entities on the platform of pure goodness, or transcendence. Until the lamp of material desire is turned off, a devotee's desire for the service of the lotus feet of Śrī Rādhā cannot materialize.

In this regard, one should contemplate the meaning of this verse:

āśā-bharair amṛta-sindhu-mayaiḥ kathañcit
kālo mayāti-gamitaḥ kila sāmprataṁ hi
tvaṁ cet kṛpāṁ mayi vidhāsyasi naiva kiṁ me
prāṇair vrajena ca varoru bakāriṇāpi

"O ravishingly beautiful Śrī Rādhe! I am passing my days and nights in torment, with the singular hope that I may obtain the ocean of immortal nectar, so kindly shower Your grace upon me. Deprived of Your mercy, of what use are my life, residence in Vraja, or even servitorship to Kṛṣṇa, the enemy of Bakāsura?" (Śrīla Raghunātha dāsa Gosvāmī's *Vilāpa-kusumāñjali* 102)

Śrī Gaurasundara has taught us that the mood of separation is the best process for relishing the mellows of ecstatic love of Kṛṣṇa.

Thus ends the translation of the Second Chapter of the Uddhava-gītā, entitled "The Story of Piṅgalā," *with the commentaries of Śrīla Viśvanātha Cakravartī Ṭhākura and chapter summary and purports by Śrīla Bhaktisiddhānta Sarasvatī Ṭhākura.*

Chapter 3

Detachment from All That is Material

CHAPTER SUMMARY

In this chapter, the *avadhūta brāhmaṇa* describes the lessons to be learned from the seven remaining spiritual masters, beginning with the kurara bird. He also describes an additional guru, one's own body.

1. The instruction of the kurara bird is that attachment is the mother of all distress. One who is unattached and has no material possessions is qualified to achieve unlimited happiness.

2. The *avadhūta brāhmaṇa* learned from a foolish, lazy boy that by becoming free from anxiety, one can nicely worship the Supreme Lord and experience transcendental bliss.

3. The instruction received from the young girl who kept only one conchshell bangle on each wrist is that one should remain alone and thus steady his mind. Only in such a condition will it be possible for one to fix his mind completely on the Supreme Lord. Once, several men arrived to ask for the hand of a young girl, whose relatives had coincidentally left the house. She went inside and began to prepare food for the unexpected guests by beating rice paddy. At that time, her conchshell bangles made a loud noise, rattling against each other. in order to stop this sound, the girl broke off the bangles, one by one, until at last, only one remained on each arm. Just as two or more bangles make noise, if two or more people live together, there is bound to be quarrel and useless gossiping.

4. The *avadhūta brāhmaṇa* also received instruction from the arrow maker, who was so absorbed in constructing an arrow that he did not even notice that the king was

passing right by him on the road. In the same way, one should worship Śrī Hari with undivided attention and a controlled mind.

5. The lesson to be learned from the serpent is that a sage should wander alone, should not live in any prearranged place, should be always careful and grave, should not reveal his movements, should take assistance from no one, and should speak little.

6. This is the lesson to be learned from the spider. Just as a spider makes its web from its own saliva and then withdraws it, the Supreme Lord creates this universe from out of Himself and then winds it up into His own body.

7. From the weak insect that assumed the form of a wasp, the *avadhūta brāhmaṇa* learned that the living entity, under the sway of affection, hatred, and fear, attains in his next life the identity of that object upon which he had fixed his attention.

8. Realizing that the temporary material body is subject to birth and death, and that this human form of body is extremely rarely achieved, a sober person should give up his attachment for the body and should properly utilize his time for acquiring knowledge so that he can attain the goal of life.

TEXT 1

श्रीब्राह्मण उवाच
परिग्रहोहिदुःखाययद्यत्प्रियतमंनृणाम् ।
अनन्तंसुखमाप्नोतितद्विद्वान् यस्त्वकिञ्चनः ॥१॥

śrī-brāhmaṇa uvāca
parigraho hi duḥkhāya yad yat priyatamaṁ nṛṇām
anantaṁ sukham āpnoti tad vidvān yas tv akiñcanaḥ

The *avadhūta brāhmaṇa* said: Everyone considers something of this world to be very dear to him. Because of such attachment, one ultimately becomes morose. One who understands this simple truth should give up the false sense of possessiveness and thus tread the path to true happiness.

COMMENTARY

This chapter describes seven spiritual masters, beginning with the kurara bird. The material body has been added as the eighth spiritual master in this chapter. In total, the lessons to be learned from twenty-five spiritual masters are described. The first two verses of this chapter deal with the lesson to be learned from the kurara bird. When one enjoys the object that is most dear to him, he will certainly face great distress later on. On the other hand, those who remain aloof from such attachment, remaining as *akiñcana*, are to be known as learned men who are qualified to achieve unlimited happiness.

PURPORT

As a result of forgetfulness of the Supreme Lord, the conditioned soul's taste for objects produced by the material modes of passion and ignorance increases unlimitedly. The conditioned souls rarely have the inclination to attain the platform of pure goodness, from which one can realize the Supreme Lord. All material miseries are produced from the influence of the modes of passion and ignorance. The momentary lack of distress experienced due to the influence of mode of goodness is not the same as genuine, spiritual happiness. Unalloyed devotees do not notice the presence of temporary distress produced by the interaction of the modes of nature because they experience unlimited happiness due to being situated on the platform of pure goodness. Conditioned souls who are under the control of their senses run after limited, ever-changing, and tempting material objects and thus become beggars to achieve their objectives. This is the cause of their distress.

TEXT 2

सामिषंकुररंजघ्नुर्बलिनोऽन्येनिरामिषाः ।
तदामिषंपरित्यज्यससुखंसमविन्दत ॥२॥

sāmiṣaṁ kuraraṁ jaghnur balino 'nye nirāmiṣāḥ
tadāmiṣaṁ parityajya sa sukhaṁ samavindata

Once a large kurara bird was very hungry, being unable to find any prey, it attacked a weaker kurara bird who had some flesh in its claws. Being in danger of his life, the weaker kurara bird gave up his meat and thereby attained actual happiness.

COMMENTARY

The word *samiṣaṁ* in this verse refers to a meat-eating kurara bird. When a kurara bird was chased by another stronger kurara bird, it dropped the flesh in its claws and thus achieved happiness.

PURPORT

Incited by the modes of nature, birds become violent and kill other birds, either to eat them or to steal meat captured by them. Hawks, vultures and eagles are in this category. A human being should give up the envious propensity to commit violence against others and should take to Kṛṣṇa consciousness, whereby one sees every living entity as equal to oneself. On this platform of actual happiness, one does not envy anyone, and thus sees no one as his enemy.

TEXT 3

नमेमानापमानौस्तोनचिन्तागेहपुत्रिणाम् ।
आत्मक्रीड आत्मरतिर्विचरामीहबालवत् ॥३॥

na me mānāpamānau sto na cintā geha-putriṇām
ātma-krīḍa ātma-ratir vicarāmīha bāla-vat

Those who are attached to family life are always anxious about their children, wealth, and reputation, but I have nothing to do with all these. I do not worry about a family, and I have no concern for praise or insult. I live the life of the eternal soul, and I experience affection on the spiritual platform. Thus I wander over the earth like a child.

PURPORT

When one has no interest in accumulating worldly praise or criticism, he can become fixed in the science of the self.

TEXT 4

द्वावेवचिन्तयामुक्तौपरमानन्द आप्लुतौ ।
योविमुग्धोजडोबालोयोगुणेभ्यःपरंगतः ॥४॥

dvāv eva cintayā muktau paramānanda āplutau
yo vimugdho jaḍo bālo yo guṇebhyaḥ paraṁ gataḥ

In this world, two types of people are free from all anxiety and merged in great happiness—one is the retarded and childish fool, and the other is an advanced transcendentalist who knows the science of the Absolute Truth.

COMMENTARY

In this verse, the lesson to be learned from a foolish boy is described. The *brāhmaṇa* said, "I don't care for honor and dishonor, I am not worried about house, children, and so on. Just like a child, I happily wander about alone in this world."

PURPORT

The more one prays for sensual enjoyment in this material world, the more his desires for such enjoyment increase, so that he becomes more and more absorbed in matter. Those who are indifferent to material pleasures are freed from material miseries and are happy.

TEXT 5

क्वचित्कुमारीत्वात्मानंवृणानान्गृहमागतान् ।
स्वयंतानर्हयामासक्वापियातेषुबन्धुषु ॥५॥

kvacit kumārī tv ātmānaṁ vṛṇānān gṛham āgatān
svayaṁ tān arhayām āsa kvāpi yāteṣu bandhuṣu

Once, a girl of marriageable age was at home alone because her parents and relatives were away. At that time, some men came to ask for her hand in marriage and so she received them with all hospitality.

COMMENTARY

The lesson to be learned from the unmarried girl is being described. Once, some men went to the house of an unmarried girl to ask for her hand in marriage. It so happened that the girl's relatives were away from home at that time. So, the unmarried girl received the guests nicely, offering them *āsanas* of *kuśa* grass and water.

TEXT 6

तेषामभ्यवहारार्थंशालीन्रहसिपार्थिव ।
अवघ्नन्त्याःप्रकोष्ठस्थाश्चक्रुःशङ्खाःस्वनंमहत् ॥६॥

teṣām abhyavahārārthaṁ śālīn rahasi pārthiva
avaghnantyāḥ prakoṣṭha-sthāś cakruḥ śaṅkhāḥ svanaṁ mahat

O King, when that unmarried girl began to beat rice paddy to prepare food for the unexpected guests, the conch shell bangles on her arms began to collide with each other and create a loud noise.

COMMENTARY

Wondering when the people of the house would return and begin to cook, the girl began to prepare rice to serve the guests. However, her conch shell bangles began to make a loud noise.

TEXT 7

सा तज्जुगुप्सितं मत्वा महती व्रीडिता ततः ।
बभञ्जैकैकशः शङ्खान्द्वौ द्वौ पाण्योरशेषयत् ॥७॥

sā taj jugupsitaṁ matvā mahatī vrīḍitā tataḥ
babhañjaikaikaśaḥ śaṅkhān dvau dvau pāṇyor aśeṣayat

The young girl was afraid that her guests would know that her family was poor because she was performing the menial task of husking the rice. Being very intelligent, the girl broke the conchshell bangles so that only two remained on each wrist.

TEXT 8

उभयोरप्यभूद्घोषो ह्यवघ्नन्त्याः स्वशङ्खयोः ।
तत्राप्येकं निरभिददेकस्मान्नाभवद्ध्वनिः ॥८॥

ubhayor apy abhūd ghoṣo hy avaghnantyāḥ sva-śaṅkhayoḥ
tatrāpy ekaṁ nirabhidad ekasmān nābhavad dhvaniḥ

Thereafter, when the young girl resumed husking the rice, the bangles once again made noise by colliding with each other. Then, the girl took off one more bangle from each arm, leaving only one, so that the noise completely stopped.

COMMENTARY

The girl was embarrassed because husking rice is the job of a servant in the house of well-to-do people. The intelligent girl then took off her bangles, one by one, leaving only two on each arm. When these bangles again began to make noise, she took one more bangle from each arm, leaving only one.

TEXT 9

अन्वशिक्षमिमं तस्या उपदेशमरिन्दम ।
लोकाननुचरन्नेतान्लोकतत्त्वविवित्सया ॥९॥

anvaśikṣam imaṁ tasyā upadeśam arindama
lokān anucarann etān loka-tattva-vivitsayā

O subduer of the enemy, I travel over the surface of the earth learning about the nature of this world. Thus, I personally witnessed the lesson taught by this girl.

COMMENTARY

The *brāhmaṇa* sage explained to King Yadu that what he was speaking was realized knowledge. By wandering over the world, he had experienced everything that he had learned from the gurus under discussion. Instead of pretending to be an all-knowing mystic, he simply described what he had learned during his wanderings.

TEXT 10

वासेबहूनांकलहोभवेद्वार्ताद्वयोरपि ।
एक एववसेत्तस्मात्कुमार्या इवकङ्कणः ॥१०॥

vāse bahūnāṁ kalaho bhaved vārtā dvayor api
eka eva vaset tasmāt kumāryā iva kaṅkaṇaḥ

When many people live together, there will undoubtedly be quarrels. Even if only two people live together, there will certainly be frivolous conversation and disagreement. That is why one should live alone, following the example of the young girl and her bangles.

COMMENTARY

The lesson to be learned from the girl who removed all her bangles but one is that one who is trying to advance on the path of *jñāna-yoga*, which involves philosophical speculation, should live alone after giving up all desires for having the association of friends and relatives. After all, whenever people live together, they quarrel over insignificant matters, and engage in much trivial talk that has no relation to their aspiration for spiritual advancement. Therefore, just to have a peaceful environment in which to practice yoga, it is recommended that one live alone. On the other hand, a princess who has been married to a qualified prince dresses herself very attractively and then appears before him to receive his love. Similarly, Bhakti-devī decorates herself with the association of Vaiṣṇavas, who assemble to chant the holy names of the Lord and dance in ecstasy. Because pure devotees do not associate with nondevotees, in that sense, they reside alone and thus take the lesson of the single bangle from the young girl. After all, pure devotees do not quarrel among themselves, nor do they engage in frivolous talks because they are fully satisfied on the platform of rendering devotional service to the Lord, without any material desires. Thus, devotees of the Lord happily associate with one another for the purpose of rendering service to the Lord.

The Supreme Lord has personally said in the *Śrīmad Bhāgavatam* (3.25.34):

naikātmatām me spṛhayanti kecin
mat-pāda-sevābhiratā mad-īhāḥ
ye 'nyonyato bhāgavatāḥ prasajya
sabhājayante mama pauruṣāṇi

A pure devotee, who is attached to the activities of devotional service and who always engages in the service of My lotus feet, never desires to become one with Me. Such a devotee, who is unflinchingly engaged, always glorifies My pastimes and activities.

PURPORT

If there is more than one person in a place, there is every possibility that there will be a quarrel, because each individual has his own idea and purpose. When the girl took away all her bangles except one on each wrist, there was no more noise as a result of colliding with each other. Similarly, one should give up the association of those who are not devoted to the Supreme Lord. The character of a Vaiṣṇava is always pure. However, in places where nondevotees congregate, there will undoubtedly be envious criticism of Vaiṣṇavas. If many people gather to glorify the Lord, there will be no conflict of interest. That is why one should worship the Lord in the association of like-minded people. This is also solitary *bhajana* as described in the system of *ekāyana.*

TEXT 11

मन एकत्रसंयुंज्ञ्ज्ञितश्वासोजितासनः ।
वैराग्याभ्यासयोगेनध्रियमाणमतन्द्रितः ॥११॥

mana ekatra saṁyuñjyāj jita-śvāso jitāsanaḥ
vairāgyābhyāsa-yogena dhriyamāṇam atandritaḥ

One should perfect his yoga sitting postures and the breathing exercises while carefully cultivating a life of renunciation. Thus, with single-minded attention, one should engage in yoga, making it the goal of his life.

COMMENTARY

One should practice concentrating his mind. This lesson is to be learned from the arrow maker. The mind is always flickering, due to material attachment, wandering here and there. Here it is recommended, to perfect a life of renunciation, one should practice *aṣṭāṅga-yoga* mixed with devotional service.

TEXT 12

यस्मिन्मनोलब्धपदंयदेतच्छनैःशनैर्मुञ्चतिकर्मरेणून् ।
सत्त्वेनवृद्धेनरजस्तमश्चविधूयनिर्वाणमुपैत्यनिन्धनम् ॥१२॥

yasmin mano labdha-padaṁ yad etac chanaiḥ śanair muñcati karma-reṇūn
sattvena vṛddhena rajas tamaś ca vidhūya nirvāṇam upaity anindhanam

The mind can be controlled when it is fixed on the Supreme Personality of Godhead. When the mind is thus applied to the service of the Lord, it becomes free from polluted desires for sense gratification so that as the mode of goodness increases in strength, one can completely give up the modes of passion and ignorance. When the mind is no longer fed the fuel of the modes of nature, the fire of material existence becomes extinguished, so that one achieves the transcendental platform of direct relationship with the object of his meditation, the Supreme Lord.

COMMENTARY

When the mind is controlled and restrained from the desire for performing fruitive activities, it becomes cleansed of the contamination of passion and ignorance through an increase of the mode of goodness. When the mind is no longer influenced by the modes of passion and ignorance, it becomes steady and as a result of being situated in the mode of goodness, one becomes joyful.

PURPORT

The three modes of material nature create conflict among one another. For that reason, those who are actually intelligent carefully control their mind. When one is freed from the influence of the modes of passion and ignorance, one achieves a life of auspiciousness. It is only possible to transcend the three modes of material nature when the mind is fully under control.

TEXT 13

तदैवमात्मन्यवरुद्धचित्तोनवेदकिञ्चिद्बहिरन्तरंवा ।
यथेषुकारोनृपतिंव्रजन्तमिषौगतात्मानददर्शपार्श्वे ॥१३॥

tadaivam ātmany avaruddha-citto na veda kiñcid bahir antaraṁ vā
yatheṣu-kāro nṛpatiṁ vrajantam iṣau gatātmā na dadarśa pārśve

There was once an arrow maker who was so absorbed in making a straight arrow that he did not even notice the king, when he passed right in front of him. When one's

consciousness is completely fixed on the Supreme Personality of Godhead, one no longer sees in terms of duality, or internal and external reality.

COMMENTARY

If one desires to concentrate his mind on the Supreme Lord, he should study the example of the arrow maker. The arrow maker was so absorbed in his work that even when the king passed by, with so much pomp and commotion, the arrow maker did not even notice him.

PURPORT

The only way to withdraw the mind from the objects of the senses is to eagerly engage in the devotional service of Lord Kṛṣṇa. When the mind is not absorbed in fervently desiring to please the Supreme Lord, it wanders on the subtle platform of accepting and rejecting the things of this world. By surrendering unto the Supreme Lord and engaging in His devotional service, one can be freed from the continuous struggle for supremacy of the three modes of material nature. For one who is thus fully engaged, the spirit of enjoying things in a mood of being separate from Kṛṣṇa will not affect him. As long as a conditioned soul wanders within the kingdom of mental speculation, having giving up Kṛṣṇa's service, he will remain fully absorbed in matter. In this regard, one should carefully consider this verse (2) of the *Upadeśāmṛta*:

atyāhāraḥ prayāsaś ca prajalpo niyamāgrahaḥ
jana-saṅgaś ca laulyaṁ ca ṣaḍbhir bhaktir vinaśyati

One's devotional service is spoiled when he becomes too entangled in the following six activities:

1. Eating more than necessary or collecting more funds than required.
2. Over endeavoring for mundane things that are very difficult to obtain.
3. Talking unnecessarily about mundane subject matters.
4. Practicing the scriptural rules and regulations only for the sake of following them, and not for the sake of spiritual advancement, or rejecting the rules and regulations of the scriptures and working independently or whimsically.
5. Associating with worldly-minded persons who are not interested in Kṛṣṇa consciousness.
6. Being greedy for mundane achievements.

TEXT 14

एकचार्यनिकेतःस्यादप्रमत्तोगुहाशयः ।
अलक्ष्यमाण आचारैर्मुनिरेकोऽल्पभाषणः ॥१४॥

eka-cāry aniketaḥ syād apramatto guhāśayaḥ
alakṣyamāṇa ācārair munir eko 'lpa-bhāṣaṇaḥ

A saintly person should wander about alone, without any companion and without a fixed residence. Indeed, just to avoid bad association, he should be careful so that he will not even be recognized by others. While traveling here and there, he should avoid speaking more than what is absolutely necessary.

COMMENTARY

The lesson to be learned from the snake is herein described. As a snake wanders about alone, out of fear of people, behaving in such a way that no one will notice it, an introspective sage should conduct his life in the same manner.

PURPORT

The propensity for material enjoyment is the cause of the living entity's distress. This propensity also covers his actual purpose in life. Instead of opposing the previously followed social etiquette, if one accepts it without attachment then gradually he will achieve auspiciousness. When one follows the *varṇāśrama* system, he takes the first step in self-realization. One should work honestly and control his propensity for sexual enjoyment, either by completely renouncing it as a *brahmacārī* or *sannyāsī*, or by accepting the concession offered to the householder. Without regulating one's life, everything will be performed whimsically, so that it will be impossible to make spiritual advancement. A person's attachment to society, friendship, and love is a great impediment on the path of spiritual elevation. If one maintains such attachments, progress will be very slow. Śrī Caitanya Mahāprabhu taught us by His personal example what a devotee should and should not do. It is simply obedience to these principles that will lead one to the perfection of life. There is no use in ways of mundane society, which simply directs us toward the path of sense gratification.

TEXT 15

गृहारम्भोहिदुःखायविफलश्चाध्रुवात्मनः ।
सर्पःपरकृतंवेश्मप्रविश्यसुखमेधते ॥१५॥

gṛhārambho hi duḥkhāya viphalaś cādhruvātmanaḥ
sarpaḥ para-kṛtaṁ veśma praviśya sukham edhate

For the living entities who possess perishable material bodies, building a house is miserable and useless. A snake enters a hole created by others and lives happily.

PURPORT

Because the snake does not build its own house, but occupies a dwelling constructed by others, it does not become entangled in the miseries of building a residence. The ass-like people of this world have accepted a great burden by providing electric lights, vehicles, fans, and so on, for the Vaiṣṇavas, and they should continue to do so. Because Vaiṣṇavas are travelers on the path of spiritual life, they do not carry the great burden of material advancement, because they abstract the essence of life. They do not undergo great inconvenience just for the comfort of their bodies but instead live in a world built by others without becoming attached to it. Expertise in the act of renovation and preserving one's family or society traditions is not the goal of those who travel on the path of spiritual life.

TEXT 16

एकोनारायणोदेवःपूर्वसृष्टंस्वमायया ।
संहृत्यकालकलयाकल्पान्तेदमीश्वरः ।
एक एवाद्वितीयोऽभूदात्माधारोऽखिलाश्रयः ॥१६॥

eko nārāyaṇo devaḥ pūrva-sṛṣṭaṁ sva-māyayā
saṁhṛtya kāla-kalayā kalpānta idam īśvaraḥ
eka evādvitīyo 'bhūd ātmādhāro 'khilāśrayaḥ

Nārāyaṇa, is the worshipable Lord of the universe and of all the living entities contained therein. Working independently, the Lord creates the cosmic manifestation by directing His potency. To enact the annihilation of the universe, the Lord employs His personal expansion, time, thus withdrawing everything to remain within Himself. Thus, the Lord is the reservoir of all potencies. The pradhāna, which is the cause of the cosmic manifestation, is conserved within the Lord and thus is nondifferent from Him. After the annihilation of the universe, the Lord alone exists as one without a second.

COMMENTARY

The *avadhūta brāhmaṇa* says, "I have learned from the spider how the Supreme Lord creates the universe. Lord Nārāyaṇa alone, without anyone's help, created the universes by manipulating His energies, under the control of time, and then annihilated them. After the annihilation, the Lord remained as one without a second. All the conditioned living entities, as well as the material energies, became merged within the Lord. Thus, He is the shelter of all energies."

TEXTS 17-18

कालेनात्मानुभावेनसाम्यंनीतासुशक्तिषु ।
सत्त्वादिष्वादिपुरुषःप्रधानपुरुषेश्वरः ॥१७॥
परावराणांपरम आस्ते कैवल्यसंज्ञितः ।
केवलानुभवानन्दसन्दोहोनिरुपाधिकः ॥१८॥

kālenātmānubhāvena sāmyaṁ nītāsu śaktiṣu
sattvādiṣv ādi-puruṣaḥ pradhāna-puruṣeśvaraḥ

parāvarāṇāṁ parama āste kaivalya-saṁjñitaḥ
kevalānubhavānanda-sandoho nirupādhikaḥ

When His material energies, such as the mode of passion, are in a neutral condition, by His influence in the form of time, the Lord remains as the supreme controller. The Supreme Personality of Godhead is the controller of the material nature, the Lord of the *puruṣāvatāras*, the only shelter of the living entities, including the demigods, headed by Brahmā. The Lord is fully transcendental, the personification of supreme bliss, the primeval Lord, and the giver of liberation.

COMMENTARY

The Supreme Lord neutralizes the material energies, such as the mode of goodness, by displaying His potencies in the form of time. Even in that neutral state, the Lord remains the controller of the material nature, as well as the *puruṣāvatāras*. He is the supremely worshipable Lord of all liberated and conditioned souls. Because there are no activities, such as the creation of the universe, in that neutral state, the Supreme Lord enjoys eternal happiness in His own mood, referred to as *yoga-nidrā*. He is called *nirupādhika* because at that time, His energy, *maya*, remains dormant. It is stated in the Third Canto of the *Śrīmad-Bhāgavatam* that when the energies of the Supreme Lord are dormant, He remains awake.

PURPORT

While trying to ascertain the nature of the Absolute Truth with the help of their speculations, conditioned souls come to the conclusion that it is impersonal. Less intelligent people, under the grips of illusion, imagine that the living entities and the Supreme Lord are one and the same. With this conclusion, they focus their attention on the impersonal feature of the Supreme Lord. According to the *Śrīmad-Bhāgavatam*, the Supreme Personality of Godhead creates, sustains, and annihilates this universe, which is under the control of time, by the three modes of material nature. The supremely independent Lord induces the conditioned living entities, who are His fragmental parts, to dance as the enjoyers of the objects of the senses. When one gains practical experience that the gross and subtle material bodies are simply coverings of the eternal soul, one gives up the foolishness of material attachment and becomes attached to the Supreme Personality of Godhead. This is actual liberation, the highest form of which is to reside in Vraja and relish supreme bliss, free from all material designations.

TEXT 19

केवलात्मानुभावेनस्वमायांत्रिगुणात्मिकाम् ।
सङ्क्षोभयनसृजत्यादौतयासूत्रमरिन्दम ॥१९॥

kevalātmānubhāvena sva-māyāṁ tri-guṇātmikām
saṅkṣobhayan sṛjaty ādau tayā sūtram arindama

O subduer of the enemies, at the time of creation, the Personality of Godhead expands His energy in the form of time and by glancing over His material energy, *maya,* which is composed of the three modes of material nature, the *mahat-tattva* becomes manifested.

COMMENTARY

After describing the annihilation, creation is now being described. By His own spiritual energy, the Supreme Lord awakens His material energy, *maya*, and agitates her by means of His glance. In this way, he creates the *mahat-tattva*, which consists of the total material ingredients and the power of creation.

PURPORT

The fully cognizant Supreme Lord is the creator of the conditioned souls, and the material world. The infinitesimal conditioned living entities can attain the ultimate goal of life, love of God, by executing practical devotional service under the guidance of a pure devotee. The conception that this material world is false, and that the infinitesimal living entities can merge in the infinite Supreme Lord at the time of liberation is not factual.

TEXT 20

तामाहुस्त्रिगुणव्यक्तिंसृजन्तींविश्वतोमुखम् ।
यस्मिन्प्रोतमिदंविश्वंयेनसंसरतेपुमान् ॥२०॥

tām āhus tri-guṇa-vyaktiṁ sṛjantīṁ viśvato-mukham
yasmin protam idaṁ viśvaṁ yena saṁsarate pumān

The compilers of the scriptures describe the *mahat-tattva,* from which the cosmic manifestation springs, to be the effect of the three modes of material nature. Indeed, this universe is resting within that *mahat-tattva,* and due to its potency, the living entity undergoes material existence.

COMMENTARY

The word *tām* in this verse indicates the *mahat-tattva*, which is the manifestation of the three modes of material nature, and which creates the various planets, with the help of the false ego. How have the varieties of planets and living entities been created? This is described in the *Vedas* as follows: "O Gautama, it is the air that sustains all the planets of the universe, and the varieties of living entities residing on them. The living entities are traveling throughout the material existence by the force of air."

PURPORT

The material creation is a manifestation of the Lord's external energy, which covers the healthy condition of the living entities, who are spiritual by nature, and induces them to become masters of the material universe, which is actually under the control of time. By thinking themselves to be the enjoyers of material nature, the insignificant living entities mistakenly imitate the Supreme Lord and thus create the misfortune of wandering within the conditional state of material existence under the control of perverted desires. Undivided devotional service to the Supreme Lord is real liberation. As soon as one is separated from the Lord's service, due to the influence of *maya*, one tries to become the master. This is the actual fault of the living entities in this material world, and it results from their aversion to the service of the Supreme Lord.

TEXT 21

यथोर्णनाभिर्हृदयादूर्णांसन्तत्यवक्त्रतः ।
तयाविहृत्यभूयस्तांग्रसत्येवंमहेश्वरः ॥२१॥

yathorṇanābhir hṛdayād ūrṇāṁ santatya vaktrataḥ
tayā vihṛtya bhūyas tāṁ grasaty evaṁ maheśvaraḥ

Just as from within himself the spider manifests thread through its mouth, plays with it for some time, and then eventually withdraws it within itself, the Supreme Lord creates this universe from His own self, utilizes it for some time, and then He eventually withdraws it within His own self.

COMMENTARY

The word *ūrṇanābhi* indicates a spider. A spider releases threads from her heart through her mouth, creates a web, and plays on it. Then again, it swallows the entire web. In the same way, the Supreme Lord creates the entire universe from His own self and then, after enjoying His pastimes, again withdraws it within His own self .

PURPORT

The spirit souls wander about in this temporary world, which was created by the Supersoul. Just as a spider manifests thread from its body and then again winds it up within itself, the Supreme Lord creates this temporary material world, which is a manifestation of His inferior energy, and then again winds it up. This temporary material world is under the control of time, it is limited, and it is full of miseries.

TEXT 22

यत्रयत्रमनोदेहीधारयेत्सकलंधिया ।
स्नेहादद्वेषाद्भयाद्वापियातितत्तत्स्वरूपताम् ॥२२॥

yatra yatra mano dehī dhārayet sakalaṁ dhiyā
snehād dveṣād bhayād vāpi yāti tat-tat-svarūpatām

Whatever a living entity concentrates his mind upon, whether out of affection, hatred, or fear, he will certainly attain in his next life.

COMMENTARY

The *avadhūta brāhmaṇa* says, "The devotees of the Supreme Lord, who are attached to meditating upon His transcendental form, easily attain the same bodily features as the Lord. This is not at all wonderful. I have learned this lesson from the wasp."

The next two verses describe the lesson to be learned from the wasp. When one's mind meditates upon a particular form without deviation, he will certainly attain that form in the future.

PURPORT

The living entity, who is embodied by gross and subtle matter, experiences affection, hatred, or fearfulness for the object of his attachment as dictated by his intelligence, which is under the control of the spirit of material enjoyment. Ultimately. one attains the form of the object upon which he meditates. If one can renounce the desire for material enjoyment and thus attract the attention of the unlimitedly affectionate Lord, while displaying anger towards those who are envious of the Lord, and fear of the consequences of absorption in sense gratification, he can attain an eternal spiritual form as a servant of the Supreme Lord in His transcendental abode.

TEXT 23

कीटःपेशस्कृतंध्यायन्कुड्यांतेनप्रवेशितः ।
यातितत्सात्मतांराजन्पूर्वरूपमसन्त्यजन् ॥२३॥

kīṭaḥ peśaskṛtaṁ dhyāyan kuḍyāṁ tena praveśitaḥ
yāti tat-sātmatāṁ rājan pūrva-rūpam asantyajan

O King, once a tiny insect was captured and kept captive in a hive of a wasp. Out of great fear, that tiny insect constantly meditated upon his captor so that, without giving up its present body, it gradually assumed the form of a wasp. There is no doubt that whatever one thinks of at the time of death, he will attain that state of existence in his next life.

COMMENTARY

The insect attained the same bodily features as the wasp, even without giving up its present body. This indicates that when one meditates on a particular form, he will gradually come to resemble the object of his meditation. A good example of this is Dhruva Mahārāja. Generally, a devotee who meditates upon the Lord gives up his material body at the time of death and then attains a spiritual form, so that materialistic persons are unable to perceive the transformation. This is enacted by the internal energy of the Supreme Lord. Sometimes, it appears that the spiritual body has been given up but such pastimes are illusory. Nārada Munī has explained that when he received the spiritual body of an associate of the Lord, his material body was instantaneously relinquished, just like a flash of lightning and its illumination occur simultaneously.

PURPORT

When a cockroach sees a bright green insect, it becomes so afraid that it begins to meditate on it and thus becomes fully absorbed in its mood. Similarly, conditioned souls can become self-realized in this very lifetime by practicing Kṛṣṇa consciousness. By being established in the devotional service of the Supreme Lord, they attain liberation even in the present life. Steady intelligence is the main criteria for achieving complete absorption in the object of one's meditation. Being bewildered by his knowledge of the external world, a person may see the body of a liberated person as meant for his enjoyment, failing to understand his own position as a servant of the Lord. Internal perfection is distinct from external appearances. Foolish people cannot understand this, and so they are unable to understand the intentions of perfected souls. If an ordinary person tries to understand the position of a *paramahaṁsa mahābhāgavata* with the help of his mundane perception, there is no doubt that he will pave his way to hell. In this regard, one should carefully consider the verse that begins *arcye viṣṇau śilā-dhī.*[3] A person's assessment of a self-realized Vaiṣṇava's external behavior becomes the cause of his inauspiciousness. That is why the [4]*api cet sudurācāraḥ* verse has been presented in the *Bhagavad-Gītā* 9.30.

TEXT 24

एवंगुरुभ्य एतेभ्य एषामेशिक्षितामतिः ।
स्वात्मोपशिक्षितांबुद्धिंशृणुमेवदतःप्रभो ॥२४॥

evaṁ gurubhya etebhya eṣā me śikṣitā matiḥ
svātmopaśikṣitāṁ buddhiṁ śṛṇu me vadataḥ prabho

O King, from these spiritual masters I have acquired great wisdom. Now, please listen to what I have learned from my own body.

COMMENTARY

Now, the *brāhmaṇa* will speak about what he learned from his own body.

---

3 *arcye viṣṇau śilā-dhīr guruṣu nara-matir vaiṣṇave jāti-buddhiḥ śrī-viṣṇor nāmni śabda-sāmānya-buddhiḥ*, etc. "One should not consider the Deity of the Lord as worshiped in the temple to be an idol, nor should one consider the authorized spiritual master an ordinary man. Nor should one consider a pure Vaiṣṇava to belong to a particular caste, etc." (*Padma Purāṇa*)

4 *api cet sudurācāro bhajate mām ananya-bhāk s*
ādhur eva sa mantavyaḥ samyag vyavasito hi saḥ

Even if a devotee sometimes seems to engage in abominable activities, he should be considered a sādhu, a saintly person, because his actual identity is that of one engaged in the loving service of the Lord. In other words, he is not to be considered an ordinary human being.

PURPORT

The *avadhūta brāhmaṇa* says, "I have provided my intelligence with many valuable lessons after seeing the activities of various spiritual masters. Now, I will tell you what I have learned from my own self."

TEXT 25

देहोगुरुर्ममविरक्तिविवेकहेतुर्बिभ्रत्स्मसत्त्वनिधनंसततार्त्युदर्कम् ।
तत्त्वान्यनेनविमृशामियाथातथापिपारक्यमित्यवसितोविचराम्यसङ्गः ॥२५॥

deho gurur mama virakti-viveka-hetur
bibhrat sma sattva-nidhanaṁ satatārty-udarkam
tattvāny anena vimṛśāmi yathā tathāpi
pārakyam ity avasito vicarāmy asaṅgaḥ

The material body is also my spiritual master because it teaches me detachment. Being a product of the material nature, it always comes to a painful end. Thus, although I use my body to acquire knowledge, I always remember that it will ultimately be consumed by others. Thus, in a mood of detachment, I wander about in this world.

COMMENTARY

The *avadhūta brāhmaṇa* says, "By the use of my power of discrimination, I have learned the lesson of detachment from my body, and so I also consider it to be a spiritual master. This body is born at a particular time and ultimately perishes. In this way, it has taught me detachment. The stomach is a part of the body, and it can remain like a mendicant without food for two or three days. This is another lesson I have learned from my body. With the help of the senses of the body, I will cultivate devotional service to the Lord by hearing and chanting. A pure devotee, despite contact with all varieties of material tastes, does not become attached to them, although he is attached to tasting the mellows of his relationship with Lord Hari. When one chews betel nuts, his tongue remains red long after the betel nuts are spit out. By this example, one should know that engagement in sense gratification will undoubtedly produce a lasting effect within the mind. Actually, the material body does not belong to us—it will ultimately be enjoyed by someone else. If it is discarded in a lonely place, dogs and jackals will eat it. If it is buried after death, it will become the food of worms and germs. After considering all this, I have given up all attachment to my body and I simply wander about freely."

PURPORT

The *avadhūta brāhmaṇa* says, "My present diseased material condition is due to my attachment for the objects of the senses. By utilizing both my gross and subtle bodies for engagement in sense gratification, I have come under the control of time. This would not be the case if my intelligence were fixed on attaining the Absolute Truth. Now, I will give up all attempts to enjoy the objects of the senses, so that I will no longer be materially absorbed, despite living in a material body." The proper utilization of one's intelligence is to extract the essence from life in this material world, instead of becoming overwhelmed by material attachment. This is the secret of serving the Supreme Lord, which is distinct from a life of material enjoyment.

TEXT 26

जायात्मजार्थपशुभृत्यगृहाप्तवर्गान्पुष्नातियत्प्रियचिकीर्षयावितन्वन् ।
स्वान्तेसकृच्छ्रमवरुद्धधनःसदेहःसृष्ट्वास्यबीजमवसीदतिवृक्षधर्मः ॥२६॥

jāyātmajārtha-paśu-bhṛtya-gṛhāpta-vargān
puṣnāti yat-priya-cikīrṣayā vitanvan
svānte sa-kṛcchram avaruddha-dhanaḥ sa dehaḥ
sṛṣṭvāsya bījam avasīdati vṛkṣa-dharmaḥ

A man who is attached to his material body accumulates money with great struggle to maintain his wife, children, property, domestic animals, servants, homes, relatives, friends, and so on. Actually, one does all this for the gratification of his own body. As a tree before dying produces the seed of a future tree, the dying body manifests the seed of one's next material body in the form of accumulated karma. Thus assuring the continuation of one's material existence, the material body sinks down and dies.

COMMENTARY

One may question, "The material body is the best of all spiritual masters because it teaches one detachment, leading to engagement in devotional service. Although it is temporary, one should take great care to preserve the material body, which enlightens one with knowledge. If one does not properly adore his material body, he must certainly incur the sin of ungratefulness. How can one remain detached from such a body?"

The answer is that the material body does not instruct one like a benevolent teacher, it teaches detachment by placing us in so much misery. A person remains busy expanding his family empire because he wants to experience pleasure from it. It is only due to attachment for his body that a person carefully maintains his family members. In due course of time, the body will lose all capacity for material enjoyment, and then lay down and die. A person's karma creates the seed of his future life, and thus forces him to continue suffering in material existence. When the seed of a tree is ripe, it falls. The same principle applies to the material body.

PURPORT

A tree creates a seed that produces another tree before dying. Similarly, a conditioned soul nourishes his wife, children, pet animals, wealth, and relatives with his hard-earned money, just to give pleasure to his own gross and subtle bodies, and these acts create the seed of his future existence. After working hard in this way, a materially attached person gives up his body at death. To see the gross and subtle material bodies as identical with the soul is ignorance. Those who cannot discriminate between matter and spirit are not on the level of intelligent people who very well understand the existence of the eternal soul beyond the temporary material body.

TEXT 27

जिह्वैकतोऽमुमपकर्षतिकर्हितर्षाशिश्नोऽन्यतस्त्वगुदरंश्रवणंकुतश्चित् ।
घ्राणोऽन्यतश्चपलदृक्क्वचकर्मशक्तिर्बह्व्यःसपत्न्य इवगेहपतिंलुनन्ति ॥२७॥

jihvaikato 'mum apakarṣati karhi tarṣā
śiśno 'nyatas tvag udaraṁ śravaṇaṁ kutaścit
ghrāṇo 'nyataś capala-dṛk kva ca karma-śaktir
bahvyaḥ sapatnya iva geha-patiṁ lunanti

As each wife of a householder who has many wives tries to attract her husband for her own purpose—the tongue, genitals, sense of touch, belly, ears, nose, restless eyes, and working senses, attract the embodied soul towards their respective objects of enjoyment.

COMMENTARY

One should feed his body only as much as is necessary to maintain it, without attachment. This is the way to serve the body as one's spiritual master. When one, due to great attachment, provides the senses with whatever they ask for, the tongue demands palatable food and engagement in gossip, thirst demands water, and the genitals demand the association of women.

PURPORT

As a landlord is attracted by his many wives to fulfill their respective self-interests, the objects of this world attract the working senses and knowledge-acquiring senses.

TEXT 28

सृष्ट्वापुराणिविविधान्यजयात्मशक्त्यावृक्षान्सरीसृपपशून्खगदन्दशूकान् ।
तैस्तैरतुष्टहृदयःपुरुषंविधायब्रह्मावलोकधिषणंमुदमापदेवः ॥२८॥

sṛṣṭvā purāṇi vividhāny ajayātma-śaktyā
vṛkṣān sarīsṛpa-paśūn khaga-dandaśūkān
tais tair atuṣṭa-hṛdayaḥ puruṣaṁ vidhāya
brahmāvaloka-dhiṣaṇaṁ mudam āpa devaḥ

The Supreme Lord first created, with the help of His energy, *māyā-śakti*, trees, insects, animals, birds, reptiles, and so on and yet, He was not satisfied. Finally, the Lord created the human body, which offers the conditioned soul sufficient intelligence to realize Him, and thus He became pleased.

COMMENTARY

This human form of body, which can award one liberation, was created by the supreme controller. Therefore, one should not misuse this body and go to hell. It is described in this verse, after creating various types of bodies, the supreme controller was not satisfied and so He finally created the human body, considering it suitable for awarding the conditioned soul the opportunity to regain His association. It is stated in the *Vedas* that after creating the human form of body, the Supreme Lord achieved immense happiness.

The *Vedas* state:

tābhyo gām ānayat tā abruvan na vai no 'yam alam iti
tābhyo 'śvam ānayat tā abruvan na vai no 'yam alam iti
tābhyaḥ puruṣam ānayat tā abruvan su-kṛtaṁ bata

After creating various types of bodies, the Lord called for a cow and asked, "Do you know the Supreme Lord?" She replied, "No. I cannot understand who is the Supreme Lord." Then, the Lord called a horse and asked it the same question. The horse gave a similar reply. Then, the Lord called for human beings and asked them the same question. They replied, "We will know You by Your mercy." (*Aitareya Upaniṣad* 1.2.2-3)

PURPORT

The Supreme Lord, with the help of His energy, creates the enjoyers and objects of enjoyment, imbuing them with their respective propensities. However, the enjoyers, the minute conditioned spirit souls, cannot be satisfied by enjoying limited and temporary inert objects. Until the conditioned soul, who is a part and parcel of the Supreme Lord, realizes that the attempt to enjoy material form, taste, sound, smell, and touch, without self-realization, is most abominable, he will continue to suffer material miseries. However, when he realizes his spiritual identity as the eternal servant of the Lord, he crosses over the influence of *maya* and accepts himself as being maintained and protected by the Lord. Such a pure devotee, being freed from false pride, never thinks of himself as the maintainer or enjoyer.

TEXT 29

लब्ध्वासुदुर्लभमिदंबहुसम्भवान्तेमानुष्यमर्थदमनित्यमपीहधीरः ।
तूर्णंयतेतनपतेदनुमृत्युयावन्निःश्रेयसायविषयःखलुसर्वतःस्यात् ॥२९॥

labdhvā su-durlabham idaṁ bahu-sambhavānte
mānuṣyam artha-dam anityam apīha dhīraḥ
tūrṇaṁ yateta na pated anu-mṛtyu yāvan
niḥśreyasāya viṣayaḥ khalu sarvataḥ syāt

After many lifetimes in lower species, one achieves the rare human form of life. Although temporary, the human body gives one the opportunity to attain the perfection of life. One who is actually intelligent should try to attain this perfection of life as long as the body remains healthy. After all, sense gratification is available in all the other species of life, whereas Kṛṣṇa consciousness can only be cultivated by a human being.

COMMENTARY

Although this body is temporary, it awards eternal benefit. Therefore, one should try to attain supreme auspiciousness as long as the body is functioning properly. One should know for certain that the body is born, then dies, and then again one accepts another birth, which are all temporary. Sense enjoyment, which is available in the human form of life, is also available for hogs, dogs, and horses.

PURPORT

The conditioned souls are subjected to the cycle of repeated birth and death. Sometimes one becomes a demigod, sometimes a human being, sometimes an animal, and sometimes a tree, or even a stone. In this way, the eternal soul identifies himself in various ways, according to the body that he receives. According to his particular type of body, a living entity is destined to enjoy a particular set of sense objects. This is also true for a human being, but the human form of life affords one the opportunity to cultivate knowledge of the Absolute Truth. Therefore, the human form of life is extremely desirable. Still, one cannot remain permanently in the human body.

Only the human form affords one the opportunity of attaining life's ultimate goal. Therefore, while situated in a human body, one should carefully consider how to attain life's perfection and not waste his valuable time gratifying his senses to no avail. Even activities meant for the temporary welfare of human society should be avoided. One should only cultivate the devotional service of the Lord because only this will afford him eternal benefit. One's supreme benefit is obtained when one follows in the footsteps of those who do not endeavor for material gain because they are always engaged in the service of the Supreme Lord. Duties to family, society, and one's occupation only seem prominent as long as one does not strive for his ultimate benefit by surrendering to the Lord. By the association of devotees, one awakens his eternal propensity for devotional service. Without taking shelter of the association of devotees, one must continue to suffer the threefold material miseries. Even when such nondevotees strive for liberation from material miseries, they generally become impersonalists.

TEXT 30

एवंसञ्जातवैराग्योविज्ञानालोक आत्मनि ।
विचरामिमहीमेतांमुक्तसङ्गोऽनहङ्कृतः ॥३०॥

evaṁ sañjāta-vairāgyo vijñānāloka ātmani
vicarāmi mahīm etāṁ mukta-saṅgo 'nahaṅkṛtaḥ

Having learned these lessons from my spiritual masters, I remain fixed in realization of the Supreme Lord, and fully renounced and enlightened by realized spiritual knowledge, I wander over the earth without mundane association or false ego.

COMMENTARY

In reply to King Yadu's question, the *brāhmaṇa* said: "I have acquired knowledge in this way. I have become detached from sense gratification, I have realized the presence of the Supersoul by practical application of my acquired knowledge, I have become freed from false ego, and I wander about this world, free from unnecessary association."

TEXT 31

नह्येकस्माद्गुरोर्ज्ञानंसुस्थिरंस्यात्सुपुष्कलम् ।
ब्रह्मैतदद्वितीयंवैगीयतेबहुधर्षिभिः ॥३१॥

na hy ekasmād guror jñānaṁ su-sthiraṁ syāt su-puṣkalam
brahmaitad advitīyaṁ vai gīyate bahudharṣibhiḥ

Although God is one, sages have described Him in different manners. For this reason, one may not be able to gain a complete understanding of God from one ordinary spiritual master.

COMMENTARY

The question may arise that since the Supreme Lord has said, *tasmād guruṁ prapadyeta jijñāsuḥ śreya uttamam*: "One should take shelter of a self-realized spiritual master who knows the science of the Absolute Truth and inquire from him about one's ultimate welfare," then how can one have more than one guru? Śvetaketu and Bṛghu are examples of those who had more than one guru.

In this regard, the *brāhmaṇa* replied, "It is true that I have only one initiating guru, but in the field of practical activity, I have found these twenty five objects as providing very good and bad examples to take lessons from, and so I have accepted them as my *śikṣā-gurus*, or instructing spiritual masters. By observing examples of good behavior one will be strengthened in devotional service, and in seeing negative examples one will be forewarned and avoid danger."

" I have learned to become detached from eight spiritual masters—the pigeon, fish, deer, young girl, elephant, snake, moth, and kurara bird. I have learned both renunciation of the temporary and acceptance of the eternal from three spiritual masters—the honeybee, the honey thief, and Piṅgalā. I have learned how to cultivate interest in the Supreme Lord from the other spiritual masters, beginning with the earth. Acceptance of many instructing spiritual masters often helps to strengthen one's convictions."

PURPORT

The most correct meaning of the word Brahman is Lord Viṣṇu. There is no worthy song or subject for hearing other than that which glorifies Lord Vāsudeva. There is nothing actually worth learning in this world other than knowledge leading to the devotional service of the Supreme Lord. Cultivating knowledge in a way that is not related to the Lord can do nothing more than enhance our material enjoyment.

TEXT 32

श्रीभगवानुवाच
इत्युक्त्वासयदुंविप्रस्तमामन्त्र्यगभीरधी : ।
वन्दितःस्वर्चितोराज्ञाययौप्रीतोयथागतम् ॥३२॥

śrī-bhagavān uvāca
ity uktvā sa yaduṁ vipras tam āmantrya gabhīra-dhīḥ
vanditaḥ sv-arcito rājñā yayau prīto yathāgatam

The Supreme Lord said: Having thus spoken to King Yadu, the wise *brāhmaṇa* accepted obeisances and worship from the king. Feeling satisfied within himself, he left exactly as he had come, after bidding the king farewell.

TEXT 33

अवधूतवचः श्रुत्वा पूर्वेषां नः सपूर्वजः ।
सर्वसङ्गविनिर्मुक्तः समचित्तो बभूव ह ॥३३॥

avadhūta-vacaḥ śrutvā pūrveṣāṁ naḥ sa pūrva-jaḥ
sarva-saṅga-vinirmuktaḥ sama-citto babhūva ha

O Uddhava, King Yadu, who was the forefather of our ancestors, became freed from all material attachment so that his mind became fixed in tranquility after hearing these statements of the *avadhūta*.

COMMENTARY

The Supreme Lord Kṛṣṇa said to Uddhava: "After the *brāhmaṇa*, Dattātreya, had instructed King Yadu, he departed out of his own sweet will, just as he had come."

Thus ends the translation of the Third Chapter of the Uddhava-gītā *entitled* **"Detachment from All That is Material"** *with the commentaries of Śrīla Viśvanātha Cakravartī Ṭhākura and chapter summary and purports by Śrīla Bhaktisiddhānta Sarasvatī Ṭhākura.*

Chapter 4

The Nature of Fruitive Activity

CHAPTER SUMMARY

In this chapter, Lord Śrī Kṛṣṇa refutes the doctrines of philosophers like Jaimini and describes to Uddhava how the conditioned souls can develop pure transcendental knowledge.

One who is fully surrendered unto the Supreme Lord should follow the Vaiṣṇava *dharma* that is described in the *Pañcarātra* and other revealed scriptures. According to his natural qualities and work, one should follow the rules of *varṇāśrama* without duplicity. So-called knowledge that is received through one's material senses, mind, and intelligence is as useless as the dreams experienced by a person attached to sense gratification. Therefore, one should give up work for sense gratification and accept work as a matter of duty.

When one has come to understand something of the truth of the self, he should give up material work performed out of duty and simply dedicate himself completely to the service of the bona fide spiritual master, who is the manifest representative of the Personality of Godhead. A disciple should have firm faith in his spiritual master, he should be anxious to learn from him the science of the soul, and he should be free from envy and the tendency to indulge in nonsense talk.

The spirit soul is separate from both the gross and subtle bodies. An embodied soul accepts different kinds of bodies according to his karma. Only a bona-fide spiritual master is able to impart the knowledge of self-realization. By refuting the philosophies of Jaimini and others, Lord Śrī Kṛṣṇa explains that the embodied soul who has come in contact with segmented material time takes upon himself a perpetual chain of births and deaths and is therefore forced to suffer the resultant happiness and distress. Thus, there is no possibility that one who is attached to the fruits of his material work can achieve any substantial goal in life. The pleasures of heaven, which are achieved by performing sacrificial rituals, can be experienced for only a short time. After one's heavenly enjoyment is finished, one must return to this mortal sphere to partake of lamentation and suffering. On the path of materialism, there is certainly no uninterrupted happiness.

TEXT 1

श्रीभगवानुवाच
मच्चोदितेष्ववहितःस्वधर्मेषुमदाश्रयः ।
वर्णाश्रमकुलाचारमकामात्मासमाचरेत् ॥१॥

śrī-bhagavān uvāca
mayoditeṣv avahitaḥ sva-dharmeṣu mad-āśrayaḥ
varṇāśrama-kulācāram akāmātmā samācaret

The Supreme Lord said: One who is surrendered unto Me should tirelessly practice *Vaiṣṇava dharma* as prescribed by Me in scriptures such as the *Pañcarātra*. He should also perform his occupational duties according to the system of *varṇāśrama*, which is a favorable condition for accepting spiritual life.

COMMENTARY

In this chapter, the cultivation of spiritual knowledge, the living entities' bondage as a result of their contact with matter, and the refutation of philosophers like Jaiminī are described. Having given Uddhava many valuable lessons by narrating the story of an *avadhūta brāhmaṇa*, the Supreme Lord now describes the process of *sādhana*. He says, "O Uddhava, you should follow the *varnāśrama dharma*, and the devotional practices described by Me in the scriptures like the *Pañcarātra*."

PURPORT

The Supreme Lord said: One should take shelter of Me and work under My direction while following the system of *varnāśrama*. If one gives up My shelter and engages in fruitive activities due to material attachment, he will never attain his ultimate welfare. When one follows *varnāśrama dharma* and family traditions simply for amassing pious merit rather than for engagement in My service, one is certainly misdirected and will never attain eternal benefit. Despite executing one's duties as prescribed by Me in the

Vedas, and rejecting all prohibited activities, if one does not take shelter of Me, then his endeavor is ultimately useless. On the other hand, if one engages in My devotional service without deviation, there is no necessity for performing the religious duties prescribed in the *Vedas*. When My unalloyed devotees fail to observe all the rules and regulations prescribed in the *Vedas*, they should never be considered as misguided.

TEXT 2

अन्वीक्षेतविशुद्धात्मादेहिनांविषयात्मनाम् ।
गुणेषुतत्त्वध्यानेनसर्वारम्भविपर्ययम् ॥२॥

anvīkṣeta viśuddhātmā dehināṁ viṣayātmanām
guṇeṣu tattva-dhyānena sarvārambha-viparyayam

A transcendentalist should see that because the conditioned souls who are dedicated to sense gratification have falsely accepted the objects of sense pleasure as reality, all of their endeavors are doomed to failure.

COMMENTARY

How is it possible to give up material desires? The reply given here is that one should see the disastrous result obtained by materialistic people who consider the temporary manifestations of this world to be ultimate reality. By such an observation, one will certainly become detached from the aspiration to enjoy such objects that will disappear in due course of time.

PURPORT

When the conditioned souls come to realize the utter futility of their endeavors to enjoy the temporary manifestations of this world, they certainly become detached.

TEXT 3

सुप्तस्यविषयालोकोध्यायतोवामनोरथः ।
नानात्मकत्वाद्विफलस्तथाभेदात्मधीर्गुणैः ॥३॥

suptasya viṣayāloko dhyāyato vā manorathaḥ
nānātmakatvād viphalas tathā bhedātma-dhīr guṇaiḥ

A sleeping person may see many objects of sense gratification in his dreams but such things are merely creations of his mind and are thus of no benefit to him. Similarly, one who is asleep to his spiritual identity sees many sense objects in this world, but they

are all creations of the Lord's illusory potency and have no permanent existence. One who meditates upon the temporary objects of the senses therefore uselessly engages his intelligence.

COMMENTARY

Because the results of material work are temporary, they cannot provide one with lasting benefit and are thus considered useless. Materialistic activities can never bring one to the perfection of life or free one from the pangs of material existence. Material intelligence, when impelled by the senses, strongly desires sense gratification, and thus separates one from one's real self-interest. Such diverted intelligence will never be able to understand the Absolute Truth, the Personality of Godhead, Śrī Kṛṣṇa. The devotees of the Lord, however, fix their intelligence upon Him by meditating upon the His form, qualities, pastimes, and devotees. In this way, their intelligence is never separated from the Absolute Truth. As stated in *Bhagavad-gītā* (2.41):

vyavasāyātmikā buddhir ekeha kuru-nandana
bahu-śākhā hy anantāś ca buddhayo 'vyavasāyinām

Those who are on this path are resolute in purpose, and their aim is one. O beloved child of the Kurus, the intelligence of those who are irresolute is many-branched.

PURPORT

The sense objects observed in one's dreams are of no value, just as the objects seen in the waking state are ultimately useless, because they are temporary.

TEXT 4

निवृत्तंकर्मसेवेतप्रवृत्तंमत्परस्त्यजेत् ।
जिज्ञासायांसम्प्रवृत्तोनादियेत्कर्मचोदनाम् ॥४॥

nivṛttaṁ karma seveta pravṛttaṁ mat-paras tyajet
jijñāsāyāṁ sampravṛtto nādriyet karma-codanām

One who has fixed his mind on Me, making Me his goal of life, should give up activities of sense gratification and should instead engage in the regulated practice of devotional service. On the other hand, when one is fully endeavoring for self-realization, he has no need to follow the scriptural injunctions regarding fruitive activities.

COMMENTARY

A materialistic person does whatever is pleasing to his senses. One who acts according to religious principles regulates his material enjoyment in a way that is prescribed in the scriptures. Those who are advancing toward the transcendental platform, however, desist from all activities of sense gratification. In *Bhagavad-gītā* (6.3-4) it is stated:

ārurukṣor muner yogam karma kāraṇam ucyate
yogārūḍhasya tasyaiva śamaḥ kāraṇam ucyate

For one who is a neophyte in the eightfold yoga system, work is said to be the means; and for one who is already elevated in yoga, cessation of all material activities is said to be the means.

yadā hi nendriyārtheṣu na karmasv anuṣajjate
sarva-saṅkalpa-sannyāsī yogārūḍhas tadocyate

A person is said to be elevated in yoga when, having renounced all material desires, he neither acts for sense gratification nor engages in fruitive activities.

PURPORT

There is no need for those who are engaged in the service of the Supreme Lord to perform fruitive activities with a desire to enhance their worldly enjoyment. One should remain aloof from the activities of sense gratification and instead engage in unalloyed devotional service to the Supreme Lord. Engagement in devotional service to the Supreme Lord is real freedom from material desires. The paths of sense gratification and renunciation are always full of contradictions whereas the service of the Supreme Lord is the doubtless path of perfection.

TEXT 5

यमानभीक्ष्णंसेवेतनियमान्मत्परःक्वचित् ।
मदभिज्ञंगुरुंशान्तमुपासीतमदात्मकम् ॥५॥

yamān abhīkṣṇaṁ seveta niyamān mat-paraḥ kvacit
mad-abhijñaṁ guruṁ śāntam upāsīta mad-ātmakam

One who has surrendered unto Me, accepting Me as the goal of life, should follow all the rules that forbid sinful activities. One should also try his best to follow all the sub-

religious principles, such as those dealing with cleanliness. One should approach a bona fide spiritual master who is intimately related to Me, and who is thus very peaceful, and is nondifferent from Me.

COMMENTARY

One should very carefully control his senses and follow the scriptural injunctions for morality, such as nonviolence and cleanliness. These rules will be more fully described later on. One who is intelligent should faithfully render service to a self-realized spiritual master, who has full knowledge of the Supreme Personality of Godhead.

PURPORT

It is the eternal duty of everyone to worship his spiritual master, who is always engaged in the service of the Supreme Lord. The devotees of the Lord are always engaged in devotional service, which is concomitantly inclusive of activities, such as *yama* and *niyama*. If one is indifferent to the service of Lord Hari, one's *guru*, and the Vaiṣṇavas, one can never achieve eternal benefit.

TEXT 6

अमान्यमत्सरोदक्षोनिर्ममोदृढसौहृदः ।
असत्वरोऽर्थजिज्ञासुरनसूयुरमोघवाक् ॥६॥

amāny amatsaro dakṣo nirmamo dṛḍha-sauhṛdaḥ
asatvaro 'rtha-jijñāsur anasūyur amogha-vāk

A disciple of the spiritual master should be freed from false pride, false ego, and laziness. He should give up all sense of proprietorship over the objects of the senses, even his wife and children, and he should have firm faith and affection for his spiritual master. He should be steady, always desiring advancement in spiritual understanding, and he should not envy anyone, and should avoid useless talk.

COMMENTARY

The duties of a disciple are being described. The disciple should not expect any respect for himself. He should not envy anyone, and he should be expert and free from material attachment. He should have firm faith in the spiritual master, as well as his worshipable Lord. He should always be eager to engage in devotional service and thus attain his goal of life. One who wants to advance in spiritual understanding should not find fault in others, and should always avoid idle talk.

TEXT 7

जायापत्यगृहक्षेत्रस्वजनद्रविणादिषु ।
उदासीनःसमंपश्यन्सर्वेष्वर्थमिवात्मनः ॥७॥

jāyāpatya-gṛha-kṣetra- svajana-draviṇādiṣu
udāsīnaḥ samaṁ paśyan sarveṣv artham ivātmanaḥ

A sincere disciple is equal to everyone. He should remain detached from his wife, children, household, property, relatives, wealth, and so on.

COMMENTARY

How can one be without a sense of proprietorship? For example, a wealthy materialist will feel equally attached as the proprietor of all his various assets but if some are taken away by thieves or the government, he gives up attachment for them. An intelligent person should understand that everything he possesses will not remain for long and thus he should cultivate a mood of detachment.

The son of Citraketu said in *Śrīmad-Bhāgavatam* (6.16.6-7):

yathā vastūni paṇyāni hemādīni tatas tataḥ
paryaṭanti nareṣv evaṁ jīvo yoniṣu kartṛṣu
nityasyārthasya sambandho hy anityo dṛśyate nṛṣu
yāvad yasya hi sambandho mamatvaṁ tāvad eva hi

Just as gold and other commodities are continually transferred from one place to another in due course of purchase and sale, so the living entity, as a result of his fruitive activities, wanders throughout the entire universe, being injected into various bodies in different species of life by one kind of father after another.

Relatively few living entities are born in the human species, and others are born as animals. Although both are living entities, the relationships they establish are impermanent. An animal may remain in the custody of a human being for some time, and then the same animal may be transferred to the possession of other human beings. As soon as the animal goes away, the former proprietor no longer has a sense of ownership. As long as the animal is in his possession, he certainly has an affinity for it, but as soon as the animal is sold, the affinity is lost.

As far as the spiritual master and the Lord are concerned, one should simply keep firm faith at their lotus feet.

PURPORT

A devotee of the Lord should not consider himself to be the enjoyer of his wife, children, house, land, friends, and other possessions, knowing them to be intended for the Lord's service, just like himself. He should not try to demand respect from others with a desire to enjoy fame and reputation. He should become free from envy, laziness, and material attachment. He should be inquisitive, devoid of pride, truthful, and steady in his determination.

TEXT 8

विलक्षणःस्थूलसूक्ष्माद्देहादात्मेक्षितास्वदृक्।
यथाग्निर्दारुणोदाह्याद्दाहकोऽन्यःप्रकाशकः ॥८॥

vilakṣaṇaḥ sthūla-sūkṣmād dehād ātmekṣitā sva-dṛk
yathāgnir dāruṇo dāhyād dāhako 'nyaḥ prakāśakaḥ

Just as a blazing fire is different from the wood it burns to provide illumination, so the knower within the material body is different from the body itself, which is pervaded by the consciousness of the soul. It should be firmly understood that the spirit soul and the body have different characteristics because they are two distinct entities.

COMMENTARY

One should not maintain the false egoistic conception of "I" and "mine" in relation to the material body. The gross and subtle bodies covering the living entities are made of the material elements, but the spirit soul is transcendental to matter. The spirit soul possesses the transcendental qualities of the Lord, but in minute quantity. In this verse the soul is described as self-enlightened. Because the conditioned soul is enlightened by the mercy of the Lord, one may question how this can be. Although the Supreme Personality of Godhead certainly furnishes the living entity with consciousness, the living entity being endowed with the potency of the Lord, has himself the capacity to revive and expand his pure consciousness.

In this regard, the soul is compared to gold and silver, which, although having no power of self-illumination, brightly reflect the rays of the sun. Thus, it may be said that gold and silver possess the power to illuminate, although not independently. This verse gives an example to illustrate how the spirit soul is distinct from the body. Just as fire is distinct from the wood it burns, the soul is distinct from the body it illuminates with consciousness. In the conditional state, the spirit soul is compared to fire that is dormant within wood. When the conditioned soul is enlightened, on the strength of his spiritual knowledge, he can burn his ignorance to ashes, just as fire burns wood.

PURPORT

Just as fire is separate from the wood it burns—one is that which burns and the other is that which is burnt—the spirit soul is distinct from the gross body and subtle mind. He is self-manifest and minutely independent.

TEXT 9

निरोधोत्पत्त्यणुबृहन्नानात्वंतत्कृतान्गुणान् ।
अन्तःप्रविष्ट आधत्त एवंदेहगुणान्परः ॥९॥

nirodhotpatty-aṇu-bṛhan-nānātvaṁ tat-kṛtān guṇān
antaḥ praviṣṭa ādhatta evaṁ deha-guṇān paraḥ

Just as fire manifested from wood takes different shapes, according to the condition of the fuel, the embodied soul enters various material bodies and thus accepts varieties of bodily characteristics.

COMMENTARY

Although fire may be sometimes visible and sometimes not, the element fire always exists. Similarly, the soul may appear within a body and then depart but still, the soul is eternal. It is a mistake to impose material conditions upon the spirit soul, who has nothing to do with the material body. As fire is sometimes blazing, some times great, sometimes small, and sometimes extinguished, the spirit soul is sometimes born, sometimes in the body of Brahmā, sometimes in the body of an ant, and sometimes departs from the body at death.

PURPORT

Fire, although separate from the object it burns, appears in various ways, as big, small, blazing, or extinguished, according to the condition of the fuel. In the same way, the spirit soul, being averse to the Supreme Lord, identifies himself with his gross and subtle bodies, although he is distinct from them and eternal.

TEXT 10

योऽसौगुणैर्विरचितोदेहोऽयंपुरुषस्यहि ।
संसारस्तन्निबन्धोऽयंपुंसोविद्याच्छिदात्मनः ॥१०॥

yo 'sau guṇair viracito deho 'yaṁ puruṣasya hi
saṁsāras tan-nibandho 'yaṁ puṁso vidyā cchid ātmanaḥ

The subtle and gross material bodies are created by the material modes of nature, which are creations of the illusory energy of the Supreme Personality of Godhead. Material existence occurs when the living entity falsely accepts the qualities of the gross and subtle bodies as being his self. This illusory state, however, can be destroyed by real knowledge.

COMMENTARY

The question may arise that since fire is produced from wood, and fire has never been seen independently of any fuel, it may be assumed that the existence of the soul is dependent upon the gross and subtle material bodies. The answer is that only through the Supreme Personality of Godhead's knowledge potency (*vidyā*) can one clearly understand the nature of the living entity. By such real knowledge, one may cut material existence to pieces and even in this lifetime experience spiritual reality. Our material existence is an artificial imposition. By the Lord's inconceivable potency of nescience, the qualities of gross and subtle material forms are imposed upon the living being, and because of misidentification with the body, he initiates a series of illusory activities. When, by the mercy of the Lord, the conditioned souls are freed from the material conception of life, having revived their original consciousness, they become free from material bondage.

PURPORT

Those living entities who are averse to the Supreme Lord forget their constitutional position and become conditioned by material existence, so that they consider their gross and subtle bodies as their selves. However, a pure spirit soul is not bewildered by material existence, which keeps the rebellious souls under a spell of illusion.

TEXT 11

तस्माज्जिज्ञासयात्मानमात्मस्थंकेवलंपरम् ।
सङ्गम्यनिरसेदेतद्वस्तुबुद्धिंयथाक्रमम् ॥११॥

tasmāj jijñāsayātmānam ātma-sthaṁ kevalaṁ param
saṅgamya nirased etad vastu-buddhiṁ yathā-kramam

Therefore, after careful consideration, one should approach the Supreme Personality of Godhead, who is the cause and effect of everything, while renouncing the false conception that this world is an independent reality.

COMMENTARY

The spirit soul is covered by gross and subtle bodies. One should understand that the spirit soul is completely distinct from these gross and subtle material bodies. Gradually, on the strength of one's *sādhana*, one should rise above the conception that the material body is the self.

PURPORT

When one comes to the platform of self-realization, he should inquire about his duty and then dedicate himself to the service of the Supreme Lord. While engaged in devotional service, one should remain detached from thoughts of enjoying the objects of the senses, which are all creations of *maya*. It is only due to a lack of inquisitiveness that a foolish person fails to attain knowledge of the Absolute Truth.

TEXT 12

आचार्योऽरणिराद्यःस्यादन्तेवास्युत्तरारणिः ।
तत्सन्धानंप्रवचनंविद्यासन्धिःसुखावहः ॥१२॥

ācāryo 'raṇir ādyaḥ syād ante-vāsy uttarāraṇiḥ
tat-sandhānaṁ pravacanaṁ vidyā-sandhiḥ sukhāvahaḥ

The spiritual master is compared to the lower kindling wood. The disciple is compared to the upper kindling wood, and the instructions imparted by the spiritual master are compared to the wood placed between these two. The fire of knowledge that is produced by the interaction of these three destroys the darkness of ignorance and gives happiness to both the spiritual master and the disciple.

COMMENTARY

The knowledge received from the spiritual master is capable of burning ignorance and its effects to ashes. When two sticks are rubbed together, the friction produces fire. Similarly, the spiritual master imparts instructions to his disciple, and this knowledge destroys the disciple's ignorance, burning his desire for material enjoyment to ashes.

PURPORT

Knowledge of self-realization is produced by linking the living entities, who are conditioned by *maya*, with a spiritual master, who is in full knowledge of the Absolute Truth. Just as fire is produced when one rubs two sticks, the knowledge of self-realization is attained by the disciple who is under the shelter of the lotus feet of the spiritual master.

TEXT 13

वैशारदीसातिविशुद्धबुद्धिर्धुनोतिमायांगुणसम्प्रसूताम् ।
गुनांश्चसन्दह्ययदात्ममेतत्स्वयंचशाम्यत्यसमिद्यथाग्निः ॥१३॥

vaiśāradī sāti-viśuddha-buddhir dhunoti māyāṁ guṇa-samprasūtām
gunāṁś ca sandahya yad-ātmam etat svayaṁ ca śāṁyaty asamid yathāgniḥ

By submissively hearing from a bonafide spiritual master, one receives perfect understanding that dispels the illusion of material existence which is due to the influence of the three modes of material nature. Ultimately, the quest for perfect knowledge ceases when one has become fully satisfied on the spiritual platform.

COMMENTARY

Perfect knowledge comes from the expert spiritual master, and it removes the bondage to material existence created by attachment to the gross and subtle bodies. After establishing one on the transcendental platform, where one becomes absorbed in thoughts of the Lord, the fire of knowledge becomes extinguished, just as fire is extinguished after all the fuel is consumed.

PURPORT

Just as fire is extinguished when there is no more supply of fuel, similarly, a disciple who receives transcendental knowledge from the expert spiritual master is able to free himself from the clutches of the three modes of material nature. Only then the intelligence is purified and one becomes inclined towards the Supreme Lord.

TEXTS 14-16

अथैषाम्कर्मकर्तृणांभोक्तृणांसुखदुःखयोः ।
नानात्वमथनित्यत्वंलोककालागमात्मनाम् ॥१४॥
मन्यसेसर्वभावानांसंस्थाह्यौत्पत्तिकीयथा ।
तत्तदाकृतिभेदेनजायतेभिद्यतेचधीः ॥१५॥
एवमप्यङ्ग सर्वेषां देहिनां देहयोगतः ।
कालावयवतःसन्तिभावाजन्मादयोऽसकृत् ॥१६॥

athaiṣām karma-kartṛṇāṁ bhoktṛṇāṁ sukha-duḥkhayoḥ
nānātvam atha nityatvaṁ loka-kālāgamātmanām

manyase sarva-bhāvānāṁ saṁsthā hy autpattikī yathā
tat-tad-ākṛti-bhedena jāyate bhidyate ca dhīḥ

evam apy aṅga sarveṣāṁ dehināṁ deha-yogataḥ
kālāvayavataḥ santi bhāvā janmādayo 'sakṛt

My dear Uddhava, I have thus imparted perfect knowledge unto you. There are other philosophers, however, who arrive at a different conclusion. They say that the conditioned souls should engage in fruitive activities because they are the enjoyers of the happiness and unhappiness that are derived from the results of their work. According to this understanding, the cosmic manifestation, including the time, the scriptures, and the souls are transforming in a perpetual cycle. Just as the objects of this world are constantly transforming, so knowledge based on such objects is also impermanent and ever-changing. My dear Uddhava, if this philosophy is accepted, there will be no escape from the cycle of repeated birth and death, accompanied by old age and disease, as the living beings accept material bodies that are subject to the influence of time.

COMMENTARY

Lord Kṛṣṇa says, "My dear Uddhava, in the instructions I have given to you, I clearly indicated the ultimate goal of life. There are those who would not agree with My teachings, however, such as the followers of Jaimini. If you are inclined to accept their materialistic philosophy instead of My instructions, then listen to what I have to say about that."

"According to the philosophy of Jaimini, the living entity is constitutionally the performer of fruitive activities, and such actions are the causes of his happiness and distress. The energy or nature that forms the world we live in, the time under which we are controlled, the revealed scriptures that lead us on the path of advancement, and the subtle bodies that are the medium through which we experience happiness and distress, although constantly being transformed, remain eternally."

"The living being need not renounce sense gratification, either due to understanding the temporary nature of existence, or by seeing the world as an illusory creation of *maya*. According to such a materialistic philosophy, the objects of this world, even the bodies of beautiful women, are temporary manifestations of an eternal nature. Thus, creation, maintenance, and destruction are the three phases of eternal existence. By executing fruitive rituals that are prescribed by the *Vedas*, one can maintain his aristocratic position, which affords him the possession of women and wealth birth after birth. In this way, one can go on enjoying sense gratification eternally."

"Such philosophers say that the universe eternally exists in some form or another and thus imply that there is no need to suppose that there is a God who created it. They claim that the cosmic manifestation is therefore real, and not illusory. In this way, they defy the conception of an eternal soul having an eternal spiritual form, which is now covered by matter. They say that knowledge is derived from sense perception and is not coming from some kind of Absolute Truth, and therefore knowledge itself is subject to change, just as are the objects that it perceives."

"In this way, materialistic philosophers conclude that although the material nature is unlimitedly transformable, it still exists eternally. By thinking in this way, such persons are more inclined to follow the path of advancing material enjoyment, instead of the path of renunciation. They see liberation as a state of pure consciousness without any activity or variety. Indeed, many such philosophers feel that liberation is an abnormal state of existence because the liberated souls would be without any activity or enjoyment. Even if we accept for the sake of argument that their philosophy is correct, we would still have to conclude that a path of regulated sense enjoyment would never provide ultimate happiness, but instead, would simply award countless miseries. For this reason, even from a materialistic point of view, detachment is in the living being's self-interest."

TEXT 17

तत्रापिकर्मणांकर्तुरस्वातन्त्र्यंचलक्ष्यते ।
भोक्तुश्चदुःखसुखयोःकोन्वर्थोविवशंभजेत् ॥१७॥

tatrāpi karmaṇāṁ kartur asvātantryaṁ ca lakṣyate
bhoktuś ca duḥkha-sukhayoḥ ko nv artho vivaśaṁ bhajet

Although the person who engages in fruitive activities hopes to become eternally happy, it is practically seen that materialists are mostly miserable and only rarely actually satisfied. This proves that the conditioned souls are not independent, nor are they in control of their destiny. When a person is always under someone else's control, how can he expect to get anywhere by acting independently?

COMMENTARY

It is practically seen that when one performs fruitive activities, he is still under the control of destiny and thus rarely achieves the fulfillment of his desires. If there was actual freedom, then who would have to suffer miseries? What intelligent person would allow himself to suffer the miseries of birth, death, old age, and disease? Therefore, the conclusion is that the living entities are dependent upon a higher authority.

PURPORT

The performer of activities enjoys happiness or distress, being under the control of time. In modern times, inventions have been created to eliminate the inconveniences of life, but the maintenance and production of such conveniences has proven to be unbearably inconvenient for hundreds of millions of people throughout the world. Only the most foolish person will propose that there is no superior controller and that one can achieve favorable results simply by expert performance of material activities.

TEXT 18

नदेहिनांसुखंकिञ्चिद्विद्यतेविदुषामपि ।
तथाचदुःखंमूढानांवृथाहङ्करणंपरम् ॥१८॥

na dehināṁ sukhaṁ kiñcid vidyate viduṣām api
tathā ca duḥkhaṁ mūḍhānāṁ vṛthāhaṅkaraṇaṁ param

It is observed within this world that sometimes even a learned person feels distressed, whereas a great fool may feel happy. Therefore, it is simply a manifestation of false ego to think that by the expert performance of *karma,* one can achieve happiness.

COMMENTARY

It can be argued that a person could continuously perform pious activities, avoiding all sinful acts, and thus never suffer, because misery is caused by acting sinfully. The answer is that you will never find anyone in this world who is always happy, or who is always distressed. Sometimes it is seen that pious men are in a miserable condition and sinful men are happy. The conclusion is that even pious men sometimes perform forbidden acts, and even sinful men sometimes perform unknown pious activities, such as traveling to a holy place or serving a saintly person.

PURPORT

The living entities who are averse to Kṛṣṇa are always under the control of the three modes of material nature. Because of this, whether they are in knowledge or in ignorance, they do not become lastingly happy.

TEXT 19

यदिप्राप्तिंविघातंचजानन्तिसुखदुःखयोः ।
तेऽप्यद्धानविदुर्योगमृत्युर्नप्रभवेद्यथा ॥१९॥

yadi prāptiṁ vighātaṁ ca jānanti sukha-duḥkhayoḥ
te 'py addhā na vidur yoga mṛtyur na prabhaved yathā

Even if someone was able to somehow achieve only happiness and completely avoid distress in this life, he still would have to succumb to all-devouring death.

COMMENTARY

Even if one is very learned, he is certainly ignorant of how to stop death.

PURPORT

Although learned people under the influence of the illusory energy of the Lord may display expertise in the field of achieving happiness and avoiding distress, they are still unable to save themselves from the hands of imminent death.

TEXT 20

कोऽन्वर्थःसुखयत्येनंकामोवामृत्युरन्तिके ।
आघातंनीयमानस्यवध्यस्येवनतुष्टिदः ॥२०॥

ko 'nv arthaḥ sukhayaty enaṁ kāmo vā mṛtyur antike
āghātaṁ nīyamānasya vadhyasyeva na tuṣṭi-daḥ

Death is certainly very horrible. Since everyone in this world is just like a prisoner condemned to be executed, what actual happiness can be derived from the objects of this world and the gratification that they offer?

COMMENTARY

If you say that there is happiness before death, the answer is that a man who is condemned to die cannot enjoy the sumptuous meal placed before him. A person who is going to be executed cannot feel happiness, even if you give him nice sweet rice or milk cakes because such things are simply a reminder that he will soon die. Therefore, this belief that wealth and sense gratification can give one happiness in this world of birth and death is herein refuted.

PURPORT

Can the temporary happiness which is available in this world protect one who knows that he is always under the control of inevitable death? Palatable food offered to a condemned person is not relished by him because of the chilling thought of imminent death.

TEXT 21

श्रुतंचदृष्टवद्दुष्टंस्पर्धासूयात्ययव्ययैः ।
बह्वन्तरायकामत्वात्कृषिवच्चापिनिष्फलम् ॥२१॥

śrutaṁ ca dṛṣṭa-vad duṣṭaṁ spardhāsūyātyaya-vyayaiḥ
bahv-antarāya-kāmatvāt kṛṣi-vac cāpi niṣphalam

The material happiness that is available in the heavenly planets is discussed in the *Vedas*, but it is simply a royal version of the happiness found on earth. Life here and life in heaven are both polluted by envy, deterioration, and death. Just as a farmer has to contend with many problems while growing crops, such as drought or the attack of insects, similarly, the attempt to become happy, whether on earth or in heaven, is fraught with many difficulties.

COMMENTARY

After concluding that there is no happiness in this world, it is being described that there is no happiness in the heavenly planets as well. The information that there is ample happiness in the heavenly planets is illusory. In heaven, there is arrogance because one person is envious of others' happiness, and there is destruction when one's accumulated piety is exhausted. As agriculture is troublesome, and sometimes unproductive, the performance of sacrifice and other pious acts, which award one heavenly residence, is ultimately of no avail.

PURPORT

When the farmer plants his crops, he has to worry about so many potential problems, such as defective seeds, drought, plagues of insects, excessive heat, and so on. Similarly, the attempt to enjoying happiness in this world, whether on earth or in heaven, is accompanied by anxiety due to jealousy, cheating, and so on. When conditioned souls interact, there is naturally competition and envy because that is the very nature of material existence. Due to the influence of time, no position within the material world is stable and so, when there are reverses, violence and intrigue create great disturbances, both here and in heaven. Even the attempt to attain a heavenly destination is also fraught with many difficulties. Therefore, one should enquire about the eternal abode of the Supreme Personality of Godhead, which is far beyond the disturbances of this material world.

TEXT 22

अन्तरायैरविहितोयदिधर्मःस्वनुष्ठितः ।
तेनापिनिर्जितंस्थानंयथागच्छतितच्छृणु ॥२२॥

antarāyair avihito yadi dharmaḥ sv-anuṣṭhitaḥ
tenāpi nirjitaṁ sthānaṁ yathā gacchati tac chṛṇu

Even if one properly performs Vedic sacrifices and fruitive rituals without committing any mistake or offense, the result of attaining the heavenly planets obtained by such activities will be destroyed in due course of time. Listen as I now explain this to you.

COMMENTARY

Even if one avoids mistakes and offenses while performing Vedic rituals, it is impossible to avoid the miseries felt at the time of destruction. This is being described in the following five verses.

PURPORT

Unless one very carefully executes religious rituals, various obstacles will come in his way. But, even if one is able to perform such rituals properly, and without encountering any obstacles, the result obtained is temporary because, whether good or bad, all material conditions are imperfect.

TEXT 23

इष्ट्वेहदेवतायज्ञैःस्वर्लोकंयातियाज्ञिकः ।
भुञ्जीतदेववत्तत्रभोगान्दिव्यान्निजार्जितान् ॥२३॥

iṣṭveha devatā yajñaiḥ svar-lokaṁ yāti yājñikaḥ
bhuñjīta deva-vat tatra bhogān divyān nijārjitān

Pious people attain the heavenly planets by worshiping the demigods with the performance of Vedic sacrifices. By means of their accumulated piety, they enjoy heavenly pleasures just like the demigods.

PURPORT

The demigods award their worshipers their desired goals. People who perform Vedic sacrifices to please the demigods attain the heavenly planets as a result of their worship and thus enjoy heavenly pleasures. Such enjoyment, however, is temporary and the worshipers of the demigods have to return to earth after exhausting their pious merit.

TEXT 24

स्वपुण्योपचितेशुभ्रेविमान उपगीयते ।
गन्धर्वैर्विहरन्मध्येदेवीनांहृद्यवेषधृक् ॥२४॥

sva-puṇyopacite śubhre vimāna upagīyate
gandharvair viharan madhye devīnāṁ hṛdya-veṣa-dhṛk

After ascending to the heavenly planets, one who had previously performed numerous sacrifices will ride in an effulgent celestial chariot, which he is awarded as the result of his past pious activities. He is glorified by the Gandharvas and dressed in gorgeous clothing as he enjoys life in the company of heavenly damsels.

COMMENTARY

The word *devī* in this verse refers to the Apśarās, or celestial women.

TEXT 25

स्त्रीभिःकामगयानेनकिङ्किनीजालमालिना ।
क्रीडन्नवेदात्मपातंसुराक्रीडेषुनिर्वृतः ॥२५॥

strībhiḥ kāmaga-yānena kiṅkinī-jāla-mālinā
krīdan na vedātma-pātaṁ surākrīḍeṣu nirvṛtaḥ

In the company of celestial women, the enjoyer of the results of sacrifice travels to heavenly gardens in a wonderful airplane, which is decorated with circles of tinkling bells and which moves according to his desire. Being relaxed, comfortable, and happy in heavenly pleasure gardens, he does not consider that he is exhausting the results of his previously-acquired piety and will soon fall down to the mortal world.

COMMENTARY

The phrase *kāma yāna* means "traveling at will in his celestial airplane."

TEXT 26

तावत्समोदतेस्वर्गेयावत्पुण्यंसमाप्यते ।
क्षीणपुन्यःपतत्यर्वागनिच्छन्कालचालितः ॥२६॥

tāvat sa modate svarge yāvat puṇyaṁ samāpyate
kṣīṇa-punyaḥ pataty arvāg anicchan kāla-cālitaḥ

For as long as his pious merit remains, the performer of sacrifice enjoys life in the heavenly planets. When his pious merit is exhausted, however, he falls down from the pleasure gardens of heaven, being moved against his will by the force of eternal time.

COMMENTARY

Being driven by time, one again falls down to this planet of birth and death.

TEXTS 27-29

यद्यधर्मरतःसङ्गादसतांवाजितेन्द्रियः ।
कामात्माकृपणोलुब्धःस्त्रैणोभूतविहिंसकः ॥२७॥
पशूनविधिनालभ्यप्रेतभूतगणान्यजन् ।
नरकानवशोजन्तुर्गत्वायात्युल्बणंतमः ॥२८॥
कर्माणिदुःखोदर्काणिकुर्वन्देहेनतैः पुनः ।
देहमाभजतेतत्रकिंसुखंमर्त्यधर्मिणः ॥२९॥

yady adharma-rataḥ saṅgād asatāṁ vājitendriyaḥ
kāmātmā kṛpaṇo lubdhaḥ straiṇo bhūta-vihiṁsakaḥ

paśūn avidhinālabhya preta-bhūta-gaṇān yajan
narakān avaśo jantur gatvā yāty ulbaṇaṁ tamaḥ

karmāṇi duḥkhodarkāṇi kurvan dehena taiḥ punaḥ
deham ābhajate tatra kiṁ sukhaṁ martya-dharmiṇaḥ

If a person engages in sinful activities, either due to bad association or his unwillingness to control his senses, he will certainly become mad due to having desires that are impossible to fulfill. Such a person hardly cares for others, is very greedy, and always seeking the opportunity to enjoy the bodies of women. When the mind is contaminated in this way, one does not hesitate to commit violence and thus he slaughters poor animals for the satisfaction of the tongue. Sometimes worshiping ghosts and spirits, such a bewildered person is not better than an animal and after death, he goes to hell, which is a manifestation of the darkest mode of material nature. Receiving a hellish body, he continues to perform horrible activities that insure his future misery. What happiness can there be for one who engages in activities that culminate in death?

COMMENTARY

There are two classes of those who perform *karma*—the pious and the impious. After describing the destination of pious persons, the destination of impious persons is now being described. One who is not self-controlled is certainly lusty, and such a person afflicted by lust becomes very miserly. Such a greedy person, who is overwhelmed by the thirst for material enjoyment, becomes henpecked due to being addicted to enjoying sex with women. He performs animal sacrifices that are opposed to the principles of religion, to fulfill his insatiable desires. The phrase *ulbaṇamtamaḥ* refers to the non-moving living entities, such as trees. Such persons who are engaged in fruitive activities never achieve tangible happiness. This is the conclusion of these verses.

PURPORT

Impious people engage in irreligious activities. Becoming addicted to sinful activities, they are intemperate, lusty, miserly, greedy, henpecked, and violent, either due to the association of other sinful people, or due to being unable to control their senses. Such impious persons indulge in unrestricted sexual enjoyment, slaughter countless animals for the satisfaction of their tongues, and try to forget their miseries by means of intoxication. In this way, they transgress all prescribed rules and regulations. Eventually such persons become influenced by ghosts and spirits, who deprive them of all ability to discriminate between right and wrong. Losing all sense of decency, they become fit candidates for entrance into the darkest modes of material existence.

Those who are ignorant of the glories of devotional service engage in fruitive activities with a desire to enjoy the flickering pleasures of sense gratification. As a result, when their duration of life comes to an end, they are transferred to another body to enjoy or suffer the results of their past fruitive activities. Considering all this, one should never aspire for material happiness. Material life is so horrible because no matter what one's duration of life might be, one will still always be afflicted with fear of death. Even Brahmā is afraid of death, and so what to speak of us, who live for no more than one hundred years. Considering this, what possible happiness can there be for the conditioned souls?

TEXT 30

लोकानांलोकपालानांमद्भयंकल्पजीविनाम् ।
ब्रह्मणोऽपिभयंमत्तोद्विपरार्धपरायुषः ॥३०॥

lokānāṁ loka-pālānāṁ mad bhayaṁ kalpa-jīvinām
brahmaṇo 'pi bhayaṁ matto dvi-parārdha-parāyuṣaḥ

In all the planetary systems, from the heavenly planets down to the hellish planets, even the demigods who live for one thousand *yuga* circles, and even Brahmā, who lives for two *parāradhas*, are afraid of Me in My form of time.

COMMENTARY

One may imagine that the heavenly planets and the pleasure experienced there are eternal, but this is being refuted in this verse. Neither the heavenly planets nor its rulers are eternal. Even Brahmā is afraid of the Supreme Lord. This is stated in the *Vedas:*

bhīṣāsmād vātaḥ pavate bhīṣodeti sūryaḥ
bhīṣāsmād agniś candraś ca mṛtyur dhāvati pañcamaḥ

It is out of fear of the Supreme Brahman that the wind is blowing, out of fear of Him that the sun regularly rises and sets, and out of fear of Him that fire acts. It is only due to fear of Him that death and Indra, the King of heaven, perform their respective duties. (*Taittirīya Upaniṣad* 2.8)

From this statement, the supreme authority of the Supreme Personality of Godhead is clearly established, and the belief that Brahmā is the supreme person is refuted.

TEXT 31

गुणाःसृजन्तिकर्माणिच्गुणोऽनुसृजतेगुणान् ।
जीवस्तुगुणसंयुक्तोभुङ्क्तेकर्मफलान्यसौ ॥३१॥

guṇāḥ sṛjanti karmāṇicguṇo 'nusṛjate guṇān
jīvas tu guṇa-saṁyukto bhuṅkte karma-phalāny asau

It is the material senses that perform pious and sinful activities, it is the three modes of material nature that inspire the senses to engage in fruitive activities, and it is the living entity who enjoys the fruit of his *karma*, with the help of his senses.

COMMENTARY

It was previously described how sinful living entities are degraded to a hellish condition of life. Now, the question may arise as to whether the living entities are helpless or are they the master of their own destiny? The answer is that it is the senses that worship the demigods and perform other ritualistic activities. It is the senses that enjoy intimate association with another's wife, and perform other abominable acts, thus creating the destiny of the living entity. It is due to being impelled by the three modes of material nature that the senses create one's future body. The minute independence of the living entity consists of how he chooses to associate with the modes of nature. It is in this way that the living entity experiences suffering or enjoyment of his pious and sinful acts.

PURPORT

According to the *Bhagavad-gītā*, one's activities are impelled by the three modes of material nature. As long as one thinks himself to be the doer of activities, he remains on the platform of false ego. Until one comes to the platform of self-realization, he continues to experience lamentation and illusion. The conditioned soul can be liberated if he gives up his separatist mentality and engages in the devotional service of the Lord. When one is under the shelter of the Supreme Personality of Godhead, he is removed from the disturbing influence of the external energy of the Lord. By the perfection of devotional service to the Lord, one realizes his original identity of eternity, knowledge, and bliss, so that he goes to reside in Vaikuṇṭha, the eternal abode of the Lord.

TEXT 32

यावत्स्याद्गुणवैषम्यंतावन्नानात्वमात्मनः ।
नानात्वमात्मनोयावत्पारतन्त्र्यंतदैवहि ॥३२॥

yāvat syād guṇa-vaiṣamyaṁ tāvan nānātvam ātmanaḥ
nānātvam ātmano yāvat pāratantryaṁ tadaiva hi

As long as the living entity remains under the control of the three modes of material nature, he will attain various forms of life, such as a demigod, animal, and so on. As long as the living entity remains in the bodily concept of life, thinking himself to be the doer, he will have to experience the good and bad results of his karma.

COMMENTARY

When the living entity is forgetful of his relationship with Kṛṣṇa, he considers this material world as ultimate reality. Thus, he wanders among various species of life, sometimes as a hog, sometimes as a bird, and sometimes as a demigod.

PURPORT

While considering himself to be the doer of activities, the conditioned soul continues to wander through varieties of material bodies, one after another. In such a condition of life, one is incapable of understanding that behind this temporary manifestation is the Supreme Personality of Godhead. Unless one is situated in his constitutional position as the eternal servant of the Lord, one will remain falsely proud of being the proprietor of all he surveys, and the performer of heroic activities. In the human form of life, the conditioned soul may begin to worship five demigods for the fulfillment of his material desires. In such a situation, one thinks of the material world, which is a creation of the Lord's external energy, as being an object of his enjoyment.

TEXT 33

यावदस्यास्वतन्त्रत्वंतावदीश्वरतोभयम् ।
य एतत्समुपासीरंस्तेमुह्यन्तिशुचार्पिताः ॥३३॥

yāvad asyāsvatantratvaṁ tāvad īśvarato bhayam
ya etat samupāsīraṁs te muhyanti śucārpitāḥ

As long as the living entities remain dependent upon fruitive activities under the control of the modes of nature, they will continue to fear, because I am the giver of the results of *karma*. Those who accept the material concept of life, taking this cosmic manifestation to be factual, will devote themselves to material enjoyment, and therefore remain absorbed in lamentation and illusion.

COMMENTARY

Here, the Supreme Lord chastises those who say that the path of material enjoyment is auspicious. Those who praise the performance of fruitive activities are themselves tormented by lamentation and illusion.

PURPORT

The living entity is trapped in a network of illusion. Even if he can understand that he is dependent upon someone superior, he is not inclined to serve the Supreme Lord. This causes him to suffer in so many ways, however. Dreaming of sense gratification, the conditioned soul always fears the destruction of the arrangements he has so carefully made. Simply engaged in trying to perfect his eating, sleeping, mating, and defending, and thus exploiting material nature, he glides down to the lower species of life.

maya has two potencies—the covering potency and the throwing potency. When one is covered by *maya*, he forgets his original consciousness, so that she throws him into the darkness of ignorance. When one foolishly thinks that he is independent of the Supreme Lord, he becomes enamored by temporary material objects, hoping to enjoy sense gratification. The result is that when a person grows older, his life becomes filled with fear and anxiety. A conditioned soul falsely considers himself to be in control of his life, but because he is not in control, he is forced to suffer against his will. Truthfully, material life is abominable. It is only due to illusion that we think it to be satisfactory.

TEXT 34

कालआत्मागमोलोकःस्वभावोधर्मएवच ।
इतिमांबहुधाप्राहुर्गुणव्यतिकरेसति ॥३४॥

kāla ātmāgamo lokaḥ svabhāvo dharma eva ca
iti māṁ bahudhā prāhur guṇa-vyatikare sati

Due to the interaction of the three modes of material nature, the conditioned souls described Me in various ways as the time, the soul, the religious principles, the universal form, one's own nature, and so on.

COMMENTARY

According to some opinion, the material nature, time, the scriptures, and the soul are eternal. The word *svabhāva* means "nature," which is attributed to a conditioned soul. When the three modes of material nature cover the intelligence of the living entity, he considers the form of the Lord, as a creation of *māyāśakti*. This misconception can be removed by the will of the Lord and thus everyone should strive to get freed from the bondage of karma and engage in the devotional service of the Lord.

PURPORT

When the intelligence of the conditioned soul is covered by the external energy of the Lord, he forgets the Supreme Personality of Godhead. In such a condition, some people refer to Him as time, some refer to Him as the Vedic literature, some refer to Him as nature, and some refer to Him as religious principles. In this way, various fragmental understandings of the potencies of the Lord are understood.

TEXT 35

श्रीउद्धव उवाच
गुणेषुवर्तमानोऽपिदेहजेष्वनपावृतः ।
गुणैर्नबध्यतेदेहीबध्यतेवाकथंविभो ॥३५॥

śrī-uddhava uvāca
guṇeṣu vartamāno 'pi deha-jeṣv anapāvṛtaḥ
guṇair na badhyate dehī badhyate vā kathaṁ vibho

Śrī Uddhava said: My dear Lord, the souls of this world are conditioned by the three modes of material nature and thus they experience the happiness and distress that results from the activities performed under their direction. How can the conditioned souls be considered as independent? One can argue that the living entity is spiritual in nature and thus has nothing to do with this material world. If this is the fact, then how has he become bound up by nature?

COMMENTARY

It appears to ordinary people that even liberated souls also eat, sleep, walk, talk, and perform other similar activities, just as they do. Considering this, how can it be said that a liberated soul is not bound by his gross and subtle bodies, which act under the direction of the three modes of material nature? It may be questioned that if the soul is like the sky in that it never mixes with anything, then how it became conditioned by material nature? Uddhava presents such arguments just to clear up the understanding of actual spiritual life.

PURPORT

Conditioned souls under the influence of the three modes of material nature describe the Absolute Truth as nonexistent, or as possessing material qualities, or as being devoid of all qualities, or as being a neuter object like a eunuch. How can a spirit soul, who is now conditioned by the modes of nature, be freed from the bodily concept of life? If the transcendental spirit soul is never actually touched by *maya*, then why is he referred to as conditioned?

TEXTS 36-37

कथंवर्तेतविहरेत्कैर्वाज्ञायेतलक्षणै ।
किंभुञ्जीतोतविसृजेच्छयीतासीतयातिवा ॥३६॥
एतदच्युतमेब्रूहिप्रश्नंप्रश्नविदांवर ।
नित्यबद्धोनित्यमुक्त एक एवेतिमेभ्रमः ॥३७॥

kathaṁ varteta viharet kair vā jñāyeta lakṣaṇaiḥ
kiṁ bhuñjītota visṛjec chayītāsīta yāti vā

etad acyuta me brūhi praśnaṁ praśna-vidāṁ vara
nitya-baddho nitya-mukta eka eveti me bhramaḥ

O Acyuta, the living entity is sometimes described as eternally conditioned and at other times as eternally liberated. Because of this, I am not able to understand the actual situation of the living entity. My Lord, You are the best of those who are expert in answering philosophical questions. Please explain to me the symptoms by which one can tell the difference between a living entity who is eternally liberated and one who is eternally conditioned. In what ways are they situated, and how do they enjoy life, eat, evacuate, lie down, sit, and move about?

COMMENTARY

Uddhava says, "As long as the living entities identify themselves as products of matter, they continue to remain conditioned by the illusory energy. As soon as they are free from this misconception, they become liberated from material bondage. If this is a fact, then how can I recognize who is liberated and who is conditioned?"

Uddhava goes on to say, "Both liberated and conditioned souls eat, pass stool and urine, sleep, sit, walk, and talk. How can I recognize who is performing these activities under the direction of the modes of nature, and who is acting free from *maya*'s influence? Personalities like Dattātreya and Bharata were eternally liberated souls, whereas Devadatta and Yajñadatta were eternally conditioned souls. Since their bodily activities appear similar, I am confused, being unable to differentiate between them. Therefore, please tell me how one can recognize an eternally conditioned soul and an eternally liberated soul."

PURPORT

In the *Caitanya-caritāmṛta* (Madhya 20:109 and 20:117) it is stated:

jīvera 'svarūpa' haya—kṛṣṇera 'nitya-dāsa'
kṛṣṇera 'taṭasthā-śakti' 'bhedābheda-prakāśa'

It is the living entity's constitutional position to be an eternal servant of Kṛṣṇa because he is the marginal energy of Kṛṣṇa and a manifestation simultaneously one with and different from the Lord.

kṛṣṇa bhuli 'sei jīva anādi-bahirmukha
ataeva māyā tāre deya saṁsāra-duḥkha

By forgetting Kṛṣṇa, the living entity has become materialistic since time immemorial. Therefore, the illusory energy of Kṛṣṇa is giving him different types of miseries in material existence.

Conditional and liberated—both these states are adjectives. These two natures, when seen from two different angles, are known by two different names. According to the difference in the propensity of service the conditioned and liberated states are ascertained. When one is manifested, the other disappears.

Thus ends the translation of the Fourth Chapter of the Uddhava-gītā entitled **"The Nature of Fruitive Activity"** *with the commentaries of Śrīla Viśvanātha Cakravartī Ṭhākura and chapter summary and purports by Śrīla Bhaktisiddhānṭa Sarasvatī Ṭhākura.*

Chapter 5

The Symptoms of Conditioned and Liberated Living Entities

CHAPTER SUMMARY

In this chapter, Lord Śrī Kṛṣṇa describes to Uddhava the difference between conditioned and liberated living entities, the characteristics of a saintly person, and the various limbs of devotional service.

In the previous chapter, Uddhava had inquired about the difference between conditioned and liberated souls. In His reply, the supremely cognizant Śrī Kṛṣṇa states that although the spirit soul is His part and parcel, on account of his infinitesimal nature, he comes in contact with the material energy, which causes him to accept covering designations of the modes of goodness, passion, and ignorance. Thus, he has been bound up since time immemorial. But, when the spirit soul cultivates spiritual knowledge and achieves the shelter of devotional service, he becomes designated as eternally liberated. Therefore, transcendental knowledge is the cause of the living entity's liberation, and ignorance is the cause of his bondage. Both knowledge and ignorance are products of the illusory energy of Lord Śrī Kṛṣṇa and thus are His eternal potencies. The living entities who are captivated by the three modes of material nature are bewildered by false ego, which causes them to see themselves as the enjoyer of miseries, illusion, happiness, distress, danger, and so on. They thus remain absorbed in thoughts of such things, although they have no existence in the spiritual world.

Both the individual spirit soul and the Supersoul reside within the same body. The difference between the two is that the Supersoul, being fully cognizant, does not indulge in enjoying the fruits of actions but rather remains as a witness, whereas the infinitesimal conditioned soul, being ignorant, suffers the consequences of his own actions. The liberated soul, in spite of being within a material body because of the remaining reactions of his past activities, does not become disturbed by the happiness and suffering of the body. He sees such bodily experiences in the same way that a person who has just awakened from a dream sees his dream experiences. On the other hand, a conditioned soul, who actually has nothing to do with bodily happiness and distress, nevertheless imagines himself the enjoyer of his bodily experiences, just as a dreaming person imagines his dream experiences to be real.

Just as the sun reflected in water is not bound up by the water, and just as the air is not confined to some particular segment of the sky, a detached person takes advantage of his broad vision of the world to cut off all his doubts with the sword of proper renunciation. Since his life force, senses, mind, and intelligence have no tendency to become fixed on sense objects, he remains liberated even while situated within the material body. Regardless of whether he is harassed or worshiped, he remains equipoised. He is therefore considered liberated even in this life. A liberated person has nothing to do with the piety and sin of this world, but rather sees everything equally. A self-satisfied sage does not praise or condemn anyone. He does not speak uselessly to anyone and does not fix his mind on material things. Rather, he is always absorbed in meditation upon the Supreme Personality of Godhead, so that in the eyes of fools, he seems to be a speechless, crazy person.

Even if one has studied and has been taught all the Vedic literatures, if he has not developed a taste for the devotional service of the Supreme Lord, he has accomplished nothing more than his own labor. One should study only those scriptures that glorify the Supreme Personality of Godhead and His transcendental pastimes, and that contain narrations of His various incarnations. By doing so, one gains the highest good fortune whereas by studying scriptures other than these, one simply acquires misfortune.

With firm determination, one should understand the true identity of the spirit soul and then give up his false identification with the material body. Thereafter, he should offer himself at the lotus feet of Lord Śrī Kṛṣṇa, who is the reservoir of all love and thus attain actual peace. The mind that is under the sway of the three modes of material nature is unable to concentrate upon the Absolute Truth. After many lifetimes, faithful persons who have performed sacrifices for the attainment of religiosity, economic development, and sense gratification can begin the process of hearing and chanting of the Supreme Lord's transcendental pastimes. Such persons then achieve the association of a bona-fide spiritual master and saintly devotees. Thereafter, by the mercy of the spiritual master, they begin following the path of the *mahājanas* and thus attain self-realization.

Having heard these instructions from Lord Śrī Kṛṣṇa, Uddhava further desired to hear about the characteristics of a saintly person, and about various aspects of devotional service. Lord Kṛṣṇa replied that one who possesses these twenty-six qualities is actually a *sadhu* or Vaiṣṇava. He is merciful, nonenvious, always truthful, self-controlled, faultless, magnanimous, gentle, clean, nonpossessive, helpful to all, peaceful, dependent on Kṛṣṇa alone, free from lust, devoid of material endeavor, steady, in control of the six enemies of the mind, moderate in eating, never bewildered, always respectful to others, never desirous of respect for himself, sober, compassionate, friendly, poetic, expert and silent. The principal characteristic of a *sādhu* is that he takes shelter of Kṛṣṇa alone. One who knows that Śrī Kṛṣṇa is the unlimited, indwelling Lord who possesses a form that is eternal, full of knowledge and bliss, and thus engages in His service without deviation, is a topmost devotee.

Lord Śrī Kṛṣṇa next described to Uddhava the sixty-four limbs of devotional service. Among these are: seeing, touching, worshiping, serving, glorifying and offering obeisances to the Deity of the Lord and His pure devotees; developing attachment for hearing the chanting of the Lord's qualities, pastimes, and so on; remaining always in meditation upon the Lord; offering everything one acquires to the Lord; accepting oneself to be the Lord's servant; offering the Lord one's heart and soul; engaging in glorification of the Lord's appearance and activities; observing holidays related to the Lord; performing festivals in the Lord's temple in the company of other devotees, with music, singing and dancing; celebrating all varieties of yearly functions; offering food to the Lord; taking initiation according to the *Vedas* and *tantras*; taking vows related to the Lord; being eager to establish Deities of the Lord; endeavoring either alone or in association with others in constructing, for the service of the Lord, vegetable and flower gardens, temples, cities, and so on; humbly cleansing the temple of the Lord; and rendering service to the Lord's house by painting it, washing it with water and decorating it with auspicious designs.

After this, the process of worshiping the Deity of the Supreme Lord is briefly described.

TEXT 1

श्रीभगवानुवाच
बद्धोमुक्तैतिव्याख्यागुणतोमेनवस्तुतः ।
गुणस्यमायामूलत्वान्नमेमोक्षोनबन्धनम् ॥१॥

śrī-bhagavān uvāca
baddho mukta iti vyākhyā guṇato me na vastutaḥ
guṇasya māyā-mūlatvānna me mokṣo na bandhanam

The Supreme Lord said: My dear Uddhava, the three modes of material nature work under My control, sometimes designating the living entities as conditioned and sometimes granting them liberation. Truthfully, the living entities are never really conditioned or liberated, just as I remain unchanged as the Supreme Absolute Truth, the master of all potencies.

COMMENTARY

In this chapter, the Lord describes to Uddhava characteristics of conditioned and liberated souls, the symptoms by which one can recognize saintly persons, and the limbs of devotional service.

The Lord tells Uddhava that his question is unnecessary because the soul is never really bound by the material nature. It is simply an illusion to think that the materal body, which is created by the influence of the three modes of material nature, is the self. Only due to such illusion does the living entity suffer, just as one experiences distress in a dream. Of course, materal nature is not an illusion—it actually exists, just as the living entities also exist, both being potencies of the Supreme Personality of Godhead. It is the dream that he is a part of the material nature that constitutes the illusion of the living entity. Thus, the soul is never actually bound because his existence is always superior to that of matter.

PURPORT

The Supreme Personality of Godhead is the master of all potencies. It is only by speculation that the ignorant conditioned souls imagine that the Lord is devoid of variegatedness. Although the living entity is part and parcel of the Lord's superior potency, he now identifies with the inferior potency of the Lord and thus experiences conditional life. The living entity is liberated when contacts the superior potency of the Lord, which has three divisions—*hlādinī*, or spiritual pleasure; *sandhinī*, or eternal existence, and *saṁvit*, or all-pervading knowledge. The Lord's existence is *sac-cid-ānanda* and He never becomes forgetful. The living entities, however being minute in quantity, are sometimes conditioned and sometimes liberated.

The neutral state of the three modes of material nature is called *pradhāna*. When the three modes of material nature interact, they compete for control over the tiny living entities, thus creating a variety of manifestations. When the conditioned soul desires to free himself from the entanglements caused by the modes of material nature, he must take to the devotional service of the Lord, which can elevate him to the spiritual world. In the spiritual sky, everyone possesses spiritual bodies that are not subject to change. In such a liberated state of existence, there is no possibility of being influenced by the three modes of material nature.

After understanding one's eternal nature, one can see that he was never really a part of this material world. On the spiritual platform, there is no existence of the conception of liberation and bondage. Being the marginal energy of the Supreme Lord, one should use his minute independence to engage in the Lord's devotional service and thus revive his original consciousness, which is eternal, full of knowledge, and full of bliss. In such a state, there is no chance of once again falling into illusion.

TEXT 2

शोकमोहौसुखंदुःखंदेहापत्तिश्चमायया ।
स्वप्नोयथात्मनःख्यातिःसंसृतिर्नतुवास्तवी ॥२॥

śoka-mohau sukhaṁ duḥkhaṁ dehāpattiś ca māyayā
svapno yathātmanaḥ khyātiḥ saṁsṛtir na tu vāstavī

Just as a dream is an illusory creation of the mind, so lamentation, illusion, happiness, distress, and the bodily concept of life are simply creations of My illusory energy. That is to say, materal existence is essentially illusory.

COMMENTARY

The nature of material bondage is being described in this verse. Lamentation, illusion, happiness, and distress, are all related to the material body. Gross bodily designations are accepted by the subtle body and thus a living entity falsely identifies himself as the enjoyer of material nature. Material existence, which is full of lamentation and illusion Is not factual reality because it is a temporary display of the Lord's external energy, just like a dream, and thus has no relation with the eternal spirit soul.

PURPORT

The illusioned soul forgets his eternal existence and imagines that there is no Supreme Truth. Even in its most advanced stages, material life is simply ignorance. Just as when one dreams, there is no question of a pleasant dream being more real than a nightmare, so heavenly and hellish material existences are equally illusory. This material world is a manifestation of the Lord's external energy, just as the eternal spiritual sky is a manifestation of His internal energy. Although material nature is infinitely mutable and thus has no stable condition, it is real and not simply an illusion, like a mirage in the desert, because it is an emanation from the Supreme Reality. It is only our mistaking the material body as the self that constitutes illusion. One should therefore wake up from the dream of bodily identification and see the reality of the eternal Supreme Personality of Godhead.

TEXT 3

विद्याविद्येममतनूविद्धयुद्धवशरीरिणाम् ।
मोक्षबन्धकरी आद्येमाययामेविनिर्मिते ॥३॥

vidyāvidye mama tanū viddhy uddhava śarīriṇām
mokṣa-bandha-karī ādye māyayā me vinirmite

O Uddhava, you should understand that both ignorance and knowledge are creations of My maya. **Being expansions of My potency, they are beginningless and are the cause of the living entity's bondage and liberation.**

COMMENTARY

It may be questioned how *maya*, being illusion, can influence the eternal spirit soul. The answer is that both knowledge and ignorance are two manifestations of the Lord's powerful energy, and which are the causes of liberation and bondage. Knowledge awards liberation and ignorance causes bondage. Being creations of the eternal energy of the Lord, knowledge and ignorance are beginningless, unlimited, and inexhaustible. In the Vedic literature, it is described that the Supreme Lord has an eternal energy known as *maya*, which manifests in three features—*vidyā*, *avidyā*, and *pradhāna*. *Pradhāna* creates the material world, *avidyā* creates the conditioned souls' misconceptions, and *vidyā* removes those misconception and awards enlightenment.

PURPORT

The living entity, being the marginal energy of the Lord, can exist under the shelter of either knowledge or ignorance. When the living entity takes shelter of *vidyā*, he remains in the liberated condition and when he takes shelter of *avidyā*, he remains in bondage. *Vidyā* and *avidyā* are the two eternal energies of the Supreme Lord. Followers of the *viśiṣṭādvaita* philosophy address the living entities as *cit* and the material world as *acit*. According to the Vedic statement, *yathābhāso yathā tamaḥ*, Śrī Jīva Gosvāmī has described the living entities as *jīvamāyā* and matter as *guṇamāyā*. It is the mistaken identification of the living entities with matter that causes illusory material existence, or ignorance. When the living entities can see himself as the superior potency of the Lord, giving up his misidentification with the inferior potency of matter, he can return to his blissful condition in the spiritual sky.

TEXT 4

एकस्यैवममांशस्यजीवस्यैवमहामते ।
बन्धोऽस्याविद्ययानादिर्विद्ययाचतथेतरः ॥४॥

ekasyaiva mamāṁśasya jīvasyaiva mahā-mate
bandho 'syāvidyayānādir vidyayā ca tathetaraḥ

O intelligent Uddhava, the eternal living entities are My parts and parcels, for I am the Supreme Personality of Godhead. Ignorance is the cause of the living entities' bondage, and knowledge is the cause of their liberation.

COMMENTARY

The two energies of the Lord, *vidyā* and *avidyā*, influence the marginal potency, or living entities. When they are under the influence of *avidyā*, the living entities are conditioned and when they are under the influence of *vidyā*, they are liberated. As stated in the *Bhagavad-gītā* (7.5):

apareyam itas tv anyāṁ prakṛtiṁ viddhi me parām
jīva-bhūtāṁ mahā-bāho yayedaṁ dhāryate jagat

Besides this inferior nature, O mighty-armed Arjuna, there is another, superior energy of Mine, consisting of all living entities who are struggling with material nature and are sustaining the universe.

There are many statements in the Vedic literature indicating that the Absolute Truth is one. Here the living entities are described as innumerable, being fragmental parts and parcels of the Lord. How can this apparent contradiction be reconciled? Lord Caitanya has informed us that the living entities are inconceivably simultaneously one with and different from the Absolute Truth. The external energy of the Lord has two features—*avidyā* and *vidyā*. Under the influence of these potencies the propensities of the *jīvaśakti* and *māyāśakti* are eternally manifest. It is stated in the *Vedas* (*Kaṭha Upaniṣad* 2.2.13):

nityo nityānāṁ cetanaś cetanānām
eko bahūnāṁ yo vidadhāti kāmān

The Lord is the prime eternal among all eternals. He is the supreme living entity of all living entities, and He alone is maintaining all life.

When the living entities are freed from the influence of *avidyā* they attain liberation. However, the liberation of merging into the existence of Brahman is condemned. A devotee, although united with the Lord, keeps his individuality intact.

As stated in the *Viṣṇu Purāṇa* (6.7.61):

viṣṇu-śaktiḥ parā proktā kṣetra-jñākhyā tathā parā
avidyā-karma-saṁjñānyā tṛtīyā śaktir iṣyate

The potency of Lord Viṣṇu is summarized in three categories—namely, the spiritual potency, the living entities and ignorance. The spiritual potency is full of knowledge; the living entities, although belonging to the spiritual potency, are subject to bewilderment; and the third energy, which is full of ignorance, is always visible in fruitive activities.

PURPORT

The Supreme Lord is one without a second and the innumerable living entities, both conditioned and liberated, are His eternal fragmental parts and parcels. The conditioned souls have been under the influence of *avidyā* since time immemorial. However, with the help of *vidyā*, they can attain liberation. Although the parts and parcels of the Lord are sometimes liberated and sometimes conditioned, there is no question of conditioning or liberation for the Lord Himself. *Avidyā* and *vidyā* can exert their supremacy over the parts and parcels of the Lord but not the Lord Himself.

TEXT 5

अथबद्धस्यमुक्तस्यवैलक्षण्यंवदामिते ।
विरुद्धधर्मिणोस्तातस्थितयोरेकधर्मिणि ॥५॥

atha baddhasya muktasya vailakṣaṇyaṁ vadāmi te
viruddha-dharmiṇos tāta sthitayor eka-dharmiṇi

O Uddhava, I shall now describe the difference between the embodied spirit soul, who possesses the two contradictory natures of misery and happiness, and the eternally liberated Supreme Personality of Godhead.

COMMENTARY

In the previous chapter, Uddhava inquired from the Lord about the symptoms by which one can understand who is a conditioned soul and who is a liberated soul. In reply, the Lord explained that the characteristics of bondage and liberation may be understood in two divisions—as the difference between the ordinary conditioned soul and the eternally liberated Personality of Godhead, or as the difference between conditioned and liberated living entities in the *jīva* category. The *Vedas* confirm that the Supersoul is untouched by material contamination. The difference between the spirit soul and the Supersoul will be described in the following verses. The conditioned soul is full of lamentation whereas the Supersoul is full of bliss. They are both situated in the same body, but one of them is fully independent and the other is completely dependent on the independent Lord.

PURPORT

When the respective symptoms of the conditioned and liberated souls are carefully considered, there appears to be two contradictory natures. The conditional state is full of lamentation, and the liberated state is the platform of boundless happiness. The Supersoul is the controller of all energies and the spirit soul, being the marginal energy, is always controlled.

TEXT 6

सुपर्णावेतौसदृशौसखायौयदृच्छयैतौकृतनीडौचवृक्षे ।
एकस्तयोःखादतिपिप्पलान्नमन्योनिरन्नोऽपिबलेनभूयान् ॥६॥

suparṇāv etau sadṛśau sakhāyau yadṛcchayaitau kṛta-nīḍau ca vṛkṣe
ekas tayoḥ khādati pippalānnam anyo niranno 'pi balena bhūyān

There are two birds, the living entity and the Supersoul, who live together in a nest (heart) of a tree (the material body). They are similar in nature, both being spiritual, and they are inseparable friends. One bird (the living entity) enjoys the fruit of the tree, whereas the other bird (the Supersoul), does not partake of the fruit because He is in a superior position, on account of His potency.

COMMENTARY

Just as a bird is separate from the tree he sits in, the spirit soul and the Supersoul are distinct from the material body, which is compared to a tree. Because both of them are of the same spiritual quality, they are naturally related as friends. While residing within the tree, one of them enjoys the fruit of that tree whereas the other one simply witnesses his friend's activities. This tree of material existence has its roots upwards and its branches down, as described in the *Bhagavad-gītā* (15.1):

śrī-bhagavān uvāca
ūrdhva-mūlam adhaḥ-śākham aśvatthaṁ prāhur avyayam
chandāṁsi yasya parṇāni yas taṁ veda sa veda-vit

The Supreme Personality of Godhead said: It is said that there is an imperishable banyan tree that has its roots upward and its branches down and whose leaves are the Vedic hymns. One who knows this tree is the knower of the *Vedas.*

Two birds live in this imperishable banyan tree. One of them is the living entity who engages in eating the fruit of the tree, and the other is the Supersoul, who does not eat the fruit but remains always self-satisfied. It is also stated in the *Vedas:*

dvā suparṇā sayujā sakhāyā samānaṁ vṛkṣaṁ pariṣasvajāte
tayor anyaḥ pippalaṁ svādy atty anaśnann anyo 'bhicākaśīti

Two companion birds sit together in the shelter of the same pippala tree. One of them is relishing the taste of the tree's berries, while the other refrains from eating and instead watches over His friend. (*Śvetāśvatara Upaniṣad* 4.6)

TEXT 7

आत्मानमन्यंचसवेदविद्वानपिप्पलादोनतुपिप्पलादः ।
योऽविद्ययायुक् सतुनित्यबद्धोविद्यामयोयःसतुनित्यमुक्तः ॥७॥

ātmānam anyaṁ ca sa veda vidvān apippalādo na tu pippalādaḥ
yo 'vidyayā yuk sa tu nitya-baddho vidyā-mayo yaḥ sa tu nitya-muktaḥ

The Supersoul, who does not taste the fruit of the tree and who is the shelter of eternal knowledge, knows all about Himself and the living entities. However, the living entity, who tastes the fruit of the tree is ignorant of both himself and the Supreme Lord. The living entity has been conditioned by the Lord's illusory energy since time immemorial, and the Supreme Lord, who is always in full knowledge, is eternally liberated.

COMMENTARY

The Supersoul knows Himself, as well as the living entities, and He does not eat the bitter fruit of the tree of material existence. The conditioned living entity, on the other hand, who tries to enjoy the fruits of his labor, neither knows himself nor the Supreme Lord. These living entities are eternally conditioned whereas the Supersoul is eternally full of knowledge. The word *vidyā* in this verse refers to the internal spiritual knowledge of the Supreme Lord, which is distinct from material knowledge. In the *Gopāla-tāpani Upaniṣad*, it is stated:

> There are two birds living as friends in the same tree—the living entity and the Supersoul. The living entity is a separated part and parcel of the Supreme Lord and he enjoys the fruits of his fruitive actions. The Supersoul is a plenary portion of the Supreme Lord, and He witnesses the actions of the living entity.

PURPORT

There is always a distinction between the Supreme Lord, who is the supreme controller, and the living entities, who are His eternal servants. The Lord is the master of all potencies and the living entities are subordinate to Him. The Lord does not enjoy the fruits of *karma*, and He is omniscient. The living entity enjoys the fruits of his own *karma*, and he is ignorant. Due to ignorance, the living entity has been conditioned since time immemorial. If he reinstates himself as a servant of the Supreme Lord, then by the influence of spiritual knowledge, he becomes eternally liberated. In his conditioned state of existence, the living entity enjoys by acting piously and suffers by acting impiously. In the liberated state of existence, there is no question of piety or impiety because one is fully devoted to the Supreme Lord and is not attached to the fruits of his *karma*.

TEXT 8

देहस्थोऽपिनदेहस्थोविद्वान् स्वप्नाद्यथोत्थितः ।
अदेहस्थोऽपिदेहस्थःकुमतिःस्वप्नदृग्यथा ॥८॥

deha-stho 'pi na deha-stho vidvān svapnād yathotthitaḥ
adeha-stho 'pi deha-sthaḥ kumatiḥ svapna-dṛg yathā

A liberated soul, although living within the material body, sees himself as distinct from the body, just as one who wakes up from a dream sees that it was not his real life. An ignorant person, however, thinks the body to be the self, just as a dreaming person takes what he sees to be his reality.

COMMENTARY

In the next nine verses, the Lord will explain the difference between the conditioned souls and the liberated souls. In a dream, one sees oneself in an imaginary body, but upon waking, one gives up all identification with that body. Similarly, one who has awakened to Kṛṣṇa consciousness no longer identifies with the gross or subtle material bodies, nor does he become affected by the happiness and distress of material life. On the other hand, a foolish person does not awaken from the dream of material existence and is afflicted with innumerable problems due to false identification with the gross and subtle material bodies. One should become situated in one's eternal spiritual identity. By properly identifying oneself as the eternal servant of Kṛṣṇa, one becomes relieved of his false material identity, and therefore the miseries of illusory existence immediately cease, just as the anxiety of a troublesome dream ceases as soon as one awakens to his normal, pleasant surroundings.

PURPORT

Although the subject matter of a dream may remain fresh in the mind of a person when he wakes up, the illusory nature of the dream is immediately realized by him. However, those who are sleeping in the lap of material nature cannot realize the illusory nature of their existence until they awaken by means of self-realization. The seer himself is eternal but his dreams at night and his experiences during the day are of no lasting importance, being no better than a phantasmagoria.

TEXT 9

इन्द्रियैरिन्द्रियार्थेषुगुणैरपिगुणेषुच ।
गृह्यमाणेष्वहंकुर्यान्नविद्वान्यस्त्वविक्रियः ॥९॥

indriyair indriyārtheṣu guṇair api guṇeṣu ca
gṛhyamāṇeṣv ahaṁ kuryān na vidvān yas tv avikriyaḥ

A learned person who has seen the futility of material desires does not think that he performs the activities of the body. Indeed, he knows that the activities of the body, which amount to the senses contacting their objects, are going on automatically by the dictation of the three modes of material nature.

COMMENTARY

One who is liberated from the bodily conception of life knows very well that he is not the doer and that nothing belongs to him. However, there are persons who claim to be transcendentally situated and yet are seen to be fully under the influence of material desire. Such persons are nothing more than cheaters and so must be considered the lowest of mankind.

PURPORT

The material body always interacts with the sense objects because in order to survive, the body must eat, drink, speak, sleep, and so on, but an enlightened person who knows the science of Kṛṣṇa consciousness never thinks, "These sense objects are my property. They are meant for my pleasure."

TEXT 10

दैवाधीनेशरीरेऽस्मिन्गुणभाव्येनकर्मणा ।
वर्तमानोऽबुधस्तत्रकर्तास्मीतिनिबध्यते ॥१०॥

daivādhīne śarīre 'smin guṇa-bhāvyena karmaṇā
vartamāno 'budhas tatra kartāsmīti nibadhyate

Under the control of his previous deeds, a foolish person accepts a material body and proudly considers himself the doer of all activities. Thus he becomes entangled in all kinds of bodily affairs as the reactions to his fruitive activities that are actually carried out by the three material qualities.

COMMENTARY

This material body is received as the result of one's previous activities. While residing in this body, one manipulates his senses and engages them in various activities. In this way, he becomes entangled in the actions and reactions of work. How does it happen? Because he is bewildered by false ego, the conditioned soul thinks himself to be the doer. This is stated in the *Bhagavad-gītā* (3.27):

prakṛteḥ kriyamāṇāni guṇaiḥ karmaṇi sarvaśaḥ
ahaṅkāra-vimūḍhātmā kartāham iti manyate

The spirit soul, bewildered by the influence of false ego, thinks himself the doer of activities that are in actuality carried out by the three modes of material nature.

PURPORT

Those who are bewildered by false ego foolishly claim to be the doers of all activities, which are actually carried out by the three modes of material nature. Accepting the material body as the self, they think that they are working independently, although their activities are fully under the control of material nature.

TEXT 11

एवंविरक्तःशयन आसनाटनमज्ज्ने ।
दर्शनस्पर्शनघ्राणभोजनश्रवणादिषु ।
नतथाबध्यतेविद्वान्तत्रतत्रादयन् गुणान् ॥११॥

evaṁ viraktaḥ śayana āsanāṭana-majjane
darśana-sparśana-ghrāṇa- bhojana-śravaṇādiṣu
na tathā badhyate vidvān tatra tatrādayan guṇān

Learned persons who are fixed in detachment engage their senses in activities such as sleeping, sitting, traveling, bathing, seeing, touching, smelling, and hearing, but they never become entangled. By simply remaining as a witness, they do not become entangled like foolish people.

COMMENTARY

A foolish person, as a result of his attachment for material objects, enjoys sense gratification but then becomes entangled in material bondage. However, according to the logic of *vādita anuvṛtti*, a liberated person is never entangled, even if he seems somewhat connected with material happiness and lamentation. One who is actually detached from matter, even though he may accept material objects for the maintenance of his body, remains aloof as the witness of his activities.

PURPORT

An intelligent and experienced person is never compelled to act under the influence of the three modes of material nature. He remains detached from activities like sleeping, sitting idly, and traveling, and is not forced to perform activities like looking, touching, smelling, and eating.

TEXTS 12-13

प्रकृतिस्थोऽप्यसंसक्तोयथाखंसवितानिलः ।
वैशारद्येक्षयासङ्गशितयाछिन्नसंशयः ॥१२॥
प्रतिबुद्धैवस्वप्नान्नानात्वाद्विनिवर्तते ॥१३॥

prakṛti-stho 'py asaṁsakto yathā khaṁ savitānilaḥ
vaiśāradyekṣayāsaṅga-śitayā chinna-saṁśayaḥ
pratibuddha iva svapnān nānātvād vinivartate

Although everything rests in space, it does not mix with anything, the sun is not affected by the water in which its reflection appears, and the wind that blows everywhere is not affected by the aromas it carries. Similarly, a self-realized soul is detached from the material body and the world he lives in. He is like someone who has awakened from a dream. With the sword of knowledge sharpened by detachment, the self-realized soul cuts to pieces all doubts born of misidentification with matter, and thus withdraws his mind from the temporary displays of *maya*.

COMMENTARY

How is such detachment possible? The answer is provided here by giving the examples of space, the air, and the sun. One who has cut-off the attachment of his senses for their objects by utilizing the sharp weapon of renunciation, can remain aloof from the material body and the material world.

PURPORT

A self-realized soul is freed of all doubts when he directly experiences his eternal spiritual identity. Lord Kṛṣṇa is the Supreme Personality of Godhead, and nothing is separate from Him. Such an understanding frees one from all doubts. As stated here, just like the sky, the sun, or the wind, one who is self-realized is not entangled, although situated within the material creation of the Lord.

TEXT 14

यस्यस्युर्वीतसङ्कल्पाःप्राणेन्द्रियमनोधियाम् ।
वृत्तयःसविनिर्मुक्तोदेहस्थोऽपिहितद्गुणैः ॥१४॥

yasya syur vīta-saṅkalpāḥ prāṇendriya-mano-dhiyām
vṛttayaḥ sa vinirmukto deha-stho 'pi hi tad-guṇaiḥ

A person is known to be actually liberated from the gross and subtle material bodies when all the functions of his body and mind are performed without material desires. Although possessing a material body, such a person is not in bondage.

COMMENTARY

Uddhava had asked, "How does a liberated person live?" The answer is that although the material body and mind are subject to lamentation, illusion, hunger, lust, greed, insanity, frustration, and so on, one who remains active in this world without attachment is considered *vinirmukta*, or completely liberated.

PURPORT

Those who have no material desires are not influenced by the three modes of material nature, even though they are situated within the material world. Their vital energy, senses, mind, and intelligence are purified when engaged in the devotional service of Lord Kṛṣṇa. Nondevotees are the servants of their material desires, whereas devotees are the servants of the Supreme Lord.

TEXT 15

यस्यात्माहिंस्यतेहिंस्त्रैर्येनकिञ्चिद्यदृच्छया ।
अर्च्यतेवाक्वचित्तत्रनव्यतिक्रियतेबुधः ॥१५॥

yasyātmā hiṁsyate hiṁsrair yena kiñcid yadṛcchayā
arcyate vā kvacit tatra na vyatikriyate budhaḥ

Sometimes, one may be tormented by a miscreant or attacked by a ferocious animal, and at other times, one may be shown all respect and worshiped. One who does not become angry when attacked, or satisfied when worshiped, is certainly most intelligent.

COMMENTARY

What are the symptoms of a liberated soul? The answer is given here and the next two verses. If one does not become angry when attacked for no apparent reason, and if one does not become enlivened when glorified or worshiped, then one has passed the test of self-realization and is considered fixed in spiritual intelligence. Yājñavalkya has said that when a person doesn't become angry when pierced by sharp thorns, and doesn't become elated when shown great respect, he must be considered actually intelligent.

PURPORT

A person who is not affected, whether he is tortured or worshiped, is a liberated soul, although living in this world.

TEXT 16

नस्तुवीतननिन्देतकुर्वतःसाध्वसाधुवा ।
वदतोगुणदोषाभ्यांवर्जितःसमदृङ् मुनिः ॥१६॥

na stuvīta na nindeta kurvataḥ sādhv asādhu vā
vadato guṇa-doṣābhyāṁ varjitaḥ sama-dṛṅ muniḥ

A saintly person views everyone with equal vision, and so he is not affected by what ordinary person considers good or bad. Although he certainly sees how others are performing beneficial or horrible work, and speaking intelligently or foolishly, he does not wish to praise or criticize anyone.

COMMENTARY

A liberated soul neither blasphemes nor praises people who are engaged on the material platform.

PURPORT

The equipoised sage who does not see material qualities and faults is liberated. He therefore neither glorifies anyone nor blasphemes anyone.

TEXT 17

नकुर्यान्नवदेत्किञ्चिन्नध्यायेत्साध्वसाधुवा ।
आत्मारामोऽनयावृत्त्याविचरेज्जडवन्मुनिः ॥१७॥

na kuryān na vadet kiñcin na dhyāyet sādhv asādhu vā
ātmārāmo 'nayā vṛttyā vicarej jaḍa-van muniḥ

For the sake of maintaining his body, a liberated soul does not act, speak, or think in terms of material duality, considering something to be good and something else to be bad. Rather, he is detached in all circumstances, taking pleasure in self-realization. Thus he wanders about in his own mood, appearing like a dullard to outsiders.

COMMENTARY

A person who does not possess the above-mentioned qualities should be understood to be a conditioned soul.

PURPORT

A self-satisfied devotee of the Lord does not divert his attention to observe the activities of materialists. Thinking how everything can be utilized in the service of the Lord, he never views material objects as meant for his gratification. He has no conception of good and bad because he sees how everything can be used for the satisfaction of the Lord. To the external vision of ordinary people, however, he may appear to be acting on the material platform.

TEXT 18

शब्दब्रह्मणिनिष्णातोननिष्णायात्परेयदि ।
श्रमस्तस्यश्रमफलोह्यधेनुमिवरक्षतः ॥१८॥

śabda-brahmaṇi niṣṇāto na niṣṇāyāt pare yadi
śramas tasya śrama-phalo hy adhenum iva rakṣataḥ

If, after thoroughly studying the Vedic literature one makes no endeavor to fix his mind on the Supreme Personality of Godhead, then his endeavor is like that of a man who works very hard to take care of a cow that gives no milk. In other words, the fruit of one's laborious study of Vedic knowledge is nothing more than the labor itself.

COMMENTARY

In this verse, the word *pare* indicates the Supreme Personality of Godhead, and not the impersonal Brahman. It will be seen later on that Lord Kṛṣṇa, the speaker of this verse, repeatedly refers to Himself as the Supreme. An impersonal interpretation of this verse would therefore be contradictory and illogical. If one's aim is opposed to pleasing the Lord, then all his endeavors are futile, just like the labor of a person who maintains a barren cow.

PURPORT

The maintainer of a cow that does not give any milk does not receive any profit in exchange for his service. Similarly, the endeavor of a person who has very strenuously studied the Vedic literature will not prove fruitful if he has not concluded that he must devote himself to the service of the Supreme Lord.

TEXT 19

गांदुग्धदोहामसतींचभार्यांदेहंपराधीनमसत्प्रजांच ।
वित्तंत्वतीर्थीकृतमङ्गवाचंहीनांमयारक्षतिदुःखदुःखी ॥१९॥

gāṁ dugdha-dohām asatīṁ ca bhāryāṁ dehaṁ parādhīnam asat-prajāṁ ca
vittaṁ tv atīrthī-kṛtam aṅga vācaṁ hīnāṁ mayā rakṣati duḥkha-duḥkhī

My dear Uddhava, that person is certainly most miserable who maintains a cow that gives no milk, an unchaste wife, a body that is completely dependent upon others, useless children, and wealth not utilized for a good purpose. Similarly, one who makes a study of the Vedic literature that is devoid of My glories is certainly most miserable.

COMMENTARY

One who is actually learned can appreciate that everything perceived through the bodily senses are expansions of the Supreme Personality of Godhead, and that nothing exists independently of Him. In this verse, through various examples, it is concluded that the power of speech is useless if not engaged in glorifying the Supreme Lord. It is a fact that in this world, a person labors uselessly while maintaining false hopes. There is the example of the cow that gives no milk. When a cow no longer gives milk, one still must work hard to protect her, because no one will purchase such a cow. The owner of the cow may hope, "Perhaps she will again become pregnant and give some milk." Then, when this hope is smashed, the owner becomes indifferent to cow, and for this, he must suffer in the next life, after going through so much trouble in this life.

Another example is that a man may discover that his wife doesn't care for him any more. Still, he may go on caring for such a useless woman, thinking, "If I work hard and supply her everything she desires, she will surely love me in return." Unfortunately, such unchaste women generally do not change their attitude and so the husband simply labors without any pleasing result.

Another example is that one who has attained wealth by the mercy of God must give in charity to the deserving persons and causes. If such an opportunity presents itself and one refused to give charity due to selfishness, one is considered a miser in this life, and in the next life, he will be poverty-stricken.

PURPORT

One who maintains a cow that does not produce milk, an unchaste wife, a body that is completely dependent upon others, sons that are not of good character, and wealth that is not used for good purposes, suffers miseries, as do those who do not hear and chant the glories of the Supreme Lord.

TEXT 20

यस्यांनमेपावनमङ्गकर्मस्थित्युद्भवप्राणनिरोधमस्य ।
लीलावतारेप्सितजन्मवास्याद्वन्ध्यांगिरंतांबिभृयान्नधीरः ॥२०॥

yasyāṁ na me pāvanam aṅga karma sthity-udbhava-prāṇa-nirodham asya
līlāvatārepsita-janma vā syād vandhyāṁ giraṁ tāṁ bibhṛyān na dhīraḥ

O Uddhava, an intelligent person should never read literature that does not describe My activities, which purify the entire universe. It is I who creates, maintains, and annihilates the cosmic manifestation. Any so-called knowledge that does not recognize

these activities of Mine is simply barren and is not acceptable to those who are actually intelligent.

COMMENTARY

In the Vedic literature, the Absolute Truth is sometimes described as Brahman, sometimes as Paramātmā, and sometimes as Bhagavān. Just to clarify the actual purpose of the Vedic literature, it is being said in this verse: "Those literatures that do not glorify the pastimes of My various incarnations, which are beneficial to all living entities throughout the universe, are to be avoided by saintly persons. Even Vedic statements that are devoid of the glorification of My transcendental pastimes, should never be studied by learned persons."

PURPORT

In this verse the Lord explains that the literatures approved for the devotees are those that glorify the Lord's pastimes as the *puruṣa-avatāra* and the *līlāvatāras*, culminating in the personal appearance of Lord Kṛṣṇa Himself. Even Vedic literatures that neglect the Supreme Personality of Godhead should be ignored. This fact was also explained by Nārada Muni to Śrīla Vyāsadeva, the author of the *Vedas*, when the great Vedavyāsa felt dissatisfied with his work.

TEXT 21

एवंजिज्ञासयापोह्यनानात्वभ्रममात्मनि ।
उपारमेतविरजंमनोमय्यर्प्यसर्वगे ॥२१॥

evaṁ jijñāsayāpohya nānātva-bhramam ātmani
upārameta virajaṁ mano mayy arpya sarva-ge

After coming to this conclusion of knowledge, you should remove the misconception that the material body is the self, and you should fix your mind upon Me, the all-pervading Lord, and thereby free yourself from material existence.

COMMENTARY

The conclusion of knowledge is herein being described. To identify with one's gross and subtle bodies, to think that the innumerable living entities are ultimately one, and to think that human beings and demigods possess different types of souls—these are all misconceptions. One should give up such misconceptions by the process of devotional service and fix his mind on the Supreme Lord. In this way, one will attain realization of the Personality of Godhead on the strength of his knowledge in devotional service. This is confirmed in the *Bhagavad-gītā* (18.55):

bhaktyā mām abhijānāti yāvān yaś cāsmi tattvataḥ
tato māṁ tattvato jñātvā viśate tad-anantaram

One can understand Me as I am, as the Supreme Personality of Godhead, only by devotional service. And when one is in full consciousness of Me by such devotion, he can enter into the kingdom of God.

PURPORT

As long as one considers the body as the self, various misconceptions will pollute his mentality. By full engagement in the devotional service of the Supreme Lord, one gains respite from the endeavors for sense gratification, being resolute in his determination to use everything for the Lord's satisfaction. The acceptance of anything as not being related to the Lord and thus meant for one's sense gratification, is the cause of material bondage. One should therefore avoid this misconception by coming to the true conclusion of knowledge, that the Supreme Lord is the sum total of everything.

TEXT 22

यद्यनीशोधारयितुंमनोब्रह्मणिनिश्चलम् ।
मयिसर्वाणिकर्माणिनिरपेक्षःसमाचर ॥२२॥

yady anīśo dhārayituṁ mano brahmaṇi niścalam
mayi sarvāṇi karmāṇi nirapekṣaḥ samācara

My dear Uddhava, if you cannot detach your mind from the objects of the senses and thus absorb it completely in Me, then offer the results of all your activities to Me, without considering the fruits of your labor to be your personal property.

COMMENTARY

If one offers the results of all activities to Lord Kṛṣṇa, one will gradually become detached from the false egoistic conception of life. When the mind becomes purified by such detachment, transcendental knowledge becomes manifest within the heart. When the mind remains absorbed in transcendental understanding, it can come to the spiritual platform, as described in *Bhagavad-gītā* (18.54):

brahma-bhūtaḥ prasannātmā na śocati na kāṅkṣati
samaḥ sarveṣu bhūteṣu mad-bhaktiṁ labhate parām

One who is thus transcendentally situated at once realizes the Supreme Brahman. He never laments nor desires to have anything; he is equally disposed to every living entity. In that state he attains pure devotional service unto Me.

It is not difficult to understand the preliminary teachings of the Lord which stress the distinction between matter and spirit—between the living entity and his material body. When one surpasses the stage of simple self-realization and begins meditation upon the Supreme Personality of Godhead and rendering service unto Him, he can enter into a personal relationship with the Absolute Truth. Such a revival of one's dormant love for God dispels all traces of illusion whereby one thinks that this world is ultimate reality. By experiencing the reality of one's relationship with the Supreme Lord, one automatically becomes detached from mundane society, friendship, and love. Ultimately, such rendering of devotional service enables one to go back home, back to Godhead and thus personally associate with the Lord.

The simple offering of the results of one's activities to the Lord certainly purifies one's existence and enables one to comprehend the preliminary instructions of the spiritual master in disciplic succession. Still, if one truly aspires to fix his mind in the service of the Lord, then he should associate with pure devotees of the Lord and render regulaged service in their association.

PURPORT

The conditioned soul, being in the bodily concept of life, is generally not inclined to offer the results of his activities to the Supreme Personality of Godhead. Being materially conditioned, he considers himself to belong to a particular family, society, and nation instead of understanding himself to be the eternal servant of the Personality of Godhead. The conditioned souls try to alleviate their suffering by exercising their minds in speculating in various ways, but such endeavors will never free them from illusion. It behooves one to begin offering the results of his activities for the service of the Lord, as this will lead him to the proper understanding of his self.

TEXT 23-24

श्रद्धालुर्मत्कथाःशृण्वन्सुभद्रालोकपावनीः।
गायन्ननुस्मरन्कर्मजन्मचाभिनयन् मुहुः॥२३॥

मदर्थेधर्मकामार्थान्आचरन्मदपाश्रयः।
लभतेनिश्चलांभक्तिंमय्युद्धवसनातने ॥२४॥

śraddhālur mat-kathāḥ śṛṇvan su-bhadrā loka-pāvanīḥ
gāyann anusmaran karma janma cābhinayan muhuḥ

mad-arthe dharma-kāmārthān ācaran mad-apāśrayaḥ
labhate niścalāṁ bhaktiṁ mayy uddhava sanātane

My dear Uddhava, My faithful devotees always hear about and glorify My all-auspicious characteristics. They meditate on Me and enact My pastimes through dramatic performances, thus taking full shelter of Me. They cultivate religiosity, economic development, and sense gratification only in relation to Me, and in this way, attain pure devotional service to Me, the Supreme Personality of Godhead.

COMMENTARY

After explaining the characteristics of *jñāna-yoga*, Śrī Kṛṣṇa now describes the characteristics of *bhakti-yoga*. In this connection, the faithful *jñānīs* have been separated from those who have no connection with Kṛṣṇa consciousness. Because the word "faithful" has been used right from the beginning of this discussion, it is to be understood that only a faithful person can come to the platform of devotional service. When one regularly engages in hearing the glories of the Lord, while offering the results of his activities for His satisfaction, one can attain perfection in devotional service. Until one becomes actually detached from matter, one should continue to perform his prescribed duties, offering the results in the devotional service of the Lord.

Lord Kṛṣṇa's pastimes of stealing butter from the elderly *gopīs*, enjoying life with His cowherd boyfriends and the young *gopīs*, playing His flute and engaging in the *rāsa* dance, and so on, are all-auspicious spiritual activities. There are many authorized songs and prayers glorifying these pastimes of the Lord, and by constantly chanting them one will automatically be fixed in *smaraṇam*, or remembrance of the Supreme Personality of Godhead. The Lord exhibited His opulences upon His birth in Kaṁsa's prison and at the birth ceremony subsequently performed by Nanda Mahārāja in Gokula. The Lord further performed many adventurous activities, such as chastising the serpent Kāliya and many other demons. One should regularly take part in the ceremonies commemorating Kṛṣṇa's pastimes, such as the Janmāṣṭamī celebration glorifying the Lord's birth. On such days one should worship the Deity of Lord Kṛṣṇa and the spiritual master and thus remember the Lord's pastimes. One should give food grains and cloth to the *brāhmaṇas* and Vaiṣṇavas. One should serve the Vaiṣṇavas by giving them *mahāprasada*, flower garlands, sandalwood paste, and cloth. One who desires to accumulate wealth should do so for the service of Lord Viṣṇu and the Vaiṣṇavas.

PURPORT

One who engages in hearing, glorifying, remembering and dramatically recreating the pastimes of the Lord will soon be freed from all material desire. One may take pleasure in spiritual festivals, performances of particular pastimes of Lord Kṛṣṇa, or activities of other devotees of the Lord. In this way, one can continually increase one's faith in the Personality of Godhead. Those who have no desire to hear, glorify, or remember the transcendental activities of the Lord are certainly materially polluted and never achieve the highest perfection. Such persons spoil the opportunity of human life by devoting themselves to fleeting mundane topics that produce no eternal benefit. The real meaning of religion is to constantly serve the Supreme Personality of Godhead, whose form is eternal, full of bliss and knowledge. One who has taken full shelter of the Lord is completely uninterested in impersonal speculations about the nature of God. He uses his time to advance more and more in the unlimited bliss of pure devotional service.

TEXT 25

सत्सङ्गलब्धयाभक्त्यामयिमांस उपासिता ।
सवैमेदर्शितंसद्भिरञ्जसाविन्दतेपदम् ॥२५॥

sat-saṅga-labdhayā bhaktyā mayi māṁ sa upāsitā
sa vai me darśitaṁ sadbhir añjasā vindate padam

One who has attained devotional service through the association of devotees always engages in worshiping Me. As a result of his devotion, he easily attains My association in My eternal abode in the spiritual sky, which was revealed to him by My devotees.

COMMENTARY

One may ask how such surrender or devotion is actually achieved. The Lord gives the answer in this verse. One must live in a society of devotees. By such association, one will be engaged twenty-four hours a day in the various processes of devotional service. The pure devotees of the Lord can reveal the spiritual world by their transcendental sound vibration, making it possible for even a neophyte devotee to experience the Lord's abode. Being thus enlivened, the neophyte makes further progress and gradually becomes qualified to personally serve the Personality of Godhead in the spiritual world.

By constantly associating with devotees and learning from them about devotional science, one quickly achieves a deep attachment for the Lord and the Lord's service, and such attachment gradually matures into pure love of Godhead.

PURPORT

Materialists often challenge that the chanting of the holy names of the Lord is simply a mundane activity. They therefore conclude that any kind of concocted *mantra* is as good as chanting the holy names of the Lord. Just to establish the truth of the matter, the Lord herein describes the genuine method for attaining His transcendental abode in the spiritual sky. One should avoid the association of impersonalists, who preach that the name and form of the Lord are products of *maya*, or illusion. Actually, the impersonalists are envious of the devotees of the Lord and so they take every opportunity to deride them, thus simply creating disturbances. It is only by hearing from the pure devotees of the Lord that one can understand the truth about the Supreme Lord and His eternal abode.

TEXTS 26-27

श्रीउद्धव उवाच
साधुस्तवोत्तमश्लोकमतःकीदृग्विधःप्रभो ।
भक्तिस्त्वय्युपयुज्येतकीदृशीसद्भिरादृता ॥२६॥
एतन्मेपुरुषाध्यक्षलोकाध्यक्षजगत्प्रभो ।
प्रणतायानुरक्तायप्रपन्नायचकथ्यताम् ॥२७॥

śrī-uddhava uvāca
sādhus tavottama-śloka mataḥ kīdṛg-vidhaḥ prabho
bhaktis tvayy upayujyeta kīdṛśī sadbhir ādṛtā

etan me puruṣādhyakṣa lokādhyakṣa jagat-prabho
praṇatāyānuraktāya prapannāya ca kathyatām

Śrī Uddhava said: O Uttama-śloka! O Lord, who is glorified by select prayers, what kind of person do You accept as a genuinely saintly person? What kind of devotional service is approved by You as worthy of being offered to Your Lordship? O Lord of Vaikuṇṭha! O master of the universe, I am fully surrendered unto You and have no shelter other than Your lotus feet. Kindly explain this to me.

COMMENTARY

The word *puruṣādhyakṣa* in this verse indicates that Lord Kṛṣṇa is the master not only of all the demigods, but of the *puruṣa-avatāras*. The word *lokādhyakṣa* indicates that Lord Kṛṣṇa is the master of Vaikuṇṭha. Uddhava also addresses Lord Kṛṣṇa as *jagat-prabhu*, because the Lord mercifully incarnates within the material world for the purpose of delivering the pious conditioned souls. The word *praṇatāya* indicates that Uddhava is a surrendered soul and not an impersonalist who refuses to bow down to the Supreme Personality of Godhead. In this verse, Uddhava says that he is *anuraktāya*, or attached to Lord Kṛṣṇa with love. Although some great devotees like Arjuna sometimes worshiped the demigods, just to acknowledge their exalted positions within the universe, Uddhava never adored anyone but the Supreme Lord.

TEXT 28

त्वंब्रह्मपरमंव्योमपुरुषःप्रकृतेःपरः ।
अवतीर्णोऽसिभगवन् स्वेच्छोपात्तपृथग्वपुः ॥२८॥

tvaṁ brahma paramaṁ vyoma puruṣaḥ prakṛteḥ paraḥ
avatīrno 'si bhagavan svecchopātta-pṛthag-vapuḥ

My dear Lord, although You are transcendental to material nature, and like the sky, You are never entangled in any way, You assume different forms of incarnation in this world, according to the desires of Your devotees.

COMMENTARY

The pure devotees of the Lord are interested in delivering the conditioned souls from their ignorance. As such, they are considered to be direct representatives of the Lord and thus nondifferent from Him. Although the Lord is fully self-satisfied and thus not at all interested in the affairs of this material world, still, by His causeless mercy, He sometimes incarnates just to propagate His devotional service for the benefit of the ignorant conditioned souls.

Thus, it must be concluded that the Lord descends in various forms as incarnations for the pleasure of His devotees. He also appears as the Deity so that His devotees can render service unto Him. The Lord is nondifferent from His devotees because He preaches devotional service through His devotees. This has been expressed by Śrī Nārada: "Having been awarded a transcendental body befitting an associate of the Personality of Godhead, I quit the body made of five material elements." Thus, the devotees are considered to be nondifferent from the Lord. The Lord is self-satisfied, and so is indifferent to this material world, and yet He incarnates to preach devotional service to Himself. By His own sweet will, He assumes various forms, such as Kapila, Dattātreya, and Nārada. Thus it is seen that although the Lord is one, He assumes many transcendental forms.

PURPORT

Uddhava said, "O Lord! You are the Supreme Brahman, the transcendental Personality of Godhead, the Lord of Vaikuṇṭha. You have personally manifested in this world, by Your own sweet will. You have assumed innumerable forms of incarnation and now You have appeared in Your eternal two-armed form of Muralidhara, which is independent of Your features of Brahman, Paramātmā, and four-armed Lord Nārāyaṇa. You have directly descended to this world from Your eternal abode, Goloka Vṛndāvana."

After reading this verse, unscrupulous people may think that Kṛṣṇa appeared in this form before Uddhava as a manifestation of Brahman, or as an expansion of Paramātmā. The devotees eternally serve the Supreme Personality of Godhead in the spiritual world in forms of full consciousness and bliss.

TEXTS 29-32

श्रीभगवानुवाच
कृपालुरकृतद्रोहस्तितिक्षुःसर्वदेहिनाम् ।
सत्यसारोऽनवद्यात्मासमःसर्वोपकारकः ॥२९॥
कामैरहतधीर्दान्तोमृदःशुचिरकिञ्चनः ।
अनीहोमितभुक् शान्तःस्थिरोमच्छरणोमुनिः ॥३०॥
अप्रमत्तोगभीरात्माधृतिमाञ्जितषड्गुणः ।
अमानीमानदःकल्योमैत्रःकारुणिकःकविः ॥३१॥
आज्ञायैवंगुणान्दोषान्मयाादिष्टानपिस्वकान् ।
धर्मान्सन्त्यज्ययःसर्वान्मांभजेतसतुसत्तमः ॥३२॥

śrī-bhagavān uvāca
kṛpālur akṛta-drohas titikṣuḥ sarva-dehinām
satya-sāro 'navadyātmā samaḥ sarvopakārakaḥ

kāmair ahata-dhīr dānto mṛduḥ śucir akiñcanaḥ
anīho mita-bhuk śāntaḥ sthiro mac-charaṇo muniḥ

apramatto gabhīrātmā dhṛtimāñ jita-ṣaḍ-guṇaḥ
amānī māna-daḥ kalyo maitraḥ kāruṇikaḥ kaviḥ

ājñāyaivaṁ guṇān doṣān mayādiṣṭān api svakān
dharmān santyajya yaḥ sarvān māṁ bhajeta sa tu sattamaḥ

The Supreme Personality of Godhead said: O Uddhava, a saintly person is merciful and so is never inclined to give pain to others. Even if others are aggressive, he is tolerant and forgiving towards all. His purpose in life comes from the truth itself, he is free from envy, and his mind is equipoised in happiness and distress. He dedicates his time to work for the welfare of others. His intelligence is never bewildered by material desires, and he has learned to control his senses. His behavior is always pleasing, never harsh and always exemplary, and he is free from possessiveness. He never endeavors like ordinary worldly people, and he strictly controls his eating and so he always remains peaceful and steady. A saintly person is thoughtful and accepts Me as his only shelter. Such a person is very cautious in the execution of his duties and is not disturbed even in a distressing situation. He has conquered over the six material qualities—hunger, thirst, lamentation, illusion, old age, and death. He is free from all desire for prestige, and he offers respect to others. He is expert in reviving the Kṛṣṇa consciousness of others, and so he never cheats anyone. Rather, he is a well-wishing friend to all, being most merciful. Such a saintly person must be considered the most learned of men. He perfectly understands that the ordinary religious duties prescribed by Me in various Vedic scriptures possess favorable qualities that purify the performer, and he knows that neglect of such duties constitutes a discrepancy in one's life. Having taken complete shelter at My lotus feet, however, a saintly person ultimately renounces such ordinary religious duties and worships Me alone. He is thus considered to be the best among all living entities.

COMMENTARY

The Supreme Lord says that there are two types of saintly persons. Those who perform devotional service mixed with *karma* or *jñāna*, and those who engage in unalloyed devotional service. The first class of saintly persons is described in the first three verses. The word *kṛpālu* indicates that one is not able to tolerate others' distress. *Akṛta-droha* indicates that a devotee does not wish misery even for his enemy. *Titikṣu* means that he tolerates others' neglect and forgives the offenses committed against him. *Satya-sāra* indicates that a devotee is always fixed in the truth. *Anavadyātmā* means that a pure devotee is devoid of envy and never unnecessarily criticizes others. *Sama* means that he is equal in both happiness and distress, as well as in honor and dishonor. *Sarvopakāraka* means that a devotee is always engaged in acts meant for the welfare of others. *Kāmair ahata-dhī* indicates that a devotee is not agitated by lusty desires because, *dānta,* his senses are completely under control. *Mṛdu* means that his heart is gentle, and *śuci* means that he is pure and always careful to observe the prescribed etiquette. The word *akiñcana* indicates that a devotee doesn't claim anything as his own because He knows that everything belongs to the Lord. The word *anīha* means detached from all worldly activities. *Mitabhuk* refers to a person who eats pure and simple food, and just enough to maintain a healthy condition of the body. *Śānta* means peaceful in mind. *Sthira* means to remain fixed in one's occupational duties and devotional activities. *Mat-śaraṇa* indicates that the devotee has taken complete shelter at the lotus feet of Śrī Kṛṣṇa. *Muni* refers to a thoughtful man. *Apramatta* means cautious, and not mad. *Gabhirātmā* means he whose nature is unfathomable. *Dhṛtimān* means one is not agitated by the urges of the tongue and genitals. *Amāni* means devoid of the desire for respect. *Mānada* means to give respect to others. *Kalya* means that the devotee is expert in preaching to others. *Maitra* indicates that by his missionary activities, a devotee is friendly to everyone. *Kāruṇika* means that a devotee mercifully tries to bring people to a sane condition of life. *Kavi* indicates that a devotee performs all of his activities expertly. These are the twenty-eight qualities of a pure devotee.

A pure devotee who possesses the above-mentioned qualities is understood to have attained the perfection of life. He no longer has any desire for liberation by merging into the existence of the Lord. In the beginning, one cultivates devotional service mixed with *karma,* and then one progresses to the practice of devotional service mixed with *jñāna.* The stage of perfection, however, is characterized as being devoid of *karma* and *jñāna.* This is the meaning of pure devotional service. One who is thus situated on the transcendental platform is called *ātmārāma,* or *śānta-bhakta,*

In the *Bhakti-rasāmṛta-sindhu* (3.1.34) it is said: "In this Dvārakā-dhāma, I am being attracted by the Supreme Personality of Godhead, Kṛṣṇa, who is personified spiritual bliss. Simply by seeing Him, I am feeling great happiness. Oh, I have wasted so much time trying to become self-realized through impersonal cultivation. This is a cause for lamentation!"

Śrīla Sukadeva Gosvāmī has said, "Being attracted by the qualities of Śrī Hari, I had heard *Śrīmad Bhāgavatam* from my father."

The cultivation of knowledge is neglected by those engaged in the process of devotional service. In the *Bhakti-rasāmṛta-sindhu* (1.1.11) it is further stated: "[5]One should render transcendental loving service to the Supreme Lord Kṛṣṇa favorably and without desire for material profit or gain through fruitive activities or philosophical speculation. That is called pure devotional service."

---

5 *anyābhilāṣitā-śūnyaṁ jñāna-karmādy-anāvṛtam*
ānukūlyena kṛṣṇānu- śīlanam bhaktir uttamā

As indicated in verse thirty-two, a pure devotee of the Lord is fully aware of the pious advantages of executing duties within the *varṇāśrama* system, and he is similarly aware of the harmful mistake of neglecting such duties. Still, having full faith in the Supreme Personality of Godhead, a devotee gives up all ordinary social and religious activities and engages fully in devotional service. He knows that Lord Kṛṣṇa is the ultimate source of everything and that all perfection comes from Lord Kṛṣṇa alone. Because of his extraordinary faith, the devotee is called *sattama*, or the best among all living beings.

In the *Śrīmad Bhāgavatam* (5.18.12) it is said:

yasyāsti bhaktir bhagavaty akiñcanā sarvair guṇais tatra samāsate surāḥ
harāv abhaktasya kuto mahad-guṇā mano-rathenāsati dhāvato bahiḥ

One who has unflinching devotion for the Personality of Godhead has all the good qualities of the demigods. But one who is not a devotee of the Lord has only material qualifications that are of little value. This is because he is hovering on the mental plane and is certain to be attracted by the glaring material energy.

PURPORT

In the first three verses, the twenty-eight qualities of a pure devotee are described. Among them, the seventeenth quality, *kṛṣṇaika śaraṇa* is the most important, and the other twenty-seven are secondary.

1. *Kṛpālu.* A devotee cannot tolerate seeing the world merged in ignorance and suffering the whiplashes of *maya.* Therefore he busily engages in distributing Kṛṣṇa consciousness and is called *kṛpālu*, or merciful.

2. *Akṛta-droha.* Even if someone tries to harm a devotee, he does not try to retaliate. Indeed, he never tries to harm any living entity. The Māyāvādīs, on the other hand, are most envious and thus try to kill God, as well as the individuality of the living entities. Thus, the impersonalists are their own worst enemies, and they are certainly the enemies of their unfortunate followers. Fruitive workers are also envious of their self because they purposely absorb themselves in material affairs so that they do not have the chance to understand their eternal existence. In this world of survival of the fittest, everyone is engaged in exploiting others. It is only the devotees of the Lord who uses his body, mind, and words, not only for his own benefit, but for the welfare of others.

3. *Titikṣu.* A devotee tolerates the offenses of others. He is detached from the material body, which is composed of skin, bones, blood, pus, urine, and so on, and so he

forgives the obnoxious behavior of those who cannot appreciate the value of a devotee of the Lord.

4. *Satyaniṣṭha.* A devotee always remains fixed in the truth. He knows very well that he is the eternal servant of the Lord and thus does not waste his time by engaging in useless, material activities.

5. *Asūyā.* A devotee is never envious. He knows that this world is a kind of phantasmagoria, so he never envies someone in any material condition. Therefore, he never unnecessarily criticizes others or causes any kind of disturbance.

6. *Samadarśī.* A devotee has equal vision. His goal is to attain the eternal Supreme Personality of Godhead, so he is not elated or disturbed by the temporary happiness or miserable conditions of this world. For him, all temporary material conditions are the same.

7. *Sarvopokāraka.* The devotee is a benefactor of all living entities. Neglecting one's own interest and working for the satisfaction of others is called *paropakāra*, whereas causing trouble to others for one's personal gratification is called *parāpakāra*. A devotee always works for the satisfaction of Lord Kṛṣṇa, who is the maintainer of all living entities, and so his activities are ultimately pleasing to everyone. Devotional service to Lord Kṛṣṇa is the perfectional stage of welfare work because Lord Kṛṣṇa is the supreme controller of everyone's happiness and distress. Foolish persons, under the influence of false egotism, considering themselves to be the benefactors of others, perform materialistic welfare work rather than attending to the eternal happiness of others. Because a devotee remains pure and engages in missionary activities, he is everyone's best friend.

8. *Vāsanā-varjita-vicāraparāyaṇa.* A devotee has no material desires. Those who have given up the service of Kṛṣṇa maintain a desire to become the master of all they survey. Thus, the conditioned soul is busily engaged in trying to lord it over material nature, although the Lord Himself is the actual enjoyer. Ordinary persons see all material things as objects for their personal gratification and thus try to acquire or control them. Ultimately a man wants to possess a woman and enjoy sex gratification with her. The Supreme Lord supplies the desired fuel that causes the fire of lust to burn painfully in one's heart, but the Lord does not give self-realization to such a misguided person. A liberated devotee, who is fully surrendered to Lord Kṛṣṇa, enjoys a blissful life of devotional service and never becomes tempted by the seductions of the external world. The devotee does not follow the example of the foolish deer, who is attracted by the hunter's sweet music and then killed. He does not become attached to sumptuous eating, nor does he spend the whole day making arrangements for bodily comfort. A fully surrendered soul, who is devoted to the service of the Supreme Personality of Godhead, who is the only enjoyer, never sacrifices his auspicious position of steady intelligence, even in the face of so-called material opportunity.

9. *Dānta.* A devotee is naturally repelled by sinful activities and controls his senses by dedicating all his acts to Kṛṣṇa.

10. *Mrdu.* A devotee is gentle. Conditioned souls invariably consider others as friends or enemies, and they justify cruel behavior meted out to their opponents. A devotee never considers others as his enemies and so never indulges in the tendency to take pleasure in the suffering of others.

11. *Śuci.* A devotee is pure, both internally and externally because impurity and abomination cannot touch him. Simply by remembering such a pure devotee, one is freed from the tendency to sin. Because of his perfect behavior, a devotee is called *śuci*, or pure.

12. *Akiñcana.* A devotee is free from possessiveness. He is not eager to enjoy or renounce anything because he considers everything to be Lord Kṛṣṇa's property. One who is *akiñcana* has no desire for religiosity, economic development, sense gratification, or liberation because he has no hankering for material enjoyment or renunciation.

13. *Anīha.* A devotee is indifferent to material acquisitions because he sees everything in relation to the Lord.

14. *Mitabhuk.* A devotee eats only as much as is required to maintain his health. Indeed, he accepts all types of material enjoyment only as much as is required. He is not feverishly attached to sense gratification, like the materialists. When necessary, a devotee can give up anything for Lord Kṛṣṇa's service, but he does not accept or reject anything for his personal prestige.

15. *Śānta.* A devotee is peaceful because he abstains from material enjoyment, which is full of disturbances. He is indifferent to material enjoyment because he is constantly engaged in the Lord's service. Peaceful does not mean inactive. Because a devotee is active in service to the Lord, material enjoyers may wrongly consider him to be restless, just like themselves.

16. *Sthira.* A devotee is fixed in his determination and is not restless. He is not situated on the platform of fearfulness because of material absorption.

17. *Śaraṇāgata.* A devotee is fully surrendered to the Lord. A devotee does not take pleasure in anything except serving Lord Kṛṣṇa, and so he is always attentive while executing his duties in devotional service.

18. *Muni.* A devotee is thoughtful and intelligent, and so he is not distracted from his path of spiritual advancement.

19. *Apramatta.* A devotee is without inebriation. Conditioned souls are more or less crazy but the devotee is sane, due to his being situated in his natural, or constitutional position.

20. *Gambhīrātmā.* A devotee is grave. Being absorbed in the Absolute Truth his mentality cannot be understood by gross materialists.

21. *Dhṛtimān.* A devotee is firm and steady in his determination because he has fully controlled his tongue and genitals. In other words, he fully possesses the power of discrimination and does not irrationally change his position.

22. *Jita-ṣaḍ-guṇa.* A devotee has conquered the six material qualities-hunger, thirst, illusion, death, fear, and lamentation.

23. *Amānī.* A devotee is not proud. Even if he is famous, he does not take it very seriously.

24. *Mānada.* A devotee is not one to brag about himself, under the influence of passion and ignorance. Rather, he offers all respects to others, since everyone is part and parcel of Lord Kṛṣṇa.

25. *Kalya*, or *dakṣa.* A devotee is expert in making people understand the truth of Kṛṣṇa consciousness.

26. *Maitra.* A devotee is a kind friend to everyone because he preaches Kṛṣṇa consciousness and never encourages anyone on the bodily platform.

27. *Kāruṇika.* A devotee is most merciful because he tries to bring everyone to the platform of sanity, or Kṛṣṇa consciousness.

28. *Kavi.* A devotee is poetic and very learned. He is expert in studying the transcendental qualities of Lord Kṛṣṇa and is able to show the harmony and compatibility of the Lord's apparently contradictory qualities. This is possible through expert knowledge of the absolute nature of the Lord.

One who fully engages in the unalloyed devotional service of the Lord is expected to develop all of these transcendental qualities. In the beginning, the devotee should cultivate the limbs of devotional service while continuing to perform the duties of his occupation according to the rules prescribed in the scriptures. As the devotee becomes fixed in devotional service and freed from material desires, he can give up these regulations so that he can intensify his engagement on the spiritual platform. Thus he will gradually become a genuinely saintly person. Kṛṣṇa consciousness has nothing to do with material enjoyment and renunciation. The conceptions that, "I am the enjoyer," and "I have renounced something," only apply to those who are in the bodily conception of life. The devotee thinks, "Nothing is mine because everything is owned and controlled by the Lord."

TEXT 33

ज्ञात्वाज्ञात्वाथयेवैमांयावान्यश्चास्मिचादृशः ।
भजन्त्यनन्यभावेनतेमेभक्ततमामताः ॥३३॥

jñātvājñātvātha ye vai māṁ yāvān yaś cāsmi yādṛśaḥ
bhajanty ananya-bhāvena te me bhaktatamā matāḥ

My devotees may or may not understand Me in truth, how I am situated beyond the cosmic manifestation, but if they possess unalloyed devotion for Me, I consider them to be great personalities.

COMMENTARY

In this verse, the word *yāvān* is used to indicate that Lord Kṛṣṇa is unlimited, beyond the jurisdiction of material existence. Still, He is captivated by the love of His pure devotees. It is said that Lord Kṛṣṇa never leaves Vṛndāvana, because of the love of the cowherd men and women. The word *yaḥ* is used to indicate that the Absolute Truth appears as the son of Vasudeva. *Yādṛśa* indicates that the Lord is completely self-satisfied, and *āpta-kāma* means, "one who has nothing to gain from anyone else." Still, being captivated by the love of His devotees, the Lord sometimes appears to be dependent on them, needing them to fulfill His desires. Actually, the Supreme Personality of Godhead is always independent, but He reciprocates the love of His devotees and thus seems to be dependent upon them. For example, Lord Kṛṣṇa appeared to be completely dependent upon Nanda Mahārāja and mother Yaśodā as a child in Vṛndāvana. The word *ajñātvā* means "ignorant" and it indicates that sometimes a devotee may seem to be philosophically naive and bereft of a proper understanding of the Lord.

PURPORT

Although a materialist or impersonalist may appear to be very highly qualified, without Kṛṣṇa consciousness, such a person will never attain the success of life. One must understand the personal feature of the Absolute Truth and surrender unto Him. Even if one is not very intelligent, if he simply accepts that he is the eternal servant of the Lord, he will certainly attain perfection. The residents of Vṛndāvana had no idea or didn't understand that Kṛṣṇa is the Supreme Personality of Godhead. They simply loved Kṛṣṇa as their most beloved, and it is for this reason that they are considered perfect.

TEXTS 34-41

मल्लिङ्गमद्भक्तजनदर्शनस्पर्शनार्चनम् ।
परिचर्यास्तुतिःप्रह्वगुणकर्मानुकीर्तनम् ॥३४॥
मत्कथाश्रवणेश्रद्धामदनुध्यानमुद्धव ।
सर्वलाभोपहरणंदास्येनात्मनिवेदनम् ॥३५॥

मज्जन्मकर्मकथनंममपर्वानुमोदनम् ।
गीतताण्डववादित्रगोष्ठीभिर्मद्गृहोत्सवः ॥३६॥
यात्राबलिविधानंचसर्ववार्षिकपर्वसु ।
वैदिकीतान्त्रिकीदीक्षामदीयव्रतधारणम् ॥३७॥
ममार्चास्थापनेश्रद्धास्वतःसंहत्यचोद्यमः ।
उद्यानोपवनाक्रीडपुरमन्दिरकर्मणि ॥३८॥
सम्मार्जनोपलेपाभ्यांसेकमण्डलवर्तनैः ।
गृहशुश्रूषणंमह्यंदासवद्यदमायया ॥३९॥
अमानित्वमदम्भित्वंकृतस्यापरिकीर्तनम् ।
अपिदीपावलोकंमेनोपयुञ्ज्यान् निवेदितम् ॥४०॥
यद्यदिष्टतमंलोकेयच्चातिप्रियमात्मनः ।
तत्तन् निवेदयेन्मह्यंतदानन्त्यायकल्पते ॥४१॥

mal-liṅga-mad-bhakta-jana-darśana-sparśanārcanam
paricaryā stutiḥ prahva-guṇa-karmānukīrtanam

mat-kathā-śravaṇe śraddhā mad-anudhyānam uddhava
sarva-lābhopaharaṇaṁ dāsyenātma-nivedanam

maj-janma-karma-kathanaṁ mama parvānumodanam
gītā-tāṇḍava-vāditra- goṣṭhībhir mad-gṛhotsavaḥ

yātrā bali-vidhānaṁ ca sarva-vārṣika-parvasu
vaidikī tāntrikī dīkṣā madīya-vrata-dhāraṇam

mamārcā-sthāpane śraddhā svataḥ saṁhatya codyamaḥ
udyānopavanākrīḍa- pura-mandira-karmaṇi

sammārjanopalepābhyāṁ seka-maṇḍala-vartanaiḥ
gṛha-śuśrūṣaṇaṁ mahyaṁ dāsa-vad yad amāyayā

amānitvam adambhitvaṁ kṛtasyāparikīrtanam
api dīpāvalokaṁ me nopayuñjyān niveditam

yad yad iṣṭatamaṁ loke yac cāti-priyam ātmanaḥ
tat tan nivedayen mahyaṁ tad ānantyāya kalpate

My dear Uddhava, one will be able to give up false pride by cultivating these limbs of devotional service. One should purify himself by seeing, touching, worshiping, serving, and offering prayers of glorification and obeisances to My form as the Deity, as well as to My pure devotees. One should hear My glories in the association of devotees and meditate upon Me. One should offer whatever he happens to possess to Me, considering himself to be My eternal servant. In this way, one should surrender unto Me. One should make arrangements for the celebration of festivals in relation to Me. These festivals should be celebrated in the temple with singing and dancing in ecstasy. One should, in the association of devotees, visit the holy places of pilgrimage that are related to Me and observe the vows meant for devotees, such as Ekādaśī. One should receive initiation from a bona fide spiritual master and if able to do so, give donations for the construction of My temples. Most importantly, one should always consider himself to be My humble servant, and thus engage for My satisfaction without duplicity. As a menial servant, one should sweep the floor of the temple and then cleanse it with water and cow dung. When the floor is dry, one should sprinkle scented water over it and then draw auspicious mandalas. **A devotee should not become proud, advertising himself as an exalted soul. If one offers to Me that which is most dear to him, that will please Me greatly and thus advance him on the path toward eternal life.**

COMMENTARY

The Supreme Lord said, "O Uddhava, you had asked Me to describe what kind of devotional service is pleasing to Me. Here is the answer—you should offer respect and worship to My deity form and to My devotees. You should offer all your possessions for My service, thinking that 'everything I have has been given to me by the Lord for use in His service.' With this attitude, one should offer to the Deity whatever he has at his disposal. One should surrender one's body and very self at the lotus feet of the Lord. One should glorify the Lord's transcendental birth and activities, and sing His glories in the association of devotees. One should observe My festivals, such as Janmāṣṭamī, with singing, dancing, and the playing of musical instruments. One should arrange for very opulent worship of the Lord by offering new clothes, ornaments, sweets, flower garlands, sandalwood paste, and so on, during festivals such as Holi.

One should observe religious vows like Ekādaśī, worship the Deity, and one should arrange flower gardens, individually or collectively, for My service. One should arrange a place for enacting the pastimes of the Lord. One should sweep the temple of the Lord and then smear it with cow dung mixed with water. Thereafter, when the temple room is dry, one should sprinkle scented water and then decorate the floor with auspicious drawings. In this way, one should engage in My temple as a menial servant. Just as a servant of the king works for his satisfaction, one should engage in My service, giving up all sense of miserliness. One should give up the desire for personal aggrandizement. One should not use a ghee lamp that has been offered to Me for his own use, such as to illuminate his own room. One should only partake of that food which was first offered to Me. As dictated by etiquette, one should distribute the remnants of My food to the Vaiṣṇavas, and then honor the *prasāda* oneself. It is stated in the *śāstra* that the merit one obtains by fasting for six months can be attained in Kali-yuga simply by partaking of one morsel of Lord Viṣṇu's remnants. One should meditate upon My form within his heart, chant My holy names, accept the remnants of My food, drink the water that has washed My feet, and touch the remnants of My flowers to one's head. One who follows all these principles is to be considered as on the same platform as the infallible Lord Viṣṇu. One should offer to Me the thing that is most dear to him in this world. However, although wine is very dear to Lord Baladeva, it should never be offered to the Deity because there is no mention of such a practice in the *śāstra*. Among all these practices, the most effective is the offering of one's most dear thing for the service of the Lord.

PURPORT

Pure devotees never consider the things of this world to be meant for their personal enjoyment, without connection to Kṛṣṇa consciousness. Pure devotees consider themselves the eternal servants of the Lord, and never make false claims of being themselves the Lord. Knowing the pure devotee to be the Lord's representative, sent into this world by His mercy, fortunate people touch his feet, have his *darśana*, worship him, serve him, glorify him, offer obeisances to him, and appreciate his transcendental qualities.

One should not consider the Deity, the Lord in the heart, and the pure devotees of the Lord to be separate from one another. One should know that the Absolute Truth is one, while manifesting in infinite varieties. One should faithfully hear about the Supreme Personality of Godhead from the spiritual master, while fully surrendering unto the Lord, offering all of one's possessions to Him in His service. Indeed, one should consider his very self as being meant for the pleasure of the Lord and for no other purpose.

The word *varṣa* refers to a period of time, as well as a tract of land. *Yātrā* refers to the performance of religious celebrations current at various places and at various times. The performance of worship is called *balividhāna*. There are two kinds of initiation, Vedic initiation and initiation conducted in pursuance of the Vedic literature. The word *dīkṣā* indicates that one should be very eager to cultivate Kṛṣṇa consciousness. The word *harivāsara* refers to the appearance day of the Lord, which should be nicely celebrated by all Vaiṣṇavas. The firm determination to engage in the Lord's service is indicated by the word *vratadhāraṇam*.

Impersonalists do not accept the supremacy of the Supreme Personality of Godhead. One should give up the association of such persons and work, either individually or collectively, to make flower gardens and fruit orchards for the service of the Deity, *āśramas* for the residence of devotees, and temples so that people in general can take part in the worship of the Lord. Giving up all false pride, one should sweep the floor of the Lord's temple, smear it with cow dung, sprinkle it with scented water, and then draw auspicious symbols, engaging just like a menial servant. One should never make such endeavors simply to enhance his prestige. One should never consider himself to be a great devotee, and one should never brag about his devotional activities. One should not employ a lamp that was offered to the Lord for serving his own purpose, such as illuminating his residence. One should never offer to the Lord something that was given to someone else, or used by him.

Being impelled by material desires, one should not utilize what is dear to him for his personal sense gratification. Rather, he should offer his favorite things for the service of the Supreme Lord. By doing so, one will attain eternal benefit. One should not become bewildered by thoughts of material enjoyment and thus forget the service of the Supreme Lord. All of one's wealth and family members should be engaged for the Lord's satisfaction, and this will save one from increasing his material bondage.

TEXT 42

सूर्योऽग्निर्ब्राह्मणागावोवैष्णवःखंमरुज्जलम् ।
भूरात्मासर्वभूतानिभद्रपूजापदानिमे ॥४२॥

sūryo 'gnir brāhmaṇā gāvo vaiṣṇavaḥ khaṁ maruj jalam
bhūr ātmā sarva-bhūtāni bhadra pūjā-padāni me

O gentle one, you may worship Me in the sun, fire, brāhmaṇas, cows, Vaiṣṇavas, sky, wind, water, earth, individual soul, and all living entities.

COMMENTARY

Uddhava had asked, "Where should I worship You? The Lord herein replies, "There are eleven places where you can worship Me, such as the sun, fire and so on."

TEXTS 43-45

सूर्येतुविद्ययात्रय्याहविषाग्नौयजेतमाम् ।
आतिथ्येनतुविप्राग्र्येगोष्वङ्गयवसादिना ॥४३॥
वैष्णवेबन्धुसत्कृत्याहृदिखेध्याननिष्ठया ।
वायौमुख्यधियातोयेद्रव्यैस्तोयपुरःसरैः ॥४४॥
स्थण्डिलेमन्त्रहृदयैर्भोगैरात्मानमात्मनि ।
क्षेत्रज्ञंसर्वभूतेषुसमत्वेनयजेतमाम् ॥४५॥

sūrye tu vidyayā trayyā haviṣāgnau yajeta mām
ātithyena tu viprāgrye goṣv aṅga yavasādinā

vaiṣṇave bandhu-sat-kṛtyā hṛdi khe dhyāna-niṣṭhayā
vāyau mukhya-dhiyā toye dravyais toya-puraḥsaraiḥ

sthaṇḍile mantra-hṛdayair bhogair ātmānam ātmani
kṣetra-jñaṁ sarva-bhūteṣu samatvena yajeta mām

My dear Uddhava, one should worship Me within the sun by chanting the *Puruṣa-sūkta mantras,* by perfoming worship, and offering obeisances. One should worship Me within fire with oblations of ghee, and one should worship the *brāhmaṇas* as representing Me by respectfully honoring them as guests. One should worship Me within the cows by offerings them grass and grains. One should worship the Vaiṣṇavas as being nondifferent from Me by showing them love and respect. I should be worshiped within the heart by meditation, and I should be worshiped within the air by the practice of *prāṇāyama.* I should be worshiped within water by offerings of water and other paraphernalia, and I should be worshiped within the earth by the chanting of *mantras.* One should worship Me within all living entities by seeing the Supersoul present within everyone, thus seeing with equal vision.

COMMENTARY

How should I adore My worshipable Lord in all these manifestations? The answer is given in these three verses.

PURPORT

It is not possible to understand the transcendental Lord simply by accumulating knowledge with the help of materially conditioned senses. Considering this, one should not think of the sun, fire, the *brāhmaṇas*, cows, Vaiṣṇavas, the sky, air, water, the earth, and the individual spirit souls as devoid of any relation with the Absolute Truth, and thus to be avoided. Rather, one should accept all these entities as being favorable for the execution of one's devotional service. As soon as one sees anything as separate from the Lord's service, one will certainly neglect it. These entities should be accepted as worshipable because of their relationship with the Lord.

The things mentioned in these verses are to be worshiped in various manners. By the hymns of *Ṛk*, *Sāma*, and *Yajur Vedas*, one should worship the sun. By offering ghee into the sacred fire, Agni is worshiped. By receiving them as honored guests, the *brāhmaṇas* are worshiped. By feeding them nice grass, the cows are worshiped. By following his orders and thinking of him as an instructor and an eternal friend, a Vaiṣṇava is worshiped. By constant meditation, the Lord within the heart is worshiped. The air is worshiped by considering the life-air to be the most important element. Water is worshiped by offerings of water and flowers. The earth is worshiped by performing the *nyāsa mantras*. The Supersoul is worshiped by offering Him one's dearest possessions, and all living entities are worshiped by treating them with equal vision.

TEXT 46

धिष्ण्येष्वित्येषुमद्रूपंशङ्खचक्रगदाम्बुजैः ।
युक्तंचतुर्भुजंशान्तंध्यायन्नर्चेत्समाहितः ॥४६॥

dhiṣṇyeṣv ity eṣu mad-rūpaṁ śaṅkha-cakra-gadāmbujaiḥ
yuktaṁ catur-bhujaṁ śāntaṁ dhyāyann arcet samāhitaḥ

In this way, you should worship My transcendental four-armed form, holding a conch, disc, club, and lotus, with fixed attention.

COMMENTARY

With a controlled mind, one should worship the Supreme Lord as being present in these entities. This worship is actually the worship of Lord Nārāyaṇa, although it appears to be the worship of many separate entities. The worshipers of Śrī Rāmacandra should also meditate on their worshipable Lord and offer worship as prescribed herein.

PURPORT

By worshiping all these as if they were independent entities, one will be considered a pantheist, or one who worships many gods. One should meditate on the form of Lord Nārāyaṇa, who holds a conch, disc, club, and lotus in His hands, as being situated within all these entities. In this way, the worship of all these entities will be in relation to Lord Hari.

TEXT 47

इष्टापूर्तेनमामेवंयोयजेतसमाहितः ।
लभतेमयिसद्भक्तिंमत्स्मृतिःसाधुसेवया ॥४७॥

iṣṭā-pūrtena mām evaṁ yo yajeta samāhitaḥ
labhate mayi sad-bhaktiṁ mat-smṛtiḥ sādhu-sevayā

One who worships Me in full concentration by performing sacrifices and activities meant for the welfare of others, attains unflinching devotional service unto Me. By rendering service to saintly persons, he achieves realized knowledge of Me.

COMMENTARY

An advanced devotee performs his service meticulously because it is his very life and soul. His austerities are never artificial because he keeps his body healthy so that he can properly execute his service to his spiritual master and the Supreme Lord.

PURPORT

The congregational chanting of the holy names of the Lord and the worship of the spiritual master are the best means for rising to the platform of pure devotional service. It is far better to chant the holy name of the Lord in the association of sincere devotees than to simply practice some form of dry renunciation or fruitive sacrifices. This is the process recommended for this age, and those who are actually intelligent will perform *kṛṣṇa-saṅkīrtana* with great enthusiasm.

TEXT 48

प्रायेणभक्तियोगेनसत्सङ्गेनविनोद्धव ।
नोपायोविद्यतेसम्यक् प्रायणंहिसतामहम् ॥४८॥

prāyeṇa bhakti-yogena sat-saṅgena vinoddhava
nopāyo vidyate samyak prāyaṇaṁ hi satām aham

O Uddhava, I am the supreme shelter and goal of life of the devotees. If one does not engage in My devotional service, which is received by the association of My pure devotees, there will be no means for his escaping material existence.

COMMENTARY

The paths of *jñāna* and *bhakti* have both been described but here it is said that deliverance from material existence is possible only by devotional service, which is to be performed in the association of devotees. Pure devotional service to the Lord is called *kevala-bhakti*, whereas devotional service mixed with speculative propensities is called *guṇa-bhūta-bhakti*, or devotional service polluted by the material modes of nature. Actually, as stated in the *Śrīmad Bhāgavatam*, pure devotional service automatically awards one knowledge and detachment. On the other hand, without devotional service, the cultivation of knowledge cannot award one perfection. Processes for spiritual perfection other than devotional service are described as being like the nipples on a goat's neck. One can never hope to get milk from such useless nipples and one cannot achieve perfection by any process other than devotional service.

In the *Śrīmad-Bhāgavatam* (11.19.9) Śrī Uddhava said:

tāpa-trayeṇābhihitasya ghore santapyamānasya bhavādhvanīśa
paśyāmi nānyac charaṇaṁ tavāṅghri-dvandvātapatrād amṛtābhivarṣāt

My dear Lord, for one who is being cruelly burned in the blazing fire of material miseries, having fallen into the network of material existence, I do not see any other possible shelter besides Your two lotus feet, which are a shower of nectar extinguishing the fire of suffering.

In the *Śrīmad-Bhāgavatam* (12.4.40) Śrī Śukadeva Gosvāmī has said:

saṁsāra-sindhum ati-dustaram uttitīrṣor
nānyaḥ plavo bhagavataḥ puruṣottamasya

līlā-kathā-rasa-niṣevaṇam antareṇa
puṁso bhaved vividha-duḥkha-davārditasya

For a person who is suffering in the fire of countless miseries and who desires to cross the insurmountable ocean of material existence, there is no suitable boat except that of cultivating devotion to the transcendental taste for the narrations of the Supreme Personality of Godhead's pastimes.

In the *Śrīmad-Bhāgavatam* (4.31.12) Nārada Muni has said:

kiṁ vā yogena sāṅkhyena nyāsa-svadhyāyayor api
kiṁ vā śreyobhir anyaiś ca na yatrātma-prado hariḥ

Transcendental practices that do not ultimately help one realize the Supreme Personality of Godhead are useless, be they mystic yoga practices, the analytical study of matter, severe austerity, the acceptance of *sannyāsa*, or the study of Vedic literature. All these may be very important aspects of spiritual advancement, but unless one understands the Supreme Personality of Godhead, Hari, all these processes are useless.

PURPORT

The Supreme Personality of Godhead alone is the ultimate goal and shelter of saintly persons. Religiosity, economic development, sense gratification, and liberation are not the ultimate goals of life. Although these are desired by the conditioned souls, they are full of inauspiciousness. By constantly engaging in the service of the Supreme Lord in the association of devotees, one certainly achieves the ultimate goal of life.

TEXT 49

अथैतत्परमंगुह्यंशृण्वतोयदुनन्दन ।
सुगोप्यमपिवक्ष्यामित्वंमेभृत्यःसुहृत्सखा ॥४९॥

athaitat paramaṁ guhyaṁ śṛṇvato yadu-nandana
su-gopyam api vakṣyāmi tvaṁ me bhṛtyaḥ suhṛt sakhā

O Uddhava, O beloved descendant of the Yadu dynasty, because you are My servant, well-wisher, and friend, I shall now reveal to you the most confidential knowledge. Please hear these confidential topics from Me.

COMMENTARY

The sages headed by Śaunaka have said in the first chapter of the *Śrīmad-Bhāgavatam* (1.1.8) *brūyuḥ snigdhasya śiṣyasya guravo guhyam apy uta*, that a bona-fide spiritual master will impart transcendental knowledge unto the heart of a sincere disciple. Uddhava had surrendered to Lord Kṛṣṇa, and in reciprocation, the Lord imparted to him transcendental understanding. It is a fact that only unto one who has absolute faith in the Supreme Lord and the spiritual master is the mystery of spiritual understanding revealed. Other processes of elevation are incapable of delivering the desired results because it is only by devotional service that the Lord becomes actually pleased. Simply by accepting the association of pure devotees and working under the direction of the spiritual master, one attains all perfection of life. This is the essential understanding gained by study of this chapter.

Thus ends the translation of the Fifth Chapter of the Uddhava-gītā entitled "The Symptoms of Conditioned and Liberated Living Entities" *with the commentaries of Śrīla Viśvanātha Cakravartī Ṭhākura and chapter summary and purports by Śrīla Bhaktisiddhānta Sarasvatī Ṭhākura.*

Chapter 6

Beyond Renunciation and Knowledge

CHAPTER SUMMARY

In this chapter, the glories of *sādhu saṅga* and the superexcellence of the Vrajavāsís' ecstatic love for Kṛṣṇa are described.

The association of saintly devotees can destroy one's attachment to material life and can even bring the Supreme Lord, Śrī Kṛṣṇa, under one's control. Neither mystic *yoga*, Sāṅkhya philosophy, following religious principles, studying the *Vedas*, performing austerities, cultivating dry renunciation, performing welfare activities, giving charity, observing vows such as fasting, worshiping the demigods, chanting secret *mantras*, nor visiting holy places of pilgrimage can give one the same result. In every age there are demons, animals, birds, and other lower classes of beings who are in the modes of passion and ignorance, as well as human beings such as *vaiśyas*, *śudras*, women, and outcastes who cannot study the *Vedas*. Nevertheless, by the association of saintly devotees, they can attain the supreme abode of the Lord. On the other hand, without such association, even those who very seriously endeavor for perfection in mystic yoga, the cultivation of knowledge, giving charity, observing vows, and practicing renunciation are generally incapable of attaining the Supreme Personality of Godhead.

The young damsels of Vraja, ignorant of the true identity of Śrī Kṛṣṇa, considered Him to be their paramour. Simply by the influence of Lord Kṛṣṇa's association, they attained the supreme Absolute Truth, which is rarely attained by even demigods like Lord Brahmā. These *gopīs* of Vraja were so deeply attached to Kṛṣṇa that they considered an entire night in His association to be just a moment. When Akrura took Kṛṣṇa and Baladeva to Mathurā, the *gopīs* considered a night in separation from Kṛṣṇa to be as long as a *kalpa*. The *gopīs*, who were afflicted by separation from Kṛṣṇa, could not imagine anything pleasant other than Kṛṣṇa's association. Therefore the *gopīs'* love for Kṛṣṇa is certainly incomparable.

After imparting these instructions to Uddhava, Lord Śrī Kṛṣṇa concluded by saying that he should give up the considerations of religion and irreligion as described in the *śrutis* and *smṛtis*, and instead take shelter of the example of the women of Vṛndāvana.

TEXTS 1-2

श्रीभगवानुवाच
नरोधयतिमांयोगोनसांख्यंधर्म एवच ।
नस्वाध्यायस्तपस्त्यागोनेष्टापूर्तंनदक्षिणा ॥१॥
व्रतानियज्ञश्छन्दांसितीर्थानिनियमायमाः ।
यथावरुन्धेसत्सङ्गःसर्वसङ्गापहोहिमाम् ॥२॥

śrī-bhagavān uvāca
na rodhayati māṁ yogo na sāṅkhyaṁ dharma eva ca
na svādhyāyas tapas tyāgo neṣṭā-pūrtaṁ na dakṣiṇā

vratāni yajñaś chandāṁsi tīrthāni niyamā yamāḥ
yathāvarundhe sat-saṅgaḥ sarva-saṅgāpaho hi mām

The Supreme Lord said: My dear Uddhava, the association of My pure devotees can destroy all one's material attachment. Such purifying association brings Me under the control of My devotees. One may perform yoga, engage in an analytical study of the material nature, practice nonviolence, follow religious principles, study the Vedas, perform austerities, cultivate renunciation, perform fire sacrifices, undertake welfare activities, give charity, carry out severe vows, worship the demigods, chant secret mantras, and control the mind, but even by performing such activities, one does not bring Me under his control.

COMMENTARY

This chapter describes the glories of the association of devotees and the Vrajavāsīs' incomparable love for Kṛṣṇa.

The Supreme Lord said, "O Uddhava, the *astāṅga-yoga* system of practicing sitting postures and controlling the mind, the *sāṅkhya-yoga* system of discriminating between matter and spirit, the practice of nonviolence, the study of the *Vedas*, the performance of severe austerities, the practice of renunciation, the performance of welfare activities like digging wells, the pious act of giving charity, the observance of vows such as *cāturmāsya*, the performance of sacrifices, the worship of the demigods, and the chanting of Vedic *mantras* cannot control Me."

The word *rodhayati* in this verse is singular, indicating that it should be applied separately to each of the processes described. It could also be the plural *rodhayanti* because of the other plural word in this verse, *vratāni*. The verb *ruddha* means "to control." The Lord therefore says, "Activities like yoga cannot control Me. I am not controlled by *astāṅga yogīs*. They cannot attain My shelter." This is purport of this verse.

The Supreme Lord said, "O Uddhava, the study of *sāṅkhya* and the following of religious principles also cannot control Me. Study of the *Vedas*, performance of austerities, and a life of renunciation do not enable one to attain My shelter. The powerful process of devotional service is the only method of controlling Me and pleasing Me. It is an established fact that I am attained only by devotional service and by no other means. One who simply associates with My pure devotees pleases Me, and so what can be said of one who renders devotional service to Me in the association of devotees? One advances on the path of devotional service in the association of devotees. Although activities like practicing yoga contain some degree of devotion, I am not controlled by the mixed devotion of such practitioners. Thus, the word *yathā* has been used in this verse, indicating that only when activities are performed in pure devotion are they fully pleasing to the Lord. Because the association of devotees destroys all of one's material attachment, it enables one to bring Me under control."

PURPORT

The relationships we establish in this temporary material world are not eternal nor are they actually beneficial. The association of the Supreme Personality of Godhead is attained by the association of His associates. The various methods for attaining perfection in life, such as the atheistic *sāṅkhya* philosophical system, the theistic *sāṅkhya* philosophical system, the performance of major and minor religious duties, the study of the *Vedas*, the performance of penances, cultivating a life of renunciation, engaging in welfare activities, giving charity, performing sacrifices, chanting Vedic *mantras*, taking bath in holy places, and controlling the mind and senses, are not as effective in pleasing the Lord as the association of His pure devotees. The Supreme Lord is unconquerable, but He is controlled by the love of His pure devotees. All methods for achieving the ultimate goal of life that are followed by nondevotees cannot purchase the favor of the Supreme Lord.

TEXTS 3-6

सत्सङ्गेनहिदैतेयायातुधानामृगाःखगाः ।
गन्धर्वाप्सरसोनागाःसिद्धाश्चारणगुह्यकाः ॥३॥
विद्याधरामनुष्येषुवैश्याःशूद्राःस्त्रियोऽन्त्यजाः ।
रजस्तमःप्रकृतयस्तस्मिंस्तस्मिन्युगेयुगे ॥४॥
बहवोमत्पदंप्राप्तास्त्वाष्ट्रकायाधवादयः ।
वृषपर्वाबलिर्बाणोमयश्चाथविभीषणः ॥५॥
सुग्रीवोहनुमान् ऋक्षोगजोगृध्रोवणिक्पथः ।
व्याधःकुब्जाव्रजेगोप्योयज्ञपत्न्यस्तथापरे ॥६॥

sat-saṅgena hi daiteyā yātudhānā mṛgāḥ khagāḥ
gandharvāpsaraso nāgāḥ siddhāś cāraṇa-guhyakāḥ

vidyādharā manuṣyeṣu vaiśyāḥ śūdrāḥ striyo 'ntya-jāḥ
rajas-tamaḥ-prakṛtayas tasmiṁs tasmin yuge yuge

bahavo mat-padaṁ prāptās tvāṣṭra-kāyādhavādayaḥ
vṛṣaparvā balir bāṇo mayaś cātha vibhīṣaṇaḥ

sugrīvo hanumān ṛkṣo gajo gṛdhro vaṇikpathaḥ
vyādhaḥ kubjā vraje gopyo yajña-patnyas tathāpare

In every *yuga*, many who are influenced by the modes of passion and ignorance, including demons, animals, birds, Gandharvas, Apsarās, Nāgas, Siddhas, Cāraṇas, Guhyakas, Vidhyādharas, *vaiśyas, śudras,* women, and others were able to come back home, back to Godhead, due to gaining the association of My devotees. Vṛtrāsura and Prahlāda Mahārāja also attained My transcendental abode due to the association of devotees, as did Vṛṣaparvā, Bali Mahārāja, Bāṇāsura, Maya, Vibhīṣaṇa, Sugriva, Hanumān, Jāmbavān, Gajendra, Jaṭāyu, Tulādhāra, Dharma-vyādha, Kubjā, the *gopīs* of Vṛndāvana, and the wives of the *brāhmaṇas* that were performing sacrifices.

COMMENTARY

These four verses describe how the Supreme Lord is directly controlled by the *gopīs* of Vraja, and indirectly by demons like King Bāṇa. There are two kinds of saintly persons—those who are engaged in activities based on devotional service, and those who are engaged in pure unalloyed devotional service. The controlling power of the former is indirect, whereas the controlling power of the latter is direct. The word *yātudhanā* refers to demons, such as Tvāṣtra and Vṛtrāsura. Prahlāda received the association of Śrī Nārada even before his birth. Soon after his birth, Vṛṣaparvā was rejected by his mother. He was then brought up by a sage and became a devotee of Lord Viṣṇu. Bali Mahārāja attained the association of Prahlāda Mahārāja. All these examples are given in the *Purāṇas*. When King Bāṇa's arms were being cut off, he received the association of Mahādeva. While constructing their assembly house, the demon, *Maya*, had the association of the Pāṇḍavas. Vibhīṣaṇa received Hanumān's association. The monkeys headed by Sugrīva received Lakṣmaṇa's association. Gajendra, the king of the elephants, received the association of Śrī Nārada in his previous life. The giant bird, Jaṭāyu had Garuḍa's and Daśaratha's association. The stories of Vaṇika or Tulādhāra are narrated in the *Mahābhārata*, but it is unclear whose association they had received. The story of Dharma-vyādha, the nonviolent hunter, was described in the *Varāha Purāṇa*. In a previous life, he somehow became a *brahma-rākṣasa*, or *brāhmaṇa* ghost, but was eventually saved. In a previous Kali-yuga he had the association of a Vaiṣṇava king named Vāsu. In the *Harivaṁśa*, it is stated that in her previous life, Kubjā had the association of Nārada. The sages of Daṇḍakāraṇya who appeared as *gopīs* in Vraja had the association of many saintly persons in their previous life, and the association of eternally perfect *gopīs* in their next life. The wives of the *brāhmaṇas* who were engaged in performing sacrifice had the opportunity to associate with Kṛṣṇa's messengers, Mālī and Tāmbulī, when they went to Mathurā on business.

PURPORT

Simply by the influence of the devotees' association, all of one's incompetence is destroyed so that one became qualified to attain the service of the Supreme Personality of Godhead.

TEXT 7

तेनाधीतश्रुतिगणानोपासितमहत्तमाः।
अव्रतातप्ततपसःमत्सङ्गान्मामुपागताः॥७॥

te nādhīta-śruti-gaṇā nopāsita-mahattamāḥ
avratātapta-tapasaḥ mat-saṅgān mām upāgatāḥ

These persons did not study the *Vedas*, worship saintly persons, or perform terrible austerities. They had attained My association simply as a result of the association of My devotees.

COMMENTARY

According to the advancement they made by means of *sādhu-saṅga*, the above-mentioned persons either achieved mixed devotional service or pure devotional service. There was no need for them to follow other *sādhanas*. They did not study the *Vedas*, which indicates that they did not approach sages who were well-acquainted with the *Vedas*. Similarly, they did not perform any austerities or execute any vows. They developed devotional service simply by the association of the Lord's devotees and thus ultimately attained His shelter.

PURPORT

Without following any other *sādhana*, simply by the influence of the devotees' association, one can attain the devotional service of Supreme Lord.

TEXT 8

केवलेनहिभावेनगोप्योगावोनगामृगाः ।
येऽन्येमूढधियोनागाःसिद्धामामीयुरञ्जसा ॥८॥

kevalena hi bhāvena gopyo gāvo nagā mṛgāḥ
ye 'nye mūḍha-dhiyo nāgāḥ siddhā mām īyur añjasā

All of the residents of Vṛndāvana—the *gopīs*, cows, trees and plants, animals, and serpents very easily attained life's perfections because of their love for Me.

COMMENTARY

The unique position of the *gopīs* is herein described. The word *kevala* means "devoid of *karma* and *jñana*," or in other words pure devotional service, without any tinge of material desire. Devotional service to the Lord is rendered in the moods of *śṛṅgāra*, *vātsalya*, *sakhya*, and *dāsya*. The *gopīs* attained the Lord by serving Him in the mood of *mādhurya rasa*, the cows in the mood of *vātsalya rasa*, Govardhana Hill and the deer in the mood of *sakhya rasa*, and the trees and creepers of Vṛndāvana, as well as the Kāliya serpent, in the mood of *dāsya rasa*. The *gopīs* referred to in this verse are the eternally perfect *gopīs*. Indeed, all the inhabitants of Vṛndāvana should be considered eternally liberated souls, as expressed by the word *siddhāḥ*, which means "having achieved the perfection of life."

PURPORT

By love and devotion, persons who appear to be incompetent can achieve the mercy of the Supreme Personality of Godhead.

TEXT 9

यंनयोगेनसांख्येनदानव्रततपोऽध्वरैः ।
व्याख्यास्वाध्यायसन्न्यासैःप्राप्नुयाद्यत्नवानपि ॥९॥

yaṁ na yogena sāṅkhyena dāna-vrata-tapo-'dhvaraiḥ
vyākhyā-svādhyāya-sannyāsaiḥ prāpnuyād yatnavān api

Even though others engaged with great endeavor in the mystic yoga system, philosophical speculation, giving charity, executing vows and penances, performing ritualistic sacrifices, teaching the Vedic mantras to others, a personal study of the *Vedas*, or the renounced order of life, they could not achieve Me.

COMMENTARY

Even if one faithfully practices the yoga system, one cannot attain the devotional service of the Lord. Association of devotees is the only criteria for attaining pure devotional service, and not any other discipline or pious activity. This is the purport of this verse.

PURPORT

Even if one carefully studies the atheistic or theistic Sāṅkhya philosophy, gives charity, observes vows, undergoes austerity, performs sacrifices, studies the *Vedas*, and explains the Vedic literature to others, one will still not attain the mercy of the Supreme Lord.

TEXT 10

रामेणसार्धंमथुरांप्रणीतेश्वाफल्किनामय्यनुरक्तचित्ताः ।
विगाढभावेननमेवियोगतीव्राधयोऽन्यंददृशुःसुखाय ॥१०॥

rāmeṇa sārdhaṁ mathurāṁ praṇīte śvāphalkinā mayy anurakta-cittāḥ
vigāḍha-bhāvena na me viyoga-tīvrādhayo 'nyaṁ dadṛśuḥ sukhāya

When Akrūra took Me to Mathurā, along with My brother, Baladeva, the *gopīs*, whose hearts were completely attached to Me, felt severe mental agony due to separation from Me. They thus could not consider any source of happiness other than My association.

COMMENTARY

That the devotional mood of the *gopīs* is the topmost form of devotional service is being stressed in these four verses. When Kṛṣṇa was brought to Mathurā by Akrūra, the *gopīs* could not see anything that would give them happiness because their love for Kṛṣṇa was so intense. The *gopīs* were situated on the platform of *adhirūḍha mahābhāva*. In such a loving condition, they felt severe mental agony due to separation from their beloved, Kṛṣṇa. Because this verse is spoken in the past tense, it is understood that the *gopīs* rejoined Kṛṣṇa after the killing of Dantavakra.

PURPORT

No one who desires actual happiness can achieve his goal of life without engaging in the devotional service of the Supreme Lord, who is eternal, full of knowledge, and full of bliss. The *gopīs*, whose attachment for Kṛṣṇa was intense, felt unlimited distress because of separation from Him, when He and Balarāma left for Mathurā with Akrūra.

TEXT 11

तास्ताःक्षपाःप्रेष्ठतमेननीतामयैववृन्दावनगोचरेण ।
क्षणार्धवत्ताःपुनरङ्गतासांहीनामयाकल्पसमाबभूवुः ॥११॥

tās tāḥ kṣapāḥ preṣṭhatamena nītā mayaiva vṛndāvana-gocareṇa
kṣaṇārdha-vat tāḥ punar aṅga tāsāṁ hīnā mayā kalpa-samā babhūvuḥ

Dear Uddhava, the nights that the *gopīs* spent with Me in Vṛndāvana appeared to them to be no more than a moment. Now, in separation from Me, a night appears to them to be longer than a *kalpa*.

COMMENTARY

On the topmost platform of love of God, there are symptoms such as *adhiruḍha mahābhāva*. Even a *kalpa* seems like a moment because of attachment for Kṛṣṇa. And, the same moment appears like a *kalpa* in separation from Kṛṣṇa. Lord Kṛṣṇa says, "Although the *gopīs* spent an entire night of Brahmā with Me enjoying the *rāsa* dance, they considered it to be less than a moment. This was their experience when they were with Me in Vṛndāvana." And yet, the *gopīs* considered the same one moment to be more than hundreds of *yugas* whenever Kṛṣṇa went to the pasturing grounds to tend the cows.

TEXT 12

तानाविदन्मय्यनुषङ्गबद्धधियःस्वमात्मानमदस्तथेदम् ।
यथासमाधौमुनयोऽब्धितोयेनद्यःप्रविष्टा इवनामरूपे ॥१२॥

tā nāvidan mayy anuṣaṅga-baddha-dhiyaḥ svam ātmānam adas tathedam
yathā samādhau munayo 'bdhi-toye nadyaḥ praviṣṭā iva nāma-rūpe

Just as sages, by means of *samādhi*, forget the names and forms of this world because of their full absorption in the self, like rivers merging into the ocean, the *gopīs* were so attached to Me that they could not even think of their own bodies, their lives in this world, or their future lives.

COMMENTARY

It is stated in *Ujjvala-nīlamaṇi* that forgetfulness without any question of illusion is a feature of *adhiruḍha mahābhāva*. This is being described in this verse, wherein it is said about the *gopīs*, "their intelligence was captivated by My association." Here, the word *baddha* or "captivated" means that the propensity of the intelligence has become more enthusiastic due to the enchanting pastimes of Śrī Kṛṣṇa. These propensities of the intelligence are just like wish-fulfilling cows that fulfill all of Kṛṣṇa's desires. The *gopīs* could not know who they were, where they were, or where had they come from while performing *rāsa* dance. They transgressed all worldly etiquette, shyness, fear, and so on, just like sages who forget everything when they realize Brahman while in *samādhi*. The *gopīs* are herein compared to sages in *samādhi* because they both exhibit single-minded concentration. Actually, the ecstatic love of the *gopīs* is far superior to the dry meditation of the sages who are trying to liberate themselves from the material body. The *gopīs* did not possess material bodies because they were personally dancing with the Supreme Lord and embracing Him. It should be very well understood that the bliss of impersonal Brahman realization hardly equals a tiny fragment of the ocean of ecstatic love of Kṛṣṇa. The Supreme Lord comes under the control of His pure devotees. The sages were not attached to the Supreme Lord and so they could not control Him with their love. Rivers enter the ocean, losing their separate identity. This is an example to illustrate how devotees become fully absorbed in thoughts of Kṛṣṇa, and thus relish the mellows of devotional service without any concern for their personal existence.

PURPORT

The *gopīs*, whose hearts were fully attached to Kṛṣṇa and who were thus in a trance of meditation upon the service of the Lord, completely forgot about their relatives, as well as their gross and subtle bodies. They forgot about their personal existence—their names, forms, and so on—just as a river loses its identity after entering the ocean.

TEXT 13

मत्कामारमणंजारमस्वरूपविदोऽबलाः ।
ब्रह्ममांपरमंप्रापुःसङ्गाच्छतसहस्रशः ॥१३॥

mat-kāmā ramaṇaṁ jāram asvarūpa-vido 'balāḥ
brahma māṁ paramaṁ prāpuḥ saṅgāc chata-sahasraśaḥ

All those hundreds of thousands of cowherd girls, although ignorant of My actual position as the Supreme Personality of Godhead, attained Me simply by desiring My association as their paramour.

COMMENTARY

Śrī Kṛṣṇa herein explains how the *gopīs* attained His shelter: "The *gopīs* desired nothing but Me, the supreme Brahman. How did they attain Me? I enjoyed pastimes with them, and thus they experienced great happiness." In the *Śrīmad Bhāgavatam*, Śrī Śukadeva Gosvāmī said, "After seeing the beauty of Vṛndāvana, Kṛṣṇa desired to enjoy His *rāsa-līlā* pastimes. Although Kṛṣṇa is self-sufficient, He enjoyed the *rāsa* dance with the *gopīs*." Did the *gopīs* enjoy Kṛṣṇa's company as a husband? No, as a paramour. What was the essential characteristic of the *gopīs*? The Supreme Personality of Godhead said, "The *gopīs* were so attracted by My sweetness and beauty that they forgot about My opulent features. Otherwise, it would not have been possible for Me to enjoy their company. Although they were the most beautiful girls in the creation, they forgot about their own beauty, being attracted by My beauty." This is what is being indicated by the word *asvarūpa-vidaḥ*, "not understanding My actual position or form."

PURPORT

Because of their strong desire to please Kṛṣṇa, the *gopīs*, who were completely absorbed in the service of the Lord, and who had only one goal in life, attained the Supreme Personality of Godhead. The *gopīs* were many and the Lord was one. Following their example, innumerable persons of a similar nature attained the association of the Absolute Truth, the Supreme Personality of Godhead, Śrī Kṛṣṇa. Although, from an external point of view, the *gopīs* may be considered as women attached to a man other than their husband, because they took shelter of the supreme enjoyer, their conduct is always to be glorified.

TEXTS 14-15

तस्मात्त्वमुद्धवोत्सृज्यचोदनांप्रतिचोदनाम् ।
प्रवृत्तिंचनिवृत्तिंचश्रोतव्यंश्रुतमेवच ॥१४॥
मामेकमेवशरणमात्मानंसर्वदेहिनाम् ।
याहिसर्वात्मभावेनमयास्याह्यकुतोभयः ॥१५॥

tasmāt tvam uddhavotsṛjya codanāṁ praticodanām
pravṛttiṁ ca nivṛttiṁ ca śrotavyaṁ śrutam eva ca

mām ekam eva śaraṇam ātmānaṁ sarva-dehinām
yāhi sarvātma-bhāvena mayā syā hy akuto-bhayaḥ

Therefore, My dear Uddhava, abandon the *mantras* of the *śrutis* and *smṛtis*, as well as the rules and regulations prescribed in the supplementary Vedic literature. Disregard all that you have heard, and all that is to be heard, and just surrender unto Me alone because I am the Supersoul of all living entities. By taking shelter of Me, you will certainly be freed from fear in all circumstances, by My mercy.

COMMENTARY

After Śrī Uddhava had inquired about the characteristics of a saintly person, the Supreme Lord, Kṛṣṇa, described the characteristics of the two classes of transcendentalists, the methods for executing devotional service in the association of devotees, and how devotional service has the power to control Him. The Lord next described the good qualities of the devotees and concluded that the *gopīs*' devotion to Him is the topmost platform of love of God. The Lord further described how, when He was being taken, along with Balarāma, by Akrūra to Mathurā, the *gopīs* shed incessant tears due to impending separation from Him. The *gopīs* were greatly agitated due to feelings of ecstatic love in separation from the Lord, and thus their devotional service could control Him. Here, Lord Śrī Kṛṣṇa is trying to inspire Uddhava to follow in the footsteps of the *gopīs* and thus render devotional service as they did. Śrī Kṛṣṇa said to Uddhava, "Give up the rules and regulations prescribed in the scriptures, and give up all recommended and prohibited activities mentioned in the *Vedas*." Does this mean that Uddhava should take *sannyāsa*? No, it means that he should give up the activities that are prescribed for both householders and *sannyāsīs*, and he should become indifferent to all that has been heard, as well as all that may be heard in the future. In this way, Uddhava should abandon all varieties of religion and just surrender to Kṛṣṇa in the mood of one of the five *rasas*. Then, he will have no fear, by Kṛṣṇa's mercy. He should not think that he will be the loser by rejecting fruitive activities and the cultivation of knowledge. The Supreme Lord is there to protect His devotees from all types of fearful conditions.

PURPORT

After carefully deliberating on that which was spoken by the Supreme Lord, one should simply surrender himself at the lotus feet of the Supreme Personality of Godhead, knowing that this will eradicate all lamentation, illusion, and fear. Taking shelter of too many persons will not award one any real benefit. Rather, by taking shelter of the son of the king of Vraja alone, who is one without a second, one will easily be liberated from the hands of all inauspiciousness.

TEXT 16

श्रीउद्धव उवाच
संशयःशृण्वतोवाचंतवयोगेश्वरेश्वर ।
ननिवर्तत आत्मस्थोयेनभ्राम्यतिमेमनः ॥१६॥

śrī-uddhava uvāca
saṁśayaḥ śṛṇvato vācaṁ tava yogeśvareśvara
na nivartata ātma-stho yena bhrāmyati me manaḥ

Śrī Uddhava said: O Lord of the foremost yogis, even after hearing Your statements, the doubt in my heart has not gone away, so my mind is bewildered.

COMMENTARY

Uddhava says, "My dear Lord Kṛṣṇa, You had first recommended that I perform my duties according to the *varṇāśrama* system, but then You advised me to give up these activities and take to the advancement of knowledge. Now, You seem to be rejecting the path of *jñāna*, and recommending that I surrender unto You and practice *bhakti-yoga*. If I accept this path, how do I not know that in the future You will not once again recommend that I perform my worldly duties." Such frank talk indicates Uddhava's intimate relationship with Lord Kṛṣṇa.

PURPORT

In the first verse of the Fourth Chapter, the Lord said that one should take shelter of Him while continuing to perform one's prescribed duties within the *varṇāśrama* system without material desire. Uddhava took this to mean *karma-miśrā bhakti*, or devotional service mixed with fruitive activities. Of course, if one has not yet realized that Lord

Kṛṣṇa is the cause of all causes, there is no question of renouncing worldly responsibilities. Such a person is encouraged to offer the fruits of his work to the Lord. In the fourth verse of the Fourth Chapter, the Lord recommended that one give up his worldly duties and engage in the cultivation of knowledge. Uddhava took this to mean *jñāna-miśrā bhakti*, or devotional service mixed with speculative knowledge. Beginning with verse thirty-five of the Fourth Chapter, Uddhava inquired about the two conditions of existence—material bondage and liberation. In response, the Lord explained that without devotional service, mere philosophical speculation cannot enable one to attain perfection. In verse eighteen of Chapter Five, faith in the Supreme Personality of Godhead was extolled, and in verse twenty-three, Kṛṣṇa recommended hearing and chanting the glories of the Lord. The Lord concluded by saying that the association of devotees is essential for spiritual advancement. In verse twenty-six of the Fifth Chapter, Uddhava inquired about the details of devotional service and the characteristics of perfection. And in verse forty-eight, Lord Kṛṣṇa stated that only engagement in devotional service awards one liberation. Finally, in verse fourteen of this chapter the Lord firmly rejected both fruitive activities and mental speculation and in verse fifteen, He recommended that one surrender unto Him unconditionally.

After receiving so many instructions, Uddhava appears to be bewildered about what he should actually do. For this reason, Uddhava requests Lord Kṛṣṇa to clearly tell him exactly what he should do.

TEXT 17

श्रीभगवानुवाच
स एषजीवोविवरप्रसूतिःप्राणेनघोषेणगुहांप्रविष्टः।
मनोमयांसूक्ष्ममुपेत्यरूपंमात्रास्वरोवर्ण इतिस्थविष्ठः॥१७॥

śrī-bhagavān uvāca
sa eṣa jīvo vivara-prasūtiḥ prāṇena ghoṣeṇa guhāṁ praviṣṭaḥ
mano-mayaṁ sūkṣmam upetya rūpaṁ mātrā svaro varṇa iti sthaviṣṭhaḥ

The Supreme Lord said: My dear Uddhava, the Supreme Lord is situated within the hearts of all living beings. It is only by His presence that the life air functions so that the physical processes continue to function. The Lord's subtle presence within the heart can be perceived by seeing how the mind is under superior control. The Lord also appears as the sound of the *Vedas*, which is composed of short and long vowels and consonants.

COMMENTARY

Uddhava was bewildered because Lord Kṛṣṇa had explained many different processes, such as devotional service, speculative knowledge, renunciation, mystic yoga, austerities, and pious duties. All of these processes are meant to help the living entities obtain the shelter of Lord Kṛṣṇa, either directly or indirectly. Thus, Lord Kṛṣṇa explained the entire Vedic system, from the beginning stages, to the most advanced. Actually, Lord Kṛṣṇa was surprised that Uddhava thought that he was meant to practice every process, as if the instructions were just meant for him. Lord Kṛṣṇa therefore wants to inform His devotee, "My dear Uddhava, when I told you that analytic knowledge is to be practiced, pious duties are to be performed, devotional service is obligatory, yoga procedures must be observed, and austerities are to be executed, I was instructing all living entities, although you were My immediate audience. Whatever I spoke in the past, have spoken now, and will speak in the future should be understood as guidance for all living entities in different situations. How could you possibly think that you were meant to practice all of the different Vedic processes? I accept you as you are now, My pure devotee. You are not supposed to execute all of these processes." In this way, with lighthearted and encouraging words, the Lord revealed to Uddhava the deep purpose behind the variety of Vedic procedures.

The Supreme Personality of Godhead is the knower of the *Vedas* and it was He who appeared from the four mouths of Brahmā in the form of the *Vedas*. This is being described in this verse. The word *jīva* indicates that it is the Supreme Lord who gives life. The Lord is speaking this verse with firm conviction while touching His chest with His index finger. The word *vivara* indicates that the *Vedas* have manifested from the womb of Brahmā's body. The word *ghoṣa* means "transcendental sound vibration." This sound vibration, along with the life air, entered the heart of Brahmā and manifested in the form of the *Vedas*, which is composed of short and long vowels, and consonants pronounced with high and low tones.

PURPORT

When Kṛṣṇa and Balarāma left for Mathurā, the *gopīs* became greatly afflicted due to the pain of separation from Kṛṣṇa. They could not imagine any other source of happiness than the association of Kṛṣṇa. This has been described in the tenth verse.

In the thirteenth verse of this chapter, the purport of all the Vedic literatures has been explained. Then, in two verses, the supremacy of the Supreme Lord has been described. The Lord is the ultimate shelter of everyone and all the Vedic *mantras* are transcendental sound vibrations that have emanated from Him.

Śrīla Śrīdhara Svāmī has described the word *vivara* as meaning "the basis of everything." This has been elaborately discussed in verses thirty-six to forty-three of the

Twenty-first Chapter of the Eleventh Canto. Transcendental sound vibration appear in two forms—gross and subtle. From the subtle form, the life air, intelligence, and mind are manifest. From the gross form, the senses, *parā*, *paśyantī*, *madhyamā*, and *vaikharī* manifest. The mind and the senses are particularly described as *parā*, or *prāṇamayī*. When subtle substance is associated with the transcendental sound vibration, it is known as *manomayī paśyantī*. When *praṇava*, or *oṁ*, is manifest, it is called *buddhimayī madhyamā*. When *praṇava* transforms into alphabets, it is called *vaikharī*. *Vaikharī* produces different meters, such as *bṛhatī*.

The tenth verse presents another meaning. The Supreme Personality of Godhead is the life and soul of Vraja. Although Lord Kṛṣṇa eternally performs His pastimes in the spiritual world, beyond the vision of the conditioned souls, He also enters within the material universe to display these same pastimes. The words *guhāṁ praviṣṭaḥ* indicates that after displaying such pastimes, the Lord withdraws them and enters into His unmanifest pastimes, or those pastimes not manifest to the conditioned souls. In this case, *mātrā* indicates the transcendental senses of the Lord, *svara* indicates the Lord's transcendental sound vibration and singing, and the word *varṇa* indicates the transcendental form of the Lord. The word *sthaviṣṭha*, or "gross manifestation," means that the Lord becomes manifest in the material world even to those devotees who are not completely advanced in Kṛṣṇa consciousness and whose vision is not completely purified. *Manomaya* indicates that somehow or other Lord Kṛṣṇa is to be kept within one's mind; and for the nondevotees Lord Kṛṣṇa is *sūkṣma*, or most subtle, because He cannot be known.

TEXT 18

यथानलःखेऽनिलबन्धुरुष्माबलेनदारुण्यधिमथ्यमानः
अणुःप्रजातोहविषासमेधतेतथैवमेव्यक्तिरियंहिवाणी

yathānalaḥ khe 'nila-bandhur uṣmā balena dāruṇy adhimathyamānaḥ
aṇuḥ prajāto haviṣā samedhate tathaiva me vyaktir iyaṁ hi vāṇī

When two pieces of wood are vigorously rubbed together, heat is produced by contact with air, so that a spark appears. Once the fire is kindled, ghee is added so that the fire blazes. Similarly, I am manifest in the sound vibration of the Vedas.

COMMENTARY

Lord Kṛṣṇa said to Uddhava, "Although there is fire within wood, it does not manifest until there is friction with another piece of wood. When two pieces of wood are vigorously rubbed together, sparks appear with the help of the air. Thereafter, it becomes a blazing fire as one continues to pour ghee upon it. Similarly, the *Vedas* are produced from Me. Who other than Me can know the confidential purport of the *Vedas*? It is I who have prescribed the process of *karma*, *jñāna*, and *bhakti*, so that the conditioned souls can become delivered from material existence. My dear Uddhava, I am now imparting the proper understanding of these processes to you because you are the person most qualified to receive this knowledge. Later on, you will enlighten the sages at Badarikāśrama, thus enabling them to achieve life's ultimate goal.

PURPORT

The pastimes of the Supreme Lord become manifest when there is glorification of the Lord in the association of devotees. Just as fire, which remains in an unmanifest state, is produced by the friction of two pieces of wood, and then becomes a blazing fire with the help of air and ghee, the manifestation of the Lord's pastimes, along with His names, forms, and qualities, is realized by means of *kīrtana*. Simply by the chanting of the holy name of Kṛṣṇa, His forms, qualities, and pastimes become manifest.

TEXT 19

एवंगदिःकर्मगतिर्विसर्गोघ्राणोरसोदृक् स्पर्शःश्रुतिश्च ।
सङ्कल्पविज्ञानमथाभिमानःसूत्रंरजःसत्त्वतमोविकारः ॥१९॥

evaṁ gadiḥ karma gatir visargo ghrāṇo raso dṛk sparśaḥ śrutiś ca
saṅkalpa-vijñānam athābhimānaḥ sūtraṁ rajaḥ-sattva-tamo-vikāraḥ

It should be understood that the functions of the working senses—the organ of speech, the hands, the legs, the genital and the anus—and the functions of the knowledge-acquiring senses—the nose, tongue, eyes, skin and ears—along with the functions of the subtle senses of mind, intelligence, consciousness, and false ego, as well as the function of the subtle *pradhāna* and the interaction of the three modes of material nature—are all My materially manifest form.

COMMENTARY

Lord Kṛṣṇa said to Uddhava, "Everything visible in this world should be known as external manifestations of Myself. The function of the hands is to work. The function of the legs is to move about. The function of the tongue is to vibrate various sounds. The functions of the genitals and anus are to pass urine and stool. These are the activities of the working senses. The function of the nose is to smell. The function of the tongue is to taste. The function of the eyes is to see. The function of the skin is to touch, and the function of the ears is to hear. These are the activities of the knowledge-acquiring senses. The function of the mind is to make plans. The function of the intelligence is to put the plans of the mind into practical action. The function of the false ego is to manifest pride, and the function of the material nature is to create transformations of the three modes.

PURPORT

The visible material variegatedness is made possible by the transformations of the three modes of material nature. This varigatedness is supported by the functions of the organs of speech, the hands, the legs, the genitals, and the anus, as well as the nose, the tongue, the eyes, the ears, the skin, the mind, the intelligence, the false ego, and the material nature, which is called *pradhāna,* from which the living entities, the senses, and the demigods have been created. The original source of all of this variegatedness is the Supreme Lord. All of these manifestations gradually help one to attain the lotus feet of the Supreme Lord, who is the complete spiritual whole, and who is the supreme shelter for all.

Those who are averse to the service of the Supreme Lord glorify the functions of the mind, as a result of being bewildered by false ego, and so cannot understand how everything is an emanation from the Supreme Personality of Godhead.

Actually, all material objects can be properly utilized in the service of the Supreme Lord. Not understanding the variegated pastimes of the supreme spirit whole, people who are absorbed in the impersonal conception of the Absolute Truth falsely consider eternal devotional service and temporary material enjoyment to be one and the same.

TEXT 20

अयंहिजीवस्त्रिवृदब्जयोनिरव्यक्त एकोवयसास आद्यः ।
विश्लिष्टशक्तिर्बहुधेवभातिबीजानियोनिंप्रतिपद्ययद्वत् ॥२०॥

ayaṁ hi jīvas tri-vṛd abja-yonir avyakta eko vayasā sa ādyaḥ
viślista-śaktir bahudheva bhāti bījāni yoniṁ pratipadya yadvat

Many seeds grow into different kinds of plants when they are placed in an agricultural field, although they arise from a single source, the soil. Similarly, the Supreme Personality of Godhead, who originally exists in an unmanifested form, who is the source of the three modes of material nature, who is eternal, and who is the source of the universal lotus flower in which the cosmic manifestation takes place, divides His material potencies and thus appears to be manifest in innumerable forms, although He is one.

COMMENTARY

Here, the Lord wishes to establish that this material world, which has emanated from Him, is nondifferent from Him. The Supreme Lord is the shelter of the three modes of material nature, and He is the original cause of the fourteen planetary systems. Before the creation, the Lord existed in His original transcendental form. He then manifested Himself in the form of the universe, so that the knowledge-acquiring senses and working senses were produced from His energy, as were the human beings and demigods.

PURPORT

The word *avyakta* indicates the Lord's transcendental form, which exists alone before the material creation. The Lord's original form, being spiritual, does not undergo birth, transformation or death. It is eternal. In the course of time, the Lord's material potencies are divided and manifest as bodies, bodily paraphernalia, sense objects, bodily expansions, false ego and false proprietorship. Thus the Lord expands His conscious living potency called *jīva-śakti*, which is manifest in innumerable material forms such as those of men, demigods, animals, and so on. Being bewildered by false ego, nondevotees indulge in material sense gratification and thus fail to understand that the internal potency of the Supreme Lord as the original source of His external potency. Only when, due to an inclination for devotional service, one develops a sense of discrimination between matter and spirit, can he understand himself to be an eternal servant of the Lord. The conditioned souls, on the other hand, being in the bodily concept of life, think that material nature has the power to create living entities, under the control of time.

TEXT 21

यस्मिन्निदंप्रोतमशेषमोतंपटोयथातन्तुवितानसंस्थः ।
य एषसंसारतरुःपुराणःकर्मात्मकःपुष्पफलेप्रसूते ॥२१॥

yasminn idaṁ protam aśeṣam otaṁ paṭo yathā tantu-vitāna-saṁsthaḥ
ya eṣa saṁsāra-taruḥ purāṇaḥ karmātmakaḥ puṣpa-phale prasūte

Just as a cloth is a manifestation of lengthwise and crosswise threads, the universe is expanded on the lengthwise and crosswise potency of the Supreme Personality of Godhead. The conditioned soul has been accepting material bodies since time immemorial, and these bodies are like trees sustaining his material existence. Just as a tree first blossoms and then produces fruit, the tree of material existence, one's material body, produces the various results of material existence.

COMMENTARY

The material universe is an expansion of the illusory potency of the Supreme Lord and is always dependent on Him and nondifferent from Him. This simple understanding can relieve the conditioned souls from endless wandering in the unhappy kingdom of *Maya*. In this verse, the example is given of a cloth, which is made of threads, and is therefore nondifferent from the threads. Similarly, this universe is a manifestation of the potency of the Lord and is therefore not different from Him. The example of a tree is also given in this verse. The tree of material existence, or the material body, produces flowers and fruit, in the form of happiness and distress.

TEXTS 22-23

द्वे अस्यबीजेशतमूलस्त्रिनालःपञ्चस्कन्धःपञ्चरसप्रसूतिः ।
दशैकशाखोद्विसुपर्णनीडस्त्रिवल्कलोद्विफलोऽर्कंप्रविष्टः ॥२२॥
अदन्तिचैकंफलमस्यगृध्राग्रामेचरा एकमरण्यवासाः ।
हंसाय एकंबहुरूपमिज्यैर्मायामयंवेदसवेदवेदम् ॥२३॥

dve asya bīje śata-mūlas tri-nālaḥ pañca-skandhaḥ pañca-rasa-prasūtiḥ
daśaika-śākho dvi-suparṇa-nīḍas tri-valkalo dvi-phalo 'rkaṁ praviṣṭaḥ

adanti caikaṁ phalam asya gṛdhrā grāme-carā ekam araṇya-vāsāḥ
haṁsā ya ekaṁ bahu-rūpam ijyair māyā-mayaṁ veda sa veda vedam

This tree of material existence has two seeds—piety and impiety. The unlimited material desires are its roots, the three modes of material nature are its trunks, the five material elements are its branches, the eleven senses are its sub-branches, and the five sense objects are its juice. Air, bile, and mucous are its three layers of bark. Happiness and distress are its fruit, and the individual soul and the Supersoul are the two birds that live in this tree. This tree extends up to the sun. Lusty householders enjoy one of the fruits of this tree (distress), and swan-like *sannyāsīs* enjoy the other fruit (happiness). One who, with the help of the worshipable spiritual master, can understand this tree to be a manifestation of the Supreme Lord actually knows the confidential meaning of the *Vedas*.

COMMENTARY

In this verse, the tree of material existence is being described. Piety and impiety are the two seeds of this tree. The unlimited material desires of the living entities are its roots, and the modes of material nature are its trunks. The five material elements are its branches, the five sense objects are its juice, the eleven senses are its sub-branches, and the individual soul and the Supersoul are two golden birds who reside in a nest in that tree. Air, bile, and mucous are the tree's three layers of bark and happiness and distress are its fruit. This tree extended up to the sun. Lusty householders enjoy one of the fruits, in the form of distress. For the conditioned souls, both heaven and hell are miserable. The swan-like *sannyāsīs* enjoy another fruit of this tree, in the form of happiness. Knowledge of the Absolute Truth is always relishable. One who, with the help of the worshipable spiritual master, understands the various manifestations of the one Supreme Lord actually realizes the confidential purport of the *Vedas*.

PURPORT

All gross and subtle forms of existence, and the tree of material existence itself, which is born from *karma* performed since time immemorial, are inseparably connected to each other, just like the horizontal and vertical threads of a cloth. The Supreme Lord is the origin of the cause of creation, in the form of Brahmā, and the effect, in the form of the universe. The tree of material existence produces flowers in the form of material happiness and distress, and fruits in the form of bondage and liberation. By the influence of *karma*, piety and impiety are created. Material desires are the cause of committing pious and sinful activities. The three trunks of this tree are the three modes of material nature, the five material elements are its branches, and the eleven senses are its sub-branches. Happiness and distress are the fruits of this tree that are tasted by the conditioned souls. There is a nest in the tree of material existence wherein two birds—the individual soul and the Supersoul—reside. Air, bile, and mucous are the coverings of bark of this tree. The material universe extends up to the sun. Those who are attracted to sense enjoyment suffer distress under the control of material desires. Those in the renounced order of life who are free from all desires for temporary sense gratification enjoy happiness even in this life. When one can see the Supreme Lord as the ultimate cause of everything, then his knowledge is perfect.

TEXT 24

एवंगुरूपासनयैकभक्त्याविद्याकुठारेणशितेनधीरः ।
विवृश्चयजीवाशयमप्रमत्तःसम्पद्यचात्मानमथत्यजास्त्रम् ॥२४॥

evaṁ gurūpāsanayaika-bhaktyā vidyā-kuṭhāreṇa śitena dhīraḥ
vivṛścya jīvāśayam apramattaḥ sampadya cātmānam atha tyajāstram

With steady intelligence, you should advance to the platform of unalloyed devotional service by faithful worship of the spiritual master. With the sharpened axe of transcendental knowledge, you should cut off the subtle material coverings of the soul. Upon realizing the Supreme Personality of Godhead, you should then give up the axe of transcendental knowledge.

COMMENTARY

Lord Kṛṣṇa said to Uddhava, "Try to understand this tree of material existence and thus make your life successful. By the sharp axe of such knowledge, you can cut to pieces your gross and subtle bodies, which are manifestations of the three modes of material nature. After attaining realization of the Supersoul, you can then discard the weapon of transcendental knowledge. Whatever I am speaking is just what I had taught Arjuna in the *Bhagavad-gītā*."

PURPORT

An intelligent person, desirous of freedom from material existence, should take shelter of a bona fide spiritual master and render service to him, considering him to be the topmost devotee of the Supreme Lord. While engaged in the devotional service of the Supreme Lord, one should destroy all obstacles with the axe of transcendental knowledge. In this way, one can come to transcend the three modes of material nature.

By awakening knowledge of one's relationship with the Supreme Lord, one can become freed from material bondage and attain all auspiciousness by engaging in the devotional service of the Supreme Lord.

Thus ends the translation of the Sixth Chapter of the Uddhava-gītā, entitled "**Beyond Renunciation and Knowledge**" *with the commentaries of Śrīla Viśvanātha Cakravartī Ṭhākura, and chapter summary and purports by Śrīla Bhaktisiddhānta Sarasvatī Ṭhākura.*

CHAPTER 7

THE HAṀSA-AVATĀRA ANSWERS THE QUESTIONS OF THE SONS OF BRAHMĀ

CHAPTER SUMMARY

In this chapter, Lord Śrī Kṛṣṇa explains how the conditioned souls become bound by the three modes of material nature due to being full of desires for sense gratification. The means for liberating the conditioned souls is also discussed. In this chapter, the Lord tells how He appeared as Lord Haṁsa before Brahmā and his sons, the four Kumāras, and spoke to them confidentially.

The three modes of material nature—goodness, passion, and ignorance—have no actual relationship with the eternal soul. One should free himself from the influence of the lower modes of nature—passion and ignorance—by cultivating the mode of goodness. Ultimately, one should transcend the mode of goodness by acting on the platform of pure goodness. The three modes of material nature influence one according to one's association with particular types of scripture, water, places, times, recipients of charity, quality of activities, births, meditations, *mantras*, rituals, and so on.

Being merged in ignorance, the conditioned soul misidentifies with the material body, so that the mode of passion conquers the mode of goodness, thus producing misery. When the mode of passion predominates, the mind becomes filled with insatiable desires for sense gratification. Those who are tormented by strong urges produced by the mode of passion become slaves of their senses. Although they can understand that this will eventually bring on all kinds of misery, they cannot resist the temptation to gratify their senses. On the other hand, one who is actually intelligent will remain detached from the objects of the senses by taking shelter of pure devotional service.

Lord Brahmā is referred to as the unborn original person within the universe. He is the secondary creator of the living entities, and he is the ultimate ruler of all the demigods. And yet even Brahmā is anxious because of his contact with material nature. Therefore, when he was questioned by his mind-born sons, headed by Sanaka, about the means for renouncing all desires for sense gratification, he couldn't conclusively reply. Therefore, for further enlightenment, he took shelter of the Supreme Personality of Godhead, so that the Lord appeared before him as the swan incarnation, Lord Haṁsa. Lord Haṁsa then instructed Brahmā about the nature of the self, the three states of consciousness (wakefulness, sleep, and deep sleep) and the means for crossing the ocean of material existence. The sages, headed by Sanaka, became enlightened by hearing the words of the Lord, and they worshiped Him in a mood of unalloyed devotion.

TEXT 1

श्रीभगवानुवाच
सत्त्वंरजस्तमइतिगुणाबुद्धेर्नचात्मनः ।
सत्त्वेनान्यतमौहन्यात्सत्त्वंसत्त्वेनचैव हि ॥१॥

śrī-bhagavān uvāca
sattvaṁ rajas tama iti guṇā buddher na cātmanaḥ
sattvenānyatamau hanyāt sattvaṁ sattvena caiva hi

The Supreme Lord said: The three modes of material nature—goodness, passion, and ignorance—pertain to material intelligence, and not to the soul. You should subdue the modes of passion and ignorance by the cultivation of the mode of goodness, Thereafter, you should conquer even the mode of material goodness by the cultivation of the transcendental mode of pure goodness.

COMMENTARY

In this chapter, Lord Śrī Kṛṣṇa explains that one should give up attachment to the three modes of material nature, and He also describes the history of the Haṁsa incarnation. In the previous chapter, the Lord concluded that one should destroy the tree mode of material existence by utilizing the axe of knowledge. Now, in the next seven verses, He will explain how one can acquire that knowledge. The three material modes—goodness, passion, and ignorance—are qualities of material intelligence. One must rise above the state of nescience, which is the cause of material bondage. One should conquer the modes of passion and ignorance by cultivating the mode of goodness, and then the mode of goodness can be transcended stepping onto the platform of pure goodness.

PURPORT

The subtle elements—the mind, intelligence, and false ego—are material, and under the influence of the three modes of material nature. The spirit soul, on the other hand, is completely aloof from matter. One should regain his original condition of life by curtailing the influence of passion and ignorance, by cultivating the mode of goodness, and then transcend the influence of mixed material goodness by taking shelter of transcendental goodness (*viśuddha-sattva*).

TEXT 2

सत्त्वाद्धर्मोभवेद्वृद्धात्पुंसोमद्भक्तिलक्षणः ।
सात्त्विकोपासयासत्त्वंततोधर्मः प्रवर्तते ॥२॥

sattvād dharmo bhaved vṛddhāt puṁso mad-bhakti-lakṣaṇaḥ
sāttvikopāsayā sattvaṁ tato dharmaḥ pravartate

When the conditioned soul becomes firmly situated in the mode of goodness, religious principles, characterized by devotional service to Me, become prominent in his life. One can strengthen the mode of goodness by cultivation of those things that are characterized by goodness.

COMMENTARY

By fixing oneself firmly in the mode of goodness, one can minimize the influence of the modes of passion and ignorance. When one is situated in the mode of goodness, he can easily accept devotional service to the Lord. However, without engagement in devotional service, the cultivation of the mode of goodness is practically useless. How can one strengthen his position in the mode of goodness? The answer is that by choosing food, attitudes, work, recreation, etc., strictly in the mode of goodness, one will become firmly situated in that mode.

PURPORT

The purified mode of goodness is called *vīśuddha-sattva*, or the transcendental platform on which there is no trace of any other quality. In pure goodness, knowledge automatically manifests and one can easily understand one's eternal loving relationship with Lord Kṛṣṇa. That is the actual meaning and purpose of *dharma*, or religious principles.

TEXT 3

धर्मोरजस्तमोहन्यात्सत्त्ववृद्धिरनुत्तमः ।
आशुनश्यतितन्मूलोह्यधर्म उभयेहते ॥३॥

dharmo rajas tamo hanyāt sattva-vṛddhir anuttamaḥ
āśu naśyati tan-mūlo hy adharma ubhaye hate

When one follows the religious principles of goodness, this practice frees one from the influence of passion and ignorance. When passion and ignorance are not present, then their original cause, irreligion, cannot be seen.

COMMENTARY

When the influence of passion and ignorance is vanquished, irreligious principles that are born of passion and ignorance are also vanquished.

PURPORT

There is no superior quality than purified goodness, which when developed, vanquishes the qualities of passion and ignorance. When passion and ignorance are destroyed, then irreligion, which is the origin of these qualities, is also destroyed.

TEXT 4

आगमोऽपःप्रजादेशःकालःकर्मचजन्मच ।
ध्यानंमन्त्रोऽथसंस्कारोदशैतेगुणहेतव" ॥४॥

āgamo 'paḥ prajā deśaḥ kālaḥ karma ca janma ca
dhyānaṁ mantro 'tha saṁskāro daśaite guṇa-hetavaḥ

Religious scriptures, water, one's association with one's children or with people in general, the particular place, the time, activities, birth, meditation, chanting of *mantras*, and purificatory rituals—these vary in quality so that by their association, the modes of nature become variously prominent.

COMMENTARY

It has already been described that by eating food in the mode of goodness, one's existence becomes purified. The next two verses describe objects on the platform of goodness. The word *āgama* means "religious scriptures", and the word *prajā* means people in general. There are three kinds of religious scriptures—those in the mode of goodness, those in the mode of passion, and those in the mode of ignorance.

PURPORT

The three material modes are prominent in varieties of people, water, children, time, place, action, *mantras*, and so on.

TEXT 5

तत्तत्सात्त्विकमेवैषांयद्यद्वृद्धाःप्रचक्षते ।
निन्दन्तितामसंतत्तद्राजसंतदुपेक्षितम् ॥५॥

tat tat sāttvikam evaiṣāṁ yad yad vṛddhāḥ pracakṣate
nindanti tāmasaṁ tat tad rājasaṁ tad-upekṣitam

Among the ten items I have just mentioned, the ones that have been praised by great sages, such as Śrīla Vyāsadeva, are those that are *sāttvika,* or in the mode of goodness. The ones that have been condemned are those that are *tāmasika,* or in the mode of ignorance, and the ones that have been neglected are those that are *rājasika,* or in the mode of passion.

COMMENTARY

The *sāttvika* scriptures have been glorified by the great sages, the *tāmasika* scriptures have been criticized, and the *rājasika* scriptures have been ignored, meaning that they have neither been praised nor criticized.

PURPORT

Among these ten items, the ones that are beneficial and admirable are *sāttvika,* the ones that are obnoxious are *tāmasika,* and the ones that simply give rise to indifference are *rājasika.*

TEXT 6

सात्त्विकान्येवसेवेतपुमान्सत्त्वविवृद्धये ।
ततोधर्मस्ततोज्ञानंयावत्स्मृतिरपोहनम् ॥६॥

sāttvikāny eva seveta pumān sattva-vivṛddhaye
tato dharmas tato jñānaṁ yāvat smṛtir apohanam

Until one attains the platform of self-realization and is thus able to give up his illusory identification with the gross and subtle bodies, which is caused by the three modes of nature, he should cultivate the mode of goodness. When one's quality of goodness is enhanced, religious principles can be practiced, leading to an awakening of one's transcendental understanding.

COMMENTARY

One should study those scriptures that are in the mode of goodness and therefore prescribe detachment from sense gratification and mental speculation. One should not study the *rājasika* and *tāmasika* scriptures that propagate the paths of sense gratification and atheism by means of religious rituals and impersonal philosophy. One should bathe and quench his thirst with pure water, and remain aloof from contaminated water in the form of perfume and wine. One should associate with those who are cultivating detachment from this material world and give up the association of those who aspire for material enjoyment, and who are sinful. One should reside in a solitary place, in the association of devotees. One should not be attracted to gambling in casinos or bars. One should worship the Supreme Lord during the auspicious time of *brāhma-muhūrta* and avoid the sinful influence of the middle of the night. One should conscientiously perform his prescribed duties, and pious activities should never be performed with a desire to fulfill one's lusty ambitions or to give trouble to others. One should receive an initiation *mantra* from a bona-fide spiritual master and not take initiation into the chanting of insignificant *śākta mantras*. One should meditate on the Supreme Personality of Godhead and His pure devotees, and not on lusty women and envious men. Following the example of Lord Caitanya, one should chant the holy names of the Lord and not songs that glorify the bondage of lust between men and women. Purificatory rituals should be accept for the purpose of actual purification, and not for the purpose of achieving material blessings.

When one tries to cultivate the mode of goodness by following the principles of religion, transcendental knowledge will awaken within the heart. This knowledge consists of the eternal nature of the individual spirit soul and the Supreme Personality of Godhead. Such knowledge frees one from the bodily concept of life and thus destroys the material designations that cover the conditioned souls. This is the path to eternal life.

PURPORT

One who diligently remains aloof from the influence of passion and ignorance can enhance the quality of goodness. Only in this way can one achieve real knowledge and thereby free oneself from the gross and subtle designations that cover his pure existence.

TEXT 7

वेणुसङ्घर्षजोवह्निर्दग्ध्वाशाम्यतितद्वनम् ।
एवंगुणव्यत्ययजोदेहःशाम्यतितत्क्रियः ॥७॥

veṇu-saṅgharṣa-jo vahnir dagdhvā śāmyati tad-vanam
evaṁ guṇa-vyatyaya-jo dehaḥ śāmyati tat-kriyaḥ

When fire is produced from the friction of bamboos in the forest, it burns the source of its birth, the bamboo forest. Thus, the fire is calmed by its own action. Similarly, the gross and subtle bodies of the living entities are created by the interactions of the material modes of nature. If one uses his gross and subtle body to cultivate knowledge of the self, then such enlightenment destroys the influence of the material modes of nature. Thus, like the fire, the body and mind are pacified by their own actions in destroying the source of their birth.

PURPORT

The term *guṇa-vyatyaya-jaḥ* indicates that the body is generated by the competition of the three modes of material nature, which exist everywhere in constantly changing proportions. As fire produced by the friction of bamboo sticks burns a forest and then becomes extinguished, The gross and subtle bodies, which are generated by the interaction of the modes of material nature, become pacified when the influence of the modes of nature is destroyed.

TEXT 8

श्रीउद्धव उवाच
विदन्तिमर्त्याःप्रायेणविषयान्पदमापदाम् ।
तथापिभुञ्जतेकृष्णतत्कथंश्वखराजवत् ॥८॥

śrī-uddhava uvāca
vidanti martyāḥ prāyeṇa viṣayān padam āpadām
tathāpi bhuñjate kṛṣṇa tat kathaṁ śva-kharāja-vat

Śrī Uddhava said: Human beings can generally understand that material life ultimately awards great misery but still, they try to enjoy it as much as they can. My

dear Lord Kṛṣṇa, how can a person who possesses genuine knowledge act just like a dog or a donkey?

PURPORT

Due to an absence of foresight, dogs, asses, and goats put themselves into great danger. A dog steals food, at the risk of being beaten or killed, and he often approaches a bitch for sex, even though she bares her teeth and snarls, threatening him with severe injury. An ass approaches a female ass for sex simply to be kicked by her hind legs. He carries a heavy burden all day long, simply for a little grass that is available everywhere. A goat is being taken to the slaughterhouse and yet, even in that situation, he happily approaches a female goat for sex. Similarly, most human beings, being without the understanding that the acts of sense gratification are the very causes of their suffering, indulge themselves without restriction. Uddhava wants to know why human beings are generally mad after sense gratification, even when they know that it will simply cause them miseries in the future.

TEXTS 9-10

श्रीभगवानुवाच
अहमित्यन्यथाबुद्धिःप्रमत्तस्ययथाहृदि ।
उत्सर्पतिरजोघोरंततोवैकारिकंमनः ॥९॥
रजोयुक्तस्यमनसःसङ्कल्पःसविकल्पकः ।
ततःकामोगुणध्यानाद्दुःसहःस्याद्धिदुर्मतेः ॥१०॥

śrī-bhagavān uvāca
aham ity anyathā-buddhiḥ pramattasya yathā hṛdi
utsarpati rajo ghoraṁ tato vaikārikaṁ manaḥ

rajo-yuktasya manasaḥ saṅkalpaḥ sa-vikalpakaḥ
tataḥ kāmo guṇa-dhyānād duḥsahaḥ syād dhi durmateḥ

The Supreme Lord said: O Uddhava, an ignorant person falsely identifies himself with the material body and mind. In this consciousness, the mode of passion, which simply causes distress, overwhelms the mind, which is born of the mode of goodness. The mind, under the influence of the mode of passion, functions by accepting and rejecting things, in the hopes of making material advancement. As a result, by constantly thinking of the products of the modes of material nature, a foolish person becomes afflicted with unbearable material longings.

COMMENTARY

The Supreme Lord says, "Those who thirst for sense gratification cannot be called learned men, although they think of themselves as very intelligent."

The process by which one is helplessly bound in illusion is clearly described herein.

PURPORT

The words *saṅkalpaḥ sa-vikalpakaḥ* in this verse indicate that materialistic people are continually making plans in the hopes of attaining happiness and avoiding suffering. Any sane person must admit that inspite of all such plans, material life is simply full of miseries. The mind is a creation of the mode of goodness and thus it is not meant for absorption in attempts to fulfill the animalistic propensities, which are impelled by the lower modes of passion and ignorance.

TEXT 11

करोतिकामवशगःकर्माण्यविजितेन्द्रियः ।
दुःखोदर्कणिसम्पश्यन्रजोवेगविमोहितः ॥११॥

karoti kāma-vaśa-gaḥ karmāṇy avijitendriyaḥ
duḥkhodarkāṇi sampaśyan rajo-vega-vimohitaḥ

One who fails to control his senses comes under the control of material desires and is thus bewildered by the strong waves of the mode of passion. Such a person performs material activities with great enthusiasm, although he clearly sees that the result will be future unhappiness.

COMMENTARY

In the hopes of increasing his material enjoyment, a person of uncontrolled senses performs many activities, although he knows very well that they will ultimately bring him misery.

PURPORT

Being driven by material desires, materialistic people who are controlled by their senses invite unlimited distress.

TEXT 12

रजस्तमोभ्यां यदपि विद्वान्विक्षिप्तधीः पुनः ।
अतन्द्रितो मनो युञ्जन्दोषदृष्टिर्न सज्जते ॥१२॥

rajas-tamobhyāṁ yad api vidvān vikṣipta-dhīḥ punaḥ
atandrito mano yuñjan doṣa-dṛṣṭir na sajjate

When the mind of an intelligent person is disturbed by the modes of passion and ignorance, he should carefully control his mind. By clearly seeing the contamination of the modes of nature, he does not become attached.

COMMENTARY

Even though learned people are sometimes disturbed by the modes of passion and ignorance, coming under their control, they do not become attached, due to understanding the inauspicious consequences.

PURPORT

Although a learned person's mind may become disturbed because of its nature of accepting and rejecting the things of this world, because he knows that he will incur sin if he indulges in acts of passion and ignorance, he does not allow himself to be deviated from his religious life.

TEXT 13

अप्रमत्तोऽनुयुञ्जीत मनो मय्यर्पयञ्छनैः ।
अनिर्विण्णो यथाकालं जितश्वासो जितासनः ॥१३॥

apramatto 'nuyuñjīta mano mayy arpayañ chanaiḥ
anirviṇṇo yathā-kālaṁ jita-śvāso jitāsanaḥ

One should be attentive and grave, and never indolent or depressed. While diligently practicing the yoga procedures of breathing and sitting postures, one should practice fixing the mind on Me at dawn, noon, and sunset. In this way, the mind will gradually become absorbed in Me.

COMMENTARY

The word *atandrita* means "cautious." One should never be diverted by sense gratification. Where should one fix his mind? The Supreme Lord is herein giving the answer: "On Me." If one is unable to fix the mind on the Lord in the beginning, don't be discouraged but continue one's practice to gradually make advancement.

PURPORT

Those who are trying to absorb their minds in thought of the Supreme Lord should give up all desires for enjoying the objects of the external world. They should remain enthusiastically engaged in the service of the Lord, while practicing *āsanas*, *prāṇāyāma*, and so on.

TEXT 14

एतावान्योग आदिष्टोमच्छिष्यैःसनकादिभिः ।
सर्वतोमन आकृष्यमय्यद्धावेश्यतेयथा ॥१४॥

etāvān yoga ādiṣṭo mac-chiṣyaiḥ sanakādibhiḥ
sarvato mana ākṛṣya mayy addhāveśyate yathā

The actual yoga system as taught by My devotees, headed by Sanaka-kumāra, can be summarized in these few words: After withdrawing the mind from all other objects, one should completely absorb it in Me without deviation.

TEXT 15

श्रीउद्धव उवाच
यदात्वंसनकादिभ्योयेनरूपेणकेशव ।
योगमादिष्टवानेतद्रूपमिच्छामिवेदितुम् ॥१५॥

śrī-uddhava uvāca
yadā tvaṁ sanakādibhyo yena rūpeṇa keśava
yogam ādiṣṭavān etad rūpam icchāmi veditum

Śrī Uddhava said: O Keśava, I would like to know—when, and in what form, did You instruct the science of yoga to the sages, headed by Sanaka?

TEXT 16

श्रीभगवानुवाच
पुत्राहिरण्यगर्भस्यमानसाःसनकादयः ।
पप्रच्छुःपितरंसूक्ष्मांयोगस्यैकान्तिकीम्गतिम् ॥१६॥

śrī-bhagavān uvāca
putrā hiraṇyagarbhasya mānasāḥ sanakādayaḥ
papracchuḥ pitaraṁ sūkṣmāṁ yogasyaikāntikīm gatim

The Supreme Lord said: Once, the sages, headed by Sanaka, who were born from the mind of Brahmā, inquired from him about the difficult subject matter of the goal of yoga.

COMMENTARY

The phrase *aikāntikīṁ gatim* means "the ultimate goal."

TEXT 17

सनकादय ऊचुः
गुणेष्वाविशतेचेतोगुणाश्चेतसिचप्रभो ।
कथमन्योन्यसन्त्यागोमुमुक्षोरतितितीर्षोः ॥१७॥

sanakādaya ūcuḥ
guṇeṣv āviśate ceto guṇāś cetasi ca prabho
katham anyonya-santyāgo mumukṣor atititīrṣoḥ

The sages headed by Sanaka said: My dear Lord, the minds of human beings are naturally attracted towards the objects of sense gratification, and the sense objects enter the mind in the form of material desires. Considering this, how can a person who desires liberation, who wants to desist from the activities of sense gratification, sever the mutual tie between the sense objects and the mind? Please explain this to us.

COMMENTARY

The sons of Brahmā said to their father: Human beings are naturally attached to sense gratification, and this attachment is firmly rooted within their minds. How is it possible for a person who wishes to conquer the urges for material enjoyment to cut off the relationship between the sense objects and the mind?

PURPORT

An intelligent person must understand that as long as he remains conditioned by material nature, the modes of nature will constantly disturb him with enticements for sense gratification. If one falls victim to such allurements, the perfection of life will remain unachieved.

TEXT 18

श्रीभगवानुवाच
एवंपृष्टोमहादेवःस्वयम्भूर्भूतभावनः
ध्यायमानःप्रश्नबीजंनाभ्यपद्यतकर्मधीः

śrī-bhagavān uvāca
evaṁ pṛṣṭo mahā-devaḥ svayambhūr bhūta-bhāvanaḥ
dhyāyamānaḥ praśna-bījaṁ nābhyapadyata karma-dhīḥ

The Supreme Lord said: My dear Uddhava, Brahmā, who is born from My body, and who is the creator of the living entities within this material world, being the best among the demigods, seriously considered how to answer the question of his sons, headed by Sanaka. The intelligence of Brahmā, however, was affected by his activities of creation and so he could not discover the essential answer to their question.

COMMENTARY

The Supreme Lord said, " Brahmā is the best among the demigods, and the creator of the living beings. And yet, even after much consideration, he could not understand the actual answer of the question placed before him by his sons. This was due to the fact that his intelligence had been affected by his activities of creation, which were performed with material attachment."

PURPORT

Because of being attached to his activities of creation, Prajāpati Brahmā, the creator of the living entities, was unable to answer the question of his sons.

TEXT 19

समामचिन्तयद्देवःप्रश्नपारतितीर्षया ।
तस्याहं हंसरूपेणसकाशमगमंतदा ॥१९॥

sa māṁ acintayad devaḥ praśna-pāra-titīrṣayā
tasyāhaṁ haṁsa-rūpeṇa sakāśam agamaṁ tadā

Brahmā, wanted to find out the answer to the question that was puzzling him and so he meditated on Me. At that time, I appeared before him in My form as Haṁsa.

COMMENTARY

The Supreme Lord said, "While thinking over the answer to his sons' question, Brahmā absorbed his mind in meditation upon Me. Just to show him mercy, I revealed Myself to Brahmā by appearing before him in My form as Haṁsa. As the *haṁsa*, or swan, is able to separate milk from water, I appeared to separate Brahmā's intelligence from the modes of material nature."

PURPORT

Being unable to answer the question of Sanaka, Brahmā began to meditate on the Supreme Lord. At that time, the Lord assumed the form of Haṁsa and appeared before Brahmā. Brahmā then inquired from Haṁsa about His identity.

TEXT 20

दृष्ट्वामाम्त उपव्रज्यकृत्वपादाभिवन्दनम् ।
ब्रह्माणमग्रतःकृत्वापप्रच्छुःकोभवानिति ॥२०॥

dṛṣṭvā mām ta upavrajya kṛtva pādābhivandanam
brahmāṇam agrataḥ kṛtvā papracchuḥ ko bhavān iti

Upon seeing My form as Haṁsa, the sages, headed by Sanaka, placing Brahmā in the lead, approached Me and worshiped My lotus feet. They then asked Me, "Who are You?"

TEXT 21

इत्यहंमुनिभिःपृष्टस्तत्त्वजिज्ञासुभिस्तदा ।
यदवोचमहंतेभ्यस्तदुद्धवनिबोध मे ॥२१॥

ity ahaṁ munibhiḥ pṛṣṭas tattva-jijñāsubhis tadā
yad avocam ahaṁ tebhyas tad uddhava nibodha me

My dear Uddhava, the sages were eager to understand the actual purpose of yoga and so they inquired from Me. Now, listen attentively as I repeat My instructions to the sages.

TEXT 22

वस्तुनोयद्यनानात्व आत्मनःप्रश्न ईदृशः ।
कथंघटेतवोविप्रावक्तुर्वामेक आश्रयः ॥२२॥

vastuno yady anānātva ātmanaḥ praśna īdṛśaḥ
kathaṁ ghaṭeta vo viprā vaktur vā me ka āśrayaḥ

My dear *brāhmaṇas*, if you believe that I am also a *jīva* soul and that there is no ultimate difference between us—because all souls are ultimately one without individuality—your question does not seem relevant. Because the spirit soul has no designations, such as caste, on what basis should I answer your question?

COMMENTARY

The Haṁsa incarnation said, "My dear *brāhmaṇas*, you ask Me, "Who are You?" because you consider Me to be a living entity like yourselves. Do you think that I possess a material body, or do you think that I am the Supreme Lord? If you consider Me to be a living entity, then as a pure spirit soul, on what basis can I distinguish Myself from you? How could you ask Me such a question?"

PURPORT

If there is no difference between the Supreme Lord and the living entities, then there is also oneness of the person who is questioning and the person who is answering. Who should ask a question and to whom? The actual purport of Lord Haṁsa's statement is that the spirit soul and the Supersoul are separate identities.

TEXT 23

पञ्चात्मकेषुभूतेषुसमानेषुचवस्तुतः ।
कोभवानितिवःप्रश्नोवाचारम्भोह्यनर्थकः ॥२३॥

pañcātmakeṣu bhūteṣu samāneṣu ca vastutaḥ
ko bhavān iti vaḥ praśno vācārambho hy anarthakaḥ

If, when You asked Me, "Who are You?" you were referring to the material body, which is made of the five gross material elements—earth, water, fire, air and ether—you should have asked, "Who are you five?" If you consider that basically all material bodies are the same, being made of the same elements, then your question cannot be taken seriously. Thus, it appears that in asking My identity, you are simply speaking words without any real meaning.

COMMENTARY

In the previous verse, the Lord indicated that if the sages accepted the impersonal philosophy that all living beings are ultimately one, then the question "Who are You?"

made no sense. In this verse, the Lord rejects the false conception that the self is the material body, which is composed of five gross material elements. The sages might argue that even among learned persons, it is a matter of courtesy to ask questions and give answers. After all, the Lord had addressed them as *brāhmaṇas*, and thus had also acted according to social conventions. To answer this argument, the Lord says, "My addressing you as *brāhmaṇas* would have no meaning if we are ultimately one. I merely reciprocated with your way of speaking to Me. If we are ultimately one, then neither of our statements has any meaning."

PURPORT

The Absolute Truth is one, but a living entity's material body, which is made of the five gross material elements, is different from other material bodies. The sages had already seen their father worship the lotus feet of the Lord and so there was no need for their question.

TEXT 24

मनसावचसादृष्ट्यागृह्यतेऽन्यैरपीन्द्रियैः ।
अहमेवनमत्तोऽन्यदितिबुध्यध्वमञ्जसा ॥२४॥

manasā vacasā dṛṣṭyā gṛhyate 'nyair apīndriyaiḥ
aham eva na matto 'nyad iti budhyadhvam añjasā

Whatever is perceived by the mind and senses is nothing but a manifestation of Me. This should be understood by an unbiased examination of the truth.

COMMENTARY

The Lord here explains that since everything is the expansion of His potency, He is not different from anything. Nothing can exist separately from the Supreme Personality of Godhead, and thus everything shares in the Lord's nature.

PURPORT

The Supreme Lord is one without a second. Therefore, whatever one perceives with his eyes and other senses must be considered in relationship with the Supreme Lord.

TEXT 25

गुणेष्वाविशतेचेतोगुणाश्चेतसिचप्रजाः ।
जीवस्यदेह उभयंगुणाश्चेतोमदात्मनः ॥२५॥

guṇeṣv āviśate ceto guṇāś cetasi ca prajāḥ
jīvasya deha ubhayaṁ guṇāś ceto mad-ātmanaḥ

My dear sons, the mind has the propensity to enter into material sense objects, and material sense objects enter into the mind. However, both the mind and the material sense objects are designations that cover the pure spirit soul, who is My eternal part and parcel.

COMMENTARY

The sons of Brahmā thought, "My dear Lord, if we are unintelligent, You definitely stated that everything is a manifestation of You alone because everything is the expansion of Your potency. It thus appears that there is an intimate relationship between the mind and the objects of the senses. We simply want to ascertain how the mind can be detached from the objects of the senses, and please be merciful and enlighten us."

The Lord replied, "My dear sons, what you say is very true. Although the living entities are My eternal parts and parcels, in conditioned life they artificially identify with the mind and thus become attracted to enjoy the objects of the senses. As long as the soul identifies with the mind, desires for sense gratification will continue to harass him. But, because the mind and sense objects actually have no connection with the soul, they should be rejected. In this way, one can become free from the dualities of material existence."

PURPORT

The conditioned living entities in the material world are under the control of the three modes of material nature, whereas the Supreme Personality of Godhead, being eternally liberated, is transcendental to the three modes of material nature. Material sense objects enter into the minds of the conditioned living entities, and their minds run after the material sense objects.

TEXT 26

गुणेषुचाविशच्चित्तमभीक्ष्णंगुणसेवया ।
गुणाश्चचित्तप्रभवामद्रूप उभयंत्यजेत् ॥२६॥

guṇeṣu cāviśac cittam abhīkṣṇaṁ guṇa-sevayā
guṇāś ca citta-prabhavā mad-rūpa ubhayaṁ tyajet

One who has thus attained Me, understanding that he is not different from Me, realizes that the material mind is absorbed within the sense objects because of constant sense gratification, and that the material objects are present within the material mind. Having understood My transcendental nature, he gives up both the material mind and its objects.

COMMENTARY

It is very difficult to restrain the mind from the object of the senses, because of the mind's false ego. Becoming detached from the mind does not mean that one stops thinking, but instead means that one must purify the mind of its material propensities by engaging it in the devotional service of the Lord. It is practically seen that the objects of the senses enter the mind at every moment, as if flowing in a continuous stream. Considering this, how is it possible to detach the mind from thoughts of sense gratification? Such an endeavor appears to be an attempt to deny the mind's very existence. What is required is to engage the objects of the senses in the proper way—for the satisfaction of the Supreme Personality of Godhead. In this way, there will be no harm of sense objects entering the mind because the intelligence will dictate that they all be used in devotional service and not for personal enjoyment. There is no question of artificial renunciation, which can serve no useful purpose. Without engagement in the devotional service of the Lord, mere renunciation is of no lasting value.

PURPORT

While residing in this material world, one engages in the service of the three modes of material nature. It is the modes of nature that capture one's mind. Therefore, one should come to understand how the individual soul and the Supersoul are both fully transcendental to the three modes of material nature.

TEXT 27

जाग्रत्स्वप्नःसुषुप्तंचगुणतोबुद्धिवृत्तयः ।
तासांविलक्षणोजीवःसाक्षित्वेनविनिश्चितः ॥२७॥

jāgrat svapnaḥ suṣuptaṁ ca guṇato buddhi-vṛttayaḥ
tāsāṁ vilakṣaṇo jīvaḥ sākṣitvena viniścitaḥ

The three functions of intelligence—wakefulness, dreaming, and deep sleep—are caused by the three modes of material nature. It has been ascertained that the spirit soul is the seer, and is completely aloof from these three states.

COMMENTARY

Actually, the pure spirit soul has no relationship with material sense objects or the materially contaminated mind. So, giving up the materially contaminated mind and the material sense objects means to give up a misconception. The state of awakening is born from the mode of goodness, the state of dreaming is born from the mode of passion, and the state of deep sleep is born from the mode of ignorance. However, the pure living entity is beyond these three states of being, which are functions of the intelligence. The living entity is actually aloof from them as a witness.

PURPORT

The three states of the living entity—wakefulness, dreaming, and deep sleep—which are functions of the intelligence, are born from material modes of goodness, passion, and ignorance, respectively. The liberated living entity is actually aloof from these three states, and is not under the control of the three modes of material nature. He is simply a witness.

TEXT 28

यर्हिसंसृतिबन्धोऽयमात्मनोगुणवृत्तिदः ।
मयितुर्येस्थितोजह्यात्त्यागस्तद्गुणचेतसाम् ॥२८॥

yarhi saṁsṛti-bandho 'yam ātmano guṇa-vṛtti-daḥ
mayi turye sthito jahyāt tyāgas tad guṇa-cetasām

Due to being bound by material intelligence, a conditioned living entity is dragged towards material sense enjoyment. I am the fourth stage of consciousness, beyond wakefulness, dreaming and deep sleep and so you should become established in Me and thus give up the bondage to material nature. In this way, you can automatically become detached from the material sense objects and the mind.

COMMENTARY

Here Lord Kṛṣṇa answers the questions that the sages had placed before Lord Brahmā. In his constitutional position, the spirit soul has nothing to do with the objects of the senses and the three modes of material nature. It is due to the conditioned soul's false identification with the material body that the modes of nature engage him in illusory activities. When this false identification is given up, the soul is freed from the illusory engagements forced upon him by the modes of nature. The conditioned souls cannot free themselves from material bondage simply by their own endeavors. They must surrender to the Supreme Personality of Godhead and depend upon His mercy.

PURPORT

Being enticed by the material sense objects, one falls into the bondage of material existence. In his constitutional position, the spirit soul is transcendental to the three modes of material nature, and when he separates himself from the influence of these modes by becoming devoted to the Supreme Lord, he can be freed from all desires for material enjoyment.

TEXT 29

अहङ्कारकृतंबन्धमात्मनोऽर्थविपर्ययम् ।
विद्वान्निर्विद्यसंसारचिन्तांतुर्येस्थितस्त्यजेत् ॥२९॥

ahaṅkāra-kṛtaṁ bandham ātmano 'rtha-viparyayam
vidvān nirvidya saṁsāra-cintāṁ turye sthitas tyajet

The living entity has been placed in bondage by the false ego, which awards him the opposite of what he had actually hoped for. Therefore, an intelligent person should give up his constant anxiety to enjoy material life and remain situated in the Supreme Lord, who exists beyond the functions of material consciousness.

COMMENTARY

A living entity's material bondage continues as long as he remains in the bodily conception of life. An intelligent person should understand this fact very carefully and then become detached from material existence, which creates many unwanted conditions, and which covers his constitutional nature of eternity, knowledge and bliss. One who transfers his attention from the objects of the senses to the Lord will no longer have to fear material existence.

PURPORT

The living entity becomes misguided from his real self-interest due to false ego. This is the cause of material entanglement. One who takes shelter of the transcendental Personality of Godhead will gradually lose interest in material life, so that he will remain steady on the transcendental platform. Being thus situated, one will take pleasure in cultivating Kṛṣṇa consciousness because the taste for material enjoyment has slackened due to an awakening of detachment within the heart. Devotional service to the Lord is the platform of transcendence.

TEXT 30

यावन्नानार्थधीःपुंसोननिवर्तेतयुक्तिभिः ।
जागर्त्यपिस्वपन्नज्ञःस्वप्नेजागरणंयथा ॥३०॥

yāvan nānārtha-dhīḥ puṁso na nivarteta yuktibhiḥ
jāgarty api svapann ajñaḥ svapne jāgaraṇaṁ yathā

As instructed by Me, one should fix the mind on Me without deviation. If one continues to have various objectives in life instead of seeing how everything can be dovetailed in My devotional service, then although believing oneself to be awake, one is actually dreaming due to lack of absorption on the transcendental platform, just as one may dream that one has awakened while still sleeping.

COMMENTARY

Until one has practically become detached from fruitive activities by engagement in devotional service, his life of sense gratification will continue. Although he may accept some path of liberation, and thus consider himself to be "saved," he will remain in material existence. Such a person is certainly in illusion and is compared to one who dreams that he has awakened, although he is still sleeping.

PURPORT

Those whose minds are absorbed in something other than the Supreme Lord, who is one without a second, will remain bound to material desires for sense gratification. Although such a person may have some understanding of his conditioned state of existence, and the means for attaining liberation, and thus proudly advertise himself as a liberated soul, he will remain attached on the material platform. While sleeping, one may dream that he has awakened, although this is not a fact. Similarly, one may understand the distinction between the body and the soul and thus think that he had become liberated, while continuing to display all the symptoms of one who is absorbed in materialistic life.

TEXT 31

असत्त्वादात्मनोऽन्येषांभावानांतत्कृताभिदा ।
गतयोहेतवश्चास्यमृषास्वप्नदृशोयथा ॥३१॥

asattvād ātmano 'nyeṣāṁ bhāvānāṁ tat-kṛtā bhidā
gatayo hetavaś cāsya mṛṣā svapna-dṛśo yathā

Any condition of life that is thought to be separate from the Supreme Personality of Godhead has no real existence, like something experienced in a dream. Just as a dreaming person sees himself engaged in many different activities, the conditioned soul imagines that he performs fruitive activities.

COMMENTARY

Although the Haṁsa-avatāra has condemned the conception of duality within the material world, the *Vedas* have prescribed *varṇāśrama-dharma*, which divides human society according to occupational duties and spiritual statuses. How can these two things be reconciled? The answer is given in this verse. The words *anyeṣām bhāvānām* refer not to the Vedic understanding, but to conception of life concocted due to false identification with the material body and mind. Of course, the divisions of the *varṇāśrama* system are also based on this illusion, but they are arranged in such a way as to gradually bring one to the point of enlightenment in spiritual understanding. Being the Lord's creation, this material world is not false, as imagined by some less-intelligent philosophers. This world is real and the living entities are real, but the identification of the living entities with this material world is false. The example is sometimes given of a rabbit with horns. Rabbits are real and horns are real but the sight of a rabbit with horns in a dream is illusion. Similarly, it is a kind of dream of the conditioned soul that he has a permanent relationship with this material world.

PURPORT

An object that was seen in a dream does not influence a person when he is awake. Similarly, when the living entity is liberated from material bondage, he no longer feels obliged to follow the principles of *varṇāśrama*, which are born from attachment to the body, nor is he attracted to enjoying heavenly pleasure, which can be obtained by performing the fruitive rituals mentioned in the *Vedas*.

TEXT 32

योजागरेबहिरनुक्षणधर्मिणोऽर्थान्भुङ्क्तेसमस्तकरणैर्हृदितत्सदृक्षान् ।
स्वप्नेसुषुप्त उपसंहरतेस एकःस्मृत्यन्वयात्त्रिगुणवृत्तिदृगिन्द्रियेशः ॥३२॥

yo jāgare bahir anukṣaṇa-dharmiṇo 'rthān
bhuṅkte samasta-karaṇair hṛdi tat-sadṛkṣān
svapne suṣupta upasaṁharate sa ekaḥ
smṛty-anvayāt tri-guṇa-vṛtti-dṛg indriyeśaḥ

While awake, the conditioned souls try to enjoy the fleeting experiences of this material world. While dreaming, he enjoys other illusory experiences within the mind, and in deep sleep, all such experiences are forgotten. By understanding these three states of wakefulness, dreaming, and deep sleep, the conditioned soul can realize that he is simply the witness and therefore transcendental.

COMMENTARY

One may first consider the three phases of consciousness mentioned above and then understand one's transcendental position as spirit soul. One experiences childhood, boyhood, adolescence, adulthood, middle age and old age, and throughout these phases, one is experiencing things while awake and while dreaming. The living entity is the same person throughout all such changes. He is the silent spectator of the three stages of consciousness. One may argue that it is actually the senses that experience during wakefulness and that it is the mind that experiences during dreams. However, the Lord here states, *indriyeśaḥ*: the living entity is actually the lord of the senses and mind, although temporarily he has become a victim of their influence. By Kṛṣṇa consciousness, one may resume one's rightful position as the master of the mind and senses.

PURPORT

The living entity experiences three stages of existence in the material world—wakefulness, dreaming, and deep sleep. While awake, the senses of the gross body are active, under the influence of time. While dreaming, although the living entity is untouched by the objects of the senses, he remains affected by them on the mental platform. In the state of deep sleep, the living entity forgets himself and the world.

TEXT 33

एवंविमृश्यगुणतोमनसस्त्र्यवस्थामन्माययामयिकृता इतिनिश्चितार्थाः ।
सञ्छिद्यहार्दमनुमानसदुक्तितीक्ष्णज्ञानासिनाभजतमाखिलसंशयाधिम् ॥३३॥

evaṁ vimṛśya guṇato manasas try-avasthā
man-māyayā mayi kṛtā iti niścitārthāḥ
sañchidya hārdam anumāna-sad-ukti-tīkṣṇa
jñānāsinā bhajata mākhila-saṁśayādhim

My dear sons, after carefully deliberating upon how these three mental states are born from the three modes of material nature, and thus created by My illusory energy, you should cut to pieces the false ego, which is the source of all doubts, with the sharpened

sword of knowledge, acquired by logical reflection upon the instructions of the sages and Vedic literatures. You should then worship Me, who am situated within the heart.

COMMENTARY

The three stages of the mind and intelligence are produced from the three modes of material nature, which are creations of the Lord's illusory energy, and thus have nothing to do with the spirit soul. By the help of the sharp sword of knowledge, acquired by logical analysis of the instructions of saintly persons and the *śāstra*, one should destroy all doubts and worship the Supreme Personality of Godhead with determination.

PURPORT

If one has attained spiritual knowledge, and is no longer influenced by the three stages of wakefulness, dreaming, and deep sleep, he vanquishes the spirit of sense enjoyment that had been directed by his materially conditioned mind, intelligence, and false ego, and engages in the devotional service of the Lord, so that all his doubts will be removed.

TEXT 34

ईक्षेतविभ्रममिदंमनसोविलासंदृष्टंविनष्टमतिलोलमलातचक्रम् ।
विज्ञानमेकमुरुधेवविभातिमायास्वप्नस्त्रिधागुणविसर्गकृतोविकल्पः ॥३४॥

īkṣeta vibhramam idaṁ manaso vilāsaṁ
dṛṣṭaṁ vinaṣṭam ati-lolam alāta-cakram
vijñānam ekam urudheva vibhāti māyā
svapnas tridhā guṇa-visarga-kṛto vikalpaḥ

One should see that the objects of this world are an illusion appearing within the mind, because material objects are temporarily manifested. They can be compared to the streaking red line created by whirling a blazing stick on fire. The spirit soul by nature exists in the single state of pure consciousness. However, in this world, the soul appears in many different forms and stages of existence. The modes of nature divide the soul's consciousness into wakefulness, dreaming, and deep sleep. All such varieties of perception, however, are actually *maya* and exist only like a dream.

COMMENTARY

After realizing that the spirit soul is distinct from the three stages of consciousness, one should carefully perceive how everything in this material world is illusory. One should give up the misconceptions of "I" and "Mine" with regards to this material world.

The conditioned soul has maintained this false misconception since time immemorial. That is why the mind is restless, making it appear like a wheel of fire. Now, the question may be raised, "If one has a vision of duality, how can he realize the Absolute Truth? The answer is, "The Absolute Truth is one but He appears to be many. The three stages of consciousness are created by the Lord's illusory energy, and so are temporary, like a dream."

PURPORT

The three states of wakefulness, dreaming, and deep sleep, which are born from the three modes of material nature, are actually illusory, and are only temporary manifestations. In the philosophy of the Māyāvādīs, these temporary manifestations are addressed as false. This understanding is false, however, because these manifestations are not false, but temporary. Until a living entity appreciates the sublime nature of the eternal spiritual pastimes of the supremely conscious person and the minutely conscious persons, his heart will remain enraptured by the mundane duality of material enjoyment and detachment.

When the remembrance of Kṛṣṇa's pastimes is awakened in the heart of a living entity, his propensity for enjoyment or renunciation is destroyed and his propensity for eternal service to the Supreme Lord is awakened.

TEXT 35

दृष्टिम्ततःप्रतिनिवर्त्यनिवृत्ततृष्णस्तूर्ष्णीभवेन्निजसुखानुभवोनिरीहः ।
सन्दृश्यतेक्वचयदीदमवस्तुबुद्धचात्यक्तंभ्रमायनभवेत्स्मृतिरानिपातात् ॥३५॥

dṛṣṭim tataḥ pratinivartya nivṛtta-tṛṣṇas
tūṣṇīṁ bhaven nija-sukhānubhavo nirīhaḥ
sandṛśyate kva ca yadīdam avastu-buddhyā
tyaktaṁ bhramāya na bhavet smṛtir ā-nipātāt

With the understanding of the temporary and illusory nature of the material world, and having pulled one's vision away from illusion, you should remain free from desires for material enjoyment. By experiencing the happiness of the soul, you should give up material speaking and activities. Even if you must be involved in material activities, like eating, you should remember that it is not ultimate reality, and that you have renounced it. By constantly living in this way, right up to the point of death, you will not again fall into illusion.

COMMENTARY

The Lord said, "Because the visible material world is illusory, and thus miserable, you should withdraw your vision from it and give up all desires for sense gratification. You should curtail material activities and talks of material subjects. You should simply take pleasure in the self within, knowing that this will free you from material bondage." Now, the question may arise, "It is impossible for an embodied soul to remain free from dealing with the external world and so will never become freed from material existence?" The answer is, "Even while performing activities of the material body, such as eating, this will not be the cause of illusion if one has given up the material conception of life, with the help of his intelligence." Therefore, until one gives up his body at the time of death, one should continue to treat material objects with a mood of detachment.

PURPORT

One who has attained the human form of life should not utilize material gain for gratifying his senses. There is no need to strive for material happiness, just as there is no point in endeavoring for distress. One should instead try to satisfy the Supreme Personality of Godhead by his execution of devotional service. One who is fully engaged in the devotional service of the Lord can understand that all kinds of material attachment simply increase material illusion. Step by step, one should detach himself from matter by fully attaching himself to the devotional service of the Lord.

TEXT 36

देहंचनश्वरमवस्थितमुत्थितंवासिद्धोनपश्यतियतोऽध्यगमत्स्वरूपम् ।
दैवादपेतमथदैववशादुपेतंवासोयथापरिकृतंमदिरामदान्धः ॥३६॥

deham ca naśvaram avasthitam utthitaṁ vā
siddho na paśyati yato 'dhyagamat svarūpam
daivād apetam atha daiva-vaśād upetaṁ
vāso yathā parikṛtaṁ madirā-madāndhaḥ

Just as a drunkard does not know whether his clothes have fallen off, or if he is still wearing them, a self-realized soul does not notice whether his temporary body is seated on an āsāna, standing, or walking about.

COMMENTARY

In these two verses, the condition of a liberated soul is described. When one has realized Brahman, he does not notice whether he is sitting, standing or walking. The example is given of an intoxicated person. He is so absorbed in himself by the influence of wine that he hardly notices even if his clothes fall off, or somebody is dressing him.

PURPORT

A self realized person has no interest in the enjoyable objects of this material world. Because he is situated in his eternal constitutional position, he sees that his temporary body and restless mind are products of matter and thus he always remains engaged in the transcendental service of the Supreme Lord. As a drunkard does not care about the state of his clothing, a self-realized soul is indifferent to and forgetful of material enjoyment.

TEXT 37

देहोऽपिदैववशगःखलुकर्मयावत्स्वारम्भकंप्रतिसमीक्षत एवसासुः ।
तंसप्रपञ्चमधिरूढसमाधियोगःस्वाप्नंपुनर्नभजतेप्रतिबुद्धवस्तुः ॥३७॥

deho 'pi daiva-vaśa-gaḥ khalu karma yāvat
svārambhakaṁ pratisamīkṣata eva sāsuḥ
taṁ sa-prapañcam adhirūḍha-samādhi-yogaḥ
svāpnaṁ punar na bhajate pratibuddha-vastuḥ

This material body, which certainly moves by the arrangement of providence, will certainly continue to exist, along with the life-air and senses, as long as one's karma is in effect. One who has attained absorption in the Lord through *samādhi*, and who is fixed in the absolute reality, will never again surrender to the material body and its manifestations, knowing it to be just like a body seen in a dream.

COMMENTARY

As long as one is destined to enjoy the results of his karma, one continues to remain within the material body, along with the life-air. The question may arise, "If a self-realized soul gives proper attention to the maintenance of his body, won't he again become attached to it?" Lord Kṛṣṇa herein states that one who is highly elevated in Kṛṣṇa consciousness, having understood Lord Kṛṣṇa to be the actual reality, never again surrenders to the illusory identification with the material body, which is just like the body seen in a dream.

PURPORT

The Supreme Lord alone is the eternal object of all kinds of relationships. As eternal servants of the Lord, His pure devotees, even while situated with their material bodies, do not forget Him. They do not become attached to the temporary activities of the insignificant states of awakening, dreaming, and deep sleep, because their only object of worship is the Supreme Personality of Godhead.

TEXT 38

मयैतदुक्तंवोविप्रागुह्यंयत्सांख्ययोगयोः ।
जानीतमागतंयज्ञंयुष्मद्धर्मविवक्षया ॥३८॥

mayaitad uktaṁ vo viprā guhyaṁ yat sāṅkhya-yogayoḥ
jānīta māgataṁ yajñaṁ yuṣmad-dharma-vivakṣayā

My dear *brāhmaṇas,* I have thus explained the confidential understanding of Sāṅkhya and *aṣṭāṅga-yoga.* You should understand that I am Lord Viṣṇu, having come here to instruct you about your actual religious duties.

COMMENTARY

To strengthen their faith in His teachings, the Lord said, "My dear *brāhmaṇas,* Sāṅkhya, or the science of the self, and *astāṅga-yoga,* the process of linking with the Supreme, have thus been revealed to you. In the future, it will be remembered that Lord Mādhava, in the form of Haṁsa, instructed Brahmā and his sons."

PURPORT

The Supreme Lord said, "I am the Supreme Absolute Truth and I have come here to reveal the confidential understandings that were incomprehensible to the misguided preachers of Sāṅkhya and Vedānta. I am the object of everyone's worship, the supreme instructor, and that which is to be known."

TEXT 39

अहंयोगस्यसांख्यस्यसत्यस्यर्तस्यतेजसः ।
परायणंद्विजश्रेष्ठाःश्रियःकीर्तेर्दमस्यच ॥३९॥

ahaṁ yogasya sāṅkhyasya satyasyartasya tejasaḥ
parāyaṇaṁ dvija-śreṣṭhāḥ śriyaḥ kīrter damasya ca

O best of *brāhmaṇas*, please know that I am the ultimate shelter of Sāṅkhya, the *yoga* system, truthfulness, influence, opulence, fame, and self-control.

COMMENTARY

The sons of Brahmā were astonished by the presentation of the Supreme Personality of Godhead. They thought, "What wonderful instructions we have just heard." The Supreme Lord thus said to them, "O best of the *brāhmaṇas*, I am the supreme shelter of Sāṅkhya yoga, truthfulness, equanimity, prowess, and influence."

PURPORT

The Lord said, "I am the ultimate goal of the various systems of *abhidheya* followed by the different sects."

TEXT 40

मांभजन्तिगुणाःसर्वेनिर्गुणंनिरपेक्षकम् ।
सुहृदंप्रियमात्मानंसाम्यासङ्गादयोऽगुणाः ॥४०॥

māṁ bhajanti guṇāḥ sarve nirguṇaṁ nirapekṣakam
suhṛdaṁ priyam ātmānaṁ sāmyāsaṅgādayo 'guṇāḥ

The best of all transcendental qualities, such as being transcendentally situated, detached from matter, the well-wisher of everyone, the most dear Supersoul of all living beings, equally disposed everywhere, and eternally liberated, are found in Me, their worshipable Lord.

COMMENTARY

Because Lord Kṛṣṇa has been describing His own nature, the sons of Brahmā might doubt that He has become proud, which is a material quality. Understanding this, the Lord clarifies His position in the present verse.

The Lord said, "My body is not material, made of the five gross elements like that of the conditioned souls. My body is completely spiritual—eternal, full of knowledge, and full of bliss. Indeed, the transcendental qualities worship Me." The Lord is called *nirapekṣakam* because He is never attached to material enjoyment, like the conditioned souls. Because He is the best well-wishing friend of His devotees, He is called *suhṛdam*. The word *priyam* indicates that the Lord is the supreme lovable person and thus has affectionate relationships with His devotees. The word *sāmya* indicates that the Lord remains neutral, even while situtated within the turmoil of the material world. It is therefore concluded that the Supreme Personality of Godhead is the reservoir of all transcendental qualities.

Śrīdhara Svāmī has also confirmed that the qualities of the Lord are transcendental and eternal. In the First Canto it is also described that all the personal characteristics of the Lord are eternally present in His form because there is no difference between the Lord and His body. This is also confirmed in the *Vedas* as follows:

na tasya kāryaṁ karaṇaṁ ca vidyate na tat-samaś cābhyadhikaś ca dṛśyate
parāsya śaktir vividhaiva śrūyate svābhāvikī jñāna-bala-kriyā ca

"The Supreme Brahman has no material senses. He has nothing to do, and there is no one equal to or greater than Him. Everything is performed naturally and systematically by His multifarious energies." (*Śvetāśvatara Upaniṣad* 6.8)

PURPORT

The Supreme Personality of Godhead said, "Do not come to a conclusion of impersonalism because it is sometimes stated that I am devoid of qualities. I possess all transcendental qualities, I am situated beyond the modes of material nature, I am the best well-wisher of My devotees, I am the shelter of all, and I am the ultimate goal of everyone. Transcendental qualities, such as equanimity, and freedom from bad association, are eternally present in Me. I cannot be understood by those who are in the bodily concept of life."

TEXT 41

इतिमेछिन्नसन्देहामुनयःसनकादयः ।
सभाजयित्वापरयाभक्त्यागृणतसंस्तवैः ॥४१॥

iti me chinna-sandehā munayaḥ sanakādayaḥ
sabhājayitvā parayā bhaktyāgṛṇata saṁstavaiḥ

Lord Kṛṣṇa continued: My dear Uddhava, all the doubts of the sages, headed by Sanaka, were thus destroyed by My words. They then worshiped Me with loving devotion and glorified Me by offering transcendental prayers.

COMMENTARY

The Supreme Lord said, "My dear Uddhava, having received My instructions, the sages, headed by Sanaka, became freed from all doubts and so they lovingly offered Me prayers and worship."

PURPORT

Those who are detached from material enjoyment have no doubts whatsoever. The sages, headed by Sanaka, attained that transcendental platform and offered prayers and worship to the Lord.

TEXT 42

तैरहंपूजितःसंयक् संस्तुतःपरमर्षिभिः ।
प्रत्येयायस्वकंधामपश्यतःपरमेष्ठिनः ॥४२॥

tair ahaṁ pūjitaḥ saṁyak saṁstutaḥ paramarṣibhiḥ
pratyeyāya svakaṁ dhāma paśyataḥ parameṣṭhinaḥ

The sages, headed by Sanaka Ṛṣi, worshiped and glorified Me to their full satisfaction. Then, as Brahmā and his sons looked on, I departed for My own abode.

COMMENTARY

The Supreme Lord said, "After I was worshiped and glorified by the great sages, I returned to My own abode, as Brahmā looked on."

Thus ends the translation of the Seventh Chapter of the Uddhava-gītā entitled "**The Haṁsa-avatāra Answers the Questions of the Sons of Brahmā**" *with the commentaries of Śrīla Viśvanātha Cakravartī Ṭhākura and chapter summary and purports by Śrīla Bhaktisiddhānta Sarasvatī Ṭhākura.*

Chapter 8

Lord Kṛṣṇa Explains the Yoga System to Śrī Uddhava

CHAPTER SUMMARY

In this chapter, Lord Kṛṣṇa explains to Uddhava that devotional service is the topmost *sādhana*. He also speaks about the process of meditation.

Śrī Uddhava wanted to know which is the best process for achieving the ultimate goal of life, and he also wanted to hear the superexcellence of pure devotional service. The Supreme Lord replied to him by explaining how the religious duties prescribed in the *Vedas* had been lost at the time of the previous annihilation. At the beginning of the new creation, the Supreme Lord instructed these religious principles to Brahmā. Brahmā repeated it to Manu, Manu spoke it to the sages, headed by Bhṛgu, who in turn instructed these eternal religious duties to the demigods and demons. Because of the living entities' varieties of material desires, religious principles were elaborately explained in different ways. Thus, different philosophies came into being, including some atheistic doctrines. Because the living entity, bewildered by illusion, is incapable of ascertaining his eternal benefit, he mistakenly identifies ordinary vows of penance, austerity, etc., to be the ultimate spiritual practice. But, the actual means of achieving happiness is to renounce material desires and become self-satisfied by surrendering everything at the lotus feet of the Supreme Lord. This drives away selfish desires for sense gratification and liberation.

The Lord then described the superior process of devotional service, which destroys countless sinful reactions and produces many ecstatic transformations, such as the standing of the bodily hairs on end. Pure devotion, having the power to purify the heart, enables one to achieve the association of the Supreme Personality of Godhead, and because the devotee is very dear to the Lord and is always close to Him, he is able in turn to purify the entire universe. Pious activities, such as giving charity and observing religious vows do not have that potency. By virtue of his unflinching devotion to the Lord, the devotee can never be completely diverted by the objects of sense enjoyment, even if he is not able to gain control over his senses in the beginning. One desiring to attain the perfection of life is advised to give up all material processes of elevation, as well as the association of women. He should then merge his mind constantly in thought of Lord Kṛṣṇa. Finally, the Lord instructed Śrī Uddhava about the true object of meditation.

TEXT 1

श्रीउद्धव उवाच
वदन्तिकृष्णश्रेयांसिबहूनिब्रह्मवादिनः ।
तेषांविकल्पप्राधान्यमुताहो एकमुख्यता ॥१॥

śrī-uddhava uvāca
vadanti kṛṣṇa śreyāṁsi bahūni brahma-vādinaḥ
teṣāṁ vikalpa-prādhānyam utāho eka-mukhyatā

Śrī Uddhava said: My dear Kṛṣṇa, learned sages who explain the Vedic literature recommend a variety of processes for achieving the ultimate goal of life. Considering the variety of viewpoints, kindly explain to me whether all of them are equally important, or if only one of them is supreme.

COMMENTARY

In this chapter, the supremacy of devotional service, which brings Śrī Kṛṣṇa under control, and the method by which devotees who desire liberation meditate upon the Supreme Lord are described.

PURPORT

Śrī Uddhava requests further clarification regarding what he has already heard from the Lord. He also wishes for the Lord to clearly state what is the foremost *sādhana*. Uddhava said, "The sages who know Brahman have propounded various paths for attaining the perfection of life. Please tell me which of those *sādhanas* is best and most effective."

TEXT 2

भवतोदाहृतःस्वामिन्भक्तियोगोऽनपेक्षितः ।
निरस्यसर्वतःसङ्गंयेनत्वय्याविशेन्मनः ॥२॥

bhavatodāhṛtaḥ svāmin bhakti-yogo 'napekṣitaḥ
nirasya sarvataḥ saṅgaṁ yena tvayy āviśen manaḥ

My dear Lord, You have clearly explained the process of unalloyed devotional service, by which one can free himself from all material association, thus enabling him to fix his mind on You without deviation.

COMMENTARY

In this chapter it is firmly established that pure devotional service is the superexcellent process for absorbing the mind in the Absolute Truth, Lord Kṛṣṇa. Next, the question will be raised whether everyone can engage in devotional service, or is such a practice limited to a select few.

PURPORT

The mind is very unsteady, and so by utilizing one's good intelligence, one must remain firmly fixed in devotional service so that one can ultimately attain the association of the Supreme Lord in His transcendental abode. This is the only intention of Lord Kṛṣṇa's speaking with Śrī Uddhava.

TEXT 3

श्रीभगवानुवाच
कालेननष्टाप्रलयेवाणीयंवेदसंज्ञिता ।
मयादौब्रह्मणेप्रोक्ताधर्मोयस्यांमदात्मकः ॥३॥

śrī-bhagavān uvāca
kālena naṣṭā pralaye vāṇīyaṁ veda-saṁjñitā
mayādau brahmaṇe proktā dharmo yasyāṁ mad-ātmakaḥ

The Supreme Lord said: In the course of time, Vedic knowledge appeared to be lost at the time of annihilation. Then, when the universe was recreated, I again imparted Vedic knowledge to Brahmā because I am the religious principles personified.

COMMENTARY

The Supreme Lord said, "O Uddhava, I am the reservoir of all pleasure, and My devotees directly engage under the direction of My *hlādinī*, or pleasure-giving, potency. Somehow or other, one must fix one's mind upon Me, and that is not possible without devotional service. One who has not developed his attraction for Me cannot restrain the senses from inferior engagements. Since other Vedic processes do not actually award Me to the practitioner, they cannot offer the highest benefit in life. The transcendental sound of the *Vedas* is itself the highest evidence, but one whose senses and mind are entangled in sense gratification and mental speculation, and whose heart is therefore covered by material dust, cannot directly receive the transcendental Vedic message. Thus one cannot appreciate the exalted position of My devotional service."

PURPORT

The transcendental objective is distinct from the objects enjoyed by material senses, and is realized by the reception of transcendental sound vibration. In the conditional state of existence, a living entity is not capable of appreciating the transcendental sound vibration of the *Vedas*. Four-headed Brahmā was instructed by the Supreme Lord about the supreme religious principles but for those who are attached to sense gratification, *bhāgavata dharma* is not easily understood.

TEXT 4

तेनप्रोक्तास्वपुत्रायमनवेपूर्वजायसा ।
ततोभृग्वादयोऽगृह्णन्सप्तब्रह्ममहर्षयः ॥४॥

tena proktā sva-putrāya manave pūrva-jāya sā
tato bhṛgv-ādayo 'gṛhṇan sapta brahma-maharṣayaḥ

Lord Brahmā instructed this Vedic knowledge to his eldest son, Manu, who in turn instructed it to the seven great sages, headed by Bhṛgu.

TEXTS 5-7

तेभ्यःपितृभ्यस्तत्पुत्रादेवदानवगुह्यकाः ।
मनुष्याःसिद्धगन्धर्वाःसविद्याधरचारणाः ॥५॥
किन्देवाःकिन्नरानागारक्षःकिम्पुरुषादयः ।
बह्व्यस्तेषांप्रकृतयोरजःसत्त्वतमोभुवः ॥६॥

याभिर्भूतानिभिद्यन्तेभूतानांपतयस्तथा ।
यथाप्रकृतिसर्वेषांचित्रावाचःस्रवन्ति हि ॥७॥

tebhyaḥ pitṛbhyas tat-putrā deva-dānava-guhyakāḥ
manuṣyāḥ siddha-gandharvāḥ sa-vidyādhara-cāraṇāḥ

kindevāḥ kinnarā nāgā rakṣaḥ-kimpuruṣādayaḥ
bahvyas teṣāṁ prakṛtayo rajaḥ-sattva-tamo-bhuvaḥ

yābhir bhūtāni bhidyante bhūtānāṁ patayas tathā
yathā-prakṛti sarveṣāṁ citrā vācaḥ sravanti hi

From the forefathers, headed by Bhṛgu Muni and other sons of Brahmā, appeared many children and descendants, who assumed different forms as demigods, demons, human beings, Guhyakas, Siddhas, Gandharvas, Vidyādharas, Cāraṇas, Kindevas, Kinnaras, Nāgas, Kimpuruṣas, and so on. All of the many universal species, along with their respective leaders, appeared with different natures and desires generated from the three modes of material nature. Therefore, because of the different natures and desires of the living entities within the universe, different statements regarding religious principles have come into existence.

COMMENTARY

Many people wonder why the Vedic literatures recommend so many different paths of advancement. The answer is given herein. Bhṛgu, Marīci, Atri, Aṅgirā, Pulastya, Pulaha, and Kratu are the seven great sages within the universe. The Kindevas are a race of human beings who are, like the demigods, are without fatigue, perspiration, and body odor. One might wonder, *kiṁ devāḥ*, "Are they demigods?" They are a species of human beings that reside on another planet within the universe. The Kinnaras are so called this because, *kiñcin narāḥ*, they are "something like human beings." The Kimpuruṣas also resemble human beings and so it might be asked, *kiṁ puruṣāḥ*: "Are these human beings?" They are a species of monkeys that are something like human beings. Why are there various paths recommended in the *Vedas*? Because people have various desires due to being under the clutches of the three modes of material nature. Hence, there are different religious systems.

PURPORT

According to the degree of aversion to the Supreme Lord, Vedic *mantras* have taken various shapes to fulfill the desires of sense enjoyers. Thus, the proliferation of Vedic processes indicates only the variety of material illusion and not a variety of ultimate purpose. The ultimate purpose of many paths recommended in the *Vedas* is one—to revive one's forgotten relationship with the Supreme Personality of Godhead.

TEXT 8

एवंप्रकृतिवैचित्र्याद्भिद्यन्तेमतयोनृणाम् ।
पारम्पर्येणकेषाञ्चित्पाषण्डमतयोऽपरे ॥८॥

evaṁ prakṛti-vaicitryād bhidyante matayo nṛṇām
pāramparyeṇa keṣāñcit pāṣaṇḍa-matayo 'pare

Thus, due to the great variety of desires among human beings, various philosophies have come into existence. These philosophies have been handed down through tradition, custom, and disciplic succession. There are other teachers who present atheistic philosophies.

COMMENTARY

The word *pāramparyeṇa* means "through disciplic succession." Atheistic philosophies are meant for those who are very foolish and opposed to the purport of the *Vedas*. Neem trees, tamarind trees, and poisonous trees are situated on the banks of the river Ganges. Although they drink the pure and sweet water of the Ganges through their roots, they produce bitter, sour, or poisonous fruit. Similarly, those who are atheistic or demoniac utilize Vedic knowledge to produce bitter or poisonous fruit in the form of atheistic or materialistic philosophies. This is the purport of this verse.

PURPORT

While viewing the variegatedness of the material world, materialistic people are distracted from the understanding of the eternal truth. Following in the footsteps of atheistic philosophers, many unfortunate people are misguided and thus miss the opportunity afforded by the human form of life. Acceptance of principles that are contrary to the *Vedas* is a prime example of misfortune.

TEXT 9

मन्मायामोहितधियःपुरुषाःपुरुषर्षभ ।
श्रेयोवदन्त्यनेकान्तंयथाकर्मयथारुचि ॥९॥

man-māyā-mohita-dhiyaḥ puruṣāḥ puruṣarṣabha
śreyo vadanty anekāntaṁ yathā-karma yathā-ruci

O best among men, the intelligence of human beings is bewildered by My illusory energy and thus, according to their inclinations, they propagate various means for attaining what they feel to be the ultimate good.

COMMENTARY

The word *anekānta* means "different kinds."

PURPORT

According to one's individual way of doing things (*yathā-karma*) and one's personal preference (*yathā-ruci*), one speaks to others about what is good for them. Everyone thinks, "What is good for me is good for everyone." Sometimes people worship five demigods for the fulfillment of their desires, and sometimes they become intoxicated by the philosophy of impersonalism. Thus, in various ways, people view life from their limited perspectives and fail to understand that service to the Supreme Personality of Godhead is the ultimate goal of life. Some of them pose as spiritual masters, and some of them assume the role of disciples. In this way, they fall into an ocean of *anarthas* because of their lack of attachment for spiritual life, being bereft of the Lord's devotional service. Being without *sādhu-saṅga*, they are unable to properly worship the Supreme Lord and this induces them to accept more and more *anarthas*. The person who has no faith in the Supreme Lord, who has no *sādhu-saṅga*, and does not worship the Lord, is certainly full of *anarthas*. Being mad after material enjoyment, they have no taste for spiritual life and are thus denied the opportunity of realizing the Absolute Truth.

TEXT 10

धर्ममेकेयशश्चान्येकामंसत्यंदमंशमम् ।
अन्येवदन्तिस्वार्थंवा ऐश्वर्यंत्यागभोजनम् ।
केचिद्यज्ञंतपोदानंव्रतानिनियमान्यमान् ॥१०॥

dharmam eke yaśaś cānye kāmaṁ satyaṁ damaṁ śamam
anye vadanti svārthaṁ vā aiśvaryaṁ tyāga-bhojanam
kecid yajñaṁ tapo dānaṁ vratāni niyamān yamān

Some say that happiness is obtained as the result of performing pious activities. Others say that fame, sense gratification, speaking the truth, control of the senses, peacefulness, fulfilling one's self interest, political influence, wealth, detachment, performance of sacrifice and austerities, giving in charity, the observance of vows, or the performance of one's occupational duties are the causes of happiness.

COMMENTARY

The *karma-mīmāṁsakas* say that one should not waste time worrying about a kingdom of God that no one has ever seen and from which no one has ever returned. Rather, one should expertly utilize the laws of *karma*, performing fruitive activities in such a way that one will always be well situated. The authors of the *kāvya* and *alaṅkāra* literatures say that as long as the glories of a person is sung in this world, he will be able to enjoy life in the heavenly planets for thousands of years. Sages like Vātsāyana preach the fulfillment of lusty desires to be the objective of life. Others propagate the idea that truthfulness, self-control, and peacefulness are the essence of religion. The materialists say that the accumulation of wealth is one's true self-interest. According to the followers of Cāvāka, eating voraciously is the true religion. The followers of the *Vedas* say that the performance of sacrifice and austerities, and observance of vows are the activities of religion. Those who are advocates of the practice of *yoga* say that controlling the mind and senses is their religion.

PURPORT

Generally, people conclude that religiosity, economic development, and sense gratification, are life's true objectives. The quest for fame is a kind of happiness enjoyed on the mental platform, and is certainly illusory. There are many people who advocate that peace can be attained by remaining aloof from the intoxication of material enjoyment. Materialists become absorbed in the attainment of prosperity, ascetics become obsessed with rejecting material prosperity, while others are concerned by accumulating huge stocks of grains and other food items, but these are all *anarthas*.

TEXT 11

आद्यन्तवन्त एवैषांलोकाःकर्मविनिर्मिताः ।
दुःखोदर्कास्तमोनिष्ठाःक्षुद्रामन्दाःशुचार्पिताः ॥११॥

ādy-anta-vanta evaiṣāṁ lokāḥ karma-vinirmitāḥ
duḥkhodarkās tamo-niṣṭhāḥ kṣudrā mandāḥ śucārpitāḥ

These people obtain the temporary results of their work. Indeed, the meager and miserable situations they achieve simply award them unhappiness, because they are based on ignorance. Even while enjoying the fruits of their labor, such persons are constantly filled with lamentation.

COMMENTARY

Although materialistic people consider the fruits of their *karma* to be desirable, their lives are based on illusion, and thus they always meet with frustration.

PURPORT

Those who simply work hard to possess the temporary things of this world, considering them to be all in all, are not actually intelligent because such endeavors keep one in constant anxiety. Material nature is infinitely mutable, so that no position in this world is permanent.

TEXT 12

मय्यर्पितात्मनःसभ्यनिरपेक्षस्य सर्वतः ।
मयात्मनासुखंयत्तत्कुतःस्याद्विषयात्मनाम् ॥१२॥

mayy arpitātmanaḥ sabhya nirapekṣasya sarvataḥ
mayātmanā sukhaṁ yat tat kutaḥ syād viṣayātmanām

O saintly Uddhava, My all-blissful form manifests in the heart of one who has freed himself from all desires for sense gratification, and who is fully surrendered unto Me. The happiness he enjoys in My association cannot be compared to the happiness one experiences by gratification of the senses.

COMMENTARY

Devotional service to the Lord is the actual purport of the *Vedas.* The Supreme Lord said, "My devotees take great pleasure in relishing My transcendental forms and qualities. The *jñānīs,* who make great endeavors to control their mind, are not purified and so they are unable to attain My lotus feet."

This is confirmed by Nārada Munī:

kiṁ vā yogena sāṅkhyena nyāsa-svādhyāyayor api
kiṁ vā śreyobhir anyaiś ca na yatrātma-prado hariḥ

Transcendental practices that do not ultimately help one realize the Supreme Personality of Godhead are useless, be they mystic yoga practices, the analytical study of matter, severe austerity, the acceptance of *sannyāsa,* or the study of Vedic literature. All these may be very important aspects of spiritual advancement, but unless one understands the Supreme Personality of Godhead, Hari, all these processes are useless." (*Śrīmad-Bhāgavatam* 4.31.12)

PURPORT

Those who have realized that this material world is a place of temporary enjoyment and have thus employed all their senses in the service of the Supreme Lord, remain situated on the platform of eternal happiness. Since material pleasure cannot entice them, they always remain devoted to the Lord's service.

TEXT 13

अकिञ्चनस्यदान्तस्यशान्तस्यसमचेतसः ।
मयासन्तुष्टमनसःसर्वाःसुखमयादिशः ॥१३॥

akiñcanasya dāntasya śāntasya sama-cetasaḥ
mayā santuṣṭa-manasaḥ sarvāḥ sukha-mayā diśaḥ

One who does not desire anything of this world, and who is peaceful, self-controlled, always equal to everyone, and self-satisfied, finds only happiness wherever he goes.

COMMENTARY

A devotee who is always meditating upon Lord Kṛṣṇa experiences transcendental sound, touch, form, flavor, and aroma by means of transcendental senses. This is due to the causeless mercy of Lord Kṛṣṇa, upon whom ones mind and senses are completely engaged. Such a person finds only happiness wherever he goes. When a very wealthy man travels all over the world, wherever he may stay, he will enjoy the same luxurious standard of comfort. Similarly, one who is advanced in Kṛṣṇa consciousness constantly experiences transcendental happiness because Lord Kṛṣṇa is all-pervading. The word *kiñcana* indicates the so-called enjoyable things of this world. One who is *akiñcana* has correctly understood that material sense gratification is simply the glare of illusion, and therefore such a person is *dāntasya*, or self-controlled, *śāntasya*, or peaceful, and *mayā santuṣṭa-manasaḥ*, or completely satisfied with his transcendental experience of the Supreme Personality of Godhead.

PURPORT

Those who are capable of controlling their senses, who are not bewildered by material desires, who do not consider anyone as inferior to them, who are always satisfied in whichever condition they are put into by the Supreme Lord, and who have no inclination to possess anything of this material world, can experience happiness everywhere. In this regard, one should carefully consider this verse from *Śrī Caitanya-candrāmṛtaṁ* (5) by Prabhodānanda Sarasvatī:

kaivalyaṁ narakāyate tridaśa-pūr ākāśa-puṣpāyate
durdāntendriya-kāla-sarpa-paṭalī protkhāta-daṁṣṭrāyate
viśvaṁ pūrṇa-sukhāyate vidhi-mahendrādiś ca kīṭāyate
yat-kāruṇya-kaṭākṣa-vaibhava-vatāṁ taṁ gauram eva stumaḥ

For those who have attained the merciful sidelong glance of Lord Caitanya, impersonal liberation becomes as palatable as going to hell, the heavenly cities of the demigods become as enticing as flowers imagined to be floating in the sky, the poisonous fangs of the untameable black snakes of the senses are broken, the whole world becomes full of joy, and Brahmā, Indra, and all the other great demigods become as insignificant as tiny insects. Let us glorify that golden-complexioned Lord Caitanya.

TEXT 14

न पारमेष्ठ्यं न महेन्द्रधिष्ण्यं न सार्वभौमं न रसाधिपत्यम् ।
न योगसिद्धीरपुनर्भवं वा मय्यर्पितात्मेच्छति मद्विनान्यत् ॥१४॥

na pārameṣṭhyaṁ na mahendra-dhiṣṇyaṁ na sārvabhaumaṁ na rasādhipatyam
na yoga-siddhīr apunar-bhavaṁ vā mayy arpitātmecchati mad vinānyat

A pure devotee whose life is dedicated to Me has no desire for even the position of Brahmā or Indra, and so what to speak of becoming a lord of this world or of the lower planets. He is not interested in achieving the perfections of mystic yoga, nor even liberation from the cycle of birth and death, because his life is simply dedicated to Me.

COMMENTARY

The Supreme Lord said, "One who is surrendered to Me does not want the position of Brahmā, nor the happiness of merging into the existence of Brahman. 'As one surrenders unto Me, I reward him accordingly.' From this statement of Mine, one can understand how My thoughts remain absorbed in My devotees. A devotee who desires nothing other than Me lives in My association and thus relishes transcendental mellows."

PURPORT

The pure devotee of the Lord has no desire other than to render devotional service. He does not cherish anything else, not even the position of Brahmā or Indra, the domain of the whole world, sovereignty over the lower planets, material opulence, the eight types of mystic perfections, or freedom from the cycle of birth and death.

TEXT 15

नतथामेप्रियतम आत्मयोनिर्नशङ्करः ।
नचसङ्कर्षणोनश्रीर्नैवात्माचयथाभवान् ॥१५॥

na tathā me priyatama ātma-yonir na śaṅkaraḥ
na ca saṅkarṣaṇo na śrīr naivātmā ca yathā bhavān

My dear Uddhava, neither Lord Brahmā, Lord Śiva, Lord Saṅkarṣaṇa, the goddess of fortune, nor even My own self is as dear to Me as you are.

COMMENTARY

If someone were to ask the Lord, "How dear is Your devotee to you?" the reply is given in this verse. The Lord says, "Brahmā is My son, Śaṅkara is My expansion and My friend, Saṅkarṣaṇa is My brother, and Lakṣmīdevī is My wife and yet, none of them, and not even My own self, is as dear to Me as you are. My dear Uddhava, you are My devotee and so you are most dear to Me." This is also confirmed by Śrīdhara Svāmi. Although personalities like Brahmā are also the Lord's devotees, they are placed in responsible positions and thus are not exactly like the fully surrendered devotees. The Lord gives preference to a helpless devotee who depends completely on His mercy. The only way to obtain the Lord's mercy is through His causeless love, and the Lord is most lovingly inclined toward those devotees who are most dependent on Him, just as ordinary mothers and fathers worry more about their helpless children than about those who are self-sufficient. Because personalities like Brahmā have a sense of their unique identity and position, they had not been addressed here as devotees. This is not the case with personalities like Nanda and Yaśodā. Although they were parents of the Supreme Lord, they acted as His great devotees and thus were very dear to Him. In His pastimes, we invariably see that the Lord is fully controlled by His devotees. This is confirmed in the *Śrīmad-Bhāgavatam* (10.9.20),

nemam viriñco na bhavo na śrīr apy aṅga saṁśrayā
prasādaṁ lebhire gopī yat tat prāpa vimuktidāt

The Supreme Lord, who can award liberation to anyone, showed more mercy toward the ***gopīs*** than to Lord Brahmā, Lord Śiva, or even the goddess of fortune, who is His own wife and is associated with His body.

It may appear from this verse that among all the devotees, Uddhava is the best, but the *gopīs* are even superior to Uddhava. The dust from the lotus feet of *gopīs* is even superior to the *gopīs* themselves, and so that is what Śrī Uddhava had hoped to receive. This is the Vaiṣṇava conclusion.

PURPORT

Pure devotees of the Supreme Personality of Godhead are most dear to Him, even more than personalities like Brahmā, Śiva, Saṅkarṣaṇa, and Lakṣmī.

TEXT 16

निरपेक्षंमुनिंशान्तंनिर्वैरंसमदर्शनम् ।
अनुव्रजाम्यहंनित्यंपूयेयेत्यङ्घ्रिरेणुभिः ॥१६॥

nirapekṣaṁ muniṁ śāntaṁ nirvairaṁ sama-darśanam
anuvrajāmy ahaṁ nityaṁ pūyeyety aṅghri-reṇubhiḥ

Thinking that I will purify the entire universe with the dust from their lotus feet, I always follow in the footstep of My devotees, who are free from material desires, rapt in thought of My pastimes, peaceful, non-envious, and equal to all living entities.

COMMENTARY

Lord Kṛṣṇa is the all-powerful creator of the universe, beyond the dualities of material existence, and thus for Him there is no conception of purity or impurity. Still, it has been seen that sometimes the Lord desires to take the dust of the lotus feet of His pure devotees upon His head. It is the statement of the scriptures that without receiving the dust of the lotus feet of the pure devotees, one cannot attain the perfection of liberation from material exiastence. Lord Kṛṣṇa considered, "I have made it the rule that one can experience transcendental happiness only as a result advancement in devotional service, which is achieved by receiving the dust of the lotus feet of My devotees. Because I also desire to experience transcendental ecstasy, I accept the dust of My devotees' lotus feet." This is the purport of this verse.

PURPORT

The Supreme Personality of Godhead sends His devotees into this world of material enjoyment for the benefit of the fallen, conditioned souls. By observing the external behavior of the devotees, it is seen that they are detached, introspective, peaceful, friendly, and equipoised. The devotees of the Lord never engage in idle talks, they are the friends of all living entities, and they are equal to everyone. However, nondevotees cannot understand the plans and activities of the pure devotees.

TEXT 17

निष्किञ्चना मय्यनुरक्तचेतसःशान्तामहान्तोऽखिलजीववत्सलाः ।
कामैरनालब्धधियोजुषन्तितेयन्नैरपेक्ष्यंनविदुःसुखंमम ॥१७॥

niṣkiñcanā mayy anurakta-cetasaḥ śāntā mahānto 'khila-jīva-vatsalāḥ
kāmair anālabdha-dhiyo juṣanti te yan nairapekṣyaṁ na viduḥ sukhaṁ mama

Those with no material possessions, who are peaceful, free from pride, affectionate to all living entities, and have no desire for personal gratification, and who serve Me with undivided attention, enjoy in Me a happiness that cannot be known by those lacking such detachment from the material world.

COMMENTARY

The happiness which is derived by realizing the transcendental qualities of the Lord while performing devotional service is being described here. Some experts say that *jñānīs* who have no material assets can also attain this platform of transcendental ecstasy. That is why the Lord has made this statement, just to distinguish the devotees from such *jñānīs*. Pure devotees always desire to give Kṛṣṇa conscious happiness to others, and therefore they are called *mahāntaḥ*, or great souls. In the course of a devotee's service, many opportunities for sense gratification may arise, but a pure devotee is not tempted, and so he does not fall down from his exalted transcendental position.

PURPORT

Sense enjoyers are always bewildered by unlimited desires for personal aggrandizement, and so they are unable to comprehend the sublime position of the pure devotees. The devotees of the Lord are free from material desires, and so they are peaceful. They don't strive for material acquisitions, and they are the best well-wishers of people in general. Because the devotees are merged in the ocean of transcendental happiness derived by engagement in pure devotional service, they can never be diverted by mundane temptations. Because they are situated on the platform of spiritual bliss, they are detached from the bodily conception of life, and thus even a learned materialist cannot understand their sublime position.

TEXT 18

बाध्यमानोऽपिमद्भक्तोविषयैरजितेन्द्रियः ।
प्रायःप्रगल्भयाभक्त्याविषयैर्नाभिभूयते ॥१८॥

bādhyamāno 'pi mad-bhakto viṣayair ajitendriyaḥ
prāyaḥ pragalbhayā bhaktyā viṣayair nābhibhūyate

My dear Uddhava, if My devotee is not fully able to control his senses, he may sometimes be attracted to material enjoyment, but because of his engagement in devotional service, he will not be diverted by sense gratification.

COMMENTARY

The Lord said, "What to speak of those devotees who have attained the platform of *rati*, even neophyte devotees are assured of success. A neophyte devotee may sometimes be attracted to material enjoyment, but because of the strength of his sincere devotional service, he will not fall down from his exalted position." If a *jñānī* commits sinful activities, he immediately falls from his elevated position. A devotee, however, even though immature, never falls from the path of devotional service. Even if he displays occasional weakness, he is still considered a devotee if his devotion to Lord Kṛṣṇa is very strong.. This is confirmed by the Lord in the *Bhagavad-gītā* (9.30):

api cet su-durācāro bhajate mām ananya-bhāk
sādhur eva sa mantavyaḥ samyag vyavasito hi saḥ

Even if one commits the most abominable action, if he is engaged in devotional service, he is to be considered saintly because he is properly situated in his determination.

In this regard, two examples can be given. Sometimes, a heroic warrior is struck by the enemy's powerful weapon, but while simply tolerating the pain, he goes on to achieve victory. In the same way, one may be afflicted by a serious disease, but can be cured by taking the prescribed medicine.

PURPORT

For the benefit of neophyte devotees who cannot fully control their senses, the Supreme Lord said, "Even though a devotee could not control his senses and thus remains attached to sense gratification, if he wants to advance in devotional service to Me and thus enthusiastically engages in *sādhana-bhakti*, so that he may gradually come to the platform of *bhāva-bhakti*, then he will never meet with defeat."

TEXT 19

यथाग्निःसुसमृद्धार्चिःकरोत्येधांसिभस्मसात् ।
तथामद्विषयाभक्तिरुद्धवैनांसिकृत्स्नशः ॥१९॥

yathāgniḥ su-samṛddhārciḥ karoty edhāṁsi bhasmasāt
tathā mad-viṣayā bhaktir uddhavaināṁsi kṛtsnaśaḥ

O Uddhava, just as a blazing fire burns firewood to ashes, devotional service executed for My pleasure completely destroys the sinful reactions of My devotees.

COMMENTARY

If a devotee fails to control his senses and accidentally engages in sinful activities, the Lord will certainly burn to ashes all his sinful reactions, just as a blazing fire reduces wood to a pile of ashes.

PURPORT

As long as we are intoxicated by material enjoyment, our propensity for serving the Supreme Lord is like smoldering ashes. But, the moment our service attitude becomes prominent, our material inclinations are destroyed, just as a blazing fire burns wood to ashes. Lord Kṛṣṇa is glorious, and one who takes exclusive shelter of the Lord receives the unique benefits of devotional service to the Supreme Personality of Godhead.

TEXT 20

नसाधयतिमांयोगोनसांख्यंधर्म उद्धव ।
नस्वाध्यायस्तपस्त्यागोयथाभक्तिर्ममोर्जिता ॥२०॥

na sādhayati māṁ yogo na sāṅkhyaṁ dharma uddhava
na svādhyāyas tapas tyāgo yathā bhaktir mamorjitā

My dear Uddhava, neither through *aṣṭāṅga-yoga,* nor through impersonal monism or an analytical study of the Absolute Truth, nor through study of the *Vedas,* nor through austerities, charity or acceptance of *sannyāsa* can one satisfy Me as much as by developing unalloyed devotional service unto Me.

COMMENTARY

Devotional service is the only means by which one can satisfy the Supreme Lord. One may make Kṛṣṇa the goal of mystic yoga, Sāṅkhya philosophy, and so on, yet such activities do not please the Lord as much as direct loving service, which one practices by hearing and chanting about the Lord and executing His mission. A devotee should simply depend on Kṛṣṇa and should not unnecessarily complicate his loving service with tendencies toward fruitive work or mental speculation.

PURPORT

Many people think that they can achieve great benefit by studying the *Vedas*, by performing austerities, by renouncing material enjoyment, by cultivating Sāṅkhya philosophy, and by study of *Vedānta*. However, all of these practices are not required for engagement in the service of the Supreme Lord. Only unalloyed devotional service is capable of satisfying the Supreme Personality of Godhead.

TEXT 21

भक्त्याहमेकयाग्राह्यःश्रद्धयात्माप्रियःसताम् ।
भक्तिःपुनातिमन्निष्ठाश्वपाकानपिसम्भवात् ॥२१॥

bhaktyāham ekayā grāhyaḥ śraddhayātmā priyaḥ satām
bhaktiḥ punāti man-niṣṭhā śva-pākān api sambhavāt

Being very dear to the devotees and *sādhus*, I am attained through unflinching faith and devotional service. This *bhakti-yoga* system, which gradually increases attachment for Me, purifies even a human being born among dog-eaters. That is to say, everyone can be elevated to the spiritual platform by the process of *bhakti-yoga*.

COMMENTARY

So that no one will have any doubt about the best process for attaining the goal of life, the Supreme Lord says, "I am only obtained by devotional service, and not by any other processes, such as *yoga*, etc." Although the goal of Brahman, attained by means of *jñāna*, is found in the *śāstras*, it is to be understood that such cultivation of knowledge must be mixed with devotional service. Pious activities, such as the cultivation of knowledge, cannot help one achieve the Supreme Lord. They can only destroy one's sinful reactions. Devotional service destroys sinful reactions in a way that other processes, such as *jñāna*, cannot. In this regard, Śrīdhara Svāmī has concluded that devotional service to the Supreme Lord automatically destroys the fault of taking birth in a family of dog-eaters and completely purifies one.

PURPORT

The propensity for material enjoyment among those who are very fond of eating dogs is so strong that they have very little faith in the service of the Supreme Lord. Devotees of the Lord are not interested in eating abominable food. They give up all varieties of sense gratification and attract the attention of the Supreme Lord by remaining completely dependent upon Him. The devotees love the Supreme Lord as their most dear friend and as such, the Lord takes pleasure in their devotional activities. Simply by developing the propensity for rendering devotional service to the Lord, the people of this world who are now engaged in acts of sense gratification can become liberated from their material conception of life.

TEXT 22

धर्मःसत्यदयोपेतोविद्यावातपसान्विता ।
मद्भक्त्यापेतमात्मानंनसम्यक् प्रपुनाति हि ॥२२॥

dharmaḥ satya-dayopeto vidyā vā tapasānvitā
mad-bhaktyāpetam ātmānaṁ na samyak prapunāti hi

Truthfulness, compassion, religious principles, austerity, and knowledge cannot completely purify a person who is bereft of devotional service to Me.

COMMENTARY

Even though following religious principles and cultivating knowledge have the power of destroying one's sinful reactions, this is to be understood as true when such activities are combined with devotional service to the Lord. Without devotional service, these activities have very little strength. The word *vidyā* in this verse refers to the cultivation of knowledge.

PURPORT

Truthfulness, trying to remove others' distress, giving in charity, performing austerities, and practicing renunciation cannot thoroughly purify one's existence. They purify one to some extent, but the seed of material desires remains so that after some time, one will again return to a life of sense gratification. However, because service to the Supreme Lord is the ultimate religious principle, it is also the topmost purifying agent.

TEXT 23

कथंविनारोमहर्षंद्रवताचेतसाविना ।
विनानन्दाश्रुकलयाशुध्येद्भक्त्याविनाशयः ॥२३॥

kathaṁ vinā roma-harṣaṁ dravatā cetasā vinā
vinānandāśru-kalayā śudhyed bhaktyā vināśayaḥ

Without the manifestation of ecstatic symptoms of devotional service, such as the hairs standing on end, how can the heart melt? If the heart does not melt, how can tears of love flow from the eyes? Without the melting of the heart, and without tears flowing from the eyes, how can one render loving devotional service? Without devotional service, how can the consciousness be purified?

COMMENTARY

Devotional service, which produces symptoms of ecstasy, such as standing of the hair of the body on end, is the only means to completely purify the heart. Only devotional service is capable of melting the heart and not any other *sādhana.* How can the heart become purified without manifesting symptoms such as tears in the eyes, the hairs standing on end, and so on? Śrī Kṛṣṇa Caitanya, who had incarnated to deliver the people of Kali-yuga, said, "Even after studying the science of the Absolute Truth, as described in the *Upaniṣads,* if one does not hear the glories of Lord Hari, then the transformations of love of God, indicating the melting of the heart, such as the shedding of tears, will not manifest." Even as one continues to engage in the activities of Kṛṣṇa consciousness, if his heart does become purified, the tinge of impurity that does not allow him to directly see the Lord will remain. This impurity is burnt to ashes only by pure devotional service, and not by the small fire of the cultivation of knowledge.

PURPORT

One's heart cannot be purified while one is constantly engaged in material enjoyment. Our desires can be purified only by dovetailing them in the service of the Supreme Lord. If we don't engage ourselves in the Lord's service, then the spirit of material enjoyment will keep us forever bound to the fruits of our actions. When the heart melts, one sheds tears of love and the hair of the body stands on end. Until that time, material enjoyment, which is always mixed with frustration, will continue to misguide us.

TEXT 24

वाग्गद्गदाद्रवतेयस्यचित्तंरुदत्यभीक्ष्णंहसतिक्वचिच्च ।
विलज्ज उद्गायतिनृत्यतेचमद्भक्तियुक्तोभुवनंपुनाति ॥२४॥

vāg gadgadā dravate yasya cittaṁ rudaty abhīkṣṇaṁ hasati kvacic ca
vilajja udgāyati nṛtyate ca mad-bhakti-yukto bhuvanaṁ punāti

A devotee who is fixed in loving service to Me, whose voice is sometimes choked up, whose heart melts, who sometimes weeps and sometimes laughs, and sometimes chants and dances without concern for others, purifies the three worlds.

COMMENTARY

One who has attained the platform of love of God can deliver the fallen conditioned souls. This is not at all surprising. Sometimes his voice becomes choked up so that he cannot speak coherently, and because his heart melts, he sometimes cries out in anxiety. The word "sometimes" should be applied to each of the ecstatic symptoms, but the heart remains melted in all situations.

PURPORT

Persons who are eternally engaged in the Lord's service sometimes sing the Lord's holy name loudly and dance in ecstasy, sometimes display the softness of their heart by speaking in a voice that is choked up, sometimes laugh, and sometimes cry, without caring for others. Only such devotees can purify the fourteen worlds.

TEXT 25

यथाग्निनाहेममलंजहातिध्मातपुनःस्वंभजतेचरूपम् ।
आत्माचकर्मानुशयंविधूयमद्भक्तियोगेनभजत्यथोमाम् ॥२५॥

yathāgninā hema malaṁ jahāti dhmātaṁ punaḥ svaṁ bhajate ca rūpam
ātmā ca karmānuśayaṁ vidhūya mad-bhakti-yogena bhajaty atho mām

Just as the gold, when smelted in fire, gives up its impurities and returns to its pure brilliant state, the spirit soul, absorbed in the fire of *bhakti-yoga*, is purified of all contamination caused by previous fruitive activities and as a result, becomes situated in his constitutional position as My eternal servant.

COMMENTARY

The Supreme Lord herein establishes the conclusion that only by devotional service can the heart be purified, and not by any other process. The example is given of gold. When gold is smelted in fire, all impurities are removed. This purification of gold cannot be obtained simply by washing it with soap and water. Similarly, a living entity can cleanse his heart of all contaminations by the fire of devotional service, and not by any superficial means. The result is that the devotee goes back home, back to Godhead, and there worships Lord Kṛṣṇa in his original spiritual body, which is compared to the original pure form of smelted gold.

PURPORT

When gold is smelted in fire, all of the impurities of base metals are removed. Similarly, when the conditioned souls, whose only engagements are those of sense gratification, put themselves in the fire of devotional service, then their aspirations for material enjoyment are reduced to nil so that they can easily traverse the path back home, back to Godhead.

TEXT 26

यथायथात्मापरिमृज्यतेऽसौमत्पुण्यगाथाश्रवणाभिधानैः ।
तथातथापश्यतिवस्तुसूक्ष्मंचक्षुर्यथैवाञ्जनसम्प्रयुक्तम् ॥२६॥

yathā yathātmā parimṛjyate 'sau mat-puṇya-gāthā-śravaṇābhidhānaiḥ
tathā tathā paśyati vastu sūkṣmaṁ cakṣur yathaivāñjana-samprayuktam

If a diseased eye is smeared with medicinal ointment, it can gradually recover its lost ability to see. Similarly, the more a living entity becomes purified by hearing and chanting the narrations of My auspicious glories, the more he can perceive My transcendental form.

COMMENTARY

The *Vedas* assure us that we can directly see the Supreme Lord and His transcendental abode if we fully surrender unto Him and agree to obey His instructions. The Lord and His name are nondifferent and as soon as one sincerely hears and chants the holy names of the Lord, the wonderful effect will be felt. The example can be given that a person who has one eye is better off than one who is blind. A person who has both eyes is better situated than a person who has only one eye, and a person whose eyes are smeared with medicinal ointment may be able to see better than one who has not taken advantage of such treatment. Similarly, according to the intensity of one's determination to achieve success in devotional service, he will be purified accordingly.

PURPORT

When one becomes too accustomed to a life of sense gratification, one loses sight of the ultimate goal of life, which is to regain the association of the Supreme Lord. By smearing medicinal ointment, diseased eyes may gradually revive their power to see. Similarly, by cultivating Kṛṣṇa consciousness, one can attain the eternal service of the Supreme Lord in transcendental love.

TEXT 27

विषयान्ध्यायतश्चित्तंविषयेषुविषज्जते ।
मामनुस्मरतश्चित्तंमय्येवप्रविलीयते ॥२७॥

viṣayān dhyāyataś cittaṁ viṣayeṣu viṣajjate
mām anusmarataś cittaṁ mayy eva pravilīyate

The mind of a person who meditates upon the objects of the senses becomes entangled in such objects, but if one constantly remembers Me, then his mind becomes absorbed in Me.

COMMENTARY

One should never think that the worship of the Lord is a mechanical process that will automatically deliver the desired result. Such a mechanical approach to constantly remembering the Lord will never stand. Constant rememberance of the Lord's transcendental name, form, qualities, and pastimes is only possible for one who has developed genuine attachment for the Lord. Just as materialists can remain absorbed in the thought of the objects of their desire, so devotees can remain in absorbed in thoughts of the Lord when they have developed transcendental attachment to His devotional service.

PURPORT

As the material senses run after sense objects, thinking them to be most desirable, by the cultivation of Kṛṣṇa consciousness, one becomes fully absorbed in hearing and chanting glorification of the Lord's transcendental name, form, qualities, and pastimes.

TEXT 28

अस्मादसदभिध्यानंयथास्वप्नमनोरथम्
हित्वामयिसमाधत्स्वमनोमद्भावभावितम्

tasmād asad-abhidhyānaṁ yathā svapna-manoratham
hitvā mayi samādhatsva mano mad-bhāva-bhāvitam

One should give up all paths for material elevation, which are no better than the creations of a dream. One should rather absorb his mind in always thinking of Me, for this will completely purify him of all material contamination.

COMMENTARY

Because other processes and their results are as illusory as things seen in a dream, the Lord instructs Uddhava to concentrate his mind on Him by engagement in pure devotional service. One should give up all other methods for making advancement in life and simply fix his mind in the thought of the Supreme Personality of Godhead.

PURPORT

The ultimate goal of life for the conditioned souls is to engage in the unalloyed devotional service of the Lord by surpassing the three stages of consciousness—wakefulness, dreaming, and deep sleep.

TEXT 29

स्त्रीणांस्त्रीसङ्गिनांसङ्गंत्यक्त्वादूरत आत्मवान् ।
क्षेमेविविक्त आसीनश्चिन्तयेन्मामतन्द्रितः ॥२९॥

strīṇāṁ strī-saṅgināṁ saṅgaṁ tyaktvā dūrata ātmavān
kṣeme vivikta āsīnaś cintayen mām atandritaḥ

One who is aware of his eternal self should give up the association of women and of those who are attached to women and fearlessly sit down in a solitary place to carefully meditate on Me.

COMMENTARY

One should particularly give up studying the *Kāma-śāstra* written by Vātsāyana Muni. If a peaceful person associates with such literature, he will lose his patience and become agitated. Therefore, one should fearlessly reside in a secluded place.

PURPORT

One should carefully give up the association of women, as well as those who are attached to women, and should fearlessly and enthusiastically cultivate Kṛṣṇa consciousness in a secluded place. Simply by thinking of a woman, one increases the desire for material life, causing one to forget the Supreme Lord. Therefore, one should completely disassociate himself from women and the desire to enjoy in their company. This is possible only by surrendering oneself to the Supreme Lord.

TEXT 30

नतथास्यभवेत्क्लेशोबन्धश्चान्यप्रसङ्गतः ।
योषित्सङ्गाद्यथापुंसोयथातत्सङ्गिसङ्गतः ॥३०॥

na tathāsya bhavet kleśo bandhaś cānya-prasaṅgataḥ
yoṣit-saṅgād yathā puṁso yathā tat-saṅgi-saṅgataḥ

Of all kinds of distress and bondage, none is greater than the suffering and bondage arising from intimate association with women, and those who attached to women.

COMMENTARY

One who desires to be delivered from material existence should renounce all intimate contact with women, as well as those who are attached to women. Any respectable gentleman will become guarded if he comes in close contact with a lusty woman. The difficulty is, however, that if one intimately associates with lusty men, their loose talk will infect one all the same. Indeed, the association of lusty men can be even more dangerous than association with women, and thus it should be avoided by all means.

PURPORT

There are innumerable verses in the *Bhāgavatam* describing the intoxication of material lust. Being forgetful of the Supreme Lord, the conditioned souls consider themselves to be the enjoyers of all they survey and thus they become bound by the three modes of material nature. This is the cause of their suffering. Because the living entities are pleasure-seeking by nature, in conditional life, they naturally endeavor to reach the peak of material happiness by enjoying the association of women. Therefore, devotees should carefully avoid the intimate association of women, as well as men who are attached to women.

TEXT 31

श्रीउद्धव उवाच
यथात्वामरविन्दाक्षयादृशंवायदात्मकम् ।
ध्यायेन्मुमुक्षुरेतन्मेध्यानंत्वंवक्तुमर्हसि ॥३१॥

śrī-uddhava uvāca
yathā tvām aravindākṣa yādṛśaṁ vā yad-ātmakam
dhyāyen mumukṣur etan me dhyānaṁ tvaṁ vaktum arhasi

Śrī Uddhava said: My dear lotus-eyed Śrī Kṛṣṇa, please describe to me how one who desires liberation should meditate upon You. Upon which form should he meditate, and what should be the nature of his meditation?

COMMENTARY

Śrī Uddhava is already on the platform of pure devotional service. Still, he is inquiring about the process of meditation, not so much for his own benefit, but for the benefit of those who are not situated in devotional service. Uddhava said: "O lotus-eyed Lord, kindly tell me how one who desires liberation should meditate on You? Upon which form should he meditate?" One may argue: "What is the need for a pure devotee like Uddhava to inquire about the process of meditation, which is to be performed by those who desire liberation?" It should simply be understood that Uddhava asked such a question not for his personal benefit, but for those who have not yet come to the platform of pure love of God.

TEXTS 32-33

श्रीभगवानुवाच
समआसनआसीनःसमकायोयथासुखम् ।
हस्तावुत्सङ्गआधायस्वनासाग्रकृतेक्षणः ॥३२॥
प्राणस्यशोधयेन्मार्गंपूरकुम्भकरेचकैः ।
विपर्ययेणापिशनैरभ्यसेन्निर्जितेन्द्रियः ॥३३॥

śrī-bhagavān uvāca
sama āsana āsīnaḥ sama-kāyo yathā-sukham
hastāv utsaṅga ādhāya sva-nāsāgra-kṛtekṣaṇaḥ

prāṇasya śodhayen mārgaṁ pūra-kumbhaka-recakaiḥ
viparyayeṇāpi śanair abhyasen nirjitendriyaḥ

The Supreme Personality of Godhead said: While seated on a level seat that is not too high or too low, keeping the body straight and yet comfortable, placing the hands on one's lap, and focusing the eyes on the tip of the nose, one should purify the pathways of

breathing by practicing the mechanical exercises of *pūraka, kumbhaka* and *recaka,* and then reverse the procedure. Having fully controlled the senses, one should thus practice *prāṇāyāma.*

COMMENTARY

To concentrate the mind, one should fix his gaze on the tip of the nose. As stated in the *yoga-śāstra, antar-lakṣyo bahir-dṛṣṭiḥ sthira-cittaḥ susaṅgataḥ*: "The eyes, which generally see externally, must be turned inward, and thus the mind is steadied and fully controlled."

TEXT 34

हृद्यविच्छिनमोंकारंघण्टानादंबिसोर्णवत् ।
प्राणेनोदीर्यतत्राथपुनःसंवेशयेत्स्वरम् ॥३४॥

hṛdy avicchinam oṁkāraṁ ghaṇṭā-nādaṁ bisorṇa-vat
prāṇenodīrya tatrātha punah saṁveśayet svaram

One should raise the life air upwards to the heart, where the sacred syllable oṁ can be heard like the sound of a bell. One should then continue raising this sacred syllable upwards until it is joined with the anusvāra vibration.

COMMENTARY

It appears that the yoga system is somewhat technical and difficult to perform. *Anusvāra* refers to a nasal vibration pronounced after the fifteen Sanskrit vowels. The complete explanation of this process is extremely complicated and obviously unsuitable for this age.

TEXT 35

एवंप्रणवसंयुक्तंप्राणमेवसमभ्यसेत्
दशकृत्वस्त्रिषवणंमासादर्वाग्जितानिलः

evaṁ praṇava-saṁyuktaṁ prāṇam eva samabhyaset
daśa-kṛtvas tri-ṣavaṇaṁ māsād arvāg jitānilaḥ

The *oṁkāra* thus being joined, one should carefully practice the *prāṇāyāma* system of *yoga* ten times at each sunrise, noon, and sunset. By doing so, after one month one will have conquered the life air.

COMMENTARY

One who diligently practices *yoga* as recommended herein will control his mind after one month.

TEXTS 36-42

हृत्पुण्डरीकमन्तःस्थमूर्ध्वनालमधोमुखम् ।
ध्यात्वोर्ध्वमुखमुन्निद्रमष्टपत्रंसकर्णिकम् ॥३६॥
कर्णिकायांन्यसेत्सूर्यसोमाग्नीन्तरोत्तरम् ।
वह्निमध्येस्मरेद्रूपंममैतद्ध्यानमङ्गलम् ॥३७॥
समंप्रशान्तंसुमुखंदीर्घचारुचतुर्भुजम् ।
सुचारुसुन्दरग्रीवंसुकपोलंशुचिस्मितम् ॥३८॥
समानकर्णविन्यस्तस्फुरन्मकरकुण्डलम् ।
हेमाम्बरंघनश्यामंश्रीवत्सश्रीनिकेतनम् ॥३९॥
शङ्खचक्रगदापद्मवनमालाविभूषितम् ।
नूपुरैर्विलसत्पादंकौस्तुभप्रभयायुतम् ॥४०॥
द्युमत्किरीटकटककटिसूत्राङ्गदायुतम् ।
सर्वाङ्गसुन्दरंहृद्यंप्रसादसुमुखेक्षनम् ॥४१॥
सुकुमारमभिध्यायेत्सर्वाङ्गेषुमनो दधत् ।
इन्द्रियाणीन्द्रियार्थेभ्योमनसाकृष्यतन्मनः ।
बुद्ध्यासारथिनाधीरःप्रणयेनमयिसर्वतः ॥४२॥

hṛt-puṇḍarīkam antaḥ-stham ūrdhva-nālam adho-mukham
dhyātvordhva-mukham unnidram aṣṭa-patraṁ sa-karṇikam

karṇikāyāṁ nyaset sūrya-somāgnīn uttarottaram
vahni-madhye smared rūpaṁmamaitad dhyāna-maṅgalam

samaṁ praśāntaṁ su-mukhaṁdīrgha-cāru-catur-bhujam
su-cāru-sundara-grīvaṁsu-kapolaṁ śuci-smitam

samāna-karṇa-vinyasta-sphuran-makara-kuṇḍalam
hemāmbaraṁ ghana-śyāmaṁśrīvatsa-śrī-niketanam

śaṅkha-cakra-gadā-padma-vanamālā-vibhūṣitam
nūpurair vilasat-pādaṁkaustubha-prabhayā yutam

dyumat-kirīṭa-kaṭaka-kaṭi-sūtrāṅgadāyutam
sarvāṅga-sundaraṁ hṛdyaṁ prasāda-sumukhekṣanam

su-kumāram abhidhyāyet sarvāṅgeṣu mano dadhat
indriyāṇīndriyārthebhyo manasākṛṣya tan manaḥ
buddhyā sārathinā dhīraḥ praṇayena mayi sarvataḥ

Keeping the eyes half closed and fixed on the tip of the nose, and being wide awake and alert, one should meditate on the lotus flower that is situated within the heart, which has eight petals and an erect stalk. One should meditate on the sun, moon, and fire, placing them one after another within the whorl of the lotus flower. Then, placing My transcendental form within the fire, one should meditate upon it as the auspicious goal of all meditation. That transcendental form is perfectly proportioned, gentle, and cheerful, and has four long arms, beautiful shoulders, a handsome forehead, a pure smile, and ears that are decorated with shark-shaped earrings. That spiritual form has a complexion that resembles that of a new rain cloud and is dressed in golden-yellowish garments. The chest of that form is the abode of Śrīvatsa and Lakṣmī, and is decorated with a conch shell, disc, club, and lotus flower. That form of Mine is decorated with a garland of forest flowers. The lotus feet are decorated with ankle bells, and this form exhibits the Kaustubha gem and an effulgent crown. The upper hips are beautified by a golden belt, and the arms are decorated with valuable bracelets. All of the limbs of this beautiful form captivate the heart, and the face is beautified by merciful glancing. Withdrawing the senses from their sense objects, one should be grave and self-controlled and should use the intelligence to fix his mind upon all of the limbs of My transcendental body. Thus one should meditate upon that most delicate transcendental form of Mine.

COMMENTARY

The lotus flower in the heart stands on an erect stalk. The word *nyaset* indicates that one should apply one's concentration to meditate on the form of the Supreme Lord. The phrase *dhyāna maṅgala* means "the auspicious object of meditation." The word *sama* indicates a similar form. The Lord is described as "peaceful," meaning that He is not harsh. The two marks of Śrīvatsa and Lakṣmī are situated on either side of Śrī Kṛṣṇa's chest. For concentrated meditation, one should fix his mind with the help of his intelligence, and in this way, one should gradually perfect his meditation upon the Supreme Lord.

TEXT 43

तत्सर्वव्यापकंचित्तमाकृष्यैकत्रधारयेत् ।
नान्यानिचिन्तयेद्भूयःसुस्मितंभावयेन्मुखम् ॥४३॥

tat sarva-vyāpakaṁ cittam ākṛṣyaikatra dhārayet
nānyāni cintayed bhūyaḥ su-smitaṁ bhāvayen mukham

Thereafter, one should withdraw the mind from the limbs of that transcendental form and fix it on the wonderful smiling face of the Lord.

COMMENTARY

The mind may be satisfied by viewing all of the limbs of the Lord's body, but for further advancement, one should withdraw and fix it on the Lord's smiling face.

TEXT 44

तत्रलब्धपदंचित्तमाकृष्यव्योम्निधारयेत् ।
तच्चत्यक्त्वामदारोहोनकिञ्चिदपिचिन्तयेत् ॥४४॥

tatra labdha-padaṁ cittam ākṛṣya vyomni dhārayet
tac ca tyaktvā mad-āroho na kiñcid api cintayet

Thereafter, one should withdraw the mind, which had been firmly fixed on the lotus face of the Lord, and establish it in the sky, which is the cause of the gross cosmic manifestation. Finally, one should relinquish that meditation as well and become fixed in Me, thus giving up the process of meditation altogether.

COMMENTARY

Uddhava had inquired about the kind of meditation that would enable one to achieve liberation from material existence. Here it is indicated that by meditating upon the lotus-like face of the Lord, one easily attains supreme liberation. It should be understood that devotional service to the Supreme Personality of Godhead is the activity of the liberated souls, and thus is fully transcendental. Simply to be a meditator is considered very insignificant for those who are engaged in the unalloyed devotional service of the Lord.

TEXT 45

एवंसमाहितमतिर्मामेवात्मानमात्मनि ।
विचष्टेमयिसर्वात्मन्ज्योतिर्ज्योतिषिसंयुतम् ॥४५॥

evaṁ samāhita-matir mām evātmānam ātmani
vicaṣṭe mayi sarvātman jyotir jyotiṣi saṁyutam

One who has fixed his mind on Me should see Me within his own self, and should see the individual soul within Me, the Supreme Personality of Godhead. He should see how he is situated within the Lord, just like rays of the sun are seen as united with the sun.

COMMENTARY

The Supreme Lord is situated within the hearts of all living entities, and the living entities are situated within the gigantic universal body of the Lord. Still, the Supreme Lord is the single maintainer of countless living entities.

TEXT 46

ध्यानेनेत्थंसुतीव्रेणयुञ्जतोयोगिनोमनः ।
संयास्यत्याशुनिर्वाणंद्रव्यज्ञानक्रियाभ्रमः ॥४६॥

dhyānenetthaṁ su-tīvreṇa yuñjato yogino manaḥ
saṁyāsyaty āśu nirvāṇaṁ dravya jñāna-kriyā-bhramaḥ

When the yogī carefully controls his mind by complete absorption in meditation, his false identification with material objects, mundane knowledge, and fruitive activities is soon dispelled.

COMMENTARY

The result of intense meditation upon the form of the Lord is that one becomes freed from all illusion, including the three-fold miseries—*ādhibhautika*, *ādhidaivika*, and *ādhyātmika*.

PURPORT

Haṭha-yoga, or *karma-yoga*, and *vicāra-yoga*, or *rāja-yoga*, are partial aspects of *bhakti-yoga*. The nondevotee *yogīs* engage in the cultivation of knowledge, but it is only partial. The meditation which is performed in pure devotional service is absorption in thought of the Supreme Lord's transcendental names, forms, qualities, associates, and pastimes. Constant meditation is the result of absorption in the glorification of the Lord, which is one of the nine processes of devotional service, known as *kīrtana.* When one is ignorant of his spiritual identity as the eternal servant of the Supreme Lord, he may be attracted to the performance of *haṭha-yoga.* Such practice will enable one to gradually come to realize his spiritual identity and so it may serve as a stepping stone to the goal of devotional service. Those who take pleasure in mental speculation to philosophically understand the Absolute Truth may, after many births and deaths, come to the conclusion that the Supreme Lord is the cause of all causes and thus begin to engage in devotional service. If one performs meditation without accepting the transcendental form of the Lord as the Absolute Truth, then his meditation will not award the results that have been described in this verse. In the *haṭha-yoga* system, one learns to control the body and in the *jñāna-yoga* system, one learns to control the mind. In either case, one works for his own elevation, being impelled by selfish desires. This kind of selfish activity is referred to in this verse as *kriyā.* One who desires the perfection of yoga must give up materialistic *dravya, jñāna* and *kriyā* and ultimately engage in the devotional service of the Lord.

Thus ends the translation of the Eighth Chapter of the Uddhava-gītā entitled "**Lord Kṛṣṇa Explains the Yoga System to Śrī Uddhava**" *with the commentaries of Śrīla Viśvanātha Cakravartī Ṭhākura and chapter summary and purports by Śrīla Bhaktisiddhānta Sarasvatī Ṭhākura.*

Chapter 9

Lord Kṛṣṇa's Description of Mystic Yoga Perfections

CHAPTER SUMMARY

This chapter describes the eight primary and ten secondary mystic perfections. These mystic perfections are developed by fixing one's mind in *yoga*, but they are ultimately detrimental to the achievement of Lord Viṣṇu's lotus feet.

Being asked by Uddhava, Lord Śrī Kṛṣṇa describes the eighteen mystic perfections, their characteristics, and what type of meditation is to be practiced for the attainment of each one. The Lord concludes by saying, "For one who desires to render pure devotional service unto the Supreme Personality of Godhead, the attainment of these mystic powers is simply a waste of time because they are impediments to the worship of the Supreme Lord. All these mystic perfections are automatically offered to a pure devotee, but he does not accept them. Unless employed in the devotional service of the Lord, these mystic perfections have no value. A devotee simply sees that the Supreme Lord is present everywhere, both externally and internally, and depends completely upon Him."

TEXT 1

श्रीभगवानुवाच
जितेन्द्रियस्ययुक्तस्यजितश्वासस्ययोगिनः ।
मयिधारयतश्चेत उपतिष्ठन्तिसिद्धयः ॥१॥

śrī-bhagavān uvāca
jitendriyasya yuktasya jita-śvāsasya yoginaḥ
mayi dhārayataś ceta upatiṣṭhanti siddhayaḥ

The Supreme Lord said: My dear Uddhava, when a *yogī* has controlled his senses, conquered his breathing process, steadied his mind, and concentrated his mind on Me, then all mystic perfections automatically appear to him.

COMMENTARY

There are eight primary mystic yoga perfections, beginning with *aṇimā-siddhi*, and ten secondary yoga perfections. In this chapter, Lord Kṛṣṇa will explain that these *yoga-siddhis* are stumbling blocks on the path of Kṛṣṇa consciousness.

TEXT 2

श्रीउद्धव उवाच
कयाधारणयाकास्वित्कथंवासिद्धिरच्युत ।
कतिवासिद्धयोब्रूहियोगिनांसिद्धिदोभवान् ॥२॥

śrī-uddhava uvāca
kayā dhāraṇayā kā svit kathaṁ vā siddhir acyuta
kati vā siddhayo brūhi yoginām siddhi-do bhavān

Śrī Uddhava said: My dear Lord Acyuta, You alone are the bestower of all types of mystic perfections. Kindly tell me—by what process can the mystic perfections be achieved, how many types of mystic perfections are there, and what is the nature of each mystic perfection?

COMMENTARY

The word *svit* is employed while inquiring.

TEXT 3

श्रीभगवानुवाच
सिद्धयोऽष्टादशप्रोक्ताधारणायोगपारगैः ।
तासामष्टौमत्प्रधानादशैवगुणहेतवः ॥३॥

śrī-bhagavān uvāca
siddhayo 'ṣṭādaśa proktā dhāraṇā yoga-pāra-gaiḥ
tāsām aṣṭau mat-pradhānā daśaiva guṇa-hetavaḥ

The Supreme Lord said: The sages, who are masters of yoga, have declared that there are eighteen kinds of *siddhi* (mystic perfection) and *dhāraṇā* (meditation). Among these, eight are primary, being sheltered in Me, and ten are secondary, appearing from the material mode of goodness.

COMMENTARY

There are eighteen kinds of *dhāraṇā* as well. The Supreme Lord is the shelter of the eight primary *dhāraṇās*, because they have been manifested from His internal potency, and are thus transcendental. The other ten meditations are mundane, being born from the material mode of goodness.

PURPORT

Among the eighteen kinds of perfection, eight are transcendental and ten are within the jurisdiction of the material modes of nature. The eight *siddhis* are *aṇimā*, *laghimā*, *mahimā*, *prāpti*, *prākāmya*, *īśitā*, *vaśitā*, and *kāmavasāyitā*. Among them, the first three pertain to the body, the fourth pertains to the senses, and the last four pertain to nature. The ten minor perfections are *anūrminattva*, *dūra-śravaṇa*, *dūradarśana*, *icchānurūpa dehera gati*, *icchānurūpa ākāra grahaṇa*, *parakāya praveśa*, *svecchāmṛtyu*, *deva krīḍā darśana*, *saṅkalpita padārtha prāpti*, and *apratihatā ājñā*, and they are all mundane.

TEXT 4-5

अणिमामहिमामूर्तेर्लघिमाप्राप्तिरिन्द्रियैः ।
प्राकाम्यंश्रुतदृष्टेषुशक्तिप्रेरणमीशिता ॥४॥
गुणेष्वसङ्गोवशितायत्कामस्तदवस्यति ।
एतामेसिद्धयःसौम्य अष्टावौत्पत्तिकामताः ॥५॥

aṇimā mahimā mūrter laghimā prāptir indriyaiḥ
prākāmyaṁ śruta-dṛṣṭeṣu śakti-preraṇam īśitā

guṇeṣv asaṅgo vaśitā yat-kāmas tad avasyati
etā me siddhayaḥ saumya aṣṭāv autpattikā matāḥ

Aṇimā, becoming smaller than the smallest; **mahimā,** becoming greater than the greatest; and **laghimā,** becoming lighter than the lightest, are mystic perfections by which one transforms one's body. **Prāpti-siddhi,** by which one acquires whatever one desires, is related to the senses. **Prākāmya-siddhi** enables one to experience any enjoyable object, in this world and in the next. **Iśitā-siddhi** enables one to manipulate the sub-potencies of Maya. **Vaśita-siddhi** enables one to be unimpeded by the three modes of nature. **Kāmāvasāyitā-siddhi** enables one to obtain anything he may desire. My dear Uddhava, these eight **siddhis** are considered as naturally existing and unexcelled within this world.

COMMENTARY

Among these eight mystic perfections, *aṇimā*, *mahimā*, and *laghimā*, are related to the body. *Prāpti-siddhi* is related to the senses, because by utilizing the senses, one can acquire anything. *Prākāmya-siddhi* awards one the power to enjoy objects that one may have heard about but cannot see, such as something buried underground. By the *īśitā-siddhi*, one can manipulate the sub-potencies of nature. By the *vaśitā-siddhi*, one can bring others under one's control, and keep oneself beyond the influence of the three modes of material nature. *Kāmāvaśāyitā-siddhi* gives one the maximum power of control, acquisition, and enjoyment. These eight mystic perfections are certainly grand accomplishments because they originally exist in the Supreme Personality of Godhead.

TEXT 6-7

अनूर्मिमत्त्वंदेहेऽस्मिन्दूरश्रवणदर्शनम् ।
मनोजवःकामरूपंपरकायप्रवेशनम् ॥६॥
स्वच्छन्दमृत्युर्देवानांसहक्रीडानुदर्शनम् ।
यथासङ्कल्पसंसिद्धिराज्ञाप्रतिहतागतिः ॥७॥

anūrmimattvaṁ dehe 'smin dūra-śravaṇa-darśanam
mano-javaḥ kāma-rūpaṁ para-kāya-praveśanam

svacchanda-mṛtyur devānāṁ saha-krīḍānudarśanam
yathā-saṅkalpa-saṁsiddhir ājñāpratihatā gatiḥ

The ten secondary mystic **siddhis** produced from the mode of material nature are the power to free oneself from hunger and thirst, to hear and see things happening in a distant place, to move one's body at the speed of the mind, to assume any form one desires, to enter the bodies of others, to die according to one's will, to witness the pastimes

of the demigods with the Apsarās, to act however one desires, and to give orders whose fulfillment is unimpeded.

COMMENTARY

The ten secondary mystic perfections are herein described. These powers award one freedom from the six urges of the body, such as hunger and thirst; seeing and hearing what is happening at a distant place; moving the body at the speed of the mind; assuming the form of one's choice; witnessing the pleasure pastimes of the demigods and celestial women; attaining whatever one desires; and the carrying out of one's orders without impediment.

TEXT 8-9

त्रिकालज्ञत्वमद्वन्द्वंपरचित्ताद्यभिज्ञता ।
अग्न्यर्कम्बुविषादीनांप्रतिष्टम्भोऽपराजयः ॥८॥
एताश्चोद्देशतःप्रोक्तायोगधारणसिद्धयः ।
ययाधारणयायास्याद्यथावास्यान्निबोधमे ॥९॥

tri-kāla-jñatvam advandvaṁ para-cittādy-abhijñatā
agny-arkāmbu-viṣādīnāṁ pratiṣṭambho 'parājayaḥ

etāś coddeśataḥ proktā yoga-dhāraṇa-siddhayaḥ
yayā dhāraṇayā yā syād yathā vā syān nibodha me

The power to know past, present, and future; tolerance of dualities, such as heat and cold; to know others' minds; checking the influence of fire, sun, water, poison and so on; and to remain undefeated by others—these constitute five perfections attained by the practice of yoga and meditation. I have simply listed them here, giving their names and characteristics. Now, please hear from Me about how one attains a particular *siddhi* by performing a specific meditation.

COMMENTARY

The following are considered to be insignificant *siddhis*—knowing past, present and future; not becoming overwhelmed by the dualities, such as heat and cold; and checking the influence of fire, sun, poison, and so on.

PURPORT

Knowledge of past, present, and future; being undisturbed by heat and cold; understanding the intentions of others; neutralization of the powers of fire, the sun, water, poison, and so on; and to be unconquerable—these are five insignificant perfections.

TEXT 10

भूतसूक्ष्मात्मनिमयितन्मात्रंधारयेन्मनः ।
अणिमानमवाप्नोतितन्मात्रोपासकोमम ॥१०॥

bhūta-sūkṣmātmani mayi tan-mātraṁ dhārayen manaḥ
aṇimānam avāpnoti tan-mātropāsako mama

One who fixes his mind on Me in My atomic form, which pervades all subtle elements, worshiping that form alone, attains the mystic perfection known as *aṇimā siddhi.*

COMMENTARY

The Supreme Lord possesses a tiny form whereby He resides within the atoms and atomic particles. One who can concentrate his mind on the Supersoul can obtain the mystic power called *aṇimā*, which enables one to enter within any material object.

PURPORT

The Supreme Lord has covered the godless living entities with gross and subtle material designations made of the illusory energy. If one desires to free his mind from the gross material designations, then he must meditate on the subtle form of the Lord. Those who worship the Lord as He is situated within the subtle forms of sense objects can achieve the *aṇimā-siddhi.*

TEXT 11

महत्तत्त्वात्मनिमयियथासंस्थंमनोदधत् ।
महिमानमवाप्नोतिभूतानांचपृथक् पृथक् ॥११॥

mahat-tattvātmani mayi yathā-saṁsthaṁ mano dadhat
mahimānam avāpnoti bhūtānāṁ ca pṛthak pṛthak

One who concentrates his mind on the Lord as He is situated in the *mahat-tattva* as the Supersoul of the total material elements can obtain the mystic perfection called

***mahimā.* By absorbing the mind in the existence of each material element, one can obtain their potencies.**

COMMENTARY

The Supreme Personality of Godhead is in one sense nondifferent from the material creation. Considering this, one can meditate upon the *mahat-tattva* as a subtle manifestation of the Lord's inferior potency. When one has actually realized that the universe is nondifferent from the Lord, he obtains the mystic perfection known as *mahimā-siddhi.* When one can realize the Lord's presence within each of the material elements, he obtains their potency.

PURPORT

One who meditates upon the Lord as the Supreme Soul of the total material existence, or *mahat-tattva,* can attain the mystic perfection called *mahimā-siddhi.* By realizing how the *mahat-tattva* is not different from the Supreme Lord, being the expansion of His energy, one can experience His presence within each of the element—earth, water, fire, air, and space. This awards one the *siddhi* of *mahimā.*

TEXT 12

परमाणुमयेचित्तंभूतानांमयिरञ्जयन्
कालसूक्ष्मार्थतांयोगीलघिमानमवाप्नुयात्

paramāṇu-maye cittaṁ bhūtānāṁ mayi rañjayan
kāla-sūkṣmārthatāṁ yogī laghimanam avāpnuyāt

By fixing the mind on Me as I am situated within everything, and thus the essence of the atomic constituents of the material elements, a yogi can attain the mystic perfection called *laghimā,* which enables him to become as light as an atom.

COMMENTARY

Kāla, or time, is the form of the Lord that moves the material world. The five gross elements are composed of atoms, and atomic particles are a subtle manifestation of the movements of time. The Personality of Godhead is more subtle than time, and it is He who expands to become the time factor. By understanding this, one obtains the mystic power known as *laghimā-siddhi,* whereby he can become lighter than the lightest.

PURPORT

If the yogi fixes his mind in meditation on the subtle characteristics of the material elements, understanding them to be energetic expansions of the Supreme Lord, he can attain the *laghimā siddhi.* Those who are not devoted to the Supreme Lord will only achieve an illusory fragment of this mystic potency, however.

TEXT 13

धारयन्मय्यहंतत्त्वेमनोवैकारिकेऽखिलम् ।
सर्वेन्द्रियाणामात्मत्वंप्राप्तिंप्राप्नोतिमन्मनाः ॥१३॥

dhārayan mayy ahaṁ-tattve mano vaikārike 'khilam
sarvendriyāṇām ātmatvaṁ prāptiṁ prāpnoti man-manāḥ

One who meditates on Me as situated within the element of false ego as generated from the mode of goodness attains the *siddhi* called *prāpti,* by which one gains mastery over everyone's senses.

COMMENTARY

The yogi who fixes his mind on the Lord as He is situated within the false ego can attain the power whereby he can acquire any object he desires.

PURPORT

By reviving one's relationship with the Absolute Personality of Godhead, all of one's senses become engaged in the service of the master of the senses. This is the essence of understanding the mystic perfection called *prāpti.* Those who try to attain mystic powers without meditating on the Supreme Lord are awarded a mere reflection of these *siddhis.* Because they are not in union with the Lord through devotion, they cannot partake of His mystic potencies, which are of cosmic proportions, and thus must be satisfied with mere reflections of those powers.

TEXT 14

महत्यात्मनियःसूत्रेधारयेन्मयिमानसम् ।
प्राकाम्यंपारमेष्ठ्यंमेविन्दतेऽव्यक्तजन्मनः ॥१४॥

mahaty ātmani yaḥ sūtre dhārayen mayi mānasam
prākāmyaṁ pārameṣṭhyaṁ me vindate 'vyakta-janmanaḥ

One who concentrates his mind on Me as the Supersoul of that aspect of the *mahat-tattva* that manifests the wheel of karma obtains from Me, who is beyond material perception, the mystic perfection called *prākāmya*.

COMMENTARY

The aspect of the *mahat-tattva* that produces the cycle of action and reaction is herein referred to as *sūtra*. By fixed meditation on the Supreme Personality of Godhead, who is the soul of the *mahat-tattva*, one can achieve the most excellent perfection called *prākāmya*. This opulence is especially employed by Brahmā. *Avyakta-janmanaḥ* indicates that the Supreme Personality of Godhead appears from the *avyakta*, or the spiritual sky, or that His birth is *avyakta*, beyond the perception of material senses.

PURPORT

Those who mistakenly consider the *mahat-tattva* to be more important than Hiraṇyagarbha claim to have achieved the mystic perfection called *prākāmya*. Those who have actually attained *prākāmya siddhi* accept Hiraṇyagarbha as the worshipable Lord of the *mahat-tattva*, lying on the ocean of milk.

TEXT 15

विष्णौत्र्यधीश्वरेचित्तंधारयेत्कालविग्रहे ।
स ईशित्वमवाप्नोतिक्षेत्रज्ञक्षेत्रचोदनाम् ॥१५॥

viṣṇau try-adhīśvare cittaṁ dhārayet kāla-vigrahe
sa īśitvam avāpnoti kṣetrajña-kṣetra-codanām

One who meditates on My form as Lord Viṣṇu, the Supersoul, the personification of time and the controller of the three modes of material nature, attains the *siddhi* called *īśitva*, by which he can control the material bodies of others, along with their designations.

COMMENTARY

The illusory energy of the Lord, which consists of the three modes of material nature, is under the control of time. By meditating on this form of the Supreme Lord, one can obtain the *īśitva siddhi*. This *siddhi* enables one to exert his influence over the bodies of other conditioned souls.

PURPORT

The Supreme Lord's illusory potency consists of three modes of material nature and it works fully under the supervision of time, which has also emanated from Him. The Supersoul of the manifested material elements is an expansion of the Supreme Personality of Godhead. Liberated souls absorbed in meditation upon the Supersoul attain the *īśitva siddhi* without separate endeavor. Those who consider the form of the Lord to be a manifestation of the three modes of material nature, and thus a product of matter under the control of eternal time, and consider themselves to be one in identity with the Supersoul, are understood to be bereft of all knowledge. Because of this, they cannot discriminate between the *māyādhīśa* Lord and the *māyāvaśa jīva*. The hopes of such persons to master the *īśitva siddhi* is simply another manifestation of illusion.

TEXT 16

नारायणेतुरीयाख्येभगवच्छब्दशब्दिते ।
मनोमय्यादधद्योगीमद्धर्मावशितामियात् ॥१६॥

nārāyaṇe turīyākhye bhagavac-chabda-śabdite
mano mayy ādadhad yogī mad-dharmā vaśitām iyāt

A yogi who meditates on My form of Nārāyaṇa, who is full of six opulences and who is fully transcendental, becomes endowed with My nature and thus achieves the *vaśitā siddhi.*

COMMENTARY

Here, the word *turīya*, or the fourth dimension, refers to the Personality of Godhead, who is beyond the influence of the three modes of material nature. He is known as Lord Nārāyaṇa and possesses all six opulences in full. By fixing one's mind on Him, one can attain the mystic perfection called *vaśitā*. The Lord is known as Bhagavān, or the possessor of unlimited opulences, principally wealth, strength, fame, beauty, knowledge, and renunciation.

PURPORT

When a yogi realizes that all the objects of this world have a relationship of service with the Supreme Lord, he surpasses materialistic conceptions, such as length, breadth, height, and so on, and becomes situated in transcendence. This is the platform of knowledge of one's eternal relationship with the Supreme Lord. While situated on the transcendental platform, such a yogi controls his senses, mind, and speech, and thus attains the *siddhi* known as *vaśitā*. Those who are servants of their bodily urges and thus come under the control of sense objects, even though they may advertise themselves as liberated souls, can never attain the *vaśitā siddhi.*

TEXT 17

निर्गुणेब्रह्मणिमयिधारयन्विशदंमनः ।
परमानन्दमाप्नोतियत्रकामोऽवसीयते ॥१७॥

nirguṇe brahmaṇi mayi dhārayan viśadaṁ manaḥ
paramānandam āpnoti yatra kāmo 'vasīyate

One who meditated upon the impersonal Brahman, which is a partial manifestation of the Absolute Truth, will attain happiness beyond material conception and all his desires will be fulfilled.

COMMENTARY

Merging into the existence of Brahman is possible only when all material desires have ceased.

PURPORT

When a conditioned living entity comes in contact with the three modes of material nature, he exhibits various kinds of material desires. When the conditioned soul engages in the devotional service of the Supreme Personality of Godhead, who is the reservoir of all transcendental qualities, and who is situated beyond the modes of material nature, then all his material desires are vanquished, just as fog is dispelled as soon as the sun rises. The *kāmāvasāyitā siddhi* is obtained when one dovetails all of his desires in the service of the eternal Kāmadeva, the Supreme Personality of Godhead.

TEXT 18

श्वेतद्वीपपतौचित्तंशुद्धेधर्ममयेमयि ।
धारयञ्छ्वेततांयातिषडूर्मिरहितोनरः ॥१८॥

śvetadvīpa-patau cittaṁ śuddhe dharma-maye mayi
dhārayañ chvetatāṁ yāti ṣaḍ-ūrmi-rahito naraḥ

One who fixes his mind on My form as the predominating Deity of the mode of goodness, the upholder of religious principles, and the Lord of Śvetadvīpa, attains a purified form and freedom from the six waves of material disturbance—hunger, thirst, decay, death, grief, and illusion.

COMMENTARY

In this verse, Lord Kṛṣṇa begins His description of how one can attain the ten secondary mystic perfections.

PURPORT

By engaging in the devotional service of the Supreme Lord, who is transcendental to the material modes of nature, who is the form of the pure religious principles, and who is the Lord of Śvetadvīpa, all of the contamination in one's heart becomes cleansed. The Absolute Truth is the embodiment of pure goodness, and He is the predominating Deity of the mode of goodness. By directing one's heart toward the service of the Lord, one becomes purified, so that the black spot of "I am God" can no longer cause contamination.

TEXT 19

मय्याकाशात्मनिप्राणेमनसाघोषमुद्वहन् ।
तत्रोपलब्धाभूतानांहंसोवाचःशृणोत्यसौ ॥१९॥

mayy ākāśātmani prāṇe manasā ghoṣam udvahan
tatropalabdhā bhūtānāṁ haṁso vācaḥ śṛṇoty asau

If a purified transcendentalist meditates on the extraordinary sound vibrations occurring within Me as the personified sky and total life air, then he is able to perceive within the sky the speaking of all living entities.

COMMENTARY

By meditating on the transcendental sound vibration, *oṁkara*, one can achieve the mystic perfection of being able to hear the words of the living entities that are spread in the sky.

PURPORT

In the *ekāyana* worship of the *paramahaṁsas*, chanting the holy name of the Lord is considered to be the most important activity. It is the duty of all living entities to receive the transcendental sound vibration of the Absolute Truth. When all words are aimed at glorifying the Supreme Lord, one becomes able to hear the speech originating from liberated living entities far beyond the material universe. Liberated souls can visualize reality simply by the reception of the transcendental sound vibration.

TEXT 20

चक्षुस्त्वष्टरि संयोज्य त्वष्टारमपि चक्षुषि ।
मां तत्र मनसा ध्यायन्विश्वं पश्यति दूरतः ॥२०॥

cakṣus tvaṣṭari saṁyojya tvaṣṭāram api cakṣuṣi
māṁ tatra manasā dhyāyan viśvaṁ paśyati dūrataḥ

While engaging in meditation on Me as existing within the combined form of the sun and vision, if one can merge one's sight into the sun, and then the sun into one's eyes, one can acquire the power to see any distant thing.

COMMENTARY

There is an intimate relationship between the sun and the process of vision. The two are inseparable and are pervaded by the presence of the Supreme Lord in His all-pervading feature as the Supersoul. Here, the process for attaining the mystic perfection that enables one to see objects even though very distant is being described.

PURPORT

While casting one's glance upon Lord Nārāyāṇa as He is situated within the sun globe, if, in reciprocation, one receives the auspicious glance of the Lord, one will see through purified vision that the objects of this world are meant for the Lord's enjoyment, and not for one's personal sense gratification. Without receiving the Lord's glance, one will see the world as either meant for one's enjoyment, or as the object of dry renunciation.

TEXT 21

मनो मयि सुसंयोज्य देहं तदनुवायुना ।
मद्धारणानुभावेन तत्रात्मा यत्र वै मनः ॥२१॥

mano mayi su-saṁyojya dehaṁ tad-anuvāyunā
mad-dhāraṇānubhāvena tatrātmā yatra vai manaḥ

When one completely absorbs his mind in Me by meditation and then utilizes the air that carries the mind, he can attain the mystic power that allows him to travel in a moment to anywhere he desires.

COMMENTARY

This verse states that there is an air that adheres to the mind. When one absorbs this air, along with the mind, in meditation upon the Supreme Lord, his gross material body will be enabled to travel at the speed of mind to any destination he desires.

PURPORT

When the yogi comes to see everything in relationship to Kṛṣṇa, then his mind will entertain no other thought than his engagement in devotional service. In that transcendental state, one loses all interest in attempts to enjoy gross material objects. This is the prerequisite for attaining genuine mystic perfections.

TEXT 22

यदामन उपादाययद्यद्रूपंबुभूषति ।
तत्तद्भवेन्मनोरूपंमद्योगबलमाश्रयः ॥२२॥

yadā mana upādāya yad yad rūpaṁ bubhūṣati
tat tad bhaven mano-rūpaṁ mad-yoga-balam āśrayaḥ

When a yogi desires to assume a particular form by applying his mind in that way, that form will appear before him. Such a mystic perfection is possible by meditating upon the inconceivable mystic potency by which I assume various transcendental forms.

COMMENTARY

If the mind desires to assume the form of a demigod, it can do so by transforming itself as the ingredient cause. If the yogi concentrates his mind on the Supreme Lord as prescribed in this verse, he can assume any form he desires.

PURPORT

Śrī Gaurasundara has said,

anyera hṛdaya—mana, mora mana—vṛndāvana,
'mane' 'vane' eka kari' jāni
tāhāṅ tomāra pada-dvaya, karāha yadi udaya,
tabe tomāra pūrṇa kṛpā māni

"For most people, the mind and heart are one, but because My mind is never separated from Vṛndāvana, I consider My mind and Vṛndāvana to be one. My mind is already Vṛndāvana, and since You like Vṛndāvana, will You please place

Your lotus feet there? I would deem that Your full mercy." (*Caitanya-caritāmṛta* Madhya 13.137)

This mystic power is called *kāma-rūpa*, or the ability to assume any form one desires. The pure devotees absorb their minds in a particular relationship with Lord Kṛṣṇa and thus a spiritual body is awarded to them for an eternal life in the Lord's association. In this age, anyone who faithfully chants the holy names of Lord Kṛṣṇa and follows the regulative principles as instructed by the spiritual master can attain an eternal form in the supreme abode of the Lord.

TEXT 23

परकायंविशन्सिद्ध आत्मानंतत्रभावयेत् ।
पिण्डंहित्वाविशेत्प्राणोवायुभूतःषडङ्घ्रिवत् ॥२३॥

para-kāyaṁ viśan siddha ātmānaṁ tatra bhāvayet
piṇḍaṁ hitvā viśet prāṇo vāyu-bhūtaḥ ṣaḍaṅghri-vat

A yogi who desires to enter another body should meditate upon himself as being situated in that body. As a bumblebee easily goes from one flower to another, a yogi, with the help of his subtle body, can enter another body through the path of the air.

COMMENTARY

To enter into the body of another person, a yogi must relinquish his gross body and with the help of his subtle body, enter that body through the pathways of external air. It is something like a bumblebee, which travels from one flower to another. The *siddhi* of entering another body is called *para-kāya-praveśanam.*

PURPORT

One may admire a heroic man or beautiful woman and desire to experience life within their extraordinary material body. One can enter the body of another person by availing himself of the mystic perfection called *para-kāya-praveśanam.* However, pure devotees are never attracted to any kind of material body, knowing that even in the topmost planet there is material misery and death. Instead, they remain satisfied on the platform of eternal life. The spiritual air transfers a devotee to Goloka Vṛndāvana, where he eternally engages in the Lord's service as a member of His entourage.

TEXT 24

पार्ष्ण्यापीड्यगुदंप्राणंहृदुरःकण्ठमूर्धसु ।
आरोप्यब्रह्मरन्ध्रेणब्रह्मनीत्वोत्सृजेत्तनुम् ॥२४॥

pārṣṇyāpīḍya gudaṁ prāṇaṁ hṛd-uraḥ-kaṇṭha-mūrdhasu
āropya brahma-randhreṇa brahma nītvotsṛjet tanum

To achieve the mystic perfection called *svacchanda-mṛtyu,* a yogi should block his anus with the heel of his foot and then gradually lift the soul, along with the life air, from the heart to the chest, then to the neck, and finally to the head. Situated within the *brahma-randhra,* the yogi then gives up his material body and guides the spirit soul to his desired destination.

COMMENTARY

One who has attained the mystic perfection of *śvecchā mṛtyu*, the ability to die at will, can guide his soul, along with the life air, to either the impersonal Brahman or to any destination within the material world, through the *brahma-randhra*, by giving up his material body while blocking the anus with the heel of the foot.

PURPORT

Since the practice of giving up the body as described in this verse, by means of perfection in the practice of *haṭha yoga*, or *rāja yoga*, cannot enable one to surpass the kingdom of mundane existence, it is sensible to accept everything favorable for the practice of Kṛṣṇa consciousness. If one cultivates Kṛṣṇa consciousness within his heart while giving up all thoughts of sense gratification, thus detaching himself from the desire for material enjoyment, and giving up the propensity for either enjoying or renouncing the fruits of his karma while engaging in the service of the Supreme Lord, he will automatically attain this mystic perfection.

TEXT 25

विहरिष्यन्सुराक्रीडेमत्स्थंसत्त्वंविभावयेत् ।
विमानेनोपतिष्ठन्तिसत्त्ववृत्तीःसुरस्त्रियः ॥२५॥

vihariṣyan surākrīḍe mat-sthaṁ sattvaṁ vibhāvayet
vimānenopatiṣṭhanti sattva-vṛttīḥ sura-striyaḥ

One who desires to enjoy life in the celestial gardens of the demigods should meditate upon the mode of purified goodness, which is situated within Me. When he becomes fixed

in this meditation, heavenly damsels that are generated from the mode of goodness will approach him, riding in their celestial chariots.

COMMENTARY

One of the mystic perfections available to the yogi enables him to enjoy with the celestial damsels in heaven.

PURPORT

In order to remain aloof from the propensity of imitating the spirit of sense enjoyment after seeing sensual activities in a movie or among the lower animals, one's heart must become captivated by the Supreme Lord's *rāsa-līlā* pastimes. Even the spirit of enjoyment that celestial women can arouse in the heart of a yogi can be transformed in this way. *Anugrahāya bhaktānāṁ mānuṣaṁ deham āsthitaḥ bhajate tādṛśīḥ krīḍa yāḥ śrutvā tat-paro bhavet* (*Śrīmad-Bhāgavatam* 10.33.36): When the Lord assumes a humanlike body to show mercy to His devotees, He engages in such pastimes as will attract those who hear about them to become dedicated to Him.

This transformation is only possible when one has come to an advanced stage of yogic perfection. In that advanced stage, there is no question of imitating the Lord for one's personal sense gratification. Rather, the perfected yogi's only desire is to serve the Supreme Lord Śrī Kṛṣṇa. This is an example of an eternal *siddhi.*

TEXT 26

यथासङ्कल्पयेद्बुद्ध्यायदावामत्परःपुमान् ।
मयिसत्येमनोयुञ्जंस्तथातत्समुपाश्नुते ॥२६॥

yathā saṅkalpayed buddhyā yadā vā mat-paraḥ pumān
mayi satye mano yuñjaṁs tathā tat samupāśnute

One who has implicit faith in Me and thus concentrates his mind upon Me, knowing that My determination is never frustrated, will have his desires fulfilled by the very means he has adopted.

COMMENTARY

If one resolves with determination to attain some particular object, then he should meditate upon the Supreme Lord, whose determination is never foiled. This will enable one to achieve his desired goal. This mystic perfection is called *saṅkalpa siddhi.*

PURPORT

One should make up his mind to revive his forgotten relationship with the Supreme Personality of Godhead by means of devotional service, which can be executed anywhere by anyone. There are many scriptures that guide one back to home, back to Godhead. Among them are *Saṅkalpa kalpa-druma* by Śrīla Jīva Gosvāmī, *Śrī Govinda-līlāmṛta* by Śrīla Kṛṣṇadāsa Kavirāja Gosvāmī, *Śrī Kṛṣṇa-bhāvanāmṛta* and *Saṅkalpa kalpa-druma* by Śrīla Viśvanātha Cakravartī, and *Śrī Gaurāṅga-smaraṇa-maṅgala* by Śrīla Bhaktivinoda Ṭhākura. By carefully studying the subjects presented in books like *Bhakti-rasāmṛta-sindhu* and *Ujjvala-nīlamaṇi*, one's eternal perfection can be awakened, saving one from the attractions of this illusory material existence, which only end in misery.

TEXT 27

योवैमद्भावमापन्न ईशितुर्वशितुःपुमान् ।
कुतश्चिन्नविहन्येततस्यचाज्ञायथामम ॥२७॥

yo vai mad-bhāvam āpanna īśitur vaśituḥ pumān
kutaścin na vihanyeta tasya cājñā yathā mama

One who perfects his meditation upon Me can imbibe My controlling power. His order, just like Mine, can never be thwarted at any time.

COMMENTARY

If a yogi perfects his meditation upon the Supersoul, he can receive from the Lord the mystic power of being able to control others so well that, like the Lord, his order can never prove futile.

PURPORT

The material nature is working under the direction of the Supreme Lord. Pure devotees are never diverted from the service of the Supreme Lord, being tempted by the temporary objects of sense gratification. The orders of such devotees can never be frustrated, just as the orders of the Supreme Lord are never counteracted.

TEXT 28

मद्भक्त्याशुद्धसत्त्वस्ययोगिनोधारणाविदः ।
तस्यत्रैकालिकीबुद्धिर्जन्ममृत्यूपबृंहिता ॥२८॥

mad-bhaktyā śuddha-sattvasya yogino dhāraṇā-vidaḥ
tasya trai-kālikī buddhir janma-mṛtyūpabṛṁhitā

One who has become purified as a result of rendering devotional service to Me, and thus has carefully controlled his mind by the practice of meditation, becomes cognizant of past, present, and future. With this understanding, he can witness the appearance and disappearance of all living beings.

COMMENTARY

The Supreme Lord knows past, present and future, and so a yogi who meditates on the Lord can receive that mystic opulence from the Lord. This is the perfection known as *trikālajñatā siddhi,* which also enables one to know about the birth and death of all people.

PURPORT

The impersonalists imagine that they have become one with the Lord, but it is the devotees who actually share the Lord's transcendental qualities. Being fully devoted to the Lord, the pure devotees are situated on the same platform as the Lord, a platform that is above the influence of time in terms of past, present, and future. Thus, the pure devotees who are liberated due to being absorbed in the service of the Lord are knowers of past, present, and future, as is the Lord.

TEXT 29

अग्न्यादिभिर्नहन्येतमुनेर्योगमयंवपुः ।
मद्योगशान्तचित्तस्ययादसामुदकंयथा ॥२९॥

agny-ādibhir na hanyeta muner yoga-mayaṁ vapuḥ
mad-yoga-śānta-cittasya yādasām udakaṁ yathā

Just as the body of an aquatic cannot be injured by water, the body of a peaceful and devoted sage whose spiritual realization has matured by the practice of yoga, cannot be injured by fire, the sun, water, poison, and so forth.

COMMENTARY

By meditating on the Supreme Lord in pure devotional service, the heart of a peaceful sage becomes saturated with transcendental experience. In that stage of perfection, one attains the *siddhi* by which his body cannot be injured by the material elements in the form of fire, the sun, water, poison, and so forth. The example of an aquatic is given here. Water cannot harm the body of aquatics—rather they enjoy life in their natural element. Similarly, the perfect yogi can easily fend off all attacks from the material elements.

PURPORT

Although the material elements cause transformations of gross objects and can effect the nature of subtle existence, the spiritually blissful body of the Lord's devotees are never affected by material conditions. Devotees are never tempted to enjoy the objects of this world in a way that is not related to the service of the Supreme Lord. Materialists condemn their misfortune when they cannot make material advancement, whereas devotees of the Lord remain joyfully engaged in the devotional service of the Lord, having given up all desires for material advancement. The example is given that aquatics enjoy living in the water, whereas terrestrials in the bodily concept of life would bring about their destruction if they tried to live in the same way. Like the aquatics in water, as long as the Lord's devotees remain situated in their natural element of devotional service, they will not become overwhelmed by the currents of material thoughts, like the conditioned souls.

TEXT 30

मद्विभूतीरभिध्यायन्श्रीवत्सास्त्रविभूषिताः ।
ध्वजातपत्रव्यजनैःसभवेदपराजितः ॥३०॥

mad-vibhūtīr abhidhyāyan śrīvatsāstra-vibhūṣitāḥ
dhvajātapatra-vyajanaiḥ sa bhaved aparājitaḥ

A devotee who constantly meditates on My incarnations, which are decorated with the mark of Śrīvatsa and hold various weapons in Their hands, and which always appear with royal grandeur, cannot be conquered by anyone.

COMMENTARY

By meditating on the various incarnations of the Lord, one becomes unconquerable in all respects. This mystic perfection is called *aparājaya siddhi.*

PURPORT

The Lord's flag, umbrella, *cāmara*, Kaustubha gem, and weapons indicate His omnipotency. Those who meditate on the Supreme Personality of Godhead in this feature attain the mystic perfection known as *aparājita*.

All of the mystic perfections obediently come to serve the devotee of the Lord. This is confirmed by Bilvamaṇgala Ṭhākura in his book, *Kṛṣṇa-karṇāmṛta* (107):

bhaktis tvayi sthiratarā bhagavan yadi syād
daivena naḥ phalati divya-kiśora-mūrtiḥ
muktiḥ svayaṁ mukulitāñjali sevate 'smān
dharmārtha-kāma-gatayaḥ samaya-pratīkṣāḥ

If I am engaged in devotional service unto You, my dear Lord, then very easily can I perceive Your presence everywhere. And as far as liberation is concerned, I think that liberation stands at my door with folded hands, waiting to serve me—and all material conveniences of *dharma* (religiosity), *artha* (economic development), and *kāma* (sense gratification) stand with her.

TEXT 31

उपासकस्यमामेवंयोगधारणयामुनेः ।
सिद्धयःपूर्वकथिता उपतिष्ठन्त्यशेषतः ॥३१॥

upāsakasya māṁ evaṁ yoga-dhāraṇayā muneḥ
siddhayaḥ pūrva-kathitā upatiṣṭhanty aśeṣataḥ

A learned sage who worships Me through *yoga* meditation certainly attains the *siddhis* that have been described by Me.

COMMENTARY

Here, the Lord concludes His explanation of the mystic powers obtained by the practice of yoga. The word *yoga-dhāraṇayā* indicates that one obtains the particular *yoga-siddha* he endeavored for.

TEXT 32

जितेन्द्रियस्यदान्तस्यजितश्वासात्मनोमुनेः ।
मद्धारणांधारयतःकासासिद्धिःसुदुर्लभा ॥३२॥

jitendriyasya dāntasya jita-śvāsātmano muneḥ
mad-dhāraṇāṁ dhārayataḥ kā sā siddhiḥ su-durlabhā

For one who has learned to control his senses, breathing, and mind, by being constantly engaged in meditation on Me, what mystic power would be very difficult for him to obtain?

COMMENTARY

The Lord herein says that anyone who can control his breathing and fix his mind on Him can achieve any mystic perfection he desires.

TEXT 33

अन्तरायान्वदन्त्येतायुञ्जतोयोगमुत्तमम् ।
मयासम्पद्यमानस्यकालक्षपणहेतवः ॥३३॥

antarāyān vadanty etā yuñjato yogam uttamam
mayā sampadyamānasya kāla-kṣapaṇa-hetavaḥ

It has been stated by learned experts in devotional service that for he who desires to achieve the wealth of My association by means of his execution of pure devotional service, the mystic perfections that I have described are actually impediments and a waste of time.

COMMENTARY

These mystic perfections can attract and excite only small boys and not mature men. These *siddhis* are actually impediments on the path of attaining shelter at the lotus feet of the Supreme Personality of Godhead. One who has the association of Lord Kṛṣṇa dwells within an unlimited ocean of mystic opulence, and so he should not waste his precious time pursuing mystic perfections independently of the Lord's service.

PURPORT

Inferior *yogas* like *haṭha-yoga* or *rāja-yoga* certainly waste the practitioner's valuable time. The devotees of the Lord consider such yoga practice to be a hindrance on the path of pure devotional service. In this regard, one should study the verse of the *Śrīmad-Bhāgavatam* (1.6.35) that begins with *yamādibhir yoga-pathaiḥ*.

TEXT 34

जन्मौषधितपोमन्त्रैर्यावतीरिहसिद्धयः ।
योगेनाप्नोतिताःसर्वानान्यैर्योगगतिंव्रजेत् ॥३४॥

janmauṣadhi-tapo-mantrair yāvatīr iha siddhayaḥ
yogenāpnoti tāḥ sarvā nānyair yoga-gatiṁ vrajet

Whatever mystic perfections can be achieved as a result of good birth, herbs, austerities, and *mantras* can be achieved by engagement in My devotional service. In fact, one cannot attain the actual perfection of yoga by any other means.

COMMENTARY

Some *siddhis* are naturally acquired from the time of one's birth. By taking birth as a demigod, one is automatically endowed with many mystic perfections. Simply by being born on Siddhaloka, one automatically acquires all of the eight principal perfections of yoga. Similarly, by being born as a fish one becomes invulnerable to water, by being born as a bird one gets the mystic perfection of flying, and by becoming a ghost one gets the mystic perfection of disappearing and entering the bodies of others. It is stated in the *Pātañjala śāstra* that mystic perfections can be achieved by good birth, medicinal herbs, austerities, *mantras*, and yoga.

PURPORT

Those who reject the devotional service of the Lord and endeavor for perfection by some other means cannot be considered very intelligent. The devotees reject all other processes to engage in the unalloyed devotional service of the Lord. So-called yogis who are interested in their personal sense enjoyment cannot understand the importance of pleasing the senses of Lord Kṛṣṇa. Any process other than the service of the Supreme Lord, which is the ultimate goal of *yoga*, will certainly award one only frustration.

TEXT 35

सर्वासामपिसिद्धीनांहेतुःपतिरहंप्रभुः ।
अहंयोगस्यसांख्यस्यधर्मस्यब्रह्मवादिनाम् ॥३५॥

sarvāsām api siddhīnāṁ hetuḥ patir ahaṁ prabhuḥ
ahaṁ yogasya sāṅkhyasya dharmasya brahma-vādinām

O Uddhava, I alone am the cause, maintainer, and Lord of all mystic perfections, all yoga processes, Sāṅkhya philosophy, devotional service, and *brahmavādīs*.

COMMENTARY

All mystic perfections are accomplished simply by meditating on the Supreme Lord. Therefore, He is the cause of all kinds of mystic perfections. He is also the maintainer of the mystic perfections, and the Lord of those perfections as well. He is the object of the yogis' meditation, by which they achieve mystic perfections. The Lord is also the objective of the cultivation of spiritual knowledge and the performance of pious activities.

PURPORT

The Supreme Lord alone is the object of the various *abhidheyas*, or paths of perfection, which are followed by all classes of human beings. The so-called perfection attained by those who have become bewildered by self-centered egoistic conceptions of life and have thus given up the service of the Supreme Lord is temporary and most insignificant. The Supreme Lord is present everywhere, and He is the ultimate goal of all processes for attaining perfection in life.

TEXT 36

अहमात्मान्तरोबाह्योऽनावृतःसर्वदेहिनाम् ।
यथाभूतानिभूतेषुबहिरन्तःस्वयंतथा ॥३६॥

aham ātmāntaro bāhyo 'nāvṛtaḥ sarva-dehinām
yathā bhūtāni bhūteṣu bahir antaḥ svayaṁ tathā

Just as the material elements are situated within and outside all material bodies, in the same way, I am also present within everything as the Supersoul and outside of everything in My all-pervading feature.

COMMENTARY

It is said that the Lord is situated within the hearts of all living beings. While considering this, one might imagine that the Lord has separated Himself into innumerable different identities. In this verse, however, the Lord explains that His existence cannot be infringed upon by some mere material conditions. He remains unchanging in spite of displaying so many manifestations. Just as the material elements are situated both within and without all material bodies, so the Lord is all-pervading.

Thus ends the translation of the Ninth Chapter of the Uddhava-gītā entitled **"Lord Kṛṣṇa's Description of Mystic Yoga Perfections,"** *with the commentaries of Śrīla Viśvanātha Cakravartī Ṭhākura and chapter summary and purports by Śrīla Bhaktisiddhānta Sarasvatī Ṭhākura.*

Chapter 10

The Lord's Opulence

CHAPTER SUMMARY

In this chapter, the Supreme Lord describes His opulence in terms of His specific potencies of knowledge, prowess, influence, and so on.

Śrī Uddhava glorified Lord Śrī Kṛṣṇa by saying, "The Supreme Lord has no beginning nor end, and He is the cause of all living entities' creation, maintenance, and destruction. He is the Supersoul of all living entities, and thus He witnesses all the activities of those in material existence by remaining within their hearts. Still, being bewildered by the Lord's external energy, the conditioned souls cannot see Him."

After offering these prayers at the lotus feet of Lord Kṛṣṇa, Śrī Uddhava expressed his desire to know about the Lord's various opulences, as exhibited in heaven, on earth, in hell, and in all directions. Lord Śrī Kṛṣṇa then described all these opulences in detail and concluded by saying that all prowess, beauty, fame, opulence, modesty, charity, wonder, good fortune, heroism, forgiveness, and wisdom that are manifest in the material world are simply portions of His splendor. It therefore cannot be truthfully said that material objects possess these opulences. Such conceptions arise from mentally combining two ideas to produce an object that exists only in the imagination, like a flower in the sky. Material objects are not essentially real, and so one should not concentrate his mind on them. By regulating their speech, mind, and vital life air, with the help of intelligence, devotees of the Lord perfect their existence in Kṛṣṇa consciousness.

TEXT 1

श्रीउद्धव उवाच
त्वंब्रह्मपरमंसाक्षादनाद्यन्तमपावृतम् ।
सर्वेषामपिभावानांत्राणस्थित्यप्ययोद्भवः ॥१॥

śrī-uddhava uvāca
tvaṁ brahma paramaṁ sākṣād anādy-antam apāvṛtam
sarveṣām api bhāvānāṁ trāṇa-sthity-apyayodbhavaḥ

Śrī Uddhava said: My dear Lord, You are beginningless and without end, the Absolute Truth Himself, uncovered by anything else. You are the protector and life-giver, as well as the destruction and creation of all things that exist.

COMMENTARY

This chapter describes the Lord's principal opulences, as well as the extent of His influence and knowledge.

The previous chapter concluded with the statement that the lotus feet of the Supreme Lord are the original cause of all mystic perfections. After hearing this, Uddhava expressed his desire to know more about Kṛṣṇa's material and spiritual opulence. Śrī Uddhava glorified Lord Kṛṣṇa as the supreme shelter of all. He said, "O Lord, You are the Supreme Personality of Godhead. Your form is eternal, You are without beginning, and Your existence is not covered by anyone or anything. Although You appear to be limited when You descend in Your humanlike form, You are all-pervading. The original creator of the cosmic manifestation, Lord Viṣṇu, is Your plenary portion. You are the protector of everyone, You sustain everyone, and You maintain all living entities."

PURPORT

The Supreme Brahman, who is the ultimate cause of the creation, maintenance, and annihilation of the visible material universe is Himself free of all kinds of material designations. He is not under the control of material time because time is one of His countless manifestations.

TEXT 2

उच्चावचेषुभूतेषुदुर्ज्ञेयमकृतात्मभिः ।
उपासतेत्वांभगवन्याथातथ्येनब्राह्मणाः ॥२॥

uccāvaceṣu bhūteṣu durjñeyam akṛtātmabhiḥ
upāsate tvāṁ bhagavan yāthā-tathyena brāhmaṇāḥ

My dear Lord, although it is difficult for those who are impious to understand how You are situated in all superior and inferior creations, the *brāhmaṇas* who actually know the Vedic conclusion, worship You in all sincerity.

COMMENTARY

Uddhava said, "Although You are the origin of the *viṣṇu-tattva*, and You are situated within all higher and lower species of life, ignorant and impious people cannot appreciate Your glories. On the other hand, *brāhmaṇas* who know the *Vedas* as Your sound representation faithfully engage in Your worship."

PURPORT

The word *uccāvaca* in this verse means "superior and inferior," "higher and lower," or "great and insignificant." When one possesses material objects, they gradually transform before one's very eyes because they are under the control of time. Therefore, to meditate on the objects of the senses will not yield a permanent result. Those who know the *Vedas* search for the origin of material time, place, and the candidate, and thus come to the conclusion that the devotional service of the Supreme Lord is life's actual goal.

TEXT 3

येषुयेषुचभूतेषुभक्त्यात्वांपरमर्षयः ।
उपासीनाःप्रपद्यन्तेसंसिद्धिंतद्वदस्वमे ॥३॥

yeṣu yeṣu ca bhūteṣu bhaktyā tvāṁ paramarṣayaḥ
upāsīnāḥ prapadyante saṁsiddhiṁ tad vadasva me

Please describe to me the perfections attained by the devotees who worship you with great and transcendental faith, and please describe the transcendental forms of Your Lordship that they worship.

COMMENTARY

By worshiping various form of the Lord, one can achieve particular mystic perfections. To hear about this is the request of Śrī Uddhava.

TEXT 4

गूढश्चरसिभूतात्माभूतानांभूतभावन
नत्वांपश्यन्तिभूतानिपश्यन्तंमोहितानिते

gūḍhaś carasi bhūtātmā bhūtānāṁ bhūta-bhāvana
na tvāṁ paśyanti bhūtāni paśyantaṁ mohitāni te

O my Lord, maintainer of the living entities, You remain hidden within the hearts of all living entities as the Supersoul. Being bewildered by Your energy, they cannot see You, although You see everyone.

COMMENTARY

For those who are conditioned by the three modes of material nature, the opulence of the Lord is incomprehensible. Uddhava said: "Despite Your presence as the Supersoul in all living entities, the conditioned souls cannot see You. Although You are the benefactor of everyone, You remain hidden within their hearts so that they cannot see You." If one reads the word *bhūtabhāvana* without the *visarga*, Uddhava addresses the Lord as, "O benefactor of all living entities."

PURPORT

The Supreme Lord is transcendentally situated, and thus beyond the reach of the material senses. The foolish conditioned souls consider God to be their order supplier. Materialistic men may sometimes appear to be very religious, but because they consider themselves to be the proprietors of God's creation, their prayers are simply that their material desires may be fulfilled. Everything within the creation is owned and controlled by the Supreme Lord. When the Lord sometimes appears as an incarnation, such bewildered materialists generally take Him to be just another product of the modes of material nature, being unable to appreciate His transcendental position.

TEXT 5

याःकाश्चभूमौदिविवैरसायांविभूतयोदिक्षुमहाविभूते ।
तामह्यमाख्याह्यनुभावितास्तेनमामितेतीर्थपदाङ्घ्रिपद्मम् ॥५॥

yāḥ kāś ca bhūmau divi vai rasāyāṁ vibhūtayo dikṣu mahā-vibhūte
tā mahyam ākhyāhy anubhāvitās te namāmi te tīrtha-padāṅghri-padmam

O Supreme Personality of Godhead, please describe to me Your inconceivable potencies, which You manifest on this earth, as well as on all other planets throughout the universe. I offer my obeisances at Your lotus feet, which are the shelter of all the holy places of pilgrimage.

COMMENTARY

Uddhava said, "Because the understanding of Your opulence is most confidential, You Yourself must reveal this knowledge. We can know about Your opulences only by Your grace." For the understanding of the conditioned souls, Uddhava requests the Lord to explain how He expands His potencies by means of His various expansions. The word *vibhūti* in this regard refers to the Lord's material and spiritual potencies, as manifested within our universe.

PURPORT

To remove the ignorance of the foolish conditioned souls, the Supreme Lord accepts a mood of magnanimity and acts as an instructor. The conditioned souls, driven by the desire to cultivate knowledge of the external world, are unable to understand the existence of the Absolute Truth.

TEXT 6

श्रीभगवानुवाच
एवमेतदहंपृष्टःप्रश्नंप्रश्नविदांवर ।
युयुत्सुनाविनशनेसपत्नैरर्जुनेन वै ॥६॥

śrī-bhagavān uvāca
evam etad ahaṁ pṛṣṭaḥ praśnaṁ praśna-vidāṁ vara
yuyutsunā vinaśane sapatnair arjunena vai

The Supreme Lord said: O best among those who inquire about the truth, at Kurukṣetra, as he prepared to confront his enemies, Arjuna asked Me this very question that you have raised.

COMMENTARY

On the battlefield of Kurukśetra, Arjuna inquired in a similar manner.

TEXT 7

ज्ञात्वाज्ञातिवधंगर्ह्यमधर्मंराज्यहेतुकम् ।
ततोनिवृत्तोहन्ताहंहतोऽयमितिलौकिकः ॥७॥

jñātvā jñāti-vadhaṁ garhyam adharmaṁ rājya-hetukam
tato nivṛtto hantāhaṁ hato 'yam iti laukikaḥ

While seated on his chariot in the midst of the battlefield, Arjuna thought that killing his relatives would be the sinful result of aspiring to fight for a kingdom to rule. He wanted to leave the battlefield, thinking, "I don't want to be the slayer of my relatives."

COMMENTARY

Arjuna inquired about the Lord's opulence at a time when he had refused to fight, considering that to kill his relatives for the sake of enjoying a kingdom would be highly irreligious. Arjuna thought of himself as the killer, and his relatives as those who would be killed. These were his mundane conceptions.

TEXT 8

सतदापुरुषव्याघ्रोयुक्त्यामेप्रतिबोधितः ।
अभ्यभाषतमामेवंयथात्वंरणमूर्धनि ॥८॥

sa tadā puruṣa-vyāghro yuktyā me pratibodhitaḥ
abhyabhāṣata mām evaṁ yathā tvaṁ raṇa-mūrdhani

I enlightened the despondent Arjuna, a tiger among men, by means of reason and argument. In the midst of the battlefield, Arjuna questioned Me just as you are now inquiring.

TEXT 9

अहमात्मोद्धवामीषांभूतानांसुहृदीश्वरः ।
अहंसर्वाणिभूतानितेषांस्थित्युद्भवाप्ययः ॥९॥

aham ātmoddhavāmīṣāṁ bhūtānāṁ suhṛd īśvaraḥ
ahaṁ sarvāṇi bhūtāni teṣāṁ sthity-udbhavāpyayaḥ

My dear Uddhava, I am the Supersoul of all living entities, and so I am naturally their benefactor. I am the supreme controller and sustainer of all living entities, and the cause of creation, maintenance, and destruction.

COMMENTARY

Lord Śrī Kṛṣṇa herein describes His opulence in general.

TEXT 10

अहंगतिर्गतिमतांकालःकलयतामहम् ।
गुनाणांचाप्यहंसाम्यंगुणिन्यौत्पत्तिकोगुणः ॥१०॥

ahaṁ gatir gatimatām kālaḥ kalayatām aham
gunāṇāṁ cāpy ahaṁ sāmyaṁ guṇiny autpattiko guṇaḥ

I am the supreme destination for those who are trying to make progress, and I am time for those who attempt to exert control over others. I am the equilibrium of the three modes of material nature, and I am the natural ability of those who possess talent.

COMMENTARY

The essential nature of all material and spiritual objects is that they are manifestations of the Lord's opulence. The Supreme Lord is the actual objective for fruitive workers and mental speculators. He is understood as time by those who delight in controlling others, and among the qualities, He is the special quality that is exhibited by those who possess some particular talent.

PURPORT

The Lord is the ultimate goal for all those who search after some kind of perfection because everything is simply a manifestation of His unlimited potencies. The results obtained by fruitive workers are awarded by the Supreme Lord through the agency of the demigods. Mental speculators may abandon the fruits of their labor, but their quest is to realize the all-pervading aspect of the Lord known as Brahman. Materialists run after the temporary objects displayed by the Lord's illusory energy and thus miss the chance for self-realization. Those who reject material variegatedness and consider the Absolute Truth to be devoid of qualities cannot understand how the Supreme Lord possesses transcendental qualities. In this way, it is seen that the Supreme Lord is the ultimate goal of all kinds of people. Those who desire to enjoy the fruits of their labor and those who desire to become one with the Supreme, are covered by the external energy of the Lord. The actual goal of life is to engage in the Lord's loving devotional service on the transcendental platform.

TEXT 11

गुणिनामप्यहंसुत्रंमहतांचमहानहम् ।
सूक्ष्माणामप्यहंजीवोदुर्जयानामहंमनः ॥११॥

guṇinām apy ahaṁ sutraṁ mahatāṁ ca mahān aham
sūkṣmāṇām apy ahaṁ jīvo durjayānām ahaṁ manaḥ

Among things that possess qualities, I am the primary manifestation of nature, and among great things, I am the *mahat-tattva,* the total material manifestation. Among subtle things, I am the spirit soul, and among things that are difficult to conquer, I am the mind.

COMMENTARY

The word *sūtra* indicates the primary manifestation of nature. Here, the Lord says, "Among things that are difficult to control, I am the mind, and among subtle things, I am the spirit soul." This is also described in the *Vedas*:

eṣo 'ṇur ātmā cetasā veditavyo yasmin prāṇaḥ pañcadhā saṁviveśa
prāṇaiś cittaṁ sarvam otaṁ prajānāṁ yasmin viśuddhe vibhavaty eṣa ātmā

The soul is atomic in size and can be perceived by perfect intelligence. The atomic soul is floating in the five kinds of air (*prāṇa, apāna, vyāna, samāna,* and *udāna*), is situated within the heart, and spreads its influence all over the body of the embodied living entities. When the soul is purified from the contamination of the five kinds of material air, its spiritual influence is exhibited. (*Muṇḍaka Upaniṣad* 3.1.9)

Elsewhere, it is stated:

bālāgra-śata-bhāgasya śatadhā kalpitasya ca
bhāgo jīvaḥ vijñeyaḥ sa cānantyāya kalpate

When the upper point of a hair is divided into one hundred parts and again each of such parts is further divided into one hundred parts, each such part is the measurement of the dimension of the spirit soul. (*Śvetāśvatara Upaniṣad* 5.9)

The dimension of the spirit soul is smaller than the tip of an arrow. Although the spirit soul is minute in size, like an atom, it is spread all over the body and its energy works throughout the body. As a precious jewel or powerful medicine, although covered by lac, manifests its effect when touched to the head, the minute size of the spirit soul does not hamper his display of prowess.

TEXT 12

हिरण्यगर्भोवेदानांमन्त्राणांप्रणवस्त्रिवृत् ।
अक्षराणामकारोऽस्मिपदानिच्छन्दुसामहम् ॥१२॥

hiraṇyagarbho vedānāṁ mantrāṇāṁ praṇavas tri-vṛt
akṣarāṇām a-kāro 'smi padāni cchandusām aham

I am the original teacher of the *Vedas*, Hiraṇyagarbha (Lord Brahmā), and among *mantras* I am the three-lettered *oṁkāra*. Among letters, I am the first letter "a" (*a-kāraḥ*), and among sacred hymns, I am the *Gāyatri mantra*.

COMMENTARY

The Lord says that among the teachers of the *Vedas*, He is Hiraṇyagarbha Brahmā, and among the sacred hymns of the *Vedas*, He is the Gāyatrī *mantra*.

TEXT 13

इन्द्रोऽहंसर्वदेवानांवसूनामस्मिहव्यवाट् ।
आदित्यानामहंविष्णूरुद्राणांनीललोहितः ॥१३॥

indro 'haṁ sarva-devānāṁ vasūnām asmi havya-vāṭ
ādityānām ahaṁ viṣṇū rudrāṇāṁ nīla-lohitaḥ

Among the demigods, I am Indra, and among the Vasus, I am Agni. Among the Ādityas, I am Viṣṇu, and among the Rudras, I am Śiva.

TEXT 14

ब्रह्मर्षीणांभृगुरहंराजर्षीणामहंमनुः ।
देवर्षीणांनारदोऽहंहविर्धान्यस्मिधेनुषु ॥१४॥

brahmarṣīṇāṁ bhṛgur ahaṁ rājarṣīṇām ahaṁ manuḥ
devarṣīṇāṁ nārado 'haṁ havirdhāny asmi dhenuṣu

Among great sages, I am Bhṛgu, and among saintly kings, I am Manu. I am Nārada Muni among saintly demigods, and among cows, I am the Kāmadhenu.

COMMENTARY

The word *havirdhāni* refers to the cow known as Kāmadhenu, or wish-fulfilling cow.

TEXT 15

सिद्धेश्वराणांकपिलःसुपर्णोऽहंपतत्रिणाम् ।
प्रजापतीनांदक्षोऽहंपितॄणामहमर्यमा ॥१५॥

siddheśvarāṇāṁ kapilaḥ suparṇo 'haṁ patatriṇām
prajāpatīnāṁ dakṣo 'haṁ pitṝṇām aham aryamā

Among perfected beings, I am Kapila, and among birds, I am Garuḍa. Among progenitors of mankind, I am Dakṣa, and among the forefathers, I am Aryamā.

TEXT 16

मांविद्धयुद्धवदैत्यानांप्रह्लादमसुरेश्वरम् ।
सोमंनक्षत्रौषधीनांधनेशंयक्षरक्षसाम् ॥१६॥

māṁ viddhy uddhava daityānāṁ prahlādam asureśvaram
somaṁ nakṣatrauṣadhīnāṁ dhaneśaṁ yakṣa-rakṣasām

My dear Uddhava, among the Daityas, I am Prahlāda Mahārāja, the king of the demons. Among the stars and medicinal herbs, I am the moon-god, and among the Yakṣas and Rākṣasas, I am the god of wealth, Kuvera.

TEXT 17

ऐरावतंगजेन्द्राणांयादसांवरुणंप्रभुम् ।
तपतांद्युमतांसूर्यंमनुष्याणांचभूपतिम् ॥१७॥

airāvataṁ gajendrāṇāṁ yādasāṁ varuṇaṁ prabhum
tapatāṁ dyumatāṁ sūryaṁ manuṣyāṇāṁ ca bhū-patim

Among lordly elephants, I am Airāvata, and among the aquatics, I am Varuṇa, the lord of the seas. Among things that heat and illuminate, I am the sun, and among human beings, I am the king.

TEXT 18

उच्चैःश्रवास्तुरङ्गाणांधातूनामस्मिकाञ्चनम् ।
यमःसंयमतांचाहम्सर्पाणामस्मिवासुकिः ॥१८॥

uccaiḥśravās turaṅgāṇāṁ dhātūnām asmi kāñcanam
yamaḥ saṁyamatāṁ cāham sarpāṇām asmi vāsukiḥ

Among horses, I am Uccaiḥśravā, and among the metals, I am gold. Among those who award punishment, I am Yamarāja, and among serpents, I am Vāsuki.

TEXT 19

नागेन्द्राणामनन्तोऽहंमृगेन्द्रःशृङ्गिदंष्ट्रिणाम् ।
आश्रमाणामहंतुर्योवर्णानांप्रथमोऽनघ ॥१९॥

nāgendrāṇām ananto 'haṁ mṛgendraḥ śṛṅgi-daṁṣṭriṇām
āśramāṇām ahaṁ turyo varṇānāṁ prathamo 'nagha

O sinless Uddhava, among the foremost of Nāgas, I am Ananta, and among those animals who have sharp horns and teeth, I am the lion. Among the ***āśramas,*** I am the fourth, the ***sannyāsa āśrama,*** and among the ***varṇas,*** I am first, the ***brāhmaṇas.***

TEXT 20

तीर्थानांस्रोतसांगङ्गासमुद्रःसरसामहम् ।
आयुधानांधनुरहंत्रिपुरघ्नोधनुष्मताम् ॥२०॥

tīrthānāṁ srotasāṁ gaṅgā samudraḥ sarasām aham
āyudhānāṁ dhanur ahaṁ tripura-ghno dhanuṣmatām

Among holy places and rivers, I am the Ganges, and among steady bodies of water, I am the ocean. Among weapons, I am the bow, and among wielders of weapons, I am Lord Śiva.

TEXT 21

धिष्ण्यानामस्म्यहंमेरुर्गहनानांहिमालयः ।
वनस्पतीनामश्वत्थ ओषधीनामहंयवः ॥२१॥

dhiṣṇyānām asmy ahaṁ merur gahanānāṁ himālayaḥ
vanaspatīnām aśvattha oṣadhīnām ahaṁ yavaḥ

Among residences, I am Mount Sumeru, and among unyielding places, I am the Himālayas. Among trees, I am the ***aśvattha,*** and among medicinal plants, I am barley.

TEXT 22

पुरोधसांवसिष्ठोऽहंब्रह्मिष्ठानांबृहस्पतिः ।
स्कन्दोऽहंसर्वसेनान्यामग्रण्यांभगवानजः ॥२२॥

purodhasāṁ vasiṣṭho 'haṁ brahmiṣṭhānāṁ bṛhaspatiḥ
skando 'haṁ sarva-senānyām agraṇyāṁ bhagavān ajaḥ

Among priests, I am Vaśiṣṭha, and among those who are well-versed in the *Vedas*, I am Bṛhaspati. Among military commanders, I am Kārtikeya, and among those who are advancing in spiritual life, I am Brahmā.

TEXT 23

यज्ञानांब्रह्मयज्ञोऽहंव्रतानामविहिंसनम् ।
वाय्वग्न्यर्काम्बुवागात्माशुचीनामप्यहं शुचिः ॥२३॥

yajñānāṁ brahma-yajño 'haṁ vratānām avihiṁsanam
vāyv-agny-arkāmbu-vāg-ātmā śucīnām apy ahaṁ śuciḥ

Among sacrifices, I am the study of the *Vedas*, among vows, I am nonviolence. Among all things that purify, I am the air, fire, the sun, water, and speech.

TEXT 24

योगानामात्मसंरोधोमन्त्रोऽस्मिविजिगीषताम् ।
आन्वीक्षिकीकौशलानांविकल्पःख्यातिवादिनाम् ॥२४॥

yogānām ātma-saṁrodho mantro 'smi vijigiṣatām
ānvīkṣikī kauśalānāṁ vikalpaḥ khyāti-vādinām

Among the eight parts of *aṣṭāṅga-yoga*, I am *samādhi*, whereby the soul is liberated from illusion. Among those who desire victory, I am good moral council, among all types of logical discrimination, I am the intelligence that allows one to discriminate between matter and spirit, and among philosophers, I am the sense of discrimination.

TEXT 25

स्त्रीणांतुशतरूपाहपुंसांस्वायम्भुवोमनुः ।
नारायणोमुनीनांचकुमारोब्रह्मचारिणाम् ॥२५॥

strīṇāṁ tu śatarūpāhaṁ puṁsāṁ svāyambhuvo manuḥ
nārāyaṇo munīnāṁ ca kumāro brahmacāriṇām

Among women, I am Śatarūpa. and among men, I am Svāyambhūva Manu. Among sages, I am Nārāyaṇa, and among *brahmacārīs*, I am Sanat-kumāra.

TEXT 26

धर्माणामस्मिसन्न्यासःक्षेमाणामबहिर्मतिः ।
गुह्यानांसुनृतंमौनंमिथुनानामजस्त्वहम् ॥२६॥

dharmāṇām asmi sannyāsaḥ kṣemāṇām abahir-matiḥ
guhyānāṁ su-nṛtaṁ maunaṁ mithunānām ajas tv aham

Among all religious principles, I am the renunciation of material enjoyment, and of all types of welfare, I am realization of the eternal soul within the material body. Among secret things, I am silence, and among those possessing sexual prowess, I am Prajāpati Brahmā.

COMMENTARY

In the *Vedas*, it is stated, *arddho vā eṣa ātmā yat patni*, which means "the wife is the better half of a man's body."

TEXT 27

संवत्सरोऽस्म्यनिमिषामृतूनांमधुमाधवौ ।
मासानांमार्गशीर्षोऽहंनक्षत्राणांतथाभिजित् ॥२७॥

saṁvatsaro 'smy animiṣām ṛtūnāṁ madhu-mādhavau
māsānāṁ mārgaśīrṣo 'haṁ nakṣatrāṇāṁ tathābhijit

Among the cycles of time, I am the year, and among seasons, I am spring. Among months, I am Mārgaśīrṣa (November-December), and among the stars, I am Abhijit.

COMMENTARY

It is stated in the *Vedas* that Abhijīt is situated between *uttarāṣaḍhā* and *śravaṇā*.

TEXT 28

अहंयुगानांचकृतंधीराणांदेवलोऽसितः ।
द्वैपायनोऽस्मिव्यासानांकवीनांकाव्य आत्मवान् ॥२८॥

ahaṁ yugānāṁ ca kṛtaṁ dhīrāṇāṁ devalo 'sitaḥ
dvaipāyano 'smi vyāsānāṁ kavīnāṁ kāvya ātmavān

Among yugas, I am Satya-yuga, the age of truth, and among sober sages, I am Devala and Asita. Among those who divided the *Vedas*, I am Kṛṣṇa Dvaipāyaṇa Vedavyāsa, and among learned scholars, I am the wise Śukrācārya, who is learned in the spiritual science.

TEXT 29

वासुदेवोभगवतांत्वंतुभागवतेष्वहम् ।
किम्पुरुषानांहनुमान्विद्याध्राणांसुदर्शनः ॥२९॥

vāsudevo bhagavatāṁ tvaṁ tu bhāgavateṣv aham
kimpuruṣāṇāṁ hanumān vidyādhrāṇāṁ sudarśanaḥ

Among personalities who are entitled to be called Bhagavān, I am Vāsudeva, and you, Uddhava, represent Me among the devotees. Among the Kimpuruṣas, I am Hanumān, and among the Vidyādharas, I am Sudarśana.

TEXT 30

रत्नानांपद्मरागोऽस्मिपद्मकोशःसुपेशसाम् ।
कुशोऽस्मिदर्भजातीनांगव्यमाज्यंहविःष्वहम् ॥३०॥

ratnānāṁ padma-rāgo 'smi padma-kośaḥ su-peśasām
kuśo 'smi darbha-jātīnāṁ gavyam ājyaṁ haviḥṣv aham

Among jewels, I am the ruby, and among beautiful things, I am the whorl of the lotus. Among grasses, I am the sacred *kuśa* grass, and among oblations meant for sacrifice, I am cow's ghee.

TEXT 31

व्यवसायिनामहंलक्ष्मीःकितवानांछलग्रहः ।
तितिक्षास्मितितिक्षूणांसत्त्वंसत्त्ववतामहम् ॥३१॥

vyavasāyinām ahaṁ lakṣmīḥ kitavānāṁ chala-grahaḥ
titikṣāsmi titikṣūṇāṁ sattvaṁ sattvavatām aham

I am the wealth of those who are enterprising, and among the cheaters, I am gambling. I am the forgiveness of those who are tolerant, and I am the good qualities of those who are situated in the mode of goodness.

TEXT 32

ओजःसहोबलवतांकर्माहंविद्धिसात्वताम् ।
सात्वतांनवमूर्तीनामादिमूर्तिरहंपरा ॥३२॥

ojaḥ saho balavatāṁ karmāhaṁ viddhi sātvatām
sātvatāṁ nava-mūrtīnām ādi-mūrtir ahaṁ parā

Of those who are exceptionally powerful, I am mental and physical strength, and I am the devotional activities of the devotees. Among the nine forms worshiped by devotees, I am Vāsudeva.

COMMENTARY

The Personality of Godhead expands as Vāsudeva, Saṅkarṣaṇa, Pradyumna, Aniruddha, Nārāyaṇa, Hayagrīva, Varāha, and Nṛsiṁha, and sometimes He accepts the post of Brahmā. It has been explained that when no one is qualified to occupy the post of Brahmā, the Lord Himself accepts this position. Lord Viṣṇu also sometimes appears as Indra. During the reign of Svāyambhūva Manu, Lord Viṣṇu appeared as Indra, and in some *kalpas*, Lord Viṣṇu appeared as Brahmā.

TEXT 33

विश्वावसुःपूर्वचित्तिर्गन्धर्वाप्सरसामहम् ।
भूधराणामहंस्थैर्यंगन्धमात्रमहंभुवः ॥३३॥

viśvāvasuḥ pūrvacittir gandharvāpsarasām aham
bhūdharāṇām ahaṁ sthairyaṁ gandha-mātram ahaṁ bhuvaḥ

Among the Gandharvas, I am Viśvāvasu, and among the Apsarās, I am Pūrvacitti. I am the immovability of mountains and I am the original fragrance of the earth.

COMMENTARY

The world *mātrā* indicates the original fragrance of the earth. In the *Bhagavad-gītā* (7.9) Lord Kṛṣṇa says, *puṇyo gandhaḥ pṛthivyāṁ ca*: "I am the original fragrance of the earth." The original fragrance of the earth is very pleasing, and it represents Lord Kṛṣṇa.

TEXT 34

अपांरसश्चपरमस्तेजिष्ठानांविभावसुः ।
प्रभासूर्येन्दुताराणांशब्दोऽहंनभसःपरः ॥३४॥

apāṁ rasaś ca paramas tejiṣṭhānāṁ vibhāvasuḥ
prabhā sūryendu-tārāṇāṁ śabdo 'haṁ nabhasaḥ paraḥ

I am the taste of water, and I am the light of the sun, moon, and stars. I am the transcendental sound vibration heard within the sky.

COMMENTARY

By the use of the word *parama*, or "excellent," other tastes, such as sour and bitter, have been rejected. The word *para* in this verse is used to indicate transcendental sound.

TEXT 35

ब्रह्मण्यानांबलिरहंवीराणामहमर्जुनः ।
भूतानांस्थितिरुत्पत्तिरहंवैप्रतिसङ्क्रमः ॥३५॥

brahmaṇyānāṁ balir ahaṁ vīrāṇām aham arjunaḥ
bhūtānāṁ sthitir utpattir ahaṁ vai pratisaṅkramaḥ

Among those who are dedicated to maintaining brahminical culture, I am Bali Mahārāja, the son of Virocana, and among heroic warriors, I am Arjuna. Indeed, I am the creation, maintenance, and annihilation of all living entities.

COMMENTARY

The word *pratisaṁkramaḥ* refers to annihilation.

TEXT 36

गत्युक्त्युत्सर्गोपादानमानन्दस्पर्शलक्षनम् ।
आस्वादश्रुत्यवघ्राणमहंसर्वेन्द्रियेन्द्रियम् ॥३६॥

gaty-ukty-utsargopādānam ānanda-sparśa-lakṣanam
āsvāda-śruty-avaghrāṇam ahaṁ sarvendriyendriyam

I am the functions of the legs, such as walking, and I am the functions of the hands, such as picking up. I am speaking, evacuation, the pleasure of the genitals, touching, seeing, tasting, hearing, and smelling. I am the potency by which each of the senses experiences its particular sense object.

COMMENTARY

The Supreme Lord Śrī Kṛṣṇa provides the potency whereby the five working senses and the five knowledge-acquiring senses can act. This is confirmed in the *Vedas*, wherein it is stated that the Lord supplies the energy whereby the senses can abstract pleasure from the sense objects.

TEXT 37

पृथिवीवायुराकाश आपोज्योतिरहंमहान् ।
विकारःपुरुषोऽव्यक्तंरजःसत्त्वंतमःपरम् ।
अहमेतत्प्रसंख्यानंज्ञानंतत्त्वविनिश्चयः ॥३७॥

pṛthivī vāyur ākāśa āpo jyotir ahaṁ mahān
vikāraḥ puruṣo 'vyaktaṁ rajaḥ sattvaṁ tamaḥ param
aham etat prasaṅkhyānaṁ jñānaṁ tattva-viniścayaḥ

I am the form, taste, smell, touch, and sound; false ego; the mahat-tattva; the five gross material elements; the eleven senses; the spirit soul, material nature, the three modes of material nature, goodness, passion and ignorance; as well as the transcendental Lord. I am all of these things, as well as the knowledge of their characteristics and the conviction brought about by this knowledge.

COMMENTARY

After giving a detailed summary of His opulences within this world, the Lord now describes the opulences that are expansions of His effulgence. The word *pṛthivī*, or earth, indicates its subtle fragrance. The word *ahaṁ* refers to *ahaṅkāra*, or false ego. The word *mahān* refers to the *mahat-tattva*. These seven are transformations of material nature. The five gross material elements are earth, water, fire, air, and sky. The eleven senses include the five working senses, the five knowledge-acquiring senses, and the mind. The word *puruṣa* refers to the living entity. Thus, the total number of items is twenty-five. In the Sāṅkhya philosophy, the three modes of material nature—goodness, passion, and ignorance—are also included. These are all opulences of the Supreme Lord.

TEXT 38

मयेश्वरेणजीवेनगुणेनगुणिनाविना ।
सर्वात्मनापिसर्वेणनभावोविद्यतेक्वचित् ॥३८॥

mayeśvareṇa jīvena guṇena guṇinā vinā
sarvātmanāpi sarveṇa na bhāvo vidyate kvacit

As the Absolute Truth, I am the origin of the living entity, the three modes of material nature, and the *mahat-tattva*. I am in one sense everything, and so nothing can exist without Me.

COMMENTARY

When the *mahat-tattva*, or total material existence, combines with the *jīvas*, or living entities, this material world becomes manifest. Everything that we experience within this world is a combination of the living entity and the material energy. The Supreme Personality of Godhead is the origin of both the living entities and matter. Thus it should be concluded that nothing can exist without the mercy of the Supreme Lord.

PURPORT

The cosmic manifestation is a combination of the Supreme Lord's two energies, the living entities and the illusory energy, *maya*. Because the energy and the energetic are ultimately one, when we speak of the Supreme Personality of Godhead, all of His energies are automatically included. One should never make the mistake of equating the temporary material nature with the eternal spiritual abode of the Lord. One should not conclude that the perverted nature of material existence also exists in the eternal realm, which is full of spiritual variegatedness. The Supreme Personality of Godhead is the entire basis of the existence of both the living entity and matter.

TEXT 39

संख्यानंपरमाणूनांकालेनक्रियतेमया ।
नतथामेविभूतीनांसृजतोऽण्डानिकोटिशः ॥३९॥

saṅkhyānaṁ paramāṇūnāṁ kālena kriyate mayā
na tathā me vibhūtīnāṁ sṛjato 'ṇḍāni koṭiśaḥ

Although it might be possible for Me to count all the atoms within the universe, I could never count all the opulences that I manifest within the innumerable universes.

COMMENTARY

In this verse, the Supreme Lord gives a hint of the extent of His opulence. The Supreme Lord said, "It is certainly possible for Me to count the number of atoms in the universe, but it is impossible for anyone to estimate the extent of My opulence. When there is no estimate of the innumerable universes that I have created, how can the opulence that is present within those innumerable universes be estimated?"

TEXT 40

तेजःश्रीःकीर्तिरैश्वर्यंह्रीस्त्यागःसौभगंभगः ।
वीर्यंतितिक्षाविज्ञानंयत्रयत्रसमेंऽशकः ॥४०॥

tejaḥ śrīḥ kīrtir aiśvaryaṁ hrīs tyāgaḥ saubhagaṁ bhagaḥ
vīryaṁ titikṣā vijñānaṁ yatra yatra sa me 'ṁśakaḥ

Whatever prowess, beauty, fame, opulence, modesty, renunciation, good fortune, mental and sensual pleasure, strength, forgiveness, and knowledge of the self one finds in existence are but manifestations of a portion of My splendor.

COMMENTARY

The word *teja* in this verse means "influence," and the word *śrī* means "opulence." The word *saubhagam* refers to that which is pleasing to the mind and the senses. The word *bhaga* means "good fortune," the word *vīrya* means "strength," and the word *aṁśaka* means "portion of."

TEXT 41

एतास्तेकीर्तिताःसर्वाःसङ्क्षेपेणविभूतयः ।
मनोविकाराएवैतेयथावाचाभिधीयते ॥४१॥

etās te kīrtitāḥ sarvāḥ saṅkṣepeṇa vibhūtayaḥ
mano-vikārā evaite yathā vācābhidhīyate

I have thus briefly described to you My manifestation of opulences, as well as some of the characteristics of the material creation that can be perceived by the conditioned souls and thus defined in various ways.

COMMENTARY

The Lord's external opulences are herein referred to as *mano-vikārāḥ*, which means that they are perceived in various ways, according to a conditioned soul's mentality. The word *vācābhidhīyate* indicates the same thing—that conditioned souls describe the nature of the universe according to their capacity, or mentality. It is for this reason that the external opulence of the Lord is considered inferior and not the direct manifestation of the Lord. The same person can evoke opposing conceptions within the mind of the conditioned soul. In a favorable state of mind, one designates someone as "my son," "my father," "my husband," "my friend," and so on, forgetting that everyone is an eternal part and parcel of the Lord. Similarly, in a negative state of mind, one may thinks, "This person is my enemy," and so on, forgetting that everyone is the Lord's eternal servant. The example can be given of the demigod Indra, who is a manifestation of the Lord's material opulence, and is thus considered in various ways. Indra's wife, mother, son, and guru naturally think of him in favorable terms, whereas the demons think of him as their enemy. It is for this reason that the Lord's material opulences are referred to here as *mano-vikāra*. Such relative perceptions are certainly material because they fail to express the truth, that all living entities are the Lord's eternal parts and parcels. When a devotee sees Lord Kṛṣṇa as the origin and proprietor of all kinds of opulence, and therefore renounces the desire to enjoy or possess them, these opulences are considered spiritual. In such consciousness, although one remains within the material world, one sees the opulences of the Lord as they are.

PURPORT

Opulence refers to the visible objects as perceived according to the transformations of the mind. Such mundane perception of opulence cannot give a clear understanding of the supremacy of the Lord's actual position. One should not wrongly assume that such insignificant material opulences occupy the same status as the Lord's plenary features in His position as the Personality of Godhead, which are qualitatively and quantitatively equal to the Lord.

TEXT 42

वाचंयच्छमनोयच्छप्राणान्यच्छेदियाणिच ।
आत्मानमात्मनायच्छनभूयःकल्पसेऽध्वने ॥४२॥

vācaṁ yaccha mano yaccha prāṇān yacchedriyāṇi ca
ātmānam ātmanā yaccha na bhūyaḥ kalpase 'dhvane

Therefore, control your speech, subdue the mind, conquer the life air, and regulate the senses, and bring your rational faculties under control by means of purified intelligence. By doing so, you will never again fall down to the path of material existence.

COMMENTARY

The Supreme Lord said, "Because everything is a manifestation of My opulence, you should respect all things by means of your body, mind, and speech. You should never chastise or blaspheme anyone out of envy."

It is stated in the *Śrīmad-Bhāgavatam* (12.6.34):

ativādāṁs titikṣeta nāvamanyeta kañcana
na cemaṁ deham āśritya vairaṁ kurvīta kenacit

One should tolerate all the insults of others, and never fail to show proper respect to any one. Avoiding identification with the material body, one should not create enmity with anyone.

PURPORT

If we carefully control the activities of our speech, mind, and senses, then we will never come under the sway of the illusory energy of the Lord, thinking of ourselves as the enjoyer. In that condition of self-control, one resides in the spiritual kingdom, which is situated beyond this material realm of anxiety.

TEXT 43

योवैवाङ्मनसीसंयगसंयच्छन्धियायतिः ।
तस्यव्रतंतपोदानंस्रवत्यामघटाम्बुवत् ॥४३॥

yo vai vāṅ-manasī saṁyag asaṁyacchan dhiyā yatiḥ
tasya vrataṁ tapo dānaṁ sravaty āma-ghaṭāmbu-vat

A transcendentalist who does not completely control his speech and mind by superior intelligence will find his vows, austerities, and charity, lost just as water flows out of an unbaked clay pot.

COMMENTARY

Despite accepting the renounced order of life, if one does not carefully control his speech and mind, then his spiritual practices, such as the execution of vows, performance of austerities, and the charity of leading others to spiritual life will be lost, just as water kept in an unbaked clay pot leaks out and is lost.

PURPORT

If a liquid is kept in a baked clay pitcher, it will not leak out, but if it is kept in an unbaked clay vessel, it will gradually flow out of the container. Similarly, for those who cannot follow the principles of the *tridaṇḍīs*, there is no possibility of achieving perfection.

TEXT 44

तस्माद्वचोमनःप्राणान्नियच्छेन्मत्परायणः ।
मद्भक्तियुक्तयाबुद्ध्याततःपरिसमाप्यते ॥४४॥

tasmād vaco manaḥ prāṇān niyacchen mat-parāyaṇaḥ
mad-bhakti-yuktayā buddhyā tataḥ parisamāpyate

A devotee who is surrendered to Me should carefully control his mind, speech, and life air. By engaging his intelligence in My loving devotional service, the devotee attains the perfection of life.

PURPORT

In this verse, it is stressed that one's intelligence should be saturated with feelings of loving devotion for the Lord. This can be developed by regularly chanting the Gāyatrī mantra, which is awarded by the spiritual master. By means of clear intelligence, one naturally becomes disinclined to perform fruitive activities, or engage in mental speculation, and one naturally becomes inclined to take shelter of the Supreme Personality of Godhead.

Thus ends the translation of the Tenth Chapter of the Uddhava-gītā, entitled **"The Lord's Opulence"** *with the commentaries of Śrīla Viśvanātha Cakravartī Ṭhākura and the chapter summary and purports by Śrīla Bhaktisiddhānta Sarasvatī Ṭhākura.*

CHAPTER 11

LORD KṚṢṆA'S DESCRIPTION OF THE VARṆĀŚRAMA SYSTEM

CHAPTER SUMMARY

Previously, Supreme Lord Śrī Kṛṣṇa had assumed the form of Haṁsa and explained to Lord Brahmā and other sages the duties of the *brahmacārī* and *gṛhastha* orders. In this chapter, the Lord further describes these matters to Uddhava.

After Uddhava inquires from Śrī Kṛṣṇa about the principles of the *varṇa* and *āśrama* orders of society, the Lord replies that in the first age, Satya-yuga, there was only one *varṇa*, called *haṁsa*. In that age, people were automatically dedicated to unalloyed devotional service right from their very birth, and since everyone was perfect in all respects, the age was called Kṛta-yuga. In that age, the *Vedas* were manifest in the form of the sacred syllable *oṁ*. The Supreme Lord was the object of everyone's meditation, and all the limbs of religion were fully manifested. There were no formal performances of Vedic sacrifices. People were naturally pious and inclined to perform austerities, and they simply engaged in meditation on the personal form the Supreme Lord.

In the following age, Tretā-yuga, the three *Vedas* became manifest from the heart of the Supreme Lord, and from them, the three forms of sacrificial fire. At that time, the system of four *varṇas* and four *āśramas*, which prescribes material and spiritual duties for the different members of society, manifested from the limbs of the Supreme Lord. According to how these divisions appeared from the higher and lower bodily limbs of the Supreme Lord, they were endowed with higher and lower qualities. After this description, the Supreme Lord, Śrī Kṛṣṇa, explains the nature of those in each of the four *varṇas*, as well as those who are outside the limits of the four *varṇas*. The Lord also describes those qualities that pertain to humanity in general.

Members of the higher social orders are qualified to take second birth. After receiving the sacred thread initiation, they should go to live in the *gurukula*, the home of the spiritual master, as *brahmacārīs*. There, the student should practice self-control and absorb himself in the study of the *Vedas*. He should keep matted hair and is forbidden to wash his teeth, prepare a nice seat for himself, talk while bathing or evacuating, cut his hair and nails, or at any time pass semen. He must regularly perform worship at the three junctures of the day and must render devotional service to his spiritual master in a spirit free from envy. A *brahmacārī* must offer to the guru whatever food and other things he collects by begging. He gladly accepts for his maintenance whatever remnants of the Lord he is granted. He should render menial service to the spiritual master by massaging his feet and worship him, and he should avoid all sense gratification and strictly maintain the vow of celibacy. He should surrender himself completely to the Supreme Lord, and engage in worshiping Him in the form of *Paramātmā*, according to the rules and regulations prescribed for him. For *brahmacārīs*, seeing or touching women, and conversations or sports in the company of women, are absolutely disallowed. Maintaining cleanliness and performing *ācamana* for purification are recommended for members of all the *āśramas*. Everyone is advised to remember that the Supreme Lord as the Supersoul is residing within all living entities.

After studying all the different aspects of the *Vedas*, a *brāhmaṇa* who has material desires may, with the permission of his spiritual master, enter household life. Otherwise, if he has no material desires, he may enter the *vānaprastha* or *sannyāsa āśrama*. The proper order of succession should be followed in changing from one spiritual order to the next. One who desires to enter household life should accept a wife who is of the same *varṇa* as himself, who is not condemnable, and who is younger than he.

The obligatory duties of the *brāhmaṇas*, *kṣatriyas*, and *vaiśyas* are worship of the Supreme Lord, study of the *Vedas*, and giving charity. Only *brāhmaṇas* have the privilege of accepting charity, teaching the Vedic scriptures to others, and conducting sacrifices. If a *brāhmaṇa* finds some fault in these three occupations, he may maintain himself by collecting grains from the agricultural fields. If a *brāhmaṇa* is extremely poverty-stricken and thus in dire need of money, he may accept the profession of a *kṣatriyas* or *vaiśya*, but he should never accept the occupation of a *śūdra*. In a similar situation, a *kṣatriya* may accept the occupation of a *vaiśya*, and a *vaiśya* that of a *śūdra*. When such an emergency has passed so that there is no more imminent danger, one should not continue to earn his livelihood by means of a lower occupation. A *brāhmaṇa* who remains fixed in performing his occupational duties while giving up insignificant material desires always remains under the protection of the Supreme Lord. The householder should study the *Vedas* daily, and maintain his family members with the wealth he has honestly earned by engaging in his occupation, and he should worship the Supreme Lord according to his capacity. Remaining unattached to family life and fixed in devotion to the Supreme Lord, a householder may finally accept the *vānaprastha āśrama*, or if he has a grown up son, he may directly take *sannyāsa* in order to completely devote his time to the worship of the Supreme Lord. But persons who are extremely lusty after women, who have no power of discrimination, and who are mad after earning wealth and amassing possessions, remain in constant anxiety over the well-being of their family members and are doomed to take their next birth in a lower species of life.

TEXTS 1-2

श्रीउद्धव उवाच
यस्त्वयाभिहितःपूर्वंधर्मस्त्वद्भक्तिलक्षणः ।
वर्णाश्रमाचारवतांसर्वेषांद्विपदामपि ॥१॥
यथानुष्ठीयमानेनत्वयिभक्तिर्नृणांभवेत् ।
स्वधर्मेणारविन्दाक्षतन्ममाख्यातुमर्हसि ॥२॥

śrī-uddhava uvāca
yas tvayābhihitaḥ pūrvaṁ dharmas tvad-bhakti-lakṣaṇaḥ
varṇāśramācāravatāṁ sarveṣāṁ dvi-padām api

yathānuṣṭhīyamānena tvayi bhaktir nṛṇāṁ bhavet
sva-dharmeṇāravindākṣa tan mamākhyātum arhasi

Śrī Uddhava said: My dear Lord, You have described the principles of devotional service that are performed by the followers of the *varnāśrama* system, as well as those who lead unregulated lives. O lotus-eyed Lord, kindly tell me how people can attain Your loving service by the execution of their prescribed duties.

COMMENTARY

After hearing from Kṛṣṇa about the processes of *jñāna-yoga*, *bhakti-yoga*, and *aṣṭāṅga-yoga*, Uddhava now inquires about the practice of *karma-yoga* as a means of attaining perfection. The Supreme Lord had previously said:

kālena naṣṭā pralaye vāṇīyaṁ veda-saṁjñitā
mayādau brahmaṇe proktā dharmo yasyāṁ mad-ātmakaḥ

The Supreme Lord said: By the influence of time, the transcendental Vedic knowledge was lost at the time of annihilation. Then, when the subsequent creation took place, I imparted the Vedic knowledge to Brahmā because I Myself am the principles of religion enunciated therein. (*Śrīmad-Bhāgavatam* 11.14.3)

Religious principles are delineated in the Vedic literature. Devotional service, which is the perfection of religion, is divided into three categories—*kevala-bhakti*, *pradhānībhūta-bhakti* and *guṇībhūta-bhakti*. Of the three, *kevala-bhakti* can be executed by members of all the *āśramas*. Indeed, even those who are outside the purview of the *varnāśrama* society can engage in unmotivated devotional service if they faithfully associate with saintly devotees. There is no other way for attaining perfection other than to attain the association of pure devotees. The Lord has confirmed this:

yaṁ na yogena sāṅkhyena dāna-vrata-tapo-'dhvaraiḥ
vyākhyā-svādhyāya-sannyāsaiḥ prāpnuyād yatnavān api

Even though one engages with great endeavor in the mystic yoga system, philosophical speculation, giving charity, executing vows and penances, performing ritualistic sacrifices, teaching the Vedic mantras to others, a personal study of the *Vedas*, or the renounced order of life, still one cannot achieve Me. (*Śrīmad-Bhāgavatam* 11.12.9)

If one associates with saintly devotees then he can attain pure devotional service, whether he follows the principles of *varnāśrama* or not.

dharmān santyajya yaḥ sarvān māṁ bhajeta sa tu sattamaḥ

One who gives up all ordinary religious principles to worship Me alone is the foremost among human beings. (*Śrīmad-Bhāgavatam* 11.11.32)

Pradhānībhūta-bhakti and *guṇībhūta-bhakti* are also awakened by the association of devotees and from the execution of one's occupational duties. The Supreme Lord alone knows how one can receive the seed of the creeper of devotional service unto Him. The word *bhakti* in this verse refers to *pradhānībhūta-bhakti* and *guṇībhūta-bhakti*.

TEXTS 3-7

पुराकिलमहाबाहोधर्मंपरमकंप्रभो ।
यत्तेनहंसरूपेणब्रह्मणेऽभ्यात्थमाधव ॥३॥

स इदानींसुमहताकालेनामित्रकर्शन ।
नप्रायोभवितामर्त्यलोकेप्रागनुशासितः ॥४॥
वक्ताकर्ताविता नान्योधर्मस्याच्युततेभुवि ।
सभायामपिवैरिञ्च्यांयत्रमूर्तिधराःकलाः ॥५॥
कर्त्राविश्राप्रवक्त्राचभवतामधुसूदन ।
त्यक्तेमहीतलेदेवविनष्टंकःप्रवक्ष्यति ॥६॥
तत्त्वंनःसर्वधर्मज्ञधर्मस्त्वद्भक्तिलक्षणः ।
यथायस्यविधीयेततथावर्णयमेप्रभो ॥७॥

purā kila mahā-bāho dharmaṁ paramakaṁ prabho
yat tena haṁsa-rūpeṇa brahmaṇe 'bhyāttha mādhava

sa idānīṁ su-mahatā kālenāmitra-karśana
na prāyo bhavitā martya-loke prāg anuśāsitaḥ

vaktā kartāvitā nānyo dharmasyācyuta te bhuvi
sabhāyām api vairiñcyāṁ yatra mūrti-dharāḥ kalāḥ

kartrāvitrā pravaktrā ca bhavatā madhusūdana
tyakte mahī-tale deva vinaṣṭaṁ kaḥ pravakṣyati

tat tvaṁ naḥ sarva-dharma-jña dharmas tvad-bhakti-lakṣaṇaḥ
yathā yasya vidhīyeta tathā varṇaya me prabho

O mighty armed-one! My dear Lord, previously, as Lord Haṁsa, You spoke to Lord Brahmā about the religious principles that bring supreme happiness to the follower. My dear Mādhava, much time has now passed, so that what You had previously instructed will soon be forgotten. O subduer of the enemy, O Lord Acyuta, You are the sole protector of religious principles. My dear Lord Madhusūdana, You are the actual propounder of religious principles. When You return to Your own abode, who will continue to propagate the true understanding of religious principles? My dear Lord, as the perfect knower of religious principles, please describe to me the path of devotional service, and tell me the qualifications of one who is to traverse this path.

COMMENTARY

There are eighteen divisions of knowledge, as described in the Vedic literature: the four *Vedas*—*Ṛg*, *Sāma*, *Yajur*, and *Atharva*—*Purāṇas*, *Nyāya-śāstra*, *Mīmamsā*, *Dharma-śāstra*, *Kalpa*, *Vyākaraṇa*, *Nirukta*, *Jyotiṣa*, *Chanḍa*, *Ayurveda*, *Dhanurveda*, *Gandharvaveda*, and *Artha-śāstra*.

PURPORT

In the beginning of creation, the first created being, Brahmā, received knowledge of the supreme religious principles from Lord Haṁsa. From Him, Brahmā and the *brāhmaṇas* attained an understanding of the *ekāyana* process of spiritual practice. In the course of time, however, misguided transcendentalists began to practice the supreme religious principles, which are based on the devotional service of the Lord, in a perverted manner. When a pure spirit soul becomes materially contaminated, he gives up the supreme religious principle of devotional service to the Lord and becomes inclined to perform fruitive activities, engage in the cultivation of knowledge, or endeavor for perfection in mystic yoga. These activities are illusory because they are based on the material conception of life and have nothing to do with the constitutional position of the living entity. *Sanātana dharma* refers to devotional service alone.

TEXT 8

श्रीशुक उवाच
इत्थंस्वभृत्यमुख्येनपृष्टःसभगवान्हरिः ।
प्रीतःक्षेमायमर्त्यानांधर्मानाहसनातनान् ॥८॥

śrī-śuka uvāca

itthaṁ sva-bhṛtya-mukhyena pṛṣṭaḥ sa bhagavān hariḥ
prītaḥ kṣemāya martyānāṁ dharmān āha sanātanān

Śrī Śukadeva Gosvāmī said: Śrī Uddhava, the foremost of devotees, thus inquired from the Lord. The Supreme Personality of Godhead, Śrī Kṛṣṇa, was pleased to hear the words of His devotee, and for the benefit of everyone, He described eternal religious principles.

TEXT 9

श्रीभगवानुवाच
धर्म्य एषतवप्रश्नोनैःश्रेयसकरोनृणाम् ।
वर्णाश्रमाचारवतांतमुद्धवनिबोधमे ॥९॥

śrī-bhagavān uvāca
dharmya eṣa tava praśno naiḥśreyasa-karo nṛṇām
varṇāśramācāravatāṁ tam uddhava nibodha me

The Supreme Lord said: My dear Uddhava, your question is glorious because it is in accordance with religious principles and thus leads the followers of *varṇāśrama* to life's ultimate goal, pure devotional service. Now, listen attentively as I talk about eternal religious principles.

COMMENTARY

The word *dharman* refers to the supreme religious principles.

PURPORT

The religious principles prescribed for ordinay men are far different from eternal religious principles prescribed for the devotees of the Lord. Ordinary persons are materialistic, and so their religious principles are simply meant to gradually elevate them to the mode of goodness. Discussion of eternal religious principles are the most auspicious topics for civilized human beings. The *varṇāśrama* system is a social order based upon religious principles that gradually leads one to the point of Kṛṣṇa consciousness.

TEXT 10

आदौकृतयुगेवर्णोनृणांहंसइतिस्मृतः ।
कृतकृत्याःप्रजाजात्यातस्मात्कृतयुगंविदुः ॥१०॥

ādau kṛta-yuge varṇo nṛṇāṁ haṁsa iti smṛtaḥ
kṛta-kṛtyāḥ prajā jātyā tasmāt kṛta-yugaṁ viduḥ

In the beginning, in Satya-yuga, there was only one social class, known as *haṁsa,* to which all human beings belonged. In that age, human beings engaged in unalloyed devotional service, right from their birth, and thus learned scholars called this first age Kṛta-yuga.

COMMENTARY

Śrī Kṛṣṇa is instructing Uddhava about *varnāśrama-dharma*, beginning from its inception.

PURPORT

The period of time when human beings were not polluted by the three modes of material nature is called Kṛta-yuga, or Satya-yuga. *Ekāyana paddhati* refers to the period of time when the *varṇas* were not divided. That undivided *varṇa* was known as *haṁsa*. The Supersoul is referred to as *haṁsa*, and the devotees are those who are maintained by the *haṁsa*.

TEXT 11

वेदःप्रणव एवाग्रेधर्मोऽहंवृषरूपधृक्।
उपासतेतपोनिष्ठाहंसंमांमुक्तकिल्बिषाः ॥११॥

vedaḥ praṇava evāgre dharmo 'haṁ vṛṣa-rūpa-dhṛk
upāsate tapo-niṣṭhā haṁsaṁ māṁ mukta-kilbiṣāḥ

In Satya-yuga, the undivided Veda is expressed by the syllable, *oṁ*, and I am manifest as the four-legged bull of religion. The pious inhabitants of that age are fixed in austerity, and with their mind and senses fully under control, they meditate on My transcendental form as Haṁsa.

PURPORT

The four legs of the bull represent the four parts of the Lord's opulence as manifested in this world. The condensed form of the Lord's holy name in the form of *oṁ* is the origin of the *Vedas*.

TEXT 12

त्रेतामुखेमहाभागप्राणान्मेहृदयात्त्रयी ।
विद्याप्रादुरभूत्तस्या अहमासंत्रिवृन्मखः ॥१२॥

tretā-mukhe mahā-bhāga prāṇān me hṛdayāt trayī
vidyā prādurabhūt tasyā aham āsaṁ tri-vṛn makhaḥ

O greatly fortunate one, at the beginning of Tretā-yuga, Vedic knowledge was manifested from My heart, which is the shelter of the life air. The *Vedas* **appeared in three divisions—the *Ṛg*, *Sāma*, and *Yajur*. From the three** *Vedas*, **I manifested three kinds of sacrifice.**

COMMENTARY

The Supreme Lord said, "From the heart of My universal form appeared the three *Vedas*, and from them appeared the three kinds of sacrifice, known as *hautra*, *ādhvaryava*, and *audgātra*." It is described in the scriptures that Lord Viṣṇu appeared in His form as Yajña.

PURPORT

When one leg of religion was lost, the three *Vedas*— *Ṛg*, *Sāma*, and *Yajur*—came into being. The three performers of Vedic sacrifices, known as *hotā*, *udgāta*, and *adhvaryyu*, also appeared.

TEXT 13

विप्रक्षत्रियविट्शूद्रामुखबाहूरुपादजाः ।
वैराजात्पुरुषाज्ञाताय आत्माचारलक्षणाः ॥१३॥

vipra-kṣatriya-viṭ-śūdrā mukha-bāhūru-pāda-jāḥ
vairājāt puruṣāj jātā ya ātmācāra-lakṣaṇāḥ

In Tretā-yuga, the four *varṇas*—the *brāhmaṇas, kṣatriyas, vaiśyas,* and śudras—along with their occupational duties and characteristics, appeared from the mouth, arms, thigh, and legs of the universal form of the Lord, respectively.

COMMENTARY

In the beginning of creation, the natural propensities of the spirit souls were manifest but gradually, in the course of time, their qualities and nature became contaminated.

PURPORT

The four social orders of human society came into existence from four parts of the Lord's universal form—His mouth, arm, thighs, and legs. In this way, human beings were divided into four classes, according to their qualities and propensities for work.

TEXT 14

गृहाश्रमोजधनतोब्रह्मचर्यंहृदोमम ।
वक्षःस्थलाद्वनेवासःसन्न्यासःशिरसिस्थितः ॥१४॥

gṛhāśramo jaghanato brahmacaryaṁ hṛdo mama
vakṣaḥ-sthalād vane-vāsaḥ sannyāsaḥ śirasi sthitaḥ

The married order of life, the *gṛhastha āśrama,* appeared from the loins of My universal form, and the celibate students, the *brahmacarya āśrama,* appeared from My heart. The forest-dwelling retired order of life, the *vānaprastha āśrama,* appeared from My chest, and the renounced order of life, the *sannyāsa āśrama,* appeared from My head.

COMMENTARY

The heart is considered to be below the chest.

TEXT 15

वर्णानामाश्रमाणांचजन्मभूम्यनुसारिणीः ।
आसन्प्रकृतयोनृणांनीचैर्नीचोत्तमोत्तमाः ॥१५॥

varṇānām āśramāṇāṁ ca janma-bhūmy-anusāriṇīḥ
āsan prakṛtayo nṝṇāṁ nīcair nīcottamottamāḥ

The four *varṇas* and four *āśramas* were then manifested according to the higher and lower natures of the conditioned souls.

COMMENTARY

The *brāhmaṇas* and *sannyāsīs* are situated on the head of the universal form of the Lord, and are thus considered to be the most important members of the social body. The *śūdras* and *gṛhasthas* are situated on the legs and abdomen of the universal form of the Lord, and so they are considered to be inferior in status. Everyone is born with a particular intelligence, and social position and in consideration of these, one is placed within the *varṇāśrama* system.

PURPORT

The *brāhmaṇa varṇa* and the *sannyāsa āśrama* are situated in the highest position of the Lord's universal form, and thus they are in the topmost positions of society. Because *kṣatriyas* and *vānaprasthas* are situated on the Lord's arms and chest, they are also considered to be in superior positions. The *vaiśya varṇa* and *brahmacarya āśrama* are situated on lower limbs of the universal form and so they are accepted as inferior statuses. The *śudras* and *gṛhasthas* are accepted as having an even lower status. This is the situation of the social and spiritual orders within the *varṇāśrama* system.

TEXT 16

शमोदमस्तपःशौचंसन्तोषःक्षान्तिरार्जवम् ।
मद्भक्तिश्चदयासत्यंब्रह्मप्रकृतयस्त्विमाः ॥१६॥

śamo damas tapaḥ śaucaṁ santoṣaḥ kṣāntir ārjavam
mad-bhaktiś ca dayā satyaṁ brahma-prakṛtayas tv imāḥ

Peacefulness, control of the senses, austerity, cleanliness, satisfaction, forgiveness, simplicity, devotion to Me, compassion, and truthfulness are the natural qualities of *brāhmaṇas.*

COMMENTARY

The phrase *mad-bhakti* refers to *guṇībhūta-bhakti.*

PURPORT

One cannot find much lust or anger in the nature of a *brāhmaṇa*. For this reason, a *brāhmaṇa* does not indulge in unrestricted sense gratification but instead, takes pleasure in discussing devotional literature. Purity, steadiness due to an absence of dissatisfaction, tolerance, simplicity, inclination toward the Lord's service, compassion for all living entities, and truthfulness—these eight characteristics are to be found in *brāhmaṇas.*

TEXT 17

तेजोबलंधृतिःशौर्यंतितिक्षौदार्यमुद्यमः ।
स्थैर्यंब्रह्मण्यमैश्वर्यंक्षत्रप्रकृतयस्त्विमाः ॥१७॥

tejo balaṁ dhṛtiḥ śauryaṁ titikṣaudāryam udyamaḥ
sthairyaṁ brahmaṇyam aiśvaryaṁ kṣatra-prakṛtayas tv imāḥ

Prowess, bodily strength, patience, heroism, tolerance, magnanimity, enthusiasm, steadiness, devotion to the *brāhmaṇas,* and leadership, are the natural qualities of the *kṣatriyas.*

PURPORT

Kṣatriyas naturally possess great prowess, patience, heroism, tolerance, magnanimity, enthusiasm, steadiness, devotion, and leadership.

TEXT 18

आस्तिक्यंदाननिष्ठाच अदम्भोब्रह्मसेवनम् ।
अतुष्टिरर्थोपचयैर्वैश्यप्रकृतयस्त्विमाः ॥१८॥

āstikyaṁ dāna-niṣṭhā ca adambho brahma-sevanam
atuṣṭir arthopacayair vaiśya-prakṛtayas tv imāḥ

Faith in Vedic culture, an inclination to give charity, freedom from pride, service to the *brāhmaṇas*, and a perpetual desire to accumulate more and more money are the natural qualities of the *vaiśyas*.

PURPORT

True *vaiśyas* are not mere businessmen. They have faith in the eternity of the soul, take pleasure in giving charity, are free from false pride, serve those who are well-versed in the Vedic literature, and have a continuous thirst for accumulating wealth.

TEXT 19

शुश्रूषणंद्विजगवांदेवानां चाप्यमायया ।
तत्रलब्धेनसन्तोषःशूद्रप्रकृतयस्त्विमाः ॥१९॥

śuśrūṣaṇaṁ dvija-gavāṁ devānāṁ cāpy amāyayā
tatra labdhena santoṣaḥ śūdra-prakṛtayas tv imāḥ

Service without duplicity to the *brāhmaṇas*, cows, demigods, and other worshipable personalities, and satisfaction with whatever is obtained by such service, are the natural qualities of *śūdras*.

COMMENTARY

In Vedic society, *śudras* are satisfied by whatever they receive as remuneration for services rendered because the higher classes of men are trained to be charitable toward those who are less fortunate, and thus they never lack the necessities of life.

TEXT 20

अशौचमनृतंस्तेयंनास्तिक्यंशुष्कविग्रहः ।
कामःक्रोधश्चतर्षश्चसभावोऽन्त्यावसायिनाम् ॥२०॥

aśaucam anṛtaṁ steyaṁ nāstikyaṁ śuṣka-vigrahaḥ
kāmaḥ krodhaś ca tarṣaś ca sa bhāvo 'ntyāvasāyinām

Lack of cleanliness, dishonesty, thievery, very little faith in God, unnecessary quarrel, lust, anger, and great hankering are the nature of the lowest among men, who are outside the *varṇāśrama* system.

COMMENTARY

This verse describes the qualities of those who live outside the *varṇāśrama* system. Such persons are referred to as *antyaja.*

TEXT 21

अहिंसासत्यमस्तेयमकामक्रोधलोभता ।
भूतप्रियहितेहाचधर्मोऽयंसार्ववर्णिकः ॥२१॥

ahiṁsā satyam asteyam akāma-krodha-lobhatā
bhūta-priya-hitehā ca dharmo 'yaṁ sārva-varṇikaḥ

Nonviolence, truthfulness, honesty, desire for the happiness and welfare of all others, and freedom from lust, anger, and greed, constitute duties for all members of society.

COMMENTARY

The phrase *sārvavarṇikaḥ* refers not only to those acting within the *varṇāśrama* system, but those outside of it as well. Every human being can practice nonviolence, restraint from stealing, the giving up of lust, anger, and greed, and a charitable disposition toward others.

PURPORT

The qualities of nonviolence, truthfulness, honesty, restraint of lust, anger, and greed, and looking after the welfare of others are held in esteem in all human societies.

TEXT 22

द्वितीयंप्राप्यानुपूर्व्याज्जन्मोपनयनंद्विजः ।
वसन्गुरुकुलेदान्तोब्रह्माधीयीतचाहूतः ॥२२॥

dvitīyaṁ prāpyānupūrvyāj janmopanayanaṁ dvijaḥ
vasan guru-kule dānto brahmādhīyīta cāhūtaḥ

The twice-born member of the *varṇāśrama* society should undergo the purificatory rituals, beginning with the *garbhādhāna* and culminating in the sacred thread initiation

ceremony. He should then reside in the *āśrama* of the spiritual master, while practicing self-control and studying the Vedic literature.

COMMENTARY

The Lord describes the qualities of the members of the four *āśramas* in the following nine verses. *Brāhmaṇas, kṣatriyas*, and *vaiśyas* are known as *dvija*, or twice-born. They observe the system of *saṁskāras*, or purificatory rites, beginning with the *garbhādhāna saṁskāra*, and later on receive the Gāyatrī mantra, which signifies their second birth through spiritual initiation. Thereafter, when they are called by the *ācārya*, they go to live in the *gurukula*, where they practice self-control and study the *Vedas*.

PURPORT

The term *dvija*, or "twice-born," here indicates the three superior classes, namely *brāhmaṇas, kṣatriyas* and *vaiśyas*. The lowest class of men, the *śūdras*, as well as those who are outside the *varṇāśrama* society do not observe the purificatory rites that are performed by the higher three classes. Because of this, their condition is full of ignorance and so they should be carefully guided so as not to become disrespectful of the higher classes of men. Those who observe the purificatory processes should give up whimisical arguments and instead become submissive to the elevated devotees of the Lord.

TEXT 23

मेखलाजिनदण्डाक्षब्रह्मसूत्रकमण्डलून् ।
जटिलोऽधौतदद्वासोऽरक्तपीठःकुशान्दधत् ॥२३॥

mekhalājina-daṇḍākṣa- brahma-sūtra-kamaṇḍalūn
jaṭilo 'dhauta-dad-vāso 'rakta-pīṭhaḥ kuśān dadhat

A *brahmacārī* should have matted hair, and he should wear a belt of kuśa grass and deerskin garments. He should carry a staff and a waterpot, and he should be decorated with *akṣa* beads and a sacred thread. He should be inclined to austerity and thus never accept an opulent sitting place. He should not take very good care of his teeth, nor should he be concerned about his clothes.

TEXT 24

स्नानभोजनहोमेषुजपोच्चारेचवाग्यतः ।
नच्छिन्द्यान्नखरोमाणिकक्षोपस्थगतान्यपि ॥२४॥

snāna-bhojana-homeṣu japoccāre ca vāg-yataḥ
na cchindyān nakha-romāṇi kakṣopastha-gatāny api

A *brahmacārī* should remain silent while bathing, eating, performing fire sacrifices, chanting *mantras,* and passing stool and urine. He should not cut his nails and hair, including the armpit and pubic hair.

COMMENTARY

A *brahmacārī* should always be seen with a waistband, deerskin, *kuśa* grass, beads, and a sacred thread. He should not be concerned about the whiteness of his teeth or the condition of his clothes. He should neither wear red cloth nor sit on a red *āśana.* He should remain silent while chanting mantras and while passing stool or urine.

TEXT 25

रेतोनावकिरेज्जातुब्रह्मव्रतधरःस्वयम् ।
अवकीर्णेऽवगाह्याप्सुयतासुस्त्रिपदांजपेत् ॥२५॥

reto nāvakirej jātu brahma-vrata-dharaḥ svayam
avakīrṇe 'vagāhyāpsu yatāsus tri-padāṁ japet

While observing the vow of celibate *brahmacārī* life, one should never pass semen. If he passes semen involuntarily, the *brahmacārī* should immediately bathe, control his breath by the practice of *prāṇāyāma,* and chant the Gāyatrī *mantra.*

TEXT 26

अग्न्यर्काचार्यगोविप्रगुरुवृद्धसुराञ्शुचिः ।
समाहित उपासीतसन्ध्येद्वेयतवाग्जपन् ॥२६॥

agny-arkācārya-go-vipra-guru-vṛddha-surāñ śuciḥ
samāhita upāsīta sandhye dve yata-vāg japan

With a purified mind and fixed attention, the *brahmacārī* should worship the fire-god, sun, *ācārya,* cows, *brāhmaṇas, guru,* elderly respectable persons, and demigods at sunrise and sunset, remaining silent while quietly chanting the appropriate *mantras.*

COMMENTARY

The *brahmacārī* should remain silent while performing his morning and evening worship, but such silence is not required when he performs his noontime rituals.

TEXT 27

आचार्यंमांविजानीयान्नवमन्येतकर्हिचित् ।
नमर्त्यबुद्ध्यासूयेतसर्वदेवमयोगुरु ॥२७॥

ācāryaṁ māṁ vijānīyān navamanyeta karhicit
na martya-buddhyāsūyeta sarva-deva-mayo guru

One should know the *ācārya* as Myself and never disrespect him in any way. One should not envy him, thinking him an ordinary man, for he is the representative of all the demigods.

COMMENTARY

The Supreme Lord said, "You should know the spiritual master as My most dear servant." For this reason, it has been stated: *guruvaraṁ mukunda preṣṭhatvena smaret*: Remember the spiritual master as the most beloved devotee of Lord Mukunda. One should never disregard the spiritual master by considering him to be an ordinary human being.

PURPORT

When the Supreme Lord takes the position of an instructor, desiring to award eternal benefit to the living entities, He becomes known as an *ācārya*. If one neglects the *ācārya*, or if a disciple considers himself as equal to his spiritual master, and thus displays envy and audacity towards him, then there is no possibility for him to become successful in his vows. This is due to a lack of faith in the spiritual master. Therefore, one who seriously aspires to attain the ultimate goal of life should properly worship the spiritual master, considering him as the supreme personality of servitor Godhead. Instead of considering the *ācārya* as the object of one's service, one should consider him a staunch servant of Lord Viṣṇu.

TEXT 28

सायंप्रातरुपानीयभैक्ष्यंतस्मैनिवेदयेत् ।
यच्चान्यदप्यनुज्ञातमुपयुञ्जीतसंयतः ॥२८॥

sāyaṁ prātar upānīya bhaikṣyaṁ tasmai nivedayet
yac cānyad apy anujñātam upayuñjīta saṁyataḥ

Every morning and evening, the *brahmacārī* should bring whatever food and other things he has received by begging door to door and offer them to his spiritual master. Thereafter, with a controlled mind, he should accept whatever is allotted to him by his spiritual master.

COMMENTARY

Whatever a *brahmacārī* collects by begging, or receives in charity, should be offered to the spiritual master. He should only eat, or utilize any object, after being permitted by the spiritual master.

PURPORT

The purpoe of human life is to revive one's forgotten relationship with the Supreme Personality of Godhead. This mission is accomplished under the direction of the bona fide spiritual master. From childhood, a boy is trained to become very submissive to his spiritual master and very austere in his lifestyle. Whatever a student has collected, he must offer to the spiritual master and then only accept what is allotted to him by his guru. One who hopes to advance in spiritual life should not want to acquire things for his personal enjoyment. Such training is imparted by the spiritual master to his disciples, and when he sees that his student has advanced, he engages him directly in the service of the Supreme Lord.

TEXT 29

शुश्रूषमाण आचार्यंसदोपासीतनीचवत् ।
यानशय्यासनस्थानैर्नातिदूरेकृताञ्जलिः ॥२९॥

śuśrūṣamāṇa ācāryaṁ sadopāsīta nīca-vat
yāna-śayyāsana-sthānair nāti-dūre kṛtāñjaliḥ

One should engage as the humble servant of the *ācārya*. When the spiritual master goes for a walk, the student should submissively follow him. When the spiritual master rests, the disciple should also rest lying down nearby, always ready to render any required service. When the spiritual master sits down, the disciple should stand nearby with folded hands, ready to execute his order.

COMMENTARY

When the spiritual master walks, a disciple should follow him like a menial servant. When the spiritual master sleeps, a disciple should sleep nearby, and when he sits on his *āśana*, a disciple should stand in front of him with folded hands, awaiting his order.

PURPORT

The only means for advancing in spiritual life is to always remain faithfully devoted to the spiritual master. In all respects, one's relationship with the spiritual master should be that of a master and servant. In this regard, one should contemplate this verse from the *Padma Purāṇa, Uttara-khaṇḍa*:

arcayitvā tu govindaṁ tadīyān nārcayet tu yaḥ
na sa bhāgavato jñeyaḥ kevalaṁ dāmbhikaḥ smṛtaḥ

One who performs worship of Lord Govinda but fails to worship His devotees should be understood to be not a devotee of the Lord, but simply a victim of false pride.

TEXT 30

एवंवृत्तोगुरुकुलेवसेद्भोगविवर्जितः ।
विद्यासमाप्यतेयावद्बिभ्रद्व्रतमखण्डितम् ॥३०॥

evaṁ-vṛtto guru-kule vased bhoga-vivarjitaḥ
vidyā samāpyate yāvad bibhrad vratam akhaṇḍitam

Until his education is completed, a *brahmacārī* should remain at the *gurukula,* faithfully engaging in the service of the spiritual master while maintaining his vow of celibacy.

PURPORT

While living at the *gurukula*, a *brahmacārī* should observe strict celibacy. He should not be driven by urges for sense gratification, and he should not think of himself as the enjoyer of the fruits of his *karma.* Only in this way can one master the spiritual knowledge that is imparted to him by the spiritual master.

TEXT 31

यद्यसौछन्दसांलोकमारोक्ष्यन्ब्रह्मविष्टपम् ।
गुरवेविन्यसेद्देहंस्वाध्यायार्थंबृहद्व्रतः ॥३१॥

yady asau chandasāṁ lokam ārokṣyan brahma-viṣṭapam
gurave vinyased dehaṁ svādhyāyārthaṁ bṛhad-vrataḥ

If a *brahmacārī* wishes to transfer himself to Maharloka, and from there to Brahmaloka, he should very thoroughly study the *Vedas* under the direction of the spiritual master while strictly observing the vow of celibacy.

COMMENTARY

After describing the characteristics of a *brahmacārī* who may later on enter the *gṛhastha āśrama*, the Lord now explains the special characteristics of a strict, lifelong *brahmacārī* in six verses. If a *brahmacārī* desires to go to Brahmaloka, he should observe strict lifelong celibacy and fully dedicate himself to his spiritual master while engaging in advanced study of the *Vedas*.

PURPORT

Anyone who desires to attain perfection in life must engage his body, mind, and words in the service of the spiritual master, without any separate interest.

TEXT 32

अग्नौगुरावात्मनिचसर्वभूतेषुमांपरम् ।
अपृथग्धीरुपसीतब्रह्मवर्चस्व्यकल्मषः ॥३२॥

agnau gurāv ātmani ca sarva-bhūteṣu māṁ param
apṛthag-dhīr upasīta brahma-varcasvy akalmaṣaḥ

Being enlightened with Vedic knowledge as a result of service to the spiritual master, and being freed from all sins and the vision of duality, one should worship Me as the Supersoul as I appear within fire, the spiritual master, one's own self, and all living entities.

COMMENTARY

The phrase *bramavarca* means "the enlightenment one attains by carefully studying the Vedic literature."

PURPORT

If a person actually becomes enlightened as a result of studying the *Vedas*, he will never again willfully indulge in sinful activities. In the state of self-realization, one does not proudly consider himself to be the enjoyer of the perishable material objects. Rather, he thinks himself to be an eternal servant of the Supreme Lord, and thus he remains engaged in the devotional service of the Lord without deviation.

TEXT 33

स्त्रीणांनिरीक्षणस्पर्शसंलापक्ष्वेलनादिकम् ।
प्राणिनोमिथुनीभूतानगृहस्थोऽग्रतस्त्यजेत् ॥३३॥

strīṇāṁ nirīkṣaṇa-sparśa-saṁlāpa-kṣvelanādikam
prāṇino mithunī-bhūtān agṛhastho 'gratas tyajet

Except householders, members of the other spiritual orders—*sannyāsīs, vānaprasthas,* and *brahmacārīs*—should never associate with women by glancing, touching, conversing, joking, or playing. Neither should they associate with any living entity who is engaged in sexual activities.

COMMENTARY

Brahmacārīs, vānaprasthas, and *sannyāsīs* should never even see birds or insects engaged in sexual intercourse.

PURPORT

With a spirit of enjoyment, if the *brahmacārī* sees, touches, intimately converses with, plays with, or jokes with a woman, then his ruination is inevitable. One should not associate with women, talk about women, or even associate or talk about those who are attached to women. This principle is particularly applicable to *brahmacārīs, vānaprasthas,* and *sannyāsīs*. If a householder does not control his senses and follow the regulative principles, he is known as *gṛha-vrata*, or an overly-attached householder. That is the danger of household life, where there are many opportunities to engage in unrestricted sense gratification. A *sannyāsī, brahmacārī,* or *vānaprastha* should strictly avoid everything related to sex and should never even gaze at an animal engaged in sexual affairs.

TEXTS 34-35

शौचमाचमनंस्नानंसन्ध्योपास्तिर्ममार्चनम् ।
तीर्थसेवाजपोऽस्पृश्याभक्ष्यासम्भाष्यवर्जनम् ॥३४॥
सर्वाश्रमप्रयुक्तोऽयंनियमःकुलनन्दन ।
मद्भावःसर्वभूतेषुमनोवाक्कायसंयमः ॥३५॥

śaucam ācamanaṁ snānaṁ sandhyopāstir mamārcanam
tīrtha-sevā japo 'spṛśyā-bhakṣyāsambhāṣya-varjanam

sarvāśrama-prayukto 'yaṁ niyamaḥ kula-nandana
mad-bhāvaḥ sarva-bhūteṣu mano-vāk-kāya-saṁyamaḥ

Cleanliness, performing *ācamana*, bathing, performing the religious duties prescribed for the morning, noon, and evening, worshiping Me, going to holy places of pilgrimage, avoiding those things that are forbidden, and cultivating the understanding that I am situated as the Supersoul within all living entities—these practices should be observed by everyone with body, mind, and speech.

TEXT 36

एवंबृहद्व्रतधरोब्राह्मणोऽग्निरिवज्वलन् ।
मद्भक्तस्तीव्रतपसादग्धकर्माशयोऽमलः ॥३६॥

evaṁ bṛhad-vrata-dharo brāhmaṇo 'gnir iva jvalan
mad-bhaktas tīvra-tapasā dagdha-karmāśayo 'malaḥ

A *brāhmaṇa* who strictly observes the vow of celibacy becomes as effulgent and powerful as fire. By the strength of his severe austerities, he burns to ashes the propensity to perform material activities. Becoming freed from all material desires, he becomes situated in pure devotional service.

COMMENTARY

This verse explains how one who observes strict celibacy becomes free from material desires.

PURPORT

As he makes advancement in spiritual life, a devotee of the Lord gradually becomes free from material desires, and thus naturally becomes austere and disinterested in mundane enjoyment. As a devotee's propensity for serving Kṛṣṇa progressively increases, his desire for enjoying or rejecting the fruits of *karma* is destroyed. Thus the moon rays of the inclination for the Lord's service illuminate the sky of the devotee's heart.

TEXT 37

अथानन्तरमावेक्ष्यन्यथाजिज्ञासितागमः ।
गुरवेदक्षिणांदत्त्वास्नायाद्गुर्वनुमोदितः ॥३७॥

athānantaram āvekṣyan yathā-jijñāsitāgamaḥ
gurave dakṣiṇāṁ dattvā snāyād gurv-anumoditaḥ

A *brahmacārī* who desires to enter the *gṛhastha āśrama* after completing his Vedic education should offer *dakṣiṇā* to his spiritual master, take permission from him, and then return home after completing the *abhyaṅgasnāna,* or sacred bath.

COMMENTARY

The Lord herein explains how a *brahmacārī* who wants to become a *gṛhastha* should return home. After duly completing his study of the *Vedas* at the *gurukula*, a *brahmacārī* who wants to enter householder life should return home after offering remuneration to his spiritual master and taking his permission, and then performing the prescribed ritualistic bath.

PURPORT

This verse describes the procedure for one who desires to return home and enter the household order of life after finishing his education at the *gurukula*. One who has not perfectly assimilated the instructions of the spiritual master is attracted to the household order of life, which is to be accepted according to the regulations prescribed by the scriptures. If one is not careful to observe the prescribed rules and regulations while in household life, he certainly becomes fallen.

TEXT 38

गृहंवनंवोपविशेत्प्रव्रजेद्वाद्विजोत्तमः ।
आश्रमादाश्रमंगच्छेन्नान्यथामत्परश्चरेत् ॥३८॥

gṛhaṁ vanaṁ vopaviśet pravrajed vā dvijottamaḥ
āśramād āśramaṁ gacchen nānyathāmat-paraś caret

If a *brahmacārī* wants to fulfill his material desires, he should accept the *gṛhastha āśrama.* If a *brāhmaṇa's* only desire is to advance on the path of spiritual realization, he should accept either the *vānaprastha āśrama* or *sannyāsa āśrama.* One who is not surrendered to Me should move progressively from one *āśrama* to another, however, and not act otherwise.

COMMENTARY

According to one's level of advancement, one should situate himself in one of the four *āśramas.* Generally, one is advised to advance from one *āśrama* to another—from the *brahmacarya āśrama* to the *gṛhastha āśrama*, then the *vānaprastha āśrama*, and finally the *sannyāsa āśrama.* In this verse it is indicated that those who are not surrendered devotees of the Lord must rigidly observe the regulations governing one's authorized social status. Here, however, it is recommended that a purified *brāhmaṇa* take to the renounced order of life (*sannyāsa*). If, however, one performs illicit activities on the strength of being transcendental to Vedic social divisions, one is revealed to be a materialistic neophyte and not an advanced devotee of the Lord.

TEXT 39

गृहार्थीसदृशींभार्यामुद्वहेदजुगुप्सिताम् ।
यवीयसींतुवयसायंसवर्णामनुक्रमात् ॥३९॥

gṛhārthī sadṛśīṁ bhāryām udvahed ajugupsitām
yavīyasīṁ tu vayasā yaṁ sa-varṇām anu kramāt

One who desires to enter the *gṛhastha āśrama* should marry a girl of his own *varṇa,* who is beyond reproach, and who is younger in age. Thereafter, if one wants more wives, they should be accepted from one of the lower *varṇas.*

COMMENTARY

One who desires to marry should select a girl from his own caste. A *brāhmaṇa* can marry girls of all the four *varṇas*, a *kṣatriya* can marry girls from three *varṇas*, a *vaiśya* can marry girls from two *varṇas*, and a *śūdra* can only marry a girl of his *varṇa.* This is the verdict of the revealed scriptures.

TEXT 40

इज्याध्ययनदानानिसर्वेषांचद्विजन्मनाम् ।
प्रतिग्रहोऽध्यापनंचब्राह्मणस्यैवयाजनम् ॥४०॥

ijyādhyayana-dānāni sarveṣāṁ ca dvi-janmanām
pratigraho 'dhyāpanaṁ ca brāhmaṇasyaiva yājanam

Those who belong to the three twice-born social orders should perform sacrifice, study the *Vedas*, and give charity. However, only *brāhmaṇas* can accept charity, teach the *Vedas*, and perform sacrifices on behalf of others.

COMMENTARY

Every member of the three higher *varṇas* should worship the Supreme Lord, study the *Vedas*, and give charity. However, acceptance of charity, teaching the *Vedas*, and acting as a priest on another's behalf can be done only by *brāhmaṇas*.

PURPORT

Those who are twice-born, who have undergone the purificatory procedures, must worship the Supreme Lord, study the Vedic literature, and give charity. Among the twice-born, only the *brāhmaṇas* are eligible to accept charity, conduct Vedic sacrifices on behalf of others, and teach the Vedic literature. Without the guidance of qualified *brāhmaṇas*, the *kṣatriyas* and *vaiśyas* will not be able to properly carry out their duties, nor will they understand the Vedic literature, properly perform sacrifices, or give in charity to deserving persons. All of these activities require the guidance of those who are in perfect knowledge of the truth. When society works under the direction of qualified *brāhmaṇas*, peace and prosperity prevail, and not otherwise.

TEXT 41

प्रतिग्रहंमन्यमानस्तपस्तेजोयशोनुदम् ।
अन्याभ्यामेवजीवेतशिलैर्वादोषदृक् तयोः ॥४१॥

pratigrahaṁ manyamānas tapas-tejo-yaśo-nudam
anyābhyām eva jīveta śilair vā doṣa-dṛk tayoḥ

A *brāhmaṇa* who considers that accepting charity from others will destroy his austerity, spiritual prowess, and fame, should maintain himself by teaching Vedic knowledge and engaging as a sacrificial priest. If he considers these two activities to also be faulty, then he should maintain himself by collecting grains from the agricultural fields.

COMMENTARY

If a *brāhmaṇa* finds fault in the occupations of a teacher of Vedic knowledge and sacrificial priest, then he should collect the grains that are found scattered in the agricultural fields.

PURPORT

A *brāhmaṇas* who is reluctant to accept charity, thinking that such an act weakens his austerity, destroys his spiritual influence, and gives him a bad reputation, should simply depend upon the Lord's mercy, and not make a great endeavor to earn wealth. A *brāhmaṇa* should simply depend upon the mercy of the Lord, and not endeavor unnecessarily for his family maintenance. The Lord has promised that He will maintain His devotee, and one who is sincere does not doubt the words of the Lord.

TEXT 42

ब्राह्मणस्यहिदेहोऽयंक्षुद्रकामायनेष्यते ।
कृच्छ्रायतपसेचेहप्रेत्यानन्तसुखाय च ॥४२॥

brāhmaṇasya hi deho 'yaṁ kṣudra-kāmāya neṣyate
kṛcchrāya tapase ceha pretyānanta-sukhāya ca

The body of a *brāhmaṇa* is not meant for enjoying insignificant sense gratification. Rather, it is meant for performing austerities in this life, so that a *brāhmaṇa* will enjoy unlimited happiness after death.

COMMENTARY

The question may arise, "Why should a *brāhmaṇa* take so much trouble performing austerities?" The answer is that the body of a *brāhmaṇa* is not meant for fulfilling insignificant material desires—it is meant for performing difficult austerities in this life, so that he will achieve unlimited happiness in the next life.

PURPORT

A *bṛāhmaṇa* who has realized the transcendental Personality of Godhead enjoys boundless spiritual happiness and so does not take pleasure in the gratification of the senses. Such a devotee does not undergo severe austerities simply for the purpose of deceiving himself. Those who consider that surrendering to the Supreme Lord involves great severe austerity think in that way because they are addicted to selfish acts of sense enjoyment. Being self-interested, they may ultimately engage in severe austerities for the purpose of attaining liberation. Devotees of the Lord, however, on the strength of their engagement in devotional service, reject the pleasures of the senses as being insignificant. It is not the duty of a *brāhmaṇa* to become either a sense enjoyer or a dry ascetic. His training is simply meant for him to understand that he is the eternal servant of the Supreme Lord.

If a *brāhmaṇa* carefully contemplates the meaning of the following three verses, he can surely come to the conclusion that human life is meant for engaging oneself in the devotional service of the Lord, and not for pursuing insignificant sense gratification.

nāhaṁ vande tava caraṇayor dvandvam advandva-hetoḥ
kumbhīpākaṁ gurum api hare nārakaṁ nāpanetum
ramyā-rāmā-mṛdu-tanu-latā nandane nāpi rantuṁ
bhāve bhāve hṛdaya-bhavane bhāvayeyaṁ bhavantam

O Lord Hari, it is not to be saved from the dualities of material existence or the grim tribulations of the Kumbhīpāka hell that I pray to Your lotus feet. Nor is my purpose to enjoy the soft-skinned beautiful women who reside in the gardens of heaven. I pray to Your lotus feet only so that I may remember You alone in the core of my heart, birth after birth. (*Mukunda-mālā-stotra* 4)

nāsthā dharme na vasu-nicaye naiva kāmopabhoge
yad bhāvyaṁ tad bhavatu bhagavan pūrva-karmānurūpam
etat prārthyaṁ mama bahu-mataṁ janma-janmāntare 'pi
tvat-pādāmbho-ruha-yuga-gatā niścalā bhaktir astu

I have no attraction for performing religious rituals or holding any earthly kingdom. I do not care for sense enjoyments; let them appear and disappear in accordance with my previous deeds. My only desire is to be fixed in devotional service to the lotus feet of the Lord, even though I may continue to take birth here life after life. (*Mukunda-mālā-stotra* 5)

na dhanaṁ na janaṁ na sundarīṁ kavitāṁ vā jagad-īśa kāmaye
mama janmani janmanīśvare bhavatād bhaktir ahaitukī tvayi

O Almighty Lord, I have no desire to accumulate wealth, nor to enjoy beautiful women. Nor do I want any number of followers. What I want only is the causeless mercy of Your devotional service in my life, birth after birth. (*Śikṣāṣṭaka* 4)

TEXT 43

शिलोञ्छवृत्यापरितुष्टचित्तोधर्मंमहान्तंविरजंजुषाणः ।
मय्यर्पितात्मागृह एवतिष्ठन्नातिप्रसक्तःसमुपैतिशान्तिम् ॥४३॥

śiloñcha-vṛttyā parituṣṭa-citto dharmaṁ mahāntaṁ virajaṁ juṣāṇaḥ
mayy arpitātmā gṛha eva tiṣṭhan nāti-prasaktaḥ samupaiti śāntim

A *brāhmaṇa* householder should remain satisfied while maintaining himself by collecting rejected grains found in the fields and marketplaces. Keeping himself free of personal desire, he should practice religious principles while fixing his mind on Me. In this way, a *brāhmaṇa* can remain at home, gradually cultivating detachment, and thus advance toward the ultimate goal of life.

COMMENTARY

The word *unchavṛtti* means "to collect rejected grains that have been left in the marketplaces and agricultural fields." The phrase *dharmaṁ mahāntaṁ* especially refers to faithfully serving guests.

PURPORT

Śrīla Narottama dāsa Ṭhākura has said that one should engage in the service of the Supreme Lord, whether one is living at home or residing in the forest. The essence of all the instructions of *śāstra* is that it is the duty of all the members of the eight *varṇas* and *āśramas* to serve the Supreme Lord, while remaining indifferent to material enjoyment. If one utilizes everything in the service of Lord Kṛṣṇa, then regardless of his position within the *varṇāśrama* social system, he must be considered a liberated soul.

In this regard, one should carefully consider the verse describing *yukta vairāgya*, beginning with *anāsaktasya*, and the verse describing *phalgu vairāgya*, beginning with *prāpañcikatayā*. By understanding the purport of these two verses, one's pure devotional service will be awakened. Without being enlightened by the instructions of the bona fide spiritual master, unrestricted material desires that are fulfilled by engagement in fruitive activities, or on a higher platform, indulgence in mental speculation, will not allow one to favorably cultivate Kṛṣṇa consciousness. *Brāhmaṇas* who are attached to ritualistic activities that are meant for enjoying material happiness, or who practice renunciation in the hopes of merging into the impersonal Brahman, invite inauspiciousness to fall upon themselves.

In this regard, one should carefully contemplate the purport of these two verses:

yadṛcchayā mat-kathādau jāta-śraddhas tu yaḥ pumān
na nirviṇṇo nātisakto bhakti-yogo 'sya siddhidaḥ

Somehow or other, if one is attracted to talks about Me and has faith in the instructions I have set forth in *Bhagavad-gītā*, and if one is actually detached from material things and material existence, his dormant love for Me will be awakened by devotional service. (*Srimad-Bhagavatam* 11.20.8)

ārādhito yadi haris tapasā tataḥ kiṁ
nārādhito yadi haris tapasā tataḥ kim
antar bahir yadi haris tapasā tataḥ kiṁ
nāntar bahir yadi haris tapasā tataḥ kim

If one is worshiping Lord Hari, what is the use of performing extraneous penances? And if one is not worshiping Lord Hari, no such penances will save one. If one can understand that Lord Hari is all-pervading, within and without, what is the need of performing penances? And if one is not able to understand that Hari is all-pervading, all his penances are useless. (*Nārada Pañcarātra*)

TEXT 44

समुद्धरन्ति ये विप्रं सीदन्तं मत्परायणम् ।
तानुद्धरिष्ये नचिरादापद्भ्यो नौरिवार्णवात् ॥४४॥

samuddharanti ye vipraṁ sīdantaṁ mat-parāyaṇam
tān uddhariṣye na cirād āpadbhyo naur ivārṇavāt

Just as a ship rescues a person who has fallen into the ocean and is drowning, I deliver My devotee *brāhmaṇa* who may be afflicted with poverty or who endeavors to deliver others from this ocean of birth and death.

COMMENTARY

When a person gives up the service of the Lord to enjoy a life of sense gratificiation, he is certainly to be considered fallen. Such a person can still benefit himself if he gives some of his hard-earned wealth for the service of the Lord. Here the example is given of a boat that rescues persons drowning in the ocean. Similarly, the Lord delivers those who are drowning in the ocean of material existence if they render service in this way.

PURPORT

If, by good fortune, one who has fallen into the ocean of material existence renders service to the pure devotees of the Supreme Lord, who are freed from all material desires, the Lord will deliver him, out of His causeless mercy. Simply by rendering service to the spiritual master and other advanced devotees, one surely receives the mercy of the Lord. It is a well-known fact that the Lord is more mercifully inclined toward those who consider themselves devotees of His devotees than those who claim to be His direct devotees.

TEXT 45

सर्वाःसमुद्धरेद् राजापितेवव्यसनात्प्रजाः ।
आत्मानमात्मनाधीरोयथागजपतिर्गजान् ॥४५॥

sarvāḥ samuddhared rājā piteva vyasanāt prajāḥ
ātmānam ātmanā dhīro yathā gaja-patir gajān

Just as the king of elephants protects all the other elephants under his shelter and also defends himself, so a king, just like a father, should afford his subjects full protection, and also defend himself from all adversaries.

COMMENTARY

The duty of a king is described in this verse. Just like a father, a king should protect his subjects from all kinds of danger.

TEXT 46

एवंविधोनरपतिर्विमानेनार्कवर्चसा ।
विधूयेहाशुभंकृत्स्नमिन्द्रेणसहमोदते ॥४६॥

evaṁ-vidho nara-patir vimānenārka-varcasā
vidhūyehāśubhaṁ kṛtsnam indreṇa saha modate

A king who protects himself and his citizens by removing all sinful activities from his kingdom will certainly enjoy with Indra in celestial airplanes that are as brilliant as the sun.

TEXT 47

सीदन्विप्रोवणिग्वृत्त्यापण्यैरेवापदंतरेत् ।
खड्गेनवापदाक्रान्तोनश्ववृत्त्याकथञ्चन ॥४७॥

sīdan vipro vaṇig-vṛttyā paṇyair evāpadaṁ taret
khaḍgena vāpadākrānto na śva-vṛttyā kathañcana

If a *brāhmaṇa* is unable to maintain himself by performing his prescribed duties, he may accept the occupation of a *vaiśya* and thus save himself from a life of poverty. If he still faces difficulty as a *vaiśya*, he can adopt the occupation of *kṣatriya*, but he should never become like a dog by accepting an ordinary man as his master.

COMMENTARY

Beginning with this verse, the Lord describes what should be done if one experiences difficulty maintaining himself by performing the duties of his *varṇa*. A *brāhmaṇa* may earn his livelihood by doing business, but he should not sell wine or salt. If in danger, a *brāhmaṇa* may also adopt the profession of a *kṣatriya*. A *brāhmaṇa* is herein recommended to adopt the profession of a merchant rather than that of a *kṣatriya*. The idea is that selling commodities as a *vaiśya* is better than killing enemies as a *kṣatriya*, but it is emphasized that a *brāhmaṇa* should never earn his livelihood by serving low-class people. This is the opinion of Lord Kṛṣṇa.

TEXT 48

वैश्यवृत्त्यातुराजन्योजीवेन्मृगययापदि ।
चरेद्वाविप्ररूपेणनश्ववृत्त्याकथञ्चन ॥४८॥

vaiśya-vṛttyā tu rājanyo jīven mṛgayayāpadi
cared vā vipra-rūpeṇa na śva-vṛttyā kathañcana

A *kṣatriya* who cannot maintain himself by his normal occupation may act as a *vaiśya*, maintain himself by hunting, or teach the *Vedas* to others, but he must never under any circumstances undertake the profession of a *śūdra*.

COMMENTARY

If a *kṣatriya* is unable to maintain himself by his own profession, he may adopt the profession of a *brāhmaṇa* by teaching Vedic knowledge.

TEXT 49

शूद्रवृत्तिंभजेद्वैश्यःशूद्रःकारुकटक्रियाम् ।
कृच्छ्रान्मुक्तोनगर्ह्येणवृत्तिंलिप्सेतकर्मणअज ॥४९॥

śūdra-vṛttiṁ bhajed vaiśyaḥ śūdraḥ kāru-kaṭa-kriyām
kṛcchrān mukto na garhyeṇa vṛttiṁ lipseta karmaṇā

A *vaiśya* who cannot maintain himself may adopt the occupation of a *śūdra,* and a *śūdra* who cannot find a master can engage in simple work, like making baskets and mats out of straw. However, all members of society who have adopted inferior occupations due to emergency situations must give them up once the difficulties have passed.

COMMENTARY

When the emergency situation that caused one to accept an inferior occupation has passed, one must return to his normal occupational duties. One must never aspire to earn wealth by performing abominable activities.

TEXT 50

वेदाध्यायस्वधास्वाहाबल्यन्नाद्यैर्यथोदयम् ।
देवर्षिपितृभूतानिमद्रूपाण्यन्वहंयजेत् ॥५०॥

vedādhyāya-svadhā-svāhā-baly-annādyair yathodayam
devarṣi-pitṛ-bhūtāni mad-rūpāṇy anv-ahaṁ yajet

According to their means, householders should daily worship the sages by studying the *Vedas,* the forefathers by offering oblations, the demigods by performing sacrifices, the living entities in general by offering them food, and human beings by offering them water and grains. They should perform the five kinds of daily sacrifices while understanding the demigods, sages, forefathers, and indeed all types of living entities to be representations of My various potencies.

COMMENTARY

After explaining what one should do in times of difficulty, the Lord once again describes the duties of a householder. A householder should repay his debt to the sages by studying the *Vedas*, his debt to the forefathers by offering them oblations, his debt to the demigods by performing sacrifices, his debt to living entities in general by offering them food, and his debt to the human beings by offering them food and water. In this way, a householder should repay the five kinds of debt.

TEXT 51

यदृच्छयोपपन्नेनशुक्लेनोपार्जितेनवा ।
धनेनापीडयन्भृत्यान् न्यायेनैवाहरेत्क्रतून् ॥५१॥

yadṛcchayopapannena śuklenopārjitena vā
dhanenāpīḍayan bhṛtyān nyāyenaivāharet kratūn

A householder should maintain his dependents by the wealth that has come to him of its own accord, as well as the wealth that he has earned by honest means. He should also utilize his wealth to perform sacrifices and other religious functions.

COMMENTARY

One should earn wealth by engaging in an honest profession, and one should not endeavor too strenuously, knowing that the Lord will supply his necessities of life. One should perform religious activities, such as sacrifices, without committing violence to other living entities.

TEXT 52

कुटुम्बेषुनसज्जेतनप्रमाद्येत्कुटुम्ब्यपि ।
विपश्चिन्नश्वरंपश्येददृष्टमपिदृष्टवत् ॥५२॥

kuṭumbeṣu na sajjeta na pramādyet kuṭumby api
vipaścin naśvaraṁ paśyed adṛṣṭam api dṛṣṭa-vat

Although a householder may have many dependents, he should not become attached to them, thinking that they have an intrinsic relation with him, nor should he become proud, considering himself to be some kind of lord. An intelligent householder should understand that all kinds of material happiness, even that which is available in heaven, is just like the temporary material happiness that he has already experienced.

COMMENTARY

In the next four verses, Lord Kṛṣṇa describes the duties of a detached householder. Even though a householder acts like a little lord, surrounded by his dependents, he should not forget the lotus feet of the Supreme Lord. He should know that his dependent family members are temporary, as are the unseen heavenly pleasures and visible pleasures of this world. The purport is that a householder should cultivate a mood of detachment so that he can guide his family members and other dependents back home, back to Godhead, for an eternal life of bliss and knowledge.

PURPORT

An intelligent person should not invite aversion to the Supreme Lord under the pretext that it is his primary duty to maintain his dependent family members by hook or by crook. Just as the things of this world are temporary manifestations, so is existence in the heavenly planets. According to one's qualities and activities, one is placed within a particular *varṇa* or *āśrama*. If there is any difficulty in the execution of one's prescribed profession, one may take up the profession of a lower *varṇa*. One should live in society and accept material enjoyment in such a way that will not cause a disturbance. One should gradually give up attachment for the material enjoyment that is available in this life and well as the next.

TEXT 53

पुत्रदाराप्तबन्धूनांसङ्गमःपान्थसङ्गमः ।
अनुदेहंवियन्त्येतेस्वप्नोनिद्रानुगोयथा ॥५३॥

putra-dārāpta-bandhūnāṁ saṅgamaḥ pāntha-saṅgamaḥ
anu-dehaṁ viyanty ete svapno nidrānugo yathā

One's society of children, wife, relatives, and friends can be compared to a meeting of travelers at an inn. Upon changing his body, one is separated from all such friends and relatives, just as when one wakes up from a dream, all that was seen is lost.

COMMENTARY

The association of wife, children, relatives, and friends, should be considered to be like the meeting of travelers at a resting place. One should cultivate a mood of detachment from everything material by carefully considering how nothing is permanent in this world. All of one's relatives will vanish one day, however affectionate they may be. All objects of this world are temporary, as are the objects one sees in a dream.

PURPORT

The relationships one has with his wife, children, kinsmen, and friends are temporary, just like the experiences of a dream. While dreaming, one comes in contact with various objects and people, but when he wakes up, all of these vanish. As long as one maintains attachment for such perishable objects, one cannot become steady on the transcendental platform of devotional service, and thus cannot relish the actual flavor of eternal happiness. One who remains attached to the bodily concept of family and friends cannot possibly give up the false egoism of "I" and "mine."

Unless a householder worships child Kṛṣṇa, his attachment for his children will remain strong. As long as the Lord's pastimes in *mādhurya rasa* do not become the subject of one's meditation, one will continue to think of his wife as the reservoir of all pleasure. Unless one becomes a pure devotee of the Lord, accepting Lord Kṛṣṇa as one's only friend, just like Śrīdāma, one will not be able to give up the hankering for temporary and superficial material relationships. Until one's propensity for rendering devotional service to Lord Kṛṣṇa is awakened, one will continue to foolishly demand service from others. One who is actually intelligent should understand that there can be no satisfaction for the self on any planet within the material world. Therefore, like a traveler who has become very tired while traveling, one should go back home, back to Godhead. Eternal peace is the condition of the faithful servant of Lord Śrī Kṛṣṇa.

TEXT 54

इत्थंपरिमृशन्मुक्तोगृहेष्वतिथिवद्वसन् ।
नगृहैरनुबध्येतनिर्ममोनिरहङ्कृतः ॥५४॥

ittham parimṛśan mukto gṛheṣv atithi-vad vasan
na gṛhair anubadhyeta nirmamo nirahaṅkṛtaḥ

A detached householder, after deeply considering his situation, should give up all pride and attachment and remain at home just like a guest. By doing so, he will never become entangled by domestic affairs.

COMMENTARY

The word *mukta* means "detached."

PURPORT

While considering how everything in this world is a temporary manifestation, one should continue to perform his occupational duties, maintain his body and the bodies of his family members, and cultivate detachment by remaining at home like a guest. By full engagement in the devotional service of the Lord, one should free himself from the false egoistic conception of thinking, "I am the enjoyer and all that I possess is mine." Such a false conception can be counteracted by thinking, "I belong to Kṛṣṇa and Kṛṣṇa belongs to me." To free oneself from attachment for one's body, friends, and so on, one should engage in the service of Lord Hari with firm determination, whether one lives at home or resides in the forest. If one remains absorbed in thinking, "I belong to this *varṇa*," "I belong to this *āśrama*," "I am a man," or "I am a woman," and so on, one will remain a *gṛha-vṛata*, a person whose life is centered around his family. Without realizing the purport of these two verses, one will either remain attached to family life, or become attached to a false concept of renunciation.

anāsaktasya viṣayān yathārham upayuñjataḥ
nirbandhaḥ kṛṣṇa-sambandhe yuktaṁ vairāgyam ucyate

prāpañcikatayā buddhyā hari-sambandhi-vastunaḥ
mumukṣubhiḥ parityāgo vairāgyaṁ phalgu kathyate

When one is not attached to anything, but at the same time accepts everything in relation to Kṛṣṇa, one is rightly situated above possessiveness. On the other hand, one who rejects everything without knowledge of its relationship to Kṛṣṇa is not as complete in his renunciation. (*Bhakti-rasāmṛta-sindhu* 1.2.255-256)

When one cultivates Kṛṣṇa consciousness favorably, without the coverings of *karma* and *jñāna*, only then will he transcend his designated position within the *varṇāśrama* system.

TEXT 55

कर्मभिर्गृहमेधीयैरिष्ट्वामामेवभक्तिमान् ।
तिष्ठेद्वनंवोपविशेत्प्रजावान्वापरिव्रजेत् ॥५५॥

karmabhir gṛha-medhīyair iṣṭvā mām eva bhaktimān
tiṣṭhed vanaṁ vopaviśet prajāvān vā parivrajet

A householder devotee who faithfully worships Me by the performance of his duties can reside at home or at a holy place of pilgrimage. If he has a grown-up son and has given up all desires for material enjoyment, he can take *sannyāsa*.

COMMENTARY

The Supreme Lord said, "A householder who is devoted to Me should perform all of his activities for My satisfaction. While doing so, he can either live at home, go to the forest, or accept the renounced order of life, *sannyāsa*."

PURPORT

The result of an attached householder's worship of the Lord is the attainment of pure devotional service. One should not remain unnecessarily entangled in family affairs, whether one lives at home, resides in the forest, or travels to holy places of pilgrimage. Remaining situated in a particular *varṇa* or *āśrama* does not constitute a hindrance to becoming an advanced devotee of the Supreme Lord. The conclusion is that everyone should engage in the service of the Lord in all respects.

TEXT 56

यस्त्वासक्तमतिर्गेहेपुत्रवित्तैषणातुरः ।
स्त्रैणःकृपणधीर्मूढोममाहमितिबध्यते ॥५६॥

yas tv āsakta-matir gehe putra-vittaiṣaṇāturaḥ
straiṇaḥ kṛpaṇa-dhīr mūḍho mamāham iti badhyate

However, a miserly householder who has strong desires to enjoy his money, lusty desires with his wife, and the association of his children, and thus thinks, "All of these are mine. I am the master of all I survey," is in the densest darkness of ignorance.

COMMENTARY

This and the next two verses describe the fault of being too attached to one's household.

PURPORT

One who does not worship Lord Hari while giving up material attachment is certainly committing an offense against the holy name of the Lord by maintaining material attachment in terms of "I" and "mine." Even though such a person may dress like a devotee, he will not be liberated from his conditional state of material existence.

TEXT 57

अहोमेपितरौवृद्धौभार्याबालात्मजात्मजाः ।
अनाथामामृतेदीनाःकथंजीवन्तिदुःखिताः ॥५७॥

aho me pitarau vṛddhau bhāryā bālātmajātmajāḥ
anāthā mām ṛte dīnāḥ kathaṁ jīvanti duḥkhitāḥ

"Alas! How will my elderly parents continue to live? Without my protection, my poor wife with her small children will suffer terribly! How can my poor family live without me?"

COMMENTARY

One may think, "How can I leave home to advance in Kṛṣṇa consciousness when I have my wife and my one-month-old son? Alas! How can I leave my sons and daughters, who are fully dependent upon me? How will they prosper—they are too young?" In this way, an attached person remains full of anxiety.

TEXT 58

एवंगृहाशयाक्षिप्तहृदयोमूढधीरयम् ।
अतृप्तस्ताननुध्यायन्मृतोऽन्धंविशतेतमः ॥५८॥

evaṁ gṛhāśayākṣipta-hṛdayo mūḍha-dhīr ayam
atṛptas tān anudhyāyan mṛto 'ndhaṁ viśate tamaḥ

Thus, as a result of his foolish mentality, a householder whose heart is overwhelmed by family attachment remains in anxiety. While constantly meditating on his family, he dies and enters the darkness of ignorance.

PURPORT

Those who engage their senses in sense gratification, instead of engaging them in the service of Lord Kṛṣṇa, think that without them, their old parents and their wives and children will suffer, or that they will be criticized for not taking proper care of their dependents. In this way, the attached householders spend their days in anxiety. As a result of their primitive mentality, after death, they will certainly be degraded to a lower species of life.

Thus ends the translation of the Eleventh Chapter of the Uddhava-gītā, *entitled* **"Lord Kṛṣṇa's Description of the Varṇāśrama System"** *with the commentaries of Śrīla Viśvanātha Cakravartī Ṭhākura and the chapter summary and purports by Śrīla Bhaktisiddhānta Sarasvatī Ṭhākura.*

CHAPTER 12

DESCRIPTION OF VARṆĀŚRAMA-DHARMA

CHAPTER SUMMARY

In this chapter, Lord Śrī Kṛṣṇa explains to Uddhava the duties and practices of those in the *vānaprastha* and *sannyāsa āśramas.*

One who accepted the *vānaprastha āśrama* should leave his wife at home in the care of his grown-up sons, or else take her with him to reside in the forest. He should then subsist upon whatever fruit and roots that are available in the forest, sometimes cooking grains when they are freely available. He should wear clothing made of tree bark, grass, and deerskin. While residing in the forest, he should not cut his hair, nails, or beard. He should bathe three times a day and sleep on the ground. During the heat of the summer, he should sit under the blazing sun, after lighting fires on all four sides. During the monsoon, he should let the rain soak him, and in the winter, he should stand in cold water up to the neck. One in the *vānaprastha āśrama* should not brush his teeth, keep left-over food, or performing any sacrifices that involve killing animals. If a *vānaprastha* faithfully follows these principles, he can attain the Tapoloka planet after death.

The fourth quarter of one's life should be spent in the renounced order of life, *sannyāsa.* When one realizes the ultimate futility of material existence, even in the endeavor to reach the heavenly planets, he should accept *sannyāsa* as an expression of his renunciation. At the time of accepting the renounced order of life, one should worship the Supreme Lord, give everything in his possession in charity, and fix his mind on the Lord with determination. For a *sannyāsī,* intimate association with women is more abominable than drinking poison. A *sannyāsī* should only wear a loin cloth, and carry nothing more than his staff and water pot. He should live a life of complete nonviolence and he should carefully control his mind, body, and speech. While remaining detached from any comfortable material situation, he should be fixed in self-realization while traveling alone to holy places of pilgrimage, as well as mountains, rivers, and forests, while constantly remembering the Supreme Lord.

A *sannyāsī* should fearlessly reside in a secluded place. He should maintain himself by begging from seven houses of those who are not fallen, selected at random. Whatever he obtains he should offer to the Supreme Lord and accept the remnants as *prasādam*. He should always remember that desires for sense gratification are the causes of bondage, whereas the utilization of everything in the service of the Lord is liberation. When a person who has failed to conquer his six enemies, headed by lust, and who has no knowledge or renunciation, accepts the renounced order of life simply for the sake of maintaining himself, the thing he will achieve is the killing of his own self.

A *paramahaṁsa* is not governed by the rules and regulations prescribed in the scriptures. He is a topmost devotee of the Lord who is fully detached from the objects of the senses and doesn't even desire liberation from material existence. Although he is the foremost learned scholar, he is devoid of pride and transcendental to praise and infamy. Although he is the most expert of all persons, he wanders about like a madman, and although he is greatly learned, he speaks like one possessed by a ghost. Although he is a master of the *Vedas*, he seems to act irresponsibly. He tolerates the harsh words of others and never tries to retaliate such insults. He never creates enmity with others, and he is never enticed into a useless argument. He sees how the Supreme Lord is situated in all living entities and how all living entities are situated in the Supreme Lord. He maintains himself with whatever food, clothing, and shelter are obtained of their own accord. As a result, he peacefully performs his worship of the Lord, without any anxiety. Although he may sometimes endeavor to get some food, just to keep body and soul together, he is never overjoyed when he receives something palatable, nor does he become dejected when he fails to receive anything. He is on the same platform as the Supreme Lord, who is not under the jurisdiction of the Vedic injunctions, but by His own free will, performs pastimes for the welfare of all. Because such a *paramahaṁsa* has transcended the dualities of material existence, as the fruit of his transcendental knowledge of the Supreme Lord, after quitting his material body, he attains the liberation known as *sārṣṭi*, whereby he becomes equal in opulence with the Lord.

A person who desires his own self-interest should take shelter of a bona fide spiritual master and faithfully serve him, considering him to be nondifferent from the Supreme Lord. The primary duty of a *brahmācārī* is to serve his spiritual master. The principal duties of a *gṛhastha* are to maintain the other classes of men and perform sacrifices. A *vānaprastha* must live a life of austerities, and a *sannyāsī* must carefully control his mind and senses. Celibacy, austerity, cleanliness, remaining satisfied, exhibiting friendship toward all living beings, and worship of the Supreme Personality of Godhead are the duties to be performed by every human being. By performing one's occupational duties under the direction of the Supreme Lord, one develops devotion for Him. One should always be cognizant of the Lord because He resides within the bodies of all creatures as the Supersoul.

Those who follow the *karma-kāṇḍa* sections of the *Vedas* ordinarily attain the planets of the forefathers, but if they become devotees of the Supreme Lord, they can rise to the platform of liberation.

TEXT 1

श्रीभगवानुवाच
वनंविविक्षुःपुत्रेषुभार्यांन्यस्यसहैववा ।
वनएव वसेच्छान्तस्तृतीयंभागमायुषः ॥१॥

śrī-bhagavān uvāca
vanaṁ vivikṣuḥ putreṣu bhāryāṁ nyasya sahaiva vā
vana eva vasec chāntas tṛtīyaṁ bhāgam āyuṣaḥ

The Supreme Lord said: One who desires to adopt the third order of life, the *vānaprastha āśrama,* should leave his wife in the care of his mature sons or else take her with him to peacefully reside in the forest.

COMMENTARY

This Twelfth Chapter describes the duties of the *vānaprastha* and *sannyāsī*, the devotees' position of not being confined to the principles of *āśrama*, and discussion of the ultimate goal of life.

The third portion of one's life, beginning at the age of fifty, and continuing up to the age of seventy-five, should be spent in the *vānaprastha āśrama*. Thereafter, one should take *sannyāsa*.

PURPORT

There are four spiritual orders in human society, of which *vānaprastha* is the third. To accept the *vānaprastha āśrama*, a householder should either leave his wife in the care of his grown up sons or take her with him and enter the forest. If one hopes to live for one hundred years, he can take *vānaprastha* at the age of fifty, and *sannyāsa* at the age of seventy-five. At present, however, very few people live to a hundred, and so one should renounce materialistic life earlier

TEXT 2

कन्दमूलफलैर्वन्यैर्मेध्यैर्वृत्तिंप्रकल्पयेत् ।
वसीतवल्कलंवासस्तृणपर्णाजिनानिवा ॥२॥

kanda-mūla-phalair vanyair medhyair vṛttiṁ prakalpayet
vasīta valkalaṁ vāsas tṛṇa-parṇājināni vā

In the forest, a *vānaprastha* should maintain himself by eating pure fruit, roots, and bulbs that grow in the forest. He should dress himself in tree bark, leaves, grass, or deerskin.

COMMENTARY

The word *vasīta* means "to dress oneself."

PURPORT

It is recommended that a member of the *vānaprastha āśrama* should subsist upon the fruit and roots that are available in the forest, and he should wear garments of deerskin, tree bark, and so on. In the fourteenth verse of the sixth chapter of the *Manu Saṁhīta*, it is stated:

varjayen madhu māṁsaṁ ca bhaumāni kavakāni ca
bhūstṛṇaṁ śigrukaṁ caiva śleṣmātakaphalāni ca

One should not partake of honey-based liquors, animal flesh, fungus, mushrooms, horseradish or any hallucinogenic or intoxicating herbs, even those taken as so-called medicine.

TEXT 3

केशरोमनखश्मश्रुमलानिबिभृयाद्दतः ।
नधावेदप्सुमज्जेतत्रिकालंस्थण्डिलेशयः ॥३॥

keśa-roma-nakha-śmaśru-malāni bibhṛyād dataḥ
na dhāved apsu majjeta tri kālaṁ sthaṇḍile-śayaḥ

A *vānaprastha* should not groom his hair or beard, manicure his nails, cleanse his teeth, or pass stool or urine at irregular times. He should be satisfied to bathe three times a day, and he should sleep on the bare ground.

PURPORT

A *vānaprastha* is prohibited to shave or brush his teeth because such activities would draw his attention to the material body. He should bathe three times a day and sleep on the ground.

TEXT 4

ग्रीष्मेतप्येतपञ्चाग्नीन्वर्षास्वासारषाड्जले ।
आकण्ठमग्नःशिशिर एवंवृत्तस्तपश्चरेत् ॥४॥

grīṣme tapyeta pañcāgnīn varṣāsv āsāra-ṣāḍ jale
ākaṇṭha-magnaḥ śiśira evaṁ vṛttas tapaś caret

While engaged in his life as a *vānaprastha,* one should execute penance during the hottest days of summer by keeping fires on four sides and the blazing sun overhead. During the rainy season, one should remain outside, subjecting himself to torrents of rain, and in the freezing winter, one should remain submerged in water up to his neck.

PURPORT

The followers of *karma-kāṇḍa* should practice the penance of tolerating the five kinds of heat during the summer. In the rainy season, they should remain outside, even when there are torrents of rain. In the winter, they should remain submerged in water up to the neck. A devotee of the Lord, however, naturally develops Kṛṣṇa consciousness and need not subject himself to such radical penances. The *Nārada-pañcarātra* confirms this:

ārādhito yadi haris tapasā tataḥ kiṁ
nārādhito yadi haris tapasā tataḥ kim
antar bahir yadi haris tapasā tataḥ kiṁ
nāntar bahir yadi haris tapasā tataḥ kim

If one is worshiping the Lord properly, what is the use of severe penance? And if one is not properly worshiping the Lord, what is the use of severe penance? If Śrī Kṛṣṇa is realized within and without everything that exists, what is the use of severe penance? And if Śrī Kṛṣṇa is not seen within and without everything, then what is the use of severe penance?

TEXT 5

अग्निपक्वंसमश्नीयात्कालपक्वमथापिवा ।
उलूखलाश्मकुट्टोवादन्तोलूखल एववा ॥५॥

agni-pakvaṁ samaśnīyāt kāla-pakvam athāpi vā
ulūkhalāśma-kuṭṭo vā dantolūkhala eva vā

One can eat cooked food, such as grains, or eat fruit that has been ripened in the course of time. One can grind grains with a stone mortar and pestle, or one can simply grind the grains with his teeth.

COMMENTARY

As a concession, one can grind food grains with a stone and mortar. Otherwise, one can simply grind his food with his teeth.

TEXT 6

स्वयंसञ्चिनुयात्सर्वमात्मनोवृत्तिकारणम् ।
देशकालबलाभिज्ञोनाददीतान्यदाहृतम् ॥६॥

svayaṁ sañcinuyāt sarvam ātmano vṛtti-kāraṇam
deśa-kāla-balābhijño nādadītānyadāhṛtam

The *vānaprastha* should go out and collect only as much as he requires for his bodily maintenance. He should not save anything for future use.

COMMENTARY

A *vānaprastha* must collect things for his maintenance in consideration of the place, the time, and his capacity, and he must not save anything for the future use, thus depending upon the mercy of the Lord. Of course, during an emergency, or if one is an invalid, this rule need not be strictly followed.

PURPORT

Unless one is an invalid, one should not depend on others for one's maintenance, because this will make one indebted so that he will have to reborn to repaid whatever he has received. In the *Manu Saṁhitā* (6.15) it is stated:

tyajedāśvayuje māsi munyannaṁ pūrvasañcitam
jīrṇāni caiva vāsāṁsi śākamūlaphalāni ca

A sage should not have the habit of accumulating things for future use. He should wear old clothes and maintain himself by eating spinach, roots, and fruit.

TEXT 7

वन्यैश्चरुपुरोडाशैर्निर्वपेत्कालचोदितान् ।
नतुश्रौतेनपशुनामांयजेतवनाश्रमी ॥७॥

vanyaiś caru-puroḍāśair nirvapet kāla-coditān
na tu śrautena paśunā māṁ yajeta vanāśramī

The *vānaprastha* should perform seasonal sacrifices by offering oblations of *caru* and sacrificial cakes prepared from rice and other grains that are found in the forest. However, he should never offer animal sacrifices to Me, even those that are mentioned in the *Vedas*.

COMMENTARY

For example, in the month of November-December, one should worship the Supreme Lord with an offering of newly harvested grains.

PURPORT

The *vānaprastha* should perform sacrifice by utilizing whatever is available in the forest during the various times of the year. However, he should never perform any sacrifice that involves killing animals.

TEXT 8

अग्निहोत्रंचदर्शश्चपौर्णमासश्चपूर्ववत् ।
चातुर्मास्यानिचमुनेराम्नातानिचनैगमैः ॥८॥

agnihotraṁ ca darśaś ca paurṇamāsaś ca pūrva-vat
cāturmāsyāni ca muner āmnātāni ca naigamaiḥ

Expert knowers of the *Vedas* have prescribed for a *vānaprastha* the performance of various sacrifices, such as the *agnihotra, darśa,* and *paurnamāsa,* as well as the vow of *cāturmāsya.*

COMMENTARY

The *vānaprastha* should observe whatever practices have been prescribed by the expert knowers of the *Vedas*.

PURPORT

1. *Agnihotra*. After marriage, a *brāhmaṇa* should perform fire sacrifice as prescribed in the *Vedas*, especially during the spring. He should make a vow to use certain ingredients for the performance of his sacrifices, and he should stick to that principle for the rest of his life. On moonless nights, one should personally perform fire sacrifice, especially with oblations of barley. On other days, he may use other ingredients. After the completion of one hundred such sacrifices, he should perform a special sacrifice for the satisfaction of the sun-god in the morning, and another special sacrifice for the satisfaction of the satisfaction of the moon-god in the evening. After commencing the performance of sacrifice during the first full moon day of the month, one should particularly perform the *darśa* and *paurṇamāsa* sacrifices. One should perform three separate fire sacrifices on the full moon day and three on the new moon day. This procedure he should observe for the remainder of his life. One who performs the *agnihotra* sacrifice in this way is assured of elevation to the heavenly planets, where he will enjoy great happiness. This has been described in the literature known as *Śatapatha Brāhmaṇa*.

2. *Darśa*. *Darśa* refers to the new moon day because on that day, the sun and the moon are in proximity. In the *Matsya Purāṇa*, it is said: *anyo 'nyaṁ candra suryo tu darśanād darśa ucyate*: On the day of *darśa*, the sun and the moon see each other.

3. *Paurṇamāsa*. There are various sacrifices to be performed on the full moon day. The procedures for performing these sacrifices are mentioned in the fourth chapter of the *Manu-saṁhitā*. In the book called *Kātāyana-śrauta-sutra*, the processes for performing these sacrifices are also described.

4. *Cāturmāsya*. *Cāturmāsya* is of two kinds—the *cāturmāsya* sacrifice and the *cāturmāsya* vow. For a description of the procedures of this sacrifice, one should refer to the *Kātāyana-śrauta-sūtra*, chapter five. The procedures for observing this vow are described in the *Matsya Purāṇa*, *Bhaviśya Purāṇa*, *Skanda Purāṇa*, and *Sanat-kumāra Saṁhitā*. One should also consult the *Hari-bhakti-vilāsa* in this connection.

TEXT 9

एवंचीर्णेनतपसामुनिर्धमनिसन्ततः ।
मांतपोमयमाराध्यऋषिलोकादुपैतिमाम् ॥९॥

evaṁ cīrnena tapasā munir dhamani-santataḥ
māṁ tapo-mayam ārādhya ṛṣi-lokād upaiti mām

When a *vānaprastha* performs severe austerities, only accepting the bare necessities of life so that he becomes so emaciated that his bones and veins are clearly seen, he will attain Maharloka and thereafter come to My supreme abode.

COMMENTARY

Maharloka is a planet of sages. After attaining the Maharloka, the *vānaprastha* who had not completed his course of Kṛṣṇa consciousness will make further advancement and thus qualify to go back home, back to Godhead.

PURPORT

After living a life of penance while observing all the required rules and regulations, an ascetic reaches the planet of the sages. If he can understand the insignificant nature of that achievement, he may cultivate his taste for worshiping the Supreme Lord. In the cultivation of unalloyed devotional service, there is no need for excessive penance. Rather, there is an abundance of worship of the Lord.

TEXT 10

यस्त्वेतत्कृच्छ्रतश्चीर्णंतपोनिःश्रेयसंमहत् ।
कामायाल्पीयसेयुंज्याद्बालिशःकोऽपरस्ततः ॥१०॥

yas tv etat kṛcchrataś cīrṇaṁ tapo niḥśreyasaṁ mahat
kāmāyālpīyase yuñjyād bāliśaḥ ko 'paras tataḥ

Who could be more foolish than a person who utilizes his exalted but painful penance, which can award ultimate liberation, for enjoying insignificant sense gratification?

COMMENTARY

In this verse, the Lord condemns those in the *vānaprastha āśrama* who are materially ambitious.

PURPORT

It is not the duty of an intelligent person to try to subdue his material desires by undergoing severe penance. Rather, he should engage in the direct service of the Supreme Lord. Penance without devotional service is the act of a fool and is glorified only in the *karma-kāṇḍa* sections of the *Vedas*.

TEXT 11

यदासौ नियमेऽकल्पो जरया जातवेपथुः ।
आत्मन्यग्नीन्समारोप्य मच्चित्तोऽग्निं समाविशेत् ॥११॥

yadāsau niyame 'kalpo jarayā jāta-vepathuḥ
ātmany agnīn samāropya mac-citto 'gniṁ samāviśet

When a *vānaprastha* approaches the old age, so that his body trembles and he can no long perform his prescribed duties, then, in a trance of meditation, he should place the sacrificial fire within his heart, fix his mind upon Me, and finally enter the fire to give up his life.

COMMENTARY

The word *akalpa* means "being incapable."

PURPORT

Only those who are attached to materialistic life, and who therefore suffer because of their enjoying spirit, need enter fire to give up their bodies. When the mind is fixed on the Supreme Lord, one does not see the need for relinquishing his body in this way. Rather, by the performance of the congregational chanting of the holy name of Kṛṣṇa, the fire of material existence becomes extinguished.

TEXT 12

यदा कर्मविपाकेषु लोकेषु निरयात्मसु ।
विरागो जायते सम्यङ् न्यस्ताग्निः प्रव्रजेत्ततः ॥१२॥

yadā karma-vipākeṣu lokeṣu nirayātmasu
virāgo jāyate samyaṅ nyastāgniḥ pravrajet tataḥ

If the *vānaprastha* develops detachment for everything material, even promotion to Brahmaloka, knowing that any situation resulting from the fruits of one's activities is miserable, he can accept the renounced order of life, *sannyāsa*.

COMMENTARY

The phrase *karma vipakeṣu* means "the result obtained by one's actions."

PURPORT

If one becomes detached from the aspiration to attain any of the higher material planets, which are obtained as the result of one's fruitive actions, then one should surrender unto the Supreme Lord and dovetail all of his propensities in His service. In this way, one can be freed from material desires without the execution of severe penance.

TEXT 13

इष्ट्वायथोपदेशंमांदत्त्वासर्वस्वमृत्विजे ।
अग्नीन्स्वप्राण आवेश्यनिरपेक्षःपरिव्रजेत् ॥१३॥

iṣṭvā yathopadeśaṁ māṁ dattvā sarva-svam ṛtvije
agnīn sva-prāṇa āveśya nirapekṣaḥ parivrajet

After worshiping Me for a long time, following the prescribed rules and regulations, one should give everything in his possession to the sacrificial priest and then place the sacrificial fire within himself. Having achieved a state of complete detachment, he should accept the renounced order of life.

COMMENTARY

At this time, one should perform eight kinds of *śrāddhā* and other rituals that are described in the *śāstra.*

PURPORT

After giving up all kinds of bad association and after giving *dakṣiṇā* to the priests, if one is fully engaged in the devotional service of the Supreme Lord, he is considered eligible to take *sannyāsa.* Lusty desires are impediments to the service of the Supreme Lord. One who aspires for liberation from material existence should give up all lusty activities and instead, accept the role of a mendicant who is only interested in rendering service to the Supreme Lord.

TEXT 14

विप्रस्यवैसन्न्यसतोदेवादारादिरूपिणः ।
विघ्नान्कुर्वन्त्ययंह्यस्मानाक्रम्यसमियात्परम् ॥१४॥

viprasya vai sannyasato devā dārādi-rūpiṇaḥ
vighnān kurvanty ayaṁ hy asmān ākramya samiyāt param

"This *sannyāsī* will surpass us and attain the supreme destination." Thinking like this, the demigods try to create obstacles on the path of the *sannyāsī* by appearing before him in the form of his former wife and other women. A *sannyāsī* should not become disturbed by this.

COMMENTARY

A *sannyāsī* should not be disturbed by the obstacles the demigods place before him. When a *brāhmaṇa* takes *sannyāsa*, the demigods enter the body of his wife and try to entangle him in sense gratification. Why do they create such impediments? Because they are envious that the *sannyāsī* will surpass them by going back home, back to Godhead.

PURPORT

The demigods are administrators of universal affairs who award the fruits of one's actions. They may be born as one's legitimate wife and children so that they can create disturbances on the path of a person who is cultivating Kṛṣṇa consciousness. When one eagerly tries to render devotional service, the demigods attempt to put obstacles on his path by posing as his wife, son, or friend. They try to misguide one from the path of spiritual life by advertising that material enjoyment is the goal of human life. In the name of religion, and on the pretext of duty, they misguide a sincere *sannyāsī* so that he falls down from the renounced order of life and gives up his desire to worship the Supreme Lord.

TEXT 15

बिभृयाच्चेन्मुनिर्वासः कौपीनाच्छादनंपरम् ।
त्यक्तंनदण्डपात्राभ्यामन्यत्किञ्चिदनापदि ॥१५॥

bibhṛyāc cen munir vāsaḥ kaupīnācchādanaṁ param
tyaktaṁ na daṇḍa-pātrābhyām anyat kiñcid anāpadi

If a *sannyāsī* desires to wear something more than a *kaupīna*, he may cover his waist and hips with another cloth. Except in the case of emergency, he should not carry anything but his *daṇḍa* and waterpot.

COMMENTARY

The duties of a *sannyāsī* are being described in this verse. He should wear only a *kaupīna*, or if he wants to wear something more, he can cover his waist and hips with another cloth. A *sannyāsī* should not carry anything more than a *daṇḍa* and a waterpot.

PURPORT

A *sannyāsī* should not think of dressing extravagantly and for that reason, he is restricted to just a *kaupīnā* and another piece of cloth. If he desires to possess something more than a *daṇḍa* and a waterpot, that thirst for accumulating many luxurious objects will certainly pollute the *sannyāsī*'s desire for worshiping the Supreme Lord.

TEXT 16

दृष्टिपूतंन्यसेत्पादंवस्त्रपूतंपिबेज्जलम् ।
सत्यपूतांवदेद्वाचंमनःपूतंसमाचरेत् ॥१६॥

dṛṣṭi-pūtaṁ nyaset pādaṁ vastra-pūtaṁ pibej jalam
satya-pūtāṁ vaded vācaṁ manaḥ-pūtaṁ samācaret

One who is trying to elevate himself to the transcendental platform should only place his foot on the ground after seeing that there are no tiny insects there, so that he may not cause any violence to any living entity. He should drink water only after straining it through a piece of cloth, and he should speak only words that possess the purity of truth. Similarly, he should only perform those activities that he has ascertained to be very pure by nature.

PURPORT

While walking, a devotee of the Lord is careful not to kill any insects that may be in his path. He strains his drinking water through a cloth just to make sure he doesn't drink any tiny creatures. Speaking lies to enhance one's sense gratification should be avoided because this is not suitable behavior for a devotee. Speech must be controlled so that it is never used to condone impersonal philosophy or heavenly sense gratification, because such sound vibrations contaminate the heart. By philosophically considering the matter very deeply, one should arrive at the conclusion that any activity other than the devotional service of the Lord is absolutely useless. In this way, one should engage in Kṛṣṇa consciousness.

TEXT 17

मौनानीहानिलायामादण्डावाग्देहचेतसाम् ।
नह्येतेयस्यसन्त्यङ्गवेणुभिर्नभवेद्यतिः ॥१७॥

maunānīhānilāyāmā daṇḍā vāg-deha-cetasām
na hy ete yasya santy aṅga veṇubhir na bhaved yatiḥ

My dear Uddhava, one who does not avoid useless speech, refrain from useless endeavors, and control his body, mind, and speech, cannot be considered a sannyāsī merely because he carries bamboo rods.

COMMENTARY

The word *mauna* means "refraining from useless speech." The word *anīha* means "refraining from useless activities." The word *anila-āyāmāḥ* means "to regulate the breathing." One who is unable to control these three internal urges cannot be accepted as a *tridaṇḍi sannyāsī.*

PURPORT

Here, the word *daṇḍa* indicates the staff carried by *sannyāsīs*, and it also means "strict discipline." Vaiṣṇava *sannyāsīs* carry a staff made of three bamboo rods that indicate the dedication of his body, mind, and words to the service of the Supreme Personality of Godhead. However, one who simply carries *daṇḍa* without disciplining the activities of his body, mind, and words, cannot be considered a true Vaiṣṇava *sannyāsī*, as indicated in this verse.

In the *Haṁsa-gītā* section of the *Mahābhārata* and in Śrīla Rūpa Gosvāmī's *Upadeśāmṛta*, there are nice instructions on how to engage in the *sannyāsa* order of life. A neophyte devotee who simply adopts the external ornaments of *tridaṇḍī-sannyāsa* will certainly fail to control his senses. One who accepts the renounced order of life simply for enhancing his false prestige, thus making a show of being an advanced devotee without actual advancement in hearing and chanting the Lord's glories, will soon become a victim of the illusory energy of the Lord.

TEXT 18

भिक्षांचतुर्षुवर्णेषुविगर्ह्यान्वर्जयंश्चरेत् ।
सप्तागारानसङ्क्लृप्तांस्तुष्येल्लब्धेनतावता ॥१८॥

bhikṣāṁ caturṣu varṇeṣu vigarhyān varjayaṁś caret
saptāgārān asaṅkḷptāṁs tuṣyel labdhena tāvatā

Leaving aside the houses of those who have fallen from the standard of Vedic culture, one should beg from seven houses and be satisfied with whatever is easily obtained. One can beg food from anyone of the four social orders.

COMMENTARY

Brāhmaṇas are qualified to accept charity, teach the *Vedas*, act as priests, or maintain themselves by collecting rejected grains from the agricultural fields. A *brāhmaṇa* should avoid begging alms from the houses of those who are cursed or who are in a wretched condition of life. He should beg alms from seven houses chosen at random, without considering who might be more favorable or generous.

PURPORT

There are three methods for begging alms—*mādhukara*, *asaṅklipta*, and *prākpraṇita*. To collect just a little food from many houses—just enough for his maintenance—is called *mādhukara*. This is the best method for a *sannyāsī* to beg alms. The process mentioned in this verse is called *asaṇklipta*, whereby one approaches seven houses and is satisfied with whatever he receives. *Prāk-praṇīta* is that process by which one establishes regular donors and collects one's maintenance from them.

In this verse it is recommended that without discriminating, one should go to seven houses and be satisfied with whatever may be obtained there. One should for one's personal maintenance only from those who sincerely observe their duties within the *varṇāśrama* system, and not from those who have neglected this culture, especially if they are atheists.

TEXT 19

बहिर्जलाशयंगत्वातत्रोपस्पृश्यवाग्यतः ।
विभज्यपावितंशेषंभुञ्जीताशेषमाहृतम् ॥१९॥

bahir jalāśayaṁ gatvā tatropaspṛśya vāg-yataḥ
vibhajya pāvitaṁ śeṣaṁ bhuñjītāśeṣam āhṛtam

Taking the food collected by begging, one should leave the populated areas and go to a reservoir of water in a solitary place. There, having taken a bath and washed one's hands thoroughly, one should distribute some of the food to those who request it. One should do this without speaking. Thereafter, one should eat whatever remains, leaving nothing for future consumption.

COMMENTARY

The *sannyāsī* should divide the food that he has collected, offering portions to Lord Viṣṇu, Brahmā, the sun-god, and others who may request it. Thereafter, he should eat whatever remains, not leaving any remnants on his plate.

PURPORT

One who is trying to advance on the path of devotional service should not get into arguments with materialistic people who may ask for a portion of one's food acquired by begging. The word *vibhajya* indicates that one should give such persons what they ask for, just to avoid a disturbance. After offering whatever remains to the Lord, one should eat everything and not save anything for the future.

TEXT 20

एकश्चरेन्महीमेतां निःसङ्गः संयतेन्द्रियः ।
आत्मक्रीड आत्मरत आत्मवान्समदर्शनः ॥२०॥

ekaś caren mahīm etāṁ niḥsaṅgaḥ saṁyatendriyaḥ
ātma-krīḍa ātma-rata ātma-vān sama-darśanaḥ

A *sannyāsī* should travel over the earth without any companion, remaining free from material desires by carefully controlling his mind and senses, and always seeing how the Supreme Lord is situated within the hearts of all living beings. With equal vision, he should remain fixed on the transcendental platform.

COMMENTARY

The word *ātmarata* indicates the state of self-satisfaction that results from realizing the Supersoul within. The word *ātmavān* indicates that the *sannyāsī* should be steady in the self.

PURPORT

One cannot remain steady in his worship of Lord Hari if he maintains material desires. When one looks towards women with thoughts of sense gratification, there is no possibility of controlling the senses. For this reason, one should engage in the cultivation of Kṛṣṇa consciousness twenty-four hours a day. When one is thus fully engaged in glorifying Lord Kṛṣṇa and engaging in His devotional service, then the desire for worldly association will certainly diminish. The association of devotees is the only remedy for curing the disease of bad association. Good association with Lord Kṛṣṇa and His devotees automatically vanquishes useless material association, and it helps one to carry out the Vedic injunctions that are meant to lift the conditioned soul out of material darkness and place him onto the liberated platform of Kṛṣṇa consciousness. In this regard, Śrīla Rūpa Gosvāmī states in his *Upadeśāmṛta* (4):

dadāti pratigṛhṇāti guhyam ākhyāti pṛcchati
bhuṅkte bhojayate caiva ṣaḍ-vidhaṁ prīti-lakṣaṇam

Offering gifts in charity, accepting charitable gifts, revealing one's mind in confidence, inquiring confidentially, accepting *prasādam* and offering *prasādam* are the six symptoms of love shared by one devotee and another.

The best association is to remain in the association of devotees, where there is always hearing and chanting of the transcendental names, forms, qualities, associates, and pastimes of the Supreme Personality of Godhead, Śrī Kṛṣṇa. The association of devotees is not bad association because in that association, there are no discussions of material topics. The devotees are all fully engaged in the devotional service of the Lord, following in the footsteps of the inhabitants of Vraja. By the influence of such devotees, one develops equal vision and sees the realized knowledge of Kṛṣṇa consciousness everywhere. As one begins to understand his eternal relationship with Lord Kṛṣṇa, he becomes *ātmavān*, situated in his constitutional position. An advanced Vaiṣṇava, constantly enjoying the mellows of loving devotional service and carrying out the mission of the Lord on the earth, is *ātma-krīḍa*, one who enjoys life within the internal potency of the Supreme Lord. The advanced devotee remains constantly attracted to the Supreme Lord and His devotees and is therefore *ātma-rata*, fully satisfied by constant engagement in devotional service. One cannot possibly develop the exalted qualities mentioned here without becoming an unalloyed devotee of Lord Kṛṣṇa.

If a devotee resides in a place where enviousness of Kṛṣṇa and His devotees is prominent, as a result of that bad association, he will be unable to control his senses and thus begin to take interest in striving for religiosity, economic development, sense gratification, and liberation. Instead of becoming fully absorbed in Kṛṣṇa consciousness, he will gradually come to resemble the nondevotees that surround him. Due to aversion to Kṛṣṇa's service, one becomes attracted to worshiping the wonderful male and female creations of the Lord's illusory energy—demigods, demigoddesses, celebrities, politicians, prostitutes, etc., considering these ordinary personalities to be equal to Kṛṣṇa. The transcendental Cupid, Kṛṣṇa, is the only object of worship. When one realizes this fact, his selfish mentality of worshiping many gods is vanquished.

TEXT 21

विविक्तक्षेमशरणोमद्भावविमलाशयः ।
आत्मानंचिन्तयेदेकमभेदेनमच्यामुनिः ॥२१॥

vivikta-kṣema-śaraṇo mad-bhāva-vimalāśayaḥ
ātmānaṁ cintayed ekam abhedena mayā muniḥ

Dwelling in a solitary place without fear, a pure-hearted devotee should realize himself as being nondifferent from Me.

COMMENTARY

To think of the spirit soul as nondifferent from the Supersoul is the essence of *sāyujya mukti.*

PURPORT

A pure devotee of the Lord is one whose only aim in life is to serve the Supreme Lord in one of the five principle relationships. He has no interest other than the service of the Lord, and he never thinks of himself as qualitatively different from Him. It is one's false identification with the temporary gross and subtle bodies that causes one to think of himself as being different from the Lord. Indeed, false identification with matter is the cause of all kinds of misery. To remedy this situation, one should render service to the Lord, who is the master of the senses, with purified senses. When the mind is distracted from the service of the Lord, being attracted by the objects of the senses, one again labors hard to fulfill his material desires under the influence of the three modes of material nature. One who is not actually fixed in devotional service, beginning with hearing and chanting the glories of the Lord, cannot be fearless, being deprived of the Lord's shelter. One should always consider how his constitutional position is that of a minute part and parcel of the Lord, and thus nondifferent from Him.

TEXT 22

अन्वीक्षेतात्मनोबन्धंमोक्षंचज्ञाननिष्ठया ।
बन्धइन्द्रियविक्षेपोमोक्ष एषांचसंयमः ॥२२॥

anvīkṣetātmano bandhaṁ mokṣaṁ ca jñāna-niṣṭhayā
bandha indriya-vikṣepo mokṣa eṣāṁ ca saṁyamaḥ

By the cultivation of spiritual knowledge, one should clearly ascertain the nature of bondage and liberation. Bondage occurs when the senses are utilized for material enjoyment, and liberation is attained when the senses are withdrawn from the enjoyment of sense objects and exclusively engaged in My service.

COMMENTARY

The word *anvīkṣeta* means "to see by careful study."

PURPORT

For one who remains absorbed in thought of the temporary objects of this world, without any care for realizing his eternal self and his relationship with the Supreme Self, his agitated senses will induce him to enjoy unrestricted gratification. If one restrains his senses from unregulated enjoyment, he can get respite from their harassment.

TEXT 23

तस्मान्नियम्यषड्वर्गंमद्भावेनचरेन्मुनिः ।
विरक्तःक्षुद्रकामेभ्योलब्ध्वात्मनिसुखंमहत् ॥२३॥

tasmān niyamya ṣaḍ-vargaṁ mad-bhāvena caren muniḥ
viraktaḥ kṣudra-kāmebhyo labdhvātmani sukhaṁ mahat

Carefully controlling the five senses and the mind by always engaging them in the devotional service of the Lord, one experiences transcendental happiness, giving one the strength to remain detached from all kinds of material sense gratification, which are, after all, quite insignificant.

COMMENTARY

The word *ṣad-vargam* refers to the six senses.

PURPORT

By the influence of cultivating attachment for the eternal, pure, complete whole, one can conquer the six enemies—lust, anger, greed, illusion, pride, and envy. If one renounces the thirst of insignificant material enjoyment and always engages in the Lord's service, he will surely experience great transcendental happiness.

TEXT 24

पुरग्रामव्रजान्सार्थान्भिक्षार्थंप्रविशंश्चरेत् ।
पुण्यदेशसरिच्छैलवनाश्रमवतींमहीम् ॥२४॥

pura-grāma-vrajān sārthān bhikṣārthaṁ praviśaṁś caret
puṇya-deśa-saric-chaila-vanāśrama-vatīṁ mahīm

One should travel to holy places of pilgrimage, or else remain by the side of rivers, or in the solitude of mountains and forests. He should go to cities, towns, and agricultural areas just to approach the materialists to beg for the bare necessities of life.

TEXT 25

वानप्रस्थाश्रमपदेष्वभीक्ष्णंभैक्ष्यमाचरेत् ।
संसिध्यत्याश्वसम्मोहःशुद्धसत्त्वःशिलान्धसा ॥२५॥

vānaprasthāśrama-padeṣv abhīkṣṇaṁ bhaikṣyam ācaret
saṁsidhyaty āśv asammohaḥ śuddha-sattvaḥ śilāndhasā

One in the *vānaprastha* order of life should be accustomed to accept charity from others because by this practice he will be freed from illusion and quickly become perfect in spiritual life. Indeed, one who subsists on food grains obtained in such a humble manner purifies his existence.

COMMENTARY

The word *śilāndhasā* means "to collect food grains scattered in the market places." By eating such food, the heart becomes purified.

PURPORT

If a materialistic sense enjoyer aspires to free himself from material entanglement, he must engage in begging alms for his subsistence because this will force him to humble himself before others. When one becomes freed from all desires for material enjoyment in this way, he no longer remains a fool. He learns to be satisfied with whatever he collects by begging, and because of the purity of his heart, he attains perfection.

TEXT 26

नैतद्वस्तुतयापश्येद्दृश्यमानंविनश्यति ।
असक्तचित्तोविरमेदिहामुत्रचिकीर्षितात् ॥२६॥

naitad vastutayā paśyed dṛśyamānaṁ vinaśyati
asakta-citto viramed ihāmutra-cikīrṣitāt

One should never think that the temporary arrangements of matter are ultimate reality. Keeping oneself free from material attachment, one should give up all kinds of endeavor meant for material betterment, both in this life and the next.

COMMENTARY

One may doubt, "How can a gentleman give up delicious food to eat dry particles of rice?" The answer is given here: "Do not see delicious food as real because in due course of time, it will be destroyed. Considering this, one should never endeavor for material gain, both in this life and in the life after death."

TEXT 27

यदेतदात्मनिजगन्मनोवाक्प्राणसंहतम् ।
सर्वंमायेतितर्केणस्वस्थस्त्यक्त्वानतत्स्मरेत् ॥२७॥

yad etad ātmani jagan mano-vāk-prāṇa-saṁhatam
sarvaṁ māyeti tarkeṇa sva-sthas tyaktvā na tat smaret

One should consider the cosmic manifestation, which includes one's physical body, mind, life-air, and speech, and which is situated within the Lord, to be a product of His illusory energy. One should remain self-situated, fully renouncing the hope that such temporary manifestations can grant him happiness.

COMMENTARY

This material world is the effect of the three modes of material nature. The word *tyaktvā* indicates that one must give up one's false identification with the material world and the material body, since both are merely products of the illusory potency of the Lord.

PURPORT

Instead of striving for material objects, if one hankers for the Lord's mercy, his material attachment will gradually diminish. According to one's previous memories, one develops a thirst for enjoying temporary objects with his body, mind, and speech. However, if one becomes inclined toward the service of the Supreme Lord, his previous memories will no longer misguide him.

TEXT 28

ज्ञाननिष्ठोविरक्तोवामद्भक्तोवानपेक्षकः ।
सलिङ्गानाश्रमांस्त्यक्त्वाचरेदविधिगोचरः ॥२८॥

jñāna-niṣṭho virakto vā mad-bhakto vānapekṣakaḥ
sa-liṅgān āśramāṁs tyaktvā cared avidhi-gocaraḥ

A learned transcendentalist who has renounced all desires for sense gratification by engaging in the cultivation of knowledge, as well as My devotee, who doesn't even desire liberation, neglect the ritualistic performances mentioned in the Vedas. They are not bound by those prescribed rules and regulation that guide persons influenced by the three modes of material nature.

COMMENTARY

Here, the *paramahaṁsa* stage is described. In such a transcendental position, one no longer bothers to perform religious rituals meant for conditioned souls. Both the *jñāna-yogī* who aspires for liberation, and the pure devotee of the Lord who does not care for liberation, are detached from all kinds of material activities. When the mind has become completely purified, there is no more chance for engagement in sinful acts. The rules and regulations that are prescribed in the *Vedas* guide those who are enamored by thoughts of gratifying the senses. One on the transcendental platform can move about freely, as herein described by the Lord. However, one who is still materially contaminated should not artificially try to imitate such an exalted position, and thus make a mockery of his spiritual life.

PURPORT

The principal duty of a *sannyāsī* is to remain disinterested in material enjoyment. The enjoyment of temporary objects by uncontrolled senses creates obstacles on the path of self-realization. The pure devotee of the Lord, being totally disinterested in material enjoyment because of being fully engaged in the service of the Lord, is beyond the range of rules and regulations, and thus can freely wander over the earth at will. Rules and regulations are meant to guide those who are still easily misguided by the urges of their uncontrolled mind and senses. It is only when one rises to the stage of *paramahaṁsa* that one can abandon the various rituals, paraphernalia and disciplines prescribed for his spiritual order. This is clearly stated in the *Caitanya-caritāmṛta* (Madhya-līlā 22.93) as follows:

eta saba chāḍi' āra varṇāśrama-dharma
akiñcana hañā laya kṛṣṇaika-śaraṇa

Without hesitation, one should take exclusive shelter of Lord Kṛṣṇa with full confidence, giving up bad association and even neglecting the regulative principles of the four *varṇas* and four *āśramas*. That is to say, one should abandon all material attachment.

TEXT 29

बुधोबालकवत्क्रीडेत्कुशलोजडवच्चरेत् ।
वदेदुन्मत्तवद्विद्वान्गोचर्यांनैगमश्चरेत् ॥२९॥

budho bālaka-vat krīḍet kuśalo jaḍa-vac caret
vaded unmatta-vad vidvān go-caryāṁ naigamaś caret

Although most wise, the *paramahaṁsa* should behave like a child, not caring for honor or dishonor. Although most expert, he should act like one who is incompetent. Although most learned, he should speak like a madman, and although well-versed in the *Vedas*, he should behave in an unrestricted manner.

COMMENTARY

A *paramahaṁsa* conceals his exalted position out of fear that the great adoration the public will offer him may disturb his equilibrium. Thus, although possessing great wisdom, he may behave in a childish manner. Although very expert, he may act like one who is incompetent. Although very learned, he may speak just like a madman, and although a great Vedic scholar, he may behave like a fool.

PURPORT

Although neglecting ordinary rules and regulations, a *paramahaṁsa* does not ever become sinful or immoral, but rather neglects ritualistic aspects of religious custom, such as dressing in a particular way, performing certain ceremonies or executing specific penances and austerities. Materialistic people, by means of their external perception, cannot understand the exalted position of a *paramahaṁsa* and thus they commit offenses that bring about their ruination. One who does not understand the purport of this verse of Śrī Rūpa Goswāmī will certainly remain fixed in a conception of materialistic *varnāśrama.*

dṛṣṭaiḥ svabhāva-janitair vapuṣaś ca doṣair
na prākṛtatvam iha bhakta janasya paśyet
gaṅgāmbhasāṁ na khalu budbuda-phena-paṅkair
brahma-dravatvam apagacchati nīra-dharmaiḥ

Being situated in his original Kṛṣṇa conscious position, a pure devotee does not identify with the body. Such a devotee should not be seen from a materialistic point of view. Indeed, one should overlook a devotee's having a body born in a low family, a body with a bad complexion, a deformed body, or a diseased or infirm body. According to ordinary vision, such imperfections may seem prominent in the body of a pure devotee, but despite such seeming defects, the body of a pure devotee cannot be polluted. It is exactly like the waters of the Ganges, which sometimes during the rainy season are full of bubbles, foam and mud. The Ganges waters do not become polluted. Those who are advanced in spiritual understanding will bathe in the Ganges without considering the condition of the water. (*Śrī Upadeśāmṛta* 6)

TEXT 30

वेदवादरतोनस्यान्नपाषण्डीनहैतुकः ।
शुष्कवादविवादेनकश्चित्पक्षंसमाश्रयेत् ॥३०॥

veda-vāda-rato na syān na pāṣaṇḍī na haitukaḥ
śuṣka-vāda-vivāde na kañcit pakṣaṁ samāśrayet

A devotee of the Lord should not divert himself to engage in the fruitive rituals recommended in the *karma-kāṇḍa* sections of the *Vedas*. Of course, he should not indulge in an atheistic mentality by speaking against the Vedic injunctions. A devotee should also avoid acting like a mundane logician, taking part in useless arguments.

COMMENTARY

Although a *paramahaṁsa* hides his actual position, he is still restrained from performing certain activities. He should not advocate fruitive activities just to conceal himself, nor should he disguise himself as an atheist or dress as a Buddhist, or member of any other atheistic cult opposing the *Vedas*.

PURPORT

The whole purpose of the *Vedas* is to understand that which is beyond material experience, so the devotees of the Lord do not become involved in dry arguments about the *Vedas*, like expert fruitive workers. They do not waste their time in useless speculation that culminates in placing the Supreme Personality of Godhead, who is the possessor of unlimited energies, in the same category as the demigods, who are subordinate to Him, being His empowered representatives. Devotees have no desire for being praised, and thus never take sides in mundane arguments. In this regard one should discuss the following verse from *Śrī Upadeśāmṛta* 2.

atyāhāraḥ prayāsaś ca prajalpo niyamāgrahaḥ
jana-saṅgaś ca laulyaṁ ca ṣaḍbhir bhaktir vinaśyati

One's devotional service is spoiled when he becomes too entangled in the following six activities: (1) eating more than necessary or collecting more funds than required; (2) over-endeavoring for mundane things that are very difficult to obtain; (3) talking unnecessarily about mundane subject matters; (4) Practicing the scriptural rules and regulations only for the sake of following them and not for the sake of spiritual advancement, or rejecting the rules and regulations of the scriptures and working independently or whimsically; (5) associating with worldly-minded persons who are not interested in Kṛṣṇa consciousness; and (6) being greedy for mundane achievements.

TEXT 31

नोद्विजेतजनाद्धीरोजनंचोद्वेजयेन्नतु ।
अतिवादांस्तितिक्षेतनावमन्येतकञ्चन ।
देहमुद्दिश्यपशुवद्वैरंकुर्यान्नकेनचित् ॥३१॥

nodvijeta janād dhīro janaṁ codvejayen na tu
ati-vādāṁs titikṣeta nāvamanyeta kañcana
deham uddiśya paśu-vad vairaṁ kuryān na kenacit

A transcendentalist should not become frightened or disturbed by others, nor should he ever act in a way that disturbs others, or makes them fearful. He should tolerate the insults others hurl at him, and he should not criticize others. He should never create enmity simply for some material advantage, for that would make him no better than an animal.

COMMENTARY

The phrase *ati-vāda* means "very harsh words."

PURPORT

A saintly person does not cause anxiety to any living entity by means of his body, mind, or speech. In this regard, one should carefully contemplate this verse, which was spoken by Śrī Caitanya Mahāprabhu.

tṛṇād api sunīcena taror api sahiṣṇunā
amāninā mānadena kīrtanīyaḥ sadā hariḥ

One should chant the holy name of the Lord in a humble state of mind, thinking oneself lower than the straw in the street. One should be more tolerant than a tree, devoid of all sense of false prestige, and ready to offer all respect to others. In such a state of mind, one can chant the holy name of the Lord constantly.

TEXT 32

एक एवपरोह्यात्माभूतेष्वात्मन्यवस्थितः ।
यथेन्दुरुदपात्रेषुभूतान्येकात्मकानिच ॥३२॥

eka eva paro hy ātmā bhūteṣv ātmany avasthitaḥ
yathendur uda-pātreṣu bhūtāny ekātmakāni ca

The one Supreme Lord is situated within the bodies of all living entities, and indeed, within their very self. Just as the moon is reflected on the surface of innumerable bodies of water, the Supersoul, although one, is present everywhere. Every material body is thus composed of the energy of the one Supreme Lord.

COMMENTARY

The understanding that frees one from enviousness is being described in this verse. The Supersoul is present within all living entities. Just as the moon, although one, is reflected in innumerable pots of water, the Supersoul, although one, is present within all living entities as the supreme director. Therefore, one should not envy anyone, knowing that the Supreme Lord is present within all material bodies, which are also manifestations of His energy.

PURPORT

An object and its reflection are certainly similar in many respects, but one should never think that they are actually equal and thus disregard the object. The material bodies of the conditioned souls may certainly be subject to criticism, but by understanding how the Supreme Lord is present within each of them, one should free himself by thoughts of duality, which are prominent in the society of animals. The devotees of the Lord are never hostile or violent toward anyone, knowing that everyone is the eternal servant of God.

TEXT 33

अलब्ध्वानविषीदेतकालेकालेऽशनंक्वचित् ।
लब्ध्वानहृष्येद्धृतिमानुभयंदैवतन्त्रितम् ॥३३॥

alabdhvā na viṣīdeta kāle kāle 'śanaṁ kvacit
labdhvā na hṛṣyed dhṛtimān ubhayaṁ daiva-tantritam

If sometimes one does not get enough food, one should not be discouraged, just as when one receives delicious food, he should not become overjoyed. Being fixed in firm determination to remain a faithful devotee, one should understand both situations to be under the control of the Supreme Lord.

COMMENTARY

The phrase *daiva tantritam* means "under the control of providence."

PURPORT

Happiness and distress come automatically in due course of time and thus one should remain undisturbed in either condition. We foolishly consider ourselves to be the doers of our activities, but due to this false ego of thinking ourselves to be the controllers, we are forced to experience happiness and distress, according to the quality of our activities.

TEXT 34

आहारार्थंसमीहेतयुक्तंतत्प्राणधारणम् ।
तत्त्वंविमृश्यतेतेनतद्विज्ञायविमुच्यते ॥३४॥

āhārārthaṁ samīheta yuktaṁ tat-prāṇa-dhāraṇam
tattvaṁ vimṛśyate tena tad vijñāya vimucyate

If required, one should endeavor to get sufficient food, because one should carefully maintain his health. By keeping the body fit, one can cultivate spiritual truth and thereby attain liberation.

COMMENTARY

If food does not come automatically, or by begging, one should make an endeavor because food is necessary to sustain one's life. If one's body is in a healthy condition, one can cultivate God consciousness without disturbance and as a result, make steady advancement.

PURPORT

One should not eat too much, nor eat too little. One should eat only as much as is required to keep the body fit for rendering devotional service to the Lord. Normally, those who are endeavoring in spiritual life cannot maintain steady concentration if their mind and body are weakened by under-eating. On the other hand, extravagant eating is a great impediment for spiritual advancement and therefore should be given up.

TEXT 35

यदृच्छयोपपन्नान्नमद्याच्छ्रेष्ठमुतापरम् ।
तथावासस्तथाशय्यांप्राप्तंप्राप्तंभजेन्मुनिः ॥३५॥

yadṛcchayopapannānnam adyāc chreṣṭham utāparam
tathā vāsas tathā śayyāṁ prāptaṁ prāptaṁ bhajen muniḥ

A transcendentalist should accept whatever food, clothing, and bedding comes of its own accord, whether they be very good or very poor.

COMMENTARY

It is best if one can obtain food without any endeavor. A sage should not discriminate between delicious and tasteless food. He should be happy with whatever he is destined to obtain.

TEXT 36

शौचमाचमनंस्नानंनतुचोदनयाचरेत् ।
अन्यांश्चनियमाञ्ज्ञानीयथाहंलीलयेश्वरः ॥३६॥

śaucam ācamanaṁ snānaṁ na tu codanayā caret
anyāṁś ca niyamāñ jñānī yathāhaṁ līlayeśvaraḥ

I am the Supreme Lord, and yet I execute regulative duties by My own free will. Similarly, one who is advancing in self-realization should wash his hands, bathe, and perform other regulative duties, just to lead others on the right path.

COMMENTARY

A devotee of the Lord is not a servant of rules and regulations, he is a servant of the Supreme Personality of Godhead. Still, he executes the regulative duties in relation to the material body by his own free will and not as a servant of the rules and regulations.

PURPORT

One who leads his life in a way that is favorable for the service of the Supreme Lord is always a liberated soul, although situated within the material world. Devotees of the Lord on the *paramahaṁsa* platform are not compelled to perform bodily activities, such as brushing the teeth or bathing, like ordinary people. Such a *paramahaṁsa* may be impure or unclean according to material estimation, because he is a servant of Lord Kṛṣṇa and not of rules and regulations.

TEXT 37

नहितस्यविकल्पाख्यायाचमद्वीक्षयाहता ।
आदेहान्तात्क्वचित्ख्यातिस्ततःसम्पद्यते मया ॥३७॥

na hi tasya vikalpākhyā yā ca mad-vīkṣayā hatā
ā-dehāntāt kvacit khyātis tataḥ sampadyate mayā

A self-realized soul does not see anything as separate from Me, because he has passed out of the dense darkness of illusion. However, because of his previous habits that absorbed his body and mind in sense gratification, he may sometimes be seen to act like an ordinary conditioned soul. Still, upon quitting his body at the time of death, such a devotee will be awarded My divine opulence.

COMMENTARY

On the strength of realized knowledge of the Lord, one gives up the illusion that anything, anywhere, at any time, can be separate from Him. Still, Lord Kṛṣṇa has said that a devotee must keep his material body and mind fit for executing devotional service. Therefore, even a self-realized soul may sometimes appear to accept or reject certain conditions within this world. Such brief apparent duality of concentration upon material conditions does not change the liberated status of a self-realized soul, however, because he never forgets to see everything in relation to the Supreme Lord.

PURPORT

A devotee does not see anything as being separate from Lord Kṛṣṇa, and he does not consider his position within the material world to be permanent. His only desire is to render service to the Supreme Personality of Godhead. Just as materialistic men are always found making arrangements for their personal enjoyment, devotees are busy throughout the day and night, planning how to best serve the Lord. Thus, they have no inclination to waste their time in the frivolous entertainments sought by the materialists. Materialistic men cannot understand this mentality of the devotee, and so they sometimes dare to criticize him, thinking him to be just like an ordinary man. At the time of death, however, the results of the devotees and the results obtained by the materialists are very different.

TEXT 38

दुःखोदर्केषुकामेषुजातनिर्वेद आत्मवान् ।
अज्ञासितमद्धर्मोमुनिंगुरुमुपव्रजेत् ॥३८॥

duḥkhodarkeṣu kāmeṣu jāta-nirveda ātmavān
ajjñāsita-mad-dharmo muniṁ gurum upavrajet

One who has become disgusted with material enjoyment, knowing that it ultimately produces only misery, and who desires spiritual perfection, but has not understood the process for attaining it, should approach a spiritual master who is fixed in the devotional service of the Supreme Lord.

COMMENTARY

The Supreme Lord said, "One who has attained wisdom and has thus become disgusted with the miserable condition of material enjoyment should inquire about Me, the Supreme Personality of Godhead. For that purpose, he should approach a bona fide spiritual master and thus receive transcendental knowledge in relation to Me."

PURPORT

One who is actually intelligent should be inquisitive to understand the cause of his suffering in this temporary world of birth and death. Thus, he should take shelter of a bona fide spiritual master, who is fully devoted to the service of the Lord and is therefore detached from desires for insignificant material enjoyment. Materialists, who are not engaged in the devotional service of the Supreme Lord, are always baffled in their attempts to enjoy the material world and as a result, they are certainly in a miserable condition of life. A sober person who has realized the futility of material existence can become freed from material bondage by taking shelter of an experienced devotee of the Lord, thus giving up all unwanted association.

TEXT 39

तावत्परिचरेद्भक्तःश्रद्धावाननसूयकः ।
यावद्ब्रह्मविजानीयान्मामेवगुरुमादृतः ॥३९॥

tāvat paricared bhaktaḥ śraddhāvān anasūyakaḥ
yāvad brahma vijānīyān mām eva gurum ādṛtaḥ

Until a devotee has practical realization of the Absolute Truth, he should continue to respectfully render service to the spiritual master, who is nondifferent from Me.

COMMENTARY

The Supreme Lord said, "The spiritual master is nondifferent from Me, being an external manifestation of My mercy."

PURPORT

A devotee who has pleased his spiritual master and is thus endowed with realization of the truth can directly engage in the service of the Supreme Personality of Godhead. It is indicated in this verse that as long as one has not become sufficiently convinced of the truth of the teachings of his spiritual master, he should remain very close to his guru, to render personal service.

TEXTS 40-41

यस्त्वसंयतषड्वर्गः प्रचण्डेन्द्रियसारथिः ।
ज्ञानवैराग्यरहितस्त्रिदण्डमुपजीवति ॥४०॥
सुरानात्मानमात्मस्थं निह्नुते मां च धर्महा ।
अविपक्वकषायोऽस्मादमुष्माच्च विहीयते ॥४१॥

yas tv asaṁyata-ṣaḍ-vargaḥ pracaṇḍendriya-sārathiḥ
jñāna-vairāgya-rahitas tri-daṇḍam upajīvati

surān ātmānam ātma-sthaṁ nihnute māṁ ca dharma-hā
avipakva-kaṣāyo 'smād amuṣmāc ca vihīyate

One who is devoid of knowledge and renunciation, who has not conquered his six enemies—lust, anger, greed, envy, false pride, and illusion—who is forcefully driven by the charioteer of his mind, who makes a show of being in the renounced order of life, sannyāsa, simply for earning his livelihood, who denies himself and the Supersoul within, is doomed both in this life and the next.

COMMENTARY

The Lord herein condemns imitation *sannyāsīs* who adopt the garb of a saintly person simply to gain material advantage. Such a person certainly cheats himself while disregarding the demigods and the Supersoul within. Such a bogus *sannyāsī* lives a most condemned existence, both in this world and in the next.

PURPORT

One who is not engaged in the devotional service of the Lord must be also devoid of genuine knowledge and renunciation. Unless the senses are fully engaged in the service of the Lord, they will restlessly drag one into inferior pursuits. Thus becoming a servant of his senses, the nondevotee fails to properly regulate his bodily activities, mind, and speech.

One who adopts the dress of a *sannyāsī* simply for filling his belly is never accepted by intelligent followers of Vedic principles. However, such a so-called *sannyāsī* who ruins all Vedic religious principles sometimes becomes famous among foolish persons, but they are simply cheating themselves and their followers. These charlatan *sannyāsīs* are never actually engaged in the loving devotional service of Lord Kṛṣṇa, and so the result they achieve is far different from that attained by genuine devotees.

TEXT 42

भिक्षोर्धर्मः शमोऽहिंसातपईक्षावनौकसः ।
गृहिणोभूतरक्षेज्याद्विजस्याचार्यसेवनम् ॥४२॥

bhikṣor dharmaḥ śamo 'hiṁsā tapa īkṣā vanaukasaḥ
gṛhiṇo bhūta-rakṣejyā dvijasyācārya-sevanam

The main religious duties of a *sannyāsī* are equanimity and nonviolence, whereas for a *vānaprastha,* austerity and the knowledge by which one can discriminate between matter and spirit are prominent. The main duties of a *gṛhastha* are to give protection to all living entities and perform sacrifices, and the duty of a *brahmacārī* is to serve the spiritual master.

COMMENTARY

The duty of a *sannyāsī* is to carefully control his mind and to remain free from envy of others. The duty of a *vānaprastha* is to perform austerities and clearly understand the difference between the body and the soul. The duty of a *gṛhastha* is to give shelter to all living entities and perform sacrifices. The duty of a *brahmacārī* is to serve the spiritual master.

PURPORT

A *brahmacārī*'s duty is to serve the spiritual master. A *gṛhastha*'s duty is to maintain all living entities and engage in the service of the Supreme Lord while carefully observing religious principles. A *vānaprastha*'s duty is to perform austerity and master the power of discrimination between matter and spirit. The duty of a *sannyāsī* is to constantly engage in the service of the Supreme Lord without causing any anxiety to any living creature by means of his body, mind, or speech.

TEXT 43

ब्रह्मचर्यंतपःशौचंसन्तोषोभूतसौहृदम् ।
गृहस्थस्याप्यृतौगन्तुःसर्वेषांमदुपासनम् ॥४३॥

brahmacaryaṁ tapaḥ śaucaṁ santoṣo bhūta-sauhṛdam
gṛhasthasyāpy ṛtau gantuḥ sarveṣāṁ mad-upāsanam

A householder should only engage in sexual intercourse with his wife at the times that are prescribed for begetting children. At other times, the householder should practice celibacy, austerity, purity of his body and mind, remaining satisfied in his position, and displaying friendship towards all living entities. Worship of Me is to be practiced by all human beings, regardless of his social or occupational status.

COMMENTARY

Generally, a householder should practice celibacy, although he may indulge in sex with his wife after her menstrual period, only for the purpose of procreation. The members of all the *varṇas* and *āśramas* are duty-bound to worship the Supreme Lord. Without this understanding, the observance of religious principles is ultimately useless. This is confirmed in these two verses from the *Śrīmad-Bhāgavatam* (11.5.2-3):

mukha-bāhūru-pādebhyaḥ puruṣasyāśramaiḥ saha
catvāro jajñire varṇā guṇair viprādayaḥ pṛthak

From the mouth of Brahmā, the *brahminical* order has come into existence. Similarly, from his arms the kṣatriyas have come, from his waist the ***vaiśyas*** have come, and from his legs the ***śūdras*** have come. These four orders and their spiritual counterparts (*brahmacarya, gṛhastha, vānaprastha,* and *sannyāsa*) combine to make human society complete.

ya eṣāṁ puruṣaṁ sākṣād ātma-prabhavam īśvaram
na bhajanty avajānanti sthānād bhraṣṭāḥ patanty adhaḥ

If one simply maintains an official position in the four ***varṇas*** and ***āśramas*** but does not worship the Supreme Lord Viṣṇu, he falls down from his puffed-up position into a hellish condition.

PURPORT

It is the duty of the members of all the four *āśramas* to serve the Supreme Lord. A householder should practice celibacy, except that he may enjoy sex with his wife at an appropriate time, only for the sake of begetting children. A householder should act for the benefit all living entities, and he should remain pure and satisfied with his position in life.

TEXT 44

इतिमांयःस्वधर्मेणभजेन्नित्यमनन्यभाक् ।
सर्वभूतेषुमद्भावोमद्भक्तिंविन्दतेदृढाम् ॥४४॥

iti māṁ yaḥ sva-dharmeṇa bhajen nityam ananya-bhāk
sarva-bhūteṣu mad-bhāvo mad-bhaktiṁ vindate dṛḍhām

One who gives up all other kinds of worship and engages in My service by the performance of his occupational duty, remembering that I am present within all living entities, achieves unflinching devotional service unto Me.

COMMENTARY

In whatever social or occupational division of human society one may be, one must be a devotee of the Supreme Personality of Godhead and worship Him alone. In the *Vedas* it is sometime prescribed that householders should worship particular demigods or forefathers. How then can such householders be considered unalloyed devotees of the Supreme Lord? The answer is that those who cannot come to the standard of pure devotional service should at least meditate upon the Personality of Godhead as being situated within the demigods and all other living entities, understanding that all religious processes are ultimately meant for the pleasure of the Lord.

PURPORT

While engaged in performing one's *varṇāśrama* duties, one should see the Lord as the basis of everything. A devotee should concentrate on pleasing the Supreme Lord by all of his activities because this alone will enable him to be elevated to the stage of life called love of God, and thus bring him to the point of actual liberation. On the other hand, those who simply execute their duties within the *varṇāśrama* system without trying to see everything in relation to Kṛṣṇa will be unable to attain the platform of devotional service to the Lord. To see how every living entity is engaged in the service of the Lord is the vision of the topmost Vaiṣṇava.

TEXT 45

भक्त्योद्धवानपायिन्यासर्वलोकमहेश्वरम् ।
सर्वोत्पत्त्यप्ययंब्रह्मकारणंमोपयातिसः ॥४५॥

bhaktyoddhavānapāyinyā sarva-loka-maheśvaram
sarvotpatty-apyayaṁ brahma kāraṇaṁ mopayāti saḥ

My dear Uddhava, I am the Supreme Lord of all creation, and I create and destroy this universe, being its ultimate cause. I am the Absolute Truth, and one who worships Me with unfailing devotional service comes to Me.

COMMENTARY

The Supreme Lord said, "One who worships Me in unalloyed devotional service achieves My shelter. I am the ultimate cause of all the universes. My pure devotee achieves the liberation known as *sārṣṭi*, whereby he achieves opulence like Mine. However, one who worships My impersonal feature attains *sāyujya mukti*, the liberation of merging into My effulgence of Brahman."

PURPORT

The Supreme Lord is the ultimate cause of this material world's creation, maintenance, and destruction. He is the supreme object of knowledge. By worshiping Him by means of unalloyed devotional service, one attains His shelter.

TEXT 46

इतिस्वधर्मनिर्णिक्तसत्त्वोनिर्ज्ञातमद्गतिः ।
ज्ञानविज्ञानसम्पन्नोनचिरात्समुपैतिमाम् ॥४६॥

iti sva-dharma-nirṇikta-sattvo nirjñāta-mad-gatiḥ
jñāna-vijñāna-sampanno na cirāt samupaiti mām

One who has purified himself by the performance of his prescribed duties, who understands My supreme position, and who has attained theoretical and practical knowledge, will soon come to Me.

COMMENTARY

In this verse, the Lord concludes His instructions.

PURPORT

If one cultivates the knowledge of his relationship with the Supreme Lord while executing his occupational duties and remaining aloof from bad association, he will gradually rise to the platform of pure goodness and thus receive the treasure of unalloyed devotional service to the Lord. This is life's ultimate goal.

TEXT 47

वर्णाश्रमवतांधर्म एष आचारलक्षणः ।
स एवमद्भक्तियुतोनिःश्रेयसकरःपरः ॥४७॥

varṇāśramavatāṁ dharma eṣa ācāra-lakṣaṇaḥ
sa eva mad-bhakti-yuto niḥśreyasa-karaḥ paraḥ

Those who are followers of this *varṇāśrama* system accept religious principles according to authorized traditions that govern proper conduct. When such religious duties are dedicated to Me in loving service, they award one the supreme perfection of life.

COMMENTARY

After describing *pradhāṇī bhūtā bhakti*, the Lord herein talks about *guṇībhūtā bhakti*. The Supreme Lord said, "If the duties entrusted to the followers of the *varnāśrama* system are dovetailed in My devotional service, they award one the supreme perfection of life."

PURPORT

The path of renunciation entails giving up all varieties of sense gratification, and so it is very difficult for ordinary people to perform. Those who are engaged in the devotional service of the Lord under proper guidance automatically achieve the result of renunciation because all of their activities are offered at the lotus feet of the Lord. Thus it should be understood that unalloyed devotion for the Supreme Lord is the ultimate fruit of engaging in the occupational and religious duties prescribed within the *varṇāśrama* system.

TEXT 48

एतत्तेऽभिहितंसाधोभवान्पृच्छतियच्चमाम् ।
यथास्वधर्मसंयुक्तोभक्तोमांसमियात्परम् ॥४८॥

etat te 'bhihitaṁ sādho bhavān pṛcchati yac ca māṁ
yathā sva-dharma-saṁyukto bhakto māṁ samiyāt param

My dear Uddhava, I have thus answered your question as you had asked Me about how a devotee, perfectly following his occupational duties can attain Me, the Supreme Personality of Godhead.

Thus ends the translation of the Twelveth Chapter of the Uddhava-gītā, entitled "**Descriptions of Varṇāśrama-dharma**" *with the commentaries of Śrīla Viśvanātha Cakravartī Ṭhākura, and the chapter summary and purports by Śrīla Bhaktisiddhānta Sarasvatī Ṭhākura.*

Chapter 13

The Perfection of Spiritual Knowledge

CHAPTER SUMMARY

This chapter describes how the *jñānīs* eventually give up their method of acquiring knowledge, whereas the pure devotees remain engaged in devotional service eternally. Also described in this chapter are the different practices of the *yogīs*, beginning with *yama*.

The Supreme Lord, Śrī Kṛṣṇa said to Uddhava, "One who is actually wise, who knows the science of the self and is endowed with spiritual insight, rejects this material world of dualities and the so-called knowledge that facilitates enjoying it. He instead engages himself in trying to satisfy the Supreme Lord, the master of all. This is called pure devotional service. Transcendental knowledge is superior to ordinary pious activities, such as the chanting of *mantras*, but pure devotional service is even superior to the cultivation of transcendental knowledge."

After this, when Śrī Kṛṣṇa was asked by Uddhava to explain in detail the processes of acquiring transcendental knowledge and devotional service, the Lord related the same instructions that the greatest of Vaiṣṇavas, Bhīṣmadeva, had imparted to Mahārāja Yudhiṣṭhira after the battle of Kurukṣetra. Following this, after being asked about *yama* and other practices of *yoga*, the Lord described the twelve kinds of *yama*, beginning with nonviolence, and twelve types of *niyama*, beginning with cleanliness.

TEXT 1

श्रीभगवानुवाच
योविद्याश्रुतसम्पन्नः आत्मवान्नानुमानिकः ।
मयामात्रमिदंज्ञात्वाज्ञानंचमयिसन्न्यसेत् ॥१॥

śrī-bhagavān uvāca
yo vidyā-śruta-sampannaḥ ātmavān nānumānikaḥ
māyā-mātram idaṁ jñātvā jñānaṁ ca mayi sannyaset

The Supreme Lord said: One who has cultivated knowledge of the self up to the point of realization of his eternity, and who has given up speculative knowledge, understanding the material universe to be a temporary illusory manifestation, should no longer endeavor to cultivate knowledge by speculative means.

COMMENTARY

This chapter describes renunciation as practiced by the *jñānīs*, and the eternal devotional service that is practiced by the pure devotees, as well as the practices of the *yogīs*, beginning with *yama* and *niyama*.

A conditioned soul must somehow free himself of his illusory existence, which has entrapped him since time immemorial. One means for accomplishing this is the practice of the eight-fold yoga system, after renouncing all material desires. By this difficult process, one can gradually lift himself above the darkness of ignorance. However, when one is actually situated on the transcendental platform, there is no more need to cultivate spiritual knowledge for the purpose of dispelling his material entanglement. For example, a man haunted by a ghost may take help from *mantras*, herbs, and other such remedial measures. However, when he is no longer possessed by the ghost, all such things have no practical value for him. Here, the word *vidyā* refers to knowledge acquired by philosophical speculation, mystic yoga practice, austerities, and so on. Such knowledge of the illusory nature of material existence certainly dispels ignorance, and there are many Vedic scriptures that impart such knowledge. After one gives up his false identification with the material body and mind, one must further advance by engaging in the loving service of the Supreme Personality of Godhead. When one becomes advanced in Kṛṣṇa consciousness, there is no more need to dispel illusion.

PURPORT

The scriptures recommend that one adopt the processes of *karma*, *jñāna*, and *bhakti*, as a means to attain the ultimate goal of life. The living entities' conditional state is due to their material conception of life. When the conditioned souls are under the influence of the three modes of material nature, they are filled with mundane conceptions and puffed up because of false ego. Because of false ego, the conditioned souls think themselves to be the enjoyers of this temporary material world. When facing competition, they attempt to defeat their opponents so that they can maintain their attempts to indulge in temporary and insignificant material enjoyment.

Whenever there is an absence of knowledge of self-realization, a conditioned soul, being under the control of false ego and devoid of devotional service to the Supreme Lord, yearns for liberation. However, such desires for liberation are another manifestation of false ego. When one's knowledge of self-realization is directed to the service of the Supreme Lord, so that one is actively engaged in the service of the Lord—that is the perfection of *karma* and *jñāna.*

A living entity that has fallen from his constitutional position is naturally covered by conceptions of *karma* and *jñāna.* The ignorance that is the result of the misuse of one's minute independence, coupled with the desire to lord it over material nature, leads one to attempt to bring the Supreme Lord under one's control. Such an illusion created by perverted knowledge induces the conditioned soul to think that he is the enjoyer of all that he surveys. Due to the absence of devotional service, such a person thinks himself to be nondifferent from the Supreme Lord, and thus readily accepts the philosophy of Māyāvāda. When under the shelter of Māyāvāda philosophy, a living entity falls into various inauspicious situations because of his ignorance of spiritual variegatedness. Although appearing to be engaged as a transcendentalist, such a person's material conception of life is evident because he sees everything in a spirit of enjoyment and thus utilizes his senses for personal sense gratification.

A self-realized soul who has crossed the boundary of inauspiciousness is not attracted to cultivating knowledge by direct perception or hypotheses, which are the domain of mundane philosophers. He is liberated from the darkness of ignorance and has graduated to the platform of pure devotional service by accepting a spiritual master in disciplic succession. Such a self-realized soul gives up the impersonal Brahman conception of the Absolute Truth, as well as all desires for fruitive activities, and thus remains fixed in unalloyed devotional service to the Lord. He directs all of his activities and whatever knowledge he possesses to the service of the Supreme Lord. The result is that he attains the blissful state of eternal existence, being situated in his eternal constitutional duty of loving devotional service to the Supreme Lord.

TEXT 2

ज्ञानिनस्त्वहमेवेष्टःस्वार्थोहेतुश्चसम्मतः ।
स्वर्गश्चैवापवर्गश्चनान्योऽर्थोमदृतेप्रियः ॥२॥

jñāninas tv aham eveṣṭaḥ svārtho hetuś ca sammataḥ
svargaś caivāpavargaś ca nānyo 'rtho mad-ṛte priyaḥ

For those who are actually *jñānīs*, I am the worshipable Lord, goal of life, means for attaining the goal of life, and ultimate aim of knowledge. I am the only object of their happiness, and I remove their unhappiness. Therefore, no one is more dear to them than Me.

COMMENTARY

Someone may question, "Should one give up the practice of devotional service at some stage, just as one gives up speculative knowledge after attaining liberation?" The Supreme Lord says, "Devotional service should never be given up. I am the ultimate object of worship, so how could one consider giving up My worship? I am the ultimate goal of truly learned transcendentalists, and I am also the means for attaining freedom from delusion. This was previously described by Me in *Bhagavad-gītā*, (18.54) which begins with *brahmabhūta prasannātma*, as well as next verse:

bhaktyā mām abhijānāti yāvān yaś cāsmi tattvataḥ
tato māṁ tattvato jñātvā viśate tad-anantaram

> One can understand Me as I am, as the Supreme Personality of Godhead, only by devotional service. And when one is in full consciousness of Me by such devotion, he can enter into the kingdom of God.

The conclusion is that one should always worship Me with love and devotion. Elevation to the heavenly planets is the cause of material happiness and attaining liberation is the negation of material distress. It is I who am the supreme goal of the *jñānīs* and the means of attaining it as well."

PURPORT

The Supreme Lord is the object of worship for all the foremost philosophers of the universe, such as the great sages, headed by Sanaka. Life's goal, the means of attaining it, and freedom from material desires are easily attained if one simply surrenders unto the Supreme Lord. Those who renounce fruitive activities and mental speculation in order to take shelter of devotional service are not interested in endeavoring for any other goal of life.

TEXT 3

ज्ञानविज्ञानसंसिद्धाःपदंश्रेष्ठंविदुर्मम ।
ज्ञानीप्रियतमोऽतोमेज्ञानेनासौबिभर्तिमाम् ॥३॥

jñāna-vijñāna-saṁsiddhāḥ padaṁ śreṣṭhaṁ vidur mama
jñānī priyatamo 'to me jñānenāsau bibharti mām

Persons who have achieved perfection by means of philosophical and realized knowledge know My lotus feet to be the supreme goal of life. Because such learned transcendentalists are always engaged in trying to please Me, they are very dear to Me.

COMMENTARY

The Lord herein establishes the truth that He is the supreme destination for all learned transcendentalists. An intelligent person knows that the Lord's lotus feet are the ultimate goal of life and not the impersonal Brahman. Those who are topmost transcendentalists know the impersonal Brahman to be the bodily effulgence of the lotus-eyed Supreme Lord. Such a person is certainly very dear to the Lord.

PURPORT

When a living entity is fixed in self-realization through devotional service and is endowed with transcendental knowledge and its practical application, he attains the perfection of life. Fortunate people serve the Supreme Lord by serving such a dear devotee. This is the actual process for pleasing the Supreme Lord. Learned transcendentalists who are always engaged in My devotional service are very dear to Me. Material knowledge, or even knowledge of impersonal Brahman, is extremely insignificant. By the cultivation of such knowledge, one attains material enjoyment and liberation, but this is not the ultimate goal of life.

TEXT 4

तपस्तीर्थंजपोदानपवित्राणीतराणिच ।
नालंकुर्वन्तितांसिद्धिंयाज्ञानकलयाकृता ॥४॥

tapas tīrthaṁ japo dānaṁ pavitrāṇītarāṇi ca
nālaṁ kurvanti tāṁ siddhiṁ yā jñāna-kalayā kṛtā

The perfection one achieves by attaining even a small fraction of spiritual understanding cannot be attained by performing austerities, chanting mantras, visiting holy places of pilgrimage, giving charity, or engaging in any other pious activity.

COMMENTARY

The word *jñāna kalayā* means "even a fraction of spiritual knowledge."

PURPORT

The position one attains by engaging his purified senses in the service of the Supreme Lord after realizing his constitutional position cannot be obtained by performing pious activities, undergoing austerities, visiting holy places, chanting *mantras*, or giving in charity.

TEXT 5

तस्माज्ज्ञानेनसहितंज्ञात्वास्वात्मानमुद्धव ।
ज्ञानविज्ञानसम्पन्नोभजमांभक्तिभावतः ॥५॥

tasmāj jñānena sahitaṁ jñātvā svātmānam uddhava
jñāna-vijñāna-sampanno bhaja māṁ bhakti-bhāvataḥ

Therefore, My dear Uddhava, you should realize the self by the cultivation of transcendental knowledge. Then, with clear realization of spiritual knowledge, you should worship Me with your heart saturated with love and devotion.

COMMENTARY

Śrī Kṛṣṇa says: "Give up everything else and simply worship Me." This is the explanation of Śrīdhara Svāmī.

PURPORT

Realized knowledge enables one to perceive his original spiritual form. Every living being has an eternal spiritual identity, which remains forgotten until revived by the practice of devotional service to the Lord. Without at least a theoretical understanding of one's spiritual self, it is not possible to advance in devotional service beyond the neophyte platform. The words *jñātvā svātmānam* in this verse indicate that everyone can realize his original spiritual identity and return to the eternal abode of the Lord.

TEXT 6

ज्ञानविज्ञानयज्ञेनमामिष्ट्वात्मानमात्मनि ।
सर्वयज्ञपतिंमांवैसंसिद्धिंमुनयोऽगमन् ॥६॥

jñāna-vijñāna-yajñena mām iṣṭvātmānam ātmani
sarva-yajña-patiṁ māṁ vai saṁsiddhiṁ munayo 'gaman

In ancient times, great sages worshiped Me through the sacrifice of Vedic knowledge and spiritual enlightenment, knowing Me to be the Supreme Lord of all sacrifice and the Supersoul in everyone's heart. As a result, these sages achieved the supreme perfection of attaining My eternal abode.

COMMENTARY

One may question, "Who possesses real knowledge and understands how to practically apply that knowledge?" In reply, Śrī Kṛṣṇa said, "By engaging in the sacrifice of cultivating transcendental knowledge, the sages of bygone age had worshiped Me as the Lord within their hearts. They worshiped Me as the Supersoul, the Lord of all sacrifices, and thus achieved the perfection of life."

PURPORT

Being covered by gross and subtle designations, the conditioned soul forgets his actual identity. When one renounces his conditional state of existence by engagement in the devotional service of the Lord, one comes to the understanding that the Supreme Lord is the only object worthy of worship. By thus worshiping the Lord in full knowledge of the self, the sages of ancient times had attained the supreme abode of the Lord.

TEXT 7

त्वय्युद्धवाश्रयतियस्त्रिविधोविकारो
मायान्तरापततिनाद्यपवर्गयोर्यत् ।
जन्मादयोऽस्ययदमीतवतस्यकिंस्युर्
आद्यन्तयोर्यदसतोऽस्ति तदेव मध्ये ॥७॥

tvayy uddhavāśrayati yas tri-vidho vikāro
māyāntarāpatati nādy-apavargayor yat
janmādayo 'sya yad amī tava tasya kiṁ syur
ādy-antayor yad asato 'sti tad eva madhye

My dear Uddhava, your eternal identity is covered by the material body and mind, which are transformations of the three modes of material nature. Although they appear very real at present, they are illusory because they have no eternal existence. How can the various stages of the body, beginning with birth, have any relationship with your eternal self? The material body is constantly changing, and it will cease to exist, just as it had not existed before. The body must be understood as only a temporary manifestation of the illusory energy of the Lord.

COMMENTARY

"By coming to the platform of realized knowledge, the *jñānīs* achieve the ultimate goal of life and yet, they remain far from attaining Me. My dear Uddhava, one who understands My nature will easily cross beyond the spell of nescience." This instruction of the Lord is not only meant for Uddhava but for everyone. The transformations of the material body, which are born of the three material modes of nature, have nothing to do with the pure spirit soul. The spell of illusion that causes one to identify with the temporary material body was not there in the beginning, nor will it remain after liberation from conditional life. The living entity is completely spiritual but at present he identifies with his mundane form, which is temporarily manifested. For the spirit soul, there is no birth and death. Under illusion, he thinks, "Now I am alive, later on I will be dead, sometimes I am happy and sometimes I am miserable. The soul has nothing to do with the transformations of the material body and when one is enlightened by spiritual knowledge, his relationship with the material body is terminated. Actually, the soul is distinct from the material body although he temporarily identifies himself with it. The example is given that a man walking in the forest may see a rope but consider it to be a snake. Such perception is *māyā*, or illusion, although the rope actually exists and a snake also exists in another place. Illusion thus refers to the false identification of one object with another. It is only due to ignorance that the living entities come in contact with *māyā*, or illusion. If his conditional state were eternal, then it would be his constitutional position and would not be dispelled by the attainment of transcendental knowledge. Saintly persons do not approve of that conception of liberation whereby one loses his individuality.

PURPORT

One cannot realize the Absolute Truth as long as he misidentifies with the gross and subtle bodies. The gross body and the subtle mind are by nature continuously changing, being under the influence of the three modes of material nature. The pure spirit soul, however, is not subjected to any change or transformation. Eternity and temporality do not go side by side.

For example, the illusion of accepting a rope as a snake is temporary. The rope is real and the snake is real but the act of mistaking a rope for a snake is illusion. When the understanding of the rope's presence is awakened, at that very moment, the temporary misconception of it being a snake is automatically dispelled. Knowledge of the eternal, which is without beginning or end is distinct from all kinds of temporary conceptions. The conclusion is that it is not desirable to praise the material body and mind while neglecting the spirit soul.

Spirit and matter are not one and the same. With their perverted understanding, the Māyāvādīs consider the Lord's variegated spiritual pastimes to be on the level of the mundane activities that are visible in this world. This mistake is caused by thinking of the self merely in terms of negating material qualities. Actually, such a conception is sheer madness born of forgetfulness of the self.

It is necessary to become freed from the control of eternal time, which has created a perverted form of the eternally present, causing the conditioned souls to see things in terms of past, present, and future. Even while living in the material world, one can absorb himself in the eternal nature by replacing the spirit of enjoyment with the spirit of service. The conclusion is that it is always profitable to give up the service of *māyā* by continually worshiping Lord Hari.

TEXT 8

श्रीउद्धव उवाच
ज्ञानंविशुद्धंविपुलंयथैतद्वैराग्यविज्ञानयुतंपुराणम् ।
आख्याहिविश्वेश्वरविश्वमूर्तेत्वद्भक्तियोगंचमहद्विमृग्यम् ॥८॥

śrī-uddhava uvāca
jñānaṁ viśuddhaṁ vipulaṁ yathaitad vairāgya-vijñāna-yutaṁ purāṇam
ākhyāhi viśveśvara viśva-mūrte tvad-bhakti-yogaṁ ca mahad-vimṛgyam

Śrī Uddhava said: O Lord of the universe! O form of the universe! Please describe the perfect eternal knowledge that results in detachment from all that is material and awards one direct perception of reality. This highly sought after knowledge describes devotional service unto You.

COMMENTARY

Not being satisfied with the knowledge of self-realization that the Lord had presented so far, Śrī Uddhava now inquires about the rarely understood process of devotional service. The Absolute Truth is beyond the reach of the empiric philosophers. Śrī Uddhava said: "O Lord of the universe! The universal form and its opulence that You manifest are temporary and therefore illusory. Now, kindly tell me about the pure and unadulterated process of devotional service that is sought after by great sages, such as Śuka and Sanaka."

PURPORT

Those who have been able to lift themselves above the illusion of material existence are called *mahat*, or very great personalities. Here, Śrī Uddhava expresses his desire to hear about that knowledge which has been sought after by such great personalities.

TEXT 9

तापत्रयेणाभिहतस्यघोरेसन्तप्यमानस्यभवाध्वनीश ।
पश्यामिनान्यच्छरणंतवाङ्घ्रिद्वन्द्वातपत्रादमृताभिवर्षात् ॥९॥

tāpa-trayeṇābhihatasya ghore santapyamānasya bhavādhvanīśa
paśyāmi nānyac charaṇaṁ tavāṅghri-dvandvātapatrād amṛtābhivarṣāt

My dear Lord, one who is caught up in the vicious cycle of repeated birth and death and thus suffers the threefold miseries of material existence—for him the only shelter is Your lotus feet, which are like an umbrella that showers nectar.

COMMENTARY

One might question, "Being satisfied with spiritual knowledge, what would one gain by inquiring about the process of devotional service?" Herein, Lord Kṛṣṇa gives a suitable reply. The lotus feet of the Supreme Lord are most pleasing to the heart and they shower nectar upon the devotee. This nectar is more relishable and sweet than the happiness derived from Brahman realization. The lotus feet of the Lord are just like an umbrella that shades one on the torturous path of material existence. Indeed, there is no other comparable shelter available in this world. Śrī Dhruva Mahārāja presented this statement, which is found in the *Śrīmad Bhāgavatam* (4.9.10):

yā nirvṛtis tanu-bhṛtāṁ tava pāda-padma-
dhyānād bhavaj-jana-kathā-śravaṇena vā syāt
sā brahmaṇi sva-mahimany api nātha mā bhūt
kiṁ tv antakāsi-lulitāt patatāṁ vimānāt

My Lord, the transcendental bliss derived from meditating upon Your lotus feet or hearing about Your glories from pure devotees is so unlimited that it is far beyond the stage of *brahmānanda*, wherein one thinks himself merged in the impersonal Brahman as one with the Supreme. Since *brahmānanda* is also defeated by the transcendental bliss derived from devotional service, then what to speak of the temporary blissfulness of elevating oneself to the heavenly planets, which is ended by the separating sword of time? Although one may be elevated to the heavenly planets, he falls down in due course of time.

In this verse, Śrī Uddhava is inquiring about the most blissful process of devotional service, which is more relishable than the happiness derived from Brahman realization which is attained by the cultivation of knowledge.

PURPORT

This formidable material existence is filled with threefold miseries. Those who are traversing the path of material existence are constantly afflicted by these miseries. The lotus feet of the Supreme Lord protect the devotees from the scorching heat of aversion to His devotional service, just like the cooling shade of an umbrella.

TEXT 10

दष्टंजनंसम्पतितंबिलेऽस्मिन्कालाहिनाक्षुद्रसुखोरुतर्षम् ।
समुद्धरैनंकृपयापवर्ग्यैर्वचोभिरासिञ्चमहानुभाव ॥१०॥

daṣṭaṁ janaṁ sampatitaṁ bile 'smin kālāhinā kṣudra-sukhoru-tarṣam
samuddharainaṁ kṛpayāpavargyair vacobhir āsiñca mahānubhāva

My dear Lord, please mercifully deliver this miserable living being who has fallen into the dark well of material existence and has thus been bitten by the snake of time. In spite of a horrible condition of life, the miserable conditioned soul is mad after attaining insignificant sense gratification. Please deliver me by Your nectarean instructions, which bring one to the path of liberation.

COMMENTARY

One should follow in the footsteps of the pure devotees of the Lord to make his life perfect. There is no necessity for cultivating knowledge that is simply a negation of material variegatedness in the hopes of attaining realization of Brahman. Even if one is not a pure or exalted devotee, he should sincerely pray for the mercy of the Supreme Lord. Without the mercy of the Supreme Lord, or His eternal servants, one's personal endeavors for liberation will yield no fruit. If one's cultivation of knowledge is free from desire for personal gain and is aimed at understanding the Absolute Personality of Godhead, it becomes fruitful. Those who have not yet attained the platform of pure devotional service may acquire such knowledge in order to free themselves from material bondage. The Lord's mercy is practically manifest by the instructions He gives, such as in the *Bhagavad-gītā* and *Uddhava-gītā*. In this verse, Uddhava prays to be bathed in the shower of the Lord's nectarean instructions. This is the purport of this verse.

PURPORT

Here, the true condition of material existence is being described. Although the happiness one gains from sense gratification is very insignificant, the conditioned soul has an insatiable desire to enjoy it. This mad desire to enjoy the dull material world is certainly due to the influence of the illusory energy of the Lord. Instead of enjoying the happiness he desires, the conditioned souls continually suffer in the dark well of material existence. It is in the best interest of everyone to renounce the false prestige based upon bodily identification and beg for the mercy of the Supreme Lord. The Lord is not a dead stone, and so He hears the sincere appeals of the conditioned souls, and mercifully helps them by His divine instructions.

TEXT 11

श्रीभगवानुवाच
इत्थमेतत्पुराराजभीष्मंधर्मभृतांवरम् ।
अजातशत्रुःपप्रच्छसर्वेषांनोऽनुशृण्वताम् ॥११॥

śrī-bhagavān uvāca
ittham etat purā raja bhīṣmaṁ dharma-bhṛtāṁ varam
ajāta-śatruḥ papraccha sarveṣāṁ no 'nuśṛṇvatām

The Supreme Lord said: My dear Uddhava, formerly, King Yudhiṣthira, who considered no one as his enemy, inquired just as you have now, from the great authority on religious principles, Bhīṣma, while We were present.

TEXT 12

निवृत्तेभारतेयुद्धेसुहृन्निधनविह्वलः ।
श्रुत्वाधर्मान्बहून्पश्चान्मोक्षधर्मानपृच्छत ॥१२॥

nivṛtte bhārate yuddhe suhṛn-nidhana-vihvalaḥ
śrutvā dharmān bahūn paścān mokṣa-dharmān apṛcchata

At the end of the battle at Kurukṣetra, King Yudhiṣthira was afflicted with grief because of the death of so many well-wishers and relatives and thus, after listening to many discussions of religious principles, he finally asked the same question regarding the path of liberation.

TEXT 13

तानहंतेऽभिधास्यामिदेवव्रतमखाच्छ्रुतान् ।
ज्ञानवैराग्यविज्ञानश्रद्धाभक्त्युपबृंहितान् ॥१३॥

tān ahaṁ te 'bhidhāsyāmi deva-vrata-makhāc chrutān
jñāna-vairāgya-vijñāna- śraddhā-bhakty-upabṛṁhitān

Now I will describe to you the religious principles governing Vedic knowledge, self-realization, renunciation, faith, and devotional service, which were heard directly from the mouth of Bhīṣma.

TEXT 14

नवैकादशपञ्चत्रीन्भावान्भूतेषुयेनवै ।
ईक्षेताथाइकमप्येषुतज्ज्ञानंममनिश्चितम् ॥१४॥

navaikādaśa pañca trīn bhāvān bhūteṣu yena vai
īkṣetāthāikam apy eṣu taj jñānaṁ mama niścitam

I approve of the various philosophical understanding that delineate a combination of nine, eleven, five, or three elements in all living entities, and ultimately one supreme element within all twenty-eight.

COMMENTARY

The knowledge by which one understands the twenty-eight elements comprising material nature—the spirit soul, *mahat-tattva*, false ego, five sense objects, eleven senses, five material elements, and three modes of material nature—to be ultimately nondifferent from the Personality of Godhead is approved by Śrī Kṛṣṇa. Actual knowledge is to understand that the Supersoul is the cause of all causes and thus the origin of these twenty-eight elements.

PURPORT

The nine elements mentioned here are material nature, the living entity, the *mahat-tattva*, false ego, and the five objects of the senses—sound, touch, form, taste and aroma. The eleven elements mentioned in this verse are the five working senses (speech, hands, legs, anus, and genitals), five knowledge-acquiring senses (ears, touch, eyes, tongue, and nostrils), and the mind. The five elements are earth, water, fire, air and ether, and the three elements are the three modes of material nature—goodness, passion, and ignorance. All of the living entities in this material world are embodied by these twenty-eight elements. The one supreme element within all twenty-eight is the all-pervading Supersoul.

TEXT 15

एतदेवहिविज्ञानंनतथैकेनयेन त् ।
स्थित्युत्पत्त्यप्ययान्पश्येद्भावानांत्रिगुणात्मनाम् ॥१५॥

etad eva hi vijñānaṁ na tathaikena yena yat
sthity-utpatty-apyayān paśyed bhāvānāṁ tri-guṇātmanām

When one no longer sees the twenty-eight material elements, but rather sees the Supersoul, from whom these elements have emanated, his understanding is called *vijñāna*, or self-realization. Every materially created form transforms in three stages— birth, existence, and destruction.

COMMENTARY

In this verse, Śrī Kṛṣṇa describes *vijñāna*, which is the mature stage of *jñāna*. On the platform of *jñāna*, one sees the material elements in relation to the Supreme Personality of Godhead but on the platform of *vijñāna*, the Supersoul is directly realized in His own abode. Upon realization of the Supersoul, who exists beyond this cosmic manifestation, one ceases to study the material elements. This is the culmination of self-realization. The objects of this material world are created by the three modes of material nature and are subjected to three phases. They come into being, remain for some time, and then are ultimately dissolved. Therefore the creation, maintenance, and annihilation of the cosmic manifestation is a temporary manifestation of the Lord's inferior potency and not ultimate reality. Those who are wise realize this on the platform of *vijñāna*.

TEXT 16

आदावन्तेचमध्येचसृज्यात्सृज्यंयदन्वियात् ।
पुनस्तत्प्रतिसङ्क्रामेयच्छिष्येततदेवसत् ॥१६॥

ādāv ante ca madhye ca sṛjyāt sṛjyaṁ yad anviyāt
punas tat-pratisaṅkrāme yac chiṣyeta tad eva sat

Creation, maintenance, and destruction are the stages of material causation. That which consistently accompanies all these material phases from one creation to another and remains alone when all material phases are annihilated is called sat, or eternal existence.

COMMENTARY

In this verse, the Supersoul, the original cause, is being further described. Although all created things can be understood in terms of cause and effect, and are temporary manifestations having a beginning, a period of manifestation, and an end, the original cause is eternal and remains even after the total annihilation of the cosmic manifestation. The *mahat-tattva* is considered to be the cause of the creation but it is not the cause of all causes. The Supreme Lord is the absolute cause of material existence. He is the unchanging reality that eternally exists while everything material goes through constant transformations. This can be understood by one who cultivates transcendental knowledge under the guidance of the bona fide spiritual master.

PURPORT

One's understanding that the Absolute Truth is one without a second should not be disturbed when one hears of the variegated pastimes of the Supreme Lord. When one is on the platform of *vijñāna*, one's resolute conviction that the Absolute Truth is the Supreme Personality of Godhead remains unshakable.

Advaya jñāna does not refer to impersonal monism, a conception that views the Absolute Truth as being devoid of variegatedness. According to such impersonal philosophy, the individuality of the living entity, the distinction between the master and the servant, and their transcendental characteristics are products of illusion. If a conditioned soul cannot appreciate the philosophy of inconceivable simultaneous oneness and distinction, he will certainly come under the spell of Māyāvāda philosophy and therefore consider the temporary material world, which is a manifestation of the three modes of material nature, to be false.

Whatever we see manifested in this world has a beginning and an end. Although the cosmic manifestation is in constant flux, the separated material energy of the Lord is eternal and therefore not false. One who stands on the platform of realization of his eternal self can, on the strength of his acquired knowledge, renounce both the aspiration for material enjoyment, which is, after all, accompanied by so many miseries, as well as dry renunciation of such enjoyment.

If one's variegated activities pertaining to life in this material world are dovetailed in the service of Lord Kṛṣṇa, one will become purified of the contamination of aversion to the Lord. This temporary material world, which covers an insignificant portion of the spiritual sky, can be realized as a place of blissful pastimes of the Lord, but the moment one sees this world as separate from the Lord and thus meant for one's personal enjoyment, one's *advaya jñāna* becomes disturbed.

The devotees of the Supreme Lord are very conversant with the understanding of how everything in this world has a beginning and an end, and so they cannot be diverted due to attraction for momentary enjoyment. As long as the devotees are fully engaged in the service of the Supreme Lord with all of their senses, material contamination cannot touch them. However, when one fails to come to the platform of seeing how everything is in relation to Kṛṣṇa, one may adopt a process of pseudo renunciation.

TEXT 17

श्रुतिःप्रत्यक्षमैतिह्यमनुमानंचतुष्टयम् ।
प्रमाणेष्वनवस्थानाद्विकल्पात्सविरज्यते ॥१७॥

śrutiḥ pratyakṣam aitihyam anumānaṁ catuṣṭayam
pramāṇeṣv anavasthānād vikalpāt sa virajyate

From the four types of evidence—Vedic oral reception, direct experience, traditional wisdom, and logical induction—one can understand the temporary nature of the material world, and thus become detached from the dualities of material existence.

COMMENTARY

After describing *jñāna* and *vijñāna*, Śrī Kṛṣṇa now discusses renunciation in this and the following verses. The evidence presented by Vedic oral reception is that the Absolute Truth is He from whom all living entities manifest, by whom they are maintained for some time, and into whom they enter at the time of annihilation. The evidence of direct perception is that a pot is made from earth and when it is broken, there will remain only clay. The evidence presented by historical or traditional wisdom is that those who declare that this material world is false did not exist previously, and thus are unauthorized and ignorant. The evidence of hypothesis is to conclude that this material world is temporary because it has a beginning and an end. Although there is sometimes disagreement between the four types of evidence, they all proclaim that material existence is temporary and therefore, one should develop *vairāgya*, or detachment, as stated here.

PURPORT

Unless one accepts direct perception, Vedic knowledge, traditional wisdom, and logical induction in relation to the Supreme Lord, one will simply engage in mental speculation while trying to understand the Absolute Truth. When any of these four kinds of evidence enhance one's spiritual cultivation, they are accepted as being worthy. Simply by utilizing any of these forms of evidence for one's personal sense gratification, one cannot attain auspiciousness. By renouncing objects that could be seen in relation to Lord Hari, one invites inauspiciousness under the banner of false renunciation. However, when one cultivates the understanding that everything can be properly utilized in the devotional service of the Lord, that is considered suitable renunciation.

TEXT 18

कर्मणांपरिणामित्वादाविरिञ्च्यादमङ्गलम् ।
विपश्चिन्नश्वरंपश्येददृष्टमपिदृष्टवत् ॥१८॥

karmaṇāṁ pariṇāmitvād ā-viriñcyād amaṅgalam
vipaścin naśvaraṁ paśyed adṛṣṭam api dṛṣṭa-vat

One who is actually intelligent should see how material nature is subject to constant transformation, so that even in the highest planet in the material world, the planet of Lord Brahmā, there is no secure position. One should understand that within the material world, everything has a beginning and an end, just as his experience has shown him.

COMMENTARY

Although heavenly enjoyment is not experienced on this earth, it can be understood that there is no real happiness there because life there is also filled with envy, lamentation, and ultimately, death. Residence on any planet within the universe is the result of one's fruitive activities. The results of *karma* are always temporary and thus an intelligent person can conclude that every situation within the material world is temporary and thus fraught with various miseries.

PURPORT

The demigods, headed by Brahmā, are under the influence of the three modes of material nature, and yet they are worshiped by those who follow the *karma-kāṇḍa* sections of the *Vedas*, and are thus a source of inauspiciousness. An intelligent person can easily understand the temporary and faulty nature of life on planet earth, and he can also conclude that life in the heavenly planets must be temporary and inauspicious.

The results of fruitive activities are not at all desirable for self-realized souls. Unless one comes to this platform, one will continue to remain entangled in temporary fruitive activities.

TEXT 19

भक्तियोगःपुरैवोक्तःप्रीयमाणायतेऽनघ ।
पुनश्चकथयिष्यामिमद्भक्तेःकारणंपरं ॥१९॥

bhakti-yogaḥ puraivoktaḥ prīyamāṇāya te 'nagha
punaś ca kathayiṣyāmi mad-bhakteḥ kāraṇaṁ paraṁ

O sinless Uddhava, because of your love for Me, I had previously explained to you the process of devotional service. I will once again impart to you that sublime means for attaining My pure devotional service.

COMMENTARY

Being requested by Uddhava, Śrī Kṛṣṇa now begins His description of devotional service. Although Uddhava had heard about many aspects of human civilization, including the *varṇāśrama-dharma* system, the processes of distinguishing between matter and spirit, renunciation of sense gratification, and so forth, he still hankered to hear specifically about pure devotional service to Lord Kṛṣṇa, and the Lord thus begins to discuss that subject.

TEXTS 20-24

रद्धामृतकथायांमेशश्वन्मदनुकीर्तनम् ।
परिनिष्ठाचपूजायांस्तुतिभिःस्तवनंमम ॥२०॥
आदरःपरिचर्यायांसर्वाङ्गैरभिवन्दनम् ।
मद्भक्तपूजाभ्यधिकासर्वभूतेषुमन्मतिः ॥२१॥
मदर्थेष्वङ्गचेष्टाचवचसामद्गुणेरणम् ।
मय्यर्पणंचमनसःसर्वकामविवर्जनम् ॥२२॥
मदर्थेऽर्थपरित्यागोभोगस्यचसुखस्यच ।
इष्टंदत्तंहुतंजप्तंमदर्थंयद्व्रतंतपः ॥२३॥
एवंधर्मैर्मनुष्याणामुद्धवात्मनिवेदिनाम् ।
मयिसञ्जायतेभक्तिःकोऽन्योऽर्थोऽस्यावशिष्यते ॥२४॥

raddhāmṛta-kathāyāṁ me śaśvan mad-anukīrtanam
pariniṣṭhā ca pūjāyāṁ stutibhiḥ stavanaṁ mama

ādaraḥ paricaryāyāṁ sarvāṅgair abhivandanam
mad-bhakta-pūjābhyadhikā sarva-bhūteṣu man-matiḥ

mad-artheṣv aṅga-ceṣṭā ca vacasā mad-guṇeraṇam
mayy arpaṇaṁ ca manasaḥ sarva-kāma-vivarjanam

mad-arthe 'rtha-parityāgo bhogasya ca sukhasya ca
iṣṭaṁ dattaṁ hutaṁ japtaṁ mad-arthaṁ yad vrataṁ tapaḥ

evaṁ dharmair manuṣyāṇām uddhavātma-nivedinām
mayi sañjāyate bhaktiḥ ko 'nyo 'rtho 'syāvaśiṣyate

Firm faith in the nectarean narrations of My pastimes, constant chanting of My transcendental glories, great attachment for My worship in the temple, praising Me by offering beautiful prayers, great respect for My devotional service, offering obeisances with the entire body, rendering service to My devotees, seeing Me within the hearts of all living entities, offering one's bodily activities in My devotional service, describing My transcendental qualities, offering one's mind to Me, renunciation of all material desires, donating one's wealth for My devotional service, giving up material sense gratification and happiness derived from it, and performing all pious activities such as giving charity, performing sacrifice, chanting *mantras*, and executing vows and austerities simply with the desire to attain Me—these constitute actual religious principles by which devotees who have actually surrendered unto Me automatically develop love for Me. What other purpose or goal could there be for such a devotee?

COMMENTARY

Discussions about Kṛṣṇa are full of nectar. Talks of Kṛṣṇa's *rāsa-līlā* pastimes are the most nectarean and should be heard with utmost faith. The worship of His devotee is more pleasing to Kṛṣṇa than His own worship. One should perform all his bodily activities, such as bathing and brushing his teeth, in relation to the service of the Lord. One should glorify the qualities and pastimes of the Lord with songs and prayers. One should give his hard-earned money to his spiritual master or the Vaiṣṇavas for arranging festivals of Kṛṣṇa consciousness. One should renounce whatever wealth creates an obstacle on his path of worshiping the Lord. One should renounce all activities of material sense gratification, of which enjoying sex is the chief. One should also give up all kinds of material happiness, such as that derived from excessive attachment to one's wife and children. One should feed rice cooked with ghee to the *brāhmaṇa* Vaiṣṇavas. One should offer oblations of sesame seeds mixed with ghee into the sacrificial fire while chanting *viṣṇave svāḥa*. One should chant the holy names of the Lord without cessation. The austerity to be performed by devotees is to observe fasting on days such as Ekādaśī. Hearing discussions of the Lord's nectarean pastimes is the ultimate fruit of all activities for a devotee who is free from all material desires. Unlike *jñānīs* who give up their *sādhana* when they attain perfection, devotees never give up the limbs of devotional service, beginning with hearing and chanting, even after attaining perfection. In the perfectional stage of Kṛṣṇa consciousness, hearing and chanting about the transcendental names, forms, qualities, and pastimes of the Lord are thousands of times more relishable than in the neophyte stage.

PURPORT

Faith in the discussion of Hari is the only qualification for chanting the holy name of the Lord. If one is attracted to mundane topics, then one's spirit of material enjoyment will increase. The more one faithfully listens to discussion of Hari, the less his taste for material sense gratification will be manifest. If one gives up hearing and chanting topics that are not related to Kṛṣṇa and always engages in glorifying the Lord, he will attain supreme auspiciousness. To hear and chant the glorification of Hari, worship the Lord, submit one's self to the Lord while offering Him prayers, offer obeisances to the Lord, worship the Lord's devotee with great care and attention, and consider all living entities to be the servants of the Supreme Lord are some of the activities by which one can quickly advance on the path of *sādhana bhakti*. If, while practicing *sādhana bhakti*, one offers all his worldly and religious activities to the Lord, glorifies the transcendental qualities of Hari, gives up activities that are not pleasing to the Lord and thus does not run after sense gratification, performs sacrifice, observes vows, undergoes austerity, chants *mantras*, and gives in charity, then gradually he will develop his dormant propensity for performing unalloyed devotional service. If one's activities are directed towards the service of the Supreme Lord, one gets respite from the false sense of false proprietorship that binds the conditioned soul. Only by complete surrender unto the Supreme Lord can one attain the platform of pure devotional service.

TEXT 25

यदात्मन्यर्पितंचित्तंशान्तंसत्त्वोपबृंहितम् ।
धर्मंज्ञानंसवैराग्यमैश्वर्यंचाभिपद्यते ॥२५॥

yadātmany arpitaṁ cittaṁ śāntaṁ sattvopabṛṁhitam
dharmaṁ jñānaṁ sa vairāgyam aiśvaryaṁ cābhipadyate

When one's peaceful mind that is enriched by the mode of goodness is fixed on the Supersoul, one attains religiosity, knowledge, renunciation, and opulence.

COMMENTARY

One might question, "What is lacking for one who is a pure devotee of the Lord?" Śrī Kṛṣṇa answers this question in this verse. One should not think that unalloyed devotional service is a limb of *jñāna*. The devotional service that is seen as a limb of *jñāna* is different from pure devotional service, which is untouched by any contamination of *karma* and *jñāna*. One who desires material enjoyment can gradually come to the platform of pure devotional service and at the same time, receive the fulfillment of all his desires. If one can fix his mind on the Supersoul, then as a result of his devotion, he can achieve all desirable perfections of life.

PURPORT

When one faithfully cultivates pure devotional service to the Supreme Lord, symptoms such as knowledge of the Supreme Lord and the individual spirit soul, detachment from all that is not related to Kṛṣṇa, dependence on the mercy of the Supreme Lord, steadiness of mind, and being firmly situated in the mode of pure goodness are observed in his character.

TEXT 26

यदर्पितंतद्विकल्पेइन्द्रियैःपरिधावति ।
रजस्वलंचासन्निष्ठंचित्तंविद्धिविपर्ययम् ॥२६॥

yad arpitaṁ tad vikalpe indriyaiḥ paridhāvati
rajas-valaṁ cāsan-niṣṭhaṁ cittaṁ viddhi viparyayam

When consciousness is fixed on the material body, family members, and other objects of sense gratification, one passes his life chasing after material objects with the help of the senses. Being under the control of the mode of passion, one becomes dedicated to impermanent things and in this way, irreligion, ignorance, attachment, and wretchedness predominate.

COMMENTARY

When one's mind contemplates the activities of the material body and household affairs, the mode of passion becomes prominent so that one becomes mad after sense gratification, even to the extent of performing prohibited activities. The mind of such a person is uncontrolled, thus becoming the cause of irreligiosity, ignorance, material attachment, and tremendous suffering.

PURPORT

Those who do not avail themselves of the opportunity to serve the Supreme Lord, being overwhelmed by desires to enjoy sense gratification, will become bound by attachment to temporary material objects, thus creating so many disturbances in their life.

TEXT 27

धर्मोमद्भक्तिकृत्प्रोक्तोज्ञानंचैकात्म्यदर्शनम् ।
गुणेस्वसङ्गोवैराग्यमैश्वर्यंचाणिमादयः ॥२७॥

dharmo mad-bhakti-kṛt prokto jñānaṁ caikātmya-darśanam
guṇesv asaṅgo vairāgyam aiśvaryaṁ cāṇimādayaḥ

The scriptures declare that real religious principles are those that lead one to devotional service to Me, real knowledge is to see everything in relation to the Supersoul, real detachment is total disinterest in the objects of material sense gratification, and real opulence is the eight mystic perfections, which includes *aṇimā-siddhi.*

COMMENTARY

Real religion means devotional service to the Supreme Lord.

PURPORT

The Supreme Lord is the personification of knowledge. Therefore, one who has been delivered from ignorance naturally engages in the devotional service of the Lord and is considered thoroughly religious. One who is detached from the three modes of material nature and the objects of sense gratification produced from them is considered to be detached. The eight mystic powers that were previously described to Uddhava are the ultimate attainments of material power and opulence.

TEXTS 28-32

श्रीउद्धव उवाच
यमःकतिविधःप्रोक्तोनियमोवारिकर्षण ।
कःशमःकोदमःकृष्णकातितिक्षाधृतिःप्रभो ॥२८॥

किंदानंकिंतपःशौर्यंकिम्सत्यमृतमुच्यते ।
कस्त्यागःकिंधनंचेष्टंकोयज्ञःकाचदक्षिणअ ॥२९॥
पुंसःकिंस्विद्बलंश्रीमन्भगोलाभश्चकेशव ।
काविद्याह्रीःपराकाश्रीःकिंसुखंदुःखमेवच ॥३०॥
कःपण्डितःकश्चमूर्खःकःपन्था उत्पथश्चकः ।
कःस्वर्गोनरकःकःस्वित्कोबन्धुरुतकिंगृहम् ॥३१॥
क आढ्यःकोदरिद्रोवाकृपणःकःकईश्वरः ।
एतान्प्रश्नान्ममब्रूहिविपरीतांश्चसत्पते ॥३२॥

śrī-uddhava uvāca
yamaḥ kati-vidhaḥ prokto niyamo vāri-karṣaṇa
kaḥ śamaḥ ko damaḥ kṛṣṇa kā titikṣā dhṛtiḥ prabho

kiṁ dānaṁ kiṁ tapaḥ śauryaṁ kim satyam ṛtam ucyate
kas tyāgaḥ kiṁ dhanaṁ ceṣṭaṁ ko yajñaḥ kā ca dakṣiṇā

puṁsaḥ kiṁ svid balaṁ śrīman bhago lābhaś ca keśava
kā vidyā hrīḥ parā kā śrīḥ kiṁ sukhaṁ duḥkham eva ca

kaḥ paṇḍitaḥ kaś ca mūrkhaḥ kaḥ panthā utpathaś ca kaḥ
kaḥ svargo narakaḥ kaḥ svit ko bandhur uta kiṁ gṛham

ka āḍhyaḥ ko daridro vā kṛpaṇaḥ kaḥ ka īśvaraḥ
etān praśnān mama brūhi viparītāṁś ca sat-pate

Śrī Uddhava said: My dear Lord Kṛṣṇa, O chastiser of the enemies, please tell me how many types of disciplinary regulations and prohibitions there are. My Lord, please define mental equilibrium, self-control, and the real meaning of tolerance and steadfastness. What are charity, austerity, and heroism, and how can truth and reality be best described? What is renunciation, and what is real wealth? What is desirable, what is sacrifice, and what is religious remuneration? My dear Keśava, O most fortunate one, how can I understand the strength, opulence, and merit of a particular person? What is the best education, what is actual humility, and what is real beauty? What are happiness and unhappiness? Who is learned, and who is a fool? What are the true and the false paths in life, and what are heaven and hell? Who is indeed a true friend, and what is one's real home? Who is a rich

man, and who is a poor man? Who is wretched, and who is actually fortunate? O Lord of the devotees, kindly explain these to me, along with their opposites.

COMMENTARY

After hearing about various kinds of religious principles, Śrī Uddhava now asks Kṛṣṇa to give authoritative definitions of the of *yamas* and *niyamas* that comprise civilized life throughout the world. The word *iṣṭa* means "most desirable." The word *śrī* means "opulence." Uddhava also wants to hear from Kṛṣṇa about that which is just the opposite of civilized life.

TEXTS 33-35

श्रीभगवानुवाच
अहिंसासत्यमस्तेयमसङ्गोह्रीरसञ्चयः ।
आस्तिक्यंब्रह्मचर्यंचमौनंस्थैर्यंक्षमाभयम् ॥३३॥
शौचंजपस्तपोहोमःश्रद्धातिथ्यंमदर्चनम् ।
तीर्थाटनंपरार्थेहातुष्टिराचार्यसेवनम् ॥३४॥
एतेयमाःसनियमा उभयोर्द्वादशस्मृताः ।
पुंसामुपासितास्तातयथाकामं दुहन्ति हि ॥३५॥

śrī-bhagavān uvāca
ahiṁsā satyam asteyam asaṅgo hrīr asañcayaḥ
āstikyaṁ brahmacaryaṁ ca maunaṁ sthairyaṁ kṣamābhayam

śaucaṁ japas tapo homaḥ śraddhātithyaṁ mad-arcanam
tīrthāṭanaṁ parārthehā tuṣṭir ācārya-sevanam
ete yamāḥ sa-niyamā ubhayor dvādaśa smṛtāḥ
puṁsām upāsitās tāta yathā-kāmaṁ duhanti hi

The Supreme Lord said: Nonviolence, truthfulness, not usurping others' property, detachment from worldly association, humility, freedom from possessiveness, faith in the principles of religion, celibacy, silence, steadiness, forgiveness, and fearlessness—these twelve are referred to as *yama*. External cleanliness, internal cleanliness, chanting the holy names of the Lord, austerity, fire sacrifice, faith, serving guests, worshiping Me, visiting holy places, engaging only in activities that are ultimately beneficial, and service to the spiritual master—these twelve are called *niyama*. My dear Uddhava, These twenty-four practices bestow all desired benedictions upon those who devotedly cultivate them.

COMMENTARY

In these three verses, the Supreme Lord defines *yama* and *niyama*. There are two types of purification—internal and external. By carefully cultivating these twenty-four *yama* and *niyama*, all of one's desires become fulfilled.

PURPORT

The twelve *yamas* are non-enviousness, remaining fixed in the truth, refraining from stealing another's property, staying aloof from all kinds of bad association, always attempting to do good to others, renunciation of unnecessary sense enjoyment, unflinching faith in the Supreme Lord, celibacy, giving up idle talks, steadiness in one's practices, tolerance of others' offenses, and fear of transgressing the prescribed rules and regulations. The twelve *niyamas* are external cleanliness such as bathing, internal cleanliness by serving Lord Hari, chanting the holy names of the Lord, observing vows such as Ekādaśī, performing sacrifice for the satisfaction of Lord Hari, maintaining faith in the discussions of the glories of Lord Hari, serving the devotees of Lord Hari, worshiping the Deity, traveling to holy places of pilgrimage, engaging in activities meant for one's ultimate welfare, remaining fixed in observing the codes of proper conduct, being satisfied in all conditions of life, and serving the spiritual master.

TEXTS 36-39

शमोमन्निष्ठताबुद्धेर्दमइन्द्रियसंयमः ।
तितिक्षादुःखसम्मर्षोजिह्वोपस्थजयोधृतिः ॥३६॥
दण्डन्यासःपरंदानंकामत्यागस्तपःस्मृतम् ।
स्वभावविजयःशौर्यंसत्यंचसमदर्शनम् ॥३७॥
अन्यच्चसुनृतावाणीकविभिःपरिकीर्तिता ।
कर्मस्वसङ्गमःशौचंत्यागःसन्न्यास उच्यते ॥३८॥
धर्मइष्टंधनंनृणांयज्ञोऽहंभगवत्तमः ।
दक्षिणाज्ञानसन्देशःप्राणायामःपरंबलम् ॥३९॥

śamo man-niṣṭhatā buddher dama indriya-saṁyamaḥ
titikṣā duḥkha-sammarṣo jihvopastha-jayo dhṛtiḥ

daṇḍa-nyāsaḥ paraṁ dānaṁ kāma-tyāgas tapaḥ smṛtam
svabhāva-vijayaḥ śauryaṁ satyaṁ ca sama-darśanam

anyac ca sunṛtā vāṇ kavibhiḥ parikīrtitā
karmasv asaṅgamaḥ śaucaṁ tyāgaḥ sannyāsa ucyate

dharma iṣṭaṁ dhanaṁ nṝṇāṁ yajño 'haṁ bhagavattamaḥ
dakṣiṇā jñāna-sandeśaḥ prāṇāyāmaḥ paraṁ balam

Full concentration of the mind on Me constitutes mental equilibrium, and complete control of the senses is self-control. Tolerance means patiently enduring distress, and steadfastness occurs when one controls the urges of the tongue and genitals. The greatest charity is to give up all envy toward others, and renunciation of sense gratification is real austerity. Real heroism is to conquer one's natural tendency to enjoy material life, and reality is seeing the Supreme Lord in everything and everything in the Supreme Lord. Truthfulness means to speak honestly in a pleasing manner, as declared by great sages. Cleanliness is attained by detachment from fruitive activities, and renunciation indicates the *sannyāsa* order of life. The true desirable wealth for human beings is religiousness, and I, the Supreme Lord, am the enjoyer of all sacrifices. Religious remuneration is devotion for the spiritual master with the desire to acquire real knowledge, and the greatest strength is the *prāṇāyāma* system of breath control.

COMMENTARY

Here, the Lord defines those qualities that should be cultivated by all who desire to advance toward the goal of human life. *Śama* means to fix the mind on Lord Kṛṣṇa because without Kṛṣṇa consciousness, peacefulness of mind is simply emptyness. *Dama* means to control the senses. One who wants to impart instructions to others without himself controlling his senses will certainly be mocked. Tolerance means to patiently endure the insults of others, as well as all kinds of distress. It is simply an artificial show if one performs some great austerity and yet is unwilling to tolerate the abuses of others. Real steadfastness is achieved when one carefully controls his tongue and genitals. Real charity is the renunciation of all kinds of violence toward others. If one contributes to charities while at the same time exploiting others by engaging them in hellish factory work—this is simply hypocrisy. Austerity means to forego all kinds of material comforts while observing the prescribed vows, such as Ekādaśī. Real austerity is not torturing the body just to achieve name and fame. Real heroism is to conquer lust, anger, and greed. If one can conquer these three enemies, he is a greater hero than one who simply vanquishes his political enemies.

Equal vision can be exhibited by one who is not envious, and who sees how the Supersoul is present along with the individual soul within all types of bodies. This vision is pleasing to the Supreme Lord, who then awards further advancement to the devotee.

Reality is only truly understood when one sees the spiritual equality of all living entities, as confirmed by Śrī Kṛṣṇa in the *Bhagavad-gītā* 6.32:

ātmaupamyena sarvatra samaṁ paśyati yo 'rjuna
sukhaṁ vā yadi vā duḥkhaṁ sa yogī paramo mataḥ

He is a perfect yogi who, by comparison to his own self, sees the true equality of all beings, in both their happiness and their distress, O Arjuna!

One who is actually an advanced soul feels compassion upon experiencing the miseries of the conditioned souls. Truthfulness means to present the facts clearly and not distort the truth to avoid offending materialistic men. However, in the name of truthfulness, one should not become a fault-finder. The truth should be spoken to elevate others to the spiritual platform, not to push forward one's limited agenda. Cleanliness is more than regular bathing. As long as the mind is absorbed in thinking of sense gratification, one must be considered contaminated, even if has taken countless baths. Therefore, real cleanliness is purification of the mind. Real renunciation involves detachment from the false egoistic conceptions that the body is the self and everything in relation to the body is a possession. If, after giving up all one's material possessions, one remains attached to family members, that renunciation is only a show. Real wealth is to possess the knowledge of self-realization and not just so much land and money. Sacrifice is one of the names of the Lord, and so one should not think that the performance of sacrifices is meant for achieving temporary rewards. The best form of remuneration to the guru is to render selfless service by distributing the knowledge one has received to others.

PURPORT

To fix one's intelligence in the service of the Supreme Lord while renouncing the natural propensity to accept and reject things for one's personal sense gratification is called *śama*. To restrain the senses from unrestrainedly enjoying their sense objects is called *dama*. To tolerate the distress that one is destined to suffer, thinking it to be the Lord's mercy, and refraining from feelings of jealousy because of another's happiness is called *titikṣā*. To abstain from all kinds of sense gratification, such as the relishing of very palatable food, is called steadfastness. To give up the mentality of unnecessarily punishing one for his faults is called *dāna*. To give up all desire for material sense enjoyment despite having such facilities is called *tapasyā*. To subdue one's natural thirst for sense enjoyment is called *śaurya*. To see everything in relation to the Supreme Lord is called *samadarśana*. This is the best form of *satya*. Speaking simply yet boldly is called *ṛta*. To remain detached from material enjoyment while utilizing everything in the service of Kṛṣṇa is called *śauca*. To refrain from enjoying the objects of the senses is called *sannyāsa*. To follow religious principles is the most desirable form of *dhana*. To serve the Supreme Lord is actual *yajña*. To instruct others in the knowledge of one's relationship with the Supreme Lord is called *dakṣina*, and to regulate the mind by breathing exercises is *prāṇāyāma*.

TEXTS 40-45

भगोम ऐश्वरोभावोलाभोमद्भक्तिरुत्तमः ।
विद्यात्मनिभिदाबाधोजुगुप्साहीरकर्मसु ॥४०॥
श्रीर्गुणानैरपेक्ष्याद्याःसुखंदुःखसुखात्ययः ।
दुःखंकामसुखापेक्षापण्डितोबन्धमोक्षवित् ॥४१॥
मूर्खोदेहाद्यहंबुद्धिःपन्थामन्निगमःस्मृतः ।
उत्पथश्चित्तविक्षेपःस्वर्गःसत्त्वगुणोदयः ॥४२॥
नरकस्तमउन्नाहोबन्धुर्गुरुरहंसखे ।
गृहंशरीरंमानुष्यंगुणाढ्योह्याढ्यउच्यते ॥४३॥
दरिद्रायस्त्वसन्तुष्टःकृपणोयोऽजितेन्द्रियः ।
गुणेष्वसक्तधीरीशोगुणसङ्गोविपर्ययः ॥४४॥
एत उद्धवतेप्रश्नाःसर्वेसाधुनिरूपिताः ।
किंवर्णितेनबहुनालक्षणंगुणदोषयोः ।
गुणदोषदृशिर्दोषोगुणस्तूभयवर्जितः ॥४५॥

bhago ma aiśvaro bhāvo lābho mad-bhaktir uttamaḥ
vidyātmani bhidā-bādho jugupsā hrīr akarmasu

śrīr guṇā nairapekṣyādyāḥ sukhaṁ duḥkha-sukhātyayaḥ
duḥkhaṁ kāma-sukhāpekṣā paṇḍito bandha-mokṣa-vit

mūrkho dehādy-ahaṁ-buddhiḥ panthā man-nigamaḥ smṛtaḥ
utpathaś citta-vikṣepaḥ svargaḥ sattva-guṇodayaḥ

narakas tama-unnāho bandhur gurur ahaṁ sakhe
gṛhaṁ śarīraṁ mānuṣyaṁ guṇāḍhyo hy āḍhya ucyate

daridro yas tv asantuṣṭaḥ kṛpaṇo yo 'jitendriyaḥ
guṇeṣv asakta-dhīr īśo guṇa-saṅgo viparyayaḥ

eta uddhava te praśnāḥ sarve sādhu nirūpitāḥ
kiṁ varṇitena bahunā lakṣaṇaṁ guṇa-doṣayoḥ
guṇa-doṣa-dṛśir doṣo guṇas tūbhaya-varjitaḥ

Actual opulence, or *bhaga,* is My own nature, in which I exhibit the six unlimited opulences. The supreme gain of life, or *lābha,* is devotional service unto Me. Actual education, or *vidyā,* is to remove the conception of duality from the mind of the conditioned soul. Real modesty, or *hrī,* is to be disgusted with abominable activities. Real beauty, or *śrī,* is to possess good qualities, such as detachment. Real happiness, or *sukha,* is to transcend material happiness and distress, whereas distress, or *duḥkha,* is the constant hankering for sex enjoyment. A learned man, or *paṇḍita,* is one who knows the process of liberation from material bondage, and a fool, or *murkha,* is one who identifies with his material body and mind. The real path, or *satpatha,* is that which ultimately leads to Me, whereas the wrong path, or *kupatha,* is sense gratification, which simply bewilders the mind. Heaven, or *svarga,* is the predominance of the mode of goodness and *naraka,* or hell, is the predominance of the mode of ignorance. I am the true friend, or *bandhu,* because I act as the spiritual master of the entire world. The body of the human being is his *gṛha,* or residence. One who is endowed with all good qualities is *ādhya,* or rich, and one who is dissatisfied with life is *daridra,* or poor. A *kṛpaṇa,* or miser, is one who cannot control his senses, whereas one who is detached from sense gratification is truly a controller, or *īśa.* One who is attached to sense gratification is just the opposite, or a slave. My dear Uddhava, I have thus elucidated all of the matters about which you inquired. There is no need for a more elaborate description of these good and bad qualities because to constantly see good and bad is itself a bad quality. The best quality is to transcend material good and evil.

COMMENTARY

Because compassion is recognized throughout the world as an exalted quality, the Lord has not described it here. Actual *bhaga*, or opulence, is possessed by the supreme controller. The controlling power of the living entities in this world, or even the demigods in heaven, cannot be considered real *bhaga*. Attainment of devotional service to the Supreme Lord is one's real asset, and not his children, home, and so on, which are all subject to destruction. Real knowledge is that which enables one to see everything in relation to the Supreme Lord, and not that which is acquired by an academic, such as knowledge of grammar and so on. The word *hrī* means to feel disgust at the mere thought of sinful activities, and not mere shyness. One's good qualities are his real decoration, and not the crown that sits on his head. One who is satisfied in Kṛṣṇa consciousness and thus does not seek material pleasure or suffer material unhappiness is considered to be actually situated in happiness. The most wretched person is one addicted to sex pleasure, and a wise man is one who knows the process of freedom from such material bondage. A fool is one who gives up his eternal friendship with Lord Kṛṣṇa and instead identifies himself with his own temporary material body, mind, society, community, and family. The real path is the path of devotional service that leads one to the Supreme Lord, and not simply a footpath that has no stones or thorns. The path of sense gratification is the wrong path because it simply leads one to utter confusion. Predominance of the mode of goodness is real heaven, and not the abode of Indra, and predominance of the mode of ignorance is hell. The spiritual master is the best friend who saves us from all danger and he is nondifferent from Kṛṣṇa, the spiritual master of the entire universe. Our material body is our real home, and not a structure of bricks and cement. One who possesses all good qualities is actually rich, and not a rascal with a big bank balance. A real lord is one who has conquered material desires and ascended to the transcendental platform, and not an aristocrat who engages in all sorts of abominable activities.

Thus being asked by Uddhava, Śrī Kṛṣṇa has nicely described the difference between good qualities and faults. The Lord concludes His analysis by stating that there is no need for further elaboration of these good and bad qualities. Indeed, the purpose of life is to transcend materially good and bad qualities and come to the liberated platform of pure Kṛṣṇa consciousness.

PURPORT

The Lord is full of six opulences—wealth, strength, beauty, fame, knowledge, and renunciation. The supreme accomplishment is when one engages in the service of the Supreme Lord. To remain aloof from the material conception of life is fruit of actual knowledge. To indulge in sinful activities unrestrictedly is the most wretched condition of life. To spontaneously abhor sinful life is the sign of true modesty. Good qualities are the actual wealth of the living entities. To give up the quest for sense gratification and achieve satisfaction due to love for the Lord is real happiness. The lust for material enjoyment produces limitless distress.

Possessing knowledge of how to free oneself from the bondage of material existence is real learning. To identify one's self as the gross and subtle material coverings is utter foolishness. The true path of life is the one shown by the spiritual master who is coming in disciplic succession and thus authorized by the Supreme Lord. The wrong path is a life of sense enjoyment, which simply leads to the bewilderment of one's mind. A predominance of the mode of goodness is real heaven and a predominance of the mode of ignorance is real hell. The Supreme Lord and the spiritual master, who is the eternal servant of the Lord, are one's real friends. The material body is one's actual place of residence. One who possesses good qualities is actually rich, and one who is dissatisfied with his position, which is the result of his previous *karma*, is actually poor. Sense enjoyers, those with uncontrolled minds and senses, and those who are overwhelmed by greed are truly misers. One whose intelligence is never swayed by the three modes of material nature is a real controller. One who acts under the influence of the three modes of material nature is controlled and dependent. To look for material qualities and faults is itself a fault. While cultivating transcendental qualities, one should give up the habit of finding fault in others.

Thus ends the translation of the Thirteenth Chapter of the Uddhava-gītā entitled **"The Perfection of Spiritual Knowledge"** *with the commentaries of Śrīla Viśvanātha Cakravartī Ṭhākura and chapter summary and purports by Śrīla Bhaktisiddhānta Sarasvatī Ṭhākura.*

Chapter 14

Pure Devotional Service Surpasses Knowledge and Detachment

CHAPTER SUMMARY

This chapter describes the processes of *karma-yoga*, *jñāna-yoga*, and *bhakti-yoga*, according to the good and bad qualities that are found in various people.

The Vedic literature propagates true religion, which are the orders of the Supreme Lord. The social structure that is put forward in the Vedic literature is known as *varṇāśrama-dharma*, which is within the realm of material duality. In other places, however, the Vedic literature advises one to rise above such a vision of duality. In this chapter, Uddhava wants this point to be cleared up, as to why the Vedic literature appears to support two contradictory positions. Just to reconcile these two conflicting positions, Śrī Kṛṣṇa describes in this chapter the processes of *karma-yoga*, *jñāna-yoga*, and *bhakti-yoga*. *Karma-yoga* is the path that is recommended for persons who are filled with material desires. *Jñāna-yoga* is the path that is recommended for those who want to retire from material activities for the purpose of understanding the Absolute Truth. *Bhakti-yoga* is recommended for those who have understood that everything in existence is owned and controlled by the Lord. As long as one desires to act fruitively, and as long as one's faith in the Supreme Lord has not matured, he should execute his prescribed duties as outlined in the *varṇāśrama* system

Those who faithfully perform their duties as prescribed by the *varṇāśrama* system of social organization, carefully avoiding the sinful acts that are forbidden by the injunctions of the scriptures, will gradually rise to the transcendental platform of absolute knowledge. Generally, transcendentalists are first attracted to the impersonal conception of the Absolute, but those who are very fortunate manifest devotion for the

Supreme Personality of Godhead. The human form of life is the special opportunity awarded to the conditioned souls to awaken their dormant spiritual awareness, and as such, such a human birth is even desired by the demigods of heaven. Although it is temporary like all other forms of life, the human body can enable one to achieve life's ultimate goal. For that reason, one who is intelligent will endeavor to gain release from the vicious cycle of birth and death before death arrives at his doorstep. The human body is compared to a boat, the spiritual master is the captain of the ship, and the injunctions of the scriptures are the favorable breezes that can carry one to his destination. One who has attained the human form of life and yet does not endeavor to cross over the ocean of material existence must be considered the killer of his own self. The mind is very restless and the senses always demand satisfaction. Therefore, by good intelligence, one should control his mind and senses by cultivation of the mode of goodness.

To help fix the mind in transcendence, one should meditate upon the creation of the universe from subtle to gross. Then, one should meditate upon the dissolution of the universe from gross to subtle. One who has understood the futility of material existence can remain detached from the objects of the senses and bodily identification by carefully putting into practice the instructions of the spiritual master. The three processes of eight-fold mystic yoga, the cultivation of transcendental knowledge, and the devotional service of the Lord can all enable one to remain fixed on the spiritual platform.

One should remained fixed in the determination to carry out one's prescribed duties. By carefully studying the scriptures, which detail exactly what is desirable and what is to be avoided in this world, one can elevate himself above the vicious modes of passion and ignorance. By directly engaging in the devotional service of the Lord, all kinds of perfection are easily achieved. Anyone who is always engaged in the service of the Supreme Lord will gradually lose his taste for the inferior engagements of sense gratification. Ultimately, when one directly perceives the Supreme Lord, his false ego is vanquished, all doubts are destroyed, and all the results of fruitive activities are burned to ashes. Thus, the devotees of the Supreme Personality of Godhead never make a separate endeavor to perform austerities, or other such similar processes. In pure devotional service, there is no question of piety or sin, because the unalloyed *bhakta* has reached the transcendental platform, where the injunctions and prohibitions of the *Vedas* no longer apply.

TEXT 1

श्रीउद्धव उवाच
विधिश्चप्रतिषेधश्चनिगमोहीश्वरस्यते ।
अवेक्षतेऽरविण्डाक्षगुणंदोषंचकर्मणाम् ॥१॥

śrī-uddhava uvāca
vidhiś ca pratiṣedhaś ca nigamo hīśvarasya te
avekṣate 'ravindākṣa guṇaṁ doṣaṁ ca karmaṇām

Śrī Uddhava said: My dear lotus-eyed Lord, the Vedic literature, which constitutes Your divine orders in terms of positive and negative injunctions, focuses on the good and bad qualities of work.

COMMENTARY

In this chapter, *jñāna*, *karma*, and *bhakti* are elaborately described, as well as those who are suitable to engage in these three processes.

PURPORT

The activities of the living entities who are averse to the service of the Supreme Lord can be divided into two categories. Some good and bad qualities are always found in such activities. The prescriptions given by the Supreme Lord are termed *vidhi*, or rules, and are always considered good. The prohibitions declared by the Supreme Lord are termed *niṣedha*, or regulations, and to transgress them is always considered faulty.

TEXT 2

वर्णाश्रमविकल्पंचप्रतिलोमानुलोमजम् ।
द्रव्यदेशवयःकालान्स्वर्गंनरकमेवच ॥२॥

varṇāśrama-vikalpaṁ ca pratilomānulomajam
dravya-deśa-vayaḥ-kālān svargaṁ narakam eva ca

The Vedic literature creates the divisions of *varṇa* and *āśrama,* and describes the good and bad qualities in relation to mixed marriages, called *pratiloma and anuloma,* according to time, ingredients, place, and age. The *Vedas* also reveal the existence of heaven and hell, which are certainly the products of piety and sin.

COMMENTARY

It was previously stated that pointing out good and bad qualities of others is in itself a fault, and so one should give up such a dualistic mentality. In the following five verses, Śrī Uddhava expresses his desire to know more about this from the Lord. Uddhava said, "My dear Lord, the Vedic literature contains Your instructions and consists of recommendations and prohibitions. The performance of prescribed duties is always beneficial and the performing of prohibited acts is always faulty. Good and bad qualities, piety and impiety, and heaven and hell are born of such recommendations and prohibitions." In the social system of *varṇa* and *āśrama*, there are good qualities and faults that are judged in terms of the various kinds of marriage. If a man marries a girl of a superior *varṇa*, then the union is termed *pratiloma*. If a man marries a girl belonging to an inferior *varṇa*, that union is termed *anuloma*. In any case, the entire Vedic social system is based on distinguishing between piety and sin, and Śrī Uddhava is encouraging the Lord to explain more elaborately His statement that one should transcend both piety and sin.

PURPORT

Divisions of *varṇa*, divisions of *āśrama*, divisions according to the nature of one's birth, various objects and places, and the existence of heaven and hell, are all the results of piety and sin.

TEXT 3

गुणदोषभिदादृष्टिमन्तरेणवचस्तव ।
निःश्रेयसंकथंनृणांनिषेधविधिलक्षणम् ॥३॥

guṇa-doṣa-bhidā-dṛṣṭim antareṇa vacas tava
niḥśreyasaṁ kathaṁ nṝṇāṁ niṣedha-vidhi-lakṣaṇam

Without differentiating between pious and sinful acts, how can one understand Your instructions in the form of the Vedic literature, which orders one to act piously and forbids one to act sinfully? Without such authorized Vedic instructions, which ultimately award liberation, how could human beings achieve the perfection of life?

COMMENTARY

All recommendations and prohibitions are presented in the Vedic literature as instructions of the Supreme Lord. In order to advance toward the perfection of life, one must discriminate between good qualities and faults. Anything prescribed by the Lord is a good quality, and anything prohibited by Him is a fault. Therefore, it is impossible to achieve any auspiciousness in this life without making a distinction between good qualities and faults.

PURPORT

Uddhava is pointing out that if a person has no interest in making a distinction between piety and sin, then it becomes impossible for him to properly understand the scriptures. Without the assistance of the scriptures, how can a human being hope to understand the Absolute Truth, or be liberated from material existence?

TEXT 4

इतृदेवमनुष्यानांवेदश्चक्षुस्तवेश्वर ।
श्रेयस्त्वनुपलब्धेऽर्थेसाध्यसाधनयोरपि ॥४॥

itṛ-deva-manuṣyānāṁ vedaś cakṣus taveśvara
śreyas tv anupalabdhe 'rthe sādhya-sādhanayor api

My dear Lord, Vedic literature in the form of Your orders is the best evidence for understanding things beyond our experience, such as liberation, the attainment of the heavenly planets, and knowledge of the ultimate goal of life. For this reason, it is imperative that the forefathers, demigods, and human beings consult the Vedic literature.

COMMENTARY

Vedic injunctions are not only beneficial for human beings, but also for the demigods and forefathers. The best way of seeing things in the right perspective is to see through the eyes of the Vedic literature, which consists of the instructions of the Supreme Lord. Vedic literature is the original source of all kinds of knowledge. One can learn about liberation, the heavenly planets, and the ultimate goal of life, as well as the process for achieving the goal of life, only from the Vedic literature.

PURPORT

Human beings, demigods, and forefathers can see everything in the right perspective, and learn about *sādhya* and the processes of *sādhana* by seeing through the eyes of the scriptures, which are the Supreme Lord's orders. All living entities, be they forefathers, demigods, or human beings, are directed by the orders of the Supreme Lord.

TEXT 5

गुणदोषभिदादृष्टिर्निगमात्तेनहिस्वतः ।
निगमेनापवादश्चभिदाया इतिहभ्रमः ॥५॥

guṇa-doṣa-bhidā-dṛṣṭir nigamāt te na hi svataḥ
nigamenāpavādaś ca bhidāyā iti ha bhramaḥ

My dear Lord, the distinction between piety and sin comes from Vedic knowledge, which emanates from You, and does not arise by itself. If it is seen that the same *Vedas* discredit attempts to distinguish between piety and sin, then surely there will be chaos.

COMMENTARY

A dilemma has apparently been created by the Vedic literature. The *Vedas*, which consist of the Lord's orders advise one to discriminate between good and bad. At the same time, it sometimes forbids us to make such distinctions. Therefore, Uddhava is confused about what is right and what is wrong and he prays to Kṛṣṇa to remove his doubt.

PURPORT

Because the Vedic statements that one should discriminate between good and bad, and other statements that one should give up such a vision of duality, are seemingly contradictory, Śrī Uddhava is herein enacting the pastime of a bewildered person by asking the Lord to resolve this apparent contradiction.

TEXT 6

श्रीभगवानुवाच
योगास्त्रयोमयाप्रोक्तानृणांश्रेयोविधित्सया ।
ज्ञानंकर्मचभक्तिश्चनोपायोऽन्योऽस्तिकुत्रचित् ॥६॥

śrī-bhagavān uvāca
yogās trayo mayā proktā nṛṇāṁ śreyo-vidhitsayā
jñānaṁ karma ca bhaktiś ca nopāyo 'nyo 'sti kutracit

The Supreme Lord said: My dear Uddhava, because I desire ultimate welfare for human beings, I created three kinds of *yoga*, or paths of advancement—*jñāna-yoga*, *karma-yoga*, and *bhakti-yoga*. Besides these three, there is no other means of elevation.

COMMENTARY

Although all the processes that are recommended in the scriptures lead one to Kṛṣṇa consciousness, it should be understood that people accept varieties of paths due to their particular inclinations and propensities. Here, Lord Kṛṣṇa describes the three paths of spiritual advancement, just to show that the ultimate goal is one. The three methods for advancement have been described in the *karma-kāṇḍa*, *jñāna-kāṇḍa*, and *upāsaṇa-kāṇḍa* sections of the *Vedas*. Whatever path one may follow, success depends upon the mercy of the Lord. Indeed, no progress in any endeavor can be made without the sanction of the Lord. It should be noted that the other Vedic prescriptions, such as the performance of austerity and the giving of charity, are contained within these three general processes. By the word *traya*, the Lord emphasizes that the fruitive activities of the *karmīs* and the mental speculation of the *jñānīs* are inferior to the surrender of the pure devotees who are engaged in *bhakti-yoga*.

PURPORT

The processes of *karma*, *jñāna*, and *bhakti*, have been described in the Vedic literature for the ultimate benefit of all human beings. Apart from engagement in these processes, there is no other way for a human being to achieve auspiciousness.

TEXT 7

निर्विण्णानांज्ञानयोगोन्यासिनामिहकर्मसु ।
तेष्वनिर्विण्णचित्तानांकर्मयोगस्तुकामिनाम् ॥७॥

nirviṇṇānāṁ jñāna-yogo nyāsinām iha karmasu
teṣv anirviṇṇa-cittānāṁ karma-yogas tu kāminām

Jñāna-yoga is recommended for those who have seen the futility of material existence, and thus want to become detached from fruitive activities. _Karma-yoga_ is recommended for those who are fond of sense gratification, failing to understand the great distress that accompanies fruitive work.

COMMENTARY

Here is a description of the various propensities that cause a person to accept a particular path of elevation. Those who have become thoroughly disgusted with the animal propensities of eating, sleeping, mating, and defending, and thus are not even interested in enjoying these things in heaven, take to the cultivation of transcendental knowledge. Those who are still very eager to enjoy a materialistic life, centered around friends and family, and who are attached to the flowery words of the *Vedas* that recommend promotion to the heavenly planets for superior sense gratification, are not fit to take to the arduous path of philosophical speculation. Materialistic men are advised to remain in family life and offer the fruits of their labor to the Supreme Lord. In this way, they can gradually attain perfection, which is dependent upon knowledge and detachment.

PURPORT

Jñāna-yoga has been prescribed for those who have become detached from worldly enjoyment, and *karma-yoga* has been recommended for those who are attached to the fruits of their work, being driven by the spirit of enjoyment.

TEXT 8

यदृच्छया मत्कथादौ जातश्रद्धस्तु यः पुमान् ।
न निर्विण्णो नातिसक्तो भक्तियोगोऽस्य सिद्धिदः ॥८॥

yadṛcchayā mat-kathādau jāta-śraddhas tu yaḥ pumān
na nirviṇṇo nāti-sakto bhakti-yogo 'sya siddhi-daḥ

Somehow or other, if one develops faith in hearing and chanting My glories, by good fortune, being neither very disgusted with nor attached to material life, he should try to achieve perfection by following the path of loving devotion to Me.

COMMENTARY

The word *yadṛcchayā* has been explained in the First Canto of the *Śrīmad-Bhāgavatam.* One develops faith in discussions of the Supreme Lord by the association of advanced devotees. This is the main criterion for developing faith in the nectarean glories of the Lord. By continuously hearing discussions of the Lord's transcendental name, fame, qualities, and pastimes, a faithful person gradually advances on the path of devotional service to the Supreme Lord. Only a faithful person is qualified to engage in *bhakti-yoga.* This faith is the actual distinction between the devotees and the *karmīs* or *jñānīs.* The word *pumāna,* which is used here, is singular and thus stresses that a devotee is very rarely found. A devotee is not overly attached to his material body, wife, and household, nor is he excessively detached. Those who are thoroughly indifferent to material life are eligible for cultivating *jñāna*, and those who are thoroughly attached to the materialistic way of life are eligible for engaging in *karma.* Those who are neither overly attached nor detached are eligible for executing *bhakti.* This is the difference between those who are suitable candidates for the three processes—*karma*, *jñāna*, and *bhakti.*

In the Eleventh Canto of the *Śrīmad-Bhāgavatam* (11.2.2) this verse is spoken by Śrī Śukadeva Gosvāmī:

ko nu rājann indriyavān mukunda-caraṇāmbujam
na bhajet sarvato-mṛtyuru pāsyam amarottamaiḥ

My dear King, in the material world the conditioned souls are confronted by death at every step of life. Therefore, who among the conditioned souls would not render service to the lotus feet of Lord Mukunda, who is worshipable even for the greatest of liberated souls?

Every conditioned soul who has received the association of a pure devotee of the Lord can become qualified to engage in the devotional service of the Supreme Lord.

PURPORT

Those who are fond of cultivating materialistic knowledge generally are devoid of faith in the descriptions of the Supreme Lord's glories. Expert linguists who study various languages and dialects, such as *brāhmī*, *kharauṣṭi*, and *sānki*, are sometimes seen to be fully absorbed in materialistic life, and sometimes seen to exhibit symptoms of extreme detachment. Neither excessive attachment nor excessive detachment can give satisfaction to the soul and so when one's faith in these practices diminishes, he can develop faith in the narrations of the Supreme Lord's pastimes. When such faith becomes firm, one can understand that devotional service alone is the ultimate goal of life.

Some commentators distort the meaning of the verse and dare to say that devotional service is only meant for those who are incapable of practicing renunciation. They say that *karma* is recommended for those who are expert at performing activities aiming at material enjoyment, and *jñāna* is recommended for those who have the strength to renounce such material enjoyment. Such false arguments are of no value, however.

In conditional life, one is sometimes absorbed in excessive material attachment, and sometimes absorbed in trying to detach himself from material association. This is something like the movements of the planets, which sometimes move forward and sometimes move in a retrograde manner. In any case, such materialists and ascetics are unable to understand the transcendental nature of devotional service. The Supreme Lord and His eternal associates exist in a realm that is distinct from the auspicious and inauspicious situations of this material world. Only those who have fallen from engagement in the service of the Absolute Truth, the Supreme Personality of Godhead, become absorbed in such positive and negative mundane considerations and thus are indifferent to the path of genuine spiritual life. In this way, they cause their own ruination. Some such persons aspire to attain the heavenly planets, where greater facilities for sense gratification are found, and some desire to enter the darkest region of nescience by merging into the existence of Brahman. When the modes of passion and ignorance predominate so that the mode of goodness appears lost, one rejects the shelter of the Lord's lotus feet, thinking himself to be the lord of material nature.

One becomes spontaneously attracted to the devotional service of the Lord simply by the causeless mercy of the Supreme Lord, or His devotee. Persons who are bewildered by false ego and so are unable to place their faith in the words of the Supreme Lord and His devotees become covered by the lower modes of nature and thus take to a non-devotional path of either excessive attachment or extreme detachment.

TEXT 9

तावत्कर्माणिकुर्वीतननिर्विद्येतयावता ।
मत्कथाश्रवणादौवाश्रद्धायावन्नजायते ॥९॥

tāvat karmāṇi kurvīta na nirvidyeta yāvatā
mat-kathā-śravaṇādau vā śraddhā yāvan na jāyate

Until one develops detachment from fruitive activities, knowing them to be the source of all miseries, and as long as a taste for hearing and chanting My glories has not awakened, one must act according to the regulative principles prescribed by the Vedic literature.

COMMENTARY

Those who are overly attached to a materialistic way of life are naturally suited for following the path of fruitive activities, or *karma*. How long such persons will continue on this path, and what will prompt them to accept the paths of *jñāna* and *bhakti* is being described in this verse. One should continue to execute the Vedic injunctions with regards to the performance of one's occupational duties as long as one is not disgusted with the materialistic life. Gradually, by the performance of *karma-yoga*, one's heart will be cleansed of the desire to enjoy the fruit of one's labor. When detachment arises within the heart, one becomes eligible for accepting the path of *jñāna-yoga*.

In whatever condition of life one finds himself in, if one becomes spontaneously attracted to hearing about the Supreme Lord as a result of receiving the mercy of a pure devotee, he can accept the path of devotional service, knowing that all kinds of responsibilities and debts are liquidated, as promised by the Lord Himself. Such a person has firm faith that simply by hearing and chanting the glories of the Lord, the perfection of life can be achieved, and not by any other process. Such a firm conviction can be attained only by the association of pure devotees of the Lord. The *śruti* and *smṛti* consists of the orders of the Lord. Therefore, anyone who transgresses these orders must be considered to be envious of the Supreme Lord, even though he may claim to be a devotee. However, for the service of the Lord, a devotee may sometimes transgress the Vedic injunctions, and for this, there is no fault.

It is the opinion of some commentators that one who has not received the mercy of a pure devotee, and who has not developed firm faith in the discussions of the Lord's glories, can also engage in the devotional service of the Supreme Lord, giving up all engagement in fruitive activities, by following the example of another Vaiṣṇava. The injunctions of the scriptures ultimately guide one to the platform of devotional service to the Lord, transcending the rules and regulations governing *varṇāśrama-dharma.* It is for this reason that the Lord has ordered: Give up all varieties of religion and simply surrender unto Me. If someone thinks, "I am a pure devotee and so there is no need for Me to follow any of the rules and regulations of the scriptures," and thus does not observe the vow of Ekādaśī, offers yogurt and milk to the Lord in a copper pot, offers coconut water in a bell metal cup, or eats food that was not first offered to the Lord—he transgresses the Lord's orders propounded in the scriptures and thus commits offenses.

There are many unalloyed devotees who appear to perform fruitive activities by the request of materialistic persons. However, such activities are performed without any attachment and thus do not produce any fruitive result. The Supreme Lord has stated in the *Bhagavad-gītā* 17.28:

aśraddhayā hutaṁ dattaṁ tapas taptaṁ kṛtaṁ ca yat
asad ity ucyate pārtha na ca tat pretya no iha

Anything done as sacrifice, charity, or penance without faith in the Supreme, O son of Pṛthā, is impermanent. It is called ***asat*** and is useless, both in this life and the next.

PURPORT

Those who are determined to enjoy sense gratification at all costs are incapable of disassociating themselves from the desire to enjoy the fruit of their *karma.* Such persons generally show very little interest in hearing the topics of the Supreme Lord. After a great deal of material enjoyment, if one becomes disgusted and thus assumes a mood of indifference, and is fortunate enough to hear the topics of the Supreme Lord from a pure devotee, his desire for sense gratification can be curbed as they engage in the devotional service of the Lord. Without developing a spontaneous attraction for hearing the topics of the Supreme Lord, one's desire for enjoying the fruit of his activities, or liberation from such entanglement, can never diminish. The only means for becoming detached from all material desires is to develop the inclination for engagement in the service of the Supreme Lord.

TEXT 10

स्वधर्मस्थोयजन्यज्ञैरनाशीःकाम उद्धव ।
नयातिस्वर्गनरकौयद्यन्यन्नसमाचरेत् ॥१०॥

sva-dharma-stho yajan yajñair anāśīḥ-kāma uddhava
na yāti svarga-narakau yady anyan na samācaret

My dear Uddhava, one who executes his occupational duties and worships the Lord by the performance of sacrifice, while not desiring to enjoy the fruitive results, and who avoids forbidden activities, will not have to spend time in the heavenly or hellish planets.

COMMENTARY

Materialists who are attached to the fruits of their work attain either heaven or hell as a result of their fruitive activities. However, one who has no desire to enjoy the fruits of his *karma* while executing his occupational duties according to the Vedic injunctions, and does not engage in prohibited activities, will neither go to the heavenly planets to enjoy celestial sense gratification, nor go to hellish planets for punishment.

PURPORT

The living entities go to hell as a result of being under the control of material desires, which force them to engage in illicit activities. The thirst for performing pious activities, such as fire sacrifices, to enjoy the results, will carry the living entities to heaven. However, those who have no desire to enjoy the fruits of their *karma* will not enjoy heavenly life nor suffer hellish conditions.

TEXT 11

अस्मिँल्लोकेवर्तमानःस्वधर्मस्थोऽनघःशुचिः ।
ज्ञानंविशुद्धमाप्नोतिमद्भक्तिंवायदृच्छया ॥११॥

asmil̐ loke vartamānaḥ sva-dharma-stho 'naghaḥ śuciḥ
jñānaṁ viśuddham āpnoti mad-bhaktiṁ vā yadṛcchayā

Those who are fixed in their occupational duties, who have renounced sinful activities, and who have become detached from the desire to enjoy the fruit of their labor, even in this life attain transcendental knowledge, or if fortunate, devotional service unto Me.

COMMENTARY

One may question, "What do *karmīs* gain?" To answer this, Śrī Kṛṣṇa says, "As a consequence of performing activities without the desire to enjoy the result, one's heart becomes purified in this very lifetime, so that he can imbibe transcendental knowledge. If he somehow or other gets the association of a pure devotee, he can come to the platform of pure devotional service, which includes liberation from material existence. One who engages in devotional service mixed with *karma* or *jñāna* can attain the platform of *śānta-rati*, but not the higher relationships in love of God."

PURPORT

Those who are fortunate are not prone to engage in sinful activities, being in a state of purified consciousness. When one factually understands his relationship with the Supreme Lord, he becomes fixed in his constitutional position of eternally engaging in the service of the Lord.

TEXT 12

स्वर्गिणोऽप्येतमिच्छन्तिलोकंनिरयिणस्तथा ।
साधकंज्ञानभक्तिभ्यामुभयंतदसाधकम् ॥१२॥

svargiṇo 'py etam icchanti lokaṁ nirayiṇas tathā
sādhakaṁ jñāna-bhaktibhyām ubhayaṁ tad-asādhakam

The inhabitants of both the hellish and heavenly planets pray to be born in the human form of life on earth, which facilitates the cultivation of transcendental knowledge and devotional service, as opposed to hellish or heavenly existence, which does not provide such a facility.

COMMENTARY

In the next six verses, the Lord glorifies the human form of life, which can award one liberation, as well as loving devotional service. It is not possible for the inhabitants of hell and heaven to cultivate spiritual knowledge or execute devotional service because of their absorption in material pleasure and pain.

PURPORT

The conditioned souls become so much absorbed in the happiness of material enjoyment in heaven that they get no opportunity to learn anything about devotional service, which is the only way to achieve supreme auspiciousness. The conditioned souls also do not get any opportunity to perform devotional service in the hellish condition because of being put into excessive pains. That is why the demigods in the heaven and the suffering living entities in hell pray to receive the human form of life on the earth planet. One can awaken one's constitutional position only in the human form of life, and he can also realize the essential characteristics of devotional service, which is his constitutional propensity. There is no possibility of cultivating *sādhana bhakti* either in heaven or in hell. Therefore, the bodies of the inhabitants of heaven and hell make them unfit for the cultivation of devotional service.

TEXT 13

ननरःस्वर्गतिंकाङ्क्षेन्नारकींवाविचक्षणः ।
नेमंलोकंचकाङ्क्षेतदेहावेशात्प्रमाद्यति ॥१३॥

na naraḥ svar-gatiṁ kāṅkṣen nārakīṁ vā vicakṣaṇaḥ
nemaṁ lokaṁ ca kāṅkṣeta dehāveśāt pramādyati

One who is intelligent should not desire promotion to the heavenly planets, nor residence in hell. One should also never become complacent, being satisfied with his human existence, because by such absorption in the bodily conception of life, one fails to attain his own self-interest.

COMMENTARY

One who is actually wise, after receiving the rare human form of life, should not engage in either pious or sinful activities that will ultimately lead him to heavenly or hellish conditions of life. One should also not desire to remain comfortable on this earth. After all, if one is too attached to his material body, it will be very difficult for him to remain fixed in devotional service.

PURPORT

An intelligent devotee desires neither heavenly pleasure nor hellish suffering. Even though he may enact the pastime of possessing a gross and subtle body and travel to various planets, he is not contaminated by material desires.

TEXT 14

एतद्विद्वान्पुरामृत्योरभवायघटेतसः ।
अप्रमत्त इदंज्ञात्वामर्त्यमप्यर्थसिद्धिदम् ॥१४॥

etad vidvān purā mṛtyor abhavāya ghaṭeta saḥ
apramatta idaṁ jñātvā martyam apy artha-siddhi-dam

Although this human body can award one liberation from material existence, one should know that it is still subject to death. Therefore, one should sincerely endeavor for attaining the perfection of life before death arrives.

COMMENTARY

The human body is a great asset because it can award one the ultimate goal of life. Knowing this perfectly well, one who is learned should relentlessly try to liberate himself from material existence before the end of life. Although the human form of body can award one the ultimate perfection of life, it is perishable just like any other body.

PURPORT

Because the human form of body helps one attain the supreme destination, an intelligent person invites his own auspiciousness by renouncing the spirit of material enjoyment before reaching the end of life.

TEXT 15

छिद्यमानंयमैरेतैःकृतनीडंवनस्पतिम् ।
खगःस्वकेतमुत्सृज्यक्षेमंयातिह्यलम्पटः ॥१५॥

chidyamānaṁ yamair etaiḥ kṛta-nīḍaṁ vanaspatim
khagaḥ sva-ketam utsṛjya kṣemaṁ yāti hy alampaṭaḥ

It is seen that a bird sometimes is forced to leave the tree where it had made its nest when the tree is cut down by heartless men who thus resemble Yamarāja, the lord of death. Still, being unattached, the bird can find happiness somewhere else.

COMMENTARY

The Lord herein gives a practical example of how one can give up attachment for his material body. The bird may live happily in its nest but when it sees that the tree is being cut by some people who are as cruel as Yamarāja, it leaves the nest without remorse. In the same way, one should not become attached to the tree of the material body.

TEXT 16

अहोरात्रैश्छिद्यमानंबुद्ध्वायुर्भयवेपथुः ।
मुक्तसङ्गःपरंबुद्ध्वानिरीह उपशाम्यति ॥१६॥

aho-rātraiś chidyamānaṁ buddhvāyur bhaya-vepathuḥ
mukta-saṅgaḥ paraṁ buddhvā nirīha upaśāmyati

Realizing that one's duration of life is also being cut down by each passing day and night, one should become detached and very afraid of material existence. By endeavoring to realize the Supreme Personality of Godhead, one will achieve perfect peace.

COMMENTARY

Knowing that the days and nights are taking away his duration of life, a sober person acts in such a way that he ultimately obtains peace and eternal residence in the Lord's abode.

PURPORT

An intelligent devotee of the Lord realizes that his duration of life is decreasing with each passing of the day and night, and thus he acts for his own welfare by giving up attachment to the objects of the senses. Just as a bird may leave its nest and go to another tree, without attachment, a devotee can live anywhere, knowing that there is no permanent residence within the material world. Instead of working hard to improve his situation more comfortable within the temporary material existence, a devotee dedicates himself to going back home, back to Godhead, where life is eternal. It is only in the spiritual world, where there is no influence of the three modes of material nature, that one can attain everlasting peace.

TEXT 17

नृदेहमाद्यंसुलभंसुदुर्लभंप्लवंसुकल्पंगुरुकर्णधारम् ।
मयानुकूलेननभस्वतेरितंपुमान्भवाब्धिंनतरेत्स आत्महा ॥१७॥

nṛ-deham ādyaṁ su-labhaṁ su-durlabhaṁ
plavaṁ su-kalpaṁ guru-karṇadhāram
mayānukūlena nabhasvateritaṁ
pumān bhavābdhiṁ na taret sa ātma-hā

The human form of life, although very rarely achieved, is automatically awarded to the conditioned soul, by the laws of nature. The human body can be compared to a boat,

having the spiritual master as the expert helmsman, and My instructions as the favorable breezes. One who does not utilize his human birth for crossing over the ocean of material existence is certainly a killer of his own soul.

COMMENTARY

Alas! One who is unfortunate may unexpectedly receive a touchstone but then throw it away. This principle is being explained herein. This human form of body is like a touchstone that can fulfill all desires. Human life is obtained after going through many millions of births and deaths. Only out of good fortune does a living entity receive the human form of life. The human body is compared to a *plava*, or boat, and the spiritual master is the helmsman who can expertly take one across the ocean of material existence. The instructions of the all-merciful Supreme Personality of Godhead are compared to favorable breezes, and by accepting them, one can quickly cross to the other side of material existence. This principle is also applicable to the *jñānīs*.

PURPORT

The human form of body is the only vehicle for a living entity to attain the ultimate goal of life. After many births and deaths, one who is fortunate attains the human form of life. The spiritual master, who is expert in the cultivation of God consciousness, acts as the boatman to take one across the ocean of material existence. The favorable wind in the form of the Lord's mercy guides the boat of the human body as he traverses the path to perfection. One who does not know that his body is a boat, the spiritual master a boatman, and the Lord's instructions a favorable wind, certainly invites his own ruination by becoming the killer of his soul.

TEXT 18

यदारम्भेषुनिर्विण्णोविरक्तःसंयतेन्द्रियः ।
अभ्यासेनात्मनोयोगीधारयेदचलंमनः ॥१८॥

yadārambheṣu nirviṇṇo viraktaḥ saṁyatendriyaḥ
abhyāsenātmano yogī dhārayed acalaṁ manaḥ

When a yogi becomes disgusted and hopeless after many endeavors for material happiness and thus completely controls his senses and develops a mood of detachment, he should fix the mind in transcendence without deviation.

COMMENTARY

After glorifying the human form of body, which awards one's real self-interest, the Lord next describes the nature of a person who is qualified to cultivate *jñāna*, in this and the following verses. One naturally becomes full of anxiety as a result of experiencing the distress that is born of material activities. If he receives the good instructions of the Lord or His devotee, he can develop a mood of detachment.

PURPORT

The mind of a conditioned soul is always restless and eager to direct the senses toward their objects. When one develops detachment from material enjoyment, which simply awards various miseries, as a result of his own experience, he will naturally want to control his senses, so that his mind will gradually become peaceful. By cultivating Kṛṣṇa consciousness, one realizes his constitutional position and thus surpasses the platform of temporary material enjoyment as his heart becomes completely purified.

TEXT 19

धार्यमाणंमनोयर्हिभ्राम्यदश्वनवस्थितम् ।
अतन्द्रितोऽनुरोधेनमार्गेणात्मवशंनयेत् ॥१९॥

dhāryamāṇaṁ mano yarhi bhrāmyad aśv anavasthitam
atandrito 'nurodhena mārgeṇātma-vaśaṁ nayet

When one is endeavoring to free himself from material existence, the restless mind should always be brought back under control by adhering to one's prescribed path.

COMMENTARY

When one first tries to control his mind, it can be very difficult. Due to past bad habits, the mind may become twice as restless when one tries to restrict it from material enjoyment. The urge for material enjoyment is so strong that the mind easily becomes carried away by such thoughts. In such a situation, one should control the mind by allowing it to have a little gratification in a way that is not contrary to religious principles.

PURPORT

Because the conditioned soul has a natural tendency to enjoy sense gratification, it is inevitable that his mind will become restless when controlled. The best thing is to divert the functions of the mind from one's personal sense enjoyment to the service of the Supreme Personality of Godhead while following the regulative principles. In this way, if one cultivates Kṛṣṇa consciousness, his mind will automatically be controlled.

TEXT 20

मनोगतिंनविसृजेज्जितप्राणोजितेन्द्रियः ।
सत्त्वसम्पन्नयाबुद्धयामन आत्मवशंनयेत् ॥२०॥

mano-gatiṁ na visṛjej jita-prāṇo jitendriyaḥ
sattva-sampannayā buddhyā mana ātma-vaśaṁ nayet

One should never allow the mind to go outside the quest for spiritual advancement. One should control the mind by engaging the senses and life-air in activities of goodness, as directed by one's good intelligence.

COMMENTARY

Although the tendency of the mind is to wander here and there, one must always bring it back to the practice of self-realization by means of one's steady intelligence. If the mind is always engaged in the activities of Kṛṣṇa consciousness, it will be restrained from thoughts of sense gratificiation. The mind is naturally attached to the objects of the senses, so unless one is careful to control the mind, advancement on the path of self-realization will be hampered.

PURPORT

Even after temporarily controlling the urges of the mind, those whose senses are not under control can easily fall down from the path of self-realization. For this reason, the mind and senses should always be engaged in the service of the all-auspicious Supreme Lord. When one comes to the platform of self-realization, the restless mind will no longer create obstacles but help one. The mind is material, and so it always hankers after the objects of the senses, and is averse to the real self-interest of the spirit soul. There is no possibility of achieving self-realization without controlling the restless mind.

TEXT 21

एषवैपरमोयोगोमनसःसङ्ग्रहःस्मृतः ।
हृदयज्ञत्वमन्विच्छन्दम्यस्येवार्वतोमुहुः ॥२१॥

eṣa vai paramo yogo manasaḥ saṅgrahaḥ smṛtaḥ
hṛdaya-jñatvam anvicchan damyasyevārvato muhuḥ

One who is expert in training wild horses will first allow a horse some freedom. Then, by pulling the reins, he will gradually control the horse. Similarly, one cannot immediately bring the mind under complete control. It must be gradually trained so that it eventually sticks to the path of yoga.

COMMENTARY

Śrī Kṛṣṇa is herein citing the example of training a horse, to show how one must check the urges of the mind. One must sometimes fulfill the demands of the mind in order to control it completely. To control the mind is the main purpose of the yoga system. One who wants to control his senses should study this example given by Lord Kṛṣṇa. A horseman, although wanting to gain full control of the horse, will in the beginning let the horse have his way for a short while. Even while doing so, he continues to hold the rope and never allows it to run completely wild.

PURPORT

If the mind, which runs towards material enjoyment like a horse, comes to know that its goal is the Supreme Absolute Truth, its functions can be properly utilized. When the consideration of worshiping Lord Hari gradually awakens in the mind, it automatically becomes controlled. Simply by engaging the functions of the mind in the service of the eternal object, a living entity attains auspiciousness. Therefore, in order to control the mind, one should follow the path of *yukta-vairāgya*, rather than that of *phalgu-vairāgya*.

TEXT 22

सांख्येनसर्वभावानांप्रतिलोमानुलोमतः ।
भवाप्ययावनुध्यायेन्मनोयावत्प्रसीदति ॥२२॥

sāṅkhyena sarva-bhāvānāṁ pratilomānulomataḥ
bhavāpyayāv anudhyāyen mano yāvat prasīdati

Until one's mind is firmly fixed in the Absolute Truth, he should carefully observe the temporary nature of all material objects, from the *mahat-tattva*, down to the gross material body. One should observe the progressive functions of creation, and the regressive functions of annihilation.

COMMENTARY

Here it is being explained how one can fix up his flickering mind. While engaging in *sānkhya-yoga*, or the analytical study of the material world, one carefully considers the varieties of creation through progressive functions and annihilation through regressive functions, until the mind becomes detached.

PURPORT

One should very carefully study the processes of creation and destruction forever being carried out in the material world, so that the mind can become steady on the path of self-realization.

TEXT 23

निर्विण्णस्यविरक्तस्यपुरुषस्योक्तवेदिनः ।
मनस्त्यजतिदौरात्म्यंचिन्तितस्यानुचिन्तया ॥२३॥

nirviṇṇasya viraktasya puruṣasyokta-vedinaḥ
manas tyajati daurātmyaṁ cintitasyānucintayā

When one finally becomes disgusted with the temporary, illusory nature of this material world and thus achieves a state of detachment, his mind, being guided by the instructions of his spiritual master, gradually gives up his false identification with matter.

COMMENTARY

The phrase *ukta vedinaḥ* refers to those who take pleasure in discussing the instructions received from the spiritual master.

PURPORT

Human beings are beset with varieties of miseries when the propensity for material enjoyment is strong due to a lack of spiritual cultivation. When the mind is engaged in the cultivation of Kṛṣṇa consciousness, it protects one from becoming absorbed in the bodily conception of life. The renunciation of false pride due to identification with the material body certainly goes a long way to curb the restlessness of the mind. Thus, one should elevate one's thinking to the eternal platform by carefully receiving the instructions of the Lord's representative, the spiritual master.

TEXT 24

यमादिभिर्योगपथैरान्वीक्षिक्याचविद्यया ।
ममार्चोपासनाभिर्वानान्यैर्योग्यंस्मरेन्मनः ॥२४॥

yamādibhir yoga-pathair ānvīkṣikyā ca vidyayā
mamārcopāsanābhir vā nānyair yogyaṁ smaren manaḥ

The mind can be fixed on the Supreme Personality of Godhead by following the path of yoga, beginning with yama, **through logic and reasoning under the guidance of a spiritual master, or by worshiping Me and meditating upon Me. There are no other means than these.**

COMMENTARY

Through reasoning and argument, one should come to the correct conclusion and thus engage oneself in worshiping the Lord. The word *vā* indicates that one who is engaged in the worship of the Personality of Godhead need not trouble himself with the disciplinary procedures of *yoga*, nor with the grueling intricacies of Vedic studies and logic. This is the opinion of Śrīdhara Svāmī.

PURPORT

One should curb his thirst for enjoying the objects of the senses by observing sacred vows. One should give up the mentality that he is the enjoyer by worshiping the Deity of the Lord according to the prescribed rules and regulations, and meditate on the Supreme Lord without deviation. One's realization of his relationship with the Supreme Lord gradually becomes established by observing Ekādaśī and chanting the holy names of the Lord. When one is situated in his constitutional position as the servant of the Supreme Lord, his thirst for enjoying the fruits of his activities diminishes as his mind distances itself from thoughts of material enjoyment. Cultivating an inclination toward the service of the Supreme Lord is the only way to curb the restless mind. One should worship the Deity throughout the day so that his mind will always remain engaged in remembering the Lord.

TEXT 25

यदिकुर्यात्प्रमादेनयोगीकर्मविगर्हितम् ।
योगेनैवदहेदंहोनान्यत्तत्रकदाचन ॥२५॥

yadi kuryāt pramādena yogī karma vigarhitam
yogenaiva dahed aṁho nānyat tatra kadācana

If a yogi, due to carelessness, performs some abominable activity, he should nullify the sinful reaction simply by continuing his engagement in yoga. He need not undergo severe penance or adopt some other method to purify himself.

COMMENTARY

The question may arise that if one who is detached from material life, along with its prescribed duties, by chance commits a sinful act then how can he be freed from the reaction of sin without undergoing atonement, which is the prescription of the *karma-kāṇḍa* sections of the *Vedas*? The answer is given here that simply by continuing his practice of yoga, all sinful reactions will be burned to ashes. Śrīdhara Svāmī has said that for a devotee, all reactions of sinful activities can be nullified simply by hearing and chanting the holy names of the Supreme Lord. It is stated in the Sixth Canto of *Śrīmad-Bhāgavatam* (6.1.15):

kecit kevalayā bhaktyā vāsudeva-parāyaṇāḥ
aghaṁ dhunvanti kārtsnyena nīhāram iva bhāskaraḥ

Only a rare person who has adopted complete, unalloyed devotional service to Kṛṣṇa can uproot the weeds of sinful actions with no possibility that they will revive. He can do this simply by discharging devotional service, just as the sun can immediately dissipate fog by its rays.

Elsewhere in the *Śrīmad Bhāgavatam* (11.5.42) it is stated:

sva-pāda-mūlaṁ bhajataḥ priyasya tyaktānya bhāvasya hariḥ pareśaḥ
vikarma yac cotpatitaṁ kathañcid dhunoti sarvaṁ hṛdi sanniviṣṭaḥ

One who has thus given up all other engagements and has taken full shelter at the lotus feet of Hari, the Supreme Personality of Godhead, is very dear to the Lord. Indeed, if such a surrendered soul accidentally commits some sinful activity, the Supreme Personality of Godhead, who is seated within everyone's heart, immediately takes away the reaction to such sin.

The word yogi in this verse refers to both the *jñāna-yogī* and *bhakti-yogī.*

PURPORT

The activities of the conditioned souls are of two kinds—pious and sinful. If an honest person accidentally commits some sinful activities, the reactions to those sins can be counteracted simply by engaging in the service of the Supreme Lord. There is no need for a devotee of the Supreme Lord to undergo atonement as a separate endeavor.

TEXT 26

स्वेस्वेऽधिकारेयानिष्ठासगुणःपरिकीर्तितः ।
कर्मणांजात्यशुद्धानामनेननियमःकृतः ।
गुणदोषविधानेनसङ्गानांत्याजनेच्छया ॥२६॥

sve sve 'dhikāre yā niṣṭhā sa guṇaḥ parikīrtitaḥ
karmaṇāṁ jāty-aśuddhānām anena niyamaḥ kṛtaḥ
guṇa-doṣa-vidhānena saṅgānāṁ tyājanecchayā

For an aspiring transcendentalist, the sincere observance of his practice constitutes piety, and the neglect of his spiritual practices constitutes sin. With this understanding of good and evil, one should detach himself from activities of sense gratification by a sincere practice of his discipline.

COMMENTARY

How can a yogi be relieved of all sinful reactions simply by continuing his practice of yoga, with no necessity for performing any other atonement? In this verse Śrī Kṛṣṇa explains the actual standard of piety. A yogi who steadfastly executes his yoga practice while remaining aloof from the duties prescribed under the jurisdiction of *karma-kāṇḍa* is actually pious, and one who gives up such practice is actually sinful. It is widely declared in the scriptures that *jñāna* and *bhakti* are competent to destroy all kinds of sinful reactions, so that *jñānīs* and *bhaktas* are never required to undergo atonement as a separate endeavor. If one does so, he commits two faults—the fault of giving up his prescribed duty and the fault of adopting another's duty. Actually, all classes of transcendentalists, and especially devotees, are devoid of the propensity to commit sinful activities. Even if by chance they do so, the powerful purifying effects of their respective processes destroy their sinful reactions without difficulty. It is the verdict of the Vedic literature that one is prohibited to see the apparent faults of one who is continuously engaged in the devotional service of the Lord, even if he accidentally commits sinful activities. A devotee is situated in the transcendental position and so he does not possess material qualities, nor is he subjected to considerations of material sins or piety. Because *jñānīs* are supposed to be firmly situated in the mode of goodness, they also are considered to be beyond the influence of the baser qualities of passion and ignorance. On the other hand, *karmīs* are by nature impure so that the *karma-*

kāṇḍa sections of the *Vedas* prescribe rules and regulations for their guidance and purification. Fruitive workers are attached to their homes and material bodies and thus have performed countless sinful activities, beginning from their birth. For this reason, the *Vedas* instruct fruitive workers to continue acting with material attachment, but in a way that will gradually elevate them to the mode of goodness. This will be more elaborately described in the next chapter.

PURPORT

The living entity must execute his duties according to his position under the three modes of material nature. When one engages in a occupation other than that which is prescribed for him, this creates a discrepancy. The performance of prescribed duties and the avoidance of forbidden acts enables attached materialists to gradually become detached from the spirit of enjoying the fruit of their labor. As soon as one performs forbidden, or sinful, acts distressful conditions are created. Just to free the conditioned soul from his distressful condition of life, the scriptures prescribe rules and regulations to guide his behavior.

As long as one fails to awaken his loving devotional service to the Supreme Lord, he will continue to desire the four objectives of human life, placing him under the control of the Vedic rules and regulations. When one is fully engaged in a process of transcendental realization, however, the mundane conceptions of good and bad no longer apply.

TEXTS 27-28

जातश्रद्धोमत्कथासुनिर्विण्णःसर्वकर्मसु ।
वेददुःखात्मकान्कामानरित्यागेऽप्यनीश्वरः ॥२७॥
ततोभजेतमांप्रीतःश्रद्धालुर्दृढनिश्चयः ।
जुषमाणश्चतान्कामान्दुःखोदर्कांश्चगर्हयन् ॥२८॥

jāta-śraddho mat-kathāsu nirviṇṇaḥ sarva-karmasu
veda duḥkhātmakān kāmān parityāge 'py anīśvaraḥ

tato bhajeta māṁ prītaḥ śraddhālur dṛḍha-niścayaḥ
juṣamāṇaś ca tān kāmān duḥkhodarkāṁś ca garhayan

Having awakened his faith in the narrations of My glories, understanding the futility of all material activities, and knowing that sense gratification ultimately leads to misery, but still being unable to renounce all kinds of sensual diversions, My devotee should remain satisfied and worship Me with great faith and conviction. Even though he is

sometimes engaged in material enjoyment, My devotee knows that such activity simply leads to a miserable result, and so he sincerely repents such activities.

COMMENTARY

Here, the Lord describes the primary characteristic of devotional service. A devotee naturally becomes indifferent to worldly activities and Vedic prescriptions because he knows that these will ultimately award him distress. He knows that material desires are sources of all miseries. If a devotee, despite understanding this, is unable to completely renounce activities of sense gratification, he should still engage in the service of the Supreme Lord with firm determination. He should not become depressed, thinking that his devotional service is inadequate. A devotee thinks, "Even if I meet with so many impediments and even though I am full of offenses, I will never for a moment give up the service of the Lord. Fruitive activities and mental speculation are useless, and so I will never accept these as my paths. I am still very attached to the objects of this world, and I know that this will only bring me misery. I must go on in this way, and simply hope for that day when the Lord will become merciful towards me." Even if, due to material sentiment, a devotee associates with his wife and children and thus indulges in sense gratification, he thinks, "Alas! This material enjoyment creates many *anarthas* because it is opposed to my advancement in the Lord's devotional service. Although I had promised many times to give up this material enjoyment, I still indulge in sense gratification from time to time."

PURPORT

By hearing discussions of the Supreme Lord's glories, one is liberated from the desire to enjoy the fruits of *karma*. Only those who are faithfully engaged in hearing and chanting the holy names of the Supreme Lord can understand that desires for material enjoyment are the causes of distress. When, even after trying to give up such distressful activities, devotees fail to completely do so, they should faithfully go on serving the Supreme Lord with determination. Devotees condemn the miserable condition that arises from material activities and while trying to give up such bad association, they engage in the service of the Supreme Lord with determination. There is actually nothing inauspicious in the devotional service of the Lord. Occasional difficulties experienced by a devotee are due to his previous material activities. On the other hand, the endeavor for sense gratification is completely inauspicious. Thus sense gratification and devotional service are directly opposed to each other. In all circumstances one should therefore remain the Lord's sincere servant, always believing in His mercy. Then one will certainly go back home, back to Godhead.

TEXT 29

प्रोक्तेनभक्तियोगेनभजतोमासकृन्मुनेः ।
कामाहृदय्यानश्यन्तिसर्वेमयिहृदिस्थिते ॥२९॥

proktena bhakti-yogena bhajato māsakṛn muneḥ
kāmā hṛdayyā naśyanti sarve mayi hṛdi sthite

When one constantly engages in My service as described by Me, his heart becomes firmly fixed in Me so that all material desires that may have been present in his heart are vanquished without separate endeavor.

COMMENTARY

One may question: "Do not the devotees of the Lord suffer material miseries just like other people?" The answer is given in this verse—definitely not. The material desires that are present within the heart of a devotee are gradually destroyed as they go on faithfully hearing the glories of the Lord and engaging in His devotional service. A devotee of the Lord situates Śrī Kṛṣṇa on a beautiful throne within his heart and there offers the Lord constant service. Just as the rising sun gradually eliminates all traces of darkness, the Lord's presence within the heart causes all material desires there to weaken and eventually disappear.

PURPORT

The senses are continuously engaged according to the proclivities of the mind, so that material desires enter the mind, one after another. Those who are devotees twenty-four hours a day engaged in the service of the Lord by hearing and chanting His glories with transcendental faith will find that such material desires gradually diminish. Instead of trying to enjoy independently, the devotees are convinced that the Lord is the supreme enjoyer and all others are meant to partake in His enjoyment.

TEXT 30

भिद्यतेहृदयग्रन्थिश्छिद्यन्तेसर्वसंशयाः ।
क्षीयन्तेचास्यकर्माणिमयिदृष्टेऽखिलात्मनि ॥३०॥

bhidyate hṛdaya-granthiś chidyante sarva-saṁśayāḥ
kṣīyante cāsya karmāṇi mayi dṛṣṭe 'khilātmani

The knot in the heart is cut asunder, all misgivings are slashed to pieces, and the chain of action and reaction is stopped when I am understood to be the Supreme Personality of Godhead.

COMMENTARY

The knot created when one's heart is bound to illusion by false identification with the material body is cut to pieces when one attains the stages of *niṣṭhā* or *ruci*, without separate endeavor. Engagement in devotional service quickly eliminates all material desires within the heart, just as fire in the stomach digests all that we eat. The word *karmāṇī* in this verse refers to sinful reactions that have not yet fructified. In this regard, the *Gopāla-tāpanī Upaniṣad* (Pūrva 15) states, *bhaktir asya bhajanaṁ tad ihāmutropādhi-nairāsyenāmuṣmin manaḥ-kalpanam, etad eva naiṣkarmyam*, "*Bhakti* means devotional service to the Lord that is free from desire for material profit, either in this life or in the next. Being devoid of such inclinations, one should fully absorb the mind in the Supreme Lord. This is the actual purpose of *naiṣkarmya*."

PURPORT

When one understands the Supreme Absolute Truth to be the ultimate shelter of everyone, one's desire for enjoying the fruits of *karma* will gradually diminish. By full engagement in the devotional service of the Supreme Lord, the knot of false ego within the heart is destroyed and all doubts are removed. The Supreme Lord is the shelter of all kinds of *rasa*. Indeed, He is the personification of all transcendental mellows. By remaining satisfied by the pleasure of engaging in devotional service, one can give up the desire for mundane enjoyment and mental speculation.

TEXT 31

तस्मान्मद्भक्तियुक्तस्ययोगिनोवैमदात्मनः ।
नज्ञानंनचवैराग्यंप्रायःश्रेयोभवेदिह ॥३१॥

tasmān mad-bhakti-yuktasya yogino vai mad-ātmanaḥ
na jñānaṁ na ca vairāgyaṁ prāyaḥ śreyo bhaved iha

For one who has fixed his mind upon Me, being constantly engaged in My devotional service, mere renunciation and the cultivation of knowledge are not considered means for attaining perfection.

COMMENTARY

Devotional service has the potency to destroy the knots of false ego within the heart without one's taking help from any other process. Therefore, the devotees of the Lord are not interested in cultivating knowledge or practicing renunciation outside the purview of devotional service. Devotional service is the only all-auspicious path, whereas the cultivation of knowledge and dry renunciation are of no value without connection to devotional service. By chanting and hearing the glories of the Lord, a devotee automatically realizes all knowledge, and as the devotee's attachment to the Lord increases, he automatically gives up attachment for the inferior material nature. Knowledge and renunciation are products of the mode of goodness, whereas devotional service is transcendental to the three modes of material nature. If one engages in devotional service, then it is a fault to separately cultivate knowledge and practice renunciation. Just as attachment and envy are byproducts of ignorance, knowledge and renunciation are naturally attained for one who is engaged in devotional service. Because knowledge of the Absolute Truth and renunciation of material enjoyment are concomitant factors of devotional service, devotees become knowledgeable and detached without separate endeavor. This is confirmed elsewhere in the *Śrīmad-Bhāgavatam* (11.2.42):

bhaktiḥ pareśānubhavo viraktir anyatra caiṣa trika eka-kālaḥ
prapadyamānasya yathāśnataḥ syus tuṣṭiḥ puṣṭiḥ kṣud-apāyo 'nu-ghāsam

Devotion, direct experience of the Supreme Lord, and detachment from other things—these three occur simultaneously for one who has taken shelter of the Supreme Personality of Godhead, in the same way that pleasure, nourishment and relief from hunger come simultaneously and increasingly, with each bite, for a person engaged in eating.

By the use of the word *prāyaḥ* (generally) in this verse, it appears that in some cases, in the primary state of *sānta bhakti*, it is not inauspicious to accept the processes of cultivation of knowledge and renunciation. Still, devotional service ensures liberation without any impediment. This is the opinion of *Bhakti-rasāmṛta-sindhu.*

PURPORT

One can never achieve real benefit simply by the cultivation of knowledge while remaining indifferent to the service of the Supreme Lord. When one is fully devoted to the Supreme Lord, he is on the platform of complete auspiciousness. There is no possibility for attaining factual benefit as long as the impersonal conception of the

Absolute Truth remains prominent. Simply by the execution of pure devotional service, genuine knowledge and proper renunciation are obtained. The constitutional duty of the spirit soul is to engage in the devotional service of the Supreme Lord. Transcendental knowledge and factual renunciation are fully manifest in those who are continuously engaged in the service of the Lord.

TEXTS 32-33

यत्कर्मभिर्यत्तपसाज्ञानवैराग्यतश्चयत् ।
योगेनदानधर्मेणश्रेयोभिरितरैरपि ॥३२॥
सर्वंमद्भक्तियोगेनमद्भक्तोलभतेऽञ्जसा ।
स्वर्गापवर्गंमद्धामकथञ्चिद्यदिवाञ्छति ॥३३॥

yat karmabhir yat tapasā jñāna-vairāgyataś ca yat
yogena dāna-dharmeṇa śreyobhir itarair api

sarvaṁ mad-bhakti-yogena mad-bhakto labhate 'ñjasā
svargāpavargaṁ mad-dhāma kathañcid yadi vāñchati

Whatever can be attained by other process of elevation that are recommended in the scriptures can be easily achieved by My devotees. If My devotee desires liberation from material existence or residence in the heavenly planets, he achieves these without difficulty.

COMMENTARY

A question may be raised: "If a devotee who is faithfully engaged in the Lord's devotional service and thus has no interest in performing *karma* or *jñāna*, and yet desires to go to heaven or attain liberation from material existence, what will he achieve?" The reply is given in these two verses. By following other auspicious paths, such as traveling to holy places of pilgrimage, one can attain *sālokya mukti*, or residence in the eternal abode of the Supreme Lord. Whatever can be gained by the various paths of perfection is easily achieved by the devotees by means of their execution of devotional service. If a devotee so desires, he can easily attain worldly happiness, purification of the heart, liberation, and even residence in the abode of the Supreme Lord, on the strength of his devotional service.

PURPORT

Whatever can be obtained as a result of performing fruitive activities, performing severe austerities, cultivating knowledge, renunciation of the objects of the senses, giving in charity, performing pious activities, and controlling the senses, are effortlessly obtained by the devotees of the Supreme Lord due to the strength of their devotional service. The devotees of the Lord can easily attain the heavenly planets, relief from material distress, the five kinds of liberation, such as *sārṣṭi*, and residence in Vaikuṇṭha.

TEXT 34

नकिञ्चित्साधवोधीराभक्ताह्येकान्तिनोमम ।
वाञ्छन्त्यपिमयादत्तंकैवल्यमपुनर्भवम् ॥३४॥

na kiñcit sādhavo dhīrā bhaktā hy ekāntino mama
vāñchanty api mayā dattaṁ kaivalyam apunar-bhavam

Even if I offer liberation from the vicious cycle of repeated birth and death to those pure devotees who are very sober, they do not accept it.

COMMENTARY

Here, the word *kathañcit* (somehow or other) of the previous verse is being explained.

PURPORT

In this verse, the words *ekāntino mama* indicate that those who are pure devotees of the Lord are cent percent engaged in the devotional service of the Lord with no separate interest. Even if the Lord offers liberation to such devotees, they do not accept it. The pure devotee is assured of going back home, back to Godhead, to reside with the Lord eternally, and so for him, mere liberation without devotional service is not at all appealing. One who engages in the devotional service of the Lord while maintaining a desire for liberation or heavenly enjoyment cannot be considered a pure devotee. The constitutional position of the living entity is that he is the eternal servant of the Lord, and that is being described herein.

TEXT 35

नैरपेक्ष्यंपरंप्राहुर्निःश्रेयसमनल्पकम् ।
तस्मान्निराशिषोभक्तिर्निरपेक्षस्यमेभवेत् ॥३५॥

nairapekṣyaṁ paraṁ prāhur niḥśreyasam analpakam
tasmān nirāśiṣo bhaktir nirapekṣasya me bhavet

The perfection of liberation is achieved when one is completely detached from matter. A devotee who has no personal ambition is eligible for engaging in My loving devotional service.

COMMENTARY

The word *nairapekṣyaṁ* means "not desiring any other process of perfection and its results." The word *nirāśiṣa* means "one who does not seek personal gain." The word *nirapekṣa* also means "to remain aloof from anything not related to Kṛṣṇa."

PURPORT

Those who are completely devoid of desires for personal sense enjoyment are the devotees of the Lord, and not those who take no interest in the Lord's devotional service, such as the impersonalists. Only those fortunate souls who have no material desires are able to achieve the platform of unalloyed devotional service to the Supreme Lord. Undoubtedly, in this age of Kali, people are generally very fallen and polluted by material lust, greed, anger, lamentation, and so forth. In this age, most people are *sarva-kāma*, or full of material desires. Still, we must understand that simply by taking shelter of Lord Kṛṣṇa we will achieve everything in life. The living entity should not engage in any process except the loving service of the Lord.

TEXT 36

नमय्येकान्तभक्तानांगुणदोषोद्भवागुणाः ।
साधूनांसमचित्तानांबुद्धेःपरमुपेयुषाम् ॥३६॥

na mayy ekānta-bhaktānāṁ guṇa-doṣodbhavā guṇāḥ
sādhūnāṁ sama-cittānāṁ buddheḥ param upeyuṣām

My unalloyed devotees, who are without material attachment, who treat all living entities equally, and who have attained Me, who am beyond the reach of material intelligence, are not subject to material piety and impiety, which arise from the good and evil of this world.

COMMENTARY

It was previously said that the mentality of finding faults and good qualities is itself faulty, and to rise above such a mentality is praiseworthy. This principle is being explained in this verse.

Unalloyed devotees of the Lord are not subject to the influence of the modes of goodness, passion, and ignorance, which give birth to all good qualities and faults. The pure devotees possess transcendental qualities. Because their intelligence is purified, they only aspire to attain the shelter of the Supreme Personality of Godhead, who is eternal, full of knowledge, and full of bliss. It will be explained later on that the mind and senses of the devotees of the Lord are fully transcendental and so devotees are not under the jurisdiction of Vedic rules and regulations. Devotees do not acquire piety by their proper conduct, nor do they incur sin by indulging in prohibited activities. While narrating the story of King Citraketu, Lord Mahādeva described the devotees' equal vision in this verse (*Śrīmad-Bhāgavatam* 6.17.28):

nārāyaṇa-parāḥ sarve na kutaścana bibhyati
svargāpavarga-narakeṣv api tulyārtha-darśinaḥ

Devotees solely engaged in the devotional service of the Supreme Personality of Godhead, Nārāyaṇa, never fear any condition of life. For them the heavenly planets, liberation and the hellish planets are all the same, for such devotees are interested only in the service of the Lord.

One should not see a devotees' intense desire to attain the lotus feet of the Supreme Lord as mundane, or as a fault. Even if some sinful activities are seen in the life of devotee, one should not see this as a fault. This has been ordered by the Supreme Lord Himself in the *Bhagavad-gītā* (9.30):

api cet su-durācāro bhajate mām ananya-bhāk
sādhur eva sa mantavyaḥ samyag vyavasito hi saḥ

Even if one commits the most abominable action, if he is engaged in devotional service, he is to be considered saintly because he is properly situated in his determination.

PURPORT

One should not find faults or discrepancies in the character of an unalloyed devotee of the Supreme Lord. The devotees of the Lord are equal to everyone and are to be considered saintly. Because they are engaged in the service of the *sac-cid-ānanda* Lord, who is situated beyond the reach of material intelligence, they are not subject to the piety and impiety that are born from the good and evil of this world. Worldly conceptions create illusion and distinctions in the minds of the living entities, and place them in the position of enjoyers. On the other hand, pure devotees who are fully engaged in the Lord's devotional service are not confined to desires for material enjoyment.

TEXT 37

एवमेतान्मयादिष्टाननुतिष्ठन्तिमेपथः ।
क्षेमंविन्दन्तिमत्स्थानंयद्ब्रह्मपरमंविदुः ॥३७॥

evam etān mayā diṣṭān anutiṣṭhanti me pathaḥ
kṣemaṁ vindanti mat-sthānaṁ yad brahma paramaṁ viduḥ

Those who follow the path of devotional service as instructed by Me attain freedom from illusion, and upon reaching My personal abode, they perfectly understand the Absolute Truth.

COMMENTARY

The Lord is herein concluding His discussion of the path of auspiciousness. Those who travel on this path that is instructed by the Lord actually achieve ultimate benefit. The devotees of the Lord reach the abode of the Lord, Vaikuṇṭha, whereas the *jñānīs* become merged in Brahman.

PURPORT

Unrestricted sense gratification, performance of fruitive activities, and engagement in mental speculation cannot be the ultimate religion for the living entities. Because these practices are born from aversion to the Lord's service, they are temporary and incomplete. The devotees who follow the instructions of the Supreme Lord become liberated from the clutches of all inauspiciousness by accepting the path of devotional service. Such devotees obtain the ultimate benefit of transferring themselves to the abode of the Supreme Lord, Vaikuṇṭha.

Thus end the translation of the Fourteenth Chapter of the Uddhava-gītā *entitled* **"Pure Devotional Service Surpasses Knowledge and Detachment"** *with the commentaries of Śrīla Viśvanātha Cakravartī Ṭhākura and chapter summary and purports by Śrīla Bhaktisiddhānta Sarasvatī Ṭhākura.*

Chapter 15

Explanation of the Vedic Path

CHAPTER SUMMARY

Some people are unfit for practicing any of the three forms of yoga—*karma*, *jñāna*, and *bhakti*. Such persons are inimical to Lord Kṛṣṇa, attached to sense gratification, and are only interested in performing fruitive activities so that they can fulfill their material desires. This chapter describes their faults in terms of place, time, substance, and beneficiary of actions.

Those who are perfect in knowledge and devotion to the Lord have no material good qualities or faults. However, for one who is acting on the platform of *karma* in the hopes of transcending material existence, the execution of his prescribed duties is good, and the failure to do so is evil. Those activities that counteract sinful reactions are also considered to be good.

When one is endeavoring to remain fixed in the mode of goodness, the cultivation of knowledge is always helpful. When one is engaged in the devotional service of the Lord, the nine practices, beginning with hearing and chanting, are most beneficial. Everything that is detrimental to one's advancement in spiritual life should be avoided. However, for those who are simply interested in engaging in fruitive work with the aim of gratifying the senses, there are innumerable considerations of what is good and what is pious and what is sinful, what is purifying and what is contaminating. All of these must be carefully considered in terms of time, place, circumstances, and the performer of the work.

Factually, virtue and fault are not absolute, but are relative to one's particular platform of advancement. Remaining fixed in the discrimination that is suitable to one's level of advancement is good, and anything contrary to that is bad. This is the basic understanding of virtue and fault. Even among objects belonging to the same category, there are different considerations of their purity or impurity in relation to performance of religious duties, worldly transactions, and the maintenance of one's life. These distinctions are described in various scriptures.

In the *varṇāśrama* society, there are very clear injunctions designating what is pure and what is contaminating. With regards to place, it is said that the presence of black deer is auspicious. Actions must be performed after considering the time as well. Purity and impurity with regards to substances is exemplified by bathing, giving in charity, and performing austerities. The mind can always be purified by remembering the Supreme Lord. There are also distinctions of purity and impurity regarding the performers of activities. When a mantra is received from the lips of a bona fide spiritual master, it is considered pure, and all work, as well as all objects, are considered purified by being offered to the Supreme Lord. For the execution of religious principles, these six factors must be considered in terms of purity and impurity.

Ultimately, there is no fixed standard by which to make distinctions of virtue and fault, because they transform according to the place, time, beneficiary, and so on. In regard to the execution of prescribed duties for sense gratification, the actual intent of all the scriptures is the subduing of materialistic propensities. This is the actual principle of religion because only this destroys sorrow, confusion, and fear, and bestows all good fortune. Work performed for sense gratification is not actually beneficial. The descriptions of such fruitive benefits described in the sections of the Vedic literature known as *phala-śruti* are actually meant to help one gradually cultivate a taste for the highest benefit. Unfortunately, those possessing inferior intelligence take the flowery benedictory verses of the scriptures to be the actual purport of the *Vedas*. However, this opinion is never upheld by those who factually know the truth of the *Vedas*. Those whose minds are agitated by the flowery words of the *Vedas* have no attraction for hearing discussions of Lord Hari. It should be understood that there is no inner purport to the *Vedas* apart from the original Personality of Godhead. The *Vedas* focus exclusively upon the Supreme Absolute Truth, the Personality of Godhead. Because this material world is simply the illusory energy of the Supreme Lord, the Vedic literature always recommends that one become aloof from material association by becoming attached to the Absolute Truth.

TEXT 1

श्रीभगवानुवाच
य एतान्मत्पथोहित्वाभक्तिज्ञानक्रियात्मकान् ।
क्षुद्रान्कामांश्चलैःप्राणैर्जुषन्तःसंसरन्तिते ॥१॥

śrī-bhagavān uvāca
Ya etān mat-patho hitvā bhakti-jñāna-kriyātmakān
kṣudrān kāmāṁś calaiḥ prāṇair juṣantaḥ saṁsaranti te

The Supreme Lord said: Those who will not follow the paths of devotional service, speculative knowledge, and fruitive activities, as prescribed by Me, and simply work to fulfill their insignificant material desires, will certainly continue in the cycle of repeated birth and death.

COMMENTARY

Here, Lord Kṛṣṇa condemns those who simply work hard for achieving sense gratification without any care for spiritual advancement. Devotional service places one directly under the shelter of the Supreme Personality of Godhead, whereas the cultivation of speculative knowledge leads one to the impersonal Brahman conception of the Absolute Truth. By executing one's duties without attachment to the results, one also becomes detached from fruitive desires. In contrast, those who work hard in the hopes of ruling a kingdom or enjoying celestial delights will certainly continue on the path of material existence.

PURPORT

Those who renounce the paths of performing fruitive activities without attachment, cultivating transcendental knowledge, and devotional service, are certainly uncontrolled and thus take pleasure in gratifying their insignificant desires for sense gratification. Unalloyed devotional service is certainly superior to devotional service mixed with *karma* and devotional service mixed with *jñāna*. Where there is no tinge of devotional service, there is only desire for sense gratification or the desire for renouncing sense gratification. Those whose aim is either material enjoyment or impersonal liberation cannot gain ultimate freedom from the cycle of repeated birth and death.

TEXT 2

स्वेस्वेऽधिकारेयानिष्ठासगुणःपरिकीर्तितः ।
विपर्ययस्तुदोषःस्यादुभयोरेषनिश्चयः ॥२॥

sve sve 'dhikāre yā niṣṭhā sa guṇaḥ parikīrtitaḥ
viparyayas tu doṣaḥ syād ubhayor eṣa niścayaḥ

To remain fixed in one's position is known as piety, or a good quality, and to deviate from one's position is known as impiety, or a fault. This is how piety and impiety should be ascertained.

COMMENTARY

Śrī Uddhava said, "My dear Lord, I had asked You how one can determine good qualities and faults. You had replied by saying that to find fault with Your devotee was itself a fault. But, what if a devotee appears to be faithfully engaged in Your service but somehow or other comes under the influence of *karmīs* or *jñānīs*, and thus deviates from his engagement in pure *bhakti*? Is it a mistake to find fault in such a devotee? What about a person who is a neophyte in spiritual life but after coming in contact with a pure devotee, decides to imitate such an exalted soul? If one prematurely gives up his occupational duties, thinking that he is situated on the liberated platform, although he is still in the bodily conception of life—isn't that also to be considered as faulty?"

In reply to this inquiry of Uddhava, the Lord said, "The characteristics of faults and piety can be understood in this way. To remain fixed in one's natural position is always to be considered a good quality. Occasionally, a neophyte devotee may become polluted by the association of those engaged in fruitive activities and mental speculation, so that he becomes affected by mundane tendencies. Similarly, an ordinary person who observes the exalted status of a pure devotee sometimes externally imitates his activities, considering himself to be on the same exalted platform of pure devotional service. These imperfect practitioners of *bhakti-yoga* are not exempt from criticism because their fruitive activities, mental speculation and false prestige are material intrusions in the pure loving service of the Lord. A pure devotee engaged exclusively in the Lord's service should not be criticized, but a devotee whose devotional service is mixed with material qualities may be corrected so that he can rise to the platform of pure devotional service."

PURPORT

One's faithfulness to his particular status is to be considered one's good quality. If, due to restlessness, one tries to imitate the position of another, that is to be understood as a fault. Different processes of self-realization exist because of people are at various stages of development. When one who is engaged in the devotional service of the Lord exhibits a spirit of enjoyment or a propensity for dry renunciation, his position is faulty. When one accepts a position that is favorable for his advancement in life that is to be considered a good quality, whereas when one accepts a position that is unfavorable for his advancement, that is a fault.

TEXT 3

शुद्ध्यशुद्धी विधीयेते समानेष्वपि वस्तुषु ।
द्रव्यस्य विचिकित्सार्थं गुणदोषौ शुभाशुभौ ।
धर्मार्थं व्यवहारार्थं यात्रार्थमिति चानघ ॥३॥

śuddhy-aśuddhī vidhīyete samāneṣv api vastuṣu
dravyasya vicikitsārthaṁ guṇa-doṣau śubhāśubhau
dharmārthaṁ vyavahārārthaṁ yātrārtham iti cānagha

O sinless Uddhava, to understand what is proper in life, one must evaluate everything, such as religious principles and considerations of economic development, in terms of its purity and impurity. Even in ordinary dealings, one must be able to distinguish between good and bad. As a matter of survival, one must be able to distinguish between that which is auspicious and that which is inauspicious.

COMMENTARY

Here, the Lord is further describing the necessity for considering qualities and faults. Uddhava has presented his doubt, and the Lord will remove it. Every doubt can be removed by good instruction, just as mosquitoes can be removed by smoke. Every material object has its good qualities or faults. For example, *bastaka* spinach is considered pure, whereas *kalami* spinach is considered impure. In this way, the faults and good qualities, or the piety and impiety, must be considered in all aspects of practical life. The same principle also applies to religion, as well as all kinds of ordinary dealings. Even though one who is well situated in terms of good behavior comes from a lower-class family, he should be considered a superior person, due to his possessing good qualities. There are also auspicious and inauspicious times to be considered while beginning a journey. Although accepting charity from an inappropriate person is a fault, in an emergency, or to save one's life, one may accept whatever is required.

PURPORT

Whether in ordinary dealing, religious practices, or basic survival, one cannot avoid making a distinction between good and bad. Religious principles must be followed for the upkeep of society and for this purpose, there must be a correct ascertainment of what is piety and what is sin, what is pure and what is impure. It is practically seen that everyone makes such distinctions with regards to food, residence, associates, and so on. Just to insure one's survival, one must distinguish between that which is healthy and that which is injurous, and that which will be profitable and that which will result in disaster. Thus it is to be concluded that even a wise man must distinguish between that which is favorable and that which is unfavorable in this material world, while at the same time understanding the transcendental position above the dualities of material existence.

TEXT 4

दर्शितोऽयंमयाचारोधर्ममुद्वहतांधुरम् ॥४॥

darśito 'yaṁ mayācāro dharmam udvahatāṁ dhuram

I have revealed these methods for making distinctions for those who bear the burden of maintaining mundane religious principles.

PURPORT

Materialistic persons, who are attached to enjoying the results of their activities, must constantly consider the purity and impurity, vice and virtue, and good qualities and faults of all their actions. Transcendentalists are not confined to such material conceptions, however. In this regard, one should discuss these two verses from the *Caitanya-caritāmṛta*:

kṛṣṇa-bhaktira bādhaka—yata śubhāśubha karma
seha eka jīvera ajñāna-tamo-dharma
'dvaite' bhadrābhadra-jñāna, saba-'manodharma'
'ei bhāla, ei manda'—saba 'bhrama'

All kinds of activities, both auspicious and inauspicious, that are detrimental to the discharge of transcendental loving service to Lord Śrī Kṛṣṇa are actions of the darkness of ignorance. (*Adi* 1.94)

In the material world, conceptions of good and bad are all mental speculations. Therefore, saying, 'This is good and this is bad,' is all a mistake. (*Antya* 4.176)

TEXT 5

भूम्यम्ब्वग्न्यनिलाकाशाभूतानांपञ्चधातवः ।
आब्रह्मस्थावरादीनांशारीरा आत्मसंयुताः ॥५॥

bhūmy-ambv-agny-anilākāśā bhūtānāṁ pañca-dhātavaḥ
ā-brahma-sthāvarādīnāṁ śārīrā ātma-saṁyutāḥ

Earth, water, fire, air and ether are the five gross elements emanating from the Supreme Lord that make up the bodies of all conditioned souls from Lord Brahmā down to the most insignificant blade of grass.

COMMENTARY

The varieties of good qualities and faults are understood from the authority of the Vedic literature. The Vedic literature makes such distinctions to help the conditioned souls on their gradual march towards progress in spiritual life. Earth, water, fire, air, and sky are the five material elements. These are the primary ingredients of the gross material bodies of all living entities, up to the standard of Brahmā.

TEXT 6

वेदेननामरूपाणिविषमाणिसमेष्वपि ।
धातुषूद्धवकल्प्यन्त एतेषांस्वार्थसिद्धये ॥६॥

vedena nāma-rūpāṇi viṣamāṇi sameṣv api
dhātuṣūddhava kalpyanta eteṣāṁ svārtha-siddhaye

My dear Uddhava, although all material bodies are constituted of these same five elements, different names are given so that one can distinguish between them and thus advance toward life's ultimate goal.

COMMENTARY

Although the bodies of all conditioned souls are made of the same five gross material elements, they are designated by various names and forms. The Vedic literature takes into account such varieties and classifies human society in terms of *varṇa* and *āśrama.* Thus, someone is a *brāhmaṇa*, someone else is a *brahmacārī*, another person is a betel nut merchant, and still another is an oil merchant. One may question, "What is the need for such diversity?" The answer is that the Vedic system is designed by the Lord so that conditioned souls may pursue their individual achievements and at the same time advance toward the ultimate goal of life, Kṛṣṇa consciousness.

TEXT 7

देशकालादिभावानांवस्तूनांममसत्तम ।
गुणदोषौविधीयेतेनियमार्थंहिकर्मणाम् ॥७॥

deśa-kālādi-bhāvānāṁ vastūnāṁ mama sattama
guṇa-doṣau vidhīyete niyamārthaṁ hi karmaṇām

O foremost of devotees, in order to regulate the activities of the living entities, I have imparted the understanding of that which is good and that which is bad in relation to time, place, and objects.

COMMENTARY

In the previous verse, the Lord explained why the Vedic literature assigns different positions to the various bodies of the living entities. In this verse, the Lord explains the Vedic evaluation regarding the entities that interact with the various classes of material bodies. The purpose of the Vedic literature is to restrict the sinful propensities of human beings by establishing proper behavior for all classes of men and defining what is improper with regards to time, place, and the objects of this world.

PURPORT

A conditioned soul falsely identifies with the gross body and thus considers anything that gives immediate satisfaction to the body to be good and anything inconvenient or disturbing for the body to be bad. By higher intelligence, however, one can recognize one's long-term self-interest and dangers. By designating and restricting the exploitation of the material world, Vedic knowledge gradually brings a conditioned soul to the platform of material goodness. At that stage, one becomes eligible to serve the Supreme Personality of Godhead.

TEXT 8

अकृष्णसारोदेशानामब्रह्मण्योऽसुचिर्भवेत् ।
कृष्णसारोऽप्यसौवीरकीकटासंस्कृतेरिणम् ॥८॥

akṛṣṇa-sāro deśānām abrahmaṇyo 'sucir bhavet
kṛṣṇa-sāro 'py asauvīra-kīkaṭāsaṁskṛteriṇam

Those places where there are no spotted deer, where respect is not given to the *brāhmaṇas*, where general cleanliness and the purificatory rites of Vedic society are

neglected, where meat-eaters predominate, and where the earth is barren, such as Kīkaṭa, are to be considered as contaminated.

COMMENTARY

In these eight verses, Śrī Kṛṣṇa describes the purity and impurity of objects, places, and times. The word *kṛṣṇasāra* means "spotted deer." Among countries, those where there is no spotted deer are considered to be impure. Besides this, any country where the inhabitants do not show respect to the *brāhmaṇas* is considered most impure. Countries where the people are uncivilized, or *asauvira*, which are inhabited by *mlechhas*, and where food grains do not grow because the land is barren are considered impure. Kīkaṭa refers to the province of Gayā.

PURPORT

While living at the *gurukula*, *brahmacārīs* dress in the hide of spotted deer. It is required to wear this during the period of learning about sacrifice. The skin of the black or spotted antelope is also used as a garment by those receiving instruction in the execution of Vedic sacrifice. Therefore, since sacrifice cannot be properly performed in areas bereft of such creatures, these places are considered impure. Even if people are advanced in terms of pious activities and the performance of sacrifice, their country is considered to be impure if they are averse to the devotional service to the Supreme Lord.

When there was no respect for devotional service to Lord Hari in countries such as Aṅga (Bihar) and Baṅga (Bengal), they were counted as impure. However, after the appearance of great Vaiṣṇavas, such as Śrī Jayadeva Gosvāmī, they have been glorified by the scriptures for their purity, even though they were also considered impure because of not having spotted deer.

TEXT 9

कर्मण्योगुणवान्कालोद्रव्यतःस्वत एववा ।
यतोनिवर्ततेकर्मसदोषोऽकर्मकःस्मृतः ॥९॥

karmaṇyo guṇavān kālo dravyataḥ svata eva vā
yato nivartate karma sa doṣo 'karmakaḥ smṛtaḥ

A time is considered to be auspicious when it facilitates the execution of one's prescribed duties, and that time which obstructs the execution of one's prescribed duties is considered inauspicious.

COMMENTARY

Now, the purity and impurity of various times is being explained. Any time that is suitable for executing one's prescribed duty is considered to be pure. The time where one obtains the ingredients necessary for performing one's work is considered pure by nature. The most auspicious time for performing *karma-yoga* is before noon. When a woman gives birth to a child, she is considered to be impure.

PURPORT

As there is consideration of purity and impurity with regards to place, there is also consideration of purity and impurity with regards to time. The time when one obtains the ingredients for performing one's occupational duty, and the time which is spent performing pious activities are naturally auspicious. Any time or condition that impedes the performance of one's occupational or religious duty must be considered as most inauspicious. The most auspicious of all times is the moment one achieves the mercy of the Supreme Personality of Godhead. If one neglects the loving service of the Lord, being carried away by sense gratification, he is certainly living in most inauspicious times. Therefore that moment in which one achieves the association of the Supreme Lord or the Lord's pure devotee is the most auspicious time, whereas the moment of losing such association is most inauspicious.

TEXT 10

द्रव्यस्यशुद्ध्यशुद्धीचद्रव्येणवचनेनच ।
संस्कारेणाथकालेनमहत्वाल्पतयाथवा ॥१०॥

dravyasya śuddhy-aśuddhī ca dravyeṇa vacanena ca
saṁskāreṇātha kālena mahatvālpatayātha vā

An object's purity or impurity is established by contact with another object, by words, by rituals, by the effects of time, or according to its magnitude.

COMMENTARY

Here, purity and impurity is being explained. The purity of pots is attained by washing them with water, and they become impure when touched by urine, or other abominable substances. The words of a saintly *brāhmaṇa* are pure, but the sound vibration of a materialistic person is contaminated by lust and envy. After the birth of a child or the death of a family member, the next ten days are considered to be impure. Water fetched by an outcaste is considered to be pure if it is from a large lake filled with lotus flowers. However, if it is brought from a small pond or well, it is considered to be impure. Impure food in the mode of ignorance is certainly to be avoided, except in the case of a dire emergency.

PURPORT

The consideration of an article's purity or impurity is determined by its proximity to other things. For example, articles touched by urine are considered to be impure, but if they are touched by Ganges water, they are considered to be pure. Although the conchshell is the bone of a dead animal, it is accepted as pure because the *Vedas* declare this as being a fact. Purity and impurity also depends on *saṁskāra*, indicating that the purity or impurity of a particular object is ascertained according to the regulations of ritualistic performances. For example, a flower to be offered to the Deity must be purified with water. Flowers or food cannot be offered to the Deity, however, if they have been contaminated by being smelled or tasted before the offering.

TEXT 11

शक्त्याशक्त्याथवाबुद्ध्यासमृद्ध्याचयदात्मने ।
अघंकुर्वन्तिहियथादेशावस्थानुसारतः ॥११॥

śaktyāśaktyātha vā buddhyā samṛddhyā ca yad ātmane
aghaṁ kurvanti hi yathā deśāvasthānusārataḥ

The contact of contaminated substances may or may not affect one with sinful contamination, depending upon one's prowess, spiritual advancement, development of intelligence, or other such conditions.

COMMENTARY

According to the laws of nature, that which is impure contaminates a particular person in accordance with that person's situation, as described here. For example, on certain occasions, such as a solar eclipse or just after childbirth, one must restrict the intake of food according to ritualistic injunctions. One who is physically weak, however, may eat without being considered impious. Ordinary persons consider the ten days following childbirth to be most auspicious, whereas one who is learned knows that this period is actually impure. Worn, dirty clothing is considered impure for a rich man but acceptable for one who is poor. The word *deśa* indicates that in a safe and peaceful place one is obligated to strictly perform religious rituals, whereas in a dangerous or chaotic situation one may be excused for occasional negligence of secondary principles. One who is physically healthy must offer obeisances to the Deities, attend religious functions and execute his prescribed duties, but a young child or sickly person may be excused from such activities, as indicated by the word *avastha*. Thus the revealed scriptures teach that one should consider purity and impurity according to the place, time, person, and circumstances.

PURPORT

The difference between purity and impurity, as well as piety and impiety, depends upon the place, circumstances, health of a person, and prosperity. One should accept everything which is favorable for the devotional service of Lord Kṛṣṇa and reject whatever is unfavorable. One must learn the process of serving God from the bona fide spiritual master and thus always maintain one's existence pure and free from anxiety. In general, however, when considering the relative purity and impurity of material things, all of the above-mentioned factors must be calculated. It can thus be concluded that the same conditions are perceived differently by swan-like personalities, and those who are no better than dogs, hogs, camels and asses.

TEXT 12

धान्यदार्वस्थितन्तूनांरसतैजसचर्मणाम् ।
कालवाय्वग्निमृत्तोयैःपार्थिवानांयुतायुतैः ॥१२॥

dhānya-dārv-asthi-tantūnāṁ rasa-taijasa-carmaṇām
kāla-vāyv-agni-mṛt-toyaiḥ pārthivānāṁ yutāyutaiḥ

Various objects such as grains, wooden utensils that are used for performing sacrifice, elephant tusks, liquid items such as oil and ghee, metal such as gold, leather, and clay pots—can all be purified by contact with time, air, fire, earth, and water.

COMMENTARY

The Lord herein explains in detail how various articles become pure by contact with certain elements. The word *asthi* refers to "elephants' tusks." The word *rasa* in this verse refers to oil or ghee. The word *taijasa* refers to gold, and other metals. All these are considered to be pure according to *śāstra* when they are combined with water, fire, and other elements, and used at a particular time. For example, a clay pitcher and bricks are considered pure, but when they are in their original form as earth they are considered impure. Metals, such as gold, can be purified by clay, water, and fire. Raw silk is purified simply by contact with the air.

TEXT 13

अमेध्यलिप्तंयद्येनगन्धलेपंव्यपोहति ।
भजतेप्रकृतिंतस्यतच्छौचंतावदिष्यते ॥१३॥

amedhya-liptaṁ yad yena gandha-lepaṁ vyapohati
bhajate prakṛtiṁ tasya tac chaucaṁ tāvad iṣyate

If a surface, a container, or cloth is contaminated by the touch of an abominable object, it can be purified by cleansing with caustic soda, acid, and water, until the smell or dirt is completely removed.

COMMENTARY

If meat, or any other abominable substance, is kept on a surface, a cloth, or in a pot, then these can be purified by scrubbing and washing with acid, detergent, clay, and water, until the contamination is removed. One should cleanse a contaminated object until the bad odor or impure coating is removed, thereby restoring it to its original condition.

TEXT 14

स्नानदानतपोऽवस्थावीर्यसंस्कारकर्मभिः ।
मत्स्मृत्याचात्मनःशौचंशुद्धःकर्माचरेद्द्विजः ॥१४॥

snāna-dāna-tapo-'vasthā-vīrya-saṁskāra-karmabhiḥ
mat-smṛtyā cātmanaḥ śaucaṁ śuddhaḥ karmācared dvijaḥ

One can purify the self by bathing, giving charity, performing austerity, undergoing purificatory rituals, as well as by personal prowess, the performance of prescribed duties, and above all, remembrance of Me. One who is twice-born should purify himself before he engages in prescribed duties.

COMMENTARY

After explaining how various objects can be purified, the Lord now describes the means for purifying the self. One can purify himself by bathing, distributing charity, and by performing the activities that are prescribed for his various stages in life. The word *saṁskāra* means "rituals, such as the sacred thread ceremony, and the chanting of *mantras*." It is necessary for the members of all *varṇas* to purify themselves before performing their prescribed duties.

PURPORT

The conditioned souls can purify themselves by bathing, giving charity, performing austerity, acting according to the rules and regulations prescribed for his situation within the *varṇāśrama* system, undergoing the fifteen kinds of *saṁskāra*, and above all, by remembering the lotus feet of the Supreme Lord, Viṣṇu. In this regard, one should carefully consider this verse from the *Garuḍa Purāṇa*:

apavitraḥ pavitro vā sarvāvasthāṁ gato 'pi vā
yaḥ smaret puṇḍarīkākṣaṁ sa bāhyābhyantare śuciḥ

Whether one is pure or contaminated, and regardless of one's external situation, simply by remembering the lotus-eyed Personality of Godhead, one can internally and externally cleanse one's existence.

TEXT 15

मन्त्रस्यचपरिज्ञानंकर्मशुद्धिर्मदर्पणम् ।
धर्मःसम्पद्यतेषड्भिरधर्मस्तुविपर्ययः ॥१५॥

mantrasya ca parijñānaṁ karma-śuddhir mad-arpaṇam
dharmaḥ sampadyate ṣaḍbhir adharmas tu viparyayaḥ

A mantra is purified when it is heard from the mouth of a bona fide spiritual master. One's activities are purified by offering the results to Me. Purified place, time, ingredients, performer, mantras, and actions constitute religion, and negligence of these six constitutes irreligion.

COMMENTARY

The purification of a mantra is being described in this verse. When mantras are received from the mouth of a bona fide spiritual master, they are considered purified. One's activities are purified when the results are offered in the service of the Supreme Lord. Purification of the place, time, ingredients, performer, mantras, and action constitutes religion, and a failure to so purify constitutes irreligion.

PURPORT

The purification of the place, time, ingredients, performer, mantra, and action constitutes religion, and the negligence of such purification is considered irreligion. If one does not receive a mantra from a bona fide spiritual master, who exhibits purified behavior, then he falls into a state of inauspiciousness because a mantra is no better than poison when it is received from a so-called spiritual master who is actually a disciple of Kali. When actions are performed for one's own sake, or for the sake of one's family or community, they are considered to be impure. Whenever an action, time, place, and so on are not in relation to the Supreme Lord, they must be considered impure and irreligious.

TEXT 16

क्वचिद्गुणोऽपिदोषःस्याद्दोषोऽपिविधिनागुणः ।
गुणदोषार्थनियमस्तद्भिदामेवबाधते ॥१६॥

kvacid guṇo 'pi doṣaḥ syād doṣo 'pi vidhinā guṇaḥ
guṇa-doṣārtha-niyamas tad-bhidām eva bādhate

Sometimes, what seems to be piety is actually sin and sometimes, what normally is sinful is to be considered as pious. Because of this, it seems that there is no clear distinction between piety and sin.

COMMENTARY

Here it is explained that piety and sin are actually relative conceptions. If a man abandons his wife and children, he must certainly be considered a rascal number one. Still, when a man gives up his family to accept the renounced order of life, *sannyāsa*, he is offered the respect due a great soul. It must therefore be concluded that piety and sin depend upon circumstances, and are therefore not easily ascertained.

PURPORT

Human beings are considered to be capable of distinguishing between good and bad and are thus responsible for their pious and sinful activities. Animals, on the other hand, being merged in ignorance, cannot be blamed for their offenses, which arise from ignorance. Human beings who act like animals, with the idea that one should not feel any guilt but should do whatever he likes, will certainly take birth as animals absorbed in ignorance.

TEXT 17

समानकर्माचरणपतितानांनपातकम् ।
औत्पत्तिकोगुणःसङ्गोनशयानःपतत्यधः ॥१७॥

samāna-karmācaraṇaṁ patitānāṁ na pātakam
Autpattiko guṇaḥ saṅgo na śayānaḥ pataty adhaḥ

Activities that would degrade an elevated person do not cause a fall down for those who are already fallen. Indeed, one who is lying on the ground cannot possibly fall any further. The material association that is dictated by one's own nature is considered a good quality. For example, association with a woman is a fault for a person in the renounced order of life, but it is a good quality for a householder.

COMMENTARY

For an elevated person, drinking wine would be the cause of his degradation but an ordinary laborer who could moderate his drinking would be considered pious. From this example, we can understand that on the material platform, piety and sin are relative. Another example is that if a *sannyāsī* intimately associates with a woman, he would be considered most abominable, whereas that same association for a householder is considered pious. The conclusion is that piety and sin on the material level are relative considerations.

PURPORT

For one who is full of faults, his actions cannot be the cause of his degradation because they are natural for him. One who is lying on the floor cannot go any lower. The possibility of falling down looms large for those who are elevated, but not for those who are already fallen. The nature of a talented person is never considered to be faulty. Because transcendentalists know that sense enjoyers and dry renunciates are fallen, they are careful to avoid their association or imitate their behavior.

TEXT 18

यतोयतोनिवर्त्तेतविमुच्येततततस्ततः ।
एषधर्मोनृणांक्षेमःशोकमोहभयापहः ॥१८॥

yato yato nivarteta vimucyeta tatas tataḥ
eṣa dharmo nṛṇāṁ kṣemaḥ śoka-moha-bhayāpahaḥ

The more one distances himself from sinful or materialistic activities, the more he is freed from their bondage. Such renunciation is the basis of religion and drives away all kinds of lamentation, illusion, and fear.

COMMENTARY

The aim of the scriptures is to encourage renunciation by means of a gradual diminishing of the enjoying propensity. This is done by prescribing rules and regulations that govern all aspects of human behavior.

PURPORT

The conception, "I am the enjoyer of this temporary, perishable material world," creates lamentation, illusion, and fear in the minds of the conditioned souls. People who renounce sense gratification and dry renunciation and engage in the worship of the Supreme Lord bring about their own auspiciousness. In this regard, one should carefully consider this verse from the *Caitanya-caritāmṛta* (*Antya* 6.220):

mahāprabhura bhakta-gaṇera vairāgya pradhāna
yāhā dekhi' prīta hana gaura-bhagavān

Renunciation is the basic principle sustaining the lives of Śrī Caitanya Mahāprabhu's devotees. Seeing this renunciation, Śrī Caitanya Mahāprabhu, the Supreme Personality of Godhead, is extremely satisfied.

TEXT 19

विषयेषुगुणाध्यासात्पुंसःसङ्गस्ततोभवेत् ।
सङ्गात्तत्रभवेत्कामःकामादेवकलिर्नृणाम् ॥१९॥

viṣayeṣu guṇādhyāsāt puṁsaḥ saṅgas tato bhavet
saṅgāt tatra bhavet kāmaḥ kāmād eva kalir nṛṇām

When one is attracted to the objects of the senses, attachment for them certainly develops within his heart. This attachment gives rise to lust, and from lust, anger and violence are generated.

COMMENTARY

In these four verses, the Supreme Lord is demonstrating the uselessness of the path of enjoyment, although it is sometimes encouraged in the *Vedas*. Desire is the cause of attachment, and from attachment, lust develops. A lusty person is easily angered and becomes inimical to anyone frustrating his lusty desires. For this reason, there is constant strife within human society.

TEXT 20

कलेर्दुर्विषहःक्रोधस्तमस्तमनुवर्तते ।
तमसाग्रस्यतेपुंसश्चेतनाव्यापिनीद्रुतम् ॥२०॥

kaler durviṣahaḥ krodhas tamas tam anuvartate
tamasā grasyate puṁsaś cetanā vyāpinī drutam

From quarrel arises unbearable anger, from anger bewilderment is produced, and from bewilderment, one quickly loses his power of discrimination.

COMMENTARY

From conflict of interest comes anger, followed by *tama*, or illusion. Due to illusion, one becomes bewildered, and this causes one to become completely bereft of any sense of discrimination.

PURPORT

From the tendency to enjoy material objects, considering them to be separate from the Supreme Lord, one develops attachment. From attachment, lust is born, and from lust, a conflict of interest arises. When there is a conflict of interest, strong anger results, and from this unbridled anger, one is covered by the dense darkness of ignorance, which robs one of the power of discrimination.

TEXT 21

तयाविरहितःसाधोजन्तुःशून्यायकल्पते ।
ततोऽस्यस्वार्थविभ्रंशोमूर्च्छितस्यमृतस्यच ॥२१॥

tayā virahitaḥ sādho jantuḥ śūnyāya kalpate
tato 'sya svārtha-vibhraṁśo mūrcchitasya mṛtasya ca

O saintly Uddhava, a person who has lost his power of discrimination is as good as dead matter. As a result of his ignorance, he loses the opportunity to achieve life's ultimate goal.

COMMENTARY

An unconscious person loses all sense of what is to be done and what is not to be done. Such a person is considered to be as good as dead because he has lost all sense of life's ultimate goal.

PURPORT

When one becomes bereft of the power of discrimination, he loses his good consciousness, almost like a dead man, and falls down from understanding life's ultimate goal.

TEXT 22

विषयाभिनिवेशेननात्मानंवेदनापरम् ।
वृक्षजीविकयाजीवन्व्यर्थंभस्त्रेवयुःश्वसन् ॥२२॥

viṣayābhiniveśena nātmānaṁ veda nāparam
vṛkṣa jīvikayā jīvan vyarthaṁ bhastreva yaḥ śvasan

One who uselessly passes his life by maintaining himself on whatever food he receives without personal endeavor is no better than a tree. Living uselessly in ignorance like a tree, his breathing is no better than that of a bellows. Such a person, who is almost like a dead man, has no understanding of himself, or anyone else.

COMMENTARY

One who lives like a tree, without making any personal endeavor, is considered to be practically unconscious. One whose breathing is therefore like that of a bellows is considered to be no better than a dead man.

PURPORT

One who is devoid of Kṛṣṇa consciousness uselessly breathes like a bellows and spoils his human birth by being absorbed in matter, just like a tree, without any enthusiasm for attaining life's ultimate goal.

TEXT 23

फलश्रुतिरियंनृणांनश्रेयोरोचनंपरम् ।
श्रेयोविवक्षयाप्रोक्तंयथाभैषज्यरोचनम् ॥२३॥

phala-śrutir iyaṁ nṛṇāṁ na śreyo rocanaṁ param
śreyo-vivakṣayā proktaṁ yathā bhaiṣajya-rocanam

The attainment of heavenly enjoyment as the result of pious activities is not the ultimate goal of life for human beings. Just as a child is promised a sweet to create his desire for taking medicine, the promise of heavenly rewards that are described in the scriptures are there to create a desire for performing pious activities.

COMMENTARY

It has been heard from the scriptures that materialistic people can go to heaven if they perform pious activities. Therefore, how can they be considered to be deviating from the ultimate goal of life? The answer is given in this verse. Such inducements to perform pious activities are not actually life's ultimate goal. The great sage, Nārada, has said, "Destruction of distress and attainment of happiness is auspicious. This cannot be achieved by the performance of fruitive activities." By this statement, the ultimate auspiciousness of *karma* is refuted. Then, what about statements found in the Vedic literature such as, "Enjoy life with the damsels of heaven?" The answer is that just to develop in the conditioned souls a taste for performing pious activities, the Vedic literature sometimes offers inducements to gradually bring them to the path of liberation. This is like the inducement given to a child so that he will take some medicine. The father may tell him, "If you drink this bitter juice of *neem* leaves, I will give you a *laddu*." Because of the inducement, the son will agree to drink the bitter medicine and thus his disease will be cured. Of course, the gift of a *laddu* is not the actual fruit of drinking bitter *neem* juice.

PURPORT

When fruitive workers hear about the tempting fruits of *karma*, they cannot resist the temptation. Actually, they are deceived by such flowery language of the *Vedas* because such fruitive work, in and of itself, cannot award one ultimate benefit.

TEXT 24

उत्पत्त्यैवहिकामेषुप्राणेषुस्वजनेषुच ।
आसक्तमनसोमर्त्या आत्मनोऽनर्थहेतुषु ॥२४॥

utpattyaiva hi kāmeṣu prāṇeṣu sva-janeṣu ca
āsakta-manaso martyā ātmano 'nartha-hetuṣu

Right from their birth, human beings naturally becomes attached to the animalistic propensities, a long duration of life, sense gratification, bodily strength, personal influence, friends, and family— all of which create *anarthas* that defeat the real purpose of life.

COMMENTARY

The question may be raised, "In the *karma-kāṇḍa* sections of the *Vedas*, there is no mention of liberation from material existence. Therefore, by what authority can one state that liberation is the goal of *karma*?" The answer is given herein: "The primary purport of the *Vedas* supports this statement. By nature, the conditioned souls are attached to material enjoyment since the moment of their birth. As a result, they become attached to their senses, strength, influence, wife, children, and other relatives. However, such attachment is simply *anartha*, or unwanted, and therefore produces only distress.

TEXT 25

नतानविदुषःस्वार्थंभ्राम्यतोवृजिनाध्वनि ।
कथंयुंज्त्पुनस्तेषुतांस्तमोविशतोबुधः ॥२५॥

natān viduṣaḥ svārthaṁ bhrāmyato vṛjinādhvani
kathaṁ yuñjyāt punas teṣu tāṁs tamo viśato budhaḥ

Those whose knowledge is covered by ignorance, and are thus acting against their self-interest, are wandering on the path of material existence. Why would the *Vedas* encourage them to enter deeper into darkness by engaging them in sense gratification?

COMMENTARY

Generally, materialistic people are ignorant of their real self-interest, the platform of ultimate happiness. Therefore, the Vedic literature does not actually encourage faithful persons to act in a way that will enable them to enjoy heavenly pleasure and thereafter be born in the lower species of life. If this were the actual intention of the *Vedas*, they could not be considered genuinely auspicious.

TEXT 26

एवंव्यवसितंकेचिदविज्ञायकुबुद्धयः ।
फलश्रुतिंकुसुमितांनवेदज्ञावदन्तिहि ॥२६॥

evaṁ vyavasitaṁ kecid avijñāya kubuddhayaḥ
phala-śrutiṁ kusumitāṁ na veda-jñā vadanti hi

Without understanding the actual intention of the Vedic literature, some evil-minded people, such as the *karma-mīmāṁsakas*, who are bewildered by the statements promising heavenly rewards that are found in the *Vedas*, propagate that such flowery statements are the supreme objective of life. However, this is not the opinion of actual authorities, such as Vyāsadeva, who know the real purport of the *Vedas*.

COMMENTARY

One may still question, "Why do the *mīmāṁsakas* declare that the aim of the *Vedas* is to transfer the living entities to heaven?" The answer is herein given: "Such people, not realizing the real intention of the *Vedas*, accept the Vedic statements that promise heavenly elevation to be the actual purport of the *Vedas*. Actually, the flowery language of the *Vedas* have bewildered these people. Due to ignorance, they consider the flowers to be the fruit. As a result of being bewildered, their intelligence has become contaminated so that they are misguided. Such persons certainly do not know the actual purport of the *Vedas*. Great sages, such as Vyāsadeva, who are conversant with the actual purport of the *Vedas*, never preach in this way.

TEXT 27

कामिनःकृपणालुब्धाःपुष्पेषुफलबुद्धयः ।
अग्निमुग्धाधूमतान्ताःस्वंलोकंनविदन्तिते ॥२७॥

kāminaḥ kṛpaṇā lubdhāḥ puṣpeṣu phala-buddhayaḥ
agni-mugdhā dhūma-tāntāḥ svaṁ lokaṁ na vidanti te

Materialistic men, who are naturally very lusty and greedy, think the flowery words of the Vedas to be their actual purpose. Being blinded by the smoke and glare of the sacrificial fire, they cannot understand their actual position.

COMMENTARY

In the next eight verses, Śrī Kṛṣṇa exposes the evil-mindedness of the *mīmāṁsakas*. Those who consider the irrelevant results of *karma* to be their aim of life become absorbed in the performance of Vedic sacrifices, which can be compared to a glaring fire. As a result, they are overcome by the smoke produced by that fire and thus lose their power of discrimination. While blinded by the smoke, they wander on the path of material existence and thus experience countless miseries.

TEXT 28

नतेमामङ्गजानन्तिहृदिस्थंयदेयतः ।
उक्थशस्त्राह्यसुतृपोयथानीहारचक्षुषः ॥२८॥

na te māṁ aṅga jānanti hṛdi-sthaṁ ya idaṁ yataḥ
uktha-śastrā hy asu-tṛpo yathā nīhāra-cakṣuṣaḥ

My dear Uddhava, those who perform the Vedic rituals in the hopes of achieving future sense gratification cannot understand that I am situated within the hearts of all living entities, and that this universe is nondifferent from Me, being a manifestation of My energy. It is as if their eyes are covered by a dense fog.

COMMENTARY

Although the Lord is situated in the hearts of the *mīmāṁsakas*, they do not know Him as the original cause of the cosmic manifestation. The false bodily concept of life, in which one ignores the eternal soul within the body, is a dense fog of ignorance that blocks our vision of God. *Mīmāṁsakas* refers to those whose eyes are covered with fog of ignorance. It is stated in the *Vedas* that the Supreme Lord is situated within the hearts of all living entities as the Supersoul. However, because people are covered by ignorance and indulge in idle talks, they cannot know Him.

PURPORT

In spite of the Lord's existence within the hearts of all living entities, they still engage in sense gratification and thus lose their power of vision.

TEXTS 29-30

तेमेमतमविज्ञायपरोक्षंविषयात्मकाः ।
हिंसायांयदिरागःस्याद्यज्ञ एवनचोदना ॥२९॥
हिंसाविहाराह्यालब्धैःपशुभिःस्वसुखेच्छया ।
यजन्तेदेवतायज्ञैःपितृभूतपतीन्खलाः ॥३०॥

te me matam avijñāya parokṣaṁ viṣayātmakāḥ
hiṁsāyāṁ yadi rāgaḥ syād yajña eva na codanā

hiṁsā-vihārā hy ālabdhaiḥ paśubhiḥ sva-sukhecchayā
yajante devatā yajñaiḥ pitṛ-bhūta-patīn khalāḥ

"If one has a propensity for violence in the form of eating meat, one may slaughter an animal during the performance of a fire sacrifice." By this statement, the *Vedas* have regulated the propensity for violence. The *Vedas* neither encourage animal slaughter nor prescribe it. Without understanding My inner intentions, fruitive workers, who are fond of violence, worship the demigods, forefathers, and leaders of ghostly creatures, with a desire to achieve heavenly pleasure, and thus they cruelly slaughter innocent animals in sacrifice.

COMMENTARY

Although the *Vedas* sometimes recommend the performance of animal sacrifices, this is actually meant to restrict the killing of animals, and not to encourage it. Because there is always a class of men who will eat meat, the *Vedas* prescribe the performance of elaborate rituals at certain prescribed times, just to discourage unrestricted animal slaughter. It is only misguided philosophers that encourage the sacrifice of animals as a means for enjoying sense gratification in this life, and attaining the planets of the demigods or forefathers after death.

PURPORT

Being influenced by the mode of ignorance, there are many people who consider the performance of sacrifices mentioned in the *Vedas* to be the their supreme religious duty. Such people generally worship the forefathers, demigods, and ghosts in order to enjoy a life of sense gratification, both in this world and the next, and thus they take pleasure in killing animals in the name of performing sacrifices.

TEXT 31

स्वप्नोपममुमुंलोकमसन्तंश्रवणप्रियम् ।
आशिषोहृदिसङ्कल्प्यत्यजन्त्यर्थान्यथावणिक् ॥३१॥

svapnopamam amuṁ lokam asantaṁ śravaṇa-priyam
āśiṣo hṛdi saṅkalpya tyajanty arthān yathā vaṇik

Just as a foolish businessman, desiring to obtain additional wealth, may cross the insurmountable ocean and invest his previously accumulated wealth speculatively, and thus lose everything, fruitive workers, desiring to experience heavenly pleasure after death, which is only like a dream, whimsically waste their time performing Vedic sacrifices.

COMMENTARY

Fruitive workers are actually very unfortunate. This is being pointed out in this verse. Both in this world and in the heavenly planets, life is temporary. Materialistic people resolve to enjoy like a king in this world, and so seek the demigods' blessings for this purpose. Still, they are always full of anxieties. They spend a huge amount of wealth for conducting Vedic sacrifices, just as a merchant takes the risk of crossing the insurmountable ocean in the hopes of accumulate great wealth. However, in the long run, both lose their hard-earned wealth while making a risky journey that does not provide eternal benefit.

PURPORT

It is the nature of material existence that causes everyone to work very hard for the purpose of enjoying sense gratification as far as possible. As eternal fragmental parts and parcels of the Lord, we can enjoy a blissful life in His association, but instead, we waste our time struggling for existence in this illusory material manifestation. It is something like a businessman who foolishly squanders all his wealth on a useless business venture that yields no profit.

TEXT 32

रजःसत्त्वतमोनिष्ठारजःसत्त्वतमोजुषः ।
उपासतेन्द्रमुख्यान्देवादीन्नयथैवमाम् ॥३२॥

rajaḥ-sattva-tamo-niṣṭhā rajaḥ-sattva-tamo-juṣaḥ
upāsata indra-mukhyān devādīn na yathaiva mām

Fruitive workers are under the influence of the three modes of material nature—goodness, passion, and ignorance—and they worship the demigods, who are also under the influence of the three modes of material nature, but they fail to worship Me, who am transcendental to the three modes of material nature. Although the demigods, headed by Indra, are parts and parcels of Me, when they are worshiped as being independent from Me, this constitutes an impropriety.

COMMENTARY

Those who are under the influence of the three modes of material nature act according to their situation under the modes of nature. Although the demigods, headed by Indra, are parts and parcels of the Supreme Lord, worshiping them is not considered to be direct worship of the Lord. Sometimes persons situated in the mode of goodness accept the supremacy of the Supreme Lord but are more attracted to the demigods, believing that through Vedic rituals they can achieve the same standard of living as the demigods. This proud tendency is certainly an obstacle in the loving service of the Supreme Lord and ultimately causes falldown. This is confirmed in the *Bhagavad-gītā* (9.24):

ahaṁ hi sarva-yajñānāṁ bhoktā ca prabhur eva ca
na tu mām abhijānanti tattvenātaś cyavanti te

I am the only enjoyer and master of all sacrifices. Therefore, those who do not recognize My true transcendental nature fall down.

PURPORT

Those who consider themselves to be servants of the demigods can overcome the influence of the modes of passion and ignorance by acting in the mode of goodness. However, although they enthusiastically worship the demigods, headed by Indra, they have no taste for worshiping the Supreme Personality of Godhead. Even the demigods, who are supposed to be situated in the mode of goodness, often oppose the worship of the Supreme Lord, creating a situation that is inauspicious.

TEXTS 33-34

इष्ट्वेहदेवतायज्ञैर्गत्वारंस्यामहेदिवि ।
तस्यान्तैहभूयास्ममहाशालामहाकुलाः ॥३३॥
एवंपुष्पितयावाचाव्याक्षिप्तमनसांनृणाम्
मानिनांचातिलुब्धानांमद्वार्तापिनरोचते

iṣṭveha devatā yajñair gatvā raṁsyāmahe divi
tasyānta iha bhūyāsma mahā-śālā mahā-kulāḥ

evaṁ puṣpitayā vācā vyākṣipta-manasāṁ nṛṇām
māninām cāti-lubdhānāṁ mad-vārtāpi na rocate

Discussions about Me are not pleasing to those who are greedy and proud, and whose minds are attracted to the flowery words of the *karma-kāṇḍa* sections of the *Vedas*. Because of their excessive pride and greed, they think, "We will go to heaven as a result of worshiping the demigods and enjoy immense happiness there. When our enjoyment is exhausted, we will return to this world, being born in a family of aristocratic householders."

COMMENTARY

The attached fruitive workers think that they will perform sacrifice in this world to please the demigods and when they finish enjoying heavenly delights, they will return to this world to become rich householders.

PURPORT

Bewildered by the flowery words of the *Vedas*, greedy and proud materialists do not have any interest in satisfying the senses of the master of the senses.

TEXT 35

वेदाब्रह्मात्मविषयास्त्रिकाण्डविषया इमे ।
परोक्षवादाऋषयःपरोक्षंममचप्रियम् ॥३५॥

vedā brahmātma-viṣayās tri-kāṇḍa-viṣayā ime
parokṣa-vādā ṛṣayaḥ parokṣaṁ mama ca priyam

The *Vedas*, which consists of three divisions, reveal that the soul is spiritual and has nothing to do with material existence. The soul is not a product of matter. Great sages explain this truth in an esoteric manner, and I approve of their confidential teachings. Those who are pure-hearted are eligible to receive Vedic knowledge, whereas those whose hearts are contaminated certainly fall down.

COMMENTARY

The *Vedas* are divided into three sections, referred to as *karma-kāṇḍa*, *brahma-kāṇḍa*, and *devatā-kāṇḍa*. The Vedic literature teaches the science of the individual spirit soul and the supreme Brahman. Human beings are supposed to worship the Supreme Personality of Godhead by chanting the *mantras* that are revealed in the Vedic literature. The question may arise, "Why do the sages and the Vedic *mantras* speak in esoteric or indirect terms?" The answer is: "The Supreme Lord does not allow Himself to be taken cheaply, and thus He is not manifest to superficial or inimical people."

PURPORT

One who depends upon material sense perception remains in gross ignorance of the Absolute Truth. One who depends upon mental and intellectual speculation may get a clue that the eternal soul and Supersoul are both within the material body. In this regard, one should study the tenth verse of the *Upadeśāmṛta* of Śrī Rūpa Gosvāmī:

karmibhyaḥ parito hareḥ priyatayā vyaktiṁ yayur jñāninas
tebhyo jñāna-vimukta-bhakti-paramāḥ premaika-niṣṭhās tataḥ
tebhyas tāḥ paśu-pāla-paṅkaja-dṛśas tābhyo 'pi sā rādhikā
preṣṭhā tadvad iyaṁ tadīya-sarasī tāṁ nāśrayet kaḥ kṛtī

In the ***śāstra*** it is said that of all types of fruitive workers, he who is advanced in knowledge of the higher values of life is favored by the Supreme Lord Hari. Out of many such people who are advanced in knowledge (***jñānīs***), one who is practically liberated by virtue of his knowledge may take to devotional service. He is superior to the others. However, one who has actually attained ***prema***, pure love of Kṛṣṇa, is superior to him. The *gopīs* are exalted above all the advanced devotees because they are always totally dependent upon Śrī Kṛṣṇa, the transcendental cowherd boy. Among the ***gopīs***, Śrīmatī Rādhārāṇī is the most dear to Kṛṣṇa. Her *kuṇḍa* (lake) is as profoundly dear to Lord Kṛṣṇa as this most beloved of the gopīs. Who, then, will not reside at Rādhā-kuṇḍa and, in a spiritual body surcharged with ecstatic devotional feelings *(aprākṛtabhāva)*, render loving service to the divine couple Śrī Śrī Rādhā-Govinda, who perform Their *aṣṭakālīya-līlā*, Their eternal eightfold daily pastimes. Indeed, those who execute devotional service on the banks of Rādhā-kuṇḍa are the most fortunate people in the universe.

TEXT 36

अब्दब्रह्मसुदुर्बोधंप्राणेन्द्रियमनोमयाम् ।
अनन्तपारंगम्भीरंदुर्विगाह्यंसमुद्रवत् ॥३६॥

śabda-brahma su-durbodhaṁ prāṇendriya-mano-mayam
ananta-pāraṁ gambhīraṁ durvigāhyaṁ samudra-vat

The transcendental sound of the *Vedas* is very difficult to comprehend and manifests on different levels within the life-air, senses, and mind. Actually, the transcendental sound of the *Vedas* is unlimited, unfathomable, and very grave like an ocean.

COMMENTARY

The transcendental sound vibration of the *Vedas* exists in four stages, as understood by those who are highly qualified *brāhmaṇas*. Three of these stages are internally situated and only the fourth stage is manifest externally as speech. Even this fourth stage of the *Vedas* is very difficult for ordinary people to understand, and so what to speak of the other three. The *prāṇa* stage of the Vedic sound vibration is located in the *ādhāra-cakra*. The mental stage is located in the region of the navel, in the *maṇipūraka-cakra*. The intellectual stage is located in the region of the heart, in the *anāhata-cakra*, and the sensory stage is referred to as *vaikharī*.

The transcendental vibration of the *Vedas* encompasses all the energies within creation and is beyond the limitations of time and space. It is so subtle and sublime that only the Lord Himself and His representatives can understand its actual purport.

PURPORT

Because foolish people consider the transcendental name of Lord Hari to be equal to ordinary mundane sound vibrations, while remaining engaged in sense enjoyment with their body, mind, and life air, the Supreme Lord appears incomprehensible to them. The transcendental name of the Supreme Lord and the Supreme Lord Himself are nondifferent. Because transcendental sound vibration and the object of transcendental sound vibration are unfathomable, no one can realize their glories without the mercy of the Supreme Lord. The four levels of transcendental sound—*parā*, *paśyantī*, *madhyamā*, and *vaikharī*—are completely transcendental, devoid of material contamination, and untouched by the spirit of mundane enjoyment. Therefore, the mentality of sense enjoyers and dry renunciates makes a distinction between transcendental sound and its object, thereby inviting inauspiciousness.

TEXT 37

मयोपबृंहितंभूम्नाब्रह्मणानन्तशक्तिना ।
भूतेषुघोषरूपेणविसेषूर्णेवलक्ष्यते ॥३७॥

mayopabṛṁhitaṁ bhūmnā brahmaṇānanta-śaktinā
bhūteṣu ghoṣa-rūpeṇa viseṣūrṇeva lakṣyate

I am the unlimitedly powerful Supreme Lord, situated within the bodies of all living beings, wherein I establish the subtle form of transcendental sound.

COMMENTARY

Transcendental sound vibration manifests in different phases, according to the inspiration of the Supreme Lord. The question may arise: "If the Supreme Lord is one without a second, how is it possible that He remains present as unlimited spiritual and material manifestations?" The answer is given in this verse: "I am the almighty Lord. I manifest innumerable forms of unlimited potency and by the expansion of these forms, I am all-pervading. For those who can perceive Me in meditation, I am realized as *oṁkāra* within the heart." In this verse, the Lord cites the example of a strand of fiber within a lotus stem.

PURPORT

Because the holy name of the Lord and the Supreme Lord Himself are identical, descriptions such as all-pervading, all-powerful, unlimited, and the Supersoul, are befitting Him and no one else. All these adjectives describe the Lord's transcendental qualities, and are devoid of any mundane tinge. As a fiber is inseparable from the stem of a lotus, the Supreme Lord is inseparable from His holy name, and thus both the Lord and His holy names are the objects of the liberated soul's worship.

TEXT 38-40

यथोर्णनाभिर्हृदयादूर्णामुद्वमतेमुखात् ।
आकाशाद्घोषवान्प्राणोमनसास्पर्शरूपिणा ॥३८॥
छन्दोमयोऽमृतमयाःसहस्रपदवींप्रभुः ।
ॐकाराद्व्यञ्जितस्पर्शस्वरोष्मान्तस्थभूषिताम् ॥३९॥
विचित्रभाषाविततांछन्दोभिश्चतुरुत्तरैः ।
अनन्तपारांबृहतींसृजत्याक्षिपतेस्वयम् ॥४०॥

yathorṇanābhir hṛdayād ūrṇām udvamate mukhāt
ākāśād ghoṣavān prāṇo manasā sparśa-rūpiṇā

chando-mayo 'mṛta-mayaḥ sahasra-padavīṁ prabhuḥ
oṁkārād vyañjita-sparśa- svaroṣmāntastha-bhūṣitām

vicitra-bhāṣā-vitatāṁ chandobhiś catur-uttaraiḥ
ananta-pārāṁ bṛhatīṁ sṛjaty ākṣipate svayam

Just as a spider produces its web from its mouth, the Supreme Lord manifests Himself as the primeval vital air, consisting of all the sacred Vedic meters and full of transcendental pleasure. The Lord, from the sky of His heart, creates the unlimited Vedic sound through the agency of His mind. The sound vibrations of the Vedas then spread in all directions, adorned with the various letters, meters, consonants, vowels, and semi-vowels. The Vedas are expressed in different meters, each having four more syllables than the previous one. Ultimately, the Supreme Lord withdraws the unlimited and unfathomable manifestation of Vedic sound within Himself.

COMMENTARY

Just as a spider brings forth its web from its heart and produces it through its mouth, the plenary portion of the Supreme Lord, who is the source of Brahmā, manifests the Vedic knowledge by means of His potency. With the support of the sky, the Vedic knowledge, along with the vital life air, then enters the heart of Brahmā. The word *ghoṣa* means "sound." Transcendental sound vibration in the form of the Vedic literature is thus revealed by the Supreme Lord in this way. It is the Supreme Lord and nothing else, that is to be realized by one's study of the *Vedas*.

TEXT 41

गायत्र्युष्णिगनुष्टुप्चबृहतीपङ्क्तिरेवच ।
त्रिष्टुब्जगत्यतिच्छन्दोह्यत्यष्ट्यतिजगद्विराट् ॥४८॥

gāyatry uṣṇig anuṣṭup ca bṛhatī paṅktir eva ca
triṣṭub jagaty aticchando hy atyaṣṭy-atijagad-virāṭ

The Vedic meters are Gāyatrī, Uṣṇik, Anuṣṭup, Bṛhatī, Paṅkti, Triṣṭup, Jagatī, Aticchanda, Atyaṣṭi, Atijagatī, and Ativirāṭ.

COMMENTARY

The Gāyatrī meter has twenty-four syllables, and the Uṣṇik meter has twenty-eight syllables. There are other meters, such as Atyaṣṭi, Atijagatī, and Ativirāṭ, all of which are defined in the *Vedas*.

TEXT 42

किंविधत्तेकिमाचष्टेकिमनूद्यविकल्पयेत् ।
इत्यस्याहृदयंलोकेनान्योमद्वेदकश्चन ॥४२॥

kiṁ vidhatte kim ācaṣṭe kim anūdya vikalpayet
ity asyā hṛdayaṁ loke nānyo mad veda kaścana

I am the actual knower of the *Vedas*, and it is Me that is to be known by the study of the *Vedas*. That which is to be known, that which is prescribed, and that which is actually revealed by the *Vedas* remains a mystery to the conditioned souls.

COMMENTARY

It is to be understood that whatever has been prescribed in the *Vedas* is meant for the ultimate benefit of all living entities. There are so many individual opinions that answer the question, "What is the actual purport of the Vedic statements? What do the *Vedas* actually teach?" The *Vedas* teach that one should chant *mantras* three times a day, offer oblations to the forefathers, and perform numerous other prescribed rituals and duties. Does this mean that the *Vedas* simply encourage the living entities to perform fruitive activities? The answer is that all Vedic formulas are preliminary stages leading to the perfect stage of Kṛṣṇa consciousness, in which one fully surrenders to the devotional service of the Lord. There are various processes recommended in the Vedic literature, such as *karma-yoga*, *jñāna-yoga*, and *bhakti-yoga*. All these processes are revealed by the Supreme Lord for the benefit of people having various qualifications.

Foolish people think that by following any of these processes one can attain the supreme perfection of life. That is why in this verse the Supreme Lord says that it is He alone who knows the actual purport of the *Vedas*.

PURPORT

Śrī Kṛṣṇa is the Supreme Personality of Godhead, who is one without a second. No one other than the Supreme Lord Śrī Kṛṣṇa knows the actual aim of the sacrifices prescribed in the *karma-kāṇḍa* section of the *Vedas*, the goal of the *mantras* that are found in the *upāsaṇa-kāṇḍa* section of the *Vedas*, and the objective of the deliberations of the *jñāna-kāṇḍa* section of the *Vedas*. The demigods, human beings, and great sages, who are all subordinate to the Supreme Lord and who have a limited capacity for transcendental understanding, cannot find out the actual intention of the *Vedas*. The Supreme Absolute Truth is the Lord Himself, who is the only shelter of all living entities and who is the only objective of all kinds of Vedic processes.

TEXT 43

मांविधत्तेऽभिधत्तेमांविकल्प्यापोह्यतेत्वहम् ।
एतावान्सर्ववेदार्थःशब्द आस्थायमांभिदाम् ।
मायामात्रमनूद्यान्तेप्रतिषिध्यप्रसीदति ॥४३॥

mām vidhatte 'bhidhatte mām vikalpyāpohyate tv aham
etāvān sarva-vedārthaḥ śabda āsthāya mām bhidām
māyā-mātram anūdyānte pratiṣidhya prasīdati

In the *karma-kāṇḍa,* the *Vedas* have described Me as the goal of all sacrifices, and in the *devatā-kāṇḍa,* the Supreme Lord of all kinds of worship. The *jñāna-kāṇḍa* elaborately analyzes all material duality as being nothing but My illusory potency, and thus not separate from Me. The transcendental sound vibration thus establishes Me as the essential meaning of all Vedic knowledge.

COMMENTARY

By all the *Vedas* the Supreme Lord is to be known. Devotional service is described as being under the guidance of the internal potency of the Supreme Lord, and it is the constitutional duty of the living entities. The recommendation to perform sacrifices is meant to ultimately bring one to the platform of devotional service. It has been stated by the Supreme Lord: "In the beginning of creation, I spoke the Vedic wisdom to Brahmā and thereafter, it became known as *bhāgavata dharma*. Indeed, I am the goal of the *Vedas*."

After elaborately propagating the various paths of wisdom, the *Vedas* concluded that the Supreme Personality of Godhead is the ultimate goal. The three *kāṇḍas* of the *Vedas* propagate *karma*, *jñāna*, and *bhakti*. At the same time, it has refuted the path of *karma*, as well as the path of *jñāna*, or the cultivation of knowledge. First, the *Vedas* advocate that one renounce the performance of activities with attachment for the results, but instead engage in *karma* without any material desires. By such a practice, one gradually comes to the platform of *jñāna*, wherein one is advised to give up all fruitive activities, even if performed without material desires. When one comes to the platform of perfection of *jñāna*, one is advised to give up the very cultivation of knowledge while attempting to merge into transcendence. However, it is to be carefully noted that nowhere in any Vedic literature has it been advised that one should renounce the devotional service of the Lord.

The teachings of the *Vedas* are based on the idea that eventually, everyone must come to the platform of devotional service to the Supreme Lord. It has been concluded that the Supreme Lord is the ultimate shelter, and that the processes of *karma* and *jñāna* are by nature illusory. The performance of *karma* takes place within the jurisdiction of the three modes of material nature, and the cultivation of knowledge causes one to be situated in the mode of goodness. Therefore, ultimately, these processes are to be abandoned because they cannot lead one to the platform of transcendence. The *Vedas* felt immense pleasure by describing the wonderfully sweet qualities of devotional service, which is transcendental to the three modes of material nature. Indeed, it is the desire of the *Vedas* that the conditioned soul may drown in the transcendentally sweet mellows of devotional service.

PURPORT

The sacrifices that are prescribed in the *karma-kāṇḍa* sections of the *Vedas* are manifestations of the Supreme Lord. The ultimate goal of all kinds of activities is certainly to satisfy the Supreme Lord. A multitude of Vedic paths of advancement have been promoted simply due to the conditioned souls' lack of love for the Supreme Lord. It is the Supreme Lord alone who is able to remove the coverings of ignorance from the minds of the living entities. He is certainly the ultimate goal of all kinds of ritualistic performances found in the *Vedas*.

In this material world, there is a distinction between an object and a sound that represents it. Because ordinary sounds are under the jurisdiction of material time and place, they are incompetent for ascertaining the nature of an object. The conditioned souls consider the objects that make up their material environment as meant for their personal enjoyment. When a person gives up this materialistic conception as being the enjoyer of all he surveys and becomes inclined toward the Lord's devotional service, the distinction between an object and the sound that represents it is vanquished. At that time, one becomes liberated from the Lord's illusory energy, *maya*, and obtains engagement in the transcendental service of the Supreme Lord. From the viewpoint of enlightenment, it can be understood that with every syllable, the *Vedas* declare the glories of the Supreme Lord and establish Him as the supreme worshipable object for all classes of living beings.

Thus end the translation of the Fifteenth Chapter of the Uddhava-gītā *entitled* **"Explanation of the Vedic Path"** *with the commentaries of Śrīla Viśvanātha Cakravartī Ṭhākura and chapter summary and purports by Śrīla Bhaktisiddhānta Sarasvatī Ṭhākura.*

CHAPTER 16

ENUMERATION OF THE ELEMENTS OF MATERIAL CREATION

CHAPTER SUMMARY

In this chapter there is a description of the material elements, the natures of male and female, and birth and death.

Various philosophies categorize the material elements in different ways. Although such differences are caused by the illusory energy of the Lord, they all are based on logic and are therefore acceptable. The material elements exist in all situations and in all places and the insurmountable illusory energy of the Lord causes them to be understood in various ways.

The knowledge acquired by the perception of the senses can determine, to some extent, the material elements, but can never penetrate to the eternal soul. There is a supreme controller of nature, and He is also the supreme enjoyer, not the controlled minute individual souls. The three modes of material nature cause the conditioned souls to appreciate different aspects of material nature. Those in the mode of goodness appreciate knowledge, those in the mode of passion appreciate activity, and those in the mode of ignorance appreciate foolishness. Time is a representation of the Supreme Personality of Godhead, and the original cause of material propensities is the *mahat-tattva*. In this chapter, twenty-five material elements are innumerated: the Supreme Lord, material nature, the *mahat-tattva*, false ego, ether, air, fire, water, earth, the eyes, ears, nose, tongue, skin, speech, the hands, feet, genitals, anus, the mind, sound, touch, form, taste, and smell.

In the beginning, the Lord glances over the material energy, so that the creation, maintenance, and destruction of the cosmic manifestation is brought into existence, under the control of the Lord. In this way, there is a distinction made between the *puruṣa* and *prakṛti*, although, in one sense, they are nondifferent as cause and effect. The universe is brought about by the interaction of the three modes of materal nature, which cause matter to be in a constant state of transformation. The rebellious living beings are then forced to accept material bodies in the cosmic manifestation as a result of their previous fruitive activites. Because his knowledge of his self is covered by the illusory energy of the Lord, the conditioned soul cannot understand his actual position. The subtle body, which is filled with desires for sense gratification, carries the helpless conditioned soul from one body to another.

The body undergoes nine stages of transformation due to being under the control of the three modes of material nature. These are impregnation, gestation within the womb, birth, childhood, youth, maturity, middle age, old age, and finally death. From the death of one's father and the birth of one's child, one can understand the temporary nature of his own body. The conscious self is distinct from the material body it identifies with. The conditioned soul is in the darkness of ignorance, being bewildered by the objects of the senses, and thus he achieves various destinations, one after another, within the cosmic manifestation. In this way, the conditioned soul wanders throughout the universe under the spell of material nature, sometimes residing in heaven due to the predominance of the mode of goodness, sometimes appearing in human society due the predominance of the mode of passion, and sometimes being forced into lower species of life due to the predominance of the mode of ignorance. The eternal soul never directly contacts the objects of the senses, but only the senses of the body. Therefore, the pleasure derived from material sense gratification is very limited and temporary. Only those who take shelter at the lotus feet of the Supreme Lord, dedicating themselves to His devotional service, attain peace, whereas all others, even great so-called scholars, are tormented by the insurmountable influence of material nature.

TEXT 1-3

श्रीउद्धव उवाच
कतितत्त्वानिविश्वेशसंख्यातान्यृषिभिः प्रभो ।
नवैकादशपञ्चत्रीण्यात्थत्वमिहशुश्रुम ॥१॥
केचित्षड्विंशतिंप्राहुरपरेपञ्चविंशतिं ।
सप्तैकेनवषट्केचिच्चत्वार्येकादशापरे ॥२॥

केचित्सप्तदशप्राहुःषोडशैकेत्रयोदश ।
एतावत्त्वंहिसंख्यानामृषयोयद्विवक्षया ।
गायन्तिपृथगायुष्मन्निदंनोवक्तुमर्हसि ॥३॥

śrī-uddhava uvāca
kati tattvāni viśveśa saṅkhyātāny ṛṣibhiḥ prabho
navaikādaśa pañca trīṇy āttha tvam iha śuśruma

kecit ṣaḍ-viṁśatiṁ prāhur apare pañca-viṁśatiṁ
saptaike nava ṣaṭ kecic catvāry ekādaśāpare

kecit saptadaśa prāhuḥ ṣoḍaśaike trayodaśa
etāvattvaṁ hi saṅkhyānām ṛṣayo yad-vivakṣayā
gāyanti pṛthag āyuṣmann idaṁ no vaktum arhasi

Uddhava said: My dear Lord, O master of the universe, how have the great sages categorized the elements of the material nature? I have heard You said that there are twenty-eight elements: the supreme controller, the spirit soul, the mahat-tattva, false ego, the five gross elements, the ten knowledge-acquiring and working senses, the mind, the five sense objects, and the three modes of nature. However, there are others who say that there are twenty-six elements, while still others point out twenty-five, seven, nine, six, four, or eleven elements, and even others who say that there are seventeen, sixteen, or thirteen. How is it that great sages categorize the material elements in different ways? Please describe to me so that I may correctly understand this.

COMMENTARY

After hearing the Lord's explanation of *karma kāṇḍa*, Śrī Uddhava now asks about some details of the *jñāna kāṇḍa* sections of the *Vedas*, desiring to gain a proper understanding. There are innumerable sages who have established their own opinions and while doing so, they have ascertained different numbers of material elements. This is not actually contradictory because various philosophers have utilized various methods of categorizing the same reality.

In these three verses, it is stated that some particular sage has ascertained that there are nine elements— the Supreme Lord, the living entities, the *mahat-tattva*, false ego, and the five gross material elements. However, besides these there are ten senses, the mind, the five sense objects, and the three modes of material nature, making a total of twenty-eight elements. The word *āyuṣman*, or "possessing eternal form," is significant in this regard. The Supreme Lord is eternal and full of knowledge of past, present, and future, and so He is the original and perfect philosopher.

PURPORT

Different philosophers have given various opinions while enumerating the number of material elements. In this verse, Uddhava states that it is the opinion of the Supreme Personality of Godhead that there are twenty-eight material elements. These are the Supreme Lord, His energy, the intelligence, false ego, the five gross elements, the mind, the five knowledge-acquiring senses, the five working senses, the five sense objects, and the three modes of material nature.

The godless Sāṅkhya philosophers, who are averse to the Supreme Lord, ascertain the number of material elements to be twenty-four. They do not accept the three modes of material nature and the supreme controller. Atheistic speculation on reality does not recognize the existence of God; consequently it is a worthless attempt to explain the truth. The Lord Himself empowers different living entities to speculate and speak on reality in different ways.

TEXT 4

श्रीभगवानुवाच
युक्तंचसन्तिसर्वत्रभाषन्तेब्राह्मणायथा ।
मायांमदीयामुद्गृह्यवदतांकिंनुदुर्घटम् ॥४॥

śrī-bhagavān uvāca
yuktaṁ ca santi sarvatra bhāṣante brāhmaṇā yathā
māyāṁ madīyām udgṛhya vadatāṁ kiṁ nu durghaṭam

Lord Kṛṣṇa said: Because all the material elements pervade the entire creation, it is justifiable that various philosophers have categorized them in different ways. All these learned men have worked under the influence of My mystic potency, thus seeing things from various perspectives.

COMMENTARY

Although there seems to be contradictions in the statements of the great sages, there is actually none. The Supreme Lord herein says that the words of the *brāhmaṇas* are all reasonable. Each of the philosophers mentioned here reveals a particular aspect of truth, and their theories are not contradictory because they are descriptions of the same phenomena with different categorical systems. Having spoken under the shelter of the Lord's mystic potency, none of the sages could ascertain the truth perfectly. As long as the sun and the moon remain, these differences of opinion will also continue to exist. This is the purport of this verse.

TEXT 5

नैतदेवंयथात्थत्वंयदहंवच्मितत्तथा ।
एवंविवदतांहेतुंशक्तयोमेदुरत्यया: ॥५॥

naitad evaṁ yathāttha tvaṁ yad ahaṁ vacmi tat tathā
evaṁ vivadatāṁ hetuṁ śaktayo me duratyayāḥ

When philosophers argue with one another, saying, "I have understood things in a way superior to you," this is simply a manifestation of My insurmountable energy.

COMMENTARY

By the influence of the modes of goodness, passion and ignorance, different philosophers are attracted to different views; and by the influence of the material atmosphere created by the Lord, these philosophers perpetually disagree with one another. As stated in *Śrīmad-Bhāgavatam* (6.4.31):

yac-chaktayo vadatāṁ vādināṁ vai vivāda-saṁvāda-bhuvo bhavanti
kurvanti caiṣāṁ muhur ātma-mohaṁ tasmai namo 'nanta-guṇāya bhūmne

"Let me offer my respectful obeisances unto the all-pervading Supreme Personality of Godhead, who possesses unlimited transcendental qualities. Acting from within the cores of the hearts of all philosophers, who propagate various views, He causes them to forget their own souls while sometimes agreeing and sometimes disagreeing among themselves. Thus He creates within this material world a situation in which they are unable to come to a conclusion. I offer my respectful obeisances unto Him."

TEXT 6

यासांव्यतिकरादासीद्विकल्पोवदतांपदम् ।
प्राप्तेशमदमेऽप्येतिवादस्तमनुशाम्यति ॥६॥

yāsāṁ vyatikarād āsīd vikalpo vadatāṁ padam
prāpte śama-dame 'pyeti vādas tam anu śāmyati

It is by the interaction of My energies that different opinions arise. However, for those who have fixed their intelligence on Me, and who have controlled their senses, differences of perception disappear so that the very cause for argument is removed.

COMMENTARY

Conflicting perceptions in the minds of various mundane philosophers is created by the Lord's external energy. Although deluded by the Lord's illusory energy, each philosopher thinks that he is correct, saying, "It may be like this and it may be like that." Although such thinking is surely rational, because of a limited view of reality, each philosopher argues and counter-argues without ever coming to a definite conclusion. Such quarreling is absent in the society of devotees, who accept the authority of the Supreme Personality of Godhead, whose vision is not limited, and who is not under the influence of the illusory energy. Being enlightened in the truth, the devotees of the Lord are in complete agreement. Even if by chance there appears to be some differences in opinion, this is not because the devotees are under the influence of false ego. On the transcendental platform, there are also varieties of perception according to one's particular relationship with the Lord.

TEXT 7

परस्परानुप्रवेशात्तत्त्वानांपुरुषर्षभ ।
पौर्वापर्यप्रसंख्यानंयथावक्तुर्विवक्षितम् ॥७॥

parasparānupraveśāt tattvānāṁ puruṣarṣabha
paurvāparya-prasaṅkhyānaṁ yathā vaktur vivakṣitam

O best among men, since the subtle and gross material elements are situated within one another, various philosophers estimate their number differently.

COMMENTARY

The creation of the universe is enacted from subtle to gross, as an effect of the inconceivable potency of the Lord. The cause is present in the effect, and so the effect is also subtly present in the cause. Considering this, it is concluded that all the elements are present in each element. It is for this reason that the elements of material nature can be categorized in various ways. That materialistic philosophers speculate according to their own propensities and limitations, they each consider their own conlusions to be the best. This is being described in these two verses.

TEXT 8

एकस्मिन्नपिदृश्यन्तेप्रविष्टानीतराणिच ।
पूर्वस्मिन्वापरस्मिन्वातत्त्वेतत्त्वानिसर्वशः ॥८॥

ekasminn api dṛśyante praviṣṭānītarāṇi ca
pūrvasmin vā parasmin vā tattve tattvāni sarvaśaḥ

The subtle material elements are present within their transformations, the gross elements, and the gross material elements are present in their subtle causes. This is true because creation is enacted from subtle to gross in a series of transformations. For this reason, all the material elements are present in each element.

COMMENTARY

The example can be given that within clay, the potentiality for a claypot exists, just as the presence of clay is within the pot. In this way, all of the material elements are present within each element, and ultimately, all elements have as their shelter the Supreme Personality of Godhead.

TEXT 9

पौर्वापर्यमतोऽमीषांप्रसंख्यानमभीप्सताम् ।
यथाविविक्तंयद्वक्त्रंगृह्णीमोयुक्तिसम्भवात् ॥९॥

paurvāparyam ato 'mīṣāṁ prasaṅkhyānam abhīpsatām
yathā viviktaṁ yad-vaktraṁ gṛhṇīmo yukti-sambhavāt

Therefore, regardless of the particular philosopher and his means of calculation, whether he includes material elements within their previous subtle causes or subsequent manifest products, I accept their conclusions as authoritative because a logical explanation can always be given for all such theories.

COMMENTARY

Even though materialistic philosophers rationally describe the universe from varying perceptions, they can never come to an ultimate understanding without hearing from the Lord or His representative. One should therefore not be proud of his limited intelligence, just because he has some partial understanding of material existence.

PURPORT

Due to misuse of their minute independence, even expert living entities come under the control of perpetual ignorance and thus enter into perpetual conflicts and arguments. One who does not misuse his good intelligence and is devoid of the propensity for material enjoyment is certainly a candidate for the pure devotional service of the Lord. Such a devotee can enlighten the entire world with the understanding of devotional service to the Supreme Lord. On the other hand, if a blind person guides another blind person, both will fall into a ditch. Non devotees, such as the *karmīs* and *jñānīs*, can never impart perfect knowledge for the simple reason that they are not self-realized.

TEXT 10

अनाद्यविद्यायुक्तस्यपुरुषस्यात्मवेदनम् ।
स्वतोनसम्भवादन्यस्तत्त्वज्ञोज्ञानदोभवेत् ॥१०॥

anādy-avidyā-yuktasya puruṣasyātma-vedanam
svato na sambhavād anyas tattva-jño jñāna-do bhavet

Because the conditioned souls, who have been covered by the illusory energy of the Lord since time immemorial, cannot effect their own liberation, there must be someone else possessing pure knowledge who can free him from materal entanglement.

COMMENTARY

Uddhava explained how some materialistic philosophers see twenty-five categories of elements, whereas others see twenty-six. Generally, this distinction is caused by a difference in spiritual understanding. Some see the individual soul and the Supreme Soul to be one and the same and so they count twenty-five, whereas others recognize the distinction between the one Supreme Lord and the many minute living entities maintained by the one Lord, and so they count twenty-six. The sixth dative case in this verse should be understood as the first dative case. Because the conditioned souls forgot their constitutional position, it is the omniscient Supreme Lord who can revive their original nature by imparting to them the knowledge of the self. This is the opinion of all the Vaiṣṇava authorities.

PURPORT

Those whose only means for acquiring knowledge is their mundane experience are unable to realize the transcendental Supreme Personality of Godhead, along with His eternal variegatedness. As a result of their mundane conceptions, such empiricists preach the philosophy of impersonalism while internally remaining sense enjoyers and externally displaying renunciation. These conditioned souls, instead of understanding themselves as minute individual spirit souls, believe themselves to be the all-pervading Supersoul. And yet, in spite of such pretensions, such mundane philosophers cannot escape the duality of lamentation and illusion. Because of rejecting their subordination to the Supreme Lord, they forever remain within the darkness of ignorance. However, if such unfortunate souls somehow take to devotional service, then all their inauspiciousness can be destroyed. When they understand that the Supreme Lord is the only enjoyer and the original source of everything, they can simultaneously realize themselves as minute particles of spirit that are the Lord's eternal servants.

TEXT 11

पुरुषेश्वरयोरत्रनवैलक्षण्यमण्वपि ।
तदन्यकल्पनापार्थाज्ञानंचप्रकृतेर्गुणः ॥११॥

puruṣeśvarayor atra na vailakṣaṇyam aṇv api
tad-anya-kalpanāpārthā jñānaṁ ca prakṛter guṇaḥ

Knowledge in the mode of goodness is characterized by the understanding that there is no qualitative difference between the Supreme Lord and the living entities. Those who imagine a qualitative difference between them are misguided.

COMMENTARY

Can the statement that there are twenty-five elements be accepted? This question is answered by the Lord in this verse. Although the individual spirit soul and the Supersoul are distinct entities, there is no qualitative difference between them. The difference between the Supreme Lord and the living entities is that the Supreme Lord is infinite whereas the living entities are infinitesimal. The Supreme Lord is the energetic source of all energies and the living entities are one of His energies. This establishes the proper understanding that the Supreme Lord and the living entities are simultaneously one with and different from each other. Any philosophical attempt to separate the living entity from the Supreme Lord and deny his eternal servitude to the Lord is thus refuted. Speculation arriving at the conclusion that the living entity has independent existence separate from the Lord is described here as *apārthā*, or useless.

PURPORT

Generally, materialists have some kind of a belief in God but because they identify with the material body as the self, they cannot appreciate the qualitative oneness of the Lord and the living beings. For this reason, genuine understanding of the Absolute Truth must begin from the understanding of the spiritual quality of the living entities, as distinct from the bodily concept of life. Lord Caitanya has described the truth as *acintya-bhedābheda-tattva*—that the Lord and the living entities are simultaneously one and different. When one cultivates the mode of goodness, this understanding develops, and by further advancement in devotional service, one can understand the variegatedness of spiritual existence.

TEXT 12

प्रकृतिर्गुणसाम्यंवैप्रकृतेर्नात्मनोगुणाः ।
सत्त्वंरजस्तमैतिस्थित्युत्पत्त्यन्तहेतवः ॥१२॥

prakṛtir guṇa-sāmyaṁ vai prakṛter nātmano guṇāḥ
sattvaṁ rajas tama iti sthity-utpatty-anta-hetavaḥ

Nature originally exists in a state of equilibrium of the three modes of material nature. When these modes are agitated, then the creation, maintenance, and dissolution of the universe takes place. Such events occur within the external energy of the Lord, and do not pertain to the eternal spirit souls.

COMMENTARY

Although the spirit souls are counted as the superior energy of the Lord, they are very tiny and thus subject to the influence of the inferior external energy of the Lord. In their original state, the three modes of material nature are in equilibrium, and later, when material nature is agitated by the glance of the Lord, creation of the universe takes place, wherein the conditioned souls are bound up. These conditioned souls are not actually the doers of activities within the cosmic manifestation. While conditioned by the modes of nature, the living entities experience various conditions of life. The mode of goodness allows one to cultivate knowledge, the mode of passion allows one to work very hard, and the mode of ignorance allows one to act foolishly. However, these qualitative distinctions have no actual relation to the spirit souls, whose actual qualities are that they are eternal, full of knowledge, and fully blissful. In the original state of material nature, the three material modes are in equilibrium. These material qualities are the causes of the creation, maintenance, and destruction of the cosmic manifestation and the spirit soul has nothing to do with them.

PURPORT

The three modes of material nature—goodness, passion, and ignorance—are the causes of the creation, maintenance, and annihilation of the material world. Unlike the material nature, the spirit soul has no material qualities. In the original condition of material nature, there is equilibrium of the three modes of material nature. The material modes have no access within the kingdom of God, in the unbounded atmosphere of which the eternal living entity is meant to live. There, the spiritual energies, which are known as *hlādinī*, *sandhinī*, and *saṁvit* are present. In the spiritual world, there is no question of creation caused by the influence of time because in that transcendental abode, time is eternally present.

TEXT 13

सत्त्वंज्ञानंरजःकर्मतमोऽज्ञानमिहोच्यते ।
गुणव्यतिकरःकालःस्वभावःसूत्रमेवच ॥१३॥

sattvaṁ jñānaṁ rajaḥ karma tamo 'jñānam ihocyate
guṇa-vyatikaraḥ kālaḥ svabhāvaḥ sūtram eva ca

Knowledge is the characteristic of the mode of goodness, activities are the characteristic of the mode of passion, and ignorance is the characteristic of the mode of darkness. Time is the product of the agītātion of the three modes of material nature, and the sum total of the conditioned souls' propensities is embodied within the *mahat-tattva.*

COMMENTARY

Knowledge can be derived from cultivation of the mode of goodness, thus leading one towards the Absolute Truth. Fruitive activities are born from the mode of passion, and the state of being devoid of knowledge is born from the mode of ignorance. These characteristics of the material nature are found in the conditioned souls who are being forced to exist under material designations. *Kāla*, or time, by which the three modes of material nature are agitated, is the impetus for the interaction of the material elements.

PURPORT

It is generally understood that knowledge is produced by the material quality of goodness, fruitive activities are enacted by the material quality of passion, and ignorance is the result of the material quality of darkness. Although there are numerous divisions of material elements within the basic divisions, the spirit soul is always to be understood as a distinct transcendental element.

TEXT 14

पुरुषः प्रकृतिर्व्यक्तमहङ्कारोनभोऽनिलः ।
ज्योतिरापःक्षितिरितितत्त्वान्युक्तानिमेनव ॥१४॥

puruṣaḥ prakṛtir vyaktam ahaṅkāro nabho 'nilaḥ
jyotir āpaḥ kṣitir iti tattvāny uktāni me nava

I have thus described the nine basic truths as the spirit soul, nature, the mahat-tattva, false ego, sky, air, fire, water, and earth.

COMMENTARY

In this and the next two verses, the Supreme Lord elucidates the twenty-five material elements. The word *vyakta* here refers to the *mahat-tattva.*

PURPORT

The nine elements— the spirit soul, nature, the material ingredients, false ego, and the five gross elements are here described as *tattva*, or truth. The material nature is originally unmanifest and later on, when it is manifest, it is known as *mahat-tattva.*

TEXT 15

श्रोत्रंत्वग्दर्शनंघ्राणोजिह्वेतिज्ञानशक्तयः ।
वाक्पाण्युपस्थपाय्वङ्घ्रिःकर्माण्यङ्गोभयंमनः ॥१५॥

śrotraṁ tvag darśanaṁ ghrāṇo jihveti jñāna-śaktayaḥ
vāk-pāṇy-upastha-pāyv-aṅghriḥ karmāṇy aṅgobhayaṁ manaḥ

My dear Uddhava, the ears, skin, eyes, nose, and tongue are the five knowledge-acquiring senses. The speech, hands, legs, anus, and genitals are the five working senses. The mind belongs to both these categories.

COMMENTARY

The word *darśana* means "eyes." The five knowledge-acquiring senses, the five working senses and the mind constitute eleven elements mentioned in this verse.

PURPORT

The five knowledge-acquiring senses, the five working senses, and the mind, which is the director of both sets of senses, are known as eleven truths.

TEXT 16

शब्दःस्पर्शोरसोगन्धोरूपंचेत्यर्थजातयः ।
गत्युक्त्युत्सर्गशिल्पानिकर्मायतनसिद्धयः ॥१६॥

śabdaḥ sparśo raso gandho rūpaṁ cety artha-jātayaḥ
gaty-ukty-utsarga-śilpāni karmāyatana-siddhayaḥ

Sound, touch, form, taste and smell are the objects of the knowledge-acquiring senses. By their transformation, the five gross material elements are created. Movement, speech, excretion, and manufacture are functions of the working senses.

COMMENTARY

The objects of the knowledge-acquiring senses are five. Thus, the Lord has enumerated twenty-five elements. Activities, such as speaking, moving about, passing stool, passing urine, and performing artistic work are the propensities of the working senses and as such, they should not be considered a separate truth.

PURPORT

The objects of the senses are sound, touch, form, taste, and smell. Activities, such as speaking, movement with the help of the legs, artistic work performed with the hands, and the releasing of bodily waste through the anus and genital are the objects of the five working senses. By counting these activities of the working senses as one, the total becomes twenty-six.

TEXT 17

सर्गादौप्रकृतिर्ह्यस्यकार्यकारणरूपिणी ।
सत्त्वादिभिर्गुणैर्धत्तेपुरुषोऽव्यक्तईक्षते ॥१७॥

sargādau prakṛtir hy asya kārya-kāraṇa-rūpiṇī
sattvādibhir guṇair dhatte puruṣo 'vyakta īkṣate

In the beginning of creation, the material nature, which consists of cause and effect, by means of the modes of goodness, passion, and ignorance, assumes its form as the embodiment of all subtle causes and gross manifestations. The Supreme Lord, who never changes His position, simply glances over material nature and remains the witness.

COMMENTARY

In the beginning of the material creation, material nature creates with the help of her three modes, goodness, passion, and ignorance. The Supreme Lord remains in His transcendental position, unaffected by the actions and reactions of the gross and subtle material elements. Therefore, the Lord is referred to as *avyakta*, or never manifest within the material creation. No matter in which way the material elements are categorized, it must be understood that the Supreme Lord is the ultimate cause of the creation, maintenance, and destruction of the cosmic manifestation.

PURPORT

The external energy of the Supreme Lord, which manifests as cause and effect, employs her three modes to perform the activities of the material world's creation, maintenance, and annihilation. The Lord personally remains unchanged as He agitates the material nature through His glance to initiate creation.

TEXT 18

व्यक्तादायोविकुर्वाणाधातवःपुरुषेक्षया ।
लब्धवीर्याःसृजन्त्यण्डंसंहताःप्रकृतेर्बलात् ॥१८॥

vyaktādāyo vikurvāṇā dhātavaḥ puruṣekṣayā
labdha-vīryāḥ sṛjanty aṇḍaṁ saṁhatāḥ prakṛter balāt

As the material elements undergo transformations, they are empowered with their particular potencies by the glance of the Lord, so that they are able to manifest the universal egg.

COMMENTARY

The universe is created from the transformation of the total material ingredients, called the *mahat-tattva.* Under the shelter of material nature, these ingredients bring about the creation of the cosmic manifestation.

TEXT 19

सप्तैवधातवइतितत्रार्थाःपञ्चखादयः ।
ज्ञानमात्मोभयाधारस्ततोदेहेन्द्रियासवः ॥१९॥

saptaiva dhātava iti tatrārthāḥ pañca khādayaḥ
jñānam ātmobhayādhāras tato dehendriyāsavaḥ

According to some philosophers, there are seven elements—earth, water, fire, air, and ether, along with the minute spirit soul and the Supreme Soul, who is the basis of both the material elements and the infinitesimal spirit soul. According to this theory, the body, senses, life air, and all material phenomena are produced from these seven elements.

COMMENTARY

The word *dhātu* in this context means "truth," or "element." The word *jñāna* in this verse refers to the living entity. These seven elements are the source of all material ingredients, beginning from the sky.

PURPORT

Those philosophers who propound the theory of seven truths accept the five gross material elements, along with the living entity and the Supersoul, to be the seven primary elements. They say that from these elements, the material body, the senses, and all other objects have become manifest.

TEXT 20

षड्इत्यत्रापिभूतानिपञ्चषष्ठः परःपुमान् ।
तैर्युइत आत्मसम्भूतैःसृष्ट्वेदंसमपाविशत् ॥२०॥

ṣaḍ ity atrāpi bhūtāni pañca ṣaṣṭhaḥ paraḥ pumān
tair yuita ātma-sambhūtaiḥ sṛṣṭvedaṁ samapāviśat

There are others who say that there are six elements—the five gross material elements and the Supersoul. According to them, the Supersoul creates the universe with the help of the elements that He has brought forth from Himself and then enters within it.

COMMENTARY

There are other philosophers that state that there are six principle truths, which include the five material elements and the Supersoul.

PURPORT

The philosophy of six truths takes consideration of the five material elements and the Supersoul.

TEXT 21

चत्वार्येवेतितत्रापितेज आपोऽन्नमात्मनः ।
जातानितैरिदंजातजन्मावयविनःखलु ॥२१॥

catvāry eveti tatrāpi teja āpo 'nnam ātmanaḥ
jātāni tair idaṁ jātaṁ janmāvayavinaḥ khalu

Some philosophers say that there are four elements, and that of these four, fire, water, and earth are created from the self, the fourth element. After manifesting, these elements combine to form the universe.

COMMENTARY

The word *anna* in this verse means "earth," the word *ātmā* means "the Supersoul," who is the source of the material ingredients.

PURPORT

The philosophers who propose that there are four truths accept fire, water, earth, and the self to be the causes of the cosmic manifestation.

TEXT 22

संख्यानेसप्तदशकेभूतमात्रेन्द्रियाणिच ।
पञ्चपञ्चैकमनसा आत्मा सप्तदशःस्मृतः ॥२२॥

saṅkhyāne saptadaśake bhūta-mātrendriyāṇi ca
pañca pañcaika-manasā ātmā saptadaśaḥ smṛtaḥ

Some calculate the existence of seventeen basic elements—the five gross material elements, the five sense objects, the five senses, the mind, and the self.

COMMENTARY

The seventeen truths propounded by some philosophers are the five gross material elements, the five sense objects, the five senses, the mind, and the self.

PURPORT

There are others who propagate the philosophy of seventeen basic truths—the five gross material elements, the five sense objects, the five senses, the mind, and the self.

TEXT 23

तद्वत्षोडशसंख्याने आत्मैवमन उच्यते ।
भूतेन्द्रियाणिपञ्चैवमन आत्मात्रयोदश ॥२३॥

tadvat ṣoḍaśa-saṅkhyāne ātmaiva mana ucyate
bhūtendriyāṇi pañcaiva mana ātmā trayodaśa

Philosophers that perceive sixteen elements differ from the previous conception only because the self is identified with the mind. Others perceive thirteen elements—the five gross elements, the five senses, the mind, the soul, and the Supreme Soul.

COMMENTARY

The soul is often addressed as the mind. In the philosophy of thirteen basic truths, the five gross elements and the five sense objects are all together counted as five, and in addition there are the five senses, the mind, the spirit soul, and the Supersoul.

PURPORT

Those who preach the philosophy of sixteen basic truths consider the soul and the mind to be one and the same. Those who propagate the philosophy of thirteen basic elements count the five gross elements and the five sense objects as five in all. In addition, they count the five senses, the mind, the spirit soul, and the Supersoul.

TEXT 24

एकादशत्व आत्मासौमहाभूतेन्द्रियाणिच ।
अष्टौप्रकृतयश्चैवपुरुषश्चनवेत्यथ ॥२४॥

ekādaśatva ātmāsau mahā-bhūtendriyāṇi ca
aṣṭau prakṛtayaś caiva puruṣaś ca navety atha

According to some philosophers, there are eleven basic truths—the five gross elements, the five senses, and the soul. There are others who propound the conception of nine basic truths—the five gross elements, the mind, intelligence, false ego, and the soul.

COMMENTARY

The propounders of eleven basic truths count the ten senses and the soul. Those who advocate the philosophy of eight basic truths count the five gross elements, mind, intelligence, and false ego. Those who advocate the philosophy of nine basic truths accept these eight, as well as the soul.

TEXT 25

इतिनानाप्रसंख्यानंतत्त्वानामृषिभिःकृतम् ।
सर्वंन्याय्यंयुक्तिमत्त्वाद्विदुषांकिमशोभनम् ॥२५॥

iti nānā-prasaṅkhyānaṁ tattvānām ṛṣibhiḥ kṛtam
sarvaṁ nyāyyaṁ yuktimattvād viduṣāṁ kim aśobhanam

Thus, philosophers have categorized the material elements in various ways. All of these categorizations are based upon logic and reason and certainly exhibit great dexterity of intelligence.

COMMENTARY

By using the word *iti* Śrī Kṛṣṇa indicates that He is concluding His explanation to Uddhava about the various estimates of material elements.

TEXT 26

श्रीउद्धव उवाच
प्रकृतिःपुरुषश्चोभौयद्यप्यात्मविलक्षणौ ।
अन्योन्यापाश्रयात्कृष्णदृश्यतेनभिदातयोः ।
प्रकृतौलक्ष्यतेह्यात्माप्रकृतिश्चतथात्मनि ॥२६॥

śrī-uddhava uvāca
prakṛtiḥ puruṣaś cobhau yady apy ātma-vilakṣaṇau
anyonyāpāśrayāt kṛṣṇa dṛśyate na bhidā tayoḥ
prakṛtau lakṣyate hy ātmā prakṛtiś ca tathātmani

Śrī Uddhava said: I have understood that the living entities and material nature are distinct existences, and yet they appear to be inextricably connected. After all, the living beings are embodied by matter and follow the ways of the modes of nature.

COMMENTARY

Uddhava is now expressing another doubt. The material nature is considered to be *prakṛti* whereas the living entity and the Supreme Lord are described as *puruṣa*, or the enjoyer of nature. It may appear difficult to discriminate between the living entity and his embodiment, or the Supreme Lord and His energy. Such distinctions must therefore be seen through the eyes of the scriptures.

PURPORT

In this material world, it appears as if life cannot exist independently of the material body. Indeed, the living entity and material nature appear to be inseparable, from the time of conception within the mother's womb, right up to the time of death. In conditional life, we cannot imagine how life can be a separate entity, without dependence upon matter for its manifestation. Of course, the material body cannot exist without the presence of the spirit soul and thus there appears to be a mutual dependence. Here, Uddhava wants the Lord to clarify all these.

TEXT 27

एवंमेपुण्डरीकाक्षमहान्तंसंशयंहृदि ।
छेत्तुमर्हसिसर्वज्ञवचोभिर्नयनैपुणैः ॥२७॥

evaṁ me puṇḍarīkākṣa mahāntaṁ saṁśayaṁ hṛdi
chettum arhasi sarva-jña vacobhir naya-naipuṇaiḥ

O lotus-eyed Lord, O omniscient one, please remove this doubt from my heart with Your words, which exhibit Your great skill in reasoning.

COMMENTARY

Śrī Uddhava said: Kindly remove my doubt by demonstrating how the material body is distinct from the soul, and how material nature is separate from the Supersoul. You can certainly do so because You are the most expert in reasoning and arguments.

TEXT 28

त्वत्तोज्ञानंहिजीवानांप्रमोषस्तेऽत्रशक्तितः ।
त्वमेवह्यात्ममायायागतिंवेत्थनचापरः ॥२८॥

tvatto jñānaṁ hi jīvānāṁ pramoṣas te 'tra śaktitaḥ
tvam eva hy ātma-māyāyā gatiṁ vettha na cāparaḥ

It is by Your mercy that the living entities obtain knowledge, and it is by Your illusory energy that they fall from knowledge. I believe that no one but You can actually understand how Your illusory energy works.

COMMENTARY

Uddhava said: You are the source of all knowledge and so it is by Your mercy that a living entity can obtain knowledge. Your energy, *vidyā*, awards one knowledge and Your energy, *avidyā*, takes away that knowledge.

PURPORT

Uddhava further inquired: By accepting subordination to the Supreme Lord, the living entities obtain knowledge. The bewildering potency of the Lord creates illusion in the minds of the rebellious living entities. Māyādevī exists under the shelter of the Supreme Lord, and she manifests her potency in two ways—the covering potency and the throwing potency. Those who are under the influence of the Lord's illusory energy cannot understand how they are being conditioned.

TEXT 29

श्रीभगवानुवाच
प्रकृतिःपुरुषश्चेतिविकल्पःपुरुषर्षभ ।
एषवैकारिकःसर्गोगुणव्यतिकरात्मकः ॥२९॥

śrī-bhagavān uvāca
prakṛtiḥ puruṣaś ceti vikalpaḥ puruṣarṣabha
eṣa vaikārikaḥ sargo guṇa-vyatikarātmakaḥ

The Supreme Lord said: O best among men, there is distinct difference between material nature and the living entities and the Supreme Lord. This manifest universe undergoes constant transformation, being acted upon by the agītātion of the modes of nature.

COMMENTARY

Material nature is subject to change, but the Supreme Lord is always unchangeable. Nature is manifold, but the Supreme Lord is one without a second. Nature is dependent, but the Supreme Lord is fully independent. Material nature is manifested with the help of others, whereas the Supreme Lord is self-manifested. In these ways, there are many differences between the material nature and the Supreme Lord. Such distinctions are being described in these four verses. The word *vikalpa* means "difference." The Supreme Lord is certainly distinct from His energy. Material bodies are products of the material nature, and all material forms are subject to transformation, being agitated by the three modes of material nature.

PURPORT

The Supreme Lord is unchanging, whereas the material nature is always subject to change. There is a manifestation of temporary variegatedness in this world produced by the illusory energy of the Lord because of the combination of the three modes of material nature. Although the material world is limited and temporary, the spiritual world, which is far beyond the material world, is full of eternal variegatedness created by the spiritual nature. In that realm, nothing is agitated or influenced by the three modes of material nature, being fully transcendental and eternal. In the transcendental abode of the Lord, there are eternal variegated pastimes of the object of service, the Supreme Lord, and the devotees of the Lord, based on loving devotional service. Because there is complete harmony in diversity in the spiritual world, there is no conflict of interest. Instead of the creation, maintenance, and annihilation that characterizes the material manifestation, there is eternity, full knowledge, and bliss.

TEXT 30

ममाङ्गमायागुणमय्यनेकधाविकल्पबुद्धीश्चगुणैर्विधत्ते ।
वैकारिकस्त्रिविधोऽध्यात्ममेकमथाधिदैवमधिभूतमन्यत् ॥३०॥

mamāṅga māyā guṇa-mayy anekadhā vikalpa-buddhīś ca guṇair vidhatte
vaikārikas tri-vidho 'dhyātmam ekam athādhidaivam adhibhūtam anyat

My dear Uddhava, My material energy, consisting of three modes by which it acts, manifests the varieties of creation along with varieties of consciousness for perceiving them. The resultant cosmic manifestation can be understood in these three aspects—*adhyātmic, adhidaivic,* and *adhibhautic.*

COMMENTARY

The diversity of nature is described herein. The various types of consciousness within the different material bodies reveals different aspects of the Lord's creation. The seemingly endless varieties of material consciousness are created by the transformation of the three modes of material nature. In this way, the multi-faceted material nature transforms into many categories, but can be simply understood in three divisions—*adhyātmic*, *adhibhautic*, and *adhidaivic*.

PURPORT

The external energy of the Lord manifests in three modes and by their interaction, all varieties of material manifestations take place. Creation, maintenance, and dissolution, are the three phases of material manifestation and these are understood in three aspects—*adhyātmika*, *ādhidaivika*, and *ādhibhautika*. The Lord's internal energy is without any tinge of the material qualities, but is manifest in three features—*sandhini*, *samvit*, and *hlādinī*.

TEXT 31

दृग्रूपमार्कंवपुरत्ररन्ध्रेपरस्परंसिध्यतियःस्वतःखे ।
आत्मायदेषामपरोय आद्यःस्वयानुभूत्याखिलसिद्धसिद्धिः ॥३१॥

dṛg rūpam ārkaṁ vapur atra randhre parasparaṁ sidhyati yaḥ svataḥ khe
ātmā 'yad eṣām aparo ya ādyaḥ svayānubhūtyākhila-siddha-siddhiḥ

The eyes of the living entities represent the *adhyātma* feature of nature, the object of vision represents the *adhibhuta* feature, and the light provided by the sun represents the *adhidaiva* feature. These three features work together to reveal one another but the sun in the sky is self-manifested. Similarly, the Supersoul is the original cause of the three features—*adhyātmic, adhibhautic,* and *adhidaivic*—but is self-sufficient, acting by the illumination of His own transcendental existence as the ultimate source of manifestation of all created objects.

COMMENTARY

The function of the eye is to recognize form, and so when there is recognition of form, the eye's presence is understood. The perception of form by the eye also depends upon light, which is supplied by the demigods, who are in charge of universal management. The demigods also depend upon those who they control, the members of human society, and thus there are three interdependent factors to be considered: *adhyātma*, represented by the senses; *adhibhūta*, represented by the sense objects; and *adhidaiva*, represented by the demigods. However, the Supersoul exists independently from all such created existences. The example is given of how the sun is situated in its orbit without any extraneous help. In this way, the Supersoul can be compared to that sun because He is the original cause of all material manifestations and yet is independent of them. He is self-illuminated by His own glories, and He enlightens all other illuminating agents. Yet He always remains aloof.

TEXT 32

एवंत्वगादिश्रवणादिचक्षुर् ।
जिह्वादिनासादिचचित्तयुक्तम् ॥३२॥

evaṁ tvag-ādi śravaṇādi cakṣur
jihvādi nāsādi ca citta-yuktam

Similarly, the skin's object of perception is touch and Vāyu is its controlling deity. The ear's object of perception is sound, and the demigods of the directions are the controlling deities. The tongue's object of perception is taste and Varuṇa is the controlling deity. The nose's object of perception is aroma and the twin Aśvinī-kumāras are the controlling deities. The mind's object of perception is thoughts and feelings, and the moon-god is the controlling deity. Intelligence is the power of discrimination, and Lord Brahmā is the controlling deity. False ego manifests pride, and Lord Rudra is the controlling deity.

COMMENTARY

Each sense has its object of perception and its controlling diety. In this way, there is an interdependence of these three features of the material manifestation. The skin's object of perception is touch and Vāyu is the controlling deity. The ears' object of perception is sound, and the demigods of the directions are its controlling deities. The tongue's object of perception is taste, and Varuṇa is the controlling diety. Aroma is the object of perception of the nose, and the twin Aśvinī-kumāras are its controlling deities. The mind's object of perception is thinking, and the moon-god is its controlling deity. The power of discrimination is the object of perception of intelligence, and its controlling deity is Brahmā. Pride is the object of perception of false ego, and its controlling deity is Rudra.

PURPORT

In the material world, sight, that which is seen, and the seer represent the three features of *adhyātma*, *adhibhuta*, and *adhidaiva*. There is no possibility of any sense perception without the cooperation of these three. The eternal soul does not have a factual relationship with the three interdependent functions: the senses, sense objects, and the demigods. There is thus a gulf of difference between the material and spiritual manifestations. As explained by the philosophy of *acintya-bhedābheda*, although there is distinction between matter and spirit, there is oneness as well due to the relationship of cause and effect. Absolute oneness can never be supported. In the material manifestation, variegatedness produces many abominable conditions whereas in the spiritual world, there are simply varieties of blissful existence.

TEXT 33

योऽसौगुणक्षोभकृतोविकारःप्रधानमूलान्महतःप्रसूतः ।
अहंत्रिवृन्मोहविकल्पहेतुर्वैकारिकस्तामस ऐन्द्रियश्च ॥३३॥

yo 'sau guṇa-kṣobha-kṛto vikāraḥ pradhāna-mūlān mahataḥ prasūtaḥ
ahaṁ tri-vṛn moha-vikalpa-hetur vaikārikas tāmasa aindriyaś ca

The Supreme Personality of Godhead in His form as time agitates the three modes of material nature. The total material ingredients, or *mahat-tattva,* thus gives rise to the false ego, which is the cause of the three kinds of illusion—*vaikārika, tāmasa,* and *aindriya.*

COMMENTARY

The cosmic manifestation is the result of the agitation of the three modes of material nature. False ego, which is born from the *mahat-tattva*, has three features, known as *vaikārikam*, *tāmasa*, and *indriyaja*. It is this illusion or ignorance that causes one to think that the cosmic manifestation is ultimate reality.

PURPORT

Due to the agitation of the three modes of material nature, the cosmic manifestation comes into being as a transformation of the total material energy, and thus the conditioned souls are put into a condition of birth and death. If the conditioned souls give up their false identification with matter by accepting their real identity as the Lord's eternal servants, they can revive their dormant original consciousness. Here, the word *moha-vikalpa-hetuḥ* indicates that false ego causes one to think of himself as the enjoyer of material nature, thus making him undergo conditions of happiness and distress. This false ego can only be overcome by accepting the real ego as the Lord's eternal servitor.

TEXT 34

आत्मापरिज्ञानमयोविवादोह्यस्तीतिनास्तीतिभिदार्थनिष्ठः
व्यर्थोऽपिनैवोपरमेतपुंसांमत्तःपरावृत्तधियांस्वलोकात्

ātmāparijñāna-mayo vivādo hy astīti nāstīti bhidārtha-niṣṭhaḥ
vyartho 'pi naivoparameta puṁsāṁ mattaḥ parāvṛtta-dhiyāṁ sva-lokāt

The speculative debates of mundane philosophers who argue, "This world is real," "No, it is not real," is based upon incomplete knowledge of the Supreme Lord and cannot go beyond understanding the actions of the material dualities. Although such arguments are useless, those who have turned their attention away from Me, their true Self, are unable to give them up.

COMMENTARY

Learned scholars are the ones who are supposed to be capable of removing all of one's doubts. However, even such philosophers are doubtful about the nature of existence. Some philosophers try to establish, by means of reasoning and arguments, that the material world is real. Then there are others who try to prove through speculative arguments that this world is false. For this reason, there is constant debate and doubt within the minds of all the mundane scholars. Such controversy is simply due to a lack of information about the Supreme Lord. When one realizes the self and Supreme Self, there is no longer any question of dispute. Duality is experienced when one accepts something other than the Supreme Lord as life's ultimate goal.

Atheists, who have no faith in the existence of the Lord, put forward various theories saying that this world is not real and has no foundation in truth. On the other hand, those who have realized the existence of the Supreme Personality of Godhead never doubt the reality of the universe because they know it to be an emanation from the Absolute Truth. Without understanding the Supreme Absolute Truth, one will never be able to ascertain the truth of the material nature.

The speculations of materially conditioned philosophers can never reach a conclusion until they take shelter of the Lord. The devotees avoid useless arguments in this regard because they are satisfied with the understanding presented by the Lord Himself.

PURPORT

One whose intelligence is under the influence of illusion falls into the pool of duality and invites the mentality of accepting something and rejecting something else. In such a condition, one doubts the very reality of his existence, and that of the world. Having fallen under the control of the Lord's external energy due to being bereft of the Lord's service, the conditioned souls become doubtful of the reality of the cosmic manifestation and thus take to the path of dry arguments. As a result of their own *karma*, and while praising the three modes of material nature, they become subject to higher and lower births, as well as lamentation, illusion, and so on.

TEXT 35-36

श्रीउद्धव उवाच

त्वत्तःपरावृत्तधियःस्वकृतैःकर्मभिःप्रभो ।
उच्चावचान्यथादेहान्गृह्णन्तिविसृजन्तिच ॥३५॥
तन्ममाख्याहिगोविन्ददुर्विभाव्यमनात्मभिः ।
नह्येतत्प्रायशोलोकेविद्वांसःसन्तिवञ्चिताः ॥३६॥

śrī-uddhava uvāca
tvattaḥ parāvṛtta-dhiyaḥ sva-kṛtaiḥ karmabhiḥ prabho
uccāvacān yathā dehān gṛhṇanti visṛjanti ca

tan mamākhyāhi govinda durvibhāvyam anātmabhiḥ
na hy etat prāyaśo loke vidvāṁsaḥ santi vañcitāḥ

Śrī Uddhava said: O Lord Govinda, please explain to me how those who are averse to understanding the Absolute Truth accept and then give up different kinds of higher and lower bodies as a result of their fruitive activities. This is very difficult for the ignorant people of this world, who are cheated by illusion, to understand.

COMMENTARY

If one's intelligence is opposed to the devotional service of the Supreme Lord, then all one's activities simply create material bondage. As a result of engaging in fruitive activities, one is forced to accept higher and lower bodies and give them up when their allotted duration of life is over. This is the case for those who are averse to the Supreme Lord. No one can be considered intelligent without understanding the science of God, which includes a description of the negative results of those who have forgotten their eternal relationship with Him. There are many so-called wise men in the world, but although considering themselves to be most intelligent, they generally do not surrender to the supreme intelligence of the Lord.

PURPORT

When the living entities fall down from the Lord's service and embrace *Maya*, they become dependent upon others for survival. Being conditioned by the external energy of the Lord, they become falsely proud, thinking themselves to be the doers of activities, and thus they are forced to suffer or enjoy the results. Due to aversion to the Supreme Lord, the living entities receive superior and inferior material bodies that force them to suffer the pangs of repeated birth and death. The conditioned souls are unable to understand their actual position due to the pride that is generated from false ego. The more one becomes attached to enjoying the fruits of his actions, the more one's aversion to the Lord becomes prominent.

TEXT 37

श्रीभगवानुवाच
मनःकर्ममचाणूणामिन्द्रियैःपञ्चभिर्युतम् ।
लोकाल्लोकंप्रयात्यन्य आत्मातदनुवर्तते ॥३७॥

śrī-bhagavān uvāca
manaḥ karma-mayaṁ nṝṇām indriyaiḥ pañcabhir yutam
lokāl lokaṁ prayāty anya ātmā tad anuvartate

Lord Kṛṣṇa said: The mind of the conditioned soul is formed by the reactions to his fruitive work (karma). Taking the conditioned soul with it, the mind travels throughout the universe. Although the soul is distinct from the material mind, it must helplessly follow it in conditional life.

COMMENTARY

The subtle body, consisting of mind, intelligence, and false ego, takes the conditioned soul from one body to another, from one planet to another, according to the results of his fruitive acts. Although the spirit soul is distinct from the material mind, it is forced to follow it to its next destination.

PURPORT

Demanding constant gratification, the material senses engage in activities under the control of the conditioned mind. The mind, whose only business is accepting and rejecting material objects for enjoyment can only act with the help of the senses. The gross and subtle bodies are simply temporary designations of the eternal spirit soul. The spirit soul views the world from within his gross and subtle coverings and as his mentality develops, he must transmigrate from one body to another. In conditional life, the tendency to accept the gross and subtle bodies as the self becomes very strong.

TEXT 38

ध्यायन्मनोऽनुविषयान्दृष्टान्वानुश्रुतानथ ।
उद्यत्सीदत्कर्मतन्त्रंस्मृतिस्तदनुशाम्यति ॥३८॥

dhyāyan mano 'nu viṣayān dṛṣṭān vānuśrutān atha
udyat sīdat karma-tantraṁ smṛtis tad anu śāmyati

The mind, which is bound by the reactions of fruitive activities, contemplates the objects of the senses that are found in this world, as well as those existing in heaven. Thus, the mind appears to come into being and then become annihilated along with its objects of perception, so that its ability to distinguish past and future is lost.

COMMENTARY

The spirit soul always accompanies the subtle body. When the living entity is separated from the gross body, this is called death. His coming in contact with another gross body is called birth. In this verse, the Supreme Lord explains the cause of loss of memory. The mind under the control of *karma* always meditates on the objects of the senses, such as the beautiful women of this world and the celestial women of the heavenly planets. When the mind becomes fully merged in thought of a particular sense object, it will force one to accept a similar form in the future. At the time of death, the mind carries the conditioned soul into a woman's womb to develop another body that will experience another set of sense objects. Death causes the forgetfulness of one's past sensual activities but it is the same mind that develops when one comes out from the womb.

PURPORT

By always remaining absorbed in thought of the objects of this material world, either directly or indirectly, one loses his transcendental memory of his relationship with God. By identifying with matter, which is always undergoing transformation, forgetfulness of the self occurs.

TEXT 39

विषयाभिनिवेशेननात्मानंयत्स्मरेत्पुनः ।
जन्तोर्वैकस्यचिद्धेतोर्मृत्युरत्यन्तविस्मृतिः ॥३९॥

viṣayābhiniveśena nātmānaṁ yat smaret punaḥ
jantor vai kasyacid dhetor mṛtyur atyanta-vismṛtiḥ

When the conditioned soul quits his body to accept another body, according to his past karma, he becomes accustomed to his new situation and forgets everything that happened in his last life. Death means the complete forgetfulness of one's previous life.

COMMENTARY

Due to full absorption in the present body, the mind does not remember the previous body, which may have been that of a demigod or a demon, according to the results of *karma*. Death means total forgetfulness of the previous gross body. When one's reactions of *karma* allotted to the present body are exhausted, death occurs.

PURPORT

Because of full absorption in the objects of the senses, one's desires for sense gratification goes on increasing. Temporary forgetfulness of the objects of the senses occurs at the time of death, which simply means that the conditioned soul is being transferred from one gross body to another.

TEXT 40

जन्मत्वात्मतयापुंसःसर्वभावेनभूरिद ।
विषयस्वीकृतिंप्राहुर्यथास्वप्नमनोरथः ॥४०॥

janma tv ātmatayā puṁsaḥ sarva-bhāvena bhūri-da
viṣaya-svīkṛtiṁ prāhur yathā svapna-manorathaḥ

O greatly charitable Uddhava, just as one may accept a dream or a fantasy as reality, the acceptance of a new body as the self is called birth.

COMMENTARY

The acceptance of a new body according to one's *karma* is called birth. Our identification with our own body and our blind acceptance of bodily relationships as permanent constitute a prolonged form of dreaming or fantasy in which one imagines oneself to be separate from the Supreme Personality of Godhead. The term birth, therefore, does not refer to the generation of a new entity but to the blind acceptance by the spirit soul of a new material body.

PURPORT

Imagination without practical action is called a daydream. The mental concoction that occurs in a sleeping state is called a dream. Dream and imagination are insignificant states of existence, and they are similar to our state of wakefulness where we accept perishable objects as being permanent. The only real difference is that our life of wakefulness lasts longer than any dream.

TEXT 41

स्वप्नंमनोरथंचेत्थंप्राक्तनंनस्मरत्यसौ ।
तत्रपूर्वमिवात्मानमपूर्वम्चानुपश्यति ॥४१॥

svapnaṁ manorathaṁ cetthaṁ prāktanaṁ na smaraty asau
tatra pūrvam ivātmānam apūrvaṁ cānupaśyati

When a person dreams at night, he forgets his waking identity. Similarly, one who accepts the material body as the self, although eternal, forgets what kind of existence he previously had, thinking his present life to be all-in-all.

COMMENTARY

Someone may claim that a dreaming person may sometimes remember a previous dream. The answer is that there are exceptions to the general rule that everyone forgets his previous lives. There is a mystic power known as *jāti-smara* whereby one can remember his previous life. Generally, however, one accepts this life as everything, having completely forgotten his past life.

PURPORT

Just as the memory of today's dream or daydream soon fades away, and is forgotten when one has another dream or daydream the next day, because one is unable to remember his previous life, his birth appears to him to be the start of a new existence.

TEXT 42

इन्द्रियायनसृष्टयेदं त्रैविध्यं भाति वस्तुनि ।
बहिरन्तर्भिदाहेतुर्जनोऽसज्जनकृद्यथा ॥४२॥

indriyāyana-sṛṣṭyedaṁ trai-vidhyaṁ bhāti vastuni
bahir-antar-bhidā-hetur jano 'saj-jana-kṛd yathā

Because the mind, which is the resting place of the senses, has created an identification with a new body, the material conceptions of high, middle, and low class appear as if pertaining to the soul. In this way, the self creates external and internal duality, just as a man might give birth to a bad son.

PURPORT

A world of enjoyment is constructed in this life by the mind, with the help of the senses. As a result of bodily identification, temporary considerations of superiority, inferiority, and intermediate arise. A father may by nature be peaceful, but because his bad son gets into trouble the father is forced to defend his son and consider his son's enemies to be enemies of the entire family. Thus the bad son implicates the father in troublesome conflicts. Similarly, the spirit soul has no intrinsic problems, but by creating a false identification with the material body the soul becomes involved in the happiness and distress of the body. With this verse the Lord summarizes His discussion of the difference between the body and the soul.

TEXT 43

नित्यदाह्यङ्गभूतानिभवन्तिनभवन्तिच ।
कालेनालक्ष्यवेगेनसूक्ष्मत्वात्तन्नदृश्यते ॥४३॥

nityadā hy aṅga bhūtāni bhavanti na bhavanti ca
kālenālakṣya-vegena sūkṣmatvāt tan na dṛśyate

My dear Uddhava, by the influence of the unseen time, material bodies are being created and annihilated at every moment. However, because time is so subtle, its actions are imperceptible.

COMMENTARY

Just as time is imperceptible, the constant creation and annihilation brought about by time is not seen by the conditioned souls due to time's subtle nature.

TEXT 44

यथार्चिषांस्रोतसांचफलानांवावनस्पतेः ।
तथैवसर्वभूतानांवयोऽवस्थादयःकृताः ॥४४॥

yathārciṣāṁ srotasāṁ ca phalānāṁ vā vanaspateḥ
tathaiva sarva-bhūtānāṁ vayo-'vasthādayaḥ kṛtāḥ

Just as, by the influence of time, the flame of a lamp, the waves of a river, and the fruit of a tree constantly change, the age and condition of the material bodies of the living entities also change.

COMMENTARY

Although one's birth and death may not be seen at present, they can be understood by hypothesis. All material transformations are caused by the influence of imperceptible time. The examples given are the flame of a lamp, the movement of waves in a river, and fruit, which are always seen as changing. In the same way, birth and death can be perceived with relation to the material body, although the action of time is practically unperceivable. By observing the changes of the body, from childhood to youth to old age, one can understand the subtle action of time.

PURPORT

Birth and death take place by the subtle influence of time. The flickering flame of a candle sometimes waxes brightly and then again becomes weak and finally dies out. The waves of a river are endlessly flowing. The fruit of a tree gradually appear, grow, ripen, sweeten, and eventually rot and die. Similarly, one can easily understand that one's own body is undergoing constant transformation, and that the body is certainly subject to old age, disease and death.

TEXT 45

सोऽयंदीपोऽर्चिषांयद्वत्स्रोतसांतदिदंजलम् ।
सोऽयंपुमानितिनृणांमृषागीर्धीर्मृषायुषाम् ॥४५॥

so 'yaṁ dīpo 'rciṣāṁ yadvat srotasāṁ tad idaṁ jalam
so 'yaṁ pumān iti nṛṇāṁ mṛṣā gīr dhīr mṛṣāyuṣām

Just as an ignorant person says, "this is the light of the lamp," and "this is the water of the river," even though the rays of light and water in the river are constantly changing, one displays his false intelligence by thinking that the particular stage of the body represents the actual person.

COMMENTARY

Someone may say, "This is the light of the lamp," but factually, there are innumerable rays emanating from the lamp at every moment. Similarly, one may speak of the water of the river, but the fact is that different water passes by at every moment. In the same way, when we think that someone is a child, that is not the fact. The body transforms through various stages and does not indicate the actual identity of the indwelling soul. Whether in the body of a child or in the body of an old man, the soul is one and the same.

PURPORT

As his body changes, a man may think that he has surpassed his previous condition. As the flame of a lamp gradually becomes dim as the fuel is burnt, and as the waves of a river take on different shapes, ignorant human beings accept the changing body as the constitutional nature of the self. Actually the constitutional nature of the living entities never changes. Mundane transformations are temporary in nature. When the spirit soul's eternal variegated pastimes are engaged in the service of the Supreme Lord, they do not create any distaste or abomination.

TEXT 46

मास्वस्यकर्मबीजेनजायतेसोऽप्ययंपुमान् ।
म्रियतेवामरोभ्रान्त्यायथाग्निर्दारुसंयुतः ॥४६॥

mā svasya karma-bījena jāyate so 'py ayaṁ pumān
mriyate vāmaro bhrāntyā yathāgnir dāru-saṁyutaḥ

Just as fire is produced from wood and then is extinguished when the wood is completely burnt, the living entities, who are eternal, mistakenly think that they have taken birth as a result of their past *karma* and then die.

COMMENTARY

When we burn some wood, it appears as if the fire is created at some point of time and then is extinguished when the fuel is spent. Actually, the element of fire continuously exists throughout the creation, although sometimes it is manifest to our eyes and sometimes not. Similarly, the living entities are eternally existing, but because of our limited vision, it appears as if someone is born and then later on dies. This illusory condition of life is imposed upon the living beings as a result of their fruitive activities, but still, the living entities themselves remain essentially unaffected.

PURPORT

Just as fire is ignited and then extinguished by contact with wood, similarly, according to his *karma*, a living entity is seen to undergo birth and death. Actually, the living entity is eternal and thus never is born nor dies. As fire is present within wood and then blazes forth and burns the wood, birth and death are manifested due to the performance of fruitive activities. In this verse, the living entities have been compared to fire, which is sometimes manifest and sometimes not. There is a difference between the activities of those who are inclined to Kṛṣṇa's service and those who are averse to the Lord. The activities of the former enable one to enjoy eternal existence, whereas the activities of the later keep one in a state of perpetual transformation.

TEXT 47

निषेकगर्भजन्मानिबाल्यकौमारयौवनम् ।
वयोमध्यंजरामृत्युरित्यवस्थास्तनोर्नव ॥४७॥

niṣeka-garbha-janmāni bālya-kaumāra-yauvanam
vayo-madhyaṁ jarā mṛtyur ity avasthās tanor nava

The nine transformations—impregnation, gestation, birth, infancy, childhood, youth, middle age, old age, and death—only relate to the material body.

COMMENTARY

The word *niṣeka* means "to enter the womb of the mother," the word *garbha* means "to grow within the womb," *janma* means "to come out of the womb," *bālya* means "childhood up to the age of five," and the periods from five to sixteen years of age are called *kaumāra*, *paugaṇḍa*, and *kaiśora*. The period from sixteen to forty-five years of age is known as *yauvana*, forty-six to sixty is called middle-age, and after that one is considered to be in old age, culminating in death.

PURPORT

The nine stages of the conditioned soul are impregnation, gestation, birth, childhood, youth, maturity, middle age, old age, and death.

TEXT 48

एतामनोरथमयीर्हान्यस्योच्चावचास्तनूः ।
गुणसङ्गादुपादत्तेक्वचित्कश्चिज्जहातिच ॥४८॥

etā manoratha-mayīr hānyasyoccāvacās tanūḥ
guṇa-saṅgād upādatte kvacit kaścij jahāti ca

The living entity foolishly considers the superior and inferior positions that he has attained as a result of activities performed in the past to be his actual self. It is very rare that someone can give up such a false conception by the grace of the Supreme Lord.

COMMENTARY

It has already been explained that birth and death are in relation to the material body and do not apply to the spirit soul. Because of being fully engrossed in material activities, the embodied soul foolishly identifies with his bodily condition. The result of one's *karma* in this life determines one's future body because it shapes one's mentality at the time of death. Only a fortunate soul who receives the Lord's mercy can give up the false egoistic conceptions of "I am this body and everything in relation to the body is mine."

PURPORT

It is only by the mercy of the Supreme Lord that one can be released from the bodily concept of life. The Lord's mercy is causeless, and so there is always a chance of gaining relief from materal existence.

TEXT 49

आत्मनःपितृपुत्राभ्यामनुमेयौभवाप्ययौ ।
नभवाप्ययवस्तूनामभिज्ञोद्वयलक्षणः ॥४९॥

ātmanaḥ pitṛ-putrābhyām anumeyau bhavāpyayau
na bhavāpyaya-vastūnām abhijño dvaya-lakṣaṇaḥ

One gains an understanding of his own birth and death by observing the death of his father and the birth of his son. In this way, when one realistically understands the birth and death of all material bodies, he will no longer be subject to these dualities.

COMMENTARY

One may question, "Is it a fact that the embodied living entity is the witness of all these changes of the material body?" The answer is that by performing the funeral rites of one's father, and by performing the rituals related to the birth of one's son, one can understand the certainty of his own birth and death. The word *bhava* in this verse refers to birth, growth, and so on. One who is self-realized is not bewildered by the birth and death of the material body, knowing himself to be eternal.

PURPORT

The eternal spirit soul is not by nature subordinate to the external energy of the Lord, nor under the control of time. However, those who are in the conditioned state of existence have artificially put themselves in such a situation. Birth and death, as described in this verse, refers only to the material body, and not the eternal soul. A sober person, knowing the soul to be eternal, therefore gives up false identification with the temporary, unreliable body and takes shelter of the devotional service of the Lord. By this process one can escape the artificial imposition of birth and death.

TEXT 50

तरोर्बीजविपाकाभ्यांयोविद्वाञ्जन्मसंयमौ ।
तरोर्विलक्षणोद्रष्टा एवंद्रष्टातनोःपृथक् ॥५०॥

taror bīja-vipākābhyāṁ yo vidvāñ janma-saṁyamau
taror vilakṣaṇo draṣṭā evaṁ draṣṭā tanoḥ pṛthak

One who observes the growth of a tree from a seed and later on, the death of the tree after maturity certainly is a distinct observer who is separate from the tree. In the same way, the witness of the birth and death of the material body is distinct from it.

COMMENTARY

Here, the word *vipāka* indicates the final transformation called death. The rice plant dies just at maturity, with no apparent dwindling as we see in the bodies of human beings and animals. One should carefully consider the nature of the material body and that of the observer, who is certainly transcendental to such changes of the body.

PURPORT

As the seer of the seed, tree, and its fruit is different from such transformations, the embodied soul is the silent and neutral spectator of the birth and death of his gross body. The liberated soul very well understands this principle whereas the conditioned soul falsely identifies with his body, even as it undergoes these transformations. The witness's distinction from all visible objects is the subject matter of the liberated soul's realization.

TEXT 51

प्रकृतेरेवमात्मानमविविच्याबुधःपुमान् ।
तत्त्वेनस्पर्शसम्मूढःसंसारंप्रतिपद्यते ॥५१॥

prakṛter evam ātmānam avivicyābudhaḥ pumān
tattvena sparśa-sammūḍhaḥ saṁsāraṁ pratipadyate

An unintelligent person, who cannot distinguish himself from material nature, considers the material manifestation to be real. By contact with it, he becomes completely bewildered and enters into the cycle of repeated birth and death.

COMMENTARY

It may be questioned, "How does a foolish person fall into material existence?" Because a foolish person identifies himself with matter, he naturally becomes attached to his body and the objects of the senses.

PURPORT

The conditioned souls, who are fully absorbed in matter, take pleasure in associating with the objects produced by material nature and thus enter deeper into material existence. Forgetfulness of the self makes him think that he is something that he actually is not. In this regard, one should carefully consider this verse from the *Śrīmad-Bhāgavatam* (1.7.5):

yayā sammohito jīva ātmānaṁ tri-guṇātmakam
paro 'pi manute 'narthaṁ tat-kṛtaṁ cābhipadyate

Due to this external energy, the living entity, although transcendental to the three modes of material nature, thinks of himself as a material product and thus undergoes the reactions of material miseries.

TEXT 52

सत्त्वसङ्गादृषीन्देवान्रजसासुरमानुषान् ।
तमसाभूततिर्यक्त्वंभ्रामितोयातिकर्मभिः ॥५२॥

sattva-saṅgād ṛṣīn devān rajasāsura-mānuṣān
tamasā bhūta-tiryaktvaṁ bhrāmito yāti karmabhiḥ

The living entities who traverse the path of material existence, being driven by the results of their karma, take birth as sages or demigods when the mode of goodness is prominent. When the mode of passion is prominent, they take birth as demons or human beings, and when the mode of ignorance is prominent, they take birth as ghosts or in the lower species.

PURPORT

By the influence of the three modes of material nature, the forgetful living entities consider themselves as enjoyers and doers and thus receive various types of bodies, such as those of demigods, sages, demons, human beings, beasts, birds, and so on.

TEXT 53

नृत्यतोगायतःपश्यन्यथैवानुकरोतितान् ।
एवंबुद्धिगुणान्पश्यन्ननीहोऽप्यनुकार्यते ॥५३॥

nṛtyato gāyataḥ paśyan yathaivānukaroti tān
evaṁ buddhi-guṇān paśyann anīho 'py anukāryate

Just as a spectator sometimes imitates a singer or dancer, the spirit soul, although not actually the doer but merely a witness, becomes captivated by material intelligence and thus imitates its activities.

COMMENTARY

One may be attracted to a professional singer or dancer and then sing the songs heard and imitate the dances seen, entering into the mood of the performer. In the same way, the conditioned soul imitates the dictations of the mind in an attempt to become an enjoyer of the material world. Such an attempt is doomed to frustration, however the conditioned soul is similarly captivated by the concoctions of the material mind and intelligence, which convince him that he can become the enjoyer of the material world. Such an attempt is doomed to frustration, however, because the soul is never the doer of activities, which are simply carried out by material nature, entailing repeated birth and death.

PURPORT

As a foolish boy may imitate a singer or dancer but fail to do a good job, the witnessing spirit soul engages his body and mind in imitating the activities of enjoyment within the material world, but fails to achieve satisfaction.

TEXT 54-55

यथाम्भसाप्रचलतातरवोऽपिचला इव ।
चक्षुसाभ्राम्यमाणेनदृश्यतेभ्रमतीवभूः ॥५४॥
यथामनोरथधियोविषय्षानुभवोमृषा ।
स्वप्नदृष्टाश्चदाशार्हतथासंसार आत्मनः ॥५५॥

yathāmbhasā pracalatā taravo 'pi calā iva
cakṣusā bhrāmyamāṇena dṛśyate bhramatīva bhūḥ

yathā manoratha-dhiyo viṣayṣānubhavo mṛṣā
svapna-dṛṣṭāś ca dāśārha tathā saṁsāra ātmanaḥ

The reflection of a tree on the water appears to quiver. When one spins around and around, the earth also appears to be spinning. While dreaming, the world that one sees appears to be real, although it is a concoction. In the same way, the soul's material life, his experience of sense gratification, is actually false, O descendant of Daśārha.

COMMENTARY

When one rides in a boat on a river, the trees on the bank of the river that are reflected in the water also appear to be moving. In the same way, the bewildered conditioned souls consider themselves to be the doers of activities which are in fact merely interactions of the external body with the modes of nature.

PURPORT

Trees appear to be swaying when reflected in agitated water, and when one is sitting on a moving boat, the trees on the shore appear to be moving. Similarly, when the living entities become attracted to the external energy of the Lord, thus deviating from their constitutional position, they become bewildered and think themselves to be the doers and enjoyers.

TEXT 56

अर्थेह्यविद्यमानेऽपिसंसृतिननिवर्तते ।
ध्यायतोविषयानस्यस्वप्नेऽनर्थागमोयथा ॥५६॥

arthe hy avidyamāne 'pi saṁsṛtir na nivartate
dhyāyato viṣayān asya svapne 'narthāgamo yathā

Just as one may experience being bitten by a snake in a dream and thus suffer, although there is no actual snake, the conditioned souls remain entangled in material existence due to absorption in sense gratification, although the objects of the senses are not real.

COMMENTARY

Although material bondage is false, the distress caused by material existence cannot easily be overcome. The Lord therefore explains here that although not factual, material life stubbornly continues for one addicted to sense gratification, just as a frightening dream continues for one who is sleeping. One who remains fully engrossed in thought of material enjoyment certainly becomes subjected to material miseries due to his contact with matter.

PURPORT

The experience of a dream has no value to the seer when he wakes up. In the same way, a liberated soul can understand that illusory material enjoyment and temporary material designation are not eternal. As a dreamer sees things that actually have no existence, the conditioned soul sees material objects as being separate from the Supreme Lord. All the transformable objects created by the external energy of the Lord are destroyed in due course of time. The spirit soul, being deprived of engagement in the devotional service of the Lord, who is the object of knowledge, as well as the opportunity to experience uninterrupted happiness, remains situated in an incompatible position while experiencing fragmented time, imperfect knowledge, and obstructed happiness. After one awakens from a dream, the remembrance of the dream may linger. Similarly, one engaging in the devotional service of the Lord may be sometimes troubled by the dim reflection of his previous sinful life. One should therefore become strong in Kṛṣṇa consciousness by hearing the Lord's instructions to Śrī Uddhava.

TEXT 57

तस्मादुद्धवमाभुंक्ष्वविषयानसदिन्द्रियैः ।
आत्माग्रहणनिर्भातंपश्यवैकल्पिकंभ्रमम् ॥५७॥

tasmād uddhava mā bhuṅkṣva viṣayān asad-indriyaiḥ
ātmāgrahaṇa-nirbhātaṁ paśya vaikalpikaṁ bhramam

Therefore, O Uddhava, do not indulge in sense gratification with your blunt material senses. Instead, understand how the illusion based on the dualities of material existence prevent one from realizing the self.

COMMENTARY

Meditation on the objects of the senses with a spirit of enjoyment is the cause of all *anarthas*. Therefore, one should give up such meditation, realizing that it is only due to ignorance that one accepts the body as the self. Attachment to the material body, which is not the self, is the cause of illusion. This is the purport of this verse.

PURPORT

The Supreme Lord instructs Uddhava that an intelligent person should realize the uselessness of trying to gratify the senses unnecessarily, seeing things as being without a relation to Lord Kṛṣṇa. If, by seeing the pathetic condition of the conditioned souls, one becomes determined to realize his constitutional position, he should be considered a genuine philosopher.

TEXT 58-59

क्षिप्तोऽवमानितोऽसद्भिःप्रलब्धोऽसूयितोऽथवा ।
ताडितःसन्निरुद्धोवावृत्त्यावापरिहापितः ॥५८॥
निष्ठुतोमूत्रितोवाज्ञैर्बहुधैवप्रकम्पित" ।
श्रेयस्कामःकृच्छ्रगत आत्मनात्मानमुद्धरेत् ॥५९॥

kṣipto'vamānito 'sadbhiḥ pralabdho 'sūyito 'tha vā
tāḍitaḥ sanniruddho vā vṛttyā vā parihāpitaḥ
niṣṭhyuto mūtrito vājñair bahudhaivaṁ prakampitaḥ
śreyas-kāmaḥ kṛcchra-gata ātmanātmānam uddharet

A devotee who actually desires to attain perfection in this very life should tolerate all kinds of difficulties. Even when insulted, ridiculed, or even beaten or confined by miscreants, or when spat upon or urinated upon by ignorant fools, with intelligence fixed in devotional service, he should remain undisturbed.

COMMENTARY

How can one live without indulging in sense gratification? These two verses provide the answer. If one is driven out, taunted, insulted, deprived of his livelihood, or spat upon, he should simply tolerate these inconveniences and protect himself with his good intelligence by remaining fixed in self-realization.

PURPORT

If one realizes the misery suffered in the field of material activities and thus become busy in trying to find a solution, either by increasing his material enjoyment or by renunciation of sense gratification, he will not be able to attain the ultimate goal of life. In this regard, Śrī Caitanya Mahāprabhu instructs us:

"One can chant the holy name of the Lord in a humble state of mind, thinking himself lower than the straw in the street. One should be more tolerant than the tree, devoid of all sense of false prestige, and ready to offer all respects to others. In such a state of mind, one can chant the holy name of the Lord constantly."

If one seriously follows this advice, then the temptation for increasing material enjoyment and the simple renunciation of the fruits of *karma* will not capture one. The best means for achieving auspiciousness is to become sober, tolerant, and free from false ego.

TEXT 60

श्रीउद्धव उवाच
यथैवमनुबुध्येयं वद नो वदतां वर ॥६०॥

śrī-uddhava uvāca
yathaivam anubudhyeyaṁ vada no vadatāṁ vara

Śrī Uddhava said: O most eloquent speaker, kindly explain these statements so that I may properly understand them.

COMMENTARY

Uddhava said: Please tell me how I can tolerate the above-mentioned disturbances and thus become advanced in spiritual life.

TEXT 61

सुदुःषहमिमंमन्य आत्मन्यसदतिक्रमम् ।
विदुषामपिविश्वात्मन्प्रकृतिर्हिबलीयसी ।
ऋतेत्वद्धर्मनिरतान्शान्तांस्तेचरणालयान् ॥६१॥

su-duḥṣaham imaṁ manya ātmany asad-atikramam
viduṣām api viśvātman prakṛtir hi balīyasī
ṛte tvad-dharma-niratān śāntāṁs te caraṇālayān

O soul of the universe, one's acquired nature in material life is very strong. Because of this, it is very difficult for even learned men to tolerate the offenses committed against them by ignorant people. I think that only Your devotees, who are fixed in Your loving service, are able to tolerate such offenses.

COMMENTARY

Even learned people who know that they should tolerate abuse are unable to do so because theoretical learning alone cannot make one saintly. On the other hand, the devotees, because they possess a similar nature to that of the Supreme Lord, remain peaceful in all conditions of life because they always reside under the shade of the Lord's lotus feet.

PURPORT

As long as one has a propensity for material enjoyment and thus is absorbed in matter, he cannot attain peace. By taking shelter of a so-called spiritual master who desires material enjoyment, liberation, or mystic perfections, one's restlessness in the form of material desires will not decrease. Only by the good influence of the devotees' association, and following their instructions, can one make tangible advancement in spiritual life.

Thus end the translation of the Sixteenth Chapter of the Uddhava-gītā *entitled* **"Enumeration of the Elements of Material Creation"** *with the commentaries of Śrīla Viśvanātha Cakravartī Ṭhākura and chapter summary and purports by Śrīla Bhaktisiddhānta Sarasvatī Ṭhākura*

Chapter 17

The Song of the Avantī Brāhmaṇa

CHAPTER SUMMARY

This chapter tells the story of a wandering mendicant *sannyāsī* from the country of Avantī as an example of how one should tolerate the disturbances created by foolish people.

The harsh words of uncultured persons pierce the heart even more painfully than arrows. Still, the mendicant *brāhmaṇa* from the city of Avantī, even while being attacked by wicked men, considered this misery to be the result of his own past misdeeds and so he tolerated it without being disturbed. Previously, the *brāhmaṇa* had been a farmer and merchant. He had been extremely greedy, miserly, and prone to anger, and so his wife, sons, daughters, relatives, and servants were deprived of a life of enjoyment and gradually came to neglect him. In due course of time, thieves, family members, and providence took away all of his wealth. Finding himself without any money and abandoned by everyone, the *brāhmaṇa* developed a deep sense of detachment.

He considered how the earning and preservation of wealth involve great effort, fear, anxiety, and confusion. Because of wealth, there arise fifteen unwanted things—thievery, violence, lying, deception, lust, anger, pride, feverishness, disagreement, hatred, distrust, conflict, attachment to women, gambling, and intoxication. When this meditation arose within his heart, the *brāhmaṇa* could understand that the Supreme Lord Śrī Hari had somehow become satisfied with him. He felt that it was because the Lord had become pleased with him that the apparently unfavorable turn of events in his life had occurred. He was grateful that a sense of detachment had arisen in his heart, and he considered it to be the factual means for his deliverance. In this condition, he became determined to engage in the worship of Lord Hari for the rest of his life and for this purpose, he accepted the order of *tridaṇḍi-sannyāsa*. Thereafter, he entered different villages to beg alms, but the people disturbed him in various ways. Still, he simply tolerated this, remaining firm like a mountain. He remained fixed in his spiritual practice and sang a song that has become famous as the *Bhikṣu-gītā*.

Neither human beings, demigods, the soul, planets, the reactions of work, nor time are the causes of one's happiness and distress. Rather, the mind alone is their cause, because it is the mind that causes the spirit soul to wander in the cycle of material life. The real purpose of all kinds of pious activities, such as charity, and the performance of religious rituals, is to bring the mind under control. One who has already conquered his mind by meditation has no need for any other process, and for one who is incapable of fixing his mind, all processes are of no practical use. The false conception of the material ego binds the eternal spirit soul to material sense objects. The Avantī *brāhmaṇa* became determined to cross over the insurmountable ocean of material existence by rendering service to the lotus feet of the Supreme Lord, Mukunda, with the same faith in the Lord that was exhibited by great devotees in the past.

Only when one can focus his intelligence on the lotus feet of the Supreme Personality of Godhead can the mind be completely controlled. This is the essence of all practices meant for spiritual advancement.

TEXT 1

श्रीबादरायणिरुवाच
स एवमाशंसित उद्धवेनभागवतमुख्येनदाशार्हमुख्यः ।
सभाजयन्भृत्यवचोमुकुन्दस्तमाबभाषेश्रवणीयवीर्यः ॥१॥

śrī-bādarāyaṇir uvāca
sa evam āśaṁsita uddhavena bhāgavata-mukhyena dāśārha-mukhyaḥ
sabhājayan bhṛtya-vaco mukundas tam ābabhāṣe śravaṇīya-vīryaḥ

Śukadeva Gosvāmī said: Lord Mukunda, the foremost of Dāśārhas, at the request of the exalted devotee, Uddhava, first praised His servant's fine statements. The Lord, whose pastimes are meditated upon by great sages, then replied.

COMMENTARY

This chapter describes how a dishonest person lost his wealth and then was insulted by miscreants, and how one can remove his distress with the help of his intelligence.

TEXT 2

श्रीभगवानुवाच
बार्हस्पत्यसनास्त्यत्रसाधुर्वैदुर्जनेरितैः ।
दुरक्तैर्भिन्नमात्मानंयःसमाधातुमीश्वरः ॥२॥

śrī-bhagavān uvāca
bārhaspatya sa nāsty atra sādhur vai durjaneritaiḥ
duraktair bhinnam ātmānaṁ yaḥ samādhātum īśvaraḥ

The Supreme Lord said: O disciple of Bṛhaspati, rare is the saintly person in this world who is capable of pacifying his mind after it has been agitated by the harsh words of a miscreant.

COMMENTARY

The Supreme Lord said: O disciple of Bṛhaspati, my dear Uddhava, your statements are most reasonable. There is a completely spiritual path that is incomprehensible even to your spiritual master, Bṛhaspati. Now, hear of this from Me.

PURPORT

Devotees try to follow in the footsteps of saintly persons, and yet nondevotees often attack them by putting forth unreasonable arguments. Upon seeing the nondevotees' life of eat, drink, and make merry, the simple-minded and peaceful devotees feel broken-hearted. Although the devotees remain aloof from sinful persons, the nondevotees' abominable mentality and their harsh words by which they insult others certainly curb the progress of the human society.

TEXT 3

नतथातप्यतेविद्धःपुमान्बाणैस्तुमर्मगैः ।
यथातुदन्तिमर्मस्थाह्यसतांपरुषेषवः ॥३॥

na tathā tapyate viddhaḥ pumān bāṇais tu marma-gaiḥ
yathā tudanti marma-sthā hy asatāṁ paruṣeṣavaḥ

The harsh and insulting words hurled by the lowest among men cause more pain than the sharp arrows that penetrate one's chest during a battle.

COMMENTARY

Harsh words are here compared to sharp arrows.

TEXT 4

कथयन्तिमहत्पुण्यमितिहासमिहोद्धव ।
तमहंवर्णयिष्यामिनिबोधसुसमाहितः ॥४॥

kathayanti mahat puṇyam itihāsam ihoddhava
tam ahaṁ varṇayiṣyāmi nibodha su-samāhitaḥ

My dear Uddhava, please listen attentively as I narrate a most pious history that the compilers of the *Purāṇas* have narrated in this regard.

TEXT 5

केनचिद्भिक्षुणागीतंपरिभूतेनदुर्जनैः ।
स्मरताधृतियुक्तेनविपाकंनिजकर्मणाम् ॥५॥

kenacid bhikṣuṇā gītāṁ paribhūtena durjanaiḥ
smaratā dhṛti-yuktena vipākaṁ nija-karmaṇām

Once there was a *sannyāsī* who was insulted in many ways by sinful men. However, with determination, he remembered that he was suffering the results of his previous actions. I shall now narrate to you his story, and that which he spoke.

COMMENTARY

Although it is common to hear harsh words these days, they are nonetheless more painful than sharp arrows. The Lord is herein narrating a story from the *Purāṇas*. The word *vipāka* means "fruits."

PURPORT

Those who try to live a renounced and saintly life are generally insulted by uncivilized men. Still, a saintly person knows that he is not simply being offended by coarse fools. He knows that whatever happiness and distress he experiences in this world are the results of his previous activities. Therefore, it is always advised that those who desire liberation from material existence, regardless of the path they cultivate, should never become angry and retaliate those who offend or insult them. In this regard, Śrī Caitanya Mahāprabhu has instructed us to be as toleranat as a tree. This instruction is for the benefit of all kinds of people because practically, in any endeavor, it is experienced that only by tolerance is conflict avoided. If one does not respond to those who offend him, one will find that such ruffians will soon leave him alone.

TEXT 6

अवन्तिषु द्विजः कश्चिदासीदाढ्यतमः श्रिया ।
वार्तावृत्तिः कदर्यस्तु कामी लुब्धोऽतिकोपनः ॥६॥

avantiṣu dvijaḥ kaścid āsīd āḍhyatamaḥ śriyā
vārtā-vṛttiḥ kadaryas tu kāmī lubdho 'ti-kopanaḥ

Long ago, in the country of Avanti, there lived a brāhmaṇa **who was wealthy and endowed with great opulence. He engaged in farming and commerce, but he was very miserly, lusty, greedy, and prone to anger.**

COMMENTARY

The city of Avantī is in the district of Malwa. This *brāhmaṇa* was a farmer and businessman by profession, but his character was abominable. One who gives abuses to his wife and children, disregards all religious principles, disrespects the demigods and guests, and torments servants is certainly an abominable person.

TEXT 7

ज्ञातयोऽतिथयस्तस्य वाङ्मात्रेणापि नार्चिताः ।
शून्यावसथ आत्मापि काले कामैरनर्चितः ॥७॥

jñātayo 'tithayas tasya vāṅ-mātreṇāpi nārcitāḥ
śūnyāvasatha ātmāpi kāle kāmair anarcitaḥ

In his home, which was devoid of religiosity and reasonable comfort, no one was given respect, be they family members or guests. Not only was the brāhmaṇa **miserly toward others, he did not even grant his own body sufficient gratification.**

COMMENTARY

The *brāhmaṇa's* householder life was completely devoid of any religious observances.

TEXT 8

दुःशीलस्यकदर्यस्यदुह्यन्तेपुत्रबान्धवाः ।
दारादुहितरोभृत्याविषण्णानाचरन्प्रियम् ॥८॥

duḥśīlasya kadaryasya druhyante putra-bāndhavāḥ
dārā duhitaro bhṛtyā viṣaṇṇā nācaran priyam

Because he was so callous and stingy, his wife, children, and other relatives, and even his servants came to hate him. Being thoroughly disgusted with him, they did not even bother to feign affection.

COMMENTARY

Neighbors always hate a wicked person.

TEXT 9

तस्यैवंयक्षवित्तस्यच्युतस्योभयलोकतः ।
धर्मकामविहीनस्यचुक्रुधुःपञ्चभागिनः ॥९॥

tasyaivaṁ yakṣa-vittasya cyutasyobhaya-lokataḥ
dharma-kāma-vihīnasya cukrudhuḥ pañca-bhāginaḥ

The five presiding deities of the five family sacrifices became angry with the brāhmaṇa who, being very frugal, protected his wealth like a Yakṣa, who was certainly cultivating inauspiciousness for both this life and the next, and who was totally devoid of religiosity and sense enjoyment.

COMMENTARY

The Yakṣas only business is to accumulate and protect wealth. They do not utilize it, either for themselves of for others. The five types of living entities who deserve a share of sacrificial offerings are the demigods, sages, forefathers, human beings, and lower classes of beings. When they are deprived of their share, they become angry at a householder.

PURPORT

If the demigods, sages, forefathers, human beings, and other living entities do not receive their respective shares of sacrificial performances, they become angry at a materialistic fruitive worker.

TEXT 10

तदवध्यानविस्रस्तपुण्यस्कन्धस्य भूरिद ।
अर्थोऽप्यगच्छन्निधनं बह्वायासपरिश्रमः ॥१०॥

tad-avadhyāna-visrasta-puṇya-skandhasya bhūri-da
artho 'py agacchan nidhanaṁ bahv-āyāsa-pariśramaḥ

O magnanimous Uddhava, as a result of disregarding the demigods in this way, the *brāhmaṇa* gradually lost his accumulated piety and soon became bereft of his hard-earned wealth.

COMMENTARY

The *brāhmaṇa* lost everything, including his hard-earned wealth, because of neglecting those upon whom he depended. Accumulating wealth by means of farming and trading is certainly very laborious.

TEXT 11

ज्ञात्यो जगृहुः किञ्चित्किञ्चिद्दस्यव उद्धव ।
दैवतः कालतः किञ्चिद्ब्रह्मबन्धोर्नृपार्थिवात् ॥११॥

ñātyo jagṛhuḥ kiñcit kiñcid dasyava uddhava
daivataḥ kālataḥ kiñcid brahma-bandhor nṛ-pārthivāt

O Uddhava, some of the wealth of that fallen *brāhmaṇa* was taken away by his relatives, some by thieves, some by providence, some by the influence of time, some by ordinary men, and some by the king.

COMMENTARY

The *brāhmaṇa* lost his wealth as a result of natural calamities, such as fire in his house, as well as due to food grains rotting under the influence of time, theft, government taxes, and pilfering by his friends and relatives. In this way, he became a poor man.

PURPORT

If a *brāhmaṇa* neglects his brahminical duties, he is referred to as *brahma-bandhu*, or a so-called *brāhmaṇa*, and not considered a genuine *brāhmaṇa*. One who takes pride in posing as a *brāhmaṇa* without making any attempt to elevate himself to the transcendental platform is not a genuine *brāhmaṇa*, but is referred to as *brahma-bandhu*, or the friend of a *brāhmaṇa*. Devotees of the Lord are not proud, thinking themselves to be the most exalted members of society. Rather, they very humbly think themselves fallen and without any qualifications. However, those who are intelligent know that such humble devotees are actually *brāhmaṇas* whose hearts are cleansed by their engagement in the devotional service of the Lord.

TEXT 12

स एवंद्रविणेनष्टेधर्मकामविवर्जितः ।
उपेक्षितश्चस्वजनैश्चिन्तामापदुरत्ययाम् ॥१२॥

sa evaṁ draviṇe naṣṭe dharma-kāma-vivarjitaḥ
upekṣitaś ca sva-janaiś cintām āpa duratyayām

At last, when all his wealth was lost, the *brahmaṇa,* who never engaged in religious practices or sense enjoyment, was totally ignored by his family. Because of this, he began to feel terrible anxiety.

TEXT 13

तस्यैवंध्यायतोदीर्घंनष्टरायस्तपस्विनः ।
खिद्यतोबाष्पकण्ठस्यनिर्वेदःसुमहानभूत् ॥१३॥

tasyaivaṁ dhyāyato dīrghaṁ naṣṭa-rāyas tapasvinaḥ
khidyato bāṣpa-kaṇṭhasya nirvedaḥ su-mahān abhūt

Being deprived of his wealth, the *brāhmaṇa* felt great fear and lamentation. Thereafter, while meditating upon his misfortune at great length, a strong feeling of detachment developed within him.

COMMENTARY

The miserly *brāhmana* had to suffer the consequences of his own faults. Finally, due to his previous training in piety, he experienced a change of heart. When he lost all his wealth, the *brāhmaṇa* had no alternative but to live like an ascetic.

TEXT 14

सचाहेदमहोकष्टंवृथात्मामेऽनुतापितः ।
नधर्मायनकामाययस्यार्थायास ईदृशः ॥१४॥

sa cāhedam aho kaṣṭaṁ vṛthātmā me 'nutāpitaḥ
na dharmāya na kāmāya yasyārthāyāsa īdṛśaḥ

The brāhmaṇa spoke as follows: O what great misfortune! I simply tormented myself uselessly, working so hard to earn money that was not utilized for religiosity or material enjoyment.

PURPORT

When one suffers a great setback on the path of his material life, one may understand that by failing to utilize everything in the service of the Supreme Lord and instead engaging in activities having no relationship with Kṛṣṇa consciousness, one gains nothing.

TEXT 15

प्रायेणाथाःकदर्याणांनसुखायकदाचन ।
इहचात्मोपतापायमृतस्यनरकायच ॥१५॥

prāyeṇāthāḥ kadaryāṇāṁ na sukhāya kadācana
iha cātmopatāpāya mṛtasya narakāya ca

Generally, the wealth of misers never affords them any happiness. In this life, it simply torments them with anxiety, and when they die, it buys their ticket to hell.

COMMENTARY

Being afraid to spend any money, misers avoid performing constitutional and conventional duties.

PURPORT

Conditioned souls who have forgotten their constitutional position accept many things in this world to be their ultimate goal of life. However, these things become the cause of their degradation, making them suffer in hell in their next life.

TEXT 16

यशोयशस्विनांशुद्धंश्लाघ्यायेगुणिनांगुणाः ।
लोभःस्वल्पोऽपितान्हन्तिश्वित्रोरूपमिवेप्सितम् ॥१६॥

yaśo yaśasvināṁ śuddhaṁ ślāghyā ye guṇināṁ guṇāḥ
lobhaḥ sv-alpo 'pi tān hanti śvitro rūpam ivepsitam

Just as even a trace of white leprosy spoils one's physical beauty, even a tinge of greed destroys a person's good reputation and sullies whatever praiseworthy qualities are found in a virtuous soul.

COMMENTARY

White leprosy certainly spoils a person's beauty.

TEXT 17

अर्थस्यसाधनेसिद्धे उत्कर्षेरक्षणेव्यये ।
नाशोपभोग आयासस्त्रासश्चिन्ताभ्रमोनृणाम् ॥१७॥

arthasya sādhane siddhe utkarṣe rakṣaṇe vyaye
nāśopabhoga āyāsas trāsaś cintā bhramo nṛṇām

People who work very hard to earn and accumulate wealth are afraid of spending it, are in anxiety about protecting it, and become bewildered when it is lost.

COMMENTARY

There are various kinds of distress experienced by one who endeavors to accumulate wealth. Such misery is experienced at all stages—while earning it, while protecting it, while spending it, and when it is somehow lost. There are fifteen types of *anarthas* born of wealth, such as gambling, drinking wine, and so on.

PURPORT

Because the means for acquiring wealth, as well as its attainment, enhancement, protection, and expenditure are under the influence of time, these are always accompanied by anxiety, hard labor, and bewilderment.

TEXT 18-19

स्तेयंहिंसानृतंदम्भःकामःक्रोधःस्मयोमदः ।
भेदोवैरमविश्वासःसंस्पर्धाव्यसनानिच ॥१८॥
एतेपञ्चदशानर्थाह्यर्थमूलामतानृणाम् ।
तस्मादनर्थमर्थाख्यंश्रेयोऽर्थीदूरतस्त्यजेत् ॥१९॥

steyaṁ hiṁsānṛtaṁ dambhaḥ kāmaḥ krodhaḥ smayo madaḥ
bhedo vairam aviśvāsaḥ saṁspardhā vyasanāni ca

ete pañcadaśānarthā hy artha-mūlā matā nṛṇām
tasmād anartham arthākhyaṁ śreyo-'rthī dūratas tyajet

Fifteen undesirable qualities arise because of wealth—theft, violence, falsehood, duplicity, lust, anger, quarrel, madness, competition, enmity, faithlessness, arrogance, and the dangers arising from attachment to women, gambling, and intoxication. Therefore, those who desire their own benefit should give up attachment to excessive wealth, which is the mother of all anarthas.

COMMENTARY

It takes great endeavor to accumulate wealth. Then, one is always afraid that his wealth will be stolen or taken away by some other means. To protect his wealth, one must lie, and excessive wealth certainly is the cause of great pride and delusion. In this way, there are fifteen kinds of *anartha* that surface because of wealth. It can be concluded that *artha* (wealth) is the cause of all *anarthas* (unwanted things).

PURPORT

One who desires his actual benefit should reject as useless that which is ascertained as beneficial according to worldly calculation. In this connection, there are fifteen unwanted things that are created by excessive wealth. The main intention of those who accumulate great wealth is sense gratification. The unwanted things that are born from excessive wealth are theft, violence, lying, pride, lust, anger, false pride, madness, duplicity, enmity, faithlessness, arrogance, and addiction to women, gambling, and intoxication. In general, gold and silver coins that are exchanged for the objects of sense gratification are known as *artha*, or wealth.

TEXT 20

भिद्यन्तेभ्रातरोदाराःपितरःसुहृदस्तथा ।
एकास्निग्धाःकाकिणिनासद्यःसर्वेऽरयःकृताः ॥२०॥

bhidyante bhrātaro dārāḥ pitaraḥ suhṛdas tathā
ekāsnigdhāḥ kākiṇinā sadyaḥ sarve 'rayaḥ kṛtāḥ

Even a man's brothers, wife, parents, and friends, who appear bound to him in love can immediately break off their affectionate relationships and become enemies due to a dispute over even an insignificant sum of money.

COMMENTARY

Even though one's brothers, father, wife, and friends may appear to be on good terms with him, they can quickly turn into enemies for the sake of a single penny.

PURPORT

The word *kākiṇi* means "twenty *barātikā*," which is the coin of the smallest denomination, or value.

TEXT 21

अर्थेनाल्पीयसाह्येतेसंरब्धादीप्तमन्यवः ।
त्यजन्त्याशुस्पृधोघ्नन्तिसहसोत्सृज्यसौहृदम् ॥२१॥

arthenālpīyasā hy ete saṁrabdhā dīpta-manyavaḥ
tyajanty āśu spṛdho ghnanti sahasotsṛjya sauhṛdam

For the sake of even an insignificant amount of money, these dear ones may become agitated and angry. Within a moment they may give up their affection and sever all ties, even up to the point of murder.

COMMENTARY

The word *spṛdhaḥ* means "audacity or arrogance."

TEXT 22

लब्ध्वाजन्मामरप्रार्थ्यंमानुष्यंतद्द्विजाग्रयताम् ।
तदनादृत्ययेस्वार्थंघ्नन्तियान्त्यशुभांगतिम् ॥२२॥

labdhvā janmāmara-prārthyaṁ mānuṣyaṁ tad dvijāgryatām
tad anādṛtya ye svārthaṁ ghnanti yānty aśubhāṁ gatim

Those who obtain this rare human form of life, which is desired even by the demigods, and take birth as *brāhmaṇas,* are extremely fortunate. If they misuse this opportunity and fail to attain their real self-interest, they come to a most unfortunate end.

PURPORT

Human life is superior to that of a demigod, ghost, animal, tree, or an inanimate stone because the demigods are absorbed in celestial pleasure while neglecting their real self-interest, and in other forms of life there is predominantly suffering. Human life affords one the opportunity of attaining the ultimate goal of life. In the human form, one has the opportunity of surpassing the concocted ideas born of a background of *anyābhilāṣa*, *karma* and *jñāna*, and engaging in the devotional service of the Supreme Lord. In the life of a *śudra*, which is generally devoid of piety, there is no possibility of contemplating one's real self-interest because a *śudra* is very busy serving the other three *varṇas*, as well as his desires for sense enjoyment. Knowledge of Brahman and Paramātmā, and the right for serving the Supreme Personality of Godhead, are the domain of the best of the twice-born. However, such a high birth has no value if one is bereft of Lord Hari's service. There is no value in simply becoming a so-called *brāhmaṇa*. In this regard one should carefully consider this verse from the *Srimad-Bhāgavatam* (11.5.3):

ya eṣāṁ puruṣaṁ sākṣād ātma-prabhavam īśvaram
na bhajanty avajānanti sthānād bhraṣṭāḥ patanty adhaḥ

Anyone who does not render service and neglects his duty unto the primeval Lord, who is the source of all living entities, will certainly fall down from his constitutional position.

The desire to become master of all one surveys checks one's advancement in spiritual life. When a *brāhmaṇa* gives up the devotional service of the Lord and works hard like a *śūdra*, simply for the prestige of his community, then lording it over material nature and the desire to enjoy the fruits of *karma* become very prominent A *brāhmaṇa*, free from false prestige, should feel himself lower than a blade of grass and offer respect to all living entities. All human beings, and especially *brāhmaṇas*, should avoid becoming killers of their own self-interest by neglecting Kṛṣṇa consciousness, the loving service of the Lord. Such neglect paves the way for future suffering.

TEXT 23

स्वर्गापवर्गयोर्द्वारंप्राप्यलोकमिमंपुमान् ।
द्रविणेकोऽनुषज्जेतमर्त्योऽनर्थस्यधामनि ॥२३॥

svargāpavargayor dvāraṁ prāpya lokam imaṁ pumān
draviṇe ko 'nuṣajjeta martyo 'narthasya dhāmani

After receiving this human form of life, which is the gateway to heaven and liberation, who would become attached to the accumulation of wealth, which brings with it all kinds of *anarthas*?

PURPORT

Objects intended for one's personal enjoyment are referred to as *draviṇa*, or material wealth. Those who desire to achieve wealth, who endeavor to transfer themselves to the heavenly planets, who practice renunciation with a desire to attain liberation, and who endeavor to attain the four objectives of human life, are unable to achieve their real self-interest because all of these desires are impediments to the attainment of the Lord's devotional service. Both material enjoyment and liberation are just like a mirage for those who have received the mercy of the Lord. Because material enjoyment and liberation are not conceived of as being in relation to Kṛṣṇa, they are considered to be *anarthas*.

TEXT 24

देवर्षिपितृभूतानिज्ञातीन्बन्धूंश्चभागिनः ।
असंविभज्यचात्मानंयक्षवित्तःपतत्यधः ॥२४॥

devarṣi-pitṛ-bhūtāni jñātīn bandhūṁś ca bhāginaḥ
asaṁvibhajya cātmānaṁ yakṣa-vittaḥ patatyadhaḥ

One who does not give his hard-earned wealth to those to whom he is obligated, such as the demigods, forefathers, great sages, family members, and living beings in general, is no better than a Yakṣa and will certainly fall down from his position.

COMMENTARY

Because the demigods, sages, forefathers, living entities in general, relatives, and friends are all interrelated, they are shareholders of one's wealth. When one deprives them of their shares and tries to enjoy alone, they will naturally become envious and thus withhold their mercy. This will create an impediment on the path of one's plans to enjoy sense gratification.

TEXT 25

व्यर्थयार्थेहयावित्तंप्रमत्तस्यवयोबलम् ।
कुशलायेनसिध्यन्तिजरठःकिंनुसाधये ॥२५॥

vyarthayārthehayā vittaṁ pramattasya vayo balam
kuśalā yena sidhyanti jaraṭhaḥ kiṁ nu sādhaye

Those who are actually intelligent are able to utilize their money, youth, and strength to achieve perfection. Unfortunately, I have feverishly squandered these assets in the

useless endeavor for accumulating wealth. Now that I have become an old man, it is too late for me to do anything auspicious.

COMMENTARY

"The very wealth for which I had become intoxicated is now gone. Intelligent people utilize their wealth in the service of the Supreme Lord and thus attain perfection. I am now an old man and so how will I be able to recover my losses?" This is the *brahmana's* lamentation.

PURPORT

The *brahmana* thought, "How will I accumulate the wealth that is required for acquiring the objects for sense gratification in my old age?"

TEXT 26

कस्मात्सङ्क्लिश्यतेविद्वान्व्यर्थयार्थेहयासकृत् ।
कस्यचिन्मcraftयानूनंलोकोऽयंसुविमोहितः ॥२६॥

kasmāt saṅkliśyate vidvān vyarthayārthehayāsakṛt
kasyacin māyayā nūnaṁ loko 'yaṁ su-vimohitaḥ

Why should an intelligent person suffer because of his useless efforts to accumulate wealth? Indeed, everyone appears to be bewildered by someone's illusory potency.

COMMENTARY

The *brāhmaṇa* thought that his misfortune must have been caused by the influence of the Lord's illusory energy, *maya*. By her influence, the whole world is bewildered.

PURPORT

Due to lack of knowledge of the Absolute Truth, the conditioned souls are overwhelmed by the Lord's illusory energy, accepting the manifestations of the Lord's energies as meant for their own enjoyment. It is for this reason that the conditioned souls remain in illusion and thus continue to suffer.

TEXT 27

किंधनैर्धनदैर्वाकिंकामैर्वाकामदैरुत ।
मृत्युनाग्रस्यमानस्यकर्मभिर्वोतजन्मदैः ॥२७॥

kiṁ dhanair dhana-dair vā kiṁ kāmair vā kāma-dair uta
mṛtyunā grasyamānasya karmabhir vota janma-daiḥ

For one who is about to die, what is the use of wealth, sense gratification, or any such thing, and what is the use of other persons who may offer them, which simply cause one to repeatedly take birth in this world?

PURPORT

Wealth, the giver of wealth, sense gratification, and the objects of the senses continuously transform by the influence of time. What then is use of being proud, thinking oneself to be the doer that awards himself the fruits of his actions?

TEXT 28

नूनंमेभगवांस्तुष्टःसर्वदेवमयोहरिः ।
येननीतोदशामेतांनिर्वेदश्चात्मनःप्लवः ॥२८॥

nūnaṁ me bhagavāṁs tuṣṭaḥ sarva-deva-mayo hariḥ
yena nīto daśām etāṁ nirvedaś cātmanaḥ plavaḥ

Śrī Hari, who is the Lord of the demigods, must have been pleased with me. It is by His mercy that I have attained this present state of suffering, and have thus developed a sense of detachment, which is the boat that will carry me across the ocean of material existence.

COMMENTARY

When the *brāhmaṇa* realized that his suffering condition enabled him to become detached, he became joyful, understanding that his so-called misfortune was actually the Lord's special mercy. Such detachment from materialistic life is a sure symptom of the Lord's causeless mercy, and the *brāhmaṇa* considered it to be the boat for crossing over the ocean of material existence.

PURPORT

The *brāhmaṇa* thought, "The demigods are empowered to award their worshipers varieties of worldly and heavenly sense pleasures. Therefore, they are only givers of imperfect benedictions. Now that all my assets have been snatched away, I think that the almighty Lord, who is my real benefactor, has mercifully given me relief from the struggle for existence that characterizes life in the material world. Now I have become detached from the four objectives of life such—religiosity, economic development, sense gratification, and liberation, which are sought after by less-intelligent people."

TEXT 29

सोऽहंकालावशेषेणशोषयिष्येऽङ्गमात्मनः
अप्रमत्तोऽखिलस्वार्थेयदिस्यात्सिद्ध आत्मनि

so 'haṁ kālāvaśeṣeṇa śoṣayiṣye 'ṅgam ātmanaḥ
apramatto 'khila-svārthe yadi syāt siddha ātmani

If I have some more time to live, then I will perform austerities while subsisting upon the bare minimum of food. Without further bewilderment, I will execute that which is actually in my self-interest, and thus remain self-satisfied.

COMMENTARY

The *brāhmaṇa* was eager to finish his life of material enjoyment at any cost. He thought that if he could spend the rest of his life thinking of the Lord's lotus feet, which are the root cause of all self-interest, then his perfection would be guaranteed.

PURPORT

The Avantī *brāhmaṇa* considered that it is useless to aspire for advancement of religiosity, economic development, and sense gratification, and also futile to try and rid one of all desires for material enjoyment by performing austerities. He thought, "To become freed from the materialistic mentality of achieving the perfection of religiosity, economic development, sense gratification, and liberation, I must take shelter of devotional service to the Lord."

TEXT 30

तत्रमामनुमोदेरन्देवास्त्रिभुवनेश्वराः ।
मुहूर्तेनब्रह्मलोकंखट्वाङ्गःसमसाधयत् ॥३०॥

tatra mām anumoderan devās tri-bhuvaneśvarāḥ
muhūrtena brahma-lokaṁ khaṭvāṅgaḥ samasādhayat

May the demigods, who are the presiding deities of the three worlds, bestow their mercy upon me. After all, Mahārāja Khaṭvāṅga was able to attain Vaikuṇṭha in just a moment.

COMMENTARY

The Avantī *brāhmaṇa* considered that if the demigods, headed by Indra, approved of his intention, then they will no longer create obstacles for him. Being near the end of his life, he carefully considered what he could do for his ultimate welfare and while doing so, he thought of King Khaṭvāṅga, who went back to Godhead simply after a moment's engagement in Kṛṣṇa consciousness.

PURPORT

King Khaṭvāṅga, who had fought on behalf of the demigods, attained the ultimate goal of life within a moment by renouncing all desires for religiosity, economic development, sense gratification, and liberation. The mendicant *brāhmaṇa* from Avantī prayed to the demigods who manage the universal affairs for the benediction of engagement in the devotional service of Lord Kṛṣṇa.

TEXT 31

श्रीभगवानुवाच
इत्यभिप्रेत्यमनसाह्यावन्त्योद्विजसत्तमः ।
उन्मुच्यहृदयग्रन्थीन्शान्तोभिक्षुरभून्मुनिः ॥३१॥

śrī-bhagavān uvāca
ity abhipretya manasā hy āvantyo dvija-sattamaḥ
unmucya hṛdaya-granthīn śānto bhikṣur abhūn muniḥ

Lord Śrī Kṛṣṇa continued: Having made up his mind in this way, the exalted Avantī *brāhmaṇa* cut asunder the knots of material attachment within his heart. In this way, he became a self-satisfied mendicant in the renounced order of life.

COMMENTARY

The phrase *hṛdaya granthīn* means "the knots in the heart." The *brāhmaṇa* was able to untie these knots in the heart, which are in the form of the misconception, "I am this body and everything in relation to this body is mine."

PURPORT

The most fortunate *brāhmaṇa* from Avantī became a *tridaṇḍi sannyāsī* devotee of the Supreme Lord by cutting the knots of desire for material enjoyment and liberation that had existed within his heart. At that time, the following verses began to appear in his heart:

jāta-śraddho mat-kathāsu nirviṇṇaḥ sarva-karmasu
veda duḥkhātmakān kāmān parityāge 'py anīśvaraḥ
tato bhajeta māṁ prītaḥ śraddhālur dṛḍha-niścayaḥ
juṣamāṇaś ca tān kāmān duḥkhodarkāṁś ca garhayan
proktena bhakti-yogena bhajato māsakṛn muneḥ
kāmā hṛdayyā naśyanti sarve mayi hṛdi sthite
bhidyate hṛdaya-granthiś chidyante sarva-saṁśayāḥ
kṣīyante cāsya karmāṇi mayi dṛṣṭe 'khilātmani

Having awakened faith in the narrations of My glories, being disgusted with all kinds of material activities, knowing that all varieties of sense gratification lead to misery, but still being unable to renounce all sense enjoyment, My devotee should remain satisfied and worship Me with great faith and conviction. Even though he is sometimes engaged in sense enjoyment, My devotee knows that this will lead to a miserable result and so he sincerely repents such activities.

When an intelligent devotee constantly engages in My loving devotional service as prescribed by Me, his heart becomes firmly situated in Me. Thus all material desires within the heart are soon destroyed.

When a living entity directly sees Me, who is the indwelling Supersoul of all living entities, then all his false ego, doubts and reactions of karma are at once destroyed. (*Śrīmad-Bhāgavatam* 11.20.27-30)

TEXT 32

सचचारमहीमेतांसंयतात्मेन्द्रियानिलः ।
भिक्षार्थंनगरग्रामानसङ्गोऽलक्षितोऽविशत् ॥३२॥

sa cacāra mahīm etāṁ saṁyatātmendriyānilaḥ
bhikṣārthaṁ nagara-grāmān asaṅgo 'lakṣito 'viśat

He wandered throughout the world, carefully controlling his senses, mind, and intelligence. To beg alms, he traveled alone through numerous towns and villages, hiding his true spiritual position so that he was not recognized by others.

PURPORT

The *brāhmaṇa* from Avantī became free from all bad association by remaining aloof from those who desire material enjoyment and liberation. He had no desire to acquire name and fame to impress others as he began to maintain himself by begging alms from door to door. In the *Caitanya-caritāmṛta* (Madhya 19.151), it is said:

brahmāṇḍa bhramite kona bhāgyavān jīva
guru-kṛṣṇa-prasāde pāya bhakti-latā-bīja

According to their karma, all living entities are wandering throughout the universe. Some of them are being elevated to the upper planetary systems, and some are going down to the lower planetary systems. Out of many millions of wandering living entities, one who is very fortunate gets an opportunity to associate with a bona fide spiritual master, by the grace of Kṛṣṇa. By the mercy of both Kṛṣṇa and the spiritual master, such a person receives the seed of the creeper of devotional service.

The acceptance of *tridaṇḍa sannyāsa* is an indication of one's complete dedication to the devotional service of the Supreme Lord. The three rods of the *sannyāsī's daṇḍa* indicate that his body, mind, and speech are fully engaged in the devotional service of the Lord. The engagement of one's body, mind, and speech in the service of the Lord enables one to manifest all good qualities, such as forgiveness, detachment, and freedom from pride and material desires. Anyone who fully engages in the service of the Lord, following in the footsteps of the previous learned devotees, will surely attain shelter at the Lord's lotus feet.

TEXT 33

तंवैप्रवयसंभिक्षुमवधूतमसज्जनाः ।
दृष्ट्वापर्यभवन्भद्रबह्वीभिःपरिभूतिभिः ॥३३॥

taṁ vai pravayasaṁ bhikṣum avadhūtam asaj-janāḥ
dṛṣṭvā paryabhavan bhadra bahvībhiḥ paribhūtibhiḥ

O gentle Uddhava, upon seeing him as an old, dirty beggar, uncultured people taunted and insulted him with many harsh words.

COMMENTARY

Mischievous persons took pleasure in reproaching the old *sannyāsī*. The word *paribhūtibhiḥ* means "various kinds of reprimands."

TEXT 34

केचित्त्रिवेणुंजगृहुरेकेपात्रंकमण्डलुम् ।
पीठंचैकेऽक्षसूत्रंचकन्थांचीराणिकेचन ।

प्रदायचपुनस्तानिदर्शितान्याददुर्मुनेः ॥३४॥

kecit tri-veṇuṁ jagṛhur eke pātraṁ kamaṇḍalum
pīṭhaṁ caike 'kṣa-sūtraṁ ca kanthāṁ cīrāṇi kecana
pradāya ca punas tāni darśitāny ādadur muneḥ

Some of these miscreants took away his *sannyāsa* rod, some took his begging bowl, some took his deerskin *āsana*, some took his chanting beads, and some took his torn, ragged clothing. Sometimes they pretended to return these things, only to conceal them once again.

COMMENTARY

Someone took away his *sannyāsa* rod and when that person was about to return it, someone else snatched it away. In this way, people mistreated the *brāhmaṇa* from Avantī.

TEXT 35

अन्नंचभैक्ष्यसम्पन्नंभुञ्जानस्यसरित्तटे ।
मूत्रयन्तिचपापिष्ठाःष्ठीवन्त्यस्यचमूर्धनि ॥३५॥

annaṁ ca bhaikṣya-sampannaṁ bhuñjānasya sarit-taṭe
mūtrayanti ca pāpiṣṭhāḥ ṣṭhīvanty asya ca mūrdhani

When the *brāhmaṇa* would sit down by the side of a river to eat the food that he collected by begging, sinful people would come and pass urine on it and then spit on his head.

COMMENTARY

These wicked people urinated on his food and spat on his head.

TEXT 36

यतवाचंवाचयन्तिताडयन्तिनवक्तिचेत् ।
तर्जयन्त्यपरेवाग्भिःस्तेनोऽयमितिवादिनः ।
बध्नन्तिरज्ज्वातंकेचिद्बध्यतांबध्यतामिति ॥३६॥

yata-vācaṁ vācayanti tāḍayanti na vakti cet
tarjayanty apare vāgbhiḥ steno 'yam iti vādinaḥ
badhnanti rajjvā taṁ kecid badhyatāṁ badhyatām iti

Although he had taken a vow of silence, foolish people would try to make him speak, and if he did not utter a word, they would beat him with sticks. There were others who would say, "This man is a thief," and then they would tie him up with a rope.

TEXT 37

क्षिपन्त्येकेऽवजानन्त एषधर्मध्वजःशठः ।
क्षीणवित्त इमांवृत्तिमग्रहीत्स्वजनोज्झितः ॥३७॥

kṣipanty eke 'vajānanta eṣa dharma-dhvajaḥ śaṭhaḥ
kṣīṇa-vitta imām vṛttim agrahīt sva-janojjhitaḥ

They would insult him by saying, "This man is a hypocrite and a cheat. He lost all his money and so his family rejected him. Now he has put on the garb of a *sannyāsī* just to fill his belly."

COMMENTARY

Some people said, "This man is a hypocrite. He earns his livelihood by showing off his *sannyāsa daṇḍa*. He is a cheater and deceives innocent people. He has dressed like a saint because he lost all his money."

TEXT 38-39

अहो एषमहासारोधृतिमान्गिरिराडिव ।
मौनेनसाधयत्यर्थंबकवद्दृढनिश्चयः ॥३८॥
इत्येकेविहसन्त्येनमेकेदुर्वातयन्ति च ।
तंबबन्धुर्निरुरुधुर्यथाक्रीडनकंद्विजम् ॥३९॥

aho eṣa mahā-sāro dhṛtimān giri-rāḍ iva
maunena sādhayaty arthaṁ baka-vad dṛḍha-niścayaḥ

ity eke vihasanty enam eke durvātayanti ca
taṁ babandhur nirurudhur yathā krīḍanakaṁ dvijam

Some would ridicule him by saying, "Just see how this powerful sage is as steadfast as the Himalaya Mountains. While remaining silent, he is pursuing his goal with great determination, like a duck." Other passed foul air on him, and some bound him with rope and kept him captive, like a pet animal.

COMMENTARY

Some people would facetiously say that the *brāhmaṇa* was very powerful and unwavering, like a mountain. Some people passed foul air in front of his mouth. Others bound him with rope and threw him into a dungeon, just as one puts a parrot in a cage.

PURPORT

As a result of giving up false pride, one acquires the quality of tolerance. Due to their deceitful mentality, nondevotees are always prone to attack the surrendered devotees of the Supreme Lord in various ways. Only those who cultivate the quality of humility, feeling themselves to be lower than the straw in the street, refuse to become entangled by engagement in gross or subtle material enjoyment.

TEXT 40

एवंसभौतिकंदुःखंदैविकंदैहिकंचयत्
भोक्तव्यमात्मनोदिष्टंप्राप्तंप्राप्तमबुध्यत

evaṁ sa bhautikaṁ duḥkhaṁ daivikaṁ daihikaṁ ca yat
bhoktavyam ātmano diṣṭaṁ prāptaṁ prāptam abudhyata

In this way, the brāhmaṇa **repeatedly suffered the threefold material miseries—** adhyātmika, adhibhautika, **and** adhidaivika**—understanding them to be allotted to him by providence, and therefore unavoidable.**

COMMENTARY

Adhibhautika miseries are those caused by other living entities, *adhyātmika* miseries are those caused by one's own body and mind, and *adhidaivika* miseries are those caused by the demigods who control the forces of nature, such as heat and cold.

PURPORT

The conditioned soul identifies with his material body and because of this misconception, it is very difficult for him to tolerate the miserable conditions of material existence. The threefold miseries can be tolerated only by one who has taken shelter of the lotus feet of Śrī Nityānanda Prabhu, the exalted elder brother of the most magnanimous Śrī Kṛṣṇa Caitanya, who is nondifferent from the son of King of Vraja. Those who are endeavoring to remain fixed in devotional service to the Lord do not become agitated by the words and actions of atheists because they know that the nondevotees' envy is a natural manifestation of their conditional life. Understanding that the atheists are acting helplessly under the control of the material nature, they consider it their duty to forgive them. That *tridaṇḍi sannyāsī* of Avantī could realize these principles within his self as a result of his sincere surrender to the Lord.

TEXT 41

परिभूतैमांगाथामगायतनराधमैः ।
पातयद्भिःस्वधर्मस्थोधृतिमास्थायसात्त्विकीम् ॥४१॥

paribhūta imāṁ gāthām agāyata narādhamaiḥ
pātayadbhiḥ sva dharma-stho dhṛtim āsthāya sāttvikīm

Even though low-class men ridiculed him in various ways in the hopes of making him fall down from his position, he remained steadfast in his determination. Keeping himself fixed in the mode of goodness, he began singing this song.

COMMENTARY

Those who were the lowest of mankind tried their best to deviate the Avantī *brāhmaṇa* from his determination to remain fixed in Kṛṣṇa consciousness. All such attempts had no effect, however, because he remained firmly fixed in his resolve while singing the song that is recorded in the following verses.

The phrase *sātvikīṁ dhṛti* is explained in *Bhagavad-gītā* (18.33):

dhṛtyā yayā dhārayate manaḥ-prāṇendriya-kriyāḥ
yogenāvyabhicāriṇyā dhṛtiḥ sā pārtha sāttvikī

O son of Pṛthā, that determination which is unbreakable, which is sustained with steadfastness by yoga practice, and which thus controls the activities of the mind, life and senses is determination in the mode of goodness.

PURPORT

Those who are envious of the Lord's devotees are certainly the lowest of men and are destined to traverse the path to hell in the near future. Indeed, atheists take pleasure in disturbing the devotees, either by jeering at them or even by becoming violent. In spite of all such torments, however, the devotees remain tolerant, being determined to stay fixed in the mode of goodness, as advised by the Lord. As described by Śrīla Rūpa Gosvāmī in *Śrī Upadeśāmṛta*(1):

vāco vegaṁ manasaḥ krodha-vegaṁ
jihvā-vegam udaropastha-vegam
etān vegān yo viṣaheta dhīraḥ
sarvām apīmāṁ pṛthivīṁ sa śiṣyāt

A sober person who can tolerate the urge to speak, the mind's demands, the actions of anger and the urges of the tongue, belly and genitals is qualified to make disciples all over the world.

TEXT 42

द्विज उवाच
नायंजनोमेसुखदुःखहेतुर्नदेवतात्माग्रहकर्मकालाः ।
मनःपरंकारणमामनन्तिसंसारचक्रंपरिवर्तयेद्यत् ॥४२॥

dvija uvāca
nāyaṁ jano me sukha-duḥkha-hetur na devatātmā graha-karma-kālāḥ
manaḥ paraṁ kāraṇam āmananti saṁsāra-cakraṁ parivartayed yat

The *brāhmaṇa* said: These people are not the cause of my happiness and distress. Neither are the demigods, my own body, the positions of the planets, my *karma,* or time. Rather, it is the mind alone that causes happiness and distress and perpetuates one's bondage to the vicious cycle of repeated birth and death.

COMMENTARY

After careful deliberation, the Avantī *brāhmaṇa* realized that it was not actually the miscreants who were the cause of his distress. Did he think that maybe they were harassing him under the instigation of someone else? The answer is given in this verse: "Neither the demigods, the body, nor the planets are causing me distress. It is the mind that is the actual cause of one's happiness and distress." It is stated in the *Vedas* that it is the mind that sees, hears, and makes one move here and there.

PURPORT

Those who are averse to the service of the Supreme Lord must live within the cycle of repeated birth and death.

īśvaraḥ sarva-bhūtānāṁ hṛd-deśe 'rjuna tiṣṭhati
bhrāmayan sarva-bhūtāni yantrārūḍhāni māyayā

The Supreme Lord is situated in everyone's heart, O Arjuna, and is directing the wanderings of all living entities, who are seated as on a machine, made of the material energy. (*Bhagavad-gītā* 18.61)

According to the purport of this verse from the *Bhagavad-gītā*, mental speculators must wander about in the cycle of birth and death, driven by the mind, under the direction of the Supreme Lord. The wheel of time causes the living entity, who is the knower of the field of activities, to experience the changing nature of material existence. The Avantī *brāhmaṇa* understood his mind alone to be the source of all inauspiciousness, despite the fact that miscreants, the demigods, planets, one's *karma*, and time are no doubt apparent causes.

In this regard, one can carefully consider this verse:

anyera hṛdaya—mana, mora mana—vṛndāvana,
'mane' 'vane' eka kari' jāni
tāhāṅ tomāra pada-dvaya, karāha yadi udaya,
tabe tomāra pūrṇa kṛpā māni

For most people, the mind and heart are one, but because My mind is never separated from Vṛndāvana, I consider My mind and Vṛndāvana to be one. My mind is already Vṛndāvana, and since You like Vṛndāvana, will You please place Your lotus feet there? I would deem that Your full mercy. (*Śrī Caitanya-caritāmṛta Madhya* 13.137)

TEXT 43

मनोगुणान्वैसृजतेबलीयस्ततश्चकर्माणिविलक्षणानि ।
शुक्लानिकृष्णान्यथलोहितानितेभ्यः सवर्णाःसृतयोभवन्ति ॥४३॥

mano guṇān vai sṛjate balīyas tataś ca karmāṇi vilakṣaṇāni
śuklāni kṛṣṇāny atha lohitāni tebhyaḥ sa-varṇāḥ sṛtayo bhavanti

The powerful mind manifests the functions of the modes of nature, from which evolve the activities of the modes of goodness, passion, and ignorance. From the interaction of the modes of nature, the various species of life evolve.

COMMENTARY

The mind is habituated to hankering after beautiful women and wealth. Even if one understands the fault of engaging in earning money for sense gratification, the mind will stubbornly insist that without wealth, even religious rituals cannot be properly performed. After all, it takes money to procure flower garlands, ghee, and sandalwood paste. In this way, the mind drives one on and on in the feverish search for money. The combination of the three modes of material natures awards one a material body whereby one sometimes identifies himself as being in a high status of life, sometimes in a low status, and sometimes somewhere in between. These conceptions are material designations generated from the modes of nature, and they arrange themselves according to the tendency of the powerful mind to enjoy temporary sense gratification.

PURPORT

The materially absorbed mind of the conditioned souls who are averse to Lord Kṛṣṇa's devotional service is under the influence of the three material qualities. When the conditioned soul is engrossed in the mode of goodness, he considers the cultivation of knowledge and his reputation as an honest man as all-important. When absorbed in the mode of passion, one's attachment to family and social position become prominent, and when one is immersed in the mode of ignorance, one simply thinks that the gratification of his senses is the be-all of his existence. All such conceptions of piety, impiety, and a mixture of both, are products of the mind. Under the influence of the material modes, one sometimes identifies oneself as a demigod, a king, a rich capitalist, a wise scholar, and so on. These bodily conceptions are illusions born from the mental qualities. Whether the materially contaminated mind is absorbed in the mood of an enjoyer, or the mood of a renunciate, in either case, the spirit soul forgets his constitutional existence.

TEXT 44

अनीह आत्मामनसासमीहताहिरण्मयोमत्सख उद्विचष्टे ।
मनःस्वलिङ्गंपरिगृह्यकामान्जुषन्निबद्धोगुणसङ्गतोऽसौ ॥४४॥

anīha ātmā manasā samīhatā hiraṇ-mayo mat-sakha udvicaṣṭe
manaḥ sva-liṅgaṁ parigṛhya kāmān juṣan nibaddho guṇa-saṅgato 'sau

Although He is present with me in this body, the Supersoul is not entangled because He exists eternally beyond the darkness of ignorance, and thus does not identify with the material body and mind. As my well-wishing friend, He simply witnesses my activities, remaining neutral. On the other hand, I, the minute spirit soul, identify the mind, which is like a mirror reflecting external reality, as my very self. In this way, I am engaged in attempting to enjoy the objects of the senses, under the dictation of the three modes of material nature.

COMMENTARY

Does this mean that only the mind suffers the material existence, and not the soul? The answer is no. There are two souls within the body, one is the Supersoul, who is untouched by the mind's influence, and the other is the infinitesimal spirit soul, who is under the influence of the materially absorbed mind. Although the Supersoul is present within the body as the controller of the mind, He is unaffected by its functions because He is full of transcendental knowledge and the master of unlimited spiritual energies. He is independent, and He is the best friend of the spirit soul. His knowledge never deteriorates as He observes everything as a witness. On the other hand, the spirit soul accepts the subtle body of mind, intelligence and false ego as the self, becomes conditioned by the mind and its resultant actions, and remains entangled in the bodily concept of life while trying to enjoy the objects of the senses. Due to the illusion created by the mind, the spirit soul suffers while remaining in material existence.

PURPORT

If a conditioned soul comes to understand that dependence on the mind simply produces misery, and is informed that service to Lord Hari is his constitutional position, the desire for material enjoyment or for renunciation of material activities, gradually diminishes. To act in our relationship with the Supreme Personality of Godhead is certainly the constitutional duty of the spirit soul. When the spirit soul gives up his constitutional engagement and becomes conditioned by the external energy of the Lord, he remains engrossed in contemplating the so-called happiness of temporary sense gratification, not realizing its insignificance.

When one advances on the path of cultivation of spiritual knowledge, lending submissive aural reception to the transcendental sound vibration, he can understand the purport of the verse beginning with *dvā suparṇā*. It is only after accepting the Supreme Personality of Godhead as the object of one of the five types of *rati* that one can distance himself from the influence of the three modes of material nature by controlling the turbulent mind.

Śrī Gaurasundara instructed that the service of the supreme transcendental personality, Śrī Kṛṣṇa, as described in the *Śrīmad-Bhāgavatam*, is the fifth dimension of human existence, to be cultivated after finishing all aspiration for attaining perfection in *dharma, artha, kāma* and *mokṣa*. The subtle body is dissolved at the time of perfection and this is technically known as *vastusiddhi*. At this time, one becomes situated on the platform of pure Kṛṣṇa consciousness, under the direction of the pure devotees of the Lord, thus enabling him to develop his particular loving relationship with the Supreme Personality of Godhead.

TEXT 45

दानंस्वधर्मोनियमोयमश्चश्रुतंच कर्माणिचसद्व्रतानि ।
सर्वेमनोनिग्रहलक्षणान्ताःपरोहियोगोमनसःसमाधिः ॥४५॥

dānaṁ sva-dharmo niyamo yamaś ca śrutaṁ ca karmāṇi ca sad-vratāni
sarve mano-nigraha-lakṣaṇāntāḥ paro hi yogo manasaḥ samādhiḥ

Giving in charity, performing prescribed duties, the observance of regulative principles, hearing from the scriptures, pious works, and purifying vows all have as their final aim the subduing of the mind. Indeed, concentration of the mind on the Supreme is the goal of *yoga*.

COMMENTARY

To make spiritual advancement, it is essential to control the mind, which creates many obstacles if allowed to roam freely. Activities such as giving charity are performed with the aim of controlling the mind. Indeed, the ultimate fruit of all kinds of *sādhana* is to regulate the mind. To control the mind is the goal of all types of *yoga* practice.

PURPORT

Pious activities, such as giving charity, fulfilling one's occupational duties, controlling the mind, controlling the senses, studying the *Vedas*, observing religious vows, and so on, are aimed at purifying and controlling the mind. Controlling the mind by meditation is essential because when the mind is undisturbed, one can gradually realize the temporary nature of even pious activities so that one becomes determined to act on the transcendental platform. Because *karma-yoga*, *haṭha-yoga*, *jñāna-yoga*, and *raja-yoga* are materialistically conceived, they do not award one factual understanding of the Absolute Truth.

TEXT 46

समाहितंयस्यमनःप्रशान्तंदानादिभिःकिंवदतस्यकृत्यम् ।
असंयतंयस्यमनोविनश्यद्दानादिभिश्चेदपरंकिमेभिः ॥४६॥

samāhitaṁ yasya manaḥ praśāntaṁ dānādibhiḥ kiṁ vada tasya kṛtyam
asaṁyataṁ yasya mano vinaśyad dānādibhiś ced aparaṁ kim ebhiḥ

If one's mind is perfectly controlled, what is the need for performing ritualistic activities, and pious works, such as giving in charity? And if one's mind remains uncontrolled, being merged in ignorance, of what use are these activities for him?

COMMENTARY

Learned transcendentalists give utmost importance to controlling the mind. If the mind is controlled, what is the use of engaging in the various processes that are meant to control it? And, if in spite of performing many religious activities, the mind is still not controlled, what was the use of performing all those activities?

PURPORT

In this connection, one should consider this verse from the *Nārada-pañcarātra*:

arādhito yadi haris tapasā tataḥ kiṁ
nārādhito yadi haris tapasā tataḥ kim
antar bahir yadi haris tapasā tataḥ kiṁ
nāntar bahir yadi haris tapasā tataḥ Kim

"If one is worshiping Lord Hari, what is the use of performing extraneous penances? And if one is not worshiping Lord Hari, no such penances will save one. If one can understand that Lord Hari is all-pervading, within and without, what is the need of performing penances? And if one is not able to understand that Hari is all-pervading, all his penances are useless."

TEXT 47

मनोवशेऽन्येह्यभवन्स्मदेवामनश्चनान्यस्यवशंसमेति ।
भीष्मोहिदेवःसहसःसहीयान्युंज्द्यद्वशेतंसहिदेवदेवः ॥४७॥

mano-vaśe 'nye hy abhavan sma devā manaś ca nānyasya vaśaṁ sameti
bhīṣmo hi devaḥ sahasaḥ sahīyān yuñjyād vaśe taṁ sa hi deva-devaḥ

The demigods, who control the senses of the conditioned souls, are also under the control of this mind, but the mind is not controlled by anyone, because it is stronger than the strongest. Indeed, the mind is the cause of fear for even mystic yogis. Therefore, anyone who can control his mind becomes the master of the senses.

COMMENTARY

One may inquire, "Besides controlling the mind, is there need for a separate endeavor to control the senses?" In this verse, the answer is given that there is no need for a separate endeavor to control the senses because one who has conquered the mind finds that his senses are automatically under control. The demigods, who control the senses of the conditioned souls are themselves under the control of the mind.

Even great yogis are afraid of the formidable mind, which is stronger than the strongest and braver than the bravest. Therefore, anyone who has learned to control his mind is certainly to be considered a great hero. It is stated in the *Vedas*, "Everything has come about by the influence of the mind, which is extremely difficult to control. The mind is like a formidable master, who is the bravest of all."

PURPORT

The materially contaminated mind is generally eager to enjoy sense gratification, although it sometimes adopts the path of dry renunciation. In order to transcend the limitations of material enjoyment and dry renunciation, one must learn to engage the mind at the lotus feet of the Supreme Lord. If the mind is controlled then all the senses are automatically controlled. The mind collects the impressions of the external world through the medium of the senses, and thus it is sensual perception that constantly disturbs the mind.

TEXT 48

तम्दुर्जयंशत्रुमसह्यवेगमरुन्तुदंतन्नविजित्यकेचित् ।
कुर्वन्त्यसद्विग्रहमत्रमर्त्यैर्मित्राण्युदासीनरिपून्विमूढाः ॥४८॥

tam durjayaṁ śatrum asahya-vegam arun-tudaṁ tan na vijitya kecit
kurvanty asad-vigraham atra martyair mitrāṇy udāsīna-ripūn vimūḍhāḥ

There are many people who fail to conquer this irrepressible enemy, the mind, whose urges are intolerable and who torments the heart. As a result, many people are completely bewildered and create useless quarrels with others, concluding that other people are either their friends, enemies, or parties indifferent to them.

COMMENTARY

The word *aru* means "the heart." Instead of controlling the mind, which gives pain to the heart and senses, a foolish person creates enmity with others, being impelled by the uncontrolled mind. Being in the bodily conception of life, he treats some people as favorable, some as unfavorable, and others as neutral.

PURPORT

The mind's business is accepting and rejecting. Attachment and hatred, as well as friendship and enmity are conceptions existing within the materially conditioned mind.

TEXT 49

देहंमनोमात्रमिमंगृहीत्वाममाहमित्यन्धधियोमनुष्याः ।
एषोऽहमन्योऽयमितिभ्रमेणदुरन्तपारेतमसिभ्रमन्ति ॥४९॥

deham mano-mātram imaṁ gṛhītvā mamāham ity andha-dhiyo manuṣyāḥ
eṣo 'ham anyo 'yam iti bhrameṇa duranta-pāre tamasi bhramanti

Persons who identify with the material body, which is a product of the mind, possess bewildered intelligence, thinking in terms of "I" and "mine." Because of their illusion of "this is I, this is my relative, and this is an outsider," they wander in endless darkness.

COMMENTARY

This verse describes how one becomes entangled in illusion. According to the dictation of the mind, one must accept a material body, thinking it to be the self, and thus one considers everything related to the body as "mine." This is how the conditioned souls wander within the formidable material existence.

PURPORT

Those who maintain a vision of duality, thinking the material body to be "I" and everything in relation to the body to be "mine" certainly continue to wander in the vast kingdom of material existence. Differentiation in behavior arises due to discrimination. Those who remain in the bodily concept of life become offenders at the lotus feet of the holy name, and thus invite aversion to the service of the Supreme Lord.

TEXT 50

जनस्तुहेतुःसुखदुःखयोश्चेत्किमात्मनश्चात्रहिभौमयोस्तत् ।
जिह्वांक्वचित्सन्दशतिस्वदद्भिस्तद्वेदनायांकतमायकुप्येत् ॥५०॥

janas tu hetuḥ sukha-duḥkhayoś cet kim ātmanaś cātra hi bhaumayos tat
jihvāṁ kvacit sandaśati sva-dadbhis tad-vedanāyāṁ katamāya kupyet

If you argue that the miscreants are the causes of my suffering then what about the eternal soul? Happiness and distress are the results of the contact of the senses with their objects, and do not affect the cternal soul. If someone bites his tongue, who can he blame for his pain?

COMMENTARY

It should be clearly understood that the mind is the cause of one's happiness and distress. Although bodily pleasure and pain are felt by the soul, one must tolerate such duality, understanding it to be a creation of one's own material mind. The gross and subtle bodies, which are transformation of material elements, are the field of activities for the soul, who is distinct from these coverings. If one accidentally bites his tongue or lip, he cannot become angry and pull out his teeth. Similarly, all living beings are individual parts and parcels of God, and thus nondifferent from each other. All of them are meant to serve the Supreme Lord in spiritual equality. If the living beings give up their master's service and instead quarrel among themselves, they will be forced to suffer by the laws of nature.

PURPORT

Just as it is not proper to pull out one's teeth if he happens to bite his tongue, one should not retaliate against an offense committed by another because every living entity is part and parcel of the supreme whole and therefore not different from one another. The servant spirit soul and the master Supersoul are always meant to live in perfect harmony. If the spirit soul exhibits opposition to his master and well-wisher, or creates conflict among his fellow souls, then he is acting against his own self-interest. It is ignorance for one to say, "I have become happy or distressed because of the activities of another person." The spirit soul is not actually subjected to temporary happiness and distress. Happiness and distress are the result of the interaction of the external objects of this world.

Because all living entities are servants of the Supreme Lord, if they somehow oppose one another, this indicates that they have become indifferent to the Lord's service, and this aversion to the performance of their respective duties will progressively become more and more prominent. Exalted devotees of the Lord are self-realized souls who know that all living entities are servants of the Supreme Lord. Servants have no other duty than service to their master. By giving up the master's service, one becomes entangled either in love or quarrel and as a result, one will have to experience either happiness or distress. The living entities' relationships with each other should be based on friendship in relationship with the Supersoul.

TEXT 51

दुःखस्यहेतुर्यदिदेवतास्तुकिमात्मनस्तत्रविकारयोस्तत् ।
यदङ्गमङ्गेननिहन्यतेक्वचित्क्रुध्येतकस्मैपुरुषःस्वदेहे ॥५१॥

duḥkhasya hetur yadi devatās tu kim ātmanas tatra vikārayos tat
yad aṅgam aṅgena nihanyate kvacit krudhyeta kasmai puruṣaḥ sva-dehe

If you say that the demigods who control the bodily senses cause suffering, still, such suffering cannot apply to the spirit soul. Acting and being acted upon are merely interactions of the senses and their presiding deities. When one limb of the body attacks another limb, with whom can the person residing in that body be angry?

COMMENTARY

Even if the demigods are considered to be responsible for one's happiness and distress, what has that got to do with the spirit soul? Actually, the demigods play a major role in human beings' happiness and distress. If the hand of a person points to the face of another and curses, "May you suffer from white leprosy," then the demigods, Indra and Agni, who are predominating deities of the face become insulted. However, this has nothing to do with the eternal soul. The example is given here of the body. If one slaps the face of another person, then it amounts to slapping the demigod, Indra, because he is the controlling deity of the face.

PURPORT

Material distress is actually a superfluous condition for the living entities. Even if the demigods are accepted as the cause of distress, there is no distress felt by self-realized souls. Self-realized persons, who are devoid of a mundane conception of life, do not invite inauspiciousness by creating rivalry with others. Rather, they are the kind friends of all living beings, irrespective of how others treat them.

If one limb of the body accidentally harms another limb, the proprietor of the body does not take revenge against the offending limb. Similarly, the Supreme Lord does not take sides in a quarrel between two of His energies. He mercifully gives them the right to serve Him, while remaining their well-wishing friend.

TEXT 52

आत्मायदिस्यात्सुखदुःखहेतुःकिमन्यतस्तत्रनिजस्वभावः ।
नह्यात्मनोऽन्यद्यदितन्मृषास्यात्क्रुध्येतकस्मान्नसुखंनदुःखम् ॥५२॥

ātmā yadi syāt sukha-duḥkha-hetuḥ kim anyatas tatra nija-svabhāvaḥ
na hy ātmano 'nyad yadi tan mṛṣā syāt krudhyeta kasmān na sukhaṁ na duḥkham

If the spirit soul is considered the cause of happiness and distress, then there is no reason to become angry with others, because happiness and distress would be the

nature of the soul. According to this theory, nothing exists besides the spirit soul. If one perceives something else besides the soul—that must be considered illusion. Therefore, what would be the cause for anger against others?

COMMENTARY

A dead body does not feel pleasure or pain, and so it must be concluded that our happiness and distress are due to our consciousness, which is the nature of the soul. It is not, however, the original function of the soul to enjoy material happiness and suffer material distress. These are produced by the ignorant conception of bodily identification, which is the action of false ego. Our involvement in sense gratification drags our consciousness into the material body, where it must experience the inevitable bodily pains and pleasures.

PURPORT

If the soul is imagined to be the cause of happiness and distress, then one should consider such happiness and distress to be his nature and therefore should not blame others. The person who gives pain and the person who suffers it are actually part and parcel of the same Supreme Person. Therefore, any conflict that arises between people on the mundane platform should be understood as superficial and due to an absence of self-realization.

Enjoyment of the objects of the senses is not the true nature of the spirit soul, but exists only in contact with matter. Knowing this very well, one should not foolishly try to maximize his material happiness while simultaneously attempting to minimize his material distress. After all, happiness and distress are concomitant factors in material existence.

The characteristics of the spirit soul only manifest in the spiritual world. In the transcendental abode of the Lord, there is no material distress, even in the case of separation from the Lord. The insignificant happiness that we experience in this world, which is actually an absence of distress, has no existence in the spiritual world. It should be understood that the pure spirit soul is naturally inclined toward the service of the Supreme Lord because that is his constitutional position.

TEXT 53

ग्रहानिमित्तंसुखदुःखयोश्चेत्किमात्मनोऽजस्यजनस्यतेवै ।
ग्रहैर्ग्रहस्यैववदन्तिपीडांक्रुध्येतकस्मैपुरुषस्ततोऽन्यः ॥५३॥

grahā nimittaṁ sukha-duḥkhayoś cet kim ātmano 'jasya janasya te vai
grahair grahasyaiva vadanti pīḍāṁ krudhyeta kasmai puruṣas tato 'nyaḥ

If we suppose that the planets are the cause of happiness and distress, then where is the relationship with the eternal spirit soul? The planets can only cause happiness and distress for that which has taken birth. Expert astrologers have explained that the planets only cause distress to one another. Therefore, because the spirit soul is distinct from the material body and the planets, against who should he vent his anger?

COMMENTARY

Even if it is accepted that the stars and planets are the cause of happiness and distress, this has nothing to do with the unborn spirit soul. The body is possessed by the soul—not that the soul is part of the body. According to expert astrologers, the positions of the stars, planets, and constellations at the time of birth influence a person's nature. Thus, it is the material body that suffers miseries caused by the planets and not the soul, which is separate from the body.

PURPORT

Astrologers say that the happiness and distress of the living entities is caused by the planets. In the spiritual realm, there is no occurrence of material distress. Therefore, the influence of the planets does not apply to the eternal spirit soul, but only to the temporary material body. Self-realized souls never become exultant or morose on account of the pleasant or unpleasant predictions of astrologers. Planetary influences are limited to the material body and mind. There is no difference between the soul of a planet and the soul of any other embodied being. Both are eternal, minute spirit souls, part and parcel of the Supreme Lord. It is only the embodiment that causes one to make a distinction between the two.

TEXT 54

कर्मास्तुहेतुःसुखदुःखयोश्चेत्किमात्मनस्तद्धिजडाजडत्वे ।
देहस्त्वचित्पुरुषोऽयंसुपर्णःक्रुध्येतकस्मैनहिकर्ममूलम् ॥५४॥

karmāstu hetuḥ sukha-duḥkhayoś cet kim ātmanas tad dhi jaḍājaḍatve
dehas tv acit puruṣo 'yaṁ suparṇaḥ krudhyeta kasmai na hi karma mūlam

If we assume that *karma* is the cause of happiness and distress, we still are not considering the eternal soul. *Karma*, or fruitive activity, takes place when there is a conscious spirit soul and a material body that undergoes the transformation of happiness and distress as a reaction to work. Because the body has no life, it cannot be the actual recipient of happiness and distress, nor can the soul, who is ultimately aloof from the

material body. Because karma has no ultimate basis in either the body or the soul, at whom can one become angry?

COMMENTARY

If we accept karma as the cause of happiness and distress, we must consider how fruitive activities are performed by the bodies of the conditioned souls and not the souls themselves. The body is a dull matter whereas the soul is pure consciousness. The pure spirit soul has no factual relationship with the material body, just as light has no connection with darkness. Considering this, at whom should one become angry?

PURPORT

If the cause of happiness and distress is attributed to the activities of the living entities, there is still no cause for anger because fruitive activities are performed under the impulse of the three modes of material nature. The owner of the body is the spirit soul, and the body itself is nothing but dead matter. Therefore, the conditioned soul's absorption in the material body is due to ignorance and cannot be considered as factual.

TEXT 55

कालस्तुहेतुःसुखदुःखयोश्चेत्किमात्मनस्तत्रतदात्मकोऽसौ ।
नाग्नेर्हितापोनहिमस्यतत्स्यात्क्रुध्येतकस्मैनपरस्यद्वन्द्वम् ॥५५॥

kālas tu hetuḥ sukha-duḥkhayoś cet kim ātmanas tatra tad-ātmako 'sau
nāgner hi tāpo na himasya tat syāt krudhyeta kasmai na parasya dvandvam

If time is accepted as the cause of happiness and distress, then that experience cannot apply to the spirit soul, because the spirit soul is an expansion of the Lord's spiritual potency and time is also a manifestation of the spiritual energy of the Supreme Lord. Certainly a fire does not burn its own flames, nor does the cold harm snow. The spirit soul is transcendental and beyond the experience of material happiness and distress. Therefore, at whom should one become angry?

COMMENTARY

If time is accepted as the cause of happiness and distress, this still cannot affect the eternal spirit soul. The spirit soul is part and parcel of the Supreme Brahman, just as much time is a representation of the Supreme Brahman. The example of fire and its flames is appropriate in this regard. Flames cannot be burnt by fire, and snow cannot be harmed by cold. Considering this, at whom should one get angry?

PURPORT

Snow cannot suffer because of cold, and flames cannot suffer on account of the heat of the fire. Similarly, the spirit soul and time are both manifestations of the internal energy of the Supreme Lord. In conditional life, there are sometimes feelings of happiness and sometimes feelings of distress, due to ignorance. When the soul is transcendentally situated in his relationship with the Supreme Lord, there is no question of happiness or distress.

TEXT 56

नकेनचित्क्वापिकथञ्चनास्यद्वन्द्वोपरागःपरतःपरस्य ।
यथाहमःसंसृतिरूपिणःस्यादेवंप्रबुद्धोनबिभेतिभूतैः ॥५६॥

na kenacit kvāpi kathañcanāsya dvandvoparāgaḥ parataḥ parasya
yathāhamaḥ saṁsṛti-rūpiṇaḥ syād evaṁ prabuddho na bibheti bhūtaiḥ

The false ego, which manifests the visible material creation, is subjected to happiness and distress. The soul, however, who is transcendental to matter, can never actually be affected by material happiness and distress in any place, under any circumstance, or by the agency of any person. When one realizes this fact, he will no longer have any fear from any material condition.

COMMENTARY

The *brāhmaṇa* has countered various philosophies regarding the happiness and distress experienced by the conditioned souls. Here, he counters any other possible explanation. Due to false ego, the conditioned soul identifies with his gross and subtle coverings and thus dreams that he is suffering or enjoying that which has no real relationship with his self. Who then is the cause of one's suffering? It is simply due to illusion that one suffers in material existence. False ego, which is one of the constituents of the subtle body, of which the mind is the leader, is the real cause of happiness and distress, and not anything else. The word *yatha* in this verse means "certainly." The word *saṁsṛti* refers to "the bondage of material existence." Normally, one who is awake is not afraid of ghosts. In the same way, one who is awake to self-realization has nothing more to fear from material existence. By nature, the soul is pure and so time or *karma* cannot be the actual cause of his distress. It is because of illusion, or the misconception of accepting the material body as the self, that the eternal soul feels temporary manifestations of happiness and distress. This is all the action of the false ego, which is born of ignorance. This is the sum and substance of this chapter.

PURPORT

The conditioned soul imagines the existence of happiness and distress as a result of his aversion to the Lord's service. However, when he wakes up from his sleep, he understands that the dream of happiness and distress does not belong to him. Under the influence of false ego, the living entities become absorbed in material existence and as a result, forget their actual identity. This condition of life is dissolved for one who is awake to the reality of Kṛṣṇa consciousness. Therefore, there is no need to be afraid of the awkward situations that arise from being absorbed on the bodily platform. The feelings of happiness, distress, and fear that are products of the material nature cannot overwhelm the self-realized souls, who are situated firmly in the devotional service of the Supreme Lord.

TEXT 57

एतांस आस्थायपरात्मनिष्ठामध्यासितांपूर्वतमैर्महर्षिभिः ।
अहंतरिष्यामिदुरन्तपारंतमोमुकुन्दाङ्घ्रिनिषेवयैव ॥५७॥

etāṁ sa āsthāya parātma-niṣṭhām adhyāsitāṁ pūrvatamair maharṣibhiḥ
ahaṁ tariṣyāmi duranta-pāraṁ tamo mukundāṅghri-niṣevayaiva

I shall cross over the insurmountable ocean of nescience by being firmly fixed in the service of the lotus feet of Kṛṣṇa. This was approved by the previous *ācāryas*, who were fixed in firm devotion to the Lord, Paramātmā, the Supreme Personality of Godhead.

COMMENTARY

Did the *brāhmaṇa* suddenly remember the pure devotion for the Lord that he had possessed in his previous life, but was obstructed for some reason? Is it for that reason that he has now developed detachment, become indifferent to happiness and distress, and resolved to serve the Lord's lotus feet while taking pleasure in chanting and dancing in ecstasy? The *brāhmaṇa* appears to exude great confidence, saying, "I will advance in self-realization, knowing that the soul is distinct from the material body, being a part and parcel of the Supersoul. There is no doubt that I will cross beyond the ocean of ignorance by being firmly fixed in the devotional service of the Supreme Lord." One might question, "Will the *brāhmaṇa* depend only on the Supreme Lord and no one else?" The answer is that he will cross over the ocean of ignorance by serving the lotus feet of Lord Kṛṣṇa, as approved by the *mahājanas.*

PURPORT

When one gives up seeing things in terms of material duality, due to cultivating an understanding of the Absolute Truth, one can realized himself as the eternal servant of the Supreme Lord. In order to cross over the formidable ocean of birth and death, the Avantī *brāhmaṇa* became determined to accept the path of devotional service to the Supreme Lord that had been traversed by the previous *ācāryas.*

TEXT 58

श्रीभगवानुवाच
निर्विद्यनष्टद्रविणेगतक्लम :प्रव्रज्यगांपर्यटमानैत्थम् ।
निराकृतोऽसद्भिरपिस्वधर्मादकम्पितोऽमूंमुनिराहगाथाम् ॥५८॥

śrī-bhagavān uvāca
nirvidya naṣṭa-draviṇe gata-klamaḥ pravrajya gāṁ paryaṭamāna ittham
nirākṛto 'sadbhir api sva-dharmād akampito 'mūṁ munir āha gāthām

Lord Śrī Kṛṣṇa said: Thus becoming detached after the loss of his wealth, the *brāhmaṇa* gave up his moroseness. He left home, taking *sannyāsa,* and began to travel over the earth. Even when insulted by uncivilized fools, he remained fixed in his duty and chanted this song.

COMMENTARY

The Supreme Personality of Godhead narrated this story to give Uddhava some very important instructions.

PURPORT

Many people consider the accumulation of worldly assets and service to family members as *svadharma*, or one's duty. However, the scriptures repeatedly advise us that human life is meant for self-realization. Those who take heed of such instructions may give up the hard labor required to amass more and more money for the satisfaction of one's wife and children, and take shelter of the association of saintly persons. By engaging in the devotional service of the Lord while remaining aloof from unwanted association, one can remain steady on the transcendental platform. Such sincere devotees should sing this song of the Avantī *sannyāsī* to further their advancement in spiritual life.

However, if one is not capable of listening to the song of this *sannyāsī*, then one will certainly remain an obedient servant of material illusion.

TEXT 59

सुखदुःखप्रदोनान्यःपुरुषस्यात्मविभ्रमः ।
मित्रोदासीनरिपवःसंसारस्तमसःकृतः ॥५९॥

sukha-duḥkha-prado nānyaḥ puruṣasyātma-vibhramaḥ
mitrodāsīna-ripavaḥ saṁsāras tamasaḥ kṛtaḥ

Nothing besides his own mental concoction makes the soul experience happiness and distress. One's perception of friends, neutral parties, and enemies, and the material life he builds around this perception, are simply created out of ignorance.

COMMENTARY

The phrase *ātma vibhrama* is in the fifth dative case, but here it has been used as first dative case. From illusion, all varieties of material manifestations emanate. Indeed, from ignorance, material existence has come into being.

PURPORT

"I am the enjoyer and I am the master." Such pride is typical of the conditioned souls, who are absorbed in the bodily conception of life, wherein the false ego dictates, "I am the material body, and everything in relation to the body is mine." Seeing everything in terms of such duality, those who are engrossed in the bodily concept of life are forgetful of their constitutional position as eternal servants of the Supreme Lord. Somehow or other, if one receives the mercy of the spiritual master and the Supreme Lord, the influence of the lower modes of nature can be vanquished to nil so that one see things in the light of pure knowledge. When one is rightly established in the devotional service of the Lord, the desires for perfection in religiosity, economic development, sense gratification, and liberation are uprooted from within the heart.

TEXT 60

तस्मात्सर्वात्मनातातनिगृहाणमनोधिया ।
मय्यावेशितयायुक्त एतावान्योगसङ्ग्रहः ॥६०॥

tasmāt sarvātmanā tāta nigṛhāṇa mano dhiyā
mayy āveśitayā yukta etāvān yoga-saṅgrahaḥ

My dear Uddhava, fixing your intelligence in Me, you should completely control your mind, because this is the essence of *yoga.*

COMMENTARY

The Supreme Lord concludes His instructions by saying that control of the mind is the essence of *yoga.*

PURPORT

Devotional service alone is capable of controlling the mind. All *yoga* systems, such as *karma-yoga, jñāna-yoga, haṭha-yoga, rāja-yoga,* as well as other godless *yogas*, simply disturb the mind. If one is bound by a particular religious system that preaches one of the previously mentioned misconceptions, he will certainly remain a nondevotee.

TEXT 61

य एतांभिक्षुणागीतांब्रह्मनिष्ठांसमाहितः ।
धारयञ्छ्रावयञ्छृण्वन्द्वन्द्वैर्नैवाभिभूयते ॥६१॥

ya etāṁ bhikṣuṇā gītāṁ brahma-niṣṭhāṁ samāhitaḥ
dhārayañ chrāvayañ chṛṇvan dvandvair naivābhibhūyate

Anyone who, with undivided attention, hears or chants this song of the Avantī *brāhmaṇa,* which contains authorized knowledge of the Absolute Truth, will soon transcend the dualities of material happiness and distress.

COMMENTARY

Even if one is unable to regulate his mind, he can achieve the same result simply by hearing the song of the Avantī *brāhmaṇa.*

PURPORT

A *tridaṇḍi-sanyāsī* who has taken shelter of the devotional service of the Lord knows that such devotion is the only process for attaining life's ultimate goal, and thus he is no longer bewildered by the illusory energy of his worshipable Lord. He engages his time in hearing and chanting the glories of the Lord and he inspires others to follow in his footsteps. Such a devotee is truly merciful because he leads others to the path of devotional service without expecting anything in return. Those who are mere imitators accept a person who is fond of the four objectives of life as their spiritual master and thus insure that they remain firmly situated in ignorance. Those who do not take shelter of devotional service must be placed in two categories—sense enjoyers and dry renunciates. Those who accept as a leader one who is a sense enjoyer or a dry renunciate will certainly remain averse to the devotional service of the Lord, who is *advaya-jñāna* Vrajendranandana.

Thus end the translation of the Seventeenth Chapter of the Uddhava-gītā entitled "**The Song of the Avantī Brāhmaṇa**" *with the commentaries of Śrīla Viśvanātha Cakravartī Ṭhākura and chapter summary and purports by Śrīla Bhaktisiddhānta Sarasvatī Ṭhākura.*

Chapter 18

The Philosophy of Sāṅkhya

CHAPTER SUMMARY

This chapter contains further instructions by the Lord dealing with Sāṅkhya, the analytical study of the elements of material nature. By the cultivation of knowledge, one can rise above the dualities of material existence so that the bewilderment of the mind can be dispelled.

Before the creation of the universe, the seer and the seen are unmanifest, being in a dormant state. The Supreme Lord then unfolds the creation of the universe, so that the conditioned souls are reawakened to activity. For creation, the three modes of material nature are agitated by the glance of the Lord, which manifests the *mahat-tattva*. When the consciousness of the conditioned souls is awakened, the false ego is generated in conjunction with the three modes of nature. False ego in the mode of ignorance creates fifteen subtle forms of sense perception, and then the fifteen physical elements. False ego in the mode of passion generates the ten senses, and false ego in the mode of goodness causes the manifestation of the mind and the eleven demigods that are the controlling deities of the senses. When all of these are amalgamated, the universal egg comes into existence. All these are enacted due to the presence of the Supersoul, who pervades the creation. Then, from the navel of the Supreme Lord sprouts a lotus, upon which Brahmā is born. Lord Brahmā then executes severe austerities under the direction of the Supreme Lord, and by the power invested in him as a result of his penance, Brahmā then recreates the universe as it was before. Within the universe are various planetary systems. The heavenly planets are the abodes of the demigods, the space between heaven and earth is the residence of ghosts and spirits, and the earth is the place for human beings and lower species of life. Above these are the planets of the great sages, and the lower regions of the universe are the residences of the demons and Nāgas. Whatever activities are performed under the direction of the three modes of material nature will carry one to these places of residence within the universe. Those who perform yoga and other types of austerity, such as accepting the renounced order of life, can reach the highest planets—Mahar, Janas, Tapas, and Satya. Devotional service is transcendental to the modes of material nature and thus the goal of the devotees is not a material planet. The destination of the devotees is the lotus feet of the Supreme Personality of Godhead in the spiritual sky. This universe is the place of fruitive activities and their reactions and is manifest under the control of time and the three modes of material nature. Whatever is seen to exist in this world is simply a product of these modes, which work under the direction of the Supreme Lord. The creation of the universe is enacted from subtle to gross, and the annihilation is enacted from gross to subtle. When all is dissolved, only the Supreme Lord remains situated in his transcendental position of self-satisfaction. When one cultivates this understanding of the Supreme Lord and His creation, the mind will rise above the dualities of material existence. This understanding is known as Sāṅkhya.

TEXT 1

श्रीभगवानुवाच
अथतेसम्प्रवक्ष्यामिसांख्यंपूर्वैर्विनिश्चितम् ।
यद्विज्ञायपुमान्सद्योजह्याद्वैकल्पिकंभ्रमम् ॥१॥

śrī-bhagavān uvāca
atha te sampravakṣyāmi sāṅkhyaṁ pūrvair viniścitam
yad vijñāya pumān sadyo jahyād vaikalpikaṁ bhramam

Lord Śrī Kṛṣṇa said: My dear Uddhava, I shall now describe to you the philosophy of Sāṅkhya, which was propounded by authorities, such as Kapila, in ancient times. By understanding this philosophy, one can immediately give up all desires for material happiness, which ultimately result in distress and which are born of duality.

COMMENTARY

This chapter describes the creation and annihilation of the cosmic manifestation. Such creation and dissolution is the subject matter of Sāṅkhya philosophy.

It has been established from the *bhikṣu-gītā* in the previous chapter that the cause of the living entities' happiness and distress is the accepting the subtle body, of which the mind is the principal component, as the self. This is the sum and substance of the material concept of life. This misunderstanding can be eliminated when the difference between matter and spirit is clearly understood. The analytical study of material nature and the difference between matter and spirit are the subject matters of the Sāṅkhya system of philosophy.

PURPORT

Those who adore the advancement of materialistic knowledge are generally averse to the service of the Supreme Lord, who is fully transcendental. Those who are satisfied to confine themselves to the material concept of life cannot understand the value of service to the transcendental Personality of Godhead. The Sāṅkhya philosophy that is presented in this chapter is the one that was propounded by Lord Kapila in the Third Canto of the *Śrīmad-Bhāgavatam* and not the atheistic Sāṅkhya taught by the imposter Kapila. The material elements are generated, one from another, from subtle to gross. One should not imagine that such a creation takes place automatically, without the superintendence of the Supreme Lord. Such a conception of evolution can only be accepted by those who are in the densest darkness of ignorance, and is never entertained by the devotees of the Lord.

TEXT 2

आसीज्ज्ञानमथो अर्थ एकमेवाविकल्पितम् ।
यदाविवेकनिपुणा आदौकृतयुगेऽयुगे ॥२॥

āsīj jñānam atho artha ekam evāvikalpitam
yadā viveka-nipuṇā ādau kṛta-yuge 'yuge

During the Kṛta-yuga, when men were very expert in spiritual understanding, and also previous to that, during the period of annihilation, the seer existed alone, nondifferent from that which is seen.

COMMENTARY

Real knowledge entails understanding of Brahman, Paramātmā, and Bhagavān. This is confirmed by Suta Gosvāmī in the *Śrīmad-Bhāgavatam* (1.2.11):

vadanti tat tattva-vidas tattvaṁ yaj jñānam advayam
brahmeti paramātmeti bhagavān iti śabdyate

Learned transcendentalists who know the Absolute Truth call this nondual substance Brahman, Paramātmā, or Bhagavān.

The word *atha* means "complete." The word *avikalpitaṁ* means "the one complete knowledge, or Brahman, who has no substitute." In Satya-yuga, however, people are *viveka-nipuṇāḥ*, or expert in intelligent discrimination, and thus there is no difference between their vision and reality. Seeing everything as the potency of the Supreme Lord, they do not artificially create duality between themselves and other living entities.

PURPORT

The Supreme Personality of Godhead is the Absolute Truth, who dissipates the darkness of ignorance. The *yuga* in which *satya*, or truth, was fully manifest is called Satya-yuga. This truth was instructed by the Lord to the heart of Brahmā. At that time, non-dual spiritual knowledge was not obscured by the material propensity of the mind to accept something and then later on reject it. In due course of time, however, understanding of the nondual truth gradually diminished.

TEXT 3

तन्मायाफलरूपेणकेवलंनिर्विकल्पितम् ।
वाङ्मनोऽगोचरंसत्यंद्विधासमभवद्बृहत् ॥३॥

tan māyā-phala-rūpeṇa kevalaṁ nirvikalpitam
vāṅ-mano-'gocaraṁ satyaṁ dvidhā samabhavad bṛhat

Thereafter, the Supreme Absolute Truth, who is beyond the jurisdiction of the mind and speech, who is one without a second, and who is completely transcendental, manifested Himself in two features—the material nature, and the living entities who are trying to enjoy the objects manifested by that nature.

COMMENTARY

The Supreme Brahman is one Absolute Truth. From Him manifested His external energy, known as *maya*, and His marginal energy, the infinitesimal spirit souls. These two manifestations are nondifferent from the one Supreme Lord. The material nature and the living entities are eternal energies of the Supreme Lord, and they are beyond the comprehension of the mind and speech.

PURPORT

The conditioned souls imagine themselves as enjoyers of the material nature because they have no understanding of its connection with the Supreme Lord. Having given up the shelter of the Supreme Lord influenced by this mundane conception, the conditioned souls try to attain knowledge by mental speculation.

TEXT 4

तयोरेकतरोह्यर्थःप्रकृतिःसोभयात्मिका ।
ज्ञानंत्वन्यतमोभावःपुरुषःसोऽभिधीयते ॥४॥

tayor ekataro hy arthaḥ prakṛtiḥ sobhayātmikā
jñānaṁ tv anyatamo bhāvaḥ puruṣaḥ so 'bhidhīyate

Of the two manifestations, one is the material nature, which embodies both the subtle causes and the products of matter, and the other is the living entity, who considers himself an enjoyer.

COMMENTARY

Among the two energies under consideration, one is the material nature and the other is the living entity. *Maya* is the form of cause and effect, and the living entity is the form of knowledge.

PURPORT

In the material creation, the knower of matter, the object of knowledge, and knowledge have appeared in three forms. The soul is the knower, or seer, who considers himself to be the enjoyer of the object of knowledge. Unadulterated devotional service is the constitutional duty of the spirit soul. When one gives up that service, he becomes a servant of ignorance by attempting to become the master of all he surveys.

TEXT 5

तमोरजःसत्त्वमितिप्रकृतेरभवन्गुणाः ।
मयाप्रक्षोभ्यमाणायाःपुरुषानुमतेनच ॥५॥

tamo rajaḥ sattvam iti prakṛter abhavan guṇāḥ
mayā prakṣobhyamāṇāyāḥ puruṣānumatena ca

When I glance over the material nature in My form as the *puruṣa* incarnation, it becomes agitated so that the three material modes—goodness, passion, and ignorance—became manifested to fulfill the desires of the conditioned souls.

COMMENTARY

The Supreme Lord agitates material nature through His plenary portion, the *puruṣa* incarnation. The creation is necessary to award an opportunity to the conditioned souls to cultivate *karma*, *jñāna*, or *bhakti*, according to their desires at the time of the previous annihilation. The living entities' fate, or destiny, necessitates the material creation.

PURPORT

After being agitated by the glance of the Lord, the three modes of material nature compete with each other for the control of the conditioned souls, so that creation, maintenance, and annihilation are also always at odds with one another. The three modes of material nature are the causes of creation, maintenance, and annihilation.

TEXT 6

तेभ्यःसमभवत्सुत्रमहान्सूत्रेणसंयुतः ।
ततोविकुर्वतोजातोयोऽहङ्कारोविमोहनः ॥६॥

tebhyaḥ samabhavat sutra mahān sūtreṇa saṁyutaḥ
tato vikurvato jāto yo 'haṅkāro vimohanaḥ

From these modes, the first transformation that takes place is the *mahat-tattva*. The transformation of the *mahat-tattva* then generated the false ego, which is the cause of the living entities' bewilderment.

COMMENTARY

The first transformation of the modes of nature is the power of action in a subtle form. This first transformation is known as *mahat-tattva*. *Mahat-tattva* is invested with activity and knowledge, for the sake of the bewildered conditioned souls.

PURPORT

The *mahat-tattva* came into existence from the three modes of material nature, and later on, the false ego manifested from the *mahat-tattva*. The false ego dictates material enjoyment or dry renunciation by covering the living entities with desires for *karma* and *jñāna*. As one's devotional service to the Lord slackens, these two tendencies automatically develop, just as the diminishing of light automatically brings an increase in darkness.

TEXT 7

वैकारिकस्तैजसश्चतामसश्चेत्यहंत्रिवृत् ।
तन्मात्रेन्द्रियमनसांकारणंचिदचिन्मयाः ॥७॥

vaikārikas taijasaś ca tāmasaś cety ahaṁ tri-vṛt
tan-mātrendriya-manasāṁ kāraṇaṁ cid-acin-mayaḥ

False ego, which encompasses both matter and spirit, manifests in three categories—*vaikārika, taijasa,* and *tāmasa*—arising from the modes of goodness, passion, and ignorance. The five sense objects, the senses, and the mind are creations of the false ego.

COMMENTARY

False ego manifests the sense objects, the mind, and the connection of the eternal spirit soul with the temporary material body. Although false ego is itself a product of matter, it remains with the spirit soul as his designation. Thus, the tight knot that binds the spirit soul to material existence is effected by the false ego.

PURPORT

The three categories of false ego are *sattvika* or *vaikārika*, *rājasa* or *taijasa*, and *tāmasika* or *tāmasa*. These three manifestations of false ego transform into the five sense objects, the five knowledge-acquiring senses, and the mind. The false ego forms the junction between the eternal soul and the material body. Desiring to lord it over the material energy of the Supreme Lord, the conditioned souls come under the control of the three modes of material nature, which causes them to assume temporary identities in the bodily concept of life.

TEXT 8

अर्थस्तन्मात्रिकाज्जज्ञेतामसादिन्द्रियाणिच ।
तैजसाद्देवता आसन्नेकादशचवैकृतात् ॥८॥

arthas tan-mātrikāj jajñe tāmasād indriyāṇi ca
taijasād devatā āsann ekādaśa ca vaikṛtāt

From false ego in the mode of ignorance, *tāmasa,* the five objects of perception and the five gross elements were generated. From false ego in the mode of passion, *rājasa,* the ten senses were generated, and from false ego in the mode of goodness, *sāttvika,* arose the eleven demigods who control the senses and the mind.

COMMENTARY

Sound, the sense of hearing and ether are the products of false ego in the mode of ignorance. Then, the sense of touch and air are produced. In this way, all of the elements and the perception of them are produced from subtle to gross. The senses are created from false ego in the mode of passion and from false ego in goodness come eleven demigods, who are controllers of the mind and senses.

PURPORT

The five material elements were created from the *tāmasa* false ego, the senses were created from the *rājasa* false ego, and the demigods controlling the senses were created from the *sattvika* false ego.

TEXT 9

मयासञ्चोदिताभावाःसर्वेसंहत्यकारिणः ।
अण्डमुत्पादयामासुर्ममायतनमुत्तमम् ॥९॥

mayā sañcoditā bhāvāḥ sarve saṁhatya-kāriṇaḥ
aṇḍam utpādayām āsur mamāyatanam uttamam

According to My will, all the elements combine to form the universal egg, which then becomes one of My transcendental abodes.

COMMENTARY

The word *bhāvāḥ* refers to all the ingredients that manifest the material universe.

PURPORT

By the combination of the elements manifested from the three modes of material nature, the universe was created.

TEXT 10

तस्मिन्नहंसमभवमण्डेसलिलसंस्थितौ ।
ममनाभ्यामभूत्पद्मंविश्वाख्यंतत्रचात्मभूः ॥१०॥

tasminn ahaṁ samabhavam aṇḍe salila-saṁsthitau
mama nābhyām abhūt padmaṁ viśvākhyaṁ tatra cātma-bhūḥ

Thereafter, I appeared within the water of the universe, in the form of Nārāyaṇa, and from My navel, a lotus flower called viśva sprouted, upon which Brahmā was born.

COMMENTARY

The Supreme Lord said: In the water within the universe, I appeared as Garbhodakaśāyī Viṣṇu. Four-headed Brahmā was then born from the lotus, called *viśva*, that grew from My navel.

PURPORT

Mahāviṣṇu, who lies on the Causal Ocean, first created the universe and then entered within it. The universe, which resembled an egg, was floating on the water of the Causal Ocean. From the navel of Lord Garbhodakaśāyī Viṣṇu sprouted a lotus called *viśva* on which Brahmā was born. This Brahmā is the original personality of the whole community of enjoyers.

TEXT 11

सोऽसृजत्तपसायुक्तोरजसामदनुग्रहात् ।
लोकान्सपालान्विश्वात्माभूर्भुवःस्वरितित्रिधा ॥११॥

so 'sṛjat tapasā yukto rajasā mad-anugrahāt
lokān sa-pālān viśvātmā bhūr bhuvaḥ svar iti tridhā

Lord Brahmā, the soul of the universe, being empowered with the mode of passion, performed great austerities, by My mercy, and thus created the three planetary systems called Bhūr, Bhuvar and Svar, along with their presiding deities.

PURPORT

By the strength of the mercy of the Supreme Personality of Godhead, Brahmā, who was born from Lord Viṣṇu's lotus-like navel, created Bhūloka, Bhuvarloka, Svargaloka, Maharloka, Janaloka, Tapoloka, and Satyaloka, as well as the seven lower planetary systems, beginning from Atala. All of these planets exist within this universe.

TEXT 12

देवानामोक आसीत्स्वर्भूतानांचभुवःपदम् ।
मर्त्यादीनांचभूर्लोकःसिद्धानांत्रितयात्परम् ॥१२॥

devānām oka āsīt svar bhūtānāṁ ca bhuvaḥ padam
martyādīnāṁ ca bhūr lokaḥ siddhānāṁ tritayāt param

Svargaloka was created for the residence of the demigods, Bhuvarloka was created for ghosts, and Bhūloka was created as the residence of human beings. Beyond these three planetary systems, other planets, beginning from Maharloka, were created as the residence of perfected beings who strive for liberation.

PURPORT

Demigods reside in Svargaloka, human beings reside in Bhūloka, and Bhuvaloka, or the sky, is a temporary residence for both classes of beings. Four higher planets were created to accommodate those who desire liberation from the material world.

TEXT 13

अधोऽसुराणांनागानांभूमेरोकोऽसृजत्प्रभुः ।
त्रिलोक्यांगतयःसर्वाःकर्मणांत्रिगुणात्मनाम् ॥१३॥

adho 'surāṇāṁ nāgānāṁ bhūmer oko 'sṛjat prabhuḥ
tri-lokyāṁ gatayaḥ sarvāḥ karmaṇāṁ tri-guṇātmanām

Lord Brahmā also created planets below the earth, beginning from Atala, as the residence for demons and the Nāga snakes. As a result of their fruitive activities performed under the modes of material nature, living entities take birth within these three worlds.

PURPORT

Planets, such as Atala, were created for the Nāgas, or serpents. Acting under the influence of the three modes of material nature, human beings are forced to suffer and enjoy the fruits of their *karma* as they are transmigrate within the limit of these three planetary systems.

TEXT 14

योगस्यतपसश्चैवन्यासस्यगतयोऽमलाः ।
महर्जनस्तपःसत्यंभक्तियोगस्यमद्गतिः ॥१४॥

yogasya tapasaś caiva nyāsasya gatayo 'malāḥ
mahar janas tapaḥ satyaṁ bhakti-yogasya mad-gatiḥ

By practice of mystic *yoga*, undergoing great austerities, and accepting the renounced order of life, the superior destinations of Maharloka, Janaloka, Tapoloka, and Satyaloka are attained. But, by executing devotional service unto Me, one attains My eternal abode, Vaikuṇṭha.

COMMENTARY

Performance of pious activities, *astāṅga yoga*, and renunciation lead one to planets such as Maharloka. Pure devotees of the Lord attain the transcendental abode of Lord, Vaikuṇṭha.

PURPORT

By the strength of their austerity, *yoga*, and renunciation, living entities obtain superior destinations like Maharloka, Janaloka, Tapoloka, and Satyaloka. Attainment of these planets is temporary because after the merit achieved by one's practice is exhausted, one must return to earth. On the other hand, by the influence of devotional service to the Supreme Lord, one attains the eternal abode, Vaikuṇṭha.

TEXT 15

मयाकालात्मनाधात्राकर्मयुक्तमिदंजगत् ।
गुणप्रवाह एतस्मिन्नुन्मज्जतिनिमज्जति ॥१५॥

mayā kālātmanā dhātrā karma-yuktam idaṁ jagat
guṇa-pravāha etasminn unmajjati nimajjati

The results of fruitive work are awarded within this world by Me, the supreme creator, acting as time. Thus, one sometimes rises up toward the surface of this mighty river of the modes of material nature, and sometimes again becomes submerged.

COMMENTARY

The destination awarded by one's fruitive activities that are performed under the influence of the modes of nature is temporary. The Supreme Lord in His form as time is the giver of the fruits of one's actions. In this world, where all activities are carried out under the influence of the three modes of nature, one sometimes rises to higher destinations, such as Satyaloka, and sometimes is submerged in the lower destinations, such as Pātālaloka.

PURPORT

Those who do not engage in the devotional service of the Supreme Lord are sometimes drowned in the river of the material modes of nature and sometimes brought to its surface. The Supreme Lord, acting as providence, causes the living entities, who suffer and enjoy the fruits of their *karma*, to wander about throughout the fourteen worlds.

TEXT 16

अणुर्बृहत्कृशःस्थूलोयोयोभावःप्रसिध्यति ।
सर्वोऽप्युभयसंयुक्तःप्रकृत्यापुरुषेणच्च ॥१६॥

aṇur bṛhat kṛśaḥ sthūlo yo yo bhāvaḥ prasidhyati
sarvo 'py ubhaya-saṁyuktaḥ prakṛtyā puruṣeṇa ca

Whatever visibly exists within the material world—whether small or great, thin or stout—certainly contains both the material nature and its enjoyer, the spirit soul.

COMMENTARY

This verse describes how the effect is present within the cause. The word *bhāva* in this verse means "effect."

PURPORT

Whatever is seen to exist within this world, whether very great or insignificant, is a combination of the conditioned souls who are acting as enjoyers, and the material nature which he is trying to enjoy.

TEXT 17

यस्तुयस्यादिरन्तश्चसवैमध्यंचतस्यसन् ।
विकारोव्यवहारार्थोयथातैजसपार्थिवाः ॥१७॥

yas tu yasyādir antaś ca sa vai madhyaṁ ca tasya san
vikāro vyavahārārtho yathā taijasa-pārthivāḥ

Gold and earth originally exist as ingredients. From gold one may make golden bracelets and earrings, and from earth one may make clay pots and plates. The original ingredients, gold and earth, exist before the products are made from them, and when the products are eventually destroyed, the original ingredients, gold and earth, will remain.

Therefore, because the ingredients are present in the beginning and at the end, they must also be present in the middle phase, taking the form of some object to which we give a particular name, such as bracelet.

COMMENTARY

In this verse, the Lord explains that the original cause is present in its effect, giving the example of gold and clay as the causal ingredients of many different products. We assign various names to such temporary products, although their essential nature continues to be that of the ingredient, and not of the temporary product, such as a bracelet or earring.

PURPORT

Under the influence of time, an element as a cause may transform into many products or effects, just as gold is transformed when we manufacture gold earrings and earth is transformed when we make clay pots. These transformations are temporary and at the beginning, in the middle, or at the end, the essential characteristic of the cause remains unchanged.

TEXT 18

यदुपादायपूर्वस्तुभावोविकुरुतेऽपरम् ।
आदिरन्तोयदायस्यतत्सत्यमभिधीयते ॥१८॥

yad upādāya pūrvas tu bhāvo vikurute 'param
ādir anto yadā yasya tat satyam abhidhīyate

A material object, which is composed of an essential ingredient, creates another material object as a transformation. Thus one created object becomes the cause and basis of another created object. Any particular object may therefore be called real in that it possesses the basic nature of another object that constitutes its origin, as well as its final state.

COMMENTARY

Although cause and effect are both accepted as factual, the *Vedas* place more stress on the cause than the effect. Earth and a clay pot must both be considered factual. For example, a potter becomes the instrumental cause, taking some earth to manufacture clay pots. Both the earth as the cause, and the clay pot as the effect, are real. The primary cause of both earth and the clay pots is material nature. Because the cause is present in the effect, they both must be real. This is called *tat satyaṁ* in the language of the *Vedas*. The Supreme Personality of Godhead has declared Himself as the original cause of everything. There is no opportunity for the impersonalists to give some other interpretation in this regard.

PURPORT

There is no objection to accepting all the objects of our perception as reality, but their temporary transformable nature must be accounted for. Still, it is never reasonable to call any materially created object false. The Supreme Personality of Godhead is the original reality and by finding that material nature is a temporary manifestation, one should not imagine Him or His actions to be false. Of course, the temporarily manifested transformations cannot be accepted as the ultimate reality, which is understood from the *Vedas* to be the eternal reality of Vaikuṇṭha.

TEXT 19

प्रकृतिर्यस्योपादानमाधारःपुरुषःपरः ।
सतोऽभिव्यञ्जकःकालोब्रह्मतत्त्रितयंत्वहम् ॥१९॥

prakṛtir yasyopādānam ādhāraḥ puruṣaḥ paraḥ
sato 'bhivyañjakaḥ kālo brahma tat tritayaṁ tv aham

Material nature, which is the original ingredient of the creation; the Supreme Lord, who is the shelter of the material nature; and time, are nondifferent from Me, the Absolute Truth.

COMMENTARY

The Supreme Lord is the cause of all causes. Mahā-Viṣṇu is His plenary portion, and time represents the Lord's activity. In this way, time and nature are always subservient to the Supreme Personality of Godhead, who creates, maintains and annihilates all that exists through the agency of His potencies and plenary portions. All followers of the *Vedas* accept that material nature is the ingredient cause of the cosmic manifestation, and that the Supreme Lord is the shelter of all energies. The Lord agitates material nature by glancing over her and then continues to superintend her activities in His form as time. Thus, material nature always works under the direction of the Supreme Lord. Although the cosmic creation is certainly a transformation of energy, the Supreme Lord Himself is unchanging and supreme.

PURPORT

It should be understood that the instrumental cause invests its potency into the ingredient cause, under the control of time, and thus they are non different from the Supreme Personality of Godhead.

TEXT 20

सर्गःप्रवर्ततेतावत्पौर्वापर्येणनित्यशः ।
महान्गुणविसर्गार्थःस्थित्यन्तोयावदीक्षणम् ॥२०॥

sargaḥ pravartate tāvat paurvāparyeṇa nityaśaḥ
mahān guṇa-visargārthaḥ sthity-anto yāvad īkṣaṇam

As long as the Supreme Personality of Godhead continues to glance upon material nature, the universe will continue to exist, manifesting through procreation of the great and variegated flow of universal creation, for the sake of the conditioned souls.

COMMENTARY

By the interactions of the three modes of material nature, various types of bodies are created, and by procreation, this process seems to go on perpetually. In order to maintain the conditioned souls, who have the spirit of material enjoyment, the creation continues to exist for as long as the Lord glances over it.

PURPORT

Material nature and time cannot function independently, they are active only as long as the Supreme Lord continues to glace over them. Time and the cosmic manifestation are created just to give the conditioned souls, who are averse to the Supreme Lord, a field of activities.

TEXT 21

विराण्मयासाद्यमानोलोककल्पविकल्पकः ।
पञ्चत्वायविशेषायकल्पतेभुवनैःसह ॥२१॥

virāṇ mayāsādyamāno loka-kalpa-vikalpakaḥ
pañcatvāya viśeṣāya kalpate bhuvanaiḥ saha

I manifest the universal form, which displays endless variety through repeated creation, maintenance, and destruction of the planetary systems. Originally containing everything

within itself, My universal form manifests the varieties of creation by arranging the coordinated combination of the five gross elements.

COMMENTARY

The Supreme Lord, in His form as time, pervades the entire universe. After creating all planets and living entities through the agency of the material nature, He finally withdraws the entire creation. The word *pañcatva* in this verse means "death."

PURPORT

The Supreme Lord, in His form as time, repeatedly creates, maintains, and annihilates the universe.

TEXT 22-27

अन्नेप्रलीयतेमर्त्यमन्नंधानासुलीयते ।
धानाभूमौप्रलीयन्तेभूमिर्गन्धेप्रलीयते ॥२२॥
अप्सुप्रलीयतेगन्ध आपश्चस्वगुणेरसे ।
लीयतेज्योतिषिरसोज्योतीरूपेप्रलीयते ॥२३॥
रूपंवायौसचस्पर्शेलीयतेसोऽपिचाम्बरे ।
अम्बरंशब्दतन्मात्रइन्द्रियाणिस्वयोनिषु ॥२४॥
योनिर्वैकारिकेसौम्यलीयतेमनसीश्वरे ।
शब्दोभूतादिमप्येतिभूतादिर्महतिप्रभुः ॥२५॥
सलीयतेमहान्स्वेषुगुणेसुगुणवत्तमः ।
तेऽव्यक्तेसम्प्रलीयन्तेतत्कालेलीयतेऽव्यये ॥२६॥
कालोमायामयेजीवेजीव आत्मनिमय्यजे ।
आत्माकेवल आत्मस्थोविकल्पापायलक्षणः ॥२७॥

anne pralīyate martyam annaṁ dhānāsu līyate
dhānā bhūmau pralīyante bhūmir gandhe pralīyate

apsu pralīyate gandha āpaś ca sva-guṇe rase
līyate jyotiṣi raso jyotī rūpe pralīyate

rūpaṁ vāyau sa ca sparśe līyate so 'pi cāmbare
ambaraṁ śabda-tan-mātra indriyāṇi sva-yoniṣu

yonir vaikārike saumya līyate manasīśvare
śabdo bhūtādim apyeti bhūtādir mahati prabhuḥ

sa līyate mahān sveṣu guṇeṣu guṇa-vattamaḥ
te 'vyakte sampralīyante tat kāle līyate 'vyaye

kālo māyā-maye jīve jīva ātmani mayy aje
ātmā kevala ātma-stho vikalpāpāya-lakṣaṇaḥ

At the time of annihilation, the bodies of the conditioned souls merge into food, food merges into grain, and grains merge into the earth. The earth merges into its quality of fragrance, fragrance merges into water, and water merges into its quality of taste. Taste merges into fire and fire merges into its quality of form, which then merges into the sky. Sky then merges into its quality of sound. The senses of the living beings merge into their predominating deities, and these demigods merges into mind. Mind merges into false ego in goodness, and sound merges into false ego in the mode of ignorance. Finally, false ego merges into the total material substance, which then merges with the modes of nature. The modes of nature then merge with the unmanifest nature and the unmanifest merges into time. Time then merges into the Supersoul, who provides inspiration to all living beings. Thus, I remain alone after the dissolution of the universe, self-satisfied in the transcendental position.

COMMENTARY

In this regard, the Vedic evidence can be cited— *tasmādvā etasmādātmana ākāśaḥ sambhūtaḥ ākāśādvāyuḥ vāyoragniḥ agnerāpaḥ adbhyaḥ pṛthivī pṛthivyā oṣadhayaḥ oṣadhībhyo'nnam annātpuruṣaḥ* "From the Supreme Personality of Godhead, ether was manifested. From ether, air was manifested. From air, fire was manifested. From fire, water was manifested. From water, earth was manifested. From earth, medicinal herbs were manifested. From herbs, grains were manifested, and the living entities subsist on food grains."

This is a description of the process of creation, and the process of annihilation is a reversal of this. It is stated that just before the time of annihilation, there will be no rainfall for one hundred years, and as a result, there will be no food grains. Because of no food grains upon which the living entities subsist, all material bodies will perish. Thus there will be complete famine, and the grains, along with their seeds, will merge into earth, and earth will merge into smell. In this way, the process of annihilation will continue. The earth will be dried up by *samvartaka* and then burnt by fire emanating from the mouth of Lord Saṅkarṣaṇa. After that, there will only be the subtle qualities of the elements, and nothing else. The senses will merge into their own cause, the *taijasa* false ego, the *taijasa* false ego will merge into the *vaikārika* false ego, the *vaikārika* false ego will merge into the mind, and the mind will merge into the supreme controller. The mind is the controller of the working senses and knowledge-acquiring senses. The sky will merge into the sense objects, the sense objects will merge into *tāmasa* false ego, the three false egos will merge into the *mahat-tattva*, the *mahat-tattva* will merge into material modes of nature, and the three modes of material nature will merge into the unmanifested material nature, *pradhāna*. The neutral state of existence of the three modes of material nature is called dissolution. In this state of neutrality, the unmanifested material nature will merge into time. Still, it is impossible to perfectly describe the dissolution of the material nature. It has therefore been stated in the *Śrīmad-Bhāgavatam* 12.4.19 as follows:

na tasya kālāvayavaiḥ pariṇāmādayo guṇāḥ
anādy anantam avyaktaṁ nityaṁ kāraṇam avyayam

The unmanifest material nature is not subjected to the six kinds of transformation caused by the influence of time. Rather, it has no beginning and no end. It is the eternal and infallible cause of creation.

Material nature has existed since time immemorial. In the story of Jayanta, when Antarikṣa described the annihilation, there is no mention of the material nature's annihilation. Therefore it is said in the *Śrīmad-Bhāgavatam* 12.4.22:

layaḥ prākṛtiko hy eṣa puruṣāvyaktayor yadā
śaktayaḥ sampralīyante vivaśāḥ kāla-vidrutāḥ

This is the annihilation called *prākṛtika*, during which the energies of the Supreme Lord and His unmanifest material nature, disassembled by the force of time, are deprived of their potencies and merge into Him.

Material nature, along with her three modes, is dissolved, so that her power of creation is withdrawn. The living entities actually are not subject to annihilation. They are eternal and inexhaustible, belonging to the Lord's superior energy known as *taṭastha śakti*. There is no question of the living entities losing their real identity and spiritual form. After annihilation of the universe, the living entities merge into the existence of the Supersoul. Although they merge, they do not lose their individuality.

PURPORT

After the temporary material manifestations are merged into their respective causes, those conditioned souls who have qualified for their liberated state of existence achieve an inclination toward the Lord's service. The segmented manifestation of time then places the liberated souls on the platform of eternal service within the realm of undivided time. Until the conditioned souls achieve shelter at the lotus feet of the Supreme Lord, they continue to remain under the control of the material nature. The influence of segmented time creates various kinds of inauspiciousness for the living entities. The conditioned souls struggle for existence under the control of the three modes of material nature. Being conditioned by the modes of nature, they swing like a pendulum, alternating between a state of material enjoyment and one of renunciation. As long as there is no resolute determination to engage in the devotional service of the Supreme Lord, such an incompatible state of being will continue to exist.

TEXT 28

एवमन्वीक्षमाणस्यकथंवैकल्पिकोभ्रमः ।
मनसोहृदितिष्ठेतव्योम्नीवार्कोदयेतमः ॥२८॥

evam anvīkṣamāṇasya kathaṁ vaikalpiko bhramaḥ
manaso hṛdi tiṣṭheta vyomnīvārkodaye tamaḥ

When the sun rises, darkness is dispelled. Similarly, when factual understanding of the universal dissolution is realized, the illusory conceptions of duality cannot remain in the mind of the serious transcendentalist. Even if such illusion enters his mind, it will not remain.

COMMENTARY

Due to illusion, one considers the material body to be the self. But, by carefully analyzing the difference between matter and spirit by studying the Sāṅkhya philosophy, such illusion will vanquish, and one will come to realize that he is a pure spirit soul.

PURPORT

Just as the rising of the sun dispels darkness, an understanding of Lord Kṛṣṇa's teachings to Uddhava dissipates one's ignorance. One who realizes the truth of these instructions will be relieved of the bodily conception of life. Even if some residual material attachment sometimes crops up, it will not remain due to the strength of one's spiritual realization.

TEXT 29

एषसांख्यविधिःप्रोक्तःसंशयग्रन्थिभेदनः ।
प्रतिलोमानुलोमाभ्यांपरावरदृशमया ॥२९॥

eṣa sāṅkhya-vidhiḥ proktaḥ saṁśaya-granthi-bhedanaḥ
pratilomānulomābhyāṁ parāvara-dṛśa mayā

Thus I, the original seer of everything material and spiritual, have imparted to you this knowledge of Sāṅkhya, which destroys the illusion of doubt by a scientific analysis of creation and annihilation.

PURPORT

The material mind accepts and rejects many different understandings of reality, generating innumerable false arguments about the actual process of perfection. But, those who have taken shelter at the lotus feet of the Supreme Lord can see everything in its right perspective. By directly and indirectly discussing these topics of the Supreme Lord and His energies, the conditioned souls can be liberated from material bondage and attain eternal service to the Supreme Personality of Godhead.

Thus end the translation of the Eighteenth Chapter of the Uddhava-gītā entitled "**The Philosophy of Sāṅkhya**" *with the commentaries of Śrīla Viśvanātha Cakravartī Ṭhākura and chapter summary and purports by Śrīla Bhaktisiddhānta Sarasvatī Ṭhākura.*

Chapter 19

The Three Modes of Nature and Beyond

CHAPTER SUMMARY

In this chapter, the effects of the influence of the three modes of material nature—goodness, passion, and ignorance—are described. Such knowledge ultimately culminates in an understanding of the transcendental nature of the Supreme Lord.

Godly qualities, such as tolerance and self control are manifestations of the mode of goodness. Material desires, feverish endeavor, and false pride are indications of the predominance of the mode of passion. Foolishness, uncontrolled anger, and insatiable greed are characteristics of the mode of ignorance. Every conditioned soul is influenced by a mixture of these thee modes, and according to one's situation under the modes of nature, the false ego of "I" and "mine" take on various aspects in terms of one's behavior, personality, concept of religion, and engagements in sense gratification.

A person primarily influenced by the mode of goodness certainly worships the Supreme Personality of Godhead as a matter of duty, without consideration of personal profit. One who worships the Supreme Lord in the hopes of some kind of material improvement is primarily influenced by the mode of passion. Crime and violence are exhibited by those who have sunk deeply into the influence of the mode of ignorance. Although these modes of nature direct the thoughts and activities of all the conditioned souls, they have no effect upon the Supreme Lord, who remains fixed in His transcendental position.

Whatever is experience in this world—the time, place, circumstances, results of karma, objects, activities, performers of activities, one's faith, development of consciousness, the destination after death, and so on—are permeated by the three modes of material nature. However, everything in relation to the Supreme Personality of Godhead—everything employed in His service, places of His pastimes, activities offered for His satisfaction, the performer of devotional service, time spent in His devotional service, and so on—is transcendental to the three modes of material nature.

The energy of the Lord is manifested in an unlimited variety of conditions of life for the living entities who are rotating within the cycle of birth and death. All such conditions of life are manifestations of the three modes of material nature, and they are the results of the conditioned souls' fruitive activities. One can free himself from the influence of the three modes of material nature by engaging in the devotional service of the Supreme Lord. Human life is the opportunity for cultivating knowledge of the Absolute Truth and any sane man will surely avail himself of this rarely obtained facility. By a careful cultivation of the mode of goodness, one can overcome the influence of the lower modes of passion and ignorance. Thereafter, one can advance even further by rising above the mode of goodness to the transcendental platform of devotional service. When one is fixed in the devotional service of the Lord, his ultimate destination is the association of the Supreme Lord in the spiritual sky, which is attained when, by His grace, the gross and subtle coverings are dissolved at the time of death.

TEXT 1

श्रीभगवानुवाच
गुणानामसम्मिश्राणांपुमान्येनयथाभवेत् ।
तन्मेपुरुषवर्येदमुपधारयशंसतः ॥१॥

śrī-bhagavān uvāca
guṇānām asammiśrāṇāṁ pumān yena yathā bhavet
tan me puruṣa-varyedam upadhāraya śaṁsataḥ

The Supreme Lord said: O foremost of men, please listen attentively as I describe how the conditioned soul is awarded his particular nature due to the association of the three modes of material nature.

COMMENTARY

This chapter describes the different natures produced by the three material modes of nature, and how these modes manifest varieties within this world. Also described are the liberated soul and the Supreme Lord, who are transcendental to the three modes of material nature.

Unless one rises above the influence of the three modes of material nature, one cannot give up the bodily concept of life. The analytical study of matter and spirit that is elaborated in the Sāṅkhya philosophy helps one rise above the influence of the modes of nature. Here, the Lord gives a more elaborate description of the characteristics of the three modes of material nature. He says: "O foremost among men, the three modes of material nature are sometimes seen in their pure condition and sometimes when they are mixed." The Supreme Lord will explain in this chapter how a person develops a particular personality according to the different manifestations of the material modes.

PURPORT

By cultivating spiritual advancement, the living entities can achieve two kinds of knowledge—that which is received in disciplic succession and that which only gradually removes ignorance. In this manifest world, we find three things in our daily experience—the speaker, the topic, and the listener. This is the nature of the world governed by the three material modes. When the transcendental spiritual objective dominates the mind of the speaker, his talks will not contain any abomination born of the three modes of material nature. Indeed, his purpose of talking is to expose the abomination that is born of the material modes. If the conditioned souls of this world simply hear topics of Vaikuṇṭha, they will gain relief from their *anarthas*, which have become temporarily manifested as a result of their material concept of life. All activities performed in this world under the control of the three modes of material nature are temporary, devoid of true knowledge, and full of misery. There is no possibility for materially conditioned people to obtain the eternal nature, which is full of knowledge and bliss, by hearing the talks of imperfect philosophers.

In this chapter, the Supreme Personality of Godhead is the speaker. Because He is fully transcendental to the material modes of nature and because He is the Supreme Personality of Godhead, He can establish the proper procedure for hearing and chanting. Because nondevotees do not hear the topics of Lord Hari from the Lord Himself, due to being averse to His devotional service, they remain covered by the Lord's illusory potency. Being bereft of oral reception in disciplic succession, they remain ignorant of the science of the self and the science of God.

TEXTS 2-5

शमोदमस्तितिक्षेक्षातपःसत्यंदयास्मृतिः ।
तुष्टिस्त्यागोऽस्पृहाश्रद्धाह्रीर्दयादिःस्वनिर्वृतिः ॥२॥

कामईहामदस्तृष्णास्तम्भ आशीर्भिदासुखम् ।
मदोत्साहोयशःप्रीतिर्हास्यंवीर्यंबलोद्यमः ॥३॥
क्रोधोलोभोऽनृतंहिंसायाञ्चादम्भःक्लमःकलिः ।
शोकमोहौविषादार्तीनिद्राशाभीरनुद्यमः ॥४॥
सत्त्वस्यरजसश्चैतास्तमसश्चानुपूर्वशः ।
वृत्तयोवर्णितप्रायाःसन्निपातमथोशृणु ॥५॥

śamo damas titikṣekṣā tapaḥ satyaṁ dayā smṛtiḥ
tuṣṭis tyāgo 'spṛhā śraddhā hrīr dayādiḥ sva-nirvṛtiḥ

kāma īhā madas tṛṣṇā stambha āśīr bhidā sukham
madotsāho yaśaḥ-prītir hāsyaṁ vīryaṁ balodyamaḥ

krodho lobho 'nṛtaṁ hiṁsā yācñā dambhaḥ klamaḥ kaliḥ
śoka-mohau viṣādārtī nidrāśā bhīr anudyamaḥ

sattvasya rajasaś caitās tamasaś cānupūrvaśaḥ
vṛttayo varṇita-prāyāḥ sannipātam atho śṛṇu

Peacefulness, self-control, tolerance, the power of discrimination, remaining fixed in one's occupational duties, truthfulness, compassion, careful study of the influence of time, satisfaction, renunciation, detachment from sense gratification, faith, modesty, giving charity, and self-satisfaction are the qualities of the mode of goodness. Lust, great endeavor, pride, thirst for material enjoyment, false ego, praying to the demigods for material wealth, discrimination between oneself and others, sense gratification, eagerness to fight, considering oneself to be supreme, fondness for flattery, the ridiculing of others, boasting of one's prowess, and justifying one's actions by dint of one's strength, are the qualities of the mode of passion. Anger, greed, falsehood, violence, envy, hypocrisy, chronic fatigue, quarrel, lamentation, illusion, moroseness, poverty, fear, and laziness, are the qualities of the mode of ignorance. Now hear about the combination of these three modes.

COMMENTARY

The characteristics of the mode of goodness are peacefulness, self control, *ikṣā*, which means the power of discrimination, tolerance, detachment, compassion, righteousness, submission, and satisfaction within one's own self. The characteristics of the mode of passion are lust, *īhā*, which means great exertion, *stambha*, which means false pride, *āśī*, which means to pray to the demigods for wealth, material enjoyment, *mada*, which means enthusiasm for fighting, flattery, desire for fame and adoration, boasting, and considering oneself to be the greatest. The characteristics of the mode of ignorance are anger, hypocrisy, moroseness, and indolence.

PURPORT

Because there is no accepting and rejecting based on the bodily concept of life in the pure mode of goodness, the mind can be easily controlled. To remain undisturbed in the face of the dualities of material existence, such as heat and cold, and happiness and distress, is called tolerance. The best use of the power of discrimination is to cultivate knowledge of the spiritual nature, which is eternal, full of knowledge, and blissful. Austerity means to accept even painful conditions that are favorable for spiritual advancement. Truthfulness refers speaking frankly about the nature of reality without distorting the facts to please others. To instruct others about the purpose of human life is the best expression of compassion. To give up activities of sense gratification by employing everything in the service of the Lord is real renunciation. To give up hankering for the possession of temporary sense objects is called detachment. To act on the order of the scriptures, and not whimsically, is termed righteousness. To patiently hear the topics of Lord Hari is called faith. To feel shame in the presence of abominable activities is termed modesty. When one engages in hearing discussions of the glories of the Lord without duplicity, for attaining self-realization and self-satisfaction in this life, this is certainly an activity that is characteristic of the mode of goodness. Those who are influenced by the mode of passion have a great desire to enjoy the objects of the senses, and they are very ambitious, intoxicated by pride, never satisfied, always eager to amass more and more wealth and possessions, very egoistic, fond of worshiping the demigods for material improvement, envious of others' success, fond of being flattered and fond of ridiculing others, thinking themselves to be the greatest. Anger due to intolerance, miserliness, falsehood and speech devoid of scriptural evidence, inclination toward violence, desiring without deserving, hypocrisy, fondness for quarrel, lamentation over previous foolishness, illusion, moroseness, laziness, dependence, selfishness, fearfulness, and lack of enthusiasm are the symptoms of people who are in the mode of ignorance.

TEXT 6

सन्निपातस्त्वहमितिममेत्युद्धवयामतिः ।
व्यवहारःसन्निपातोमनोमात्रेन्द्रियासुभिः ॥६॥

sannipātas tv aham iti mamety uddhava yā matiḥ
vyavahāraḥ sannipāto mano-mātrendriyāsubhiḥ

My dear Uddhava, all the combinations of the modes of nature manifest the mentality of "I" and "mine," which is present in all conditioned souls. The ordinary transactions of this world, which are impelled by the mind, the objects of perception, the senses, and the vital within the body, are also derived from the combination of the modes of material nature.

COMMENTARY

The conceptions of "I" and "mine" are transitory and subject to transformation. All kinds of ordinary dealings impelled by the mind having such a conception are also illusory. The sense of "I" and "mine" is applicable to the conditioned souls, and has nothing to do with the pure spirit soul. One who is very peaceful is not expected to become blinded by lust or anger, nor would he be found to be falsely proud.

PURPORT

"I am the material body, which is a product of matter, and everything in relation to the body is mine." Such an illusory concept occurs by the mixture of the three modes of material nature. It should also be understood that material objects that the mind accepts with the help of the senses are a result of the mixture of the modes of nature.

TEXT 7

धर्मेचार्थेचकामेचयदासौपरिनिष्ठितः ।
गुणानांसन्निकर्षोऽयंश्रद्धारतिधनावहः ॥७॥

dharme cārthe ca kāme ca yadāsau pariniṣṭhitaḥ
guṇānāṁ sannikarṣo 'yaṁ śraddhā-rati-dhanāvahaḥ

When a person devotes himself to religiosity, economic development, and sense gratification, the faith, sensual enjoyment, and wealth that is obtained are the results of the interactions of the three modes of nature.

COMMENTARY

Religiosity, economic development, and sense gratification are engagements impelled by the modes of nature, and the faith, wealth, and enjoyment obtained by them clearly reveal the situation of a person within the modes of nature. When one is attached to religiosity, the quality of faith becomes predominant. When one is attached to sense gratification, or lust, conjugal affairs become prominent, and when one is attached to economic development, desires for prosperity become prominent.

PURPORT

Because of the interaction of the three modes of nature, those who desire advancement in religiosity, economic development, and sense gratification, develop faith in religious practices, attachment to wealth, and a great hankering impelled by lust.

TEXT 8

प्रवृत्तिलक्षणेनिष्ठापुमान्यर्हिगृहाश्रमे ।
स्वधर्मेचानुतिष्ठेतगुणानांसमितिर्हिसा ॥८॥

pravṛtti-lakṣaṇe niṣṭhā pumān yarhi gṛhāśrame
sva-dharme cānu tiṣṭheta guṇānāṁ samitir hi sā

When one has a strong desire for sense gratification, he enters family life and subsequently engages in occupational and religious duties. Such a condition is evidence of the interaction of the three modes of material nature.

COMMENTARY

When a person has strong desires for sense gratification and thus enters family life, he performs his occupational and religious duties with great enthusiasm.

PURPORT

The principles of *āśrama dharma* arise from the interaction of the three modes of material nature. That is why Śrī Gaursundara, while discussing the constitutional position of the living entities, declared *varṇāśrama-dharma* to be external and therefore irrelevant. Different natures of the conditioned souls are born from various combinations of the modes of nature. The servants of the Supreme Lord, instead of desiring sense enjoyment, display attachment for the beauty of the spiritual nature and the pastimes of the Supreme Personality of Godhead.

TEXT 9

पुरुषंसत्त्वसंयुक्तमनुमीयाच्छमादिभिः ।
कामादिभीरजोयुक्तंक्रोधाद्यैस्तमसायुतम् ॥९॥

puruṣaṁ sattva-saṁyuktam anumīyāc chamādibhiḥ
kāmādibhī rajo-yuktaṁ krodhādyais tamasā yutam

One who exhibits qualities such as self-control is understood to be predominantly in the mode of goodness. Similarly, a passionate person is recognized by his lust, and one in ignorance is recognized by qualities such as anger.

COMMENTARY

In this verse, the Lord describes the characteristics of those who are under the influence of the various modes of material nature.

PURPORT

Qualities such as self-control that were described in the second verse of this chapter belong to a person who is situated in the mode of goodness. Qualities such as lust that were described in the third verse belong to a person situated who is situated in the mode of passion, and the qualities described in the fourth verse belong to a person who is situated in the mode of ignorance.

TEXT 10

यदाभजतिमांभक्त्यानिरपेक्षःस्वकर्मभिः ।
तंसत्त्वप्रकृतिंविद्यात्पुरुषंस्त्रियमेववा ॥१०॥

yadā bhajati māṁ bhaktyā nirapekṣaḥ sva-karmabhiḥ
taṁ sattva-prakṛtiṁ vidyāt puruṣaṁ striyam eva vā

Any man or woman who worships Me with devotion, offering the results of his activities unto Me without attachment is to be known as in the mode of goodness.

COMMENTARY

When a person is situated in a particular mode of nature and renders service to the Supreme Lord, his service is saturated with that particular mode. This is being explained in these two verses.

PURPORT

Those who are in the mode of goodness, whether male or female, become inspired to worship the Supreme Lord by offering the results of their occupational duties.

TEXT 11

यदा आशिष आशास्यमांभजेतस्वकर्मभिः ।
तंरजःप्रकृतिंविद्यात्हिंसामाशास्यतामसम् ॥११॥

yadā āśiṣa āśāsya māṁ bhajeta sva-karmabhiḥ
taṁ rajaḥ-prakṛtiṁ vidyāt hiṁsām āśāsya tāmasam

When a person serves Me with a desire to achieve sense gratification, he should be understood to be in the mode of passion, and when he worships Me with a desire to harm others, he should be understood to be in the mode of ignorance.

COMMENTARY

The word *hiṁsā* means "destroying one's enemies."

PURPORT

Materialistic people hope to achieve some temporary benefit as a result of their actions. One should know that worship of the Supreme Lord with such a desire is to be considered in the mode of passion, and activities performed with an intention of harming others are understood to be impelled by the mode of ignorance. Desire for wealth, followers, and fame is in the mode of passion, and the desire for achieving victory over others by means of violence is in the mode of ignorance.

TEXT 12

सत्त्वंरजस्तमैतिगुणाजीवस्यनैवमे ।
चित्तजायैस्तुभूतानांसज्ञमानोनिबध्यते ॥१२॥

sattvaṁ rajas tama iti guṇā jīvasya naiva me
citta-jā yais tu bhūtānāṁ sajjamāno nibadhyate

The three modes of material nature—goodness, passion, and ignorance—influence the conditioned souls but not Me. Manifesting within the mind, the modes of nature induce the living entity to become attached to their material bodies and the objects of the senses, causing him to be bound to material nature.

COMMENTARY

The three modes of material nature bind the living entities but not the Supreme Lord. The material modes act within the mind of the living entities, manifesting themselves as material designations. By the influence of the modes of nature, the living entities become conditioned, thinking the material body to be the self and material objects as meant for their enjoyment. However, the Supreme Lord is never conditioned by nature's modes because the material nature works under His direction. Although He is the origin of the cosmic manifestation, He eternally remains in His transcendental position.

PURPORT

The speaker of this chapter, as the supreme instructor, while describing the living entities' entanglement in material nature, revealed to Uddhava that He Himself is never overwhelmed by the combination of nature's three modes.

TEXT 13

यदेतरौजयेत्सत्त्वंभास्वरंविशदंशिवम् ।
तदासुखेनयुज्येतधर्मज्ञानादिभिःपुमान् ॥१३॥

yadetarau jayet sattvaṁ bhāsvaraṁ viśadaṁ śivam
tadā sukhena yujyeta dharma-jñānādibhiḥ pumān

When the pure, illuminating, and auspicious mode of goodness predominates over passion and ignorance, one become endowed with happiness, knowledge, piety, and other good qualities.

COMMENTARY

Conditioned souls and the three modes of material nature are forced and the imposers of force, respectively. How the living entities become conditioned is being explained in these three verses. When the mode of goodness conquers the modes of passion and ignorance, one becomes bright, pure, peaceful, auspicious, noble, pious, and wise. These qualities are the source of happiness for a person in the mode of goodness.

PURPORT

In the material conception of life, male and female are considered the enjoyer and the enjoyed. When a person is able to minimize the influence of the modes of passion and ignorance by cultivation of the mode of goodness, qualities such as peacefulness, give him a sense of satisfaction.

TEXT 14

यदाजयेत्तमःसत्त्वंरजःसङ्गंभिदाचलम् ।
तदादुःखेनयुज्येतकर्मणायशसाश्रिया ॥१४॥

yadā jayet tamaḥ sattvaṁ rajaḥ saṅgaṁ bhidā calam
tadā duḥkhena yujyeta karmaṇā yaśasā śriyā

When the mode of passion, which causes attachment, separatism, and activity, overwhelms the mode of ignorance and goodness, a man works hard to acquire wealth and fame. Thus, in the mode of passion, he struggles hard and experiences anxiety.

COMMENTARY

When, by acting in the mode of passion, the modes of ignorance and goodness are subdued, one suffers various forms of distress. It is stated in the Vedic literature that one experiences fear due to absorption in matter. Under the influence of the mode of passion, one performs fruitive activities to achieve wealth and fame.

PURPORT

When the mode of passion becomes prominent, subduing the influence of the modes of ignorance and goodness, one desires to become famous by lording it over material nature, but this ultimately brings him great unhappiness.

TEXT 15

यदाजयेद्रजःसत्त्वंतमोमूढंलयंजडम् ।
युज्येतशोकमोहाभ्यांनिद्रयाहिंसयाशया ॥१५॥

yadā jayed rajaḥ sattvaṁ tamo mūḍhaṁ layaṁ jaḍam
yujyeta śoka-mohābhyāṁ nidrayā hiṁsayāśayā

When the mode of ignorance defeats the modes of goodness and passion, it covers a person's consciousness so that he is deprived of all sense of discrimination. Falling into lamentation and illusion, a person in the mode of ignorance sleeps excessively, indulges in false hopes, and is violent toward others.

COMMENTARY

When the modes of goodness and passion are overtaken by the mode of ignorance, which destroys the power of discrimination and covers the spirit soul, one exhibits grief, illusion, envy, laziness, lack of enthusiasm, and impractical ambitions. However, when, by engagement in the devotional service of the Supreme Lord, one transcends the influence of the three material modes, one simply feels transcendental ecstasy. This will be described later on. When the mode of ignorance becomes firmly seated in one's heart, having subdued the modes of goodness and passion, one becomes a reservoir of lamentation, illusion, lethargy, envy, and agression.

TEXT 16

यदाचित्तंप्रसीदेतेन्द्रियाणांचनिर्वृतिः ।
देहेऽभयंमनोऽसङ्गंतत्सत्त्वंविद्धिमत्पदम् ॥१६॥

yadā cittaṁ prasīdeta indriyāṇām ca nirvṛtiḥ
dehe 'bhayaṁ mano-'saṅgaṁ tat sattvaṁ viddhi mat-padam

When consciousness becomes clear and the senses are detached from their objects, one becomes fearless, even within the material body, and detached from the workings of the material mind. You should understand this situation to be the predominance of the mode of goodness, in which one has the opportunity to realize Me.

COMMENTARY

When the heart becomes pure, one's thirst for sense gratification diminishes almost to nil. As the mind becomes detached from the three modes of material nature it can find satisfaction, being fixed at the lotus feet of the Supreme Lord.

PURPORT

When one is nurturing the mode of goodness, detachment from sense gratification relieves one of the hard labor required to maintain an opulent material position and enables one to devote himself to the service of the Supreme Lord.

TEXT 17

विकुर्वन्क्रियायाचाधीरनिवृत्तिश्चचेतसाम् ।
गात्रास्वास्थ्यमनोभ्रान्तंरज एतैर्निशामया ॥१७॥

vikurvan kriyayā cā-dhīr anivṛttiś ca cetasām
gātrāsvāsthyaṁ mano bhrāntaṁ raja etair niśāmaya

You should understand the influence of the mode of passion by its symptoms—the clouding of intelligence because of too much activity, the great attachment of the perceiving

senses to their objects, an unhealthy condition of the working physical organs, and great disturbance within the mind.

COMMENTARY

When the heart is always disturbed by unlimited desires for acquiring that which attracts it, and when the senses constantly urge one for gratification, it is to be understood that the mode of passion is prominent.

PURPORT

Varieties of material attachment, as well as insatiable greed, and continous thirst for material enjoyment are found in a person who is agitated by the mode of passion.

TEXT 18

सीदच्चित्तंविलीयेतचेतसोग्रहणेऽक्षमम् ।
मनोनष्टंतमोग्लानिस्तमस्तदुपधारय ॥१८॥

sīdac cittaṁ vilīyeta cetaso grahaṇe 'kṣamam
mano naṣṭaṁ tamo glānis tamas tad upadhāraya

When one's higher awareness fails and one is unable to focus his attention, his mind becomes dull, manifesting ignorance and depression. You should understand this to be caused by a predominance of the mode of ignorance.

COMMENTARY

When the heart becomes practically inert and one is unable to concentrate his mind, it is to be understood that the mode of ignorance has become prominent. However, whatever one's situation may be under the influence of the modes of nature, if he begins to cultivate the devotional service of the Lord, beginning with hearing and chanting, the slackening of the modes will immediately begin to take place.

PURPORT

Those who are deeply entrenched in the mode of ignorance find it very difficult to apply themselves to any sort of regulated existence. Being overwhelmed by inertia, foolishness, and even madness, such persons risk falling down into the lower species of life.

TEXT 19

एधमानेगुणेसत्त्वेदेवानांबलमेधते ।
असुराणांचरजसितमस्युद्धवरक्षसाम् ॥१९॥

edhamāne guṇe sattve devānāṁ balam edhate
asurāṇāṁ ca rajasi tamasy uddhava rakṣasām

O Uddhava, with the increase of the mode of goodness, the strength of the demigods also increases. When the mode of passion is enhanced, those who are demoniac become strong, and with the rise of the mode of ignorance, the strength of wicked persons increases.

COMMENTARY

By the increase of the modes of goodness, passion and ignorance, the influence of the demigods, *asuras*, and Rakṣasas also increases, respectfully. When the mode of pure goodness is enhanced due to the execution of devotional service, the prowess of the devotees flourishes.

PURPORT

The demigods have the tendency to enhance the mode of goodness, the *asuras* have the tendency to enhance the mode of passion, and the Rakṣasas have the tendency to enhance the mode of ignorance.

TEXT 20

सत्त्वाज्ञागरणंविद्याद्रजसास्वप्नमादिशेत् ।
प्रस्वापंतमसाजन्तोस्तुरीयंत्रिषुसन्ततम् ॥२०॥

sattvāj jāgaraṇaṁ vidyād rajasā svapnam ādiśet
prasvāpaṁ tamasā jantos turīyaṁ triṣu santatam

It should be understood that alertness is caused by the mode of goodness, sleep with dreaming is caused by the mode of passion, and deep dreamless sleep is caused by the mode of ignorance. The fourth state of consciousness, which is transcendental, continually exists even as the other three are manifest.

COMMENTARY

The three states of material consciousness are herein described in relation to the three modes of material nature. The fourth or the transcendental state of consciousness is not affected by the three material modes.

PURPORT

Those who are in the mode of goodness are awake to their real self-interest. Those who are predominantly in the mode of passion are sleeping on the lap of the material nature, dreaming of becoming happy by means of sense gratification. Those who are in the mode of ignorance are in the deep slumber of nescience, which is practically a state of unconsciousness. However, those who cultivate the mode of pure goodness are always under the shelter of the Supreme Personality of Godhead, where there is no influence of mundane goodness, passion, or ignorance

TEXT 21

उपर्युपरिगच्छन्तिसत्त्वेनब्राह्मणाजनाः ।
तमसाधोऽध आमुख्याद्रजसान्तरचारिणः ॥२१॥

upary upari gacchanti sattvena brāhmaṇā janāḥ
tamasādho 'dha ā-mukhyād rajasāntara-cāriṇaḥ

Those who are dedicated to Vedic culture go to the higher planets, such as Brahmaloka, being absorbed in the mode of goodness. Those who are in the mode of ignorance take birth in the lower species of life, and those who in the mode of passion continue to transmigrate from one human body to another.

COMMENTARY

The mode of goodness carries one to the upper planetary systems, up to Brahmaloka. The mode of passion causes one to transmigrate in human society. The mode of pure goodness, which is cultivated by those engaged in devotional service, carries one to the lotus feet of the Supreme Lord.

PURPORT

By the influence of the mode of goodness, knowers of Brahman surpass the *śudra's* lamentation, the *vaiśya's* desire for wealth, and the *kṣatriya's* thirst for power and influence. Those who are firmly situated in the mode of ignorance gradually go down to the status of non-moving entities, such as trees. When one is influenced by the mode of passion, he will sometimes advance to a higher status of human birth and sometimes degrade to an uncivilized one.

TEXT 22

सत्त्वेप्रलीनाःस्वर्यान्तिनरलोकंरजोलयाः ।
तमोलयास्तुनिरयंयान्तिमामेवनिर्गुणाः ॥२२॥

sattve pralīnāḥ svar yānti nara-lokaṁ rajo-layāḥ
tamo-layās tu nirayaṁ yānti mām eva nirguṇāḥ

Those who leave this world in the mode of goodness go to the heavenly planets, those who die in the mode of passion remain in the society of human beings, and those who pass away from the material body in the mode of ignorance go to hell. But those who are free from the influence of the three modes of material nature, attain My supreme abode.

COMMENTARY

What happens to those who die while absorbed in a particular mode of nature is explained in this verse. Whenever a particular mode is prominent, it determines his destination after death. If one dies in the mode of goodness, he ascends to the heavenly planets. If one dies in the mode of passion, he remains within human society on this earth. If one dies in the mode of ignorance, he traverses the path to hell. The Supreme Lord has not said "at the time of death" regarding those who are situated on the transcendental platform because they attain shelter at His lotus feet even before quitting their present body.

PURPORT

One who is situated in the mode of goodness goes to the heavenly planets when he leaves his present body. One predominantly in the mode of passion, with a touch of goodness, remains on this earthly planet, and one in the mode of ignorance goes to the hellish planets. But persons situated beyond the influence of the three modes of material nature are transcendentally situated and therefore traverse the path to Vaikuṇṭha.

TEXT 23

मदर्पणंनिष्फलंवासात्त्विकंनिजकर्मतत् ।
राजसंफलसङ्कल्पंहिंसाप्रायादितामसम् ॥२३॥

mad-arpaṇaṁ niṣphalaṁ vā sāttvikaṁ nija-karma tat
rājasaṁ phala-saṅkalpaṁ hiṁsā-prāyādi tāmasam

Work done as an offering to Me, without attachment to the result, is in the mode of goodness. Work performed with the desire to enjoy the results is in the mode of passion, and violent work impelled by envy is in the mode of ignorance.

COMMENTARY

The fruits of one's actions should be offered to the Supreme Lord. Śrī Nārada Muni has said that if the fruits of one's activities are not offered to the Lord, then they bind one to the cycle of birth and death. The word *madarpana* can also be taken to mean that if activities performed in the modes of passion and ignorance are offered to the Supreme Lord, they transform into activities in the mode of goodness. If activities are performed with an intention to enjoy its fruits, they are considered to be in the mode of passion. Sinful activities performed with the intention of harming others are in the mode of ignorance. The word *ādi*, indicating pride and violence, refers to activities in the mode of ignorance. Activities of devotion, such as chanting and hearing the glories of the Lord, are transcendental forms of work beyond the modes of nature.

PURPORT

Those on the platform of goodness renounce material enjoyment that is contrary to religious principles and surrender to the Supreme Lord. Those in the mode of passion desire sense gratification and work very hard to achieve it. Those in the mode of ignorance manifest pride and envy.

TEXT 24

कैवल्यंसात्त्विकंज्ञानंरजोवैकल्पिकंचयत् ।
प्राकृतंतामसंज्ञानंमन्निष्ठंनिर्गुणंस्मृतम् ॥२४॥

kaivalyaṁ sāttvikaṁ jñānaṁ rajo vaikalpikaṁ ca yat
prākṛtaṁ tāmasaṁ jñānaṁ man-niṣṭhaṁ nirguṇaṁ smṛtam

Knowledge of the distinction between matter and spirit is in the mode of goodness, knowledge based on the dualities of material existence is in the mode of passion, and knowledge that simply results in foolishness is in the mode of ignorance. Knowledge of Me, however, is transcendental.

COMMENTARY

Here the Supreme Lord describes four types of knowledge. Three of these are within the jurisdiction of the modes of nature, and one is transcendental. The word *kaivalyaṁ* means "that which has nothing to do with the material body," and such knowledge is considered to be *sāttvika*. Speculative knowledge about the nature of the self is considered to be in the mode of passion, and knowledge of eating, sleeping, mating, and defending is in the mode of ignorance.

PURPORT

By rendering service to the Supreme Lord, who is one without a second, the knowledge of a person who is situated in the mode of goodness is gradually raised to the transcendental platform. A devotee is one who accepts Viṣṇu as his only worshipable Lord and concludes that pleasing Lord Vīṣṇu is the ultimate goal of life. Being deprived of spiritual knowledge, those who are in the mode of passion desire varieties of material enjoyment and thus sometimes work feverishly for that end, and sometimes, becoming disgusted, strive for renunciation. People in the mode of ignorance become intoxicated while performing all sorts of abominable activities, and they consider self-ruination to be the goal of life. The devotees of the Supreme Lord dedicate themselves to the favorable cultivation of Kṛṣṇa consciousness, knowing that love of Kṛṣṇa is the ultimate goal of life.

TEXT 25

वनंतुसात्त्विकोवासोग्रामोराजस उच्यते ।
तामसंद्यूतसदनंमन्निकेतंतुनिर्गुणम् ॥२५॥

vanaṁ tu sāttviko vāso grāmo rājasa ucyate
tāmasaṁ dyūta-sadanaṁ man-niketaṁ tu nirguṇam

Residence in the forest is in the mode of goodness, residence in a town is in the mode of passion, residence in a gambling house is in the mode of ignorance, and residence in My abode is transcendental.

COMMENTARY

"To live in a temple or in a holy place is transcendental because the Lord is present there." These are the words of Śrīdhara Swamī. "As a touchstone turns iron into gold, similarly the presence of the Supreme Lord turns any place into a transcendental abode." These are the words of Jīva Gosvāmī.

PURPORT

Many people, desiring to cultivate the mode of goodness, go to reside in the forest after giving up a life of material enjoyment. On the path of gradual advancement, such persons, if they are fortunate, can ultimately realize the transcendental beauty of Vṛndāvana. Those who are in the mode of passion are busy establishing their name and fame while either living a life of material pleasure, or attempting to detach themselves from such a life. Those who are in the mode of ignorance take pleasure in gambling, and other such abominable activities. In these verses the Lord clearly explains that all material phenomena may be divided into three divisions, according to the modes of nature, and that there also exists a fourth, or transcendental, division—Kṛṣṇa consciousness—which elevates all aspects of human culture to the liberated platform.

TEXT 26

सात्त्विकःकारकोऽसङ्गीरागान्धोराजसःस्मृतः ।
तामसःस्मृतिविभ्रष्टोनिर्गुणोमदपाश्रयः ॥२६॥

sāttvikaḥ kārako 'saṅgī rāgāndho rājasaḥ smṛtaḥ
tāmasaḥ smṛti-vibhraṣṭo nirguṇo mad-apāśrayaḥ

A detached worker is in the mode of goodness, a worker blinded by attachment is in the mode of passion, and a worker with no conception of what is to be done and what is not to be done in the mode of ignorance. A worker who has taken shelter of Me is transcendental to the three material modes.

COMMENTARY

The performer of work who is unattached is *sāttvika*. The performer of work who is blinded by material attachment is *rājasika*, and the performer of work who has no sense of discrimination is *tāmasika*. However, the performer of work who is surrendered to the Supreme Lord is *nirguṇa*.

PURPORT

Those who are in the mode of goodness are inclined to solitary worship of the Lord, giving up all kinds of bad association. Those who are in the mode of passion are fully engrossed in sense gratification, and those who are in the mode of ignorance act whimsically, having no sense of discrimination. But pure devotees of the Lord are transcendental to the three modes of material nature, being under the shelter of the Supreme Personality of Godhead.

Those who live a life of seclusion, as well as those who mingle with sense enjoyers—if they associate with the devotees of the Supreme Lord while maintaining their separatist mentalities, remain far from the platform of pure devotional service.

TEXT 27

सात्त्विक्याध्यात्मिकीश्रद्धाकर्मश्रद्धातुराजसी ।
तामस्यधर्मेयाश्रद्धामत्सेवायांतुनिर्गुणा ॥२७॥

sāttviky ādhyātmikī śraddhā karma-śraddhā tu rājasī
tāmasy adharme yā śraddhā mat-sevāyāṁ tu nirguṇā

Faith in the existence of the eternal self is in the mode of goodness, faith that one's real self-interest lies in fruitive activities is in the mode of passion, and faith in sinful activities is in the mode of ignorance, whereas faith in My devotional service is transcendental.

PURPORT

One who desires his eternal benefit possesses faith in the mode of goodness. One who is bewildered by false ego possesses faith in the mode of passion, and one who takes pleasure in performing sinful acts possesses faith in the mode of ignorance. Those whose faith is transcendental to the three modes of material nature never forget their constitutional position. While remaining aloof from material enjoyment, they constantly engage themselves in the service of Lord Kṛṣṇa, and thus become decorated with transcendental qualities.

TEXT 28

पथ्यंपूतमनायस्तमाहार्यंसात्त्विकंस्मृतम् ।
राजसंचेन्द्रियप्रेष्ठंतामसंचार्तिदाशुचि ॥२८॥

pathyaṁ pūtam anāyastam āhāryaṁ sāttvikaṁ smṛtam
rājasaṁ cendriya-preṣṭhaṁ tāmasaṁ cārti-dāśuci

Food that is nourishing, pure, and obtained without difficulty is in the mode of goodness. Food that gives immediate pleasure to the senses is in the mode of passion, and food that is unclean and causes distress is in the mode of ignorance. Food that has been offered to Me is transcendental.

COMMENTARY

The word *anāyāstaṁ* means "that which is obtained without much endeavor." The word *ca* indicates that food which is offered to the Lord is spiritual.

PURPORT

Those who are in the mode of goodness only accept food that is wholesome and pure, and which is obtained without excessive endeavor. Food that titillates the senses is in the mode of passion, and food such as meat, fish, and eggs, which ultimately causes distress, is in the mode of ignorance.

TEXT 29

सात्त्विकंसुखमात्मोत्थंविषयोत्थंतुराजसम् ।
तामसंमोहदैन्योत्थंनिर्गुणंमदपाश्रयम् ॥२९॥

sāttvikaṁ sukham ātmotthaṁ viṣayotthaṁ tu rājasam
tāmasaṁ moha-dainyotthaṁ nirguṇaṁ mad-apāśrayam

Happiness based on satisfaction is in the mode of goodness, happiness derived from sense gratification is in the mode of passion, and happiness derived from degraded activities is in the mode of ignorance. But that happiness which is in relationship to Me is transcendental.

COMMENTARY

Happiness derived from self-realization is in the mode of goodness, and that which is relished by the devotees of the Lord by hearing and chanting His glories is transcendental.

PURPORT

Sāttvika happiness is that which is derived from the practices of self-realization. *Rājasika* happiness is derived from enjoying sense gratification, and *tāmasika* happiness is of a perverse nature and is derived from foolishness. *Nirguṇa*, or transcendental happiness, is derived under the shelter of the Supreme Lord after surpassing the three modes of material nature.

TEXT 30

द्रव्यंदेशःफलंकालोज्ञानंकर्मचकारकः ।
श्रद्धावस्थाकृतिर्निष्ठात्रैगुण्यःसर्व एवहि ॥३०॥

dravyaṁ deśaḥ phalaṁ kālo jñānaṁ karma ca kārakaḥ
śraddhāvasthākṛtir niṣṭhā trai-guṇyaḥ sarva eva hi

Therefore, material substance, place, result of work, time, knowledge, activities, performers of activities, faith, state of consciousness, species of life, and destination are all based on the three material modes of nature.

COMMENTARY

The Supreme Lord is herein concluding His instructions. It is the influence of the three modes of material nature that causes the living entities' bondage. Objects, such as pure food, and places, such as the forest, are *sāttvika*. Knowledge about the self, action without attachment, and the state of awakening, are also in the mode of goodness. If one leaves his body at the time of death in the mode of goodness, he attains the heavenly planets. In this way, all activities and states of being are under the influence of the three modes of material nature.

PURPORT

Material substance, place, result, time, knowledge, activity, performer of work, faith, species, and destination are based on the three modes of material nature. If all these are utilized for the service of the Supreme Lord, they transform into spiritual existence.

TEXT 31

सर्वेगुणमयाभावाःपुरुषाव्यक्तधिष्ठिताः ।
दृष्टंश्रुतंनुध्यातंबुद्ध्यावापुरुषर्षभ ॥३१॥

sarve guṇa-mayā bhāvāḥ puruṣāvyakta-dhiṣṭhitāḥ
dṛṣṭaṁ śrutaṁ anudhyātaṁ buddhyā vā puruṣarṣabha

O best of human beings, all states of being that are heard, seen, or thought of, are the results of the interaction of the soul with the three modes of material nature.

COMMENTARY

It is practically experienced that anyone who has not taken shelter of the Supreme Lord, no matter what his situation may be, is surely in the grips of the three modes of material nature.

PURPORT

Those who have detached themselves from the objects of sense gratification, may imagine themselves to be liberated from material entanglement. However, the mind, intelligence, and false ego, including their functions of thinking, feeling, and willing, are also products of matter, and thus not free from the influence of the three modes of material nature.

TEXT 32

एताःसंसृतयःपुंसोगुणकर्मनिबन्धनाः ।
येनेमेनिर्जिताःसौम्यगुणाजीवेनचित्तजाः ।
भक्तियोगेनमन्निष्ठोमद्भावायप्रपद्यते ॥३२॥

etāḥ saṁsṛtayaḥ puṁso guṇa-karma-nibandhanāḥ
yeneme nirjitāḥ saumya guṇā jīvena citta-jāḥ
bhakti-yogena man-niṣṭho mad-bhāvāya prapadyate

O gentle one, the living entities' conditions of material existence are caused by their activities performed under the influence of the three modes of material nature. One who conquers these modes, born from the mind, can dedicate himself to Me by executing devotional service and thus attain pure love for Me.

COMMENTARY

The three modes of material existence as the cause of material existence is herein being described. One who has conquered these modes of nature by practice of devotional service is a transcendental devotee of the Supreme Lord. He is reinstated in one of the five relationships with the Supreme Lord—*śānta, dāsya, sakhya, vātsalya* and *mādhurya*. A devotee of the Lord is situated transcendentally, like the Supreme Lord Himself. In this regard, one should consider the statement of Lord Kapiladeva, who said, "I have thus described the symptoms of devotional service." Here it is also stated that the influence of the three modes of material nature is subdued by the process of devotional service. Therefore, it must be concluded that the practice of devotional service is fully transcendental. Material entities, such as incense, sandalwood paste, flowers, ghee lamps, an umbrella, or a *cāmara*, when used in the worship of the Supreme Lord, are also considered transcendental. The faith with which a devotee executes devotional service is also transcendental. The Supreme Lord has thus confirmed that all objects related to His service are to be considered transcendental, and not products of the three modes of material nature.

PURPORT

The activities of the conditioned souls and the creation that takes place by the interaction of the three modes of material nature are the sum and substance of conditional life. Those who are engaged in the eternal service of the Supreme Lord defeat the influence of the three modes of material nature by their execution of devotional service, and ultimately go to reside in the transcendental abode of the Lord as self-realized souls. There, they serve the Supreme Lord, according to their particular devotional sentiments.

TEXT 33

तस्माद्देहमिमंलब्ध्वाज्ञानविज्ञानसम्भवम् ।
गुणसङ्गंविनिर्धूयमांभजन्तुविचक्षणाः ॥३३॥

tasmād deham imaṁ labdhvā jñāna-vijñāna-sambhavam
guṇa-saṅgaṁ vinirdhūya māṁ bhajantu vicakṣaṇāḥ

Therefore, intelligent persons, having received the human form of body, which enables one to cultivate spiritual knowledge and its practical application, should give up the association of the three material modes of nature and continuously engage in My service.

COMMENTARY

The human form of life is the opportunity to cultivate spiritual knowledge and its practical application, engagement in the devotional service of the Supreme Personality of Godhead.

PURPORT

As long as one considers devotional service to the Supreme Lord to be a product of matter, one will be forced to accept either the path of material enjoyment or dry renunciation. Only in the human form of life is the opportunity to worship the Supreme Lord attained, after surpassing the influence of the three modes of material nature. That is why the Supreme Lord instructs the conditioned souls to rise above the three modes of material nature.

TEXT 34

निःसङ्गोमांभजेद्विद्वानप्रमत्तोजितेन्द्रियः ।
रजस्तमश्चाभिजयेत्सत्त्वसंसेवयामुनिः ॥३४॥

niḥsaṅgo māṁ bhajed vidvān apramatto jitendriyaḥ
rajas tamaś cābhijayet sattva-saṁsevayā muniḥ

One who is actually intelligent, who is free from all material association and not bewildered, should subdue his senses and worship Me. He should conquer the modes of passion and ignorance by engaging himself only in relation to the mode of goodness.

COMMENTARY

The Supreme Lord describes the process of *bhajana.* The word *niḥsaṅga* means "without any tinge of *karma, jñāna,* and so on." One may question, "What should one do if he has faith in the Supreme Lord, but also possesses *sāttvika, rājasika,* or *tāmasika* faith? The answer is that if one is exclusively engaged in devotional service, by the strength of that transcendental activity, he will be able to conquer the three modes of material nature. The Supreme Lord Himself has earlier confirmed this. If one's activities are all engaged for the satisfaction of the Lord, one can rise above the three modes of material nature. One should carefully cultivate the mode of goodness and thus subdue the modes of passion and ignorance.

PURPORT

After abandoning all endeavors for material enjoyment and dry renunciation, he can certainly defeat the influence of the modes of passion and ignorance, with the help of the mode of goodness, by engaging himself in the devotional service of the Lord.

TEXT 35

सत्त्वंचाभिजयेद्युक्तोनैरपेक्ष्येणशान्तधीः ।
सम्पद्यतेगुणैर्मुक्तोजीवोजीवंविहायमाम् ॥३५॥

sattvaṁ cābhijayed yukto nairapekṣyeṇa śānta-dhīḥ
sampadyate guṇair mukto jīvo jīvaṁ vihāya mām

Being fixed in devotional service, one should then conquer the mode of goodness by means of indifference. Being pacified within his mind, the spirit soul, freed from the modes of nature, thus gives up the very cause of his conditioned life and attains Me.

COMMENTARY

The platform of pure goodness is transcendental to the three modes of material nature. By the execution of devotional service, one automatically develops detachment from the three modes of material nature. When one attains this transcendental stage, he discards his subtle body and goes back to Godhead.

TEXT 36

जीवोजीवविनिर्मुक्तोगुणैश्चाशयसम्भवैः ।
मयौवब्रह्मणापूर्णोनबहिर्नान्तरश्चरेत् ॥३६॥

jīvo jīva-vinirmukto guṇaiś cāśaya-sambhavaiḥ
mayaiva brahmaṇā pūrṇo na bahir nāntaraś caret

Being freed from the conditioning of the mind, as well as from the modes of nature born of material consciousness, the living entity becomes completely satisfied by experiencing My transcendental existence, so that he no longer searches for enjoyment in the external energy.

COMMENTARY

Internal enjoyment refers to that enjoyment which is experienced by the subtle body. Feelings of lust, anger, happiness, and illusion are in this category. External enjoyment refers to the activities of the gross senses.

PURPORT

Being situated on the platform of transcendental satisfaction, when a devotee transcends even the mode of goodness, he is situated on the platform of pure devotional service to the Supreme Lord. Simply by the influence of devotional service, the two propensities of material enjoyment and detachment which are exhibited on the platform of goodness are dispelled. When a liberated soul is engaged in the transcendental service of the *sac-cid-ānanda* Lord, the modes of material nature cannot touch him. In this chapter, Lord Kṛṣṇa enumerated the characteristics of the three modes of material nature and described the devotional service of the Lord as being transcendental to these modes. Lord Caitanya has recommended that in this age, one should incessantly chant the holy names of the Lord as the best means of engaging in devotional service and thus transcending the modes of material nature.

Thus end the translation of the Nineteenth Chapter of the Uddhava-gītā *entitled* **"The Three Modes of Nature and Beyond"** *with the commentaries of Śrīla Viśvanātha Cakravartī Ṭhākura and chapter summary and purports by Śrīla Bhaktisiddhānta Sarasvatī Ṭhākura.*

CHAPTER 20

THE AILA-GĪTĀ

CHAPTER SUMMARY

This chapter explains how unfavorable association is a threat to one's position in devotional service, and how by associating with saintly persons one can easily advance in devotional service.

The *jīva* who has received a human body, which is a very favorable condition for achieving the Supreme Personality of Godhead, and who has situated himself in the devotional service to the Lord becomes capable of realizing His transcendental nature. Such a person, fully dedicated to the Supreme Personality, becomes liberated from the influence of *maya*, even while continuing to reside in this world created by illusory energy of the Lord. Those souls, on the other hand, who are bound up by *maya*, are devoted only to their bellies and genitals. They are impure, and by associating with them, one will fall down into the dark well of ignorance.

The emperor, Purūravā, who was bewildered by the association of the heavenly damsel, Urvaśī, later became renounced after being separated from her. He thus sang a song expressing his contempt for intimate association with a woman. He said that men who are attached to the body of a woman, which is simply a combination of skin, flesh, blood, sinew, brain tissue, marrow, and bones, are not much different from worms. What is the value of one's education, austerity, renunciation, study of the *Vedas*, solitude and silence, if one's mind becomes stolen away by the body of a woman? Learned men should distrust their six enemies, headed by lust, and thus avoid associating with women, or with men who are controlled by women. After declaring these facts, King Purūravā, now freed from the illusion of material existence, attained realization of the Supreme Lord as the Supersoul.

In conclusion, one who is intelligent should give up bad association and instead take to the company of saintly persons. By their transcendental instructions, the saintly devotees of the Lord can break the false attachments that dwell within one's mind. Real saints are liberated and devoted to the Supreme Personality of Godhead. In their association, there are constant discussions of the Supreme Lord, who by serving, the spirit soul can eradicate his material sins and obtain pure devotional service. When one is engaged in the devotional service of the Supreme Personality of Godhead, who is the original ocean of unlimited qualities, what else remains to be gained?

TEXT 1

श्रीभगवानुवाच
मल्लक्षणमिमंकायंलब्ध्वामद्धर्म आस्थितः ।
आनन्दंपरमात्मानमात्मस्थंसमुपैति माम् ॥१॥

śrī-bhagavān uvāca
mal-lakṣaṇam imaṁ kāyaṁ labdhvā mad-dharma āsthitaḥ
ānandaṁ paramātmānam ātma-sthaṁ samupaiti mām

The Supreme Personality of Godhead said: Having attained the human form of life, which enables one to realize Me, and being engaged in My devotional service, one can achieve Me, the reservoir of all pleasure and the Supreme Soul of all existence who resides within the heart of every living entity.

COMMENTARY

In this chapter, the Lord explains to Uddhava how attachment to a woman can bewilder even an exalted soul and that association of advanced devotees awakens one's Kṛṣṇa consciousness.

Lord Kṛṣṇa had previously advised that a learned person should worship Him while avoiding the association of nondevotees, and in this chapter, the danger of bad association is illustrated by a practical example. One who is intelligent should carefully avoid bad association, because it can be a great impediment to the execution of devotional service. The association of women is especially dangerous. Therefore, even those in this world who are liberated should be afraid of intimately associating with a woman. In this verse, the Lord says that after obtaining the human form of life, which gives one the opportunity to realize Him, one should remain on the path of devotional service to achieve the association of the Lord, who is the Supersoul dwelling within the hearts of all living entities.

PURPORT

The human form of life is a golden opportunity to become established in the devotional service of the Supreme Lord. When one renounces the bodily concept of life and all attempts at mental speculation, and wholeheartedly engages in the devotional service of the Supersoul, he revives his original love of God. The conception of impersonalism, as well as desires to enjoy the fruits of one's *karma*, in this life and the next, simply create disturbances within the mind.

TEXT 2

गुणमय्याजीवयोन्याविमुक्तोज्ञाननिष्ठया ।
गुणेषुमायामात्रेषुदृश्यमानेष्ववस्तुतः ।
वर्तमानोऽपिनपुमान्युज्यतेऽवस्तुभिर्गुणैः ॥२॥

guṇa-mayyā jīva-yonyā vimukto jñāna-niṣṭhayā
guṇeṣu māyā-mātreṣu dṛśyamāneṣv avastutaḥ
vartamāno 'pi na pumān yujyate 'vastubhir guṇaiḥ

One who is fixed in transcendental knowledge becomes freed from conditioned life by giving up his false identification with the products of the three modes of material nature. Seeing these products as illusion, he avoids entanglement in the modes of nature, although constantly surrounded by them. Because the modes of nature and their products are not eternal facts, he does not accept them as ultimate reality.

COMMENTARY

The material designations of the living entities are born from the three modes of material nature. One who has become detached from all material forms, qualities, and objects has attained the perfection of life. Even though a self-realized soul remains within the material world, which is manifested by the modes of nature, he, unlike the conditioned soul, does not become attached to any object, knowing everything to be the property of the Supreme Lord.

PURPORT

Those who have knowledge of the Supreme Lord and who are engaged in His devotional service, do not consider the objects of the material world to be meant for their personal sense gratification. Those who are fond of voracious eating and sense gratification consider all the objects of this world as being meant for their enjoyment. It is essential for one who desires to advance in spiritual life to give up the association of such people. As a result of associating with people whose aim in life is to satisfy the urges of the belly and genitals, one becomes either a sense enjoyer or a dry renunciate, both of which cause one to continue in material bondage. The devotees of the Lord are indifferent to such material enjoyment and pseudo renunciation. They renounce their personal sense gratification to assist the Supreme Lord in His eternal pastimes. Those who accept as a spiritual master a person who is blinded by material enjoyment, certainly enters the darkest regions of ignorance. The Māyāvādīs are in this category. One should therefore carefully avoid the association of sense enjoyers and pseudo renunciates.

TEXT 3

सङ्गं न कुर्यादसतां शिश्नोदरतृपां क्वचित् ।
तस्यानुगस्तमस्यन्धे पतत्यन्धानुगान्धवत् ॥३॥

saṅgaṁ na kuryād asatāṁ śiśnodara-tṛpāṁ kvacit
tasyānugas tamasy andhe pataty andhānugāndha-vat

One should never associate with nondevotees, who are only interested in satisfying their bellies and genitals. By following them, one will fall into the densest regions of darkness, just as a blind man falls into a ditch when led by another blind man.

COMMENTARY

One should not indulge in bad association at any stage of life. There is nothing more detrimental to spiritual life than the association of nondevotees. Who are nondevotees? Whose association is undesirable? Those whose aim in life is simply to gratify their bellies and genitals. What to speak of associating with many such people, even by the association of one sense enjoyer, one can become degraded.

TEXT 4

ऐलः सम्राडिमां गाथामगायत बृहच्छ्रवाः ।
उर्वशीविरहान्मुह्यन्निर्विण्णः शोकसंयमे ॥४॥

ailaḥ samrāḍ imāṁ gāthām agāyata bṛhac-chravāḥ
urvaśī-virahān muhyan nirviṇṇaḥ śoka-saṁyame

The glorious King Purūravā became bewildered due to separation from the Apsarā, Urvaśī. Later on, however, he regained her association at Kurukṣetra. Thereafter, he performed a sacrifice with the help of the Gandharvas and thus pleased the demigods. Finally, when he attained the planet of Urvaśī, so that the cause of his lamentation was vanquished, he sang the following song.

COMMENTARY

The Supreme Personality of Godhead, Lord Kṛṣṇa, narrates the history of Aila, or King Purūravā, in this chapter. Purūravā had become overwhelmed with grief due to separation from Urvaśī but later, at Kurukṣetra, he regained her association. He then performed a sacrifice with fire given to him by the Gandharvas and thus attained the planet of Urvaśī. When he became free from lamentation, and his desire for sense gratification was vanquished, he revived his forgotten attraction for devotional service, spiritual knowledge, and renunciation, which had been impeded due to strong attachment. He then sang the following song. This history is also related in the Ninth Canto of the *Śrīmad-Bhāgavatam.*

TEXT 5

त्यक्त्वात्मानंव्रयन्तींतांनग्न उन्मत्तवन् नृपः ।
विलपन्नन्वगाज्जायेघोरेतिष्ठेतिविक्लवः ॥५॥

tyaktvātmānaṁ vrayantīṁ tāṁ nagna unmatta-van nṛpaḥ
vilapann anvagāj jāye ghore tiṣṭheti viklavaḥ

When Urvaśī was leaving the king for her own abode, even though he was naked, he ran after her like a madman with great affliction, crying out, "O dear one, please wait!"

COMMENTARY

As Urvaśī was leaving the king, he lamented, "O dear one, why are you going? You are killing me. Please wait!"

TEXT 6

कामानतृप्तोऽनुजुषन्क्षुल्लकान्वर्षयामिनीः ।
नवेदयान्तीर्नायान्तीरुर्वश्याकृष्टचेतनः ॥६॥

kāmān atṛpto 'nujuṣan kṣullakān varṣa-yāminīḥ
na veda yāntīr nāyāntīr urvaśy-ākṛṣṭa-cetanaḥ

Although for many years Purūravā had enjoyed sex with Urvaśī, he was still not satisfied by such insignificant enjoyment. Indeed, he was so captivated by Urvaśī that he did not notice how the days and nights were passing.

COMMENTARY

The king was overwhelmed by material desires.

TEXT 7

ऐल उवाच
अहोमेमोहविस्तारःकामकश्मलचेतसः ।
देव्यागृहीतकण्ठस्यनायुःखण्डा इमेस्मृताः ॥७॥

aila uvāca
aho me moha-vistāraḥ kāma-kaśmala-cetasaḥ
devyā gṛhīta-kaṇṭhasya nāyuḥ-khaṇḍā ime smṛtāḥ

King Aila said: Alas! Just see how I have become illusioned! The goddess captured me by her embraces, so that, being enamored, I could not even tell how time was passing.

COMMENTARY

The king lamented, "I spent so many years of my life simply gratifying my senses."

TEXT 8

नाहंवेदाभिनिर्मुक्तःसूर्योवाभ्युदितोऽमुया ।
मूषितोवर्षपूगानांबताहानिगतान्युत ॥८॥

nāhaṁ vedābhinirmuktaḥ sūryo vābhyudito 'muyā
mūṣito varṣa-pūgānāṁ batāhāni gatāny uta

I was cheated by that lady so that I did not even notice the rising or setting of the sun. So many years of my life have thus been wasted!

COMMENTARY

The king's bewilderment is herein explained. He lamented, "I was so engrossed in sense gratification that I did not even notice how the sun was rising and setting." Although the word *surya* is used in the second dative case, it indicates the meaning of the first dative case. The word *veda*, although used in the past tense, is supposed to be in the present tense—the first dative case. When one is fast asleep, he is in darkness, whether it be day or night. The king thought, "Why did I not know this? Because my power of discrimination was stolen by Urvaśī, I was not aware of how many days and nights were passing."

PURPORT

Due to absorption in sense gratification, King Pururavā forgot about the service of the Supreme Lord. He abandoned the worship of the Supreme Lord, which was his practice, so that he could enjoy the intimate association of Urvaśī. Realizing that he has wasted his valuable time, the king became repentant. The *sādhana-siddha* devotees, who are on the platform of love of God, cannot bear to waste even a second.

TEXT 9

अहोमे आत्मसम्मोहोयेनात्मायोषितांकृतः
क्रीडामृगश्चक्रवर्तीनरदेवशिखामणिः

aho me ātma-sammoho yenātmā yoṣitāṁ kṛtaḥ
krīḍā-mṛgaś cakravartī naradeva-śikhāmaṇiḥ

Alas! Although I was the mighty emperor, the crown jewel of all the kings of the earth, due to bewilderment I became just like a pet animal in the hands of a woman!

COMMENTARY

The mighty king lamented how he had become no better than a pet animal engaged in satisfying the whims of a woman.

TEXT 10

सपरिच्छदमात्मानंहित्वातृणमिवेश्वरम् ।
यान्तींस्त्रियंचान्वगमंनग्न उन्मत्तवदुदन् ॥१०॥

sa-paricchadam ātmānaṁ hitvā tṛṇam iveśvaram
yāntīṁ striyaṁ cānvagamaṁ nagna unmatta-vad rudan

Although I am a mighty emperor with great opulence, that woman left me as if I were no better than a blade of grass. Without shame and naked, I cried out like a madman while following her.

COMMENTARY

The king lamented that although he was the undisputed emperor of the world, she had abandoned him as if he were an insignificant straw, even though he followed her while crying out piteously.

PURPORT

By giving up the service of the Supreme Lord, the conditioned souls become intoxicated by the spirit of enjoyment and forget their own self-interest. When one realizes his constitutional position, he immediately understands that his enthusiasm for material activities is actually of no consequence.

TEXT 11

कुतस्तस्यानुभावःस्यात्तेज ईशत्वमेववा ।
योऽन्वगच्छंस्त्रियंयान्तींखरवत्पादताडितः ॥११॥

kutas tasyānubhāvaḥ syāt teja īśatvam eva vā
yo 'nvagaccham̐ striyam̐ yāntīm̐ khara-vat pāda-tāḍitaḥ

Where were my great influence, prowess, and sovereignty? Just like an ass being kicked in the face by a she-ass, I ran after that woman, although she had already given me up.

COMMENTARY

One might question the king: "Being the undisputed ruler of the entire earth, how could you fall into such a pathetic condition?" The answer is: "What was the use of my opulence, prowess, and influence? Even after being rejected by Urvaśī, I ran after her, just like an ass being kicked in the face by a she-ass."

PURPORT

For the pleasure of the association of a female ass, a male ass may receive only kicks in his face. Similarly, because the spirit of enjoyment is very strong in conditioned souls, who sometimes must face unbearable insults and inconveniences, he remains attached to the objects of the senses, especially the form of a beautiful woman.

TEXT 12

किंविद्ययाकिंतपसाकिंत्यागेनश्रुतेनवा ।
किंविविक्तेनमौनेनस्त्रीभिर्यस्यमनोहृतम् ॥१२॥

kiṁ vidyayā kiṁ tapasā kiṁ tyāgena śrutena vā
kiṁ viviktena maunena strībhir yasya mano hṛtam

What is the use of a comprehensive education, the practice of austerities and renunciation, a lengthy study of the religious scriptures, or living in solitude if, after all that, one's mind is stolen by a woman?

COMMENTARY

King Aila thought, "All kinds of endeavors are useless for a person like me."

PURPORT

One's power of discrimination, performance of austerities, receiving instructions for spiritual advancement, residing in a solitary place, and detachment from sense gratification can be destroyed in a moment by the association of a beautiful woman.

If one follows the example of the *gopīs* of Vṛndāvana, who accepted Lord Śrī Kṛṣṇa as their paramour, one can free one's mind from the contamination of lust.

TEXT 13

स्वार्थस्याकोविदंधिङ्मांमूर्खंपण्डितमानिनम् ।
योऽहमीश्वरतांप्राप्यस्त्रीभिर्गोखरवज्जितः ॥१३॥

svārthasyākovidaṁ dhiṅ māṁ mūrkhaṁ paṇḍita-māninam
yo 'ham īśvaratāṁ prāpya strībhir go-khara-vaj jitaḥ

Shame on Me! I was ignorant of my real self-interest, although I considered myself to be highly learned. Although I achieved the exalted position of being the lord of the earth, I was controlled by a woman, just like a bullock or an ass.

COMMENTARY

Being maddened by desires for sense enjoyment, foolish people, although they consider themselves to be very intelligent and learned, actually suffer while serving their animalistic propensities while enjoying the company of women. Only by the mercy of the spiritual master and saintly persons can one gradually understand that such an engagement is actually abominable. The condition of those who are intoxicated by material enjoyment so that they have become menial servants of lust is undoubtedly pathetic.

TEXT 14

सेवतोवर्षपूगान्मे उर्वश्या अधरासवम् ।
नतृप्यत्यात्मभूःकामोवह्निराहुतिभिर्यथा ॥१४॥

sevato varṣa-pūgān me urvaśyā adharāsavam
na tṛpyaty ātma-bhūḥ kāmo vahnir āhutibhir yathā

Even after I had tasted the nectar of Urvaśī's lips for many years, my lusty desires kept rising within my heart because they were never satisfied, just like a fire, which is never extinguished by the oblations of ghee poured into its flames.

COMMENTARY

King Aila lamented, "The lusty desires within my heart never became satiated, even after enjoying the association of Urvaśī for many years."

TEXT 15

पुंश्चल्यापहृतंचित्तंकोन्वन्योमोचितुंप्रभुः ।
आत्मारामेश्वरमृतेभगवन्तमधोक्षजम् ॥१५॥

puṁścalyāpahṛtaṁ cittaṁ ko nv anyo mocituṁ prabhuḥ
ātmārāmeśvaram ṛte bhagavantam adhokṣajam

Who but the Supreme Lord of all self-satisfied transcendentalists, who exists beyond the purview of the material senses, could redeem my fallen soul that was captured by a prostitute? Therefore, I shall become serious about worshiping the Supreme Personality of Godhead.

COMMENTARY

How did this change of heart take place? How did King Aila become detached from the desire to drink the nectar of Urvaśī's lips? The answer is given herein. He thought, "Who other than the Supreme Lord would be able to deliver me? Even self-satisfied sages cannot change the heart of a person like me, who is extremely fond of sensual pleasures. But, the master of all self-realized souls, the Supreme Personality of Godhead, certainly can accomplish this."

PURPORT

Those who depend upon their knowledge gained by sense perception are always disturbed in mind. As long as one does not experience satisfaction in the self in his relationship with the Supreme Lord, one's attraction for the objects of the senses will continue. However, such an ignorant condition of life is immediately dissipated when one acts under the guidance of a bona fide spiritual master. However, those who are sense enjoyers have a weakness of heart that causes them to take shelter of women, posing themselves as enjoyers. By being tempted by material enjoyment and thus avoiding the service of the Supreme Lord, one will never achieve freedom from the bondage of material existence.

TEXT 16

बोधितस्यापिदेव्यामेसूक्तवाक्येनदुर्मतेः ।
मनोगतोमहामोहोनापयात्यजितात्मनः ॥१६॥

bodhitasyāpi devyā me sūkta-vākyena durmateḥ
mano-gato mahā-moho nāpayāty ajitātmanaḥ

Because I allowed my intelligence to become stunted, and because I failed to control my senses, my mind remained bewildered, even though Urvaśī personally warned me with her intelligent instructions.

COMMENTARY

In the Ninth Canto of the *Śrīmad-Bhāgavatam*, it is seen that Urvaśī frankly instructed Purūravā that he should never place his faith in a woman. Still, he became attached to her and as a result, he suffered.

PURPORT

The uncontrolled sense enjoyer, Purūravā, could not seriously take the good advice of Urvaśī. Until one realizes that the Supreme Personality of Godhead is the only enjoyer and that all women should be regarded as spiritual masters, one's mentality will not be purified of the contamination of lust.

TEXT 17

किमेतयानोऽपकृतंरज्ज्वावासर्पचेतसः ।
द्रष्टुःस्वरूपाविदुषोयोऽहंयदजितेन्द्रियः ॥१७॥

kim etayā no 'pakṛtaṁ rajjvā vā sarpa-cetasaḥ
draṣṭuḥ svarūpāviduṣo yo 'haṁ yad ajitendriyaḥ

How can I blame her for my difficulties when it is I who acted out of ignorance? I did not control my senses, and so I am like a person who mistakes a rope for a snake.

COMMENTARY

It was said that Purūravā's heart had been captured by the prostitute. Now, the king says, "Whatever happened was my fault and not hers. One who mistakes a rope for a snake suffers fear and anxiety due to being deluded. Because I considered her to be enjoyable by me, it was my ignorance that was the cause of my suffering, and not her personally."

PURPORT

To consider the objects of material nature to be meant for one's enjoyment instead of being employed in the service of the master of nature, the Supreme Lord, is an example of illusion. Such an illusion is like accepting a rope as a snake. Although a rope cannot bite and thus is not an actual cause of fear, one who mistakes a rope for a snake becomes frightened. Similarly, the misconception of considering one's self to be the lord of all he surveys creates bewilderment in the mind of the conditioned soul. The Supreme Lord and His energies are worshipable for the living entities, but the conditioned souls invite inauspiciousness by seeing everything as enjoyable for themselves. The constitutional position of the living entity is to serve the senses of the master of the senses with one's purified senses. One should be cognizant of his fallen position and thus remain humbler than a blade of grass so that the allurements of temporary enjoyment will no longer hamper his advancement in Kṛṣṇa consciousness.

TEXT 18

क्वायंमलीमसःकयोदौर्गन्ध्याद्यात्मकोऽशुचिः ।
क्वगुणाःसौमनस्याद्याह्यध्यासोऽविद्ययाकृतः ॥१८॥

kvāyaṁ malīmasaḥ kayo daurgandhyādy-ātmako 'śuciḥ
kva guṇāḥ saumanasyādyā hy adhyāso 'vidyayā kṛtaḥ

What is this material body, which is so contaminated and full of bad odors? I was attracted by a woman's beauty and fragrance, without considering that these are simply coverings of an obnoxious body. Thus I was under the spell of illusion.

COMMENTARY

King Aila thought, "The so-called beauty, sweetness, and other attractive qualities possessed by Urvaśī were not the cause of my illusion. Such qualities were imagined by me because of ignorance. This material body, which is subject to transformation, cannot be ultimate reality. The sweet aroma, fresh youth, and other attractive qualities are simply illusions created by material nature, and yet I foolishly attributed such characteristics to Urvaśī herself."

PURPORT

The material body is awarded to one who desires to enjoy independently from the Supreme Lord, and it is stated herein that it is impure and essentially disgusting. When the living entity, by misuse of his minute independence, deviates from his constitutional duty, he is placed in ignorance and becomes afflicted with material miseries. Thus the mind, which is either engaged in sense gratification, distressed due to a lack of it, or in a mood of renunciation as a result of frustration, is certainly overcome by delusion. When one withdraws his senses from their objects, knowing that everything in existence is owned and controlled by the Lord, who is the supreme enjoyer, one comes to the platform of auspiciousness.

TEXTS 19-20

पित्रोःकिंस्वंनुभार्यायाःस्वामिनोऽग्नेःश्वगृध्रयोः ।
किमात्मनःकिंसुहृदामितियोनावसीयते ॥१९॥
तस्मिन्कलेवरेऽमेध्येतुच्छनिष्ठेविषज्जते ।
अहोसुभद्रंसुनसंसुस्मितंचमुखंस्त्रियः ॥२०॥

pitroḥ kiṁ svaṁ nu bhāryāyāḥ svāmino 'gneḥ śva-gṛdhrayoḥ
kim ātmanaḥ kiṁ suhṛdām iti yo nāvasīyate

tasmin kalevare 'medhye tuccha-niṣṭhe viṣajjate
aho su-bhadraṁ su-nasaṁ su-smitaṁ ca mukhaṁ striyaḥ

It can never be understood whose property the body is. Does the body belong to the parents, who enabled one to take birth? Does the body belong to one's wife, who gives it pleasure, or to one's master? Does it belong to the funeral pyre, or to the dogs that may one day devour it? Does it belong to the spirit soul who experiences its pleasures and pains, or does it belong to one's friends, who provide comfort? Although one can never understand who is the proprietor of the body, one certainly becomes very attached to it. Although the material body is destined to become ashes, worms, or stool, a man gazing at the face of a beautiful woman and thinks, "Oh! She is very attractive! What a charming nose she has, and just see her beautiful smile!"

COMMENTARY

Attachment for material body is simply due to ignorance. This is being stressed in these verses. Does the body belong to the parents, who gave birth to it? Does it belong to one's wife, who supplies it sense gratification? Does it belong to the husband who enjoys it? After death, the body is burnt—does that mean that it belongs to the fire? If the body is not burnt, it may be thrown to the jackals and vultures. Does the body belong to them? Or, does it belong to the soul who is responsible for its pleasant and unpleasant conditions? Does this body belong to one's well-wishers because they encourage it? This material body is temporary, insignificant, and abominable, and ultimately abandoned. Therefore, glorification of the material body is certainly an act of foolishness.

PURPORT

The relationships established between one person and another in this material world are based upon the material body. All such relationships, such as those of parents and children, wife and husband, fire and the burning body, dogs and jackals and their food—the dead body, as well as one's relationship with well-wishers and enemies, are temporarily manifested.

TEXT 21

त्वङ्मांसरुधिरस्नायुमेदोमज्जास्थिसंहतौ ।
विण्मूत्रपूयेरमतांकृमीणांकियदन्तरम् ॥२१॥

tvaṅ-māṁsa-rudhira-snāyu-medo-majjāsthi-saṁhatau
viṇ-mūtra-pūye ramatāṁ kṛmīṇāṁ kiyad antaram

What difference is there between worms and those who take pleasure in the material body, which is composed of skin, flesh, blood, nerves, pus, bone, marrow, stool and urine?

COMMENTARY

King Aila thought, "What is the difference between me and the worm that enjoys the material body, which is composed of obnoxious substances, such as stool, urine, and pus?"

PURPORT

What is the distinction between worms and human beings who consider the material body, which is a bag of stool, urine, blood, bones, pus, and so forth, as the self and are attached to sense gratification?

TEXT 22

अथापिनोपसज्जेतस्त्रीषुस्त्रैणेषुचार्थवित् ।
विषयेन्द्रियसंयोगान्मनःक्षुभ्यतिनान्यथा ॥२२॥

athāpi nopasajjeta strīṣu straiṇeṣu cārtha-vit
viṣayendriya-saṁyogān manaḥ kṣubhyati nānyathā

After carefully considering the nature of the material body, one who is wise should neither associate with women, nor those who are addicted to women. After all, as soon as there is proximity between the senses and their objects, the mind is sure to become agitated.

COMMENTARY

Although the body of a woman is composed of abominable substances, a man becomes attached to it. Therefore, the Supreme Lord is herein recommending that one should not intimately associate with members of the opposite sex. One who is wise, being aware of his real self-interest, should not allow himself to become attached to the body of a woman. Even if one must see women in the course of one's daily activities, he should stay aloof from their intimate association. As soon as the senses come in contact with their objects, the mind becomes agitated.

PURPORT

Sense enjoyers are always busy directing their minds to the objects of gratification. When one renders practical devotional service to the Supreme Lord, objects related to the Lord's service will become the subject of one's attention rather than objects meant for one's personal gratification. In this way, by diverting the mind to the service of the Lord, the inclination for material enjoyment or false renunciation will be subdued.

TEXT 23

अदृष्टादश्रुताद्भावान्नभाव उपजायते ।
असम्प्रयुञ्जतःप्राणान्शाम्यतिस्तिमितंमनः ॥२३॥

adṛṣṭād aśrutād bhāvān na bhāva upajāyate
asamprayuñjataḥ prāṇān śāmyati stimitaṁ manaḥ

The mind does not become agitated by things that are unknown or unheard of, and so the minds of those who control their senses become steady and peaceful.

COMMENTARY

One may question, "Doesn't the mind of a sage who lives in a solitary forest sometimes become agitated while contemplating sense gratification?" This is true but such an experience is due to previous sense gratification that one repeatedly experienced, saw, or heard about. If a person withdraws his senses from their objects, especially from intimate association with women, the mind will gradually become steady as material desires become extinguished, like a fire without fuel.

PURPORT

The mind always engages its servant, the eyes, in seeing beautiful forms, and engages the ears in hearing pleasant sounds, and so forth. If one refrains from hearing the glories of the master of the senses, Lord Kṛṣṇa, being induced by the material conception of life, one will be forced to act as the servant of his senses, which act under the dictation of the restless mind.

TEXT 24

तस्मात्सङ्गो न कर्तव्यः स्त्रीषु स्त्रैणेषु चेन्द्रियैः ।
विदुषां चाप्यविस्रब्धः षड्वर्गः किमु मादृशाम् ॥२४॥

tasmāt saṅgo na kartavyaḥ strīṣu straiṇeṣu cendriyaiḥ
viduṣāṁ cāpy avisrabdhaḥ ṣaḍ-vargaḥ kim u mādṛśām

Therefore, one should not let his senses freely associate with women, or those who are attached to women. Even learned persons cannot trust the six enemies of the mind, headed by lust, anger, and greed, and so what to speak of a foolish person like me.

COMMENTARY

The six enemies of the mind are lust, anger, greed, pride, illusion, and envy, and they are never to be trusted.

PURPORT

Materialistic people are attached to the objects of sense gratification, headed by women. The knowledge that is acquired by sense perception and mental speculation is unsteady. If this is the case of even learned persons, then what can be said of unabashed sense enjoyers? Therefore, it is herein advised that one completely give up the association of women, and those who are attached to women. The thinking, feeling, and willing of the mind must be employed in enhancing one's devotional service to Lord Kṛṣṇa.

TEXT 25

श्रीभगवानुवाच
एवंप्रगायन्नृपदेवदेवःसउर्वशीलोकमथोविहाय ।
आत्मानमात्मन्यवगम्यमांवै उपारमज्ज्ञाअनविधूतमोहः ॥२५॥

śrī-bhagavān uvāca
evaṁ pragāyan nṛpa-deva-devaḥ sa urvaśī-lokam atho vihāya
ātmānam ātmany avagamya māṁ vai upāramaj jñāana-vidhūta-mohaḥ

The Supreme Personality of Godhead said: After chanting this song, Mahārāja Purūravā, foremost among the demigods and human beings, gave up his position in the planet of Urvaśī. His illusion dispelled by transcendental knowledge, he understood Me to be the Supreme Soul within his heart, and so finally achieved peace.

COMMENTARY

The Supreme Lord said: King Purūravā, the best of kings and demigods, realized Me to be the object of love and thereafter left his body.

PURPORT

While singing the Aila-gītā, Purūravā made up his mind to leave the abode of Urvaśī. Realizing the Supreme Personality of Godhead to be the shelter of all *rasa*, and understanding that attachment to imperfect mundane *rasa* is an act of ignorance, King Purūravā gave up all aspirations for material enjoyment.

TEXT 26

ततोदुःसङ्गमुत्सृज्यसत्सुसज्जेतबुद्धिमान् ।
सन्त एवास्यछिन्दन्तिमनोव्यासङ्गमुक्तिभिः ॥२६॥

tato duḥsaṅgam utsṛjya satsu sajjeta buddhimān
santa evāsya chindanti mano-vyāsaṅgam uktibhiḥ

An intelligent person should therefore should give up all bad association and instead associate with saintly devotees, whose instructions destroy the material attachment within the mind.

COMMENTARY

Material attachment must be renounced, and the association of devotees must be pursued. It is the instructions of the devotees of the Lord that are able to vanquish one's strong attachment to sense gratification. Pious acts, visits to holy places, the demigods, and knowledge of the scriptures do not have such power.

PURPORT

For the benefit of those who would follow in the footsteps of Uddhava in the future, the Supreme Lord narrated the history of how Purūravā became a servant of Urvaśī, desiring to enjoy her attractive feminine features, and yet this put him into great danger. Here, we see how the king obtained auspiciousness by renouncing the mentality of being an enjoyer. The conclusion is that an intelligent person should free himself from the thirst for material enjoyment by receiving the pure and powerful instructions of saintly persons. Such instructions help one to become strongly situated in Kṛṣṇa consciousness and thus automatically rise above the platform of duality, which is based on ignorance.

TEXT 27

सन्तोऽनपेक्षामच्चित्ताःप्रशान्ताःसमदर्शिनः ।
निर्ममानिरहङ्कारानिर्द्वन्द्वानिष्परिग्रहाः ॥२७॥

santo 'napekṣā mac-cittāḥ praśāntāḥ sama-darśinaḥ
nirmamā nirahaṅkārā nirdvandvā niṣparigrahāḥ

My devotees fix their minds on Me, and do not depend upon any material conditions. They are always peaceful, free from possessiveness, false ego, duality and greed, and they view others with equal vision.

COMMENTARY

Devotees do not depend upon *karma*, *jñāna*, or other human beings and demigods, who are, after all, concerned with their own self-interest. One may question, "Do not the devotees depend upon someone?" Here, the Lord gives the reply by saying, "Saintly persons are those whose hearts are fixed on Me." Someone may say, "Kaṁsa's mind was also fixed upon Kṛṣṇa, but he is not considered a devotee." Therefore, the Lord clarifies: "The devotees are peaceful. They have conquered anger. They do not retaliate, even if they are attacked. This is because they treat all living entities equally, whether they be so-called friends, enemies, or neutral parties. This is because they have conquered the false ego. They are thus free from envy, false proprietorship, and false pride. They are equal both in honor and in dishonor because they have transcended the dualities of this material world." Someone may then question, "Is it possible for householders to become devotees?" The answer is, "Yes. Devotees are those who have renounced material attachment and it does not matter whether they are in household life or reside in the forest."

PURPORT

Many people think that simply by artificially renouncing coveted things they can become peaceful, transcendentally situated above duality, and free from false ego, material ambition, and proprietorship. However, such an artificial mental adjustment does not remain fixed. It is only on the strength of one's favorable cultivation of Kṛṣṇa consciousness that qualities such as freedom from envy and possessiveness manifest within the purified heart. When one gives up the service of his material senses and engages in the cultivation of God consciousness, he gradually becomes free from dualities, false proprietorship, and false ego, and becomes endowed with equal vision.

TEXT 28

तेषुनित्यंमहाभागमहाभागेषुमत्कथाः ।
सम्भवन्तिहितानृणांजुषतांप्रपुनन्त्यघम् ॥२८॥

teṣu nityaṁ mahā-bhāga mahā-bhāgeṣu mat-kathāḥ
sambhavanti hi tā nṛṇāṁ juṣatāṁ prapunanty agham

O greatly fortunate Uddhava, in the association of saintly devotees there is constant discussion of Me. Those who engage in hearing and chanting My glories are certainly purified of all sins.

COMMENTARY

The instructions of the saintly persons contain nothing but the instructions of the Supreme Personality of Godhead.

TEXT 29

तायेशृण्वन्तिगायन्तिह्यनुमोदन्तिचादृताः ।
मत्पराःश्रद्दधानाश्चभक्तिंविन्दन्तितेमयि ॥२९॥

tā ye śṛṇvanti gāyanti hy anumodanti cādṛtāḥ
mat-parāḥ śraddadhānāś ca bhaktiṁ vindanti te mayi

Whoever hears, chants, and respectfully takes to heart the discussions of Me becomes dedicated to Me and thus achieves My devotional service.

PURPORT

Generally, material knowledge is gained by hearing. Because the transcendental names, forms, qualities, and pastimes of the Supreme Lord, Śrī Kṛṣṇa, are always discussed by saintly persons, the conditioned souls get an opportunity to hear about them. As a result of this, their propensity for sinful activities can slacken. Simply by hearing the talks of an exalted personality, one can acquire transcendental knowledge and thereby free himself from the thirst for sense gratification. One who diligently follows the instructions of the devotees becomes situated in his constitutional duty of serving Lord Hari. When a living entity is thus engaged in the devotional service of the Lord, he naturally develops attachment for glorifying the Lord and residing in the abode of the Lord. As a result, he soon manifests divine qualities, such as tolerance, detachment, and freedom from envy and false ego. The polluted workings of the mind are checked, one sees things in a new light, and there blossoms the propensity for selfless loving service to the Lord, which ultimately awards one the fruit of love of Godhead.

TEXT 30

भक्तिंलब्धवतःसाधोःकिमन्यदवशिष्यते ।
मय्यनन्तगुणेब्रह्मण्यानन्दानुभवात्मनि ॥३०॥

bhaktiṁ labdhavataḥ sādhoḥ kim anyad avaśiṣyate
mayy ananta-guṇe brahmaṇy ānandānubhavātmani

I am the Supreme Brahman, the reservoir of unlimited transcendental qualities, and the embodiment of spiritual bliss. After attaining My devotional service, there is nothing more to be achieved.

COMMENTARY

One may question, "After attaining devotional service to the Supreme Lord, is there anything remaining to be achieved?" In this verse, the Lord clearly replies, "No, there is nothing more to be attained because devotional service awards one the perfection of everything." The impersonalists' conception of liberation entails giving up their individual identity, and thus does not award complete satisfaction of the self.

PURPORT

The sects that the self-worshiping Māyāvādīs create, by accepting four Vedic statements as conclusive evidence, without understanding the actual intention of the *Vedas*, are mundane and unauthorized.

One should reject such deviant *sampradāyas* and hear and chant the glories of Lord Hari. One should understand that engagement in such hearing and chanting is the ultimate conclusion of the *Vedas*. By hearing and chanting the glories of the Lord, one becomes firmly situated in devotional service so that one renounces whatever is not in relation to Kṛṣṇa, knowing that he has already attained that which leaves nothing further to be gained. Rather than becoming a servant of the objects of sense gratification that are produced by the interactions of the three modes of material nature, by acceptance of subordination to the Supreme Personality of Godhead, who is the embodiment of unlimited transcendental qualities, one certainly attains all good fortune. By faithfully hearing and chanting the glories of the Lord, which is the best form of worship, one is freed from the results of fruitive activities, and the ultimate goal of life is achieved.

Religious rituals prescribed in the *karma kāṇḍa* sections of the *Vedas* are distinct from the favorable cultivation of Kṛṣṇa consciousness. Being deceived by the flowery words of the *karma kāṇḍa*, foolish people uselessly spend their lives trying to enjoy the fruits of their activities. However, when such unfortunate persons associate with devotees and hear their divine instructions, their desire for enjoying the fruits of their actions can become purified if they offer the results of their work in the service of the eternally blissful Personality of Godhead.

TEXT 31

यथोपश्रयमाणस्यभगवन्तंविभावसुम् ।
शीतंभयंतमोऽप्येतिसाधून्संसेवतस्तथा ॥३१॥

yathopaśrayamāṇasya bhagavantaṁ vibhāvasum
śītaṁ bhayaṁ tamo 'pyeti sādhūn saṁsevatas tathā

Just as cold, fear, and darkness are eradicated as soon as one approaches the sacrificial fire, so fear and ignorance are dispelled when one is engaged in serving the devotees of the Lord.

COMMENTARY

Those who approach a blazing fire are surely relieved of cold, fear of the unknown, and darkness. Similarly, attachment to fruitive activities, fear of material existence, and obstacles on the path of spiritual life are destroyed when one engages in the service of saintly devotees, who aspire to attain the perfection of spiritual life.

PURPORT

Just as by approaching a fire, one is relieved of cold, darkness is dissipated, and fear of wild animals lurking in the dark is removed, simply by taking shelter of the lotus feet of those who are engaged in the favorable cultivation of Kṛṣṇa consciousness, one becomes relieved of his engagement in fruitive activities and mental speculation. The association of devotees is very powerful, like a blazing fire, and it frees one from all undesirable qualities, which are based on enviousness.

TEXT 32

निमज्ज्योन्मज्जतांघोरेभवाब्धौपरमायणम् ।
सन्तोब्रह्मविदःशान्तानौर्दृढेवाप्सुमज्जताम् ॥३२॥

nimajjyonmajjatāṁ ghore bhavābdhau paramāyaṇam
santo brahma-vidaḥ śāntā naur dṛḍhevāpsu majjatām

The devotees of the Lord, who are fixed in absolute knowledge, are the only real shelter for those who are repeatedly rising and falling within the fearful ocean of material existence. Such devotees are just like a strong boat that comes to rescue persons who are floundering within the sea.

COMMENTARY

The devotees are the safest shelter for those who are traversing the path of material existence, accepting lower and higher forms of bodies, one after another.

PURPORT

The association of devotees, wherein one hears about one's relationship with the Supreme Personality of Godhead, and then renders service to the Supreme Lord, gives shelter to the fallen conditioned souls, who are drowning in the ocean of material existence, just as a boat rescues persons who are drowning in the sea. The bodily conception of life submerges the conditioned souls deep into the ocean of material existence. Sometimes, by performing pious activities, one is brought to the surface so that he gains momentary relief, but once again, when the fruits of such actions are exhausted, he is pushed down within the water once again. Only if the conditioned souls are placed within the boat of the association of devotees can their threefold material miseries become mitigated.

TEXT 33

अन्नंहिप्राणिनांप्राण आर्तानांशरणंत्वहम् ।
धर्मोवित्तंनृणांप्रेत्यसन्तोऽर्वाग्बिभ्यतोऽरणम् ॥३३॥

annaṁ hi prāṇināṁ prāṇa ārtānāṁ śaraṇaṁ tv aham
dharmo vittaṁ nṛṇāṁ pretya santo 'rvāg bibhyato 'raṇam

Just as food grains are the life of all living entities, just as I am the shelter of those who are distressed, and just as religion is the wealth of those who are on the verge of death, My devotees are the only shelter for those who are fearful of falling into a miserable condition of life.

COMMENTARY

All living entities subsist on food grains. Without grains, one could not maintain his body in a healthy condition. In the same way, for those who desire to advance in the devotional service of the Lord, saintly devotees are their only support because without the association of advanced devotees, one cannot attain perfection in devotional service. Just as the Supreme Lord is the ultimate shelter of all kinds of distressed people, pure devotees are the only shelter for those who desire to advance in devotional service. Just as religion is the only savior from the punishment of Yamarāja, the devotees are the only shelter for those who are trying to traverse the path of spiritual life, and are afraid of falling down into an abominable condition of life due to uncontrolled lust, anger, and greed.

PURPORT

Just as food grains are the shelter for the hungry, and a policeman is the refuge for one who is being attacked, saintly devotees who are devoid of envy protect those living entities who are frightened of the fearful conditions of material existence.

TEXT 34

सन्तोदिशन्तिचक्षूंसिबहिरर्कः समुत्थितः ।
देवताबान्धवाःसन्तःसन्त आत्माहमेवच ॥३४॥

santo diśanti cakṣūṁsi bahir arkaḥ samutthitaḥ
devatā bāndhavāḥ santaḥ santa ātmāham eva ca

My devotees can award one transcendental vision, whereas the sun only enables the gross eyes to function, and only after rising in the morning. My devotees are one's real worshipable lords and well-wishers. They are as good as one's self, being nondifferent from Me.

COMMENTARY

Pure devotees are just like eyes by which one can see God, because they impart to one the nine processes of devotional service. The physical eyes have no power to see without the presence of the sun. Similarly, pure devotees are like the rising sun in that they enable one to perceive the light of transcendental knowledge. Pure devotees are the actual demigods for those who are traveling the path of devotional service, and not Indra and his followers. Devotees are therefore one's real relatives and well-wishers, and not one's father, mother, and paternal or maternal uncles. Devotees are one's real life and soul, and not one's material body. Saintly devotees are one's real worshipable Lord. Without them, the Supreme Personality of Godhead will not appear in His form as the Deity.

PURPORT

Sinful persons take great pleasure in nonsensical activities, being satisfied to remain in the darkness of ignorance, just like animals. The devotees of the Lord are like the sun because their enlightening instructions awaken the transcendental senses of the people in general, so that the darkness of ignorance is dissipated. Thus it is concluded that the Lord's devotees are one's real well-wishing friends, and so they are the proper recipients of one's service, and not the material senses, which are never satisfied. Saintly devotees are those who have firmly accepted the path of devotional service. Nondevotees cannot rightfully be termed friends or saintly.

TEXT 35

वैतसेनस्ततोऽप्येवमुर्वश्यालोकनिष्पृहः ।
मुक्तसङ्गो महीमेतामात्मारामश्चचारह ॥३५॥

vaitasenas tato 'py evam urvaśyā loka-niṣpṛhaḥ
mukta-saṅgo mahīm etām ātmārāmaś cacāra ha

Thus losing all desire to live on the same planet as Urvaśī, King Purūravā began to travel over the earth, free from material desires and thus satisfied in the self.

COMMENTARY

The Supreme Lord thus concludes this chapter by saying that King Purūravā, the son of Sudyumna, as mentioned in the Ninth Canto of the *Śrīmad-Bhāgavatam*, left the planet of Urvaśī and began to travel over the earth, being free from all material connection.

PURPORT

Even if one possesses a material body, if he is in the association of liberated devotees in this world, he will not be disturbed by desires for material enjoyment or dry renunciation if he strictly follows their instructions. Until the entire world is understood as a manifestation of the energy of Vāsudeva, and until all activities are performed for the satisfaction of Vāsudeva, understanding that the Lord is one without a second, the perfection of devotional service cannot be obtained. The vision of the devotees and that of the *karmīs*, *jñānīs*, and *anyābhilāṣīs* are not the same. An exalted devotee does not see this world as a place for his personal enjoyment, nor does he consider the objects of this world as meant for his sense gratification. He knows that everyone is a member of Kṛṣṇa's family and thus sees everyone to be always situated in the service of the Supreme Lord. His eyes, ears, nose, tongue, sense of touch, and mind, do not deviate from the service of the master of the senses. In this way, there is a great difference between the conditioned souls and the liberated or self-realized souls. The former are servants of their restless mind and beggars of material happiness and wealth, whereas the latter are those who have attained perfection of life.

Thus end the translation of the Twentieth Chapter of the Uddhava-gītā entitled "**The Aila-gītā**" *with the commentaries of Śrīla Viśvanātha Cakravartī Ṭhākura and chapter summary and purports by Śrīla Bhaktisiddhānta Sarasvatī Ṭhākura.*

CHAPTER 21

LORD KṚṢṆA'S INSTRUCTIONS ON THE PROCESS OF DEITY WORSHIP

CHAPTER SUMMARY

In this chapter, the Supreme Personality of Godhead explains the process of Deity worship.

Worshiping the Deity form of the Supreme Lord purifies the mind and awards one satisfaction. Indeed, it is the source of all desirable gains. One who does not engage himself in worshiping the Deity will certainly remain attracted to material sense gratification, and he will have no scope for giving up bad association. In the Sātvata scriptures, the Supreme Lord has given instructions on the process of worshiping Him as the Deity. Brahmā, Śiva, Nārada, Vyāsa, and all other sages have recommended this process as being most beneficial for the members of all *varṇas* and *āśramas*, including women and *śūdras*.

There are three varieties of *arcana*, or Deity worship, based on either the original *Vedas*, the secondary *tantras*, or a combination of these. The Deity form, the ground, fire, the sun, water, and the heart of the worshiper are all places where the Deity can be present. The Deity that is to be worshiped may be made of any one of eight substances—stone, wood, metal, clay, paint, sand (drawn upon the ground), the mind, or jewels. These categories are further subdivided into two: temporary and permanent.

The details of the worshiping process are as follows: The devotee should bathe, both physically and by chanting *mantras*, and then utter the Gāyatrī *mantra* at the prescribed junctures of the day. He should arrange a seat, facing either east or north, or else directly facing the Deity, and should bathe the Deity. He should then decorate the Deity with clothing and ornaments, sprinkle water on the vessels and other paraphernalia to be used for the worship, and offer water for bathing the Deity's lotus feet, *arghya*, water for washing His mouth, fragrant oils, incense, lamps, flowers, and food preparations. After this, one should worship the Lord's personal servants and bodyguards, His consort, His energies, and the spiritual masters, by chanting their respective *mūla-mantras*. The worshiper should recite prayers from the *Purāṇas* and other scriptures, offer obeisances by falling flat onto the ground, beg for the Lord's benediction, and accept the remnants of the Lord's flower garlands.

Included in this method of Deity worship are the proper installation of the Deity and the construction of a temple, and also the conducting of processions and other festivals. By worshiping Lord Śrī Hari with unconditional devotion in this manner, one is sure to advance toward pure loving service to His lotus feet. But if one steals things that had been given for the service of the Deity, or the *brāhmaṇas*, whether given by himself or by others, he will have to take his next birth as a stool-eating worm.

TEXT 1

श्रीउद्धव उवाच
क्रियायोगंसमाचक्ष्वभवदाराधनंप्रभो ।
यस्मात्त्वांयेयथार्चन्तिसात्वताःसात्वतर्षभ ॥१॥

śrī-uddhava uvāca
kriyā-yogaṁ samācakṣva bhavad-ārādhanaṁ prabho
yasmāt tvāṁ ye yathārcanti sātvatāḥ sātvatarṣabha

Śrī Uddhava said: O Lord, please describe the procedures for worshiping You in Your form as the Deity in the temple. What qualifications must a devotee possess to worship You in this way, and what are the rules and regulations to be observed?

COMMENTARY

In this chapter, Lord Śrī Kṛṣṇa gives instructions to Uddhava about the principles of Deity worship, its ingredients, the various Deity forms, and the rules and regulations that are to be observed by the worshipers. The Lord had previously said: "It is very rare to find one who is attached to his wife and children that is trying to cultivate devotional service in the association of saintly persons." With this in mind, Uddhava inquired about Deity worship, as prescribed in the Vedic literature.

TEXT 2

एतद्वदन्तिमुनयोमुहुर्निःश्रेयसंनृणाम् ।
नारदोभगवान्व्यास आचार्योऽङ्गिरसःसुतः ॥२॥

etad vadanti munayo muhur niḥśreyasaṁ nṛṇām
nārado bhagavān vyāsa ācāryo 'ṅgirasaḥ sutaḥ

All the great sages, such as Nārada Muni, Vyāsadeva, and Bṛhaspati, the spiritual master of the demigods, have declared that such worship is supremely beneficial for all members of human society.

TEXTS 3-4

निःसृतंतेमुखाम्भोजाद्यदाहभगवानजः ।
पुत्रेभ्योभृगुमुख्येभ्योदेव्यैचभगवान्भवः ॥३॥
एतद्वैसर्ववर्णानामाश्रमाणांचसम्मतम् ।
श्रेयसामुत्तमंमन्येस्त्रीशूद्राणांचमानद ॥४॥

niḥsṛtaṁ te mukhāmbhojād yad āha bhagavān ajaḥ
putrebhyo bhṛgu-mukhyebhyo devyai ca bhagavān bhavaḥ

etad vai sarva-varṇānām āśramāṇāṁ ca sammatam
śreyasām uttamaṁ manye strī-śūdrāṇāṁ ca māna-da

O most magnanimous Lord, You first gave instructions on the process of Deity worship to Lord Brahmā. Then, they were passed on by him to his sons, headed by Bhṛgu, and Lord Śiva instructed his wife, Pārvatī. Therefore, I consider that worship of You in Your form as the Deity is the best spiritual practice for the members of all the *varṇas* and *āśramas*, even for women and *śudras*.

COMMENTARY

The glories of worshiping the Deity form of the Supreme Lord is herein being described.

TEXT 5

एतत्कमलपत्राक्षकर्मबन्धविमोचनम् ।
भक्तायचानुरक्तायब्रूहिविश्वेश्वरेश्वर ॥५॥

etat kamala-patrākṣa karma-bandha-vimocanam
bhaktāya cānuraktāya brūhi viśveśvareśvara

O lotus-eyed one, O Lord of the demigods, please explain to me, Your surrendered servant, this process by which one can be delivered from the bondage of material existence.

COMMENTARY

The Lord might question Uddhava: "You are My surrendered devotee and are attached to Me in love and so, what is the need for your knowing about Deity worship?" Uddhava might answer: "I am concerned for the welfare of all living entities. Therefore, kindly reveal the glories of this process to Your surrendered servant."

PURPORT

When one engages in the service of the Lord, renouncing all sense of false proprietorship, if one acts without desiring to enjoy the fruits of his work, he is to be considered a pure devotee. However, as long as one remains within this world, embodied by gross and subtle coverings, one's nature born of the interactions of the three modes of material nature remains prominent. In the material condition of life, which is temporary, full of ignorance, and thoroughly miserable, one considers himself to be the doer of all activities, being bound by his false ego. Only by receiving instructions from a pure devotee of the Lord can one give up the materialistic conception of life. When, under the instruction of the spiritual master, one dovetails his designated existence in the service of the Supreme Personality of Godhead, who is one without a second, the false conception of being the enjoyer of nature gradually diminishes.

In order to gain relief from the materialistic conception of life, which consists of the knower of matter, material knowledge, and the object of material knowledge, one must engage in the service of the Supreme Lord. When nondevotees, who are fully absorbed in the mundane conception of life, become inclined toward the service of the Supreme Lord and His devotees then, as they surrender unto the Supreme Lord and His dear devotees, they can realize the transcendental nature of devotional service.

TEXT 6

श्रीभगवानुवाच
नह्यन्तोऽनन्तपारस्यकर्मकाण्डस्यचोद्धव ।
सङ्क्षिप्तंवर्णयिष्यामिचाथावदनुपूर्वशः ॥६॥

śrī-bhagavān uvāca
na hy anto 'nanta-pārasya karma-kāṇḍasya coddhava
saṅkṣiptaṁ varṇayiṣyāmi yathāvad anupūrvaśaḥ

The Supreme Lord said: My dear Uddhava, the procedures prescribe in the karma-kāṇḍa sections of the Vedic literature are innumerable, and so I shall explain this subject to you briefly, from the beginning.

COMMENTARY

There are innumerable Vedic methods of worship, or *arcana*, prescribed in the *karma kāṇḍa* sections of the *Vedas*.

PURPORT

All religious ritualistic activities and worldly activities that are performed with the aim of attaining material enjoyment or dry renunciation must be considered as perishable activities. In this material world, there are countless methods employed for sense gratification and renunciation. Similarly, in the spiritual world of Vaikuṇṭha, there are an unlimited variety of pastimes of the Supreme Personality of Godhead. There are innumerable prescriptions given in the *karma-kāṇḍa* sections of the *Vedas*, dealing with material enjoyment and renunciation.

TEXT 7

वैदिकस्तान्त्रिकोमिश्रैतिमेत्रिविधोमखः ।
त्रयाणामीप्सितेनैवविधिनामांसमर्चरेत् ॥७॥

vaidikas tāntriko miśra iti me tri-vidho makhaḥ
trayāṇām īpsitenaiva vidhinā māṁ samarcaret

There are three methods for worshiping Me—Vedic, Tāntrika, and mixed. One should select the method that is suited for him and then worship Me according to the prescribed rules and regulations.

COMMENTARY

The Vedic method of worshiping the Supreme Lord is by chanting the prescribed *mantras*. The *tāntrika* method of worshiping the Supreme Lord is by reciting the *mantras*, such as the eighteen-syllable *mantra*, that are given in literature such as the *Gautamiya-*

tantra. Utilization of both literatures is the mixed way of worshiping the Supreme Lord. One should choose the method that is suitable for one's condition of life.

PURPORT

There are three methods of performing sacrifice. Materialistic people are generally unwilling to perform sacrifice because of their duplicitous nature and their strong desire to enjoy material happiness. Sacrifice for the satisfaction of the Supreme Lord is performed according to the Vedic injunctions, or those prescribed in the *Pāñcarātra*. The Vedic, *Pāñcarātrika*, and a combination of both, are the three methods to properly worship the Supreme Lord.

TEXT 8

यदास्वनिगमेनोक्तंद्विजत्वंप्राप्यपूरुषः ।
यथायजेतमांभक्त्याश्रद्धयातन्निबोधमे ॥८॥

yadā sva-nigamenoktaṁ dvijatvaṁ prāpya pūruṣaḥ
yathā yajeta māṁ bhaktyā śraddhayā tan nibodha me

Now please listen faithfully as I explain to you how one who has become twice-born by observing the relevant Vedic prescriptions should worship Me with devotion.

COMMENTARY

There are particular Vedic injunctions relevant to one's social and occupational status. Members of the *brāhmaṇa, kṣatriya* and *vaiśya* communities achieve the status of twice-born by initiation into the Gāyatrī *mantra*. In this chapter, the Supreme Lord explains how such a person should worship Him with faith and devotion.

PURPORT

Vedic scriptures are divided into two categories—*ekāyana* and *bahvayana*. One must receive initiation into the practices of one of these two categories and then faithfully worship the Supreme Lord, which culminates in achievement of life's ultimate goal, the attainment of love for God.

The process of worship that is performed when one is still in the bodily conception of life, considering himself to be the enjoyer of this material world, is called *arcana*. Without being twice-born by undergoing the purificatory rituals, it is not possible to worship the Supreme Lord properly. When one makes such an attempt, the result is that he either remains a sense enjoyer or becomes a dry renunciate after giving up such worship. Those who observe the Vedic purificatory processes, or the *Pāñcarātrika* purificatory processes, undergo second birth in the *ekāyana* category. One cannot become twice-born if he is blinded by intense desires for material enjoyment. Therefore, it is essential for one to undergo second birth by following the prescribed rules and regulations of the Vedic literature.

There are three types of birth—*śaukra*, or seminal; *sāvitrya*, or becoming twice-born; and *daikśa*, or spiritual initiation. The material body, which is produced by the combined effort of the father and mother can be sanctified by undergoing the appropriate purificatory rituals. In this way, one becomes eligible to rise to the platform of transcendental bliss. False ego, which checks the flow of transcendental happiness, and which is born of ignorance, is indicative of a seminal birth. Devotional service is awakened within the heart only after one takes initiation from a bona fide spiritual master.

The object of worship, pure devotional service, and unalloyed devotees—these three exist eternally in a state of full knowledge and bliss, and such a condition becomes manifest when one develops firm faith in the instructions of the spiritual master. It is at this point that one can begin the process of worship as described in this chapter. The Vedic *saṁskāras* are considered complete when one undergoes the *Pāñcarātrika saṁskāras*. Otherwise, simply by performing the rituals of the *karma-kāṇḍa* sections of the *Vedas*, one cannot rise above the influence of the three modes of material nature.

TEXT 9

अर्चायांस्थण्डिलेऽग्नौवासूर्येवाप्सुहृदिद्विजः ।
द्रव्येणभक्तियुक्तोऽर्चेत्स्वगुरुंमाममायया ॥९॥

arcāyāṁ sthaṇḍile 'gnau vā sūrye vāpsu hṛdi dvijaḥ
dravyeṇa bhakti-yukto 'rcet sva-guruṁ mām amāyayā

A twice-born person should sincerely worship Me, his worshipable Lord, by offering appropriate paraphernalia in loving devotion to My Deity form, or to My form appearing upon the ground, in fire, in the sun, in water, or within his heart.

COMMENTARY

The word *arcā* refers to the Deity of the Supreme Lord.

PURPORT

When the eternal soul misuses his minute independence, he is placed within the material nature and accepts temporary material bodies, one after another. The

Absolute Truth possesses two principles—*aparā prakṛti* and *parā prakṛti*. The *aparā prakṛti* manifests the visible universe with five gross material elements. The three modes of material nature engage the living entities in activities of the gross and subtle bodies and by covering their knowledge, keep them far from the *parā prakṛti*. Without understanding of the characteristics of the Lord's superior nature, the conditioned souls reside in the material world as sense enjoyers or false renunciates. It is only by the mercy of the Supreme Lord or His pure devotee that a conditioned soul can understand how he is being manipulated by the three material modes, and that only the Supreme Lord has the ability to liberate him from the clutches of the material nature. With such an understanding, one realizes the complete futility of trying to become liberated from the insurmountable material energy by relying upon one's limited senses and polluted mind.

The spiritual master also belongs to the marginal potency of the Supreme Lord, but he is empowered to deliver the conditioned souls by engaging them in devotional service. The spiritual master is the incarnation of the Lord's mercy and as such, he is considered to be the external manifestation of the Supersoul. By his instructions and personal examples, he inspires the conditioned souls to renounce their foolish endeavors of lording it over the material energy of the Supreme Lord, which only awards them varieties of miserable conditions. The spiritual master engages his disciple in the worship of the Deity of the Lord because it is the practical way to employ their mind and senses in devotional service.

The word *arcā* refers to the incarnation of the Supreme Lord's mercy. It is one of the five eternal manifestations of the Lord that is comprehensible for the conditioned souls. Those who are neophytes in devotional service, who still cling to the bodily concept of life, can easily be purified when they are engaged in the worship of the Deity in the temple.

A particular place that has been purified by the chanting of *mantras* is called *sthandila*. Fire, the sun, water, and the heart of the living entity are also places for worshiping the Supreme Lord. Although Lord Viṣṇu is one, He is present in different forms. He appears as the Deity and becomes worshipable Lord for neophytes devotees. Neophyte devotees are recommended to become attached to Deity worship. By serving the Supreme Lord in this manner, they utilize all kinds of paraphernalia for His service, rather than considering such things to be material, and thus meant for their enjoyment. Gradually, while engaging in the worship of the Deity under the direction of the spiritual master, a neophyte devotee will be elevated to the platform of *madhyama adhikārī*. At this time, the devotee becomes more concerned with reviving his transcendental *rasa* instead of cultivating the five kinds of mundane *rasa*, knowing the Supreme Lord to be the reservoir of all *rasa*. At this level of advancement, one is fit to understand the purport of this verse from the *Padma Purāṇa*:

yena janma-śataiḥ pūrvaṁ vāsudevaḥ samārcitaḥ
tan-mukhe hari-nāmāni sadā tiṣṭhanti bhārata

O descendant of Bharata, the holy names of Lord Viṣṇu are always vibrating on the tongue of one who had previously worshiped Lord Vāsudeva with faith and devotion for hundreds of lifetimes.

One who is advanced in devotional service does not consider the Lord to be an order supplier. Such a second-class devotee offers his love to the Supreme Personality of Godhead, is a sincere friend to all the devotees of the Lord, shows mercy to ignorant people who are innocent, and disregards those who are envious of the Supreme Personality of Godhead.

As the devotee makes advancement in devotional service, he can come to realize that the *mantras* he is chanting are not like the mundane vibrations of this material world. When his absorption in devotional service becomes complete, so that there no longer remains any scope for his engagement in sense gratification, the devotee comes to the platform of first-class devotional service as a *mahā-bhāgavata*. Becoming thus liberated from the clutches of the Lord's external energy, the devotee realizes his original constitutional relationship with the Supreme Personality of Godhead, which is paramount to seeing the Lord face-to-face.

The spiritual master is on the same platform as the Supreme Lord, who is the maintainer of the universe and the destroyer of the conditioned soul's false spirit of enjoyment. Being one in interest with the Lord, the spiritual master is known as the dearest servant of the Lord. Enviousness will surely arise within the heart of a person who considers the spiritual master to be a mortal human being. If such a misconception is not indulged in, however, by the mercy of the Lord, one will perceive how the spiritual master is nondifferent from the Supreme Personality of Godhead.

TEXT 10

पूर्वंस्नानंप्रकुर्वीतधौतदन्तोऽङ्गशुद्धये ।
उभयैरपिचस्नानंमन्त्रैर्मृद्ग्रहणादिना ॥१०॥

pūrvaṁ snānaṁ prakurvīta dhauta-danto 'ṅga-śuddhaye
ubhayair api ca snānaṁ mantrair mṛd-grahaṇādinā

First, one should clean his teeth and bathe. Then a second cleansing of the body should be performed by by smearing it with earth and chanting mantras from both the *Vedas* and tantras.

COMMENTARY

One can also bathe by chanting Vedic and *tāntrika mantras.*

PURPORT

By the recitation of prescribed *mantras*, the contamination of considering oneself to be the enjoyer of nature can be purified.

TEXT 11

सन्ध्योपास्त्यादिकर्माणिवेदेनाचोदितानिमे ।
पूजांतैःकल्पयेत्सम्यक्सङ्कल्पःकर्मपावनीम् ॥११॥

sandhyopāstyādi-karmāṇi vedenācoditāni me
pūjāṁ taiḥ kalpayet samyak-saṅkalpaḥ karma-pāvanīm

Concentrating the mind on Me, one should worship Me by the performance of his prescribed duties, such as chanting the Gāyatrī mantra three times a day. Such performances are enjoined by the Vedas and they purify the worshiper of all reactions of karma.

COMMENTARY

One should engage in the worship of the Supreme Lord by following the rules and regulations enjoined by the scriptures. This will purify one's existence and free one from the bondage of fruitive activities.

PURPORT

After completing one's prescribed duties, such as the chanting of mantras, which are enjoined by the *Vedas*, one should engage in the worship of the Supreme Lord. As soon as one abandons the materialistic propensity for sense enjoyment by strengthening his resolve to worship Lord Hari, one becomes freed from the bondage of *karma.*

TEXT 12

शैलीदारुमयीलौहीलेप्यालेख्याचसैकती ।
मनोमयीमणिमयीप्रतिमाष्टविधास्मृता ॥१२॥

śailī dāru-mayī lauhī lepyā lekhyā ca saikatī
mano-mayī maṇi-mayī pratimāṣṭa-vidhā smṛtā

The Deity form of the Lord appears in eight varieties—stone, wood, metal, earth, paint, sand, the mind, and jewels. This is the verdict of the scriptures.

COMMENTARY

The different kinds of Deities are being described in this verse. The word *śaili* means "a Deity made of stone," the word *lauhi* indicates "a Deity made of metal," such as gold.

PURPORT

Actual worship of the Supreme Lord begins when one gives up all attempts at mental speculation, on the strength of the transcendental instructions received from the spiritual master, and thus renounces the materialistic conception that the Supreme Lord is the object of one's enjoyment. For the benefit of such a devotee, the Lord appears in eight varieties of forms. The Supreme Lord is always prepared to fulfill the desires of His devotees, as long as they will not cause him to fall into a miserable condition of life. It is only for the benefit of neophyte devotees that the Lord appears in these eight forms. However, one should never make the mistake of considering the Deity of the Lord to be made of material elements, such as marble or brass. Such a mentality is certainly suitable for placing one on the path to hell. Unless one receives initiation from a spiritual master coming in disciplic succession, it is not possible to understand the transcendental nature of Lord Vāsudeva and for that reason, the eight kinds of Deities may appear mundane to the imperfect senses of the conditioned soul. Such a misunderstanding is indicative of the ignorance that is caused by the controlling power of *maya*.

TEXT 13

चलाचलेतिद्विविधाप्रतिष्ठाजीवमन्दिरम् ।
उद्वासावाहनेनस्तःस्थिरायामुद्धवार्चने ॥१३॥

calācaleti dvi-vidhā pratiṣṭhā jīva-mandiram
udvāsāvāhane na staḥ sthirāyām uddhavārcane

My dear Uddhava, The Deity form of the Lord, who is the shelter of all living entities, can be established in two ways: movable or immovable. A permanent Deity, having been installed, can never be sent away or immersed in a body of water.

COMMENTARY

The Supreme Lord is directly present as the Deity. He is also present within the temple of the living entities' heart. Indeed, He is the shelter of all living entities. An example of His stationary form is Lord Jagannātha in Puri, and an example of His moving form is child Kṛṣṇa. Materialistic persons of whatever stripe consider the Lord to be their order supplier, and so they make temporary arrangements for religious ceremonies to achieve temporary material sense gratification. This temporary mode of worship is favored by those desiring to exploit the Personality of Godhead for their personal ends, whereas the loving devotees in Kṛṣṇa consciousness eternally engage in worship of the Personality of Godhead. They install permanent Deities meant to be worshiped perpetually.

PURPORT

The devotees of the Lord install the Deity form of their worshipable Lord in two different ways—temporary and permanent. However, there is no procedure for inviting and then immersing the permanent form of the Supreme Lord. These Deities are permanently installed and their worship goes on perpetually. Invoking and then immersing the Deity is the practice of materialists who want to exploit the Supreme Lord for the fulfillment of their personal ambitions. The impersonalists regard the eternal form of the Lord as a temporary manifestation created by the illusory energy, *maya*. In fact, they regard the Deity as a mere stepping-stone in their ambitious endeavor to become God.

TEXT 14

अस्थिरायांविकल्पःस्यात्स्थण्डिलेतुभवेद्द्वयम् ।
स्नपनंत्वविलेप्यायामन्यत्रपरिमार्जनम् ॥१४॥

asthirāyāṁ vikalpaḥ syāt sthaṇḍile tu bhaved dvayam
snapanaṁ tv avilepyāyām anyatra parimārjanam

The Deity that is temporarily established can be invited and sent away, but these two rituals should always be performed when the Deity is traced upon the ground. The Deity should be bathed with water except if the Deity is made of clay, paint, or wood, in which cases a thorough cleansing without water is enjoined.

COMMENTARY

One may invoke and then immerse a Deity made of sand from a riverbank, or painted, as desired. However, the *śālagrāma-śilā* should never be immersed. Invocation and immersion is recommended for Deities made of earth or clay, as well as sand. Except for paintings of the Lord, and Deities made of clay or sandalwood, all the other Deities should be bathed with water. The Deities of clay or wood should be carefully cleansed without the use of water.

PURPORT

There is no need for one to waste so many ingredients for worship if he considers the Deity of Lord Viṣṇu to be made of stone. The Deities that are painted or made from clay should not be bathed with water. Wiping with a dry cloth to remove the dust is sufficient.

TEXT 15

द्रव्यैःप्रसिद्धैर्मद्यागःप्रतिमादिष्वमायिनः ।
भक्तस्यचयथालब्धैर्हृदिभावेनचैवहि ॥१५॥

dravyaiḥ prasiddhair mad-yāgaḥ pratimādiṣv amāyinaḥ
bhaktasya ca yathā-labdhair hṛdi bhāvena caiva hi

One should worship Me in My Deity form by offering the most excellent paraphernalia. But, an unalloyed devotee, who is free from material desires, can worship Me with whatever is easily obtainable, or even within the mind.

COMMENTARY

If one has an abundance of wealth, he should worship the Deity with offerings of the most excellent ingredients, such as sugar candy, ghee, sandalwood paste, *kuṅkuma*, and so forth. However, an impoverished devotee can worship the Deity with whatever he may have in his possession, offering it with love and devotion. He may even offer sweet rice or fried rice within his mind, if he has nothing suitable to offer to the Lord.

PURPORT

A neophyte, or materialistic devotee who is filled with material desires, simply dreams of gaining the opportunity of gratifying his senses. Such a devotee may simply think of the Lord as His benefactor, without understanding his actual position as eternal servitor of the Lord. On the other hand, an advanced devotee knows that the Deity is identical to the Supreme Personality of Godhead, and so all the ingredients for worship that he offers are actually properly utilized. The internal mood of a devotee is the principal ingredient of his worship.

TEXT 16-17

स्नानालङ्करणंप्रेष्ठमर्चायामेवतूद्धव ।
स्थण्डिलेतत्त्वविन्यासोवह्नावाज्यप्लुतंहविः ॥१६॥
सूर्येचाभ्यर्हणंप्रेष्ठंसलिलेसलिलादिभिः ।
श्रद्धयोपाहृतंप्रेष्ठंभक्तेनममवार्यपि ॥१७॥

snānālaṅkaraṇaṁ preṣṭham arcāyām eva tūddhava
sthaṇḍile tattva-vinyāso vahnāv ājya-plutaṁ haviḥ

sūrye cābhyarhaṇaṁ preṣṭhaṁ salile salilādibhiḥ
śraddhayopāhṛtaṁ preṣṭhaṁ bhaktena mama vāry api

My dear Uddhava, while worshiping the Deity, bathing and decorating with beautiful clothes, ornaments, and flowers are the most pleasing offerings. When the Deity is drawn on a sanctified surface, the offering of *tattva-vinyāsa* is most important. Oblations of sesame seeds and barley soaked in ghee are the best oblations poured into the sacrificial fire. Worship consisting of *upasthāna* and *arghya* is the best worship of the sun. One should worship Me in the form of water by offerings of water. Whatever My devotee offers to Me, even if it is just a little water, is most dear to Me.

COMMENTARY

The Lord should be invoked and established on sanctified ground by the chanting of *mantras.* One should worship the Lord in fire by offerings of sesame seeds and barley mixed in ghee poured into the sacrificial fire. One should worship the Lord in the sun by offering *arghya.* To worship the form of the Lord in water, one should simply offer water.

PURPORT

A neophyte devotee should offer opulent paraphernalia to the Deity so that he may constantly remember that the Supreme Lord is the supreme enjoyer and that he, the neophyte, is meant for the Deity's pleasure. An advanced devotee can worship the Lord with whatever he has in his possession, offered with love and devotion. One who makes a show of great pomp while performing ritualistic worship but displays miserliness while collecting the ingredients of worship diminishes his propensity for service to the Lord. Bathing the Deity on a mirror, decorating the Deity with ornaments, performing appropriate rituals on the ground, offering oblations into the sacrificial fire, offering *arghya* to the sun, and worshiping the *puruṣa* incarnation who lies in the water, are herein recommended. Whatever a devotee offers to the Deity with faith and devotion satisfies the Supreme Lord, whereas even abundance of wealth offered without faith by nondevotees fails to attract the attention of the Lord.

TEXT 18

भूर्यप्यभक्तोपाहृतंनमेतोषायकल्पते ।
गन्धोधूपःसुमनसोदीपोऽन्नाद्यंचकिंपुनः ॥१८॥

bhūry apy abhaktopāhṛtaṁ na me toṣāya kalpate
gandho dhūpaḥ sumanaso dīpo 'nnādyaṁ ca kiṁ punaḥ

I do not accept even the most opulent offerings if they are given by nondevotees, but I am very pleased to accept even the most insignificant thing offered with love by the hand of My devotee. I am certainly most pleased when nice fragrant oil, incense, flowers, and palatable foods are offered to Me with love.

COMMENTARY

The word *sumanaso* refers to the flower known as *sumanasa.*

TEXT 19

शुचिःसम्भृतसम्भारःप्राग्दर्भैःकल्पितासनः ।
आसीनःप्रागुदग्वार्चेदर्चायांत्वथसम्मुखः ॥१९॥

śuciḥ sambhṛta-sambhāraḥ prāg-darbhaiḥ kalpitāsanaḥ
āsīnaḥ prāg udag vārced arcāyāṁ tv atha sammukhaḥ

After purifying himself and collecting all the paraphernalia for worship, one should sit down on a mat of kuśa grass, facing either east or north. If the Deity is permanently installed, the worshiper should sit facing the Deity.

COMMENTARY

Now, the beginning of the process of Deity worship is being described. One should first purify himself and then sit down facing either east or north. However, one who worships an immovable Deity should sit directly in front of the Deity.

TEXT 20

कृतन्यासःकृतन्यासांमदर्चांपाणिनामृजेत् ।
कलशंप्रोक्षणीयंचयथावदुपसाधयेत् ॥२०॥

kṛta-nyāsaḥ kṛta-nyāsāṁ mad-arcāṁ pāṇināmṛjet
kalaśaṁ prokṣaṇīyaṁ ca yathāvad upasādhayet

Thereafter, the devotee should perform the ritual known as *nyāsa* (the process of purifying oneself by touching the various parts of the body while chanting *mantras*) on his own body, and on that of the Deity. He should then take from the Deity the remnants of previous offerings, such as flowers and flower garlands. He should then prepare a pitcher of water for cleansing the Deity.

COMMENTARY

Before beginning one's worship of the Deity, one should take permission from the spiritual master by offering him obeisances. Then, according to his instructions, one should perform *aṅga-nyāsa* on his own body, perform *nyāsa* on the body of the Deity while chanting the *mūlā mantras*, and cleanse the altar and the Deity by removing the previously-offered flowers and so on. One should keep a pot of water for sprinkling, and one should then decorate the Deity with flowers, and so forth.

TEXT 21

तदद्भिर्देवयजनंद्रव्याण्यात्मानमेवच ।
प्रोक्ष्यपात्राणित्रीण्यद्भिस्तैस्तैर्द्रव्यैश्चसाधयेत् ॥२१॥

tad-adbhir deva-yajanaṁ dravyāṇy ātmānam eva ca
prokṣya pātrāṇi trīṇy adbhis tais tair dravyaiś ca sādhayet

He should then sprinkle the water of that vessel on the place of worship, the paraphernalia for worship, and his own body. Next, he should decorate three pitchers of water with sandalwood paste and flowers, which will be used for offering *pādya* to the Deity.

COMMENTARY

Next, one should sprinkle the purified water on the place of worship and the ingredients for worship. In the container of *pādya*, one should place water, black *dūrvā* grass, lotus petals, and an *aparajitā* flower. In the container of *arghya*, there should be eight items—sandalwood paste, flowers, *ātapa*, rice, barley, tips of *kuśa* grass, sesame seeds, mustard seeds, and *dūrvā* grass. In the container of *ācamanīya*, there should be three items—nutmeg, clove, and *kakkola*.

TEXT 22

पाद्यार्घ्याचमनीयार्थंत्रीणिपात्राणिदेशिकः ।
हृदाशीर्ष्णाथशिखयागायत्र्याचाभिमन्त्रयेत् ॥२२॥

pādyārghyācamanīyārthaṁ trīṇi pātrāṇi deśikaḥ
hṛdā śīrṣṇātha śikhayā gāyatryā cābhimantrayet

Next, the worshiper should purify the three vessels. He should sanctify the vessel holding water for *pādya,* (washing the Lord's lotus feet) by chanting *hṛdayāya namaḥ,* the vessel containing water for *arghya* by chanting *śirase svāhā,* and the vessel containing water for *ācamanīya* (washing the Lord's mouth) by chanting *śikhāyai vaṣaṭ.* The Gāyatrī mantra should also be chanted for all three vessels.

COMMENTARY

The worshiper should purify the three containers by chanting the *hṛdaya mantra*, and so on, as well as the *Gāyatri mantra*.

PURPORT

After chanting the Gāyatri mantra, the worshiper should purify the container of *pādya* by chanting *hṛdayāya namaḥ*, the container of *arghya* by chanting *sirase svāhā*, and the container of *ācamanīya* by chanting *śikhayai vaṣaṭ*. One should purify the ingredients for *pādya*, *arghya*, and *ācamanīya* by sprinkling water on them while remembering the Supreme Lord. The ingredients of *arghya* are water, milk, tips of *kuśa* grass, yogurt, ghee, *ātapa* rice, and barley, or simply barley water and yogurt, as prescribed by the followers of the *Sāma Veda*. *Brāhmaṇas* who follow the *Sāma Veda* use the word *arghyaṁ* with a "y" in the neuter gender, but the followers of the other *Vedas* use the word *arghyaḥ* without the "y" and in the masculine gender.

TEXT 23

पिण्डेवाय्वग्निसंशुद्धेहृत्पद्मस्थांपरांमम ।
अण्वींजीवकलांध्यायेन्नादान्तेसिद्धभाविताम् ॥२३॥

piṇḍe vāyv-agni-saṁśuddhe hṛt-padma-sthāṁ parāṁ mama
aṇvīṁ jīva-kalāṁ dhyāyen nādānte siddha-bhāvitām

Thereafter the worshiper should dry his body with the air from his stomach, burn his body with fire, and then revive it by showering nectar from the moon, which is situated on his forehead. He should then meditate on My subtle transcendental form of Śrī Nārāyaṇa, which is situated on the lotus of the heart, by the vibration of the sacred syllable oṁ. This form is meditated upon by perfected sages.

COMMENTARY

Thereafter, one should dry his body with the air from the stomach, burn it with fire, and then revive it by showering nectar from the moon, which is situated on his forehead. In this way, one should meditate on My form as Nārāyaṇa, which is situated on the lotus of the heart. The *praṇava*, or *oṁ*, has five parts— A, U, M, the nasal *bindu*, and the reverberation (*nāda*). After chanting *oṁ*, one should meditate on the transcendental form of Lord Nārāyaṇa. It is stated in the *Vedas* that the Supreme Lord Himself is the transcendental sound vibration of the *Vedas*, and the ultimate goal of Vedānta.

PURPORT

This ritual is called *bhutaśuddhi*, or purifying oneself. Before worshiping the Lord, one must perform *bhutaśuddhi.*

TEXT 24

तयात्मभूतयापिण्डेव्यासेसम्पूज्यतन्मयाः ।
आवाह्यार्चादिषुस्थाप्यन्यस्ताङ्गंमांप्रपूजयेत् ॥२४॥

tayātma-bhūtayā piṇḍe vyāpte sampūjya tan-mayaḥ
āvāhyārcādiṣu sthāpya nyastāṅgaṁ māṁ prapūjayet

When My transcendental form, which pervades his body, is perceived by the worshiper, he should worship Me within his mind, and then externally invoke Me in the Deity with full concentration. He should then perform nyāsa **on My transcendental body before beginning his worship.**

COMMENTARY

The Supersoul illuminates the entire body of the devotee, just as the light of a lamp illuminates a room. One should first worship the Lord mentally and then, with full concentration, invoke the Supreme Lord within the Deity. In this way, one installs the Deity and then performs *nyāsa* on his own body, as well as that of the Deity.

TEXTS 25-26

पाद्योपस्पर्शार्हणादीनपचारान्प्रकल्पयेत् ।
धर्मादिभिश्चनवभिःकल्पयित्वासनंमम ॥२५॥
पद्ममष्टदलंतत्रकर्णिकाकेसरोज्ज्वलम् ।
उभाभ्यांवेदतन्त्राभ्यांमह्यंतूभयसिद्धये ॥२६॥

pādyopasparśārhaṇādīn upacārān prakalpayet
dharmādibhiś ca navabhiḥ kalpayitvāsanaṁ mama

padmam aṣṭa-dalaṁ tatra karṇikā-kesarojjvalam
ubhābhyāṁ veda-tantrābhyāṁ mahyaṁ tūbhaya-siddhaye

The worshiper should mentally place an *āsana* that is decorated with the personified deities of religion, knowledge, renunciation, opulence, and My nine spiritual energies. He should think of My sitting place as an effulgent lotus flower with eight petals with saffron filaments within the whorl. Then, following the regulations of the *Vedas* and *tantras,* he should offer Me *pādya, arghya, ācamanīya,* and other items of worship. By following this procedure, one is awarded material enjoyment in this life, and attains liberation after death.

COMMENTARY

What should one do before offering *arghya* and *ācamanīya* to the Deity? One should imagine a *yogapiṭha āsana* for the Lord, consisting of religion, knowledge, renunciation, and opulence, and he should mentally place it on an eight-petal lotus flower. He should then worship the Lord by offering various paraphernalia while following the rules and regulations laid down in the *Vedas* and *tantras.* As a result of this worship, one obtains material enjoyment and liberation.

TEXT 27

सुदर्शनंपाञ्चजन्यंगदासीषुधनुर्हलान् ।
मुषलंकौस्तुभंमालांश्रीवत्संचानुपूजयेत् ॥२७॥

sudarśanaṁ pāñcajanyaṁ gadāsīṣu-dhanur-halān
muṣalaṁ kaustubhaṁ mālāṁ śrīvatsaṁ cānupūjayet

One should then worship, in order, the Lord's Sudarśana *cakra,* Pāñcajanya conch shell, flower garland, sword, arrows, bow, plow, *muṣala* weapon, Kaustubha gem, and Śrīvatsa.

COMMENTARY

One should worship the Sudarśana *cakra* and plow that are in the Lord's hands, the eight weapons on the eight sides of the Lord, the Kaustubha gem around the Lord's neck, and the curl of hair, Śrīvatsa, on His chest.

PURPORT

The name of the four-armed Lord Nārāyāṇa's *cakra* is Sudarśana, His conch shell is named Pāñcajanya, His club is named Kaumudakī, His lotus is named Śrīvasa, His bow is named Śarāṅga, His sword is named Nandaka, His gem around His neck is named Kaustubha, and the curl of hair on His chest is named Śrīvatsa.

TEXT 28

नन्दंसुनन्दंगरुडंप्रचण्डंचण्डं एवच ।
महाबलंबलंचैवकुमुदंकमुदेक्षणम् ॥२८॥

nandaṁ sunandaṁ garuḍaṁ pracaṇḍaṁ caṇḍaṁ eva ca
mahābalaṁ balaṁ caiva kumudaṁ kamudekṣaṇam

Thereafter, one should worship the eight associates of the Lord—Nanda, Sunanda, Pracaṇḍa, Caṇḍa, Mahābala, Bala, Kumuda, and Kumudekṣaṇa—in the eight directions, and worship Garuḍa in front.

TEXT 29

दुर्गांविनायकंव्यासंविष्वक्षेनंगुरून्सुरान् ।
स्वेस्वेस्थानेत्वभिमुखान्पूजयेत्प्रोक्षणादिभिः ॥२९॥

durgāṁ vināyakaṁ vyāsaṁ viṣvakṣenaṁ gurūn surān
sve sve sthāne tv abhimukhān pūjayet prokṣaṇādibhiḥ

Thereafter, with offerings such as *arghya,* one should worship Durgā, Vināyaka, Vyāsa, Visvaksena, the spiritual masters, and the demigods, headed by Indra. All these personalities should be in their proper places, facing the Deity.

PURPORT

All of these personalities are the associates of Lord Nārāyaṇa in Vaikuṇṭha. One must worship them while performing worship of Lord Nārāyaṇa. This Durgā and

Vināyaka (Ganeśa) are not the Durgā and Ganeśa of the *devi-dhāma* (material world) who award material enjoyment.

TEXT 30-31

चन्दनोशीरकर्पूरकुङ्कुमागुरुवासितैः ।
सलिलैःस्नापयेन्मन्त्रैर्नित्यदाविभवेसति ॥३०॥
स्वर्णघर्मानुवाकेनमहापुरुषविद्यया ।
पौरुषेणापिसूक्तेनसामभीराजनादिभिः ॥३१॥

candanośīra-karpūra-kuṅkumāguru-vāsitaiḥ
salilaiḥ snāpayen mantrair nityadā vibhave sati

svarṇa-gharmānuvākena mahāpuruṣa-vidyayā
pauruṣeṇāpi sūktena sāmabhī rājanādibhiḥ

As opulently as his wealth permits, a worshiper should bathe the Deity daily with water mixed with sandalwood paste, camphor, *uśīra* root, *kuṅkuma*, and *aguru*. While bathing the Deity, he should recite Vedic hymns, such as the *Svarṇa-gharma, Mahāpuruṣa-vidyā, Puruṣa-sūkta,* and *Rājana*.

COMMENTARY

One should worship the associates of the Lord in their respective places, facing the altar from the eight directions. Garuḍa should be worship in front of the altar, Durgā and others in their specified places, the spiritual masters to the left, and the demigods, headed by Indra, toward the east. One should worship all these personalities by sprinkling purified water and then offering *arghya*. One should recite the *Svarna-gharma* mantra beginning with *svarnaṁ gharma parivedanaṁ*, the *Mahāpuruṣa-vidyā* mantra beginning with *jitante puṇḍarikākṣa namaste viśvabhāvana*, the *Puruṣa-sukta* mantra beginning with *sahasra śīrṣā*, and the *Rājana* mantra from the *Sāma* Veda. Devotional songs should also be sung. The word *ādi* also means mantras, such as the *Rohini* mantras, and these should also be chanted.

PURPORT

The *Puruṣa-sukta mantras* from the *Ṛg Veda* begin with *oṁ sahasra śirṣā puruṣaḥ sahasrākṣa sahasrapāt.*

TEXT 32

वस्त्रोपवीताभरणपत्रस्रग्गन्धलेपनैः ।
अलङ्कुर्वीतसप्रेममद्भक्तोमांयथोचितम् ॥३२॥

vastropavītābharaṇa-patra-srag-gandha-lepanaiḥ
alaṅkurvīta sa-premamad-bhakto māṁ yathocitam

My devotees should then lovingly decorate Me with fine clothing, ornaments, a sacred thread, marks of *tilaka*, a flower garland, a garland of *tulasī* leaves, sandalwood paste, and other scented substances.

COMMENTARY

The word *patra-srag* refers to a garland of *tulasī* leaves.

TEXT 33

पाद्यमाचमनीयचगन्धंसुमनसोऽक्षतान् ।
धूपदीपोपहार्याणिदद्यान्मेश्रद्धयार्चकः ॥३३॥

pādyam ācamanīyaṁ ca gandhaṁ sumanaso 'kṣatān
dhūpa-dīpopahāryāṇi dadyān me śraddhayārcakaḥ

The worshiper should faithfully offer Me *pādya, arghya, ācamaṇīya,* sandalwood pulp, incense, a ghee lamp, *ātapa* rice, and flowers.

TEXT 34

गुडपायससर्पींषिशष्कुल्यापूपमोदकान् ।
संयावदधिसूपांश्चनैवेद्यंसतिकल्पयेत् ॥३४॥

guḍa-pāyasa-sarpīṁṣi śaṣkuly-āpūpa-modakān
saṁyāva-dadhi-sūpāṁś ca naivedyaṁ sati kalpayet

Within his means, the devotee should offer Me sugar candy, sweet rice, ghee, *śaṣkulī* (rice-flour cakes), *āpūpa* (various sweet cakes), *modaka* (steamed rice-flour dumplings filled with sweet coconut and sugar), *saṁyāva* (wheat cakes made with ghee and milk and covered with sugar and spices), yogurt, vegetable soups, and other palatable food.

COMMENTARY

Preparations made with *gur* and sugar candy, as well as sweet rice, fried rice made with ghee, milk cakes, sweets made with wheat flour, pancakes, and other palatable food should be offered to the Lord if one has the capacity.

TEXT 35

अभ्यङ्गोन्मर्दनादर्शदन्तधावाभिषेचनम् ।
अन्नाद्यगीतनृत्यानिपर्वणिस्युरुतान्वहम् ॥३५॥

abhyaṅgonmardanādarśa-danta-dhāvābhiṣecanam
annādya-gītā-nṛtyāni parvaṇi syur utānv-aham

On special days, such as Ekādaśī, and every day, if possible, the Deity should be massaged with scented oil, shown a mirror, offered a eucalyptus stick for brushing His teeth, bathed with the five kinds of nectar, offered varieties of opulent foods, and entertained with singing and dancing.

COMMENTARY

In the early morning, one should wake up the Deity and offer Him a small twig for brushing His teeth. One should then massage the Deity's body with scented oil, remove the oil from His body by applying *kuṅkuma* and camphor, bathe the Deity with milk, yogurt, ghee, honey, and scented water. Thereafter, one should decorate the Deity with fine silk clothing and valuable ornaments, apply sandalwood paste, offer a flower garland, display a mirror, and offer incense, flowers, a ghee lamp, and *ācamanīya*. Next, one should offer four kinds of food—those that are chewed, licked, sucked, and drunk. One should then offer scented water, betel nuts, a flower garland, and finally *ārati*. Thereafter, one should arrange a bed that is decorated with flowers, place the Deity upon it, and fan Him with a *cāmara* and a peacock feather fan. One should then sing, play musical instruments, and dance before the Deity. All of these aspects of Deity worship should be performed on special days, such as Ekādaśī, or if one has the means, on a daily basis.

TEXT 36

विधिनाविहितेकुण्डेमेखलागर्तवेदिभिः ।
अग्निमाधायपरितःसमूहेत्पाणिनोदितम् ॥३६॥

vidhinā vihite kuṇḍe mekhalā-garta-vedibhiḥ
agnim ādhāya paritaḥ samūhet pāṇinoditam

After constructing an arena as enjoined by the scriptures, utilizing a sanctified belt, a sacrificial pit, and a raised altar, the devotee should perform a fire sacrifice. He should ignite the sacrificial fire with wood that he has personally collected.

COMMENTARY

Here, the procedure for worshiping the Lord in fire is being described. Three *mekhalā*, each about four inches long, should be used. The depth of the pit should be about one foot. An altar mound should be prepared around the pit. In this way, one should make preparations for performing a fire sacrifice.

TEXT 37

परिस्तीर्याथपर्युक्षेदन्वाधाययथाविधि ।
प्रोक्षण्यासाद्यद्रव्याणिप्रोक्ष्याग्नौभावयेतमाम् ॥३७॥

paristīryātha paryukṣed anvādhāya yathā-vidhi
prokṣaṇyāsādya dravyāṇi prokṣyāgnau bhāvayeta mām

First, one should spread kuśa grass on the ground and sprinkle water over it. Then, one should perform the ritual of placing wood into the sacrificial fire while chanting the prescribed mantras. Thereafter, one should purify all of the items to be offered as oblations by sprinkling water upon them. After doing this, one should meditate upon Me as being situated within the sacrificial fire.

COMMENTARY

Thereafter, the sacrificial pit should be filled and covered with dry *kuśa* grass, and water should be sprinkled in the four directions, beginning from the north. One should then sit down and meditate on the Lord as the Supersoul, situated within the fire.

TEXT 38-41

तप्तजाम्बूनदप्रख्यंशङ्खचक्रगदाम्बुजैः ।
लसच्चतुर्भुजंशान्तंपद्मकिञ्जल्कवाससम् ॥३८॥
स्फुरत्किरीटकटककटिसूत्रवराङ्गदम् ।
श्रीवत्सवक्षसंभ्राजत्कौस्तुभंवनमालिनम् ॥३९॥
ध्यायन्नभ्यर्च्यदारूणिहविषाभिघृतानिच ।
प्रास्याज्यभागावाघारौदत्त्वाचाज्यपुतंहविः ॥४०॥

जुहुयान्मूलमन्त्रेणषोडशर्चावदानतः ।
धर्मादिभ्योयथान्यायंमन्त्रैःस्विष्टिकृतंबुधः ॥४१॥

tapta-jāmbūnada-prakhyaṁ śaṅkha-cakra-gadāmbujaiḥ
lasac-catur-bhujaṁ śāntaṁ padma-kiñjalka-vāsasam

sphurat-kirīṭa-kaṭaka kaṭi-sūtra-varāṅgadam
śrīvatsa-vakṣasaṁ bhrājat-kaustubhaṁ vana-mālinam

dhyāyann abhyarcya dārūṇi haviṣābhighṛtāni ca
prāsyājya-bhāgāv āghārau dattvā cājya-plutaṁ haviḥ

juhuyān mūla-mantreṇa ṣoḍaśarcāvadānataḥ
dharmādibhyo yathā-nyāyaṁ mantraiḥ sviṣṭi-kṛtaṁ budhaḥ

The intelligent devotee should thereafter meditate on the form of the Lord, whose complexion is the color of molten gold, whose four arms are decorated with the conch shell, disc, club, and lotus flower, and whose appearance is peaceful, and who is dressed in garments the color of the filaments within a lotus flower. His helmet, bracelets, belt, and ornaments decorating His arms shine brilliantly. The symbol of Śrivatsa is on His chest, along with the Kaustubha gem, and a garland of forest flowers. Thereafter, the devotee should worship Me by taking firewood soaked in ghee and placing it in the sacrificial fire. He should then offer as oblations into the sacrificial fire various items soaked in ghee. He should then offer oblations to sixteen demigods, beginning with Yamarāja, while reciting the *mantras* of each deity and the sixteen-line *Puruṣa-sūkta* hymn, ending each line with *svāḥā*. While pouring one oblation after each line of the *Puruṣa-sūkta*, he should utter the particular *mantra* naming each deity.

COMMENTARY

After igniting the sacrificial fire, one should place wood soaked in ghee into the fire. One should also offer ghee and other articles, such as sesame seeds, into the sacrificial fire while chanting the sixteen lines of the *Puruṣa-sukta* hymn. While chanting the *Puruṣa-sūkta*, one should pour ghee into the sacrificial fire and chant *svāḥā* at the end of each line.

TEXT 42

अभ्यर्च्याथनमस्कृत्यपार्षदेभ्योबलिंहरेत् ।
मूलमन्त्रंजपेद्ब्रह्मस्मरन्नारायणात्मकम् ॥४२॥

abhyarcyātha namaskṛtya pārṣadebhyo baliṁ haret
mūla-mantraṁ japed brahma smaran nārāyaṇātmakam

Having thus worshiped the Lord within the sacrificial fire, the devotee should offer his obeisances and then worship the Lord's personal associates, headed by Nanda. He should then chant the *mūla-mantra* of the Deity and meditate on the Supreme Lord, Nārāyaṇa.

TEXT 43

दत्त्वाचमनमुच्छेषंविष्वक्षेनायकल्पयेत् ।
मुखवासंसुरभिमत्ताम्बूलाद्यमथार्हयेत् ॥४३॥

dattvācamanam ucchesaṁ viṣvaksenāya kalpayet
mukha-vāsaṁ surabhimat tāmbūlādyam athārhayet

Next, one should offer *ācamanīya* to the Deity and then offer the remnants of His food to Viṣvaksena. Thereafter, he should offer perfumed betel nuts to the Lord.

COMMENTARY

One should meditate on Lord Nārāyaṇa, the Supreme Brahman. One should then chant the *mūla-mantra* and offer the remnants of the Lord's food to Viṣvaksena. Finally, after taking permission from the Lord and Viṣvaksena, one should honor the *prasāda*. This is the opinion of Śrīdhara Svāmī.

TEXT 44

उपगायन्गृणन्नृत्यन्कर्माण्यभिनयन्मम ।
मत्कथाःश्रावयन्शृण्वन्मुहूर्तंक्षणिकोभवेत् ॥४४॥

upagāyan gṛṇan nṛtyan karmāṇy abhinayan mama
mat-kathāḥ śrāvayan śṛṇvan muhūrtaṁ kṣaṇiko bhavet

Thereafter, one should hear and chant narrations about Me, perform dramas depicting My pastimes, and sing and dance in ecstasy. In this way, the devotee should absorb himself in the festivities.

COMMENTARY

From time to time, one should ecstatically engage in hearing about the Lord and glorifying Him, as well as chanting and dancing with great enthusiasm.

TEXT 45

स्तवैरुच्चावचैःस्तोत्रैःपौराणैःप्राकृतैरपि ।
स्तुत्वाप्रसीदभगवन्नितिवन्देतदण्डवत् ॥४५॥

stavair uccāvacaiḥ stotraiḥ paurāṇaiḥ prākṛtair api
stutvā prasīda bhagavann iti vandeta daṇḍa-vat

A devotee should offer prayers from the *Purāṇas* and other scriptures, as well prayers composed by himself, and traditional prayers. He should pray: "O my Lord, please be merciful to me!" and offer his obeisances by falling flat onto the ground like a rod.

COMMENTARY

One should offer the prayers to the Lord that are found in the *Purāṇas*, which were spoken long ago by great sages and elevated devotees. One should appeal to the Lord by praying, "My dear Lord, kindly be pleased with me." After praying in this way, one should bow down before the Lord with great respect.

TEXT 46

शिरोमत्पादयोःकृत्वाबाहुभ्यांचपरस्परम् ।
प्रपन्नंपाहिमामीशभीतमृत्युग्रहार्णवात् ॥४६॥

śiro mat-pādayoḥ kṛtvā bāhubhyāṁ ca parasparam
prapannaṁ pāhi māṁ īśa bhītaṁ mṛtyu-grahārṇavāt

One should place his head at the lotus feet of the Deity, catching hold of the Lord's lotus feet with both hands while praying, "O my Lord, I am most fearful of material existence, where birth and death take place. Please protect me, who am surrendered unto You." After praying in this way, one should offer his obeisances by falling flat before the Lord.

COMMENTARY

The procedure for offering obeisances is herein being described. One should place his head at the lotus feet of the Deity and then catch hold of the lotus feet of the Lord.

While doing so, he should pray, "O supreme controller, please protect me, because I am greatly frightened by this vast ocean of material existence." One should not chant *mantras*, perform fire sacrifice, or offer obeisances just in front of the Deity, to His left, or within the Deity room. It is prohibited to offer obeisances while facing the Deity, or in back of the Deity, and so one should offer obeisances by falling flat onto the ground, keeping the Deity to one's left. One should then join his palms while offering his prayers of submission.

TEXT 47

इतिशेषांमयादत्तांशिरस्याधायसादरम् ।
उद्वासयेच्चेदुद्वास्यंज्योतिर्ज्योतिषितत्पुनः ॥४७॥

iti śeṣāṁ mayā dattāṁ śirasy ādhāya sādaram
udvāsayec ced udvāsyaṁ jyotir jyotiṣi tat punaḥ

After praying in this way, the devotee should place the remnants of My flower garland, and so on, upon his head. If the Deity is meant to be sent away at the end of the worship, the effulgence of the Deity's presence should be withdrawn and placed within the lotus of one's heart.

COMMENTARY

After offering prayers, one should gratefully consider how the Lord has mercifully given him the remnants of His flower garland, and so on. If the Deity is made of sand, or other such material, and must be immersed, one should withdraw the effulgence of the Deity's presence and merge it within the effulgence of the lotus within one's heart.

TEXT 48

अर्चादिषुयदायत्रश्रद्धामांतत्रचार्चयेत् ।
सर्वभूतेष्वात्मनिचसर्वात्माहमवस्थितः ॥४८॥

arcādiṣu yadā yatra śraddhā māṁ tatra cārcayet
sarva-bhūteṣv ātmani ca sarvātmāham avasthitaḥ

Among My various manifestations, such as the Deity, one should worship Me in the particular form that he has developed faith in. As the Supreme Soul of all, I exist within all created beings, as well as separately in My original form.

COMMENTARY

The main criteria for Deity worship is faith. It is due to the faith of the worshiper that the Supreme Lord appears within the Deity. The Lord's appearance as the Deity is His mercy upon the conditioned souls, who cannot perceive Him with their blunt material senses. Those who are very materialistic are advised to meditate upon the Lord as the universal form. The Deity form, *arcā*, is specifically mentioned in this verse because Deity worship is essential for making further spiritual progress. With strong faith, when one becomes further advanced, he can realize the presence of the Lord everywhere.

PURPORT

The Supreme Personality of Godhead is the worshipable Lord of all living entities. As the Supersoul, He is situated within the heart of all living entities. One should faithfully worship the Lord in those forms in which he can feel the Lord's presence. The Deity form of the Lord is considered one of His incarnations. The Deity attracts the faith of His worshiper and awards him auspiciousness. Inexperienced persons may think that the Deity is meant for the sense gratification of the worshiper, because superficially, the Deity is made of external substances, such as marble or brass. If one makes a show of worshiping the Supreme Lord while considering Him an order supplier of one's sense enjoyment, it is to be understood that he is devoid of faith. It is one's duty to faithfully serve the Deity by offering various items, to the best of one's capacity. One's faith will never develop if he thinks that the Deity is different from the Lord Himself. The Supreme Lord is present within all living entities, and so the conception that other living entities and objects are meant for our personal enjoyment will distract one from the path of spiritual advancement. Indeed, such a materialistic conception is an indication of one's lack of faith in the Supreme Lord. By faithfully worshiping the Deity, one can gradually become freed from such materialistic conceptions. Because neophyte devotees, or *kaniṣṭha adhikārīs*, have such a materialistic conception of life, they cannot understand the position of an advanced devotee and thus their faith is limited to the Deity. While faithfully worshiping the Deity, when one realizes that the Deity is directly the Supreme Personality of Godhead, he can understand the distinction between the three classes of devotees—*uttama*, *madhyama*, and *kaniṣṭha*. The Supreme Lord continuously resides within the body of a devotee who is merged in ecstatic love and never considers a Vaiṣṇava according to his bodily designations.

TEXT 49

एवंक्रियायोगपथैःपुमान्वैदिकतान्त्रिकैः ।
अर्चन्नुभयतःसिद्धिंमत्तोविन्दत्यभीप्सिताम् ॥४९॥

evaṁ kriyā-yoga-pathaiḥ pumān vaidika-tāntrikaiḥ
arcann ubhayataḥ siddhiṁ matto vindaty abhīpsitām

By worshiping Me according to the various methods prescribed in the Vedas and tantras, one achieves his desired perfection from Me, both in this life and the next.

COMMENTARY

The word *ubhayataḥ* means "both in this life and the next."

PURPORT

If one worships the Supreme Lord according to the rules and regulations prescribed in the *Vedas* and *Pañcarātras*, the Lord fulfills all of his desires. Simply by the practice of chanting Vedic and *Pāñcarātrika mantras*, one attains the mercy of the Supreme Lord.

TEXT 50

मदर्चांसम्प्रतिष्ठाप्यमन्दिरंकारयेद्दृढम् ।
पुष्पोद्यानानिरम्याणिपूजायात्रोत्सवाश्रितान् ॥५०॥

mad-arcāṁ sampratiṣṭhāpya mandiraṁ kārayed dṛḍham
puṣpodyānāni ramyāṇi pūjā-yātrotsavāśritān

The devotee should more firmly establish My Deity worship by constructing a beautiful temple, along with flower gardens. These gardens should be set aside to provide flowers for the daily worship of the Deity, as well as for festival occasions.

COMMENTARY

There are many festivals to be observed for the satisfaction of the Lord, such as Janmastamī and Vasanta Pañcamī. On these days, one should worship the Supreme Lord with special offerings and great pomp. Wealthy, pious persons should be engaged in constructing temples and gardens for the pleasure of the Deity.

TEXT 51

पूजादीनांप्रवाहार्थंमहापर्वस्वथान्वहम् ।
क्षेत्रापणपुरग्रामान्दत्त्वामत्सार्ष्टितामियात् ॥५१॥

pūjādīnāṁ pravāhārthaṁ mahā-parvasv athānv-aham
kṣetrāpaṇa-pura-grāmān dattvā mat-sārṣṭitām iyāt

One who offers the Deity gifts of land, shops, towns, and villages, so that the regular worship and special festivals may continue in a grand manner, will achieve opulence equal to My own.

COMMENTARY

Those who are rich and pious will attain incomparable merit if they donate land, marketplaces, villages, or towns for the service of the Lord, so that His service can go on very nicely. Indeed, such persons will attain opulence like that of the Lord Himself.

PURPORT

After installing the Deity of the Lord, one should construct a majestic temple and arrange for flower gardens, so that opulent worship, regular processions, and festivals can be properly maintained. It is essential to hold festivals on the days of the Lord's appearance, and so on. If one donates land, marketplace, or other assets, and constructs residences for pilgrims so that with the income the worship of the Deity can be maintained with great pomp, he will achieve opulence that is as good as that of the Supreme Lord.

TEXT 52

प्रतिष्ठयासार्वभौमंसद्मनाभुवनत्रयम् ।
पूजादिनाब्रह्मलोकंत्रिभिर्मत्साम्यतामियात् ॥५२॥

pratiṣṭhayā sārvabhaumaṁ sadmanā bhuvana-trayam
pūjādinā brahma-lokaṁ tribhir mat-sāmyatām iyāt

By installing the Deity of the Lord, one becomes the ruler of the entire earth. By constructing a temple for the Lord, one becomes the ruler of the three worlds. By worshiping and serving the Deity, one attains residence in Brahmaloka, and by performing all three, one achieves a transcendental form like My own.

COMMENTARY

The result of building a temple, either by one's own endeavor or with the help of others, is herein described. Those who arrange for the installation of the Deity of the Lord, the construction of a temple, and engage in the Deity's worship, attain a transcendental form like that of the Lord.

PURPORT

By installing a Deity of the Lord one becomes the ruler of the earth, by constructing a temple one conquers the three worlds, by worshiping the Deity one achieves Brahmaloka, and by performing all three activities one attains a transcendental form similar to that of the Supreme Lord. Mixed devotional service has been recommended for those who desire such exalted positions. By careful consideration of the following verse, one can understand that it is also possible to construct a temple and worship the Deity of the Lord without expecting anything in return.

sālokya-sārṣṭi-sāmīpya-sārūpyaikatvam apy uta
dīyamānaṁ na gṛhṇanti vinā mat-sevanaṁ janāḥ

A pure devotee does not accept any kind of liberation—*sālokya, sārṣṭi, sāmīpya, sārūpya or ekatva*—even though they are offered by the Supreme Personality of Godhead. (*Śrīmad-Bhāgavatam* 3.29.3)

By worshiping Lord Hari without any material desire, even while engaging in worldly activities while living within the material world, one is sure to attain the highest destination.

TEXT 53

मामेवनैरपेक्ष्येणभक्तियोगेनविन्दति ।
भक्तियोगंसलभत एवंयःपूजयेतमाम् ॥५३॥

mām eva nairapekṣyeṇa bhakti-yogena vindati
bhakti-yogaṁ sa labhata evaṁ yaḥ pūjayeta mām

But one who simply engages in devotional service without consideration of receiving anything in return, attains Me. Thus, whoever worships Me according to the process I have described will ultimately attain pure devotional service unto Me.

COMMENTARY

One who worships the Supreme Lord without any ambition, renouncing all desires for *karma* and *jñāna*, certainly attains the platform of loving devotional service. One who gives wealth, land, marketplaces, and so on, for the service of the Lord, without any expectation of reward, will surely achieve all-auspiciousness.

PURPORT

The previous two verses were spoken by the Lord to attract those who are interested in fruitive results. In this verse, the ultimate purpose of worshiping the Supreme Lord is described. The ultimate goal is Lord Kṛṣṇa Himself. Love for the Lord is the highest attainment, although materialistic people cannot understand this. When one engages in the congregational chanting of the holy names of the Lord, it should be considered that worship of the Lord is perfectly accomplished, even without engaging so much paraphernalia. The platform of unalloyed devotional service cannot be attained by those who have a desire to accumulate wealth, enjoy beautiful women, and gain name and fame. Pleasing the Supreme Lord, Kṛṣṇa, is the actual purpose of devotional service.

TEXT 54

यःस्वदत्तांपरैर्दत्तांहरेतसुरविप्रयोः ।
वृत्तिंसजायतेविड्भुग्वर्षाणामयुतायुतम् ॥५४॥

yaḥ sva-dattāṁ parair dattāṁ hareta sura-viprayoḥ
vṛttiṁ sa jāyate viḍ-bhug varṣāṇām ayutāyutam

One who steals the property of the demigods or *brāhmaṇas,* whether donated by him or someone else, will have to suffer as a worm in stool for one hundred million years.

COMMENTARY

After describing the glorious position of those who help in the worship of the Supreme Lord, the Lord now describes the fate of a person who steals the property of the demigods, or the *brāhmaṇas.*

PURPORT

When one employs the things that were given for the Lord's service for one's personal sense gratification, he paves his way to hell and thereafter, birth as a worm in stool.

TEXT 55

कर्तुश्चसारथेर्हेतोरनुमोदितुरेवच ।
कर्मणांभागिनःप्रेत्यभूयोभूयसितत्फलम् ॥५५॥

kartuś ca sārather hetor anumoditur eva ca
karmaṇāṁ bhāginaḥ pretya bhūyo bhūyasi tat-phalam

Not only the performer of such a theft, but also anyone who assists, intigates, or simply approves of such an act must share the sinful reaction. According to the degree of their participation, they must suffer proportionate consequences.

COMMENTARY

Those who help a person usurp the property of the Lord and the *brāhmaṇas* must share the sinful reactions after death because they are directly or indirectly responsible. Those who provide direct assistance suffer the worst consequences.

PURPORT

Those who utilize money given to the Lord for His worship for their personal enjoyment, or who approve of such an act, are liable to be punished by Yamarāja after death.

Thus end the translation of the Twenty-first Chapter of the Uddhava-gītā entitled **"Lord Kṛṣṇa's Instructions on the Process of Deity Worship"** *with the commentaries of Śrīla Viśvanātha Cakravartī Ṭhākura and chapter summary and purports by Śrīla Bhaktisiddhānta Sarasvatī Ṭhākura.*

Chapter 22

Jñāna-yoga

CHAPTER SUMMARY

This chapter give a summary of *jñāna-yoga*, which had been elaborately described in previous chapters.

Everything within the cosmic manifestation is a product of the three modes of material nature. Although such products are perceived by the material senses, they are illusory by nature. Similarly, the conditioned souls' conceptions of "good" and "bad" that are given to such products and activities within the universe are illusory. It is better to avoid condemning or praising anyone, because this confines one to the bodily concept of life and thus negates superior spiritual understanding. The spirit souls pervade the entire universe and their nature is transcendental to mundane duality. By cultivating such an understanding, one can remain detached even while in material existence.

As long as the conditioned soul desires the gratification of his material senses, the bodily conception of life will continue. Although material existence is illusory, like a dream, those attached to fruitive action remain entangled in the cycle of repeated birth and death. All conditions of material existence, such as birth, death, happiness, and distress are experienced by the false ego, and not the eternal soul. By distinguishing between matter and spirit, one can gradually renounce the false sense of bodily identification.

While the material manifestation goes through stages of creation, maintenance, and annihilation, the changeless Absolute Truth remains undisturbed. While manifested, the universe rests in the Absolute Truth, which is all-pervading in time and space. The

Absolute Truth is not transformed, but this cosmic manifestation is made possible by a transformation of the mode of passion.

By the mercy of a bona fide spiritual master, one can understand illusory nature of the material body, and thus distinguish the Absolute Truth from such temporary existence. When a person renounces all desires for sense enjoyment, he can become satisfied in the self alone. Just as the sun is undisturbed by the movement of clouds in the atmosphere, the liberated soul is unaffected by the activities of the material body. Still, when one is a neophyte in the practice of the devotional service of the Lord, one should carefully restrict his contact with the objects of the senses. Until one's determination becomes fixed, one may fall down as a result of obstacles placed before him on the path of spiritual advancement. Still, there is no loss for one who is engaged in devotional service, because in his next life, he will be given a chance to continue his spiritual practice from where he left off. When one is actually liberated from material existence, he will never desire to indulge in insignificant material sense pleasures, knowing that his eternal self is distinct from the illusory material body.

While one is on the path of spiritual realization, if one suffers from disease or other disturbance, he should not neglect to take proper remedial measures. The best means for lust and the other enemies of the mind is meditation on the Supreme Personality of Godhead, especially by the performance of congregational chanting of the Lord's holy names. The false ego can best be conquered by rendering selfless service to the pure devotees of the Lord.

By the practice of yoga, materialistic men hope to keep their body fit for sense gratification, up to the limit of the attainment of mystic powers and an extended duration of life. These achievements have no lasting value, however, because they are in relation to the material body, which is temporary. The devotees of the Lord are therefore uninterested in attaining the mystic perfections of yoga. Instead, they are keen to take shelter at the lotus feet of the Supreme Personality of Godhead, knowing this to be the cause of the eternal cessation of material miseries and engagement in every-blissful devotional service.

TEXT 1

श्रीभगवानुवाच
परस्वभावकर्माणिनप्रशंसेन्नगर्हयेत् ।
विश्वमेकामकंपश्यन्प्रकृत्यापुरुषेणच ॥१॥

śrī-bhagavān uvāca
para-svabhāva-karmāṇi na praśaṁsen na garhayet
viśvam ekāmakaṁ paśyan prakṛtyā puruṣeṇa ca

The Supreme Lord said: One should neither praise nor criticize the nature and activities of others. Rather, one should understand the material world to be working as a combination of material nature and the conditioned souls, and resting in the Absolute Truth.

COMMENTARY

After describing different philosophical systems, Lord Śrī Kṛṣṇa now discusses the philosophy of impersonalism, which preaches that the material creation is false.

What is this material creation? Is it factual or is it false? Does it exist or is it merely an illusion? The answer to all these questions will be given in this chapter. Impersonal philosophers are divided into two categories—*vivartavāda* and *pariṇāmavāda*. The Supreme Lord is both the cause and effect of this universe. If the theory that that the Absolute Truth transforms to become the material universe (*pariṇāmavāda*) is accepted, then it would appear that the Supreme Lord is changeable. On the other hand, those who propagate the philosophy of *vivartavāda* say that the Absolute Truth is unchangeable, and that this material world is false. According to another opinion, since the material nature is the energy of the Absolute Truth, even if it is accepted that the material energy is subject to transformation, the Absolute Truth, being transcendental to material nature, remains unchanged. There is no objection if the followers of *pariṇāmavāda* accept this opinion. Indeed, this is what has been described by the Supreme Lord, who says that He is the ingredient cause of this universe, the Supersoul, and time.

Although there is certainly a distinction between the energetic and the energy, the Supreme Lord, despite manifesting innumerable forms, remains one without a second. Of the two categories of impersonalists, the Supreme Lord approves the second category. In this chapter, the Lord describes this understanding of *vivartavāda* and *pariṇāmavāda*.

The word *asat* is used by the followers of *vivartavāda* to mean "illusion," but it is used by the followers of *pariṇāmavāda* to mean "temporary existence." The *vivartavādīs* say that all activities are false whereas the *pariṇāmavādīs* say that they are temporary. This is the subtle difference between the two groups of impersonalists.

PURPORT

In material existence, we create distinctions between one another due to bodily designations, sometimes praising and sometimes showing disdain. Those who are trying to situate themselves on the transcendental platform, however, should not indulge in such praises and criticisms, knowing that the distinctions between the conditioned souls are simply a creation of the interaction of the three modes of material nature. Those who are impersonalists try to nullify the distinction between the seer, the seen, and the act of seeing, considering the Absolute Truth to be without variegatedness. In this material world, all varieties are manifestations of the interaction of the three modes of material nature, but in the transcendental abode of the Lord, Vaikuṇṭha, there is no existence of the modes of nature. There, the Lord's spiritual energies have manifested a world of spiritual variegatedness. Because of the competition of the three modes of material nature the polluted distinctions between superiority and inferiority predominate. Therefore, the material atmosphere is permeated with praise and condemnation, but in the transcendental abode of Vaikuṇṭha, where there is no influence of the material energy, there are no such distinctions.

TEXT 2

परस्वभावकर्माणि यः प्रशंसति निन्दति ।
स आशु भ्रश्यते स्वार्थादसत्यभिनिवेशतः ॥२॥

para-svabhāva-karmāṇi yaḥ praśaṁsati nindati
sa āśu bhraśyate svārthād asaty abhiniveśataḥ

One who indulges in praising or criticizing others' natures and activities will deviate from his own best interest because of his absorption on the platform of duality.

COMMENTARY

One who glorifies or criticizes others' natures and activities remains absorbed on the temporary, material platform and thus becomes forgetful of the eternal, spiritual reality.

PURPORT

One who becomes habituated to finding fault with others instead of chanting the glories of Lord Hari in the association of devotees will surely exhibit great pride in himself while belittling others. The act of praising and criticizing others falls within the jurisdiction of the interaction of the three modes of material nature. The conditioned souls, being absorbed in duality, have brought about their condition of inauspiciousness. When one pursues his actual self-interest, which is to elevate one to the spiritual platform, he avoids thinking of others in terms of material designations and thus refrains from criticizing or praising others. The activities of this material world are temporary, full of ignorance, and produce misery, and can never be considered constitutional in nature. As long as one maintains the habit of criticizing or praising others in the bodily conception of life, he will never be elevated to the spiritual platform, having deviated from his real self-interest.

TEXT 3

तैजसेनिद्रयापन्नेपिण्डस्थोनष्टचेतनः ।
मायांप्राप्नोतिमृत्युंवातद्वन्नानार्थदृक्पुमान् ॥३॥

taijase nidrayāpanne piṇḍa-stho naṣṭa-cetanaḥ
māyāṁ prāpnoti mṛtyuṁ vā tadvan nānārtha-dṛk pumān

Just as one loses external consciousness when his senses, which are born of the rājasika ahaṅkāra, **are overcome by the illusion of dreaming, or deathlike state of deep sleep, so a person absorbed in material duality must experience illusion and death.**

COMMENTARY

He who thinks in terms of material duality, and thus glorifies or condemns others' natures and activities is deviated from his real self-interest. This verse provides and example to illustrate this point. The senses are produced from false ego in the mode of passion. When the senses are dormant as the living entity sleeps, his mind is plunged into the illusion of dreaming. And when the mind becomes inactive, the living entity loses all external consciousness and remains in a deathlike state of deep sleep. Similarly, one who discriminates according to material designations covers his original consciousness, becoming almost like inert matter.

PURPORT

Being enthusiastically engaged on the bodily platform, the conditioned souls remain indifferent to the service of the Lord as they continue dreaming of themselves as lords of the material nature. Such material absorption is the result of forgetting one's constitutional position as the eternal part and parcel of the Supreme Lord. Although materialistic sense enjoyers endeavor for achieving high positions within this world, they ultimately meet with destruction, under the control of the laws of nature. Being bewildered by false ego, although the conditioned souls are struggling hard for existence while failing to worship the Supreme Personality of Godhead, they become very proud of their temporary designations, thinking themselves to be the lords of all they survey.

TEXT 4

किंभद्रंकिमभद्रंवाद्वैतस्यावस्तुनःकियत् ।
वाचोदिततदनृतमनसाध्यातमेवच ॥४॥

kiṁ bhadraṁ kim abhadraṁ vā dvaitasyāvastunaḥ kiyat
vāceditaṁ tad anṛtaṁ manaṣā dhyātam eva ca

That which the conditioned souls express by their words or meditate upon by their mind is not ultimate truth. Considering this, what is actually good or bad within this illusory world of duality?

COMMENTARY

In these verses, the Lord elaborately describes how it is foolish to glorify or criticize material conditions, because anything seen as not related to the Supreme Lord is an illusion. The holy names, forms, abode, and devotees of the Supreme Lord are all transcendental, and thus as good as Him. All dualities of this world—whether spoken by material words or meditated upon by the material mind—are illusory.

The word *asat* means "that which has no factual existence." So, praise and criticism of objects that are seen to be separate from the Supreme Lord is itself an activity of illusion. On the other hand, anything seen in relation to the Supreme Lord is to be considered transcendental. The Supreme Lord is eternal, full of knowledge, unlimited, and full of bliss. He is the reservoir of all transcendental pleasure. He has many transcendental names, such as Gopāla, and these names are fully spiritual. Those who glorify the Supreme Lord are on the path to liberation. Even before the devotee relinquishes his material body, he is awarded a spiritual body by the mercy of the Lord. The abode of the Lord is transcendental, and His associates are also transcendental. Anything that is not in relation to the Lord is mundane, illusory, and fit to be rejected.

PURPORT

The Absolute Truth is reflected in the objects manifested by material nature. However, one should know that a mere shadow or reflection of the Absolute Truth, as found in material objects, cannot bring about genuine auspiciousness. Sometimes the mind accepts something as favorable and sometimes it accepts the same thing as unfavorable. Perverted existence cannot be accepted as ultimate reality, although it may appear similar. All actions performed in the perverted reflection of material existence, such as speaking and meditating, are self-centered in nature, being nourished by the false ego. Those who are absorbed in thought of temporary material objects, and those who take pleasure in discussing the temporary manifestations of matter, are averse to the service of the Absolute Personality of Godhead, although they pose as being very expert in discriminating between that which is seemingly good and that which is apparently bad. When the eternal constitutional activities of the spirit soul are thus dormant, the mind assumes the role as the master. The mind's false ego considers itself as the enjoyer and thus becomes subjected to happiness and distress while interacting with the sense objects of form, taste, smell, touch, and sound, with the help of the senses. When such sense enjoyers experience frustration, they imagine themselves as renouncing sense gratification while remaining engaged in propagating the philosophy of impersonalism. While such people remain deviated from the path of devotional service because of their materialistic mentality, they attribute mundane abomination to the Supreme Absolute Truth, having no understanding of the spiritual energies—*hlādinī*, *sandhinī*, and *samvit*. Being impersonalists, they consider the temporary material manifestation as false, and the eternal kingdom of God as a similar mundane existence. Those who are conversant with the truth know that it is unreasonable to equate this temporary cosmic manifestation with the eternal abode of the Lord.

TEXT 5

छायाप्रत्याह्वयाभासाह्यसन्तोऽप्यर्थकारिणः ।
एवंदेहादयोभावायच्छन्त्यामृत्युतोभयम् ॥५॥

chāyā-pratyāhvayābhāsā hy asanto 'py artha-kāriṇaḥ
evaṁ dehādayo bhāvā yacchanty ā-mṛtyuto bhayam

Although shadows, echoes, and the acceptance of a seashell as silver are only illusory reflections of real things, such reflections do cause meaningful perception. In the same way, although the identification of the conditioned soul with his material body and mind is illusory, this identification creates fear within him, right up to the time of death.

COMMENTARY

If temporary material objects are not reality, then how can pots and pitchers be of use? The answer is that, just as a shadow, echo, reflection, or the acceptance of a seashell as silver produces an emotional response, although illusory, so material objects, although temporary and illusory, are still considered as useful by the conditioned soul. Although the material body is temporary and illusory, it creates fear of material existence for the living entities, up until the time of death.

PURPORT

A reflection, shadow, and echo, and the mistake of accepting a seashell as silver are illusory existences. Although they resemble the objects they imitate, they are distinct from them. The living entities' conditional state is a temporary and illusory manifestation of reality. Nondevotees, being bereft of the service of the Lord's lotus feet, which award fearlessness, experience fear, illusion, lamentation, and so forth, in relation to illusory material manifestations. Forgetfulness of one's constitutional position makes one identify with his gross and subtle bodies, which are temporary and thus subject to annihilation, causing great fear and anxiety.

TEXT 6-7

अत्मैवतदिदंविश्वंसृज्यतेसृजतिप्रभुः ।
त्रायतेत्रातिविश्वात्माह्रियतेहरतीश्वरः ॥६॥
तस्मान्नह्यात्मनोऽन्यस्मादन्योभावोनिरूपितः ।
निरूपितेऽयंत्रिविधानिर्मूलभातिरात्मनि ।
इदंगुणमयांविद्धित्रिविधंमाययाकृतम् ॥७॥

atmaiva tad idaṁ viśvaṁ sṛjyate sṛjati prabhuḥ
trāyate trāti viśvātmā hriyate haratīśvaraḥ

tasmān na hy ātmano 'nyasmād anyo bhāvo nirūpitaḥ
nirūpite 'yaṁ tri-vidhā nirmūla bhātir ātmani
idaṁ guṇa-mayaṁ viddhi tri-vidhaṁ māyayā kṛtam

The Supersoul is the supreme controller and creator of this world, and thus He is also that which is created. Thus, the Soul of all existence maintains and is also maintained, withdraws and is also withdrawn. No entity should be ascertained as being separate from Him, the Supreme Soul, who nonetheless remains distinct from everything. When the truth has been ascertained in this manner, it should be understood that the three conditions of material existence, *adhyātmika, adhidaivika,* and *adhibautika,* are illusory, being manifestations of *maya*.

COMMENTARY

The *Vedas* have ascertained that the material creation is a manifestation of the separated energy of the Supreme Lord. How then can it be considered false? The answer is given here: "The Supreme Lord is both the cause and effect. Therefore, the material manifestation is not separate from Him. He maintains the entire universe in His form as Paramātmā. Nothing seen as without relationship with the Supersoul can be accepted as reality. The three features of material existence—*adhyātmika*, *adhidaivika*, and *adhibautika*— are thus manifestations of illusion." If the Supersoul is the actual form of the universe, then from where did these three features come? The answer is herein given: "If there is no original, then how can there be an imitation? The cosmic manifestation is a creation of the inconceivable energy of the Lord. This is the doctrine of the followers of *pariṇāmavāda*. The followers of *vivartavāda* say that these three features are illusions born of ignorance."

PURPORT

The material world has emanated from the energy of the Supreme Lord, it is maintained by Him for some time, and then it again merges within Him. The temporary cosmic manifestation is meant for the inhabitation of those who are averse to the service of the Supreme Lord. The Lord divides the time factor and empowers the material energy, which possesses the power to cover the consciousness of the living entities, and to throw them into the darkest regions of nescience. The external energy, which manifests the material world, has no existence separate from the Supreme Lord, whose nature is eternal, full of knowledge, and full of bliss. He is very dear to His devotees. The objects of the senses have been created for the enjoyment of those who have turned their backs on the Supreme Lord. The great variety of conditions that have manifested within material existence are designed to capture the conditioned souls, whose only engagement is the gratification of their senses. The abominable conditions of birth, death, old age, and disease are absent in the eternal abode of the Lord, Vaikuṇṭha, or Goloka. Thus, there is a gulf of difference between the manifestations of the internal and external potencies. All the objects of the material world are products of the three modes of material nature, which are manifested from the external energy of the Lord. Just as an echo is similar to the original sound it mirrors, the activities of the material world bear some resemblance to those enacted in the eternal abode of the Lord. Materialistic people generally consider the form of the Lord to be a manifestation of the modes of material nature, and such a conception is a product of the darkness of nescience. The Supreme Personality of Godhead is pure, transcendental existence, devoid of all kinds of abomination that is experienced in this world. The Lord is unlimited and absolute.

TEXT 8

एतद्विद्वान्मदुदितंज्ञानविज्ञाननैपुणम् ।
ननिन्दतिनचस्तौतिलोकेचरतिसूर्यवत् ॥८॥

etad vidvān mad-uditaṁ jñāna-vijñāna-naipuṇam
na nindati na ca stauti loke carati sūrya-vat

One who has become firmly fixed in the understanding that I have imparted, and its practical application, will not be concerned with honor or dishonor. Like the sun, he wanders unimpeded throughout the world.

COMMENTARY

After realizing this knowledge and its application, as instructed by the Supreme Lord, learned devotees treat everyone equally, like the sun, which distributes its heat and light to all without discrimination.

PURPORT

The living entities are eternally parts and parcels of the Supreme Lord, and thus they are by nature full of knowledge. However, involvement in mundane activities, which naturally involves praising and criticizing others, covers one's pure and original consciousness. Just as a devotee should not be attached to anything material, so he should also not be hateful of anything. He should simply accept everything favorable for the service of the Lord and reject everything that is unfavorable, as directed by the spiritual master.

TEXT 9

प्रत्यक्षेणानुमानेननिगमेनात्मसंविदा ।
आद्यन्तवदसज्ज्ञात्वानिःसङ्गोविचरेदिह ॥९॥

pratyakṣeṇānumānena nigamenātma-saṁvidā
ādy-antavad asaj jñātvā niḥsaṅgo vicared iha

By means of sensual perception, reason and logic, the evidence of the scriptures, and one's own understanding, one should know that this world has a beginning and an end and thus has no ultimate reality. Keeping this always in mind, one should live in this world without attachment.

COMMENTARY

Anything that has a beginning also has an end. Through direct perception, one can see the beginning and end of material objects, such as clay cooking pots. Through deduction, one can conclude that there is a beginning and an end to this visible world.

From the Vedic statements, one can hear about the beginning and end of the material elements, such as the sky, and by means of one's personal realization, one can understand that the cosmic manifestation is temporarily manifested by the Lord as a concession for the conditioned souls, who desire material enjoyment.

PURPORT

A self-realized soul can understand through direct perception, deduction, and the evidence of the transcendental sound vibration, that this material world is always changing, and has a beginning and an end. A realized soul could never accept this world as eternally existent and unchanging, knowing it to be a transformation of the absolute truth. Transformable nature is distinct from eternal nature. The *Vedas* inform us that the cosmic manifestation is a transformation of the Lord's illusory energy, and therefore temporary. Only those who have cultivated spiritual knowledge, which is the fruit of their practice of yoga and meditation, can live in this world without attachment, having realized its temporary nature by means of direct perception, deduction, and scriptural evidence. The word *niḥsaṅga*, however, does not indicate that such a person gives up the association of devotees and the worship of the Supreme Personality of Godhead.

TEXT 10

श्रीउद्धव उवाच
नैवात्मनोनदेहस्यसंसृतिर्द्रष्टृदृश्ययोः ।
अनात्मस्वदृशोरीशकस्यस्यादुपलभ्यते ॥१०॥

śrī-uddhava uvāca
naivātmano na dehasya saṁsṛtir draṣṭṛ-dṛśyayoḥ
anātma-sva-dṛśor īśa kasya syād upalabhyate

Śrī Uddhava said: My dear Lord, it cannot be that this material existence is the experience of either the soul, who is the seer, or the body, which is seen. On the one hand, the spirit soul is innately endowed with perfect knowledge, and on the other hand, the material body is not a conscious entity. To whom, then, does this experience of material existence pertain?

COMMENTARY

Śrī Uddhava said: "The living entity is a pure spirit soul, full of knowledge and bliss, whereas the material body is a machine without consciousness. Who or what is actually experiencing the ignorance of material existence?" The conscious experience of material life cannot be denied, and thus Uddhava asks Lord Kṛṣṇa this question to elicit a more precise understanding of the process by which illusion occurs. Although this material creation is temporary, as long as it exists, who is it that experiences happiness and distress? The material body is a product of matter and therefore inert by nature, so that it cannot feel material happiness and distress. The spirit soul is by nature full of knowledge. Therefore, how could he lose such constitutional knowledge" How has the spirit soul been placed into illusion?

PURPORT

Inert matter cannot see, and the soul, being fully spiritual, has nothing to do with matter. How then can these two have a relationship as the seer and the seen?

TEXT 11

आत्माव्ययोऽगुणःशुद्धःस्वयंज्योतिरनावृतः ।
अग्निवद्दारुवदचिद्देहःकस्येहसंसृतिः ॥११॥

ātmāvyayo 'guṇaḥ śuddhaḥ svayaṁ-jyotir anāvṛtaḥ
Agni-vad dāru-vad acid dehaḥ kasyeha saṁsṛtiḥ

The spirit soul is transcendental, eternal, pure, self-illuminating, and unaffected by material conditions. It is like fire, whereas the material body is dead matter, like firewood. So, in this world, who is it that actually experiences material existence?

COMMENTARY

The spirit soul is imperishable, transcendental, pure, self-illuminating, full of knowledge, and unaffected by material conditions, being the superior energy of the Supreme Lord. In this verse, the example of wood and fire is given. Fire is self-illuminating and wood is illuminating only when it is associated with fire. The material body is dead matter, like wood, and the spirit soul is self-illuminating, like fire. Fire exists independently of wood and wood cannot itself illuminate. The soul exists beyond matter and matter itself is devoid of consciousness. So, who or what actually experiences the happiness and distress of material existence?

TEXT 12

श्रीभगवानूवाच
यावद्देहेन्द्रियप्राणैरात्मनःसन्निकर्षणम् ।
संसारःफलवांस्तावदपार्थोऽप्यविवेकिनः ॥१२॥

śrī-bhagavān uvāca
yāvad dehendriya-prāṇair ātmanaḥ sannikarṣaṇam
saṁsāraḥ phalavāṁs tāvad apārtho 'py avivekinaḥ

The Supreme Personality of Godhead said: As long as the ignorant spirit soul maintains his relationship with the material body, senses, and life air, his illusory material existence will continue to flourish, although it is actually meaningless.

COMMENTARY

Ignorance is the cause of the living entities' bondage to material existence. This is being explained in this and the following verses. One's material existence continues to flourish as long as the soul maintains his relationship with its temporary material products. How does a living entity establish a relationship with a temporary material body? It is simply due to ignorance.

PURPORT

As long as the spirit soul remains attracted to his material body, senses, and life air, the material world appears to be a very fruitful place, even though it is actually insignificant. The cultivation of knowledge that is based upon ignorance is not factual. Because such knowledge is based on the bodily concept of life, it is faulty and therefore useless.

TEXT 13

अर्थेह्यविद्यमानेऽपिसंसृतिर्ननिवर्तते ।
ध्यायतोविषयानस्यस्वप्नेऽनर्थागमोयथा ॥१३॥

arthe hy avidyamāne 'pi saṁsṛtir na nivartate
dhyāyato viṣayān asya svapne 'narthāgamo yathā

The living entity is transcendental to material existence, but because of his mentality of lording it over material nature, his material existence continues, so that, just as in a dream, he is affected by all sorts of inconveniences.

COMMENTARY

If the material body is an illusory manifestation of the external energy of the Lord, then how did the pure spirit soul become attached to it? Even though the objects of this material world are not factual, they continue to affect the conditioned souls. Such a condition is just like a dream, wherein the dreaming person sees many things that actually have no real existence and yet, because of them, he suffers. When one becomes frightened by seeing a snake or tiger in a dream, such a feeling is certainly based on illusion.

PURPORT

As a sleeping person accepts the objects seen in dreams as reality, so until one attains the stage of self-realization, his propensity for material enjoyment will continue.

TEXT 14

यथाह्यप्रतिबुद्धस्यप्रस्वापोबह्वनर्थभृत् ।
स एवप्रतिबुद्धस्यनवैमोहायकल्पते ॥१४॥

yathā hy apratibuddhasya prasvāpo bahv-anartha-bhṛt
sa eva pratibuddhasya na vai mohāya kalpate

While dreaming, a person may experience many undesirable things, but upon awakening, he is no longer troubled by such dreams, even though he may remember them.

COMMENTARY

A dream produces varieties of undesirable circumstances, but after awakening, one ceases to be troubled by them because of understanding the dream's illusory nature.

PURPORT

A dreaming person takes his experiences to be factual, although they are illusory. After waking up, however, one is no longer affected by whatever he might have experienced in his dreams. In the same way, a self-realized soul can understand that this visible world is illusory, and therefore insignificant. When one understands the nature of reality, the temporary and illusory experiences of material existence seem insubstantial.

TEXT 15

शोकहर्षभयक्रोधलोभमोहस्पृहादयः ।
अहङ्कारस्यदृश्यन्तेजन्ममृत्युश्चनात्मनः ॥१५॥

śoka-harṣa-bhaya-krodha-lobha-moha-spṛhādayaḥ
ahaṅkārasya dṛśyante janma-mṛtyuś ca nātmanaḥ

Lamentation, jubilation, fear, anger, greed, delusion, and hankering, and so on, are experiences of the false ego and not of the pure soul.

COMMENTARY

Feelings, such as lamentation and fear, are not experiences of the soul. Such feelings are due to the false ego, which is the pure soul's illusory identification with the subtle material mind and the gross material body. A self-realized person knows that whatever emotions are experienced on the material platform have no relation to the pure soul, whose eternal mood is engagement in the devotional service of the Supreme Lord.

PURPORT

As a result of his illusory identification with the gross body and subtle mind, the conditioned soul feels lamentation for things lost, jubilation over things gained, fear of impending danger, anger at the frustration of his desires, and greed for sense gratification. Being bewildered by such false attractions and aversions, the conditioned soul must accept further material bodies, thus forcing him to undergo repeated births and deaths. However, a self-realized soul considers all such experiences as illusory.

TEXT 16

देहेन्द्रियप्राणमनोऽभिमानोजीवोऽन्तरात्मागुणकर्ममूर्तिः ।
सूत्रंमहानित्युरुधेवगीतःसंसार आधावतिकालतन्त्रः ॥१६॥

dehendriya-prāṇa-mano-'bhimāno jīvo 'ntar-ātmā guṇa-karma-mūrtiḥ
sūtraṁ mahān ity urudheva gītāḥ saṁsāra ādhāvati kāla-tantraḥ

The conditioned soul is awarded a form according to his situation under the modes of nature and his work, and due to ignorance, he identifies with his body and mind. In this way, he receives material designations under the strict control of supreme time, and is thus forced to travel within this material world.

COMMENTARY

One might question: "If lamentation, hankering, happiness and distress, and so on are the nature of the false ego and not of the spirit soul, why does the spirit soul accept such a nature and suffer? Why would anyone accept another's nature and bring about his own suffering?" In this verse, the answer is given: The living entity never acts independently. The conditioned souls have been enticed by the false ego to become enjoyers of this material world. After accepting the false ego, the living entity runs after material sense gratification, being influenced by the three modes of material nature, under the control of time, which represents the Supreme Lord. It is for this reason that the living entity suffers by false identification, and thus accepts material bodies repeatedly in the cycle of birth and death.

PURPORT

There are two classes of living entities—those that are eternally conditioned and those that are eternally liberated. The eternally liberated associates of the Lord reside in His supreme abode, Vaikuṇṭha, which is a manifestation of the spiritual potency. There, the liberated souls are eternally engaged in the blissful service of the Supreme Lord, being situated in their original, transcendental forms. Being part and parcel of Kṛṣṇa, they naturally remain as if members of His family. The eternally conditioned souls wander about within this material world, which is under the control of time. Posing themselves as sense enjoyers, they accept the material body and mind, so that they can interact with the objects of the senses, and all these are transformations of the *mahat-tattva.*

TEXT 17

अमूलमेतद्बहुरूपरूपितंमनोवचःप्राणशरीरकर्म ।
ज्ञानासिनोपासनयाशितेनच्छित्त्वामुनिर्गांविचरत्यतृष्णः ॥१७॥

amūlam etad bahu-rūpa-rūpitaṁ mano-vacaḥ-prāṇa-śarīra-karma
jñānāsinopāsanayā śitena cchittvā munir gāṁ vicaraty atṛṣṇaḥ

Although the false ego has no factual basis in reality, it is perceived by the conditioned soul in many forms—as the functions of the mind, speech, life air, and bodily faculties. With the sharpened sword of transcendental knowledge, received from the bona fide spiritual master, one who is sober should cut off this false identification and live within this world free from material attachment.

COMMENTARY

How is it possible to give up the false egoistic conception of life, which is actually illusory? The false ego manifests in many forms, such as the activities of the mind, speech, life air, and senses. One must cut off one's attachment to the false ego with the sharpened weapon of knowledge, which is received from the spiritual master, by engagement in the devotional service of the Supreme Lord. In this way, one can live within this world without attachment.

PURPORT

Sober devotees, who are not intoxicated by desires for material enjoyment, live within this world as mendicants by cutting off the illusory false ego and its products—the body, mind, speech, and life air. The conditioned souls, who are averse to the service of Lord Hari, misuse their valuable human form of life to become either whimsical sense enjoyers or dry renouncers. The heart of the conditioned soul thus becomes covered by the dust of sense gratification, or filled with the broom of renunciation. On the strength of the association of saintly persons, and by their transcendental instructions, one can gradually be relieved of both kinds of mundane abomination, thus losing all interest in mundane sense gratification and impersonal liberation.

TEXT 18

ज्ञानंविवेकोनिगमस्तपश्चप्रत्यक्षमैतिह्यमथानुमानम् ।
आद्यन्तयोरस्ययदेवकेवलंकालश्चहेतुश्चतदेवमध्ये ॥१८॥

jñānaṁ viveko nigamas tapaś ca pratyakṣam aitihyam athānumānam
ādy-antayor asya yad eva kevalaṁ kālaś ca hetuś ca tad eva madhye

Real spiritual knowledge is based on the discrimination between spirit and matter, and it is cultivated by scriptural evidence, austerity, direct perception, and logical inference. The Supreme Lord exists alone before the material creation and after its annihilation. He is the cause of all causes and it is He who assumes the form of time. Even in the middle period of universal maintenance, the Supreme Lord alone is the only reality.

COMMENTARY

Actual knowledge refers to that which is gained by the power of discrimination between matter and spirit. The means for cultivating this knowledge are hearing from the *Vedas*, one's own realizations, the instructions of the great sages of the past, and logical inference. Such knowledge culminates in the realization of the Supreme Brahman, who alone existed before the creation of the universe, who will alone exist after the destruction of the universe, and who is the actual reality during the interim period of universal maintenance.

PURPORT

Direct perception, logical deduction, historical evidence, austerity, speech, wisdom, and time, are all situated in the Absolute Truth, who alone exists before the creation, after the annihilation, and during the interim period of maintenance. Knowledge of the Supreme Lord includes knowledge of Brahman and Paramātmā and thus it is perfect. Paramātmā is the plenary portion of the Supreme Lord and Brahman is His bodily effulgence.

TEXT 19

यथाहिरण्यंस्वकृतंपुरस्तात्पश्चाच्चसर्वस्यहिरणमचास्य ।
तदेवमध्येव्यवहार्यमाणंनानापदेशैरहमस्यतद्वत् ॥१९॥

yathā hiraṇyaṁ sv-akṛtaṁ purastāt paścāc ca sarvasya hiraṇ-mayasya
tad eva madhye vyavahāryamāṇaṁ nānāpadeśair aham asya tadvat

Gold is present before the manufacture of gold bangles, earrings, and so on; and gold remains after the destruction of these products. Thus, gold alone is the essential reality while it is being utilized under various designations. Similarly, I alone exist before the creation of this universe, after its destruction, and during its period of maintenance.

COMMENTARY

Golden bangles and earrings are nothing but gold. Before and after their manufacture, they existed as gold, and for as long as they remain, they are simply gold. Similarly, the Supreme Lord alone exists before the creation, He alone exists after its destruction, and in the interim, whatever is manifested, is actually Him alone.

PURPORT

Just as the influence of time transforms manufactured objects such as earrings, back to their original state as the ingredient, gold, similarly, the Supreme Lord directs His energy to create a seeming distinction between the created universe and Himself, although after annihilation, only He remains. The forms of the created objects are eternal and factual but because the material manifestations are mere reflections of these eternal objects, they are illusory.

TEXT 20

विज्ञानमेतत्त्रियवस्थमङ्गगुणत्रयंकारणकर्यकर्तृ ।
समन्वयेनव्यतिरेकतश्चयेनैवतुर्येणतदेवसत्यम् ॥२०॥

vijñānam etat triy-avastham aṅgaguṇa-trayaṁ kāraṇa-karya-kartṛ
samanvayena vyatirekataś ca yenaiva turyeṇa tad eva satyam

O Uddhava, the mind manifests in three phases of consciousness—wakefulness, sleep and deep sleep—which are products of the three modes of material nature. The mind further appears in three different roles—*ādhyātmika, ādhibhautika,* and *ādhidaivika*—which are the perceiver, the perceived, and the regulator of perception. However, it is the fourth factor, existing separately from all this, that alone constitutes the Absolute Truth.

COMMENTARY

The word *vijñāna* in this verse indicates the three states of existence—wakefulness, dreaming, and deep sleep, which are products of the three modes of material nature. The threefold manifestation of *ādhibhautika, ādhidaivika,* and *ādhyātmika,* are also the result of the interactions of the three material modes, as are the three planetary systems. However, the Absolute Truth is fully transcendental to the modes of material nature, and it is under His subordination that everything becomes manifest. Vedic evidence is found in this regard:

tam eva bhāntam anu bhāti sarvaṁ
tasya bhāsā sarvam idaṁ vibhāti

It is by the reflection of the spiritual sky's effulgence that everything else gives light, and thus through its radiance, this entire universe becomes luminous. (*Śvetāśvatara Upaniṣads* 6.14)

cakṣuṣaś cakṣur uta śrotrasya śrotram
annasyānnaṁ manaso ye mano viduḥ.

The Supreme Truth is understood to be the life air sustaining everyone's life air, the vision of everyone's eyes, the hearing power of the ear, and the sustenance of food itself. (*Bṛhad-āraṇyaka Upaniṣad* 4.4.18)

PURPORT

There are two causes—the immediate cause and the ingredient cause. All actions take place by the combination of these two. When the living entities become conditioned by matter, they directly and indirectly take shelter of the three material modes of goodness, passion and ignorance, which are the cause of three states of existence—

wakefulness, dreaming, and deep sleep. The words "reality" and "illusion" have been used to indicate the eternal abode of the Lord, Vaikuṇṭha, and the temporary material world, respectively.

TEXT 21

नयत्पुरस्तादुतयन्नपश्चान्मध्येचतन्नव्यपदेशमात्रम् ।
भूतंप्रसिद्धंचपरेणयद्यत्तदेवतत्स्यादितिमेमनीषा ॥२१॥

na yat purastād uta yan na paścān madhye ca tan na vyapadeśa-mātram
bhūtaṁ prasiddhaṁ ca pareṇa yad yat tad eva tat syād iti me manīṣā

That which did not exist before creation and will not exist after annihilation has no real existence during the period of its manifestation, but is only a superficial designation. In My opinion, whatever is produced from something else is nothing more than that thing.

COMMENTARY

Although the temporary forms manifested by the material nature are illusory, the material nature itself is not false, being a manifestation of the Lord's potency. The material nature is thus nondifferent from the Lord, although the temporary designations of the conditioned souls are illusion. Everything should be properly understood in terms of the Personality of Godhead, who is the essential reality of the cosmic manifestation.

PURPORT

The objects of material enjoyment did not exist in the beginning, will not exist at the end, and remain manifest only for a brief period during the interim. This material world is a creation of cause and effect and the original cause is the Supreme Personality of Godhead. Thus, it can only be concluded that everything in existence is nothing but the Supreme Lord, at any phase of its manifestation. The energy of the Lord is simultaneously one with and different from the Lord, just as the heat and light emanating from the sun are simultaneously one with and distinct from the sun. In the ultimate issue, however, it must be concluded that everything is actually the Supreme Lord, who is one without a second.

There is a tendency for the conditioned soul to consider the temporary objects of this world as ultimate reality. However, when one who is in ignorance gradually realizes that such temporary manifestations are actually unwanted impositions upon the pure soul, he can renounce his false position as an enjoyer of the material nature and become inclined toward the service of the Supreme Personality of Godhead. When one comes to the platform of devotional service, there is no longer a need to declare that the material world is false, or separate from the Supreme Lord.

TEXT 22

अविद्यमानोऽप्यवभासतेयोवैकारिकोराजससर्ग एसः ।
ब्रह्मस्वयंज्योतिरतोविभातिब्रह्मेन्द्रियार्थात्मविकारचित्रम् ॥२२॥

avidyamāno 'py avabhāsate yo vaikāriko rājasa-sarga esaḥ
brahma svayaṁ jyotir ato vibhāti brahmendriyārthātma-vikāra-citram

Although thus not existing as an eternal reality, this cosmic manifestation, which is a transformation of the mode of passion, appears to be real because it is the self-manifested, self-luminous Absolute Truth that has exhibited Himself in the form of the material senses, sense objects, mind, and elements.

COMMENTARY

That this material world is nondifferent from the Supreme Lord is being explained in this verse. All visible objects, and their transformations, are born from the *mahat-tattva*, or the total material nature. By agītāting the dormant material nature, the Lord creates through the agency of the mode of passion. The Supreme Personality of Godhead is thus the cause of all causes. Indeed, it is because the senses, sense objects, mind, five material elements, and all other manifestations in this world are expansions of the energy of the Absolute Truth that they appear to be real.

PURPORT

The Supreme Brahman is unchanging and thus the material nature is not a transformation of His primordial personality, but rather, a transformation of His energy. Simply because the external energy of the Lord manifests material variegatedness, one should not hastily conclude that the spiritual realm is without variety. Spiritual variegatedness is a fact and the material varieties that we experience are simply reflections of the original objects. The material variegatedness is temporarily manifest by the action of the mode of passion and later on, is dissolved by the mode of ignorance. While such creation and annihilation repeatedly takes place within the material nature, the supreme abode of the Lord, Vaikuṇṭha, remains unaffected.

TEXT 23

एवंस्फुतंब्रह्मविवेकहेतुभिःपरापवादेनविशारदेन ।
छित्त्वात्मसन्देहमुपारमेतस्वानन्दतुष्टोऽखिलकामुकेभ्यः ॥२३॥

evaṁ sphutaṁ brahma-viveka-hetubhiḥ parāpavādena viśāradena
chittvātma-sandeham upārameta svānanda-tuṣṭo 'khila-kāmukebhyaḥ

Thus clearly understanding, by means of discrimination, the position of the Absolute Truth, one should give up his false identification with matter and thus remove all doubts regarding his identity. One should remain satisfied with the soul's inherent ecstasy on the spiritual platform and carefully avoid engaging in useless acts of mundane sense enjoyment.

COMMENTARY

To consider the body as the self is an illusion. One should remove this illusion by understanding the unique and transcendental position of the Absolute Truth. There are various methods for acquiring knowledge of the Absolute Truth. A person of discrimination should remove all misgivings regarding the self and remain satisfied in his natural ecstasy, while keeping sense gratification at a distance.

PURPORT

It is imperative for one who desires to realize his eternal self to detach himself from the activities of sense gratification beyond the bare necessities of the body. One who understands that the Supreme Lord is the cause of all causes can accept that the objects of the senses are not actually meant for his personal enjoyment. Taking the opposite stance, when one tries to engage everything at his disposal in the service of the master of the senses, his doubts are destroyed as he rises to the platform of satisfaction in the self. This material world is not a fit place for a liberated soul. The only duty of the liberated soul is service to the transcendental Cupid, the Supreme Personality of Godhead.

TEXT 24

नात्मा वपुःपार्थिवमिन्द्रियाणिदेवाह्यसुर्वायुर्जलम्हुताशः ।
मनोऽन्नमात्रंधिषणाचसत्त्वमहङ्कृतिःखंक्षितिरर्थसाम्यम् ॥२४॥

nātmā vapuḥ pārthivam indriyāṇi devā hy asur vāyur jalam hutāśaḥ
mano 'nna-mātraṁ dhiṣaṇā ca sattvam ahaṅkṛtiḥ khaṁ kṣitir artha-sāmyam

The material body, which is predominantly made of earth, is not the true self—nor are the senses, their presiding demigods, the air of life, the external air, water, fire, or one's mind. All these are simply matter. Similarly, neither one's intelligence, material consciousness, ego, ether, the objects of sense perception, nor even the primeval state of material equilibrium can be considered the actual identity of the soul.

COMMENTARY

This material body is not the self. Indeed, it is simply a product of matter, just like a pot. Similarly, the senses, their controlling deities, the mind, life air, intelligence, heart, and false ego are not the identity of the soul, because they depend on food grains. The five gross material elements—earth, water, fire, air, and ether—the five sense objects—sound, form, taste, smell, and touch—do not pertain to the soul because they are all products of matter.

PURPORT

The material body, senses, demigods, life air, mind, intelligence, and false ego are all gross and subtle products of matter and thus are distinct from the conscious self. It is only due to ignorance that one identifies the eternal spirit soul with any of these temporary manifestations of matter.

TEXT 25

समाहितैःकःकरणैर्गुणात्मभिर्गुणोभवेन्मत्सुविविक्तधाम्नः ।
विक्षिप्यमाणैरुतकिंनुदूषणंघनैरुपेतैर्विगतैरवेःकिम् ॥२५॥

samāhitaiḥ kaḥ karaṇair guṇātmabhir guṇo bhaven mat-suvivikta-dhāmnaḥ
vikṣipyamāṇair uta kiṁ nu dūṣaṇaṁ ghanair upetair vigatai raveḥ kim

For one who has properly realized My personal identity as the Supreme Personality of Godhead, what credit is there if his senses, which are products of the modes of nature, are perfectly concentrated in meditation, and what blame is incurred if his senses happen to become agitated? What does it mean to the sun when the clouds come and go in the sky?

COMMENTARY

The pure devotees of the Lord are not to be criticized or praised simply on the basis of a materialist's perception of the activities of their senses. The senses of pure devotees are fully engaged in the service of the Lord and their minds are absorbed in meditation upon Him. Such exalted devotees never deviate from their Kṛṣṇa consciousness, even if their senses are sometimes agitated.

PURPORT

When it is cloudy so that we cannot see the sun, it is not that the sun is covered—it is our imperfect eyes that are covered. Similarly, it may appear to the vision of a materialistic person that the activities of a liberated devotee of the Lord are performed under the influence of the three modes of material nature, and thus faulty. However, the fact is that the Supreme Lord, His dedicated servants, and the process of devotional service cannot be hampered by material conditions because they are under the jurisdiction of the Lord's internal potency.

TEXT 26

यथानभोवाय्वनलाम्बुभूगुणैर्गतागतैर्वर्तुगुणैर्नसज्जते ।
तथाक्षरंसत्त्वरजस्तमोमलैरहंमतेःसंसृतिहेतुभिःपरम् ॥२६॥

yathā nabho vāyv-analāmbu-bhū-guṇair gatāgatair vartu-guṇair na sajjate
tathākṣaraṁ sattva-rajas-tamo-malair ahaṁ-mateḥ saṁsṛti-hetubhiḥ param

The sky is never affected by the various qualities of the air, fire, water, and earth that pass through it, as well as such qualities as heat and cold, which continually come and go with the seasons. Similarly, the Supreme Absolute Truth is never tinged by the contaminations of the modes of goodness, passion, and ignorance, which cause the transformations of false ego.

COMMENTARY

A liberated soul is not to be judged in terms of so-called material good qualities or faults. The example of the sky is given in this regard. The sky never mixes with anything. It is not dried by the air, burnt by fire, covered by dust, or influenced by the seasons, such as the heat of the summer or the cold of winter. Similarly, the Supreme Lord is never contaminated by the three material modes of nature.

PURPORT

The Absolute Truth is unchanging and unaffected by material conditions, as is the liberated soul. Although the air blows everywhere and the elements of fire, earth, and water contact the sky, it never mixes with any of them The unlimited Supreme Lord is the master of material nature, whereas the infinitesimal living entities are covered by *maya*.

TEXT 27

तथापिसङ्गःपरिवर्जनीयोगुणेषुमायारचितेषुतावत् ।
मद्भक्तियोगेनदृढेनयावद्रजोनिरस्येतमनःकषायः ॥२७॥

tathāpi saṅgaḥ parivarjanīyo guṇeṣu māyā-raciteṣu tāvat
mad-bhakti-yogena dṛḍhena yāvad rajo nirasyeta manaḥ-kaṣāyaḥ

Still, until one has completely eliminated from his mind all material contamination, by undivided engagement in My devotional service, one must very carefully avoid associating with the modes of material nature, which are products of My illusory energy.

COMMENTARY

A neophyte *jñānī* should not whimsically try to imitate the behavior of a liberated soul. This warning is given in this and the next verses. The word *rajo* means "attachment." The word *guṇeṣu* means "in material objects."

PURPORT

Although the material nature is nondifferent from the Supreme Lord, one who has yet to conquer material desire should not unrestrictedly associate with the objects of the senses, declaring them to be nondifferent from the Lord. One who is aspiring to be Kṛṣṇa conscious should not loosely associate with women, claiming them to be nondifferent from the Personality of Godhead, for by such imitation of the most advanced devotees, one will simply remain on the platform of material sense gratification. A neophyte devotee who presumes himself to be liberated is impelled by the mode of passion to become falsely proud of his position. As a result, he neglects the actual process of devotional service to the Lord. The conclusion is that devotees should always carefully avoid bad association. If one who is not firmly fixed in devotional service claims to be a liberated soul, he should be considered a pseudo devotee who is driven by the mode of passion. Pseudo devotees gradually become self-worshipers. This is the meaning of *sahajiya*, or one who takes things very cheaply.

TEXT 28

यथामयोऽसाधुचिकित्सितोनृणांपुनःपुनःसन्तुदतिप्ररोहन् ।
एवंमनोऽपक्वकषायकर्मकुयोगिनंविध्यतिसर्वसङ्गम् ॥२८॥

yathāmayo 'sādhu cikitsito nṛṇāṁ punaḥ punaḥ santudati prarohan
evaṁ mano 'pakva-kaṣāya-karma kuyoginaṁ vidhyati sarva-saṅgam

Just as a disease that is not treated repeatedly recurs, causing one great distress, if the mind is not purified of all material contamination, then it will remain attached to material things and repeatedly torment the imperfect yogī.

COMMENTARY

The conditional state of material existence is considered to be diseased condition of life which requires treatment by the expert physician, the bona fide spiritual master. The disease of the heart is material attachment and as long as this condition remains, one will continue to suffer the pangs of material existence. Even those who are supposedly engaged in the service of the Supreme Lord, if they stubbornly remain attached to wife, children, and so on, their material condition of life will continue.

PURPORT

Under the shelter of a pseudo spiritual master, nondevotees embrace mental speculation and gross sense gratification under the influence of bad association. If one is treated by a physician who is not experienced, although the symptom of the disease may temporarily disappear, there is every possibility of a relapse. The conclusion is that it is essential to completely give up the association of sense enjoyers and those making a show of false renunciation. When one's offense against the holy name of the Lord in the form of maintaining the false egoistic conception of "I" and "mine" is very prominent, the result is that one remains attached to his sons, wife, relatives, father, mother, wealth, and country. The practice of pseudo devotional service cannot cure one's material disease. Even while serving Lord Hari, such a pseudo devotee will find that his attachment for wife, children, and so on simply increases.

TEXT 29

कुयोगिनोयेविहितान्तरायैर्मनुष्यभूतैस्त्रिदशोपसृष्टैः ।
तेप्राक्तनाभ्यासबलेनभूयोयुञ्जन्तियोगंनतुकर्मतन्त्रम् ॥२९॥

kuyogino ye vihitāntarāyair manuṣya-bhūtais tridaśopasṛṣṭaiḥ
te prāktanābhyāsa-balena bhūyo yuñjanti yogaṁ na tu karma-tantram

Sometimes the progress of a neophyte transcendentalist is impeded due to excessive attachment to family members or others, who are sent by envious demigods. However, on the strength of their spiritual advancement, such imperfect transcendentalists will resume

their practice of yoga in the next life. They will never again be bound, like ordinary materialists, in the network of karma.

COMMENTARY

Sometimes *sannyāsīs* and others become bewildered by friends, well-wishers, or flattering disciples that are sent by the demigods to embarrass them. Therefore, in the *Śrīmad-Bhāgavatam* (10.87.39) it has been stated:

yadi na samuddharanti yatayo hṛdi kāma-jaṭā

Members of the renounced order who fail to uproot the last traces of material desire in their hearts remain impure.

It is to be understood that a *sannyāsī's* position is completely distinct from that of others who are engaged in devotional service. This is confirmed in the *Vedas*: *yasmāt tadeṣam na priyam yadetan manuṣyā viduḥ*: No human being is dear to a *sannyāsī.*

PURPORT

The conditioned souls, who work hard for the satisfaction of their senses, are tightly bound by the network of fruitive activities. When such conditioned souls take to the practice of yoga, the envious demigods may place obstacles on their path by sending flattering disciples or bodily relations. Although an imperfect transcendentalist may thus fall down from yoga practice, he will resume it in his next life, on the strength of his accumulated merit.

TEXT 30

करोतिकर्मक्रियतेचजन्तुःकेनाप्यसौचोदित आनिपतात् ।
नतत्रविद्वान्प्रकृतौस्थितोऽपिनिवृत्ततृष्णःस्वसुखानुभूत्या ॥३०॥

karoti karma kriyate ca jantuḥ kenāpy asau codita ā-nipatāt
na tatra vidvān prakṛtau sthito 'pi nivṛtta-tṛṣṇaḥ sva-sukhānubhūtyā

The conditioned living entity performs fruitive work and suffers and enjoys the reactions to his karma. Thus, he continues to work fruitively right up to the very moment of his death. One who is wise, however, after experiencing transcendental ecstasy, gives up all material desires and refrains from engaging in fruitive work.

COMMENTARY

Unlike *karmīs*, *jñānīs* do not allow themselves to become entangled in the bondage of fruitive work. This is being explained in this verse. All conditioned souls are working hard in this world, under the direction of the three modes of material nature. By their activities, they determine their future body, whether that of a demigod, human being, dog, or hog. Although there is great risk of becoming degraded, fruitive workers go on with their self-centered activities up until the point of death. However, those who are actually wise renounce fruitive activities, even while living in the material world, and thus they free themselves from the bondage of *karma*.

PURPORT

Materialistic persons engage in fruitive activities so that they can enjoy sense gratification On the other hand, one who is on the platform of self-realization does not regard himself as an enjoyer of the material world. Rather, he regards the entire creation as an expansion of the Lord's potency, and he sees himself as the Lord's humble servant.

TEXT 31

तिष्ठन्तमासीनमुतव्रजन्तंशयानमुक्षन्तमदन्तमन्नम् ।
स्वभावमन्यत्किमपीहमानमात्मानमात्मस्थमतिर्नवेद ॥३१॥

tiṣṭhantam āsīnam uta vrajantaṁ śayānam ukṣantam adantam annam
svabhāvam anyat kim apīhamānam ātmānam ātma-stha-matir na veda

One whose consciousness is absorbed in thought of the Lord does not even understand how his body is acting. While walking, sitting, standing, lying down, passing urine, eating, or doing anything else, he simply thinks that the body is acting according to its acquired nature.

COMMENTARY

One who is wise remains aloof from the functions of the material body. This is what is being explained in this verse. One who is fully absorbed in Kṛṣṇa consciousness would hardly notice even if someone passed urine on his body. One whose intelligence is fixed on the Supreme Lord hardly remembers that he has a material body.

PURPORT

A self-realized soul does not take part in the activities of material enjoyment or artificial renunciation because all of his activities are dovetailed in the service of

Lord Kṛṣṇa. Although he is detached from the functions of the material body, he enthusiastically engages his material body in the service of the Lord.

TEXT 32

यदिस्मपश्यत्यसदिन्द्रियार्थंनानानुमानेनविरुद्धमन्यत् ।
नमन्यतेवस्तुतयामनीषीस्वाप्नंयथोत्थायतिरोदधानम् ॥३२॥

yadi sma paśyaty asad-indriyārthaṁ nānānumānena viruddham anyat
na manyate vastutayā manīṣī svāpnaṁ yathotthāya tirodadhānam

Although a self-realized soul encounters material objects and activities, which are temporary, he does not accept them as reality, just as a man awakening from sleep views his fading dream as an illusory manifestation of the mind.

COMMENTARY

Although a self-realized soul is absorbed in Kṛṣṇa consciousness, he must perform routine duties in relation to the material body but he does not consider such activities as factual, just as one has awakened from sleep does not consider his dreams to be reality.

PURPORT

While dreaming, one experiences various emotions but when one awakens, he can understand that such feelings have no basis in reality. Similarly, one who is actually wise understands that the objects he experiences while awake, and the activities he performs for the maintenance of his material body, have no basis in ultimate reality, which exists apart from this temporary material manifestation. Indeed, the pleasures and pains of material existence are simply the result of being in the bodily concept of life, forgetting one's identity as pure spirit soul. For a self-realized soul, reality is his engagement in the devotional service of the Supreme Lord, which is distinct from the day dreams and night dreams of the conditioned souls.

TEXT 33

पूर्वंगृहीतंगुणकर्मचित्रमज्ञानमात्मन्यविविक्तमङ्ग ।
निवर्ततेतत्पुनरीक्षयैवनगृह्यतेनापिविसृज्य आत्मा ॥३३॥

pūrvaṁ gṛhītaṁ guṇa-karma-citram ajñānam ātmany aviviktam aṅga
nivartate tat punar īkṣayaiva na gṛhyate nāpi visṛjya ātmā

My dear Uddhava, material nescience, which expands into many varieties by the activities, is wrongly accepted by the conditioned soul to be the actual condition of the self. But, through the cultivation of spiritual knowledge, this nescience fades away as one proceeds towards liberation. The eternal self is never wrongly accepted nor rejected at any stage, however.

COMMENTARY

Knowledge is the destroyer of ignorance. All activities performed under the influence of the three modes of material nature during the conditional state of existence are born of ignorance. Although illusory, such activities appear to be real to the conditioned soul. One should try to vanquish his ignorance by the cultivation of spiritual knowledge. Ignorance is only accepted due to lack of proper understanding, and so it is rejected when one becomes enlightened with the knowledge of the self, which is changeless and eternal.

PURPORT

The visible objects of this world are always subject to transformation. The knowledge that is cultivated by a seer whose senses are imperfect is another side of ignorance. The pure spirit soul, on the other hand, is unchanging and without the four defects that are characteristic of conditional life. Whatever activities the conditioned soul performs under the direction of false ego, which is the creation of the modes of nature, have a foundation of ignorance. When spiritual knowledge is awakened, one regards his previous experiences as inconsequential. This is the symptom of self-realization. One should never mistakenly equate temporary material existence with liberated existence in the spiritual realm. It is only by identification with the temporary material body and subtle mind that one engages in the meaningless activities of sense gratification or artificial renunciation.

TEXT 34

यथाहिभानोरुदयोनृचक्षुषांतमोनिहन्यान्नतुसद्विधत्ते ।
एवंसमीक्षानिपुणासतीमेहन्यात्तमिस्रंपुरुषस्यबुद्धेः ॥३४॥

yathā hi bhānor udayo nṛ-cakṣuṣāṁ tamo nihanyān na tu sad vidhatte
evaṁ samīkṣā nipuṇā satī me hanyāt tamisraṁ puruṣasya buddheḥ

Just as, when the sun rises, it destroys the darkness covering men's eyes, but it does not create the objects they perceive, so factual realization of Me destroys the ignorance covering one's pure consciousness.

COMMENTARY

One who is self-realized understands that the soul is not subject to material transformation. It is changeless and eternal. Attributing material designations to the spirit soul is simply a result of ignorance. When the sun rises, the darkness covering one's eyes is removed so that one can see things as they are. Similarly, realization of the self dispels the darkness of ignorance, which covers his real knowledge.

PURPORT

The contamination of an object is a temporary imposition. When the contamination is removed, the object displays its original purity. When one's intelligence is fully engaged in the service of the Supreme Lord, the propensities for material enjoyment and artificial renunciation leave his association. When one's contaminated material concept of life is vanquished, he regains his natural and healthy state of serving the Supreme Lord. Just as, when the sun rises, one can see things as they are, similarly when the darkness of ignorance is dispelled by realization of the self, one can engage in his natural condition as the eternal servant of the Supreme Lord.

TEXT 35

एषस्वयंज्योतिरजोऽप्रमेयोमहानुभूतिःसकलानुभूतिः ।
एकोऽद्वितीयोवचसांविरामेयेनेषितावागसवश्चरन्ति ॥३५॥

eṣa svayaṁ-jyotir ajo 'prameyo mahānubhūtiḥ sakalānubhūtiḥ
eko 'dvitīyo vacasāṁ virāme yeneṣitā vāg-asavaś caranti

The Supreme Lord is self-luminous, unborn, and immeasurable. He is pure transcendental consciousness, all-pervading knowledge, and one without a second. He is realized only after ordinary words cease. By Him the power of speech and the life airs are set into motion.

COMMENTARY

The Supersoul is compared to the sun, whereas the individual souls are compared to the rays of the sun. The distinction between the Supersoul and the innumerable spirit souls is being described in this verse. The Supersoul is self-manifest and self-effulgent, but the living entities are manifested by Him. The Lord is unborn, but the living entities become subject to material designations. The Lord is immeasurable, or all pervading, whereas the living entities are localized. The Supersoul is the supreme spirit whole, and the living entities are His minute parts and parcels. He is omniscient, whereas the living entity is only aware of his limited experience. The Supreme Lord is one, whereas the living entities are many. Any description of the Supreme Lord is beyond the power of the words of the conditioned souls. It is said in the *Vedas*, *yato vāco nivartante aprāpya manasā saha*: The descriptive power of speech fails in the realm of the Supreme Truth, and the speculative power of the mind cannot achieve Him.

PURPORT

The Supreme Lord is unborn, beyond the range of the material senses, fully spiritual, not bound by time, space, or circumstances, omniscient, and one without a second. When the limit of one's speech is attained within this world, the Supreme Lord remains far beyond reach. Rather, by the influence of the Supreme Lord, the power of speech comes to life. It is the Lord who awards the power of the senses to the conditioned souls and when He desires, that power is withdrawn. The relationship of the independent Lord with the minute living entities is technically called *svajātīya-bheda*. The living entities' relationship with the material nature is technically called *vijātīya-bheda*. The Lord's relationship with the spiritual nature is termed *svagata-bheda*. Being influenced by the external energy of the Lord, there is confusion in the minds of the Māyāvādīs regarding *svagata-bheda*, *svajātīya-bheda*, and *vijātīya-bheda*. The enlightened view of these words is that they establish the supremacy of the Lord, whereas the unenlightened view misconstrues a meaning that there is an existence separate from the Supreme Lord.

TEXT 36

एतावानात्मसम्मोहोयद्विकल्पस्तुकेवले ।
आत्मन् ऋतेस्वमात्मानमवलम्बोनयस्यहि ॥३६॥

etāvān ātma-sammoho yad vikalpas tu kevale
ātman ṛte svam ātmānam avalambo na yasya hi

Whatever duality appears to be applicable to the self is simply a manifestation of the mind's bewilderment. There is no factual basis of such duality except the fact that it is imagined by the conditioned soul.

COMMENTARY

One may question: How can the Supersoul be one without a second when we can directly see that this visible world is separate from Him? The answer is: There is no duality present in the soul, and so what to speak of the Supreme Soul. Whatever is perceived as being separate from the Lord is not because everything in existence is the Lord and His energies. The perception of duality is simply due to a state of delusion within the mind. That the Supersoul is one without a second is stated in the *Vedas*: *neha nānāsti kiñcana*: Besides this, nothing exists.

PURPORT

The soul is pure spiritual existence, without any tinge of matter. After comprehending the illusory nature of material variegatedness, one should not foolishly conclude that there is no difference between the minute souls and the Supreme Personality of Godhead. The Lord is always in a superior position and the living entities are eternally subordinate. The soul is naturally free from material association but by misuse of his minute independence, he becomes conditioned by *Maya*. Transcendental reality has nothing to do with material variegatedness. It is most unreasonable to try to attribute the characteristics of this material world to the Lord's eternal characteristics and pastimes. The conception of duality that is born from the deluded mind of the conditioned soul can never cover the effulgent glory of spiritual variegatedness.

TEXT 37

यन्नामाकृतिभिर्ग्राह्यंपञ्चवर्णमबाधितम् ।
व्यर्थेनाप्यर्थवादोऽयंद्वयंपण्डितमानिनाम् ॥३७॥

yan nāmākṛtibhir grāhyaṁ pañca-varṇam abādhitam
vyarthenāpy artha-vādo 'yaṁ dvayaṁ paṇḍita-māninām

The duality that is applied to the five gross material elements is understood by their names and forms. Those who claim that such a dualistic conception is reality are mundane scholars who proudly put forward their theories without actual realization of the truth.

COMMENTARY

Cotton is the cause of cloth, and cloth is the effect of cotton. Cloth could not exist without the existence of cotton. No genuinely learned man could fail to understand this. This visible world of names and forms, composed of the five gross elements, is perceivable by the material senses. All such manifestations have a beginning and an end and so are not ultimate reality. The Supreme Personality of Godhead had previously stated in this chapter:

pratyakṣeṇānumānena nigamenātma-saṁvidā
ādy-antavad asaj jñātvāniḥsaṅgo vicared iha

By direct perception, logical deduction, scriptural authority, and personal realization, one should know that this world has a beginning and an end and so is not the ultimate reality. Thus, one should live in this world without attachment.

PURPORT

Material names and forms, having a beginning and an end, have no permanent existence and so do not constitute essential reality. This cosmic manifestation is a transformation of one of the energies of the Supreme Lord. The Lord is the Absolute Truth and His potencies are also truth, but the names and forms that are temporarily manifested in this material world have no eternal existence. There are two kinds of pseudo-scholars—those who accept matter as ultimate reality, and those who imagine spirit to be devoid of variegatedness. Neither group accepts the transcendental pastimes of the Supreme Lord, and so they are not fit to be addressed as actually learned. The cultivation of knowledge devoid of the service of the Supreme Lord, who is beyond the reach of mundane sense perception, is the only asset of such pseudo-scholars.

TEXT 38

योगिनोऽपक्वयोगस्ययुञ्जतःकाय उत्थितैः ।
उपसर्गैर्विहन्येततत्रायंविहितोविधिः ॥३८॥

yogino 'pakva-yogasya yuñjataḥ kāya utthitaiḥ
upasargair vihanyeta tatrāyaṁ vihito vidhiḥ

The physical body of a neophyte yogi, who has not yet achieved maturity in his practice, may sometimes be afflicted by various disturbances, such as disease. For them, the following process is recommended.

COMMENTARY

After outlining the process of *jñāna-yoga,* the Lord herein gives instructions to those who are disturbed by disease or other impediments. Yogis who are still on the material platform, due to incomplete realization, are given some suggestions by the Lord in this regard.

PURPORT

Often, *haṭha-yogīs* and *raja-yogīs,* who disregard devotional service to the Lord, cannot complete their yoga practice, due to remaining in the bodily conception of life. The process of devotional service to the Lord, which is the constitutional duty of the soul, has been prescribed to elevate such imperfect yogis to the transcendental platform.

TEXT 39

योगधारणयाकांश्चिदासनैर्धारणान्वितैः ।
तपोमन्त्रौषधैःकांश्चिदुपसर्गान्विनिर्दहेत् ॥३९॥

yoga-dhāraṇayā kāṁścid āsanair dhāraṇānvitaiḥ
tapo-mantrauṣadhaiḥ kāṁścid upasargān vinirdahet

Some disturbances, such as heat and cold, can be counteracted by meditating on the sun and moon. Illnesses, such as gastric disorders, can be restrained by practicing sitting postures and breath control. Performance of penance, chanting of mantras, and the application of medicinal herbs can counteract inauspicious planetary positions, fear of snakebite, and so on.

COMMENTARY

By practicing yoga and meditating on the sun and the moon, one can get relief from the miseries caused by excessive heat and cold. By practicing *āsanas* and *praṇāyāma*, one can cure gastric ailments. By the performance of penance, the chanting of *mantras*, and ingestion of medicinal herbs, one can neutralize inauspiciousness caused by planetary positions and the threat of snakebites.

PURPORT

For the removal of obstacles on the path of *karma yoga* and *haṭha-yoga*, various practices have been advised. Such remedial measures are only for those who are not surrendered to the Supreme Personality of Godhead.

TEXT 40

कांश्चिन्ममानुध्यानेननामसङ्कीर्तनादिभिः ।
योगेश्वरानुवृत्त्यावाहन्यादशुभदान्शनैः ॥४०॥

kāṁścin mamānudhyānena nāma-saṅkīrtanādibhiḥ
yogeśvarānuvṛttyā vā hanyād aśubha-dān śanaiḥ

One can destroy disturbances such as lust by always thinking of Me, and by congregationally chanting My holy names. One can destroy the obstacles of pride and false ego by following in the footsteps of the masters of mystic yoga.

COMMENTARY

One should overcome lust by meditating on the Supreme Lord. One should subdue his pride by following in the footsteps of great souls.

PURPORT

By engaging in the practice of devotional service to the Supreme Lord, beginning with hearing and chanting the Lord's holy names, and meditating upon His transcendental pastimes, all inauspiciousness within the heart, which are impediments to one's advancement, will gradually diminish.

TEXT 41

केचिद्देहमिमंधीराःसुकल्पंवयसिस्थिरम् ।
विधायविविधोपायैरथयुञ्जन्तिसिद्धये ॥४१॥

kecid deham imaṁ dhīrāḥ su-kalpaṁ vayasi sthiram
vidhāya vividhopāyair atha yuñjanti siddhaye

There are methods by which yogis can remain free from disease, and keep themselves in a youthful condition of life, without experiencing the distresses of old age. Thus they practice yoga for the purpose of achieving mystic perfections.

COMMENTARY

Some yogis employ various methods to keep their body fit and youthful, desiring to attain mystic perfections. They try to master the mystic perfection of entering another's body so that they can utilize it for sense enjoyment. Such practices are not to be accepted as devotional service to the Supreme Lord.

PURPORT

The practice of *haṭha-yoga* is generally accepted with a desire to attain the eighteen kinds of mystic perfection. Such practices cannot be counted as limbs of devotional service.

TEXT 42

नहितत्कुशलादृत्यंतदायासोह्यपार्थकः ।
अन्तवत्त्वाच्छरीरस्यफलस्येववनस्पतेः ॥४२॥

na hi tat kuśalādṛtyaṁ tad-āyāso hy apārthakaḥ
antavattvāc charīrasya phalasyeva vanaspateḥ

Learned persons who are expert in transcendental knowledge do not very highly value these mystic perfections because the soul, like a tree, is permanent, and the body, like the tree's fruit, is perishable.

COMMENTARY

Those who have actually realized the eternal nature of the self are not tempted by the allurements that mystic powers offer. The spirit soul is permanent, like a tree that may live for a very long time, but the material body is soon to perish, like the fruit of the tree that quickly spoils.

PURPORT

A tree produces seasonal fruit but even after the fruit is gone, the tree remains for a very long time. Self-realized souls, knowing perfectly well that the gross and subtle bodies, which are temporary manifestations of material nature, are perishable, do not undergo the severe penance required to obtain mystic powers.

TEXT 43

योगंनिषेवतोनित्यंकायश्चेत्कल्पतामियात् ।
तच्छ्रद्दध्यान्नमतिमान्योगमुत्सृज्यमत्परः ॥४३॥

yogaṁ niṣevato nityaṁ kāyaś cet kalpatām iyat
tac chraddadhyān na matimān yogam utsṛjya mat-paraḥ

Although the physical body may be improved by the practice of yoga, an intelligent person who has dedicated his life to Me does not place his faith in such a prospect, and in fact shuns such practices.

COMMENTARY

Even if there is the prospect of achieving a duration of life of one *kalpa* by the practice of mystic yoga, an intelligent person will not place his faith in such a thing but rather dedicate himself to Lord Kṛṣṇa's devotional service.

PURPORT

Although in the scriptures there are recommendations for the performance of *haṭha-yoga*, *rāja-yoga*, and *praṇāyama*, ultimately, it is advised that one become freed from all types of material bondage by faithfully worshiping the Supreme Lord in the association of devotees. The devotees of the Supreme Lord cannot place their faith in any process for overcoming lust, anger, and so on, other than devotional service to Lord Mukunda. In this connection, one should consider this verse from the *Śrīmad-Bhāgavatam* 1.6.36):

sarvaṁ tad idam ākhyātaṁ yat pṛṣṭo 'haṁ tvayānagha
janma-karma-rahasyaṁ me bhavataś cātma-toṣaṇam

O Vyāsadeva, you are freed from all sins. Thus I have explained my birth and activities for self-realization, as you asked. All this will be conducive for your personal satisfaction also.

TEXT 44

योगचर्यामिमांयोगीविचरन्मदपाश्रयः ।
नान्तरायैर्विहन्येतनिःस्पृहःस्वसुखानुभूः ॥४४॥

yoga-caryām imāṁ yogī vicaran mad-apāśrayaḥ
nāntarāyair vihanyeta niḥspṛhaḥ sva-sukhānubhūḥ

My unalloyed devotee is without material hankering because he is satisfied within the self, and thus experiences unlimited happiness. Thus, while executing this process of yoga, he is never deterred by impediments.

PURPORT

Although the followers of *haṭha-yoga* and *raja-yoga* make some progress in their respective practices, they generally fail to gain success because they are confronted by numerous obstacles. However, one who surrenders to the Supreme Lord, who is the transcendental Cupid, will certainly come out victorious on his path back home, back to Godhead.

Thus ends the translation of the Twenty-second Chapter of the Uddhava-gītā *entitled,* "**Jñāna-yoga**," *with the commentaries of Śrīla Viśvanātha Cakravartī Ṭhākura and chapter summary and purports by Śrīla Bhaktisiddhānta Sarasvatī Ṭhākura.*

Chapter 23

Bhakti-yoga

CHAPTER SUMMARY

Uddhava thought that the process of *jñāna-yoga* that the Lord had described was too difficult, and so he asked about an easier means of self-realization. In reply the Lord briefly described the process of devotional service.

Karmīs and yogīs, who are still under the inflence of the illusory energy of the Lord and thus are very proud of their meager accomplishments, are not inclined to take shelter at the lotus feet of the Lord. On the other hand, the swanlike men who can discriminate between matter and spirit take shelter of the Lord without reservation. The Supreme Lord resides within the hearts of all living entities, as the overseer and permitter, and sometimes appears externally as the spiritual master, who teaches by example. He dispels the living entities' misfortune by revealing His eternal form.

One should perform all activities in the service of the Supreme Lord, keeping one's mind fixed upon Him in all circumstances. One should reside in the holy places of pilgrimage that are related to the Supreme Lord, where many pure devotees of the Lord reside, and one should take part in the festivals that celebrate the Lord's appearance, and so on. One should at least theoretically understand that all living entities are places of the Lord's residence as the Supersoul, and thus cultivate equal vision so that material prejudices will be vanquished. One should avoid intimate association with nondevotees, and renounce desires for material enjoyment. In this frame of mind, one should offer obeisances to all, even the lowest of men and animals. As long as one cannot factually perceive the Supreme Lord present within all beings, one should continue to use his body, mind, and speech in the service of the Lord.

Because devotional service to the Supreme Lord is the eternal function of the spirit soul, and is preached by the Lord Himself, it is always auspicious and successful. When one surrenders to the Lord without duplicity, the Lord becomes satisfied. As a result, the devotee attains eternal residence with the Lord in the spiritual sky and enjoys opulence on the level of that of the Lord.

After contemplating the Lord's instructions, Uddhava went to Badarikāśrama, as ordered by the Lord. By perfectly carrying out the orders of the Lord, he ultimately attained the transcendental abode of the Lord. Indeed, anyone who faithfully assimilates and then practices these instructions of the Lord will be freed from material existence.

TEXT 1

श्रीउद्धव उवाच
सुदुस्तरामिमांमन्येयोगचर्यामनात्मनः ।
यथाञ्जसापुमान्सिद्ध्येत्तन्मेब्रूह्यञ्जसाच्युत ॥१॥

śrī-uddhava uvāca
su-dustarām imāṁ manye yoga-caryām anātmanaḥ
yathāñjasā pumān siddhyet tan me brūhy añjasācyuta

Śrī Uddhava said: O infallible Lord, I think that it is very difficult for ordinary persons who are not self-controlled to practice the yoga system described by You. Therefore, please tell me more simply how one can easily attain perfection.

COMMENTARY

Taking shelter of exalted devotees and holy places that are associated with the Lord enhances one's devotional service. This will be described in this chapter. Uddhava had difficulty imagining how anyone could follow the procedures of yoga that the Supreme Lord had imparted to him. This is being explained in this verse. The process of yoga, which teaches one to completely give up all attachment for the material body, was described in the previous chapter, but Uddhava thinks that this practice is too difficult for the majority of people. He therefore requests the Lord to describe a process whereby human beings can easily attain success. Although the word *añjasā* has been spoken twice in this verse, the fault of redundancy does not arise because each indicates a separate cause.

TEXT 2

प्रायशःपुण्दरीकाक्षयुञ्यन्तोयोगिनोमनः ।
विषीदन्त्यसमाधानान्मनोनिग्रहकर्शिताः ॥२॥

prāyaśaḥ puṇdarīkākṣa yuñyanto yogino manaḥ
viṣīdanty asamādhānān mano-nigraha-karśitāḥ

O lotus-eyed Lord, yogis who try to steady the mind generally experience frustration because of their inability to do so. As a result, they become weary of their attempt to bring the mind under control.

COMMENTARY

The practice of yoga as described in previous chapter is extremely difficult to perform. How this is so is being explained in this verse. In the course of trying to concentrate their minds on Brahman, those who practice yoga often become frustrated, being unable to do so.

TEXT 3

अथात आनन्ददुघंपदाम्बुजंहंसाःश्रयेरन्नरविन्दलोचन ।
सुखंनुविश्वेश्वरयोगकर्मभिस्त्वन्माययामीविहतानमानिनः ॥३॥

athāta ānanda-dughaṁ padāmbujaṁ haṁsāḥ śrayerann aravinda-locana
sukhaṁ nu viśveśvara yoga-karmabhis tvan-māyayāmī vihatā na māninaḥ

Therefore, O lotus-eyed Lord of the universe, swanlike men joyfully take shelter of Your lotus feet, the source of all transcendental ecstasy. However, those who do not surrender to You, being proud of their practice of yoga and *karma*, are defeated by Your illusory energy.

COMMENTARY

Uddhava desires that the Lord explain the essence of yoga, which is understood by men who are like swans, who can extract the milk from a mixture of milk and water. Those who are very proud of their positions as *karmīs*, *jñānīs*, and yogis are actually bewildered by the illusory energy of the Lord, and therefore undergo great difficulty.

PURPORT

The processes of yoga leading to spiritual perfection that are accepted by the nondevotees do not provide the satisfaction experienced by those who render service unto the lotus feet of the Supreme Lord. Actual happiness is relished in the service of the all-blissful Supreme Lord, and distress results from posing as an enjoyer in the bodily concept of life.

TEXT 4

किंचित्रमच्युततवैतदशेषबन्धोदासेष्वनन्यशरणेसुयदात्मसात्त्वम् ।
योऽरोचयत्सहमृगैःस्वयमीश्वराणांश्रीमत्किरीटतटपीडितपादपीठः ॥४॥

kiṁ citram acyuta tavaitad aśeṣa-bandho dāseṣv ananya-śaraṇesu yad ātma-sāttvam
yo 'rocayat saha mṛgaiḥ svayam īśvarāṇāṁ śrīmat-kirīṭa-taṭa-pīḍita-pāda-pīṭhaḥ

My dear infallible Lord, it is not at all astonishing that You intimately relate with Your devotees who have taken shelter of You, such as Nanda Mahārāja, the *gopīs*, and Bali Mahārāja. After all, during Your appearance as Lord Rāmacandra, when even great personalities such as Brahmā desired to place the tips of their crowns at Your lotus feet, You nevertheless showed more affection for monkeys, such as Hanuman, because they had taken exclusive shelter of You.

COMMENTARY

It is not surprising that those who serve the Supreme Lord receive His favor. The word *ananyaśaranaṁ* indicates that the Supreme Lord fully protects His servants who are completely free from the contamination of *karma* and *jñāna*, and even takes a position of subordination to them. This is not at all astonishing. Although the king is the ruler of society, he is directed by the *brāhmaṇas*. In the same way, the Supreme Lord is controlled by His dear servants. In other words, the Lord allows Himself to come under the control of His devotees. The Supreme Personality of Godhead, as Lord Rāmacandra, established friendship with monkeys, and as Kṛṣṇa, He enjoyed tending the cows in the pasturing grounds of Vṛndāvana, and would steal butter and distribute it to the monkeys. Such devotees of the Lord have no need for the elaborate *jñāna-yoga* system or the process for achieving mystic powers. All these devotees are represented here by Śrī Uddhava, who frankly informs the Lord that the sophisticated systems of philosophical speculation and mystic yoga are not appealing for one who has developed a taste for direct loving service to the Lord.

PURPORT

Unalloyed devotees in all species of life became successful in establishing a relationship of friendship with the Lord, although even great personalities, such as Brahmā, could not do so.

TEXT 5

तंत्वाखिलात्मदयितेश्वरमाश्रितानांसर्वार्थदंस्वकृतविद्विसृजेतकोनु ।
कोवाभजेत्किमपिविस्मृतयेऽनुभूत्यैकिंवाभवेन्नतवपादरजोजुषांनः ॥५॥

taṁ tvākhilātma-dayiteśvaram āśritānāṁ sarvārtha-daṁ sva-kṛta-vid visṛjeta ko nu
ko vā bhajet kim api vismṛtaye 'nu bhūtyai kiṁ vā bhaven na tava pāda-rajo-juṣāṁ naḥ

Who could even think of rejecting You, the Supreme Soul, the most dear object of worship, and the Supreme Lord of all, who awards all possible perfections to the devotees who take shelter of You? Who could be so ungrateful, knowing the great mercy You bestow? Who would reject You and accept something for the sake of material enjoyment, which simply leads to a miserable condition of life? What is there lacking for us who are engaged in the service of the dust of Your lotus feet?

COMMENTARY

The Lord is the well-wishing friend of all living entities, and for their benefit, He imparts instructions on devotional service to His empowered representatives, such as Nārada Muni. The Lord is the bestower of the fruits of everyone's activities because He is the supreme controller, but He particularly fulfills all the desires of His devotees. The Lord showered great compassion upon devotees such as Bali and Prahlāda. Knowing this, who would want to abandon Him? Only the most fallen, dry, and ungrateful yogis reject the service of the Supreme Personality of Godhead. How can an unalloyed devotee of the Lord desire elevation to the heavenly planets or liberation? How is it that devotees such as Bali and Prahlāda, who were free from material desires, attained such a status of material enjoyment, and even liberation? The answer to this dilemma is found in the *Nārāyaṇīya* of the *Mokṣa-dharma* section of the *Mahābhārata*:

yā vai sādhana-sampattiḥ puruṣārtha-catuṣṭaye
tayā vinā tad āpnoti naro nārāyaṇāśrayaḥ

Whatever among the four goals of human life can be achieved by various spiritual practices is automatically achieved without such endeavors by the person who has taken shelter of Lord Nārāyaṇa, the refuge of all persons.

Material enjoyment and liberation are simply by-products of the Lord's inconceivable mercy.

TEXT 6

नैवोपयन्त्यपचितिं कवयस्तवेश ब्रह्मायुषापि कृतमृद्धमुदः स्मरन्तः ।
योऽन्तर्बहिस्तनुभृतामशुभं विधुन्वन्नाचार्यचैत्त्यवपुषा स्वगतिं व्यनक्ति ॥६॥

naivopayanty apacitiṁ kavayas taveśa
brahmāyuṣāpi kṛtam ṛddha-mudaḥ smarantaḥ
yo 'ntar bahis tanu-bhṛtām aśubhaṁ vidhunvann
ācārya-caittya-vapuṣā sva-gatiṁ vyanakti

My dear Lord, those who are learned scholars in the transcendental science could never properly express their indebtedness to You, even with a lifetime of Brahmā, because You manifest Yourself externally as the *ācārya* and internally as the Supersoul, to deliver the conditioned souls by instructing them how to return to You.

COMMENTARY

"As all surrender unto Me, I reward them accordingly." This reward of the Lord is not artificial—it is natural. It is ultimately the Lord who is the bestower of the results of everyone's activities. Even by rendering devotional service for a duration of one thousand *kalpas*, a devotee cannot repay the debt he feels to the Lord for having awarded him loving service to His lotus feet. The word *āpaciti* indicates that a devotee could not repay his debt to the Lord, even by rendering service to Him for the duration of Brahmā's life. The Lord guides the living entities from without as the *mantra guru* and *śikṣā guru*, and by imparting instructions of devotional service, and from within, He guides the living entities as the Supersoul. The Lord has personally stated this in the *Bhagavad-gītā* (10.10):

teṣāṁ satata-yuktānāṁ bhajatāṁ prīti-pūrvakam
dadāmi buddhi-yogaṁ taṁ yena mām upayānti te

To those who are constantly devoted to serving Me with love, I give the understanding by which they can come to Me.

PURPORT

Expert and sober devotees, despite being very qualified and having a lifespan like that of Brahmā, cannot repay the Lord's favor upon them by awarding them auspiciousness while remaining seated within their hearts as the Supersoul.

TEXT 7

श्रीशुक उवाच
इत्युद्धवेनात्यनुरक्तचेतसापृष्टोजगत्क्रीडनकःस्वशक्तिभिः ।
गृहीतमूर्तित्रय ईश्वरेश्वरोजगादसप्रेममनोहरस्मितः ॥७॥

śrī-śuka uvāca
Ity uddhavenāty-anurakta-cetasā pṛṣṭo jagat-krīḍanakaḥ sva-śaktibhiḥ
gṛhīta-mūrti-traya īśvareśvaro jagāda sa-prema-manohara-smitaḥ

Śukadeva Gosvāmī said: Being thus questioned by the most affectionate Uddhava, Lord Kṛṣṇa, the master of the demigods, who considers the entire universe as His plaything, and assumes the three forms of Brahmā, Viṣṇu and Śiva, began to reply while lovingly displaying His all-attractive smile.

COMMENTARY

This material world is also a place for the Lord's eternal pastimes. He enjoys in this world with His internal, marginal, and external energies as the Supersoul within the hearts of all living entities. He inspired Uddhava from within to place before Him these inquiries for the benefit of future devotees. The Lord exhibits His pastimes within this material world, just to distribute the transcendental mellows of devotional service. Here, Uddhava is the audience and Lord Kṛṣṇa is the speaker. Similarly, Śukadeva Gosvāmī became the speaker and Mahārāja Parikṣit became the listener. These conversations shower the nectar for which all living entities are hankering. Śrī Kṛṣṇa alone is capable of bestowing actual mercy, which only brings unmixed auspiciousness. He is the controller of all the universal controllers. He spoke to Uddhava while displaying His most enchanting smile.

TEXT 8

श्रीभगवानुवाच
हन्ततेकथयिष्यामिममधर्मान्सुमङ्गलान् ।
यान्श्रद्धयाचरन्मर्त्योमृत्युंजयतिदुर्जयम् ॥८॥

śrī-bhagavān uvāca
hanta te kathayiṣyāmi mama dharmān su-maṅgalān
yān śraddhayācaran martyo mṛtyuṁ jayati durjayam

The Supreme Personality of Godhead said: Yes, I shall describe to you the religious principles of devotion to Me, by executing which a mortal human being can conquer unconquerable death.

COMMENTARY

Out of compassion, Lord Kṛṣṇa will explain the principles of devotional service unto Him. These principles are very auspicious and should be followed by all human beings with great faith. It is only in this way that the conditioned souls can conquer unconquerable death.

TEXT 9

कुर्यात्सर्वाणिकर्माणिमदर्थंशनकैःस्मरन् ।
मय्यर्पितमनश्चित्तोमद्धर्मात्ममनोरतिः ॥९॥

kuryāt sarvāṇi karmāṇi mad-arthaṁ śanakaiḥ smaran
mayy arpita-manaś-citto mad-dharmātma-mano-ratiḥ

While always remembering Me, one should perform his devotional and daily duties for My satisfaction, without becoming impetuous. With mind and intelligence offered to Me, one should cultivate attraction for My devotional service.

COMMENTARY

The Lord will herein describes devotional service that is unmixed with *karma* and *jñāna.* One should keep his body clean by brushing his teeth and bathing. One should keep his existence in a purified state by hearing and chanting the glories of the Supreme Lord. Ordinary human beings should follow the principles of *varṇāśrama,* and while performing all activities, they should remember the Supreme Lord. One whose heart is always fixed in meditation upon the Lord and His characteristics is a first-class devotee.

TEXT 10

देशान्पुण्यानाश्रयेतमद्भक्तैःसाधुभिः श्रितान् ।
देवासुरमनुष्येषुमद्भक्ताचरितानिच ॥१०॥

deśān puṇyān āśrayeta mad-bhaktaiḥ sādhubhiḥ śritān
devāsura-manuṣyeṣu mad-bhaktācaritāni ca

One should reside in a holy place that is inhabited by My saintly devotees, and one should follow in their footsteps. Such devotees appear among the demigods, demons, and human beings.

COMMENTARY

What is unalloyed devotional service? What is *vaidhī-bhakti* and *rāgānugā-bhakti*? These are being explained, one after another. One should live in a holy place, such as Dvārākā. One should follow the instructions and exemplary behavior of exalted personalities like Nārada Muni, Prahlāda Mahārāja, and King Ambariṣa. This is called *vaidhi-bhakti*, or regulative devotional service. To reside in a holy place, like Gokula, Govardhana, or Vṛndāvana, and follow in the footsteps of the *gopīs*, like Candrakānti and Vṛndā, is called *rāgānuga-bhakti*, or devotional service in attachment.

TEXT 11

पृथक् सत्रेणवामह्यंपर्वयात्रामहोत्सवान् ।
कारयेद्गीतनृत्याद्यैर्महाराजविभूतिभिः ॥११॥

pṛthak satreṇa vā mahyaṁ parva-yātrā-mahotsavān
kārayed gītā-nṛtyādyair mahārāja-vibhūtibhiḥ

Whether alone or in an assembly of devotees, one should sing, dance, and spend lavishly to celebrate My appearance days, as well as other ceremonies and festivals that are especially meant for My worship.

COMMENTARY

These basic principles apply to all types of devotional processes.

TEXT 12

मामेवसर्वभूतेषुबहिरन्तरपावृतम् ।
ईक्षेतात्मनिचात्मानंयथाखममलाशयः ॥१२॥

mām eva sarva-bhūteṣu bahir antar apāvṛtam
īkṣetātmani cātmānaṁ yathā kham amalāśayaḥ

With a purified heart, one should see Me as being situated within his own self, as well as within the hearts of all living entities, unblemished and all-pervading, like the sky.

COMMENTARY

After describing the duties of unalloyed devotees, Lord Kṛṣṇa now speaks in a way so as to attract the *jñānīs*. Those who are philosophically searching for the Absolute Truth should understand how the Lord is transcendentally situated, without any tinge of matter, although He is all-pervading and situated within the hearts of all living entities.

TEXT 13-14

इतिसर्वाणिभूतानिमद्भावेनमहाद्युते ।
सभाजयन्मन्यमानोज्ञानंकेवलमाश्रितः ॥१३॥
ब्राह्मणेपुक्कसेस्तेनेब्रह्मण्येऽर्केस्फुलिङ्गके ।
अक्रूरेक्रूरकेचैवसमदृक्पण्डितोमतः ०।१४॥

iti sarvāṇi bhūtāni mad-bhāvena mahā-dyute
sabhājayan manyamāno jñānaṁ kevalam āśritaḥ

brāhmaṇe pukkase stene brahmaṇye 'rke sphuliṅgake
akrūre krūrake caiva sama-dṛk paṇḍito mataḥ

O most-intelligent Uddhava, one who cultivates the understanding that I am present in the heart of all living beings, and who offers respect to everyone, is to be considered actually wise. Such a person sees equally the *brāhmaṇa* and the outcaste, the thief and the person who gives charity to the *brāhmaṇas*, the sun and tiny sparks, the gentle and the cruel.

COMMENTARY

Lord Kṛṣṇa said, "O Uddhava, you should regard all living entities as My parts and parcels and offer them due respect. Indeed, such consciousness is the symptom of an actually learned person."

The word *kevalam* is an adjective of the verb *āśraya*, and not the adjective of *jñāna*, because *jñāna* without devotional service is to be condemned. This could also be taken to mean, "taking shelter of the non-dual Brahman, who is full of transcendental knowledge."

Although there is a social distinction between a *brāhmaṇa* and a *caṇḍāla*, a behavioral distinction between a thief and a charitable man, a distinction between a professional *brāhmaṇa* and a devotee *brāhmaṇa*, a quantitative distinction between the sun and a spark of fire, and a qualitative distinction between a ruffian and a gentleman, one should see all of them with equal vision, because the Supreme Lord is situated within each one. One who sees like this is a truly wise person, and who does not is certainly ignorant.

PURPORT

In this regard, one should consider this verse from the *Bhagavad-gītā* (5.18):

vidyā-vinaya-sampanne brāhmaṇe gavi hastini
śuni caiva śva-pāke ca paṇḍitāḥ sama-darśinaḥ

The humble sages, by virtue of true knowledge, see with equal vision a learned and gentle *brāhmaṇa*, a cow, an elephant, a dog, and a dog-eater [outcaste].

If one can see this material world in relation to the Supreme Personality of Godhead, then his liberation is guaranteed. As soon as one sees the material nature as separate from the Lord, his constitutional spirit of service is transformed into the spirit of enjoyment. In this world, there is a superficial difference between those who are exalted and those who are fallen, between the truthful and the liars, between the fire of the sun and that of a small spark, and between gentle person and a cruel ruffian. When one ignores such differences of behavior and nature, considering them inconsequential in comparison with their actual spiritual identities, then one's vision of duality transforms into equanimity. A learned person is he who is not diverted from the truth while viewing the distinctions of this world of perverted enjoyment.

TEXT 15

नरेष्वभीक्ष्णंमद्भावंपुंसोभावयतोऽचिरात् ।
स्पर्धासूयातिरस्काराःसाहङ्कारावियन्तिहि ॥१५॥

nareṣv abhīkṣṇaṁ mad-bhāvaṁ puṁso bhāvayato 'cirāt
spardhāsūyā-tiraskārāḥ sāhaṅkārā viyanti hi

For one who constantly meditates on Me as being situated within all living entities, all bad qualities such as rivalry, abusiveness, and arrogance, along with their cause, false ego, are quickly vanquished.

COMMENTARY

One should practice seeing how the Supreme Lord is situated everywhere so that his polluted qualities, such as arrogance, can be destroyed. In material consciousness, one engages in rivalry with his equals, is envious of superiors, and belittles those who are inferior.

TEXT 16

विसृज्यस्मयमानान्स्वान्दृशंव्रीडांचदैहिकीम् ।
प्रणमेद्दण्डवद्भूमावाश्वचाण्डालगोखरम् ॥१६॥

visṛjya smayamānān svān dṛśaṁ vrīḍāṁ ca daihikīm
praṇamed daṇḍa-vad bhūmāv ā-śva-cāṇḍāla-go-kharam

Ignoring the ridicule of one's companions, one should renounce the bodily conception of life and its concomitant embarrassments, and offer obeisances to all living beings, even dogs, cows, donkeys, and untouchables, falling flat upon the ground just like a stick.

COMMENTARY

How one can cultivate equal vision, seeing everything in relation to the Supreme Lord, is described in this verse. The purport is that one should learn how to see with spiritual vision, and not remain satisfied with simply studying the bodily designations, which, after all, are temporary. Instead of showing respect or contempt according to external circumstances, one should show respect to all classes of living entities, even dogs and dog-eaters, knowing that the Supreme Personality of Godhead is present within each of them as the Supersoul.

PURPORT

One should ignore the ridicule of envious people, while showing suitable respect for all living beings, even dogs, dog-eaters, and asses. Śrī Caitanya Mahāprabhu has instructed us to consider ourselves lower than a straw in the street and to be more tolerant than a tree, offering respect to all others while not expecting any respect for oneself. This is the secret of success in the matter of chanting the holy name of the Lord.

TEXT 17

यावत्सर्वेषुभूतेषुमद्भावोनोपजायते ।
तावदेवमुपासीतवाङ्मनःकायवृत्तिभिः ॥१७॥

yāvat sarveṣu bhūteṣu mad-bhāvo nopajāyate
tāvad evam upāsīta vāṅ-manaḥ-kāya-vṛttibhiḥ

Until one is actually able to see Me within all living beings, one should worship Me in the prescribed manner with his body, mind, and speech.

COMMENTARY

Until one has gained the realization that the Supreme Lord is residing within the hearts of all living entities, it is recommended that one offer obeisances to varieties of creatures as a means for elevating one to that highest platform. Although one may not actually fall flat before every dog and donkey, at least one should carefully respect all forms of life, knowing them to be part and parcel of the Supreme Lord, Thus, one should show respect to all with one's body, mind, and words.

PURPORT

While worshiping the Supreme Lord with one's body, mind, and speech, one should think oneself to be lower than a blade of grass, one should be more tolerant than a tree, and one should be ready to give respect to all living entities without desiring any respect in return. In such a state of mind, one can continuously engage in *bhajana*, or worship of the Lord.

TEXT 18

सर्वंब्रह्मात्मकंतस्यविद्ययात्ममनीषया ।
परिपश्यन्नुपरमेत्सर्वतोमुइतसंशयः ॥१८॥

sarvaṁ brahmātmakaṁ tasya vidyayātma-manīṣayā
paripaśyann uparamet sarvato muita-saṁśayaḥ

By the cultivation of such transcendental knowledge, one should become free from all doubts by seeing the Supreme Lord everywhere and within all living entities, thus remaining aloof from all kinds of fruitive activities.

COMMENTARY

By the advancement of transcendental knowledge, one should come to see the Supreme Lord everywhere. It is a fact that everything in existence is owned and controlled by the Lord and being well aware of this, one should refrain from fruitive activities.

PURPORT

The more one advances in Kṛṣṇa consciousness, the more one becomes freed from all doubts. By constant engagement in devotional service, one can free oneself from all reactions of fruitive work. In devotional service, one works under the direction of the Supreme Lord and His representative, the spiritual master, whereas fruitive activities are impelled by the three modes of material nature. The conditioned souls exhibit many unfavorable qualities because their activities are based on envy. Such envy can only be removed by dedicated worship of the Lord with one's body, mind, and speech.

TEXT 19

अयंहिसर्वकल्पानांसध्रीचीनोमतोमम ।
मद्भावःसर्वभूतेषुमनोवाक्कायवृत्तिभिः ॥१९॥

ayaṁ hi sarva-kalpānāṁ sadhrīcīno mato mama
mad-bhāvaḥ sarva-bhūteṣu mano-vāk-kāya-vṛttibhiḥ

I consider this process of utilizing one's mind, words, and bodily functions for realizing My presence within all living entities to be the best method of spiritual enlightenment.

COMMENTARY

For the *jñānīs*, realization of impersonal Brahman is life's ultimate goal.

TEXT 20

नह्यङ्गोपक्रमेध्वंसोमद्धर्मस्योद्धवाण्वपि ।
मयाव्यवसितःसम्यङ्निर्गुणत्वादनाशिषः ॥२०॥

na hy aṅgopakrame dhvaṁso mad-dharmasyoddhavāṇv api
mayā vyavasitaḥ samyaṅ nirguṇatvād anāśiṣaḥ

My dear Uddhava, because the process of devotional service has been established by Me, it is transcendental and free from any material considerations. There is no doubt that a devotee will never suffer even the slightest loss by taking to this process.

COMMENTARY

After explaining the essence of *jñāna* in eight verses, the Lord now presents the essence of *bhakti*. Although the compilers of the scriptures have advocated various methods for elevation, this system of *bhakti-yoga*, or devotional service, was introduced by the Lord Himself. However, a neophyte can easily be diverted from the other processes so that no benefit is accrued, whereas the devotional service of the Lord never goes in vain. This is stated in this verse—that the process of devotional service is the best means of spiritual realization and such engagement can never be considered a loss.

Lord Kṛṣṇa said, "My dear Uddhava, if one begins the process of devotional service to Me and becomes diverted before reaching perfection, there is still no loss or diminution because *bhakti-yoga* is transcendental and is executed under My shelter. This supreme religious practice is perfect in all respects because I am the fuly independent Supreme Personality of Godhead."

The word *mad-dharma* in this verse refers to the principles of devotional service, and not to the cultivation of knowledge. *Jñāna*, or the cultivation of knowledge, is not fully transcendental and awards the successful performer impersonal liberation in Brahman, and not the association of the Supreme Personality of Godhead.

PURPORT

The desire for material enjoyment is the root cause of all *anarthas*. Only liberated souls who have renounced material enjoyment are actually qualified to worship Lord Hari.

TEXT 21

योयोमयिपरेधर्मःकल्प्यतेनिष्फलायचेत् ।
तदायासोनिरर्थःस्याद्भयादेरिवसत्तम ॥२१॥

yo yo mayi pare dharmaḥ kalpyate niṣphalāya cet
tad-āyāso nirarthaḥ syād bhayāder iva sattama

O most pious Uddhava, when faced with a dangerous situation, an ordinary person cries, becomes fearful, and laments, although such useless emotions do not change the situation. However, activities offered to Me without personal motivation, even if they are apparently useless, amount to the highest process of religion.

COMMENTARY

If devotional service to the Lord is performed without desire for personal gain, it will help elevate one to the spiritual platform. If devotional service, beginning with hearing and chanting, is engaged in for the sake of achieving worldly or heavenly sense gratification, as well as name and fame in this life or liberation in the next, it will act, but only gradually.

Devotional service is the supremely powerful process of self-realization and is capable of awarding one the ultimate goal of life, and so what to speak of other, lesser achievements. The scriptures advise that a Vaiṣṇava need not worry about his maintenance, such as food and clothing. The Lord is known as Viśvambhara, the maintainer of the entire universe, and so how could He neglect His devotees? Still, if a devotee cries to the Lord for protection or maintenance, desiring to continue his devotional service without impediment, the Lord accepts such apparently unnecessary appeals as the highest religious process, as stated in this verse.

PURPORT

One who performs devotional service to the Supreme Lord is never the loser. Whatever endeavor a devotee makes to serve the Lord never goes in vain, even if he cannot complete the process in this lifetime. Being transcendental, service rendered to the Lord is never forgotten or lost.

TEXT 22

एषाबुद्धिमतांबुद्धिर्मनीषाचमनीषिणाम् ।
यत्सत्यमनृतेनेहमर्त्येनाप्नोतिमामृतम् ॥२२॥

eṣā buddhimatāṁ buddhir manīṣā ca manīṣiṇām
yat satyam anṛteneha martyenāpnoti māmṛtam

This process is the supreme intelligence of the intelligent and the cleverness of the cleverest, because by following it, one can make use of that which is temporary and illusory to achieve Me, the eternal reality.

COMMENTARY

Why do people often execute devotional service in the hopes of gaining fame, and other personal advantages? The reason is that they are not actually intelligent. This is the purport of this verse. One who poses as a great devotee to enjoy immense prestige is not actually intelligent. Simply to imagine oneself to be a great preacher of devotional service, or a great relisher of transcendental *rasas*, simply for enjoying fame and reputation, is also not the sign of good intelligence.

One who has taken birth in Bhāratavarṣa should try to attain the eternal Supreme Lord with the help of his temporary material body. One can obtain the eternal with the help of the temporary. Conditioned souls can utilize their abominable material bodies to achieve a sublime eternal form like that of the Supreme Lord.

According to the material conception, one who can earn thousands of coins by investing just a few coins is considered intelligent. Especially in this age, those who possess the most wealth are considered to be the cleverest persons in society. However, if one could somehow possess a touchstone or a wish-fulfilling cow, he would certainly be considered even more clever and intelligent. Still, it must be understood that all such possessions are temporary and thus ultimately useless.

If those who have been born in Bhāratavarṣa engage their temporary material bodies, which are composed of disgusting substances, prone to dwindle, full of disease, and ultimately destroyed, in the service of the Supreme Lord, they can come to relish the best of all possessions, love of God. The Lord gives His very self to those who are devoted to Him without personal motivation. How wonderful such an attainment is! How intelligent are the inhabitants of Bhāratavarṣa who engage in unmotivated devotional service by hearing about the Lord, chanting His glories, and rendering all sorts of service to Him. The tongue should always be engaged in chanting the holy name of the Lord, the ears should be continuously engaged in hearing the Lord's glories, and the hands should be employed in rendering menial service to Him. Even by fully engaging in only one of the nine processes of devotional service, one can achieve the perfection of life. Considering this, what actually intelligent and clever person will fail to do so?

PURPORT

Those who are the most clever and intelligent will engage themselves in the devotional service of the Lord. It is only due to good fortune that a conditioned soul, who is bewildered on account of material attachment, decides to utilize whatever may be in his possession for the service of the Supreme Personality of Godhead. By such dovetailing of one's material body and possessions in the service of the Lord, one comes to the platform of eternality.

TEXT 23

एषतेऽभिहितःकृत्स्नोब्रह्मवादस्यसङ्ग्रहः ।
समासव्यासविधिनादेवानामपिदुर्गमः ॥२३॥

eṣa te 'bhihitaḥ kṛtsno brahma-vādasya saṅgrahaḥ
samāsa-vyāsa-vidhinā devānām api durgamaḥ

I have thus described to you, both briefly and in detail, the essence of spiritual knowledge, which is incomprehensible even to the demigods.

COMMENTARY

The Supreme Lord thus concludes His description of the processes of transcendental realization.

PURPORT

The word *devānām* in this verse not only refers to the demigods, but to all those who are situated in the mode of goodness. Those who are elevated in this way but still are not fully surrendered to the Supreme Lord are to be considered on the level of the demigods.

TEXT 24

अभीक्ष्णशस्ते गदितं ज्ञानं विस्पष्टयुक्तिमत् ।
एतद्विज्ञाय मुच्येत पुरुषो नष्टसंशयः ॥२४॥

abhīkṣṇaśas te gaditaṁ jñānaṁ vispaṣṭa-yuktimat
etad vijñāya mucyeta puruṣo naṣṭa-saṁśayaḥ

I have repeatedly spoken this knowledge to you within a logical manner. Anyone who properly understands this knowledge will become free from all doubts and attain liberation.

TEXT 25

सुविविक्तं तव प्रश्नं मयैतदपि धारयेत् ।
सनातनं ब्रह्मगुह्यं परं ब्रह्माधिगच्छति ॥२५॥

su-viviktaṁ tava praśnaṁ mayaitad api dhārayet
sanātanaṁ brahma-guhyaṁ paraṁ brahmādhigacchati

Anyone who carefully considers these clear answers to your questions will attain the confidential goal of the *Vedas*—the Supreme Absolute Truth.

COMMENTARY

The Supreme Lord said: I have elaborately replied to your questions. Anyone who attentively hears these answers will attain the Supreme Brahman, who is the confidential goal of the *Vedas*.

TEXT 26

य एतन्ममभक्तेषुसम्प्रदद्यात्सुपुष्कलम् ।
तस्याहंब्रह्मदायस्यददाम्यात्मानमात्मना ॥२६॥

ya etan mama bhakteṣu sampradadyāt su-puṣkalam
tasyāhaṁ brahma-dāyasya dadāmy ātmānam ātmanā

One who liberally imparts these instructions to My devotees is the bestower of the Absolute Truth, and to him I give My very self.

COMMENTARY

Although the phrase *brahmadāyasya* is in the sixth dative case, it should be understood to be in the fourth dative case, so that it indicates one who gives the Supreme Brahman to others.

PURPORT

Devotees of the Supreme Lord are well aware of the science of devotional service. When they mercifully distribute that knowledge to others and thus bring them to the service of the Supreme Lord, the Lord reciprocates such magnanimity by giving His very self to such devotees. On the other hand, those who are engrossed in their plans for material enjoyment cannot possibly achieve such mercy of the Lord.

TEXT 27

य एतत्समधीयीतपवित्रंपरमंशुचि ।
सपूयेताहरहर्मांज्ञानदीपेनदर्शयन् ॥२७॥

ya etat samadhīyīta pavitraṁ paramaṁ śuci
sa pūyetāhar ahar māṁ jñāna-dīpena darśayan

One who loudly recites this supreme knowledge, which is purifying for both the hearer and the chanter, becomes steadily purified as he reveals Me to others with the lamp of transcendental knowledge.

PURPORT

Those who are expert in the understanding of devotional service to the Lord are able to dissipate the darkness of ignorance with the light of transcendental knowledge. The conditioned souls are in a contaminated state of existence but when they take to the Lord's service, they quickly become sanctified. The darkness of ignorance cannot remain in the presence of the sun-like Supreme Personality of Godhead.

TEXT 28

य एतच्छ्रद्धयानित्यमव्यग्रःशृणुयान्नरः ।
मयिभक्तिंपरांकुर्वन्कर्मभिर्नसबध्यते ॥२८॥

ya etac chraddhayā nityam avyagraḥ śṛṇuyān naraḥ
mayi bhaktiṁ parāṁ kurvan karmabhir na sa badhyate

One who regularly hears My instructions with faith and attention while constantly engaging in My pure devotional service will never become bound by the reactions of karma.

TEXT 29

अप्युद्धवत्वयाब्रह्मसखेसमवधारितम् ।
अपितेविगतोमोहःशोकश्चासौमनोभवः ॥२९॥

apy uddhava tvayā brahma sakhe samavadhāritam
api te vigato mohaḥ śokaś cāsau mano-bhavaḥ

My dear Uddhava, have you fully understood these transcendental insturctions? Has your illusion and lamentation now been dispelled from your mind?

COMMENTARY

Uddhava's lamentation arose because he thought himself to be separated from Lord Kṛṣṇa. It is understood that Uddhava is an eternal associate of the Lord who was put into illusion so that this wonderful conversation known as *Uddhava-gītā* could be spoken. Lord Kṛṣṇa is herein indicating that if Uddhava did not perfectly understand His instructions, He would happily repeat them. Uddhava is an intimate associate of the Lord and so this question is somewhat playful in nature. After all, the all-knowing Lord could understand Uddhava's perfect understanding of Kṛṣṇa consciousness.

PURPORT

By achieving the Lord's mercy, the living entities' ignorance in the form of the material conception of life is dispelled. In the liberated condition, there is no possibility of becoming subjected to lust or lamentation.

TEXT 30

नैतत्त्वयादाम्भिकायनास्तिकायशठायच ।
अशुश्रूषोरभक्तायदुर्विनीतायदीयताम् ॥३०॥

naitat tvayā dāmbhikāya nāstikāya śaṭhāya ca
aśuśrūṣor abhaktāya durvinītāya dīyatām

You should not instruct this knowledge to anyone who is hypocritical, atheistic, or dishonest, or with anyone who will not listen faithfully, who is not a devotee, or who is simply not humble.

COMMENTARY

Spiritual knowledge should not be distributed to those who have no faith.

PURPORT

The confidential knowledge of devotional service to the Supreme Lord should not be presented to nondevotees, those who are falsely proud, cheaters, those who are arrogant, atheists, those who are faithless, and those who have no interest in hearing the truth. In this context, one should remember the ninth offense against the chanting of the holy name of the Lord.

TEXT 31

एतैर्दोषैर्विहीनायब्रह्मण्यायप्रियायच ।
साधवेशुचयेब्रूयाद्भक्तिःस्याच्छूद्रयोषिताम् ॥३१॥

etair doṣair vihīnāya brahmaṇyāya priyāya ca
sādhave śucaye brūyād bhaktiḥ syāc chūdra-yoṣitām

This knowledge should be taught to one who is devoid of these faults, who is dedicated to the welfare of the *brāhmaṇas,* and who is kindly disposed, saintly, and pure. And if *śūdrās* and women are devoted to the Supreme Lord, they can also be accepted as qualified to receive these instructions.

COMMENTARY

If *śudras* and women have devotion for the Lord, they should also be instructed about the process of devotional service.

PURPORT

The members of all the four *varṇas* can be instructed in the confidential understanding of devotional service if they maintain a condition of purity and honesty. Indeed, anyone can give up his duties within the *varṇāśrama* society and fully dedicate himself to the devotional service of the Lord.

TEXT 32

नैतद्विज्ञायजिज्ञासोर्ज्ञातव्यमवशिष्यते ।
पीत्वापीयूषममृतंपातव्यंनावशिष्यते ॥३२॥

naitad vijñāya jijñāsor jñātavyam avaśiṣyate
pītvā pīyūṣam amṛtaṁ pātavyaṁ nāvaśiṣyate

When a person who thirsts after the truth gains an understanding of this transcendental knowledge, he has reached the completion of his education. When someone drinks nectar, no more thirst will remain.

COMMENTARY

A pure devotee is fully satisfied with his engagement in the devotional service of the Lord. Outside of such engagement, he does not desire to cultivate knowledge. And, even if a pure devotee desires some particular understanding, he will receive dictation from the Lord within his heart. One who knows the Supreme Lord is the knower of everything. If one drinks celestial nectar, how can he thirst for something else?

TEXT 33

ज्ञानेकर्मणियोगेचवार्तायांदण्डधारणे ।
यावानर्थोनृणांतातत तावांस्तेऽहंचतुर्विधः ॥३३॥

jñāne karmaṇi yoge ca vārtāyāṁ daṇḍa-dhāraṇe
yāvān artho nṛṇāṁ tāta tāvāṁs te 'haṁ catur-vidhaḥ

My dear Uddhava, by means of *karma, jñāna,* yoga, mundane business, political rule, and the acceptance of *tridaṇḍa,* people try to make advancement in the four objectives of life—religiosity, economic development, sense gratification, and liberation. But because you are My devotee, whatever can be accomplished in these ways, you will very easily find within Me.

COMMENTARY

Should a devotee accept the processes of *karma* or *jñāna* if he desires material advancement or liberation? Here, the Lord says that He awards the four objectives of human life to the devotees that desire them. I am the goal of their cultivation of knowledge. The cultivation of knowledge culminates in liberation, the performance of fruitive activities depends on the principles of religiosity, and yoga awards one mystic perfections. All such accomplishments can easily be attained by the mercy of the Lord. This is confirmed in the *Nārāyaṇīya* of the *Mokṣa-dharma*, in *Śrī Mahābhārata*:

yā vai sādhana-sampattiḥ puruṣārtha-catuṣṭaye
tayā vinā tad āpnoti naro nārāyaṇāśrayaḥ

Whatever among the four goals of human life can be achieved by various spiritual practices is automatically achieved without such endeavors by the person who has taken shelter of Lord Nārāyaṇa, the refuge of all persons.

The purport of this verse is that one should not divert his attention to other process because one who is devoted to the Supreme Personality can attain all the benefits derived from the practice of yoga, philosophical speculation, the performance of religious rituals and sacrifices, the giving of charity, and so on. That is the specific benediction of devotional service to the Supreme Lord.

PURPORT

Because devotees obtain the perfection of yoga by their execution of devotional service, they never consider undergoing various disciplines, such as *jñāna-yoga*, *karma-yoga*, severe austerities, or ritualistic religious performances.

TEXT 34

मर्त्योयदात्यक्तसमस्तकर्मानिवेदितात्माविचिकीर्षितो मे ।
तदामृतत्वंप्रतिपद्यमानोमयात्मभूयायचकल्पतेवै ॥३४॥

martyo yadā tyakta-samasta-karmā niveditātmā vicikīrṣito me
tadāmṛtatvaṁ pratipadyamāno mayātma-bhūyāya ca kalpate vai

One who gives up all fruitive activities and surrenders unto Me, sincerely desiring to render service unto Me, achieves liberation from birth and death and while residing in My supreme abode, shares My opulence.

COMMENTARY

Uddhava might have said: "I have heard Your opinion on this matter but what is the opinion of Your devotees?" The Lord would reply: "My dear Uddhava, the opinion of pious persons has been described in the eighteenth chapter, and the opinion of sinful men has been given in the twenty-second chapter. My devotees are truthful, saintly, and undisturbed by material duality. A surrendered soul is one who, by the mercy of My devotee, has given up all varieties of religiosity to engage in My unalloyed service. Such a surrendered devotee has taken shelter at the lotus feet of a bona fide spiritual master, who is nondifferent from Me. The spiritual master initiates his disciple into the chanting of Kṛṣṇa *mantras* and the disciple offers everything in his possession, including his body, mind, and power of speech, for the service of the Lord. When a devotee sincerely surrenders unto Me, even once, I personally take charge of him. My activities, and the activities of My devotees, are transcendental and factual, having nothing to do with *maya*, the illusory energy. As a result of his engagement in My service, a devotee comes to associate with Me as one of My loving associates."

PURPORT

When the conditioned souls renounce fruitive activities and the cultivation of knowledge and surrender to the Supreme Personality of Godhead—it is not that they will feel any scarcity. The Supreme Lord is perfect and complete and everything in relationship with Him is also complete, or in other words, without any deficiency.

TEXT 35

श्रीशुक उवाच
स एवमादर्शितयोगमार्गस्तदोत्तमःश्लोकवचोनिशम्य ।
बद्धाञ्जलिःप्रीत्युपरुद्धकण्ठोनकिञ्चिदूचेऽश्रुपरिप्लुताक्षः ॥३५॥

śrī-śuka uvāca
sa evam ādarśita-yoga-mārgas tadottamaḥśloka-vaco niśamya
baddhāñjaliḥ prīty-uparuddha-kaṇṭho na kiñcid ūce 'śru-pariplutākṣaḥ

Śukadeva Gosvāmī said: Having been instructed by Lord Śrī Kṛṣṇa about the complete path of yoga, Uddhava, his voice choked due to ecstatic love and his eyes filled with tears, folded his hands and stood silently, unable to say anything.

TEXT 36

विष्टभ्यचित्तंप्रणयावघूर्णंधैर्येणराजन्बहुमन्यमानः ।
कृताञ्जलिःप्राहयदुप्रवीरंशीर्ष्णास्पृशंस्तच्चरणारविन्दम् ॥३६॥

viṣṭabhya cittaṁ praṇayāvaghūrṇaṁ dhairyeṇa rājan bahu-manyamānaḥ
kṛtāñjaliḥ prāha yadu-pravīraṁ śīrṣṇā spṛśaṁs tac-caraṇāravindam

O King, with great patience, Uddhava pacified his mind, which was agitated by ecstatic love. Feeling most grateful to Lord Kṛṣṇa, the greatest hero of the Yadu dynasty, he bowed down to touch the lotus feet of the Lord with his head and then spoke with folded hands.

COMMENTARY

Due to fear of impending separation, Uddhava felt very anxious, but just to steady his mind, he remembered how Śrī Kṛṣṇa had bestowed great mercy upon him.

TEXT 37

श्रीउद्धव उवाच
विद्रावितोमोहमहान्धकारोय आश्रितोमेतवसन्निधानात् ।
विभावसोःकिंनुसमीपगस्यशीतंतमोभीःप्रभवन्त्यजाद्य ॥३७॥

śrī-uddhava uvāca
vidrāvito moha-mahāndhakāro ya āśrito me tava sannidhānāt
vibhāvasoḥ kiṁ nu samīpa-gasya śītaṁ tamo bhīḥ prabhavanty ajādya

Śrī Uddhava said: O primeval Lord, I was born in the darkness of ignorance but by Your merciful association, my delusion is now dispelled. For one who stands in the sunlight, how can cold, darkness, or fear continue to oppress him?

COMMENTARY

Śrī Uddhava said: "I had fallen into the darkness of illusion. Although I am surrounded by the Yādavas, headed by Śrī Kṛṣṇa, I considered Dvārakā to be a limited and temporary material place."

In the Third Canto of *Śrīmad-Bhāgavatam*, Lord Śrī Kṛṣṇa revealed the confidential conclusions of transcendental knowledge to Uddhava, which were unknown to others, but He withheld the most confidential part, which He has now imparted to him.

PURPORT

Just as, by the rising of the sun, darkness is automatically vanquished, so when one takes to the devotional service of the Supreme Lord, the darkness of ignorance cannot remain. The processes of *karma*, *jñana*, and yoga are incapable of entirely removing the darkness of ignorance.

TEXT 38

प्रत्यर्पितोमेभवतानुकम्पिनाभृत्यायविज्ञानमयाःप्रदीपः ।
हित्वाकृतज्ञस्तवपादमूलंकोऽन्यंसमीयाच्छरणंत्वदीयम् ॥३८॥

pratyarpito me bhavatānukampinā bhṛtyāya vijñāna-mayaḥ pradīpaḥ
hitvā kṛta-jñas tava pāda-mūlaṁ ko 'nyaṁ samīyāc charaṇaṁ tvadīyam

As reciprocation for my surrender at Your lotus feet, You have mercifully illuminated me with transcendental knowledge. What devotee of Yours who has any gratitude at all could give up the shelter of Your lotus feet and accept another master?

COMMENTARY

Uddhava said, "I have surrendered my body, soul, mind, intelligence, and senses unto You and in return You have enlightened me with the knowledge that removes all darkness of ignorance. My dear Lord, I am fully satisfied at every moment by the realization of Your unfathomable glories. Now, You may do whatever You wish to Your surrendered servant. You may keep me here or send me wherever You desire. I am ever grateful to You, and I simply wish to remain Your eternal servant. I have no personal desire to go anywhere, even a holy place of pilgrimage, leaving aside Your lotus feet. I am happy to reside anywhere as long as I am fully absorbed in Your devotional service. Whatever You wish me to do—I will carry out Your order." This is the purport of this verse.

PURPORT

When one takes shelter of the lotus feet of the Supreme Lord, all of the darkness born of ignorance is dispelled so that one becomes free from all doubts. Such a devotee accepts the lotus feet of the Lord as his only refuge.

TEXT 39

वृक्णश्चमेसुदृढःस्नेहपाशोदाशार्हवृष्ण्यन्धकसात्वतेषु ।
प्रसारितःसृष्टिविवृद्धयेत्वयास्वमाययाह्यात्मसुबोधहेतिना ॥३९॥

vṛkṇaś ca me su-dṛḍhaḥ sneha-pāśo dāśārha-vṛṣṇy-andhaka-sātvateṣu
prasāritaḥ sṛṣṭi-vivṛddhaye tvayā sva-māyayā hy ātma-subodha-hetinā

With a desire to increase the population, You extended the rope of my affection towards the Dāśārhas, Andhakas, Vṛṣṇis, and Yādavas. But today, You have cut that rope with the weapon of transcendental knowledge.

COMMENTARY

Uddhava might wonder, "How can I sever my affection for the Yādavas and go elsewhere? He would answer that as follows: I am tied to the Yādavas with the rope of affection. My dear Lord, You expanded Your family, the Yādavas, and have thus increased the population, by means of Your own potency. Your family is still expanding through the agency of Your sons and grandsons. Thus, my social prestige has also spread in all directions. You should now cut off the rope of my family affection and prestige with the weapon of transcendental knowledge. Let me instead be tied by the rope of affection to those who relish hearing and chanting Your transcendental names, as well as descriptions of Your transcendental forms, qualities, and pastimes. Let that affection remain as my ornament. I wish to remain in Your association, and that of the Yādavas forever. This is my prayer."

TEXT 40

नमोऽस्तुतेमहायोगिन्प्रपन्नमनुशाधिमाम् ।
यथात्वच्चरणाम्भोजेरतिःस्यादनपायिनी ॥४०॥

namo 'stu te mahā-yogin prapannam anuśādhi mām
yathā tvac-caraṇāmbhoje ratiḥ syād anapāyinī

O greatest of mystic yogis, I offer my obeisances unto You. Please instruct me, who am surrendered unto You, so that I may have unflinching attachment for Your lotus feet.

COMMENTARY

Uddhava said, "O greatest of all mystics, You have so graciously allowed me to realize Your transcendental nature and characteristics, and thus have awarded me complete satisfaction."

TEXT 41-44

श्रीभगवानुवाच
गच्छोद्धवमयादिष्टोबदर्याख्यंममाश्रमम् ।
तत्रमत्पादतीर्थोदेस्नानोपस्पर्शनैःशुचिः ॥४१॥
ईक्षयालकनन्दायाविधूताशेषकल्मषः ।
वसानोवल्कलान्यङ्गवन्यभुक् सुखनिःस्पृहः ॥४२॥
तितिक्षुर्द्वन्द्वमात्राणांसुशीलःसंयतेन्द्रियः ।
शान्तःसमाहितधियाज्ञानविज्ञानसंयुतः ॥४३॥
मत्तोऽनुशिक्षितंयत्तेविविक्तमनुभावयन् ।
मय्यावेशितवाक्चित्तोमद्धर्मनिरतोभव ।
अतिव्रज्यगतीस्तिस्रोमामेष्यसिततःपरम् ॥४४॥

śrī-bhagavān uvāca
gacchoddhava mayādiṣṭo badary-ākhyaṁ mamāśramam
tatra mat-pāda-tīrthode snānopasparśanaiḥ śuciḥ

īkṣayālakanandāyā vidhūtāśeṣa-kalmaṣaḥ
vasāno valkalāny aṅga vanya-bhuk sukha-niḥspṛhaḥ

titikṣur dvandva-mātrāṇāṁ suśīlaḥ saṁyatendriyaḥ
śāntaḥ samāhita-dhiyā jñāna-vijñāna-saṁyutaḥ

matto 'nuśikṣitaṁ yat te viviktam anubhāvayan
mayy āveśita-vāk-citto mad-dharma-nirato bhava
ativrajya gatīs tisro mām eṣyasi tataḥ param

The Supreme Personality of Godhead said: "My dear Uddhava, follow My order and go to Badrikāśrama. Purify yourself by bathing and performing *ācamana* with the water that has emanated from My lotus feet. Free yourself of all sinful reactions by having *darśana* of the sacred Alakanandā River. Dress yourself in tree bark and eat the fruit and roots that are easily available in the forest. Thus, you should remain self-satisfied and free of all desires, tolerant of all dualities, good-natured, self-controlled, peaceful, and endowed with transcendental knowledge and realization. With fixed attention, constantly contemplate these instructions that I have imparted to you, and thus assimilate their

essence. Fix your mind and words upon Me, and in this way, you will be able to surpass the influence of the three modes of material nature and finally come back to Me.

COMMENTARY

The Supreme Personality of Godhead said, "O Uddhava, You are as good as Me and thus, among all the members of the Yadu dynasty, you are My personal representative. I had previously declared, 'Uddhava is not inferior to Me in any way.' Therefore, you should remain in this world, just to preach My instructions. Distribute this transcendental knowledge to everyone. Whatever I wish to accomplish in this world can be done by you. As I had previously sent you to Vraja, I will now send you to Badarikāśrama. There, the foremost of sages, Śrī Nārāyaṇa, as well as others, aspire to see Me. Previously, I traveled to Mithilā, and many other places on this earth, and satisfied all My devotees who desired to see Me, by giving them My *darśana* and imparting to them transcendental knowledge. Now, however, I am unable to go to Badarikāśrama. I am now one hundred and twenty-five years old, and the time for My disappearance has arrived. You said to Me, "I am Your surrendered servant and so kindly order me. What should I do?" So, this is My order. Your name, Uddhava, is suitable because you give pleasure to everyone. Now, go to Badarikāśrama and give everyone joy by displaying your knowledge, renunciation, and other sublime characteristics. This is My mission. Indeed, simply by your glance, you will nullify all the sinful reactions that have become stocked in the river Alkanandā. After you execute My order, you will return to Me in the spiritual sky."

PURPORT

Instead of working under the direction of the three modes of material nature, if one works under the direction of the spiritual master in devotional service, which is transcendental to the material modes, he certainly becomes qualified to attain the ultimate destination. Others cannot go back to Godhead because they try to attain insignificant and temporary material objects.

TEXT 45

श्रीशुक उवाच
स एवमुक्तोहरिमेधसोद्धवःप्रदक्षिणंतंपरिसृत्यपादयोः ।
शिरोनिधायाश्रुकलाभिरार्द्रधीर्न्यषिञ्चदद्वन्द्वपरोऽप्यपक्रमे ॥४५॥

śrī-śuka uvāca
sa evam ukto hari-medhasoddhavaḥ pradakṣiṇaṁ taṁ parisṛtya pādayoḥ
śiro nidhāyāśru-kalābhir ārdra-dhīr nyaṣiñcad advandva-paro 'py apakrame

Śukadeva Gosvāmī said: After being thus instructed by the supremely intelligent Lord Śrī Kṛṣṇa, Uddhava circumambulated Him and then bowed down to offer his obeisances, placing his head upon the lotus feet of the Lord. Although Uddhava was free from the influence of all material dualities, he became afflicted by feelings of separation so that he drenched the Lord's lotus feet with his tears.

COMMENTARY

Śukadeva Gosvāmī said, "After receiving instructions from Śrī Kṛṣṇa, Uddhava, whose heart was always filled with ecstatic love for the Lord, felt great lamentation due to impending separation and thus shed incessant tears."

TEXT 46

सुदुस्त्यजस्नेहवियोगकातरोनशक्नुवंस्तंपरिहातुमातुरः ।
कृच्छ्रंययौमूर्धनिभर्तृपादुकेबिभ्रन्नमस्कृत्यययौपुनःपुनः ॥४६॥

su-dustyaja-sneha-viyoga-kātaro na śaknuvaṁs taṁ parihātum āturaḥ
kṛcchraṁ yayau mūrdhani bhartṛ-pāduke bibhran namaskṛtya yayau punaḥ punaḥ

Greatly fearing separation from the Lord, for whom he felt such great affection, Uddhava was distraught, so that he could not give up the Lord's association. Finally, feeling great agony, he repeatedly bowed down to the Lord, placed His wooden shoes upon his head, and departed.

COMMENTARY

The Lord mercifully extended His lotus feet to Uddhava, who clasped them with great love and devotion and placed them on his head. Thereafter, Uddhava left for Badarikāśrama, in order to carry out the mission of the Supreme Lord. It is said in *Śrīmad-Bhāgavatam* (3.4.5), that while Uddhava was going to Badarikāśrama, he heard that the Lord had traveled to Prabhāsa. Uddhava then retraced his steps so that he could find Lord Kṛṣṇa, and it so happened that he came to where the Lord was sitting alone after the annihilation of the Yadu dynasty. Uddava was once again instructed by the Lord, and after his transcendental understanding was reawakened, on the order of the Lord, he again departed for Badarikāśrama.

TEXT 47

ततस्तमन्तर्हृदिसन्निवेश्यगतोमहाभागवतोविशालाम् ।
यथोपदिष्टांजगदेकबन्धुनातपःसमास्थायहरेरगाद्गतिम् ॥४७॥

tatas tam antar hṛdi sanniveśya gato mahā-bhāgavato viśālām
yathopadiṣṭāṁ jagad-eka-bandhunā tapaḥ samāsthāya harer agād gatim

Thereafter, the exalted devotee, Uddhava, placed Śrī Kṛṣṇa upon the lotus of his heart and went to Badrikāśrama. By engaging in austerities, he attained the Lord's eternal abode, which had been described to him by the only friend of the conditioned souls, Lord Kṛṣṇa.

COMMENTARY

The word *vīracandra viśālāṁ* refers to Badarikāśrama. After residing there, Uddhava attained the eternal abode of the Lord in the spiritual sky, Dvārakā.

TEXT 48

य एतदानन्दसमुद्रसम्भृतंज्ञानामृतंभागवतायभाषितम् ।
कृष्णेनयोगेश्वरसेविताङ्घ्रिणासच्छ्रद्धयासेव्यजगद्विमुच्यते ॥४८॥

ya etad ānanda-samudra-sambhṛtaṁ jñānāmṛtaṁ bhāgavatāya bhāṣitam
kṛṣṇena yogeśvara-sevitāṅghriṇā sac-chraddhayāsevya jagad vimucyate

Thus Lord Kṛṣṇa, whose lotus feet are served by all the great masters of yoga, spoke to His devotee this transcendental knowledge, which comprises the entire ocean of spiritual ecstasy. Anyone who receives this narration with great faith and devotion is assured of liberation in the very near future.

COMMENTARY

If one faithfully hears this conversation between the Lord and His devotee, which is like an ocean of bliss, he becomes a fit candidate for executing loving devotional service of the Lord. Indeed, by his association, the entire world can become engaged in the service of the Lord.

PURPORT

By faithfully serving the devotees of the Supreme Lord, one can attain freedom from material bondage and engagement in the devotional service of the Supreme Lord.

TEXT 49

भवभयमपहन्तुंज्ञानविज्ञानसारंनिगमकृदुपजह्रेभृङ्गवद्वेदसारम् ।
अमृतमुदधितश्चापाययद्भृत्यवर्गान्पुरुषमृषभमाद्यंकृष्णसंज्ञंनतोऽस्मि ॥४९॥

bhava-bhayam apahantuṁ jñāna-vijñāna-sāraṁ
nigama-kṛd upajahre bhṛṅga-vad veda-sāram
amṛtam udadhitaś cāpāyayad bhṛtya-vargān
puruṣam ṛṣabham ādyaṁ kṛṣṇa-saṁjñaṁ nato 'smi

I offer my obeisances unto the Supreme Personality of Godhead, the origin of everything, Lord Śrī Kṛṣṇa. He is the author of the Vedas, and just to destroy His devotees' fear of material existence, like a bee, He collected the essence of all knowledge and self-realization and then awarded it to His devotees, who, by His mercy, have drunk it.

COMMENTARY

To conclude this chapter, Śrī Śukadeva Gosvāmī offers his obeisances to the spiritual master of the whole universe, Śrī Kṛṣṇa. It is Kṛṣṇa who churned the *Vedas* to extract the essence. Other philosophers have also tried to extract the essence from the Vedic literature, but without knowing the confidential purport of the *Vedas*, being devoid of implicit faith in the Supreme Lord. Being the author of the *Vedas*, it is the Supreme Lord who understands their true purpose. The Supreme Lord, like a bee, collected honey from the garden of Vedic flowers and distributed it to His devotees. However, while favoring the devotees, the Lord has simultaneously cheated the nondevotee demons. For example, during the churning of ocean, the Lord took the pot of nectar after assuming the form of Mohinī and then distributed it to the demigods, while tactfully deceiving the demons. Let us bow down to that Supreme Lord, Śrī Kṛṣṇa.

PURPORT

Śrī Kṛṣṇa is the Supreme Personality of Godhead, without beginning and without end. As the supreme instructor, He removes the living entities' fear of repeated birth and death. He mercifully distributes love of Himself, which is the essence of all Vedic knowledge, to all conditioned souls who are otherwise averse to His service. He is the compiler of the Vedic literature, and He distributed its essence to the swan-like Vaiṣṇavas. It is the foremost duty of all living entities to surrender unto the Supreme Personality of Godhead, giving up all varieties of religiosity.

Thus end the translation of the Twenty-third Chapter of the Uddhava-gītā *entitled* **"Bhakti-yoga"** *with the commentaries of Śrīla Viśvanātha Cakravartī Ṭhākura and chapter summary and purports by Śrīla Bhaktisiddhānta Sarasvatī Ṭhākura.*

End of Uddhava-Gītā

APPENDIX

GLOSSARY

A

Abhidheya : Activities involved in developing one's relationship with the Supreme Lord.

Acintya-bhedābheda : Inconceivable simultaneous oneness and difference.

Aśvattha : Banyan tree, considered very holy.

Aśvinī-kumāras : The twin demigods, who are the controlling deities of the object of sense perception.

Adhibautika : Miseries of material existence caused by other living entities.

Adhidaivika : Miseries of material existence caused by higher authorities or the demigods.

Adhirūḍha mahābhāva : Severe agony felt due to separation from one's beloved.

Adhyātmika : Miseries of material existence caused by one's mind or body.

Advaya jñāna : The conception of the Supreme Lord as non-dual, one without a second.

Aṇimā-siddhi : First of the eighteen mystic perfections that can be attained by a yogi. In this perfection, a yogi can become smaller than the smallest.

Agnihotra : One of Vedic sacrifices which a twice-born person must perform after marriage.

Airāvata : Lord Indra's elephant.

Akṛta-droha : The devotional quality of never using one's mind. A devotee never uses his mind, body or words to perform any act that is harmful to the welfare of any living entity.

Akiñcana : Freedom from possessiveness. A devotee is not eager to enjoy or renounce anything because he considers everything to be Lord Kṛṣṇa's property.

Alaṅkāra : Literary ornaments.

Amānī : Not proud. A devotee is not proud. Even if he is famous, he does not take it very seriously.

Anāptakāma : The Lord's merciful reciprocation with His loving devotees of being unable to achieve His desire without the cooperation of His devotees.

Anartha : Unneccessary habits or unwanted traits that impede spiritual advancement.
Anātmārāma : Being affected by the love of His devotees, the Lord sometimes appears dependent on the love of His devotees.
Anavadyātmā : The devotional quality of freedom from envy and unnecessary criticism.
Aniha : Detached from all worldly activities.
Aṣṭāṅga-yoga : Eightfold system of yoga practice.
Aṣṭakālīya-līlā : The eternal eightfold daily pastimes of the Divine Couple.
Anuloma : Mixed marriage systems in Vedic culture. If a man marries a girl belonging to an inferior caste, that union is termed *anuloma*.
Anusvāra : Nasal vibration pronounced after the fifteen Sanskrit vowels.
Aparājaya siddhi : The mystic perfection of becoming unconquerable in all respects.
Apramatta : Being cautious, not mad.
Apsarās : Heavenly damsels.
Āpta-kāma : Supreme Lord automatically fulfills all of His own desires.
Asaṅklipta : One of three methods of begging alms by the mendicants. This is whereby one approaches seven houses and is satisfied with whatever he receives.
Ātma-krīḍa : An advanced Vaiṣṇava, constantly enjoying the mellows of loving devotional service and carrying out the mission of the Lord on the earth, and enjoying life within the internal potency of the Supreme Lord.
Ātma-rata : Being fully satisfied by constant engagement in devotional service.
Ātmārāma : Self satisfied. One finds pleasure only in the self.
Ātmavān : Situated in one's eternal constitutional position.
Avadhūta : A careless or mad person. Also an advanced state of spiritual practice.
Avidyā : Ignorance.
Avyakta : The Lord who is not materially manifest at any stage of cosmic evolution.

B

Bṛhaspati : Chief priest or the spiritual master of the demigods.
Bahvayana : One of the two categories into which the Vedic scriptures are divided.
Bhagavān : The Supreme Personality of Godhead, complete with six opulence.
Bhāgavata dharma : Devotional service to the Lord.
Bhakti-devī : Goddess of devotion.
Bhāva-bhakti : The advance stage of bhakti whereby one experiences loving feelings towards the Supreme Lord.
Bhūmi : Mother earth.
Bhūtabhāvana : The Lord, who is the benefactor of all living entities.

C

Caitya-guru : The Lord as the spiritual master situated within.

D

Dakṣiṇa : An offering of gratitude to one's preceptor.
Dāna : Giving charity to others or being compassionate toward inferiors.
Dānta : The devotional qualification of being sense controlled.
Darśa : New moon day when the sun and the moon are in proximity.
Daridra : One who is dissatisfied with life or is poor.
Dāsya : The mood of being the Lord's servant in loving devotional service.
Devatā-kāṇḍa : One of three sections of the *Vedas*. The *Vedas* have three divisions.
Dhana : Wealth.
Dhāraṇā : Meditation.
Dharma : Occupational duties.
Dhṛtimāna : One who is not agitated by the urges of the tongue and genitals.
Dhātu : Truth or element.
Dikṣā : Spiritual initiation.

E

Ekāyana : One of two categories into which the *Vedas* are divided. This category aims at sole meditation on the Supreme Lord. This is the method adopted by the topmost devotee of the Lord who firmly believe that chanting the holy names of the Lord is the only way of achieving the ultimate goal of life.

G

Gabhirātmā : He whose nature is unfathomable.
Gṛha-vrata : An attached householder who cannot control his senses.
Garbhādhāna : Purificatory rites performed while a child is in the womb of the mother.
Guṇa-bhūta-bhakti : Devotional service mixed with speculative propensities, or performed under the influence of the modes of material nature.
Guṇamāyā : Mundane qualitative potency.
Guṇībhūtā-bhakti : Devotional service that is performed based on the execution of occupation's duties.

H

Harivāsara : The appearance day of the Lord.
Hrī : Actual modesty, which is, to be disgusted with abominable activities.

I

Iṣṭa : Most desirable. The Supreme Lord is the only most desirable object.
Īśa : A controller. Also pertains to one who is detached from sense gratification.
Īśitā : A mystic perfection that enables one to manipulate the sub-potencies of *Maya*.
Īśitva : The mystic perfection that enables one to exert his influence over the bodies of others.

J

Jāti-smara : The mystic power that enables one to remember his previous birth.
Jīvaśakti : The potency of the Lord that manifests living entities.
Jīvamāyā : The living potency of the living entities.

K

Kāma-rūpa : A mystic perfection of the ability to assume any form that one desires, even the form of a demigod.
Kāmair ahata-dhī : A devotee who is not agitated by lusty desires.
Kāmāvasāyitā : A mystic perfection that enables one to obtain anything he may desire.
Kṛpaṇa : A miserly person.
Kṛpālu : A devotee is always merciful.
Kāruṇika : A devotee if fully magnanimous to all.
Kāvya : Poetic.
Kevala-bhakti : Unalloyed devotional service to the Lord.
Kimpuruṣas : A race of monkeys who are almost like human beings.
Kindevas : A race of human beings who are, like the demigods, completely free from fatigue, sweat and body odor.
Kinnaras : A race of beings who are a little like human. They have either a human head or human body (but not both) combined with a nonhuman form.
Kriyā : Activities that one performs, usually under the influence of material energy.
Kupatha : The wrong path, which leads to sense gratification and simply bewilders the mind.

L

Lābha : Greed.
Laghimā : A mystic perfection that enables to become as light as an atom.

M

Mādhukara : A method of begging by a mendicant where he collects little from each household, just like a honeybee.

Mṛdu : The devotional qualification of being gentle-hearted.
Mahāntaḥ : A great soul.
Mahat-tattva : The combined material nature.
Mahimā-siddhi : The mystic perfection whereby a yogi meditates upon the total material existence as a manifestation of the external potency of the Lord and thus firmly realized that the material creation is not different from the Lord. By therefore realizing the Lord's presence in each individual element, the yogi acquires the greatness of each element.
Maitra : The devotional qualification of being friendly to everyone.
Mānada : The devotional qualification of giving respect to everyone.
Mano-javaḥ : A mystic perfection that enables one's body to follow his mind wherever it goes.
Manomaya : Lord Kṛṣṇa is to be kept within one's mind.
Mārgaśīrṣa : Lunar month that falls between November and December.
Māyāśakti : Illusory potency.
Mitabhuk : A devotee eats enough only to sustain his body.

N

Niṣedha : Regulations.
Niṣṭhā : Fixed.
Niḥsaṅga : Without any tinge of karma, jñāna, and so on.

P

Para-kāya-praveśanam : The mystic perfection that enables to enter the body of another person.
Pariṇāmavāda : The philosophy of transformation.
Paurnamāsa : Full moon day.
Pradhāna : The totality of material ingredients.
Pradhānībhūtā-bhakti : Devotional service performed according to principles delineated by the Supreme Lord in the scriptures.
Prākpraṇita : One of three methods for begging alms. This is a process by which one establishes regular donors and collects one's maintenance from them.
Prāpti : A mystic perfection by which one gains mastery over everyone's senses.
Pratiloma : Vedic system of marriage where a man marries a girl of the higher caste.
Priyam : Dear most. The Lord is the supreme lovable object, and He establishes wonderful affectionate relationships with His devotees.

R

Rāga-mārga : The path of intimate devotion to the Lord.
Rasa : Mellow or relishable relationship.

S

Saṁskāra : Purificatory rites.
Saṅkalpa siddhi : A mystic perfection that enables one to achieve his goal.
Sālokya mukti : Liberation of being able to be on the same planet as the Lord.
Sama : Equal in happiness and distress, as well as in honor and dishonor.
Samadarśana : Equal vision. A learned person sees the equality of all beings.
Sandhinī : The potency of eternal existence.
Sānta : The devotional qualification of being always peaceful.
Sārṣṭi : The liberation of achieving the same opulence as the Lord.
Sarvopakāraka : The devotional qualification of being always engaged in acts meant for the welfare of others.
Satpatha : True path that leads to liberation.
Satya-sāra : The devotional qualification of being always fixed in the truth.
Sāyujya mukti : The liberation of merging into the personal effulgence of the Lord.
Sthira : The devotional qualification of being always fixed.
Svacchanda-mṛtyu : The mystic perfection of the ability to die at will.
Svagata-bheda : The Lord's relationship with the spiritual nature.
Śṛṅgāra : The intimate loving mood by which devotional service is rendered.
Śākta : Possessor of the energy. Usually refers to Lord Śiva.
Śānta-bhakta : A devotee who has attained the first stage of loving association with the Lord, which is a position of neutrality.
Śānta-rati : The mood of neutrality in the perfection of devotional service.
Śauca : To remain detached from material enjoyment while utilizing everything in the service of Kṛṣṇa.
Śaurya : To subdue one's natural thirst for material sense enjoyment.
Śrīvatsa : Tuft of hair on the chest of the Lord.
Śuci : Cleanliness and purity.
Śvetadvīpa : White island. Spiritual abode of the Lord situated within this material world.

T

Tattva-vinyāsa : A procedure in Deity worship whereby the Lord is invoked and established on sanctified ground by the chanting of *mantras*.
Titikṣu : The devotional qualification of being always tolerant, even in the midst of adversities.

Titikṣā : To tolerate the distress that one is destined to suffer, thinking it to be the Lord's mercy, and refraining from feelings of jealousy because of another's happiness.

Trikālajñatā siddhi : The mystic perfection that enables one to know past, present, and future, as well as knowing about the birth and death of all people.

V

Vastusiddhi : When the subtle body is dissolved at the time of spiritual perfection.

Vātsalya : Parental relationship with the Lord.

Vātsāyana : The author of Kama sutra.

Viśiṣṭādvaita : This philosophy addresses the living entities as *cit* and the material world as *acit*. This was propounded by Śrī Rāmānuja.

Viśuddha-sattva : Pure existence of the Lord, free from the modes of material nature.

Vidhi : Rules, which are in regard to the activities of the living entities that are always good.

Vidyā : Knowledge.

Vijātīya-bheda : The living entities' relationship with the material nature.

Vijñāna : Wisdom or realization of knowledge.

Vivartavāda : The impersonal philosophy that says that the Absolute Truth is unchangeable, and that this material world is false.

Vratadharaṇa : The firm determination to engage in the Lord's service.

GENERAL INDEX